S0-ADB-359

Bernard Shaw

SHAW'S MUSIC

VOLUME III

Bernard Shaw

SHAW'S MUSIC

The complete musical criticism

in three volumes

Edited by

Dan H. Laurence

VOLUME III

1893–1950

Biographical and General
Indexes to the Entire Edition

Dodd, Mead & Company
NEW YORK

First published in the United States of America in 1981
by Dodd Mead & Company, Inc.
79 Madison Avenue, New York, N.Y. 10016

Vol. III: ISBN 0–396–07962–8
3 vol. set ISBN 0–396–07967–9
Library of Congress Catalog Number: 80–70541

Printed and bound in Great Britain for
Max Reinhardt, The Bodley Head Ltd.
9 Bow Street, London WC2E 7AL
by William Clowes (Beccles) Ltd.
Set in Clowes Plantin Light by CCC

CONTENTS

Shaw's Music

is published in three volumes
Volume I: 1876–1890
Volume II: 1890–1893
Volume III: 1893–1950 and
biographical and general indexes
to the entire edition

HALF A CENTURY BEHIND

The World, 25 October 1893

Comic opera is still trying to mend its luck, apparently with some success. The Mascotte has been transferred from the Gaiety to the Criterion, where Miss St John still keeps it going with ease, though from the middle of the last act onwards it is certainly as crazy a piece of dramatic botchwork as the worst enemy of the human intelligence could desire. What it would be without the *prima donna* I dare not imagine; rather let me sit quietly in my stall and wonder whether Miss St John's next speech will be delivered in the prettiest serious manner of Miss Ellen Terry, or in cockney, Irish, or Yankee, as the mood of the moment may suggest. But, however it comes, it comes with genuine comic force; and the opera does not flag for a moment while Miss St John is on the stage. Her singing is as good as ever; and though her voice is a shade less fresh than it was twenty years ago, it is in much better condition than most voices are after twenty months' stage wear. Mr Wallace Brownlow is unfortunate in having to impersonate a youth who is accepted by a traveling dramatic company as a nimble comedian, which is exactly what he is not; but his singing pulls him through. Mr Conyers, the tenor, does not improve, the fault being, not his, but his method's. Mr Fred Emney is condemned to enact one of those zany kings of *opéra bouffe* whose tyranny, I hope, must be as heavy on the player as on the audience. Miss Phyllis Broughton, rather at a discount in the earlier scenes, brought off her song and dance in the last act triumphantly; and Miss Mabel Love, who with the natural expansion of her view of life has quite relaxed the tragic aspect which distinguished her in her teens, was left breathless by a double *encore* for a tarantella which was really a dance, and not one of the arrant impostures which have lately got into currency under the pretext of "skirt dancing."

Mr Hollingshead's venture at the Princess's is chiefly notable for the new departure downward in prices. Whether Miami succeeds or not, Mr Hollingshead is certainly sound in his economic reasoning. The notion that you can keep on increasing the supply of places of entertainment in London without affecting prices can only be defended on the hypothesis that the demand at the old prices far exceeded the supply. Considering that theatrical business has been falling off in all directions for some time past at the old prices, whilst the music halls, at lower prices, hold their own, the hypothesis seems contradicted by the facts. Obstinately high prices and obstinately high salaries on the one hand, with closing theatres and the most desperate precariousness of employment on the other, have been the rule for the last few years. It is not certain even that the theatres which have kept open have paid.

Actor-managers find "backers" to subsidize experiments with expensively mounted plays which are assumed to be successful because they are persisted in for some months; but in such cases there is no satisfactory evidence to shew that the backer has escaped a loss, much less come out with his capital intact, plus the ordinary interest on it. Meanwhile hundreds of half-crowns are paid every night at the pit-door by men who would pay five shillings for an orchestra or balcony stall if it were to be had so cheap; whilst hundreds of others stay at home or go to the music halls because theatre managers will not make them comfortable at a reasonable rate. Whether the stalls are always filled by persons who pay half a guinea apiece is best known to the managers.

My own observation leads me to suspect that, under circumstances of no more than ordinary attractiveness, it is difficult to fill even three rows of stalls without the assistance of deadheads—and as I am a professional deadhead myself, I may perhaps be excused for hinting a doubt as to whether the tone given to the stalls by the courtiers of the boxoffice is so very much more elevated from the fashionable point of view than that which might be expected to prevail among plain persons good for hard cash to the extent of five shillings. On the whole, I agree cordially with Mr Hollingshead that there is room for his Volkstheater in London, and can testify, having tried the experiment, to the sense of economic satisfaction produced by a comfortable balcony stall costing a modest extravagance of three shillings.

At the same time, I must confess I do not in the least believe in the success of Mr Hollingshead's extraordinary freak of combining the most advanced arrangements before the curtain with an attempt to revive the Crummles repertory behind it. I daresay Miami will draw a certain number of veteran playgoers who will go to see Green Bushes* again just as they might go to see their birthplace, or their old school, or anything else likely to recall the sensations of "auld lang syne." Such gnawing pleasures reassure and freshen the man who fears that he has lost his youthful power of feeling thoroughly maudlin. The veterans, combined with the devotees of Miss Violet Cameron and Mr Courtice Pounds, will, no doubt, keep Miami going for a time;

* John Hollingshead's melodramatic opera Miami was founded on a highly successful melodrama The Green Bushes (1845) by J.B. Buckstone, which had starred Mme Céleste (d. 1882), French dancer and actress popular in England and America, and Paul Bedford (d. 1871), who had toured in the work for years afterwards.

but I am sceptical as to its enjoying any great vogue on the strength of its artistic merits. The fact is, it has no such merits, and never had.

I do not speak altogether as a modern: these eyes have seen the great Céleste as Miami, and also as the heroine of a melodrama* in which she was eighteen in the first act, thirty in the second, forty in the third, sixty in the fourth, and eighty in the fifth; after which I came away wondering how old Madame really was, as she had looked like a made-up old woman in the early stages, and like a made-up young woman in the later ones, never by any chance presenting a convincing appearance of being near the age indicated by the dramatist. She was, I took it, a clever lady who had taken the measure of that huge section of the playgoing public which is enormously credulous of everything except the truth, highly susceptible to the instinctive emotions, entirely uncritical as to the reasonableness of what it is used to, and mutinously indisposed to face the painful and unaccustomed exertion of thought or artistic perception, though not without a certain practical shrewdness as to the worth of its money, which makes it very necessary to give good value for it in amusement, excitement, and, above all, in that moral satisfaction produced by the spectacle of punishment spread over crime like jam over butter.

The melodramas of Buckstone and the acting of Céleste had no other purpose in the world that I could ever discover beyond the exploitation of this stratum of the playgoing world to the uttermost farthing. Considered in relation to any other purpose, Green Bushes is foolish and Miami-Céleste impossible. This is apparent to everybody now that the purpose is no longer fulfilled,

* J. S. Coyne's The Woman in Red (1868). Shaw had seen this play and The Green Bushes in Dublin in his teens.

the falling-off in the efficiency of the play being due, not, I regret to say, to any elevation of the taste of its audience, but simply to a change of fashion in stage folly. Green Bushes now looks dowdy, and it is accordingly found out and cut by the very people who would sedulously chatter its praises in order to prove their culture if it were up to date in externals. This, I apprehend, is why Mr Hollingshead has not ventured to revive it as it originally stood. Instead, he has, by a happy thought, changed it into an opera, thereby securing for its absurdities the benefit of the unwritten law by which the drama which is sung is allowed to lag half a century behind that which is spoken.

If the experiment succeeds, we shall perhaps have The Wreck Ashore set to music by Mr Haydn Parry and revived. I shall not object, for Miami entertained me more than most comic operas do, the obvious reason being that Buckstone was a playwright without genius trying to be popularly sentimental, an attempt in which a man of ordinary sense and sympathy may attain a tolerable measure of success, wheras your modern comic opera librettist is mostly a man without brains trying to be clever, which is out of the question. This is the most that can be said for the Green Bushes basis of Miami; and I think that if Mr Hollingshead will rub the glamor of old times out of his eyes, and contemplate that last act gravely from the point of view of the rational stranger who never heard of Madame Céleste or Paul Bedford, he will agree with me that its day is happily past.

And before he changes that attitude, he might as well take the opportunity to forget that Grinnidge is a notoriously funny part, and Mr. George Barrett a notoriously funny actor; so that, escaping for a moment from the foregone conclusion that Mr Barrett's Grinnidge is a screamingly funny performance, he may be able to give him a friendly hint that it is a noisy, slovenly business, unworthy of a comedian of Mr Barrett's standing. Mr Barrett himself, indeed, continues to intimate, by an expressive gag, that he considers the part an impossible one. All the more reason why he should take it quietly.

The cast does credit to Mr Hollingshead's judgment. Miss Jessie Bond did not appear on the night of my visit; but the lady who took her place sang pleasantly, and would no doubt have spoken equally well if she had frankly given up her hopeless attempt at a brogue. Miss Violet Cameron played Miami with a wholehearted loyalty to the management, which stopped at nothing but the firing off of a Martini rifle, a weapon unknown to Céleste and Fenimore Cooper. Her voice is in excellent preservation, sound and sympathetic in the middle, as a properly used voice of its age ought to be. Miami's songs are all encored; and the audience does not laugh at her when she is not singing, a fact which speaks volumes for Miss Cameron's earnestness. Miss Isabella Girardot celebrates the virtues and misfortunes of Geraldine in song; and Mr Courtice Pounds struggles bravely to avoid the throaty habits which seemed at one time likely to cost him his voice. The score, which was probably composed originally to some other libretto, is pretty in a well-established way, with plenty of bright and tender orchestral color; but it has been considerably shorn on the comic side, the numbers for Jack Gong and Grinnidge appearing only in the program—which, by the way, costs nothing, and is full of instruction and amusement. Miss Clara Jecks enters into the humors of the Mrs Gong, *née* Tigertail, much further than I could; but the opera is certainly none the heavier for her. Each act contains at least one effective *coup de théâtre* in the way of a *finale* or a dance. *Matinées* are promised of Cavalleria, Suppé's Galatea, Handel's Rinaldo (!), Dr Arne's Artaxerxes (good heavens!), and an original operetta by Mr Squiers, not to mention a Christmas play for children. I am sure I wish Mr Hollingshead every success.

I have said my say so often about Gounod, our XIX century Fra Angelico, that I need not add to the burden of the obituary notices that have been laid upon us since his death on Wednesday last. In his honor the program of the Saturday concert at the Crystal Palace was altered so as to include his Religious March and the overture to Mireille. The march was only nominally appropriate: it is, in truth, an uninspired affair, with a trio that would not surprise anyone in a second-rate comic opera. That exquisite little funeral march from Roméo, called Juliet's Last Sleep, would have been far better. Mireille was altogether charming: the beautiful smoothness of its lines and the transparent richness and breadth of its orchestral coloration were admirably reproduced by the Crystal Palace band. In the sixties the Parisian critics found it Wagnerian: nowadays the abyss of erroneousness—not to say downright ignorance—revealed by such an opinion makes one giddy.

After the Gounod numbers came an orchestral prelude to The Eumenides of Eschylus, by Mr W. Wallace, whose Passing of Beatrice made some mark last year. Like that work, it shewed that Mr Wallace knows how to use every instrument except the scissors. It is all that a young man's work ought to be, imaginative, ambitious, impetuous, romantic, prodigal, and most horribly indiscriminate. Mr Wallace's imagination is so susceptible, and his critical faculty so unsuspicious, that when he once gets exalted he will keep pegging away at a figure long after it has been worn threadbare, or he will remind you, in the thick of The Eumenides, of the bathers' chorus in Les Huguenots, because he cannot resist a few rushing bassoon scales. If every bar in the overture were as good as the best, it would be very good;

and if every bar were as bad as the worst, it would be very bad: further than that I decline to go, as there is no saying what Mr Wallace would be at next if he were rashly encouraged. Mr Manns and the band covered themselves with glory in Schumann's first symphony, which was very welcome after Saint-Saëns' violin concerto in B minor, with its trivially pretty scraps of serenade music sandwiched between pages from the great masters. Miss Frida Scotta failed to interest me either in the concerto or in her own certainly very surprising technical skill. The vocal part of the concert was unusually strong, Miss Emma Juch very nearly vanquishing the difficulties of Softly Sighs, and shewing herself at any rate a highly cultivated singer; whilst Mr David Bispham attacked a still more difficult song—Purcell's Mad Tom—and was completely victorious.

BEETHOVEN'S *UNSTERBLICHE GELIEBTE*

The World, 1 November 1893

Those who are interested in everything concerning Beethoven, even in his music, will perhaps be interested by Mariam Tenger's Recollections of Countess Theresa Brunswick, translated by Gertrude Russell, and just published by Fisher Unwin. Theresa was one of the noble Viennese ladies with whom Beethoven fell in love. According to Frau Tenger the two were engaged for four years, and the Countess was the "unsterbliche Geliebte" to whom he wrote the famous letter of July 6th, 1806, which was found among his papers after his death, having been presumably returned when the "All is over between us" stage of the adventure was reached—unless, indeed, we are to suppose that Beethoven, like

Mr Toots,* amused himself by imaginary correspondences. For my part, I find the letter too idiotic to be other than a genuine love letter. The prodigious literary vogue which these tender episodes enjoy is due to the fact that very few people in the world have ever had a love affair.

Larochefoucauld was of the opinion that most of us would never fall in love if we had never read anything about it; but I go further: I affirm that in spite of our reading, and the ambition it gives us to have an affair of the heart, the great majority never realize that ambition, and have to marry with a guilty consciousness of falling considerably short of the ardent condition in which the other party seems an *unsterbliche Geliebte.* We take an interest in love stories by the law of nature which Richelieu turned to account when he hung one side of his ante-room with battle pictures and the other with domestic subjects in order to keep the soldier apart from the bourgeois, each, of course, crowding to the side which shewed him the romance of his life, and turning his back on the reality.

Let no one, then, rashly set me down as unsympathetic because I cannot gush with Frau Tenger over the Countess Theresa. You have only to think for a moment to see that the first qualification of a good art critic is extreme susceptibility to beauty, a fatal gift which exposes its possessor professionally to actions for libel, and privately to suits for breach of promise. Unlike the general reader, I have been in love, like Beethoven, and have written idiotic love letters, many of which, I regret to say, have *not* been returned; so that instead of turning up among my papers after my death, they will probably be published by inconsiderate admirers during my lifetime, to my utter confusion. My one comfort is, that

* Character in Dickens's Dombey and Son.

whatever they may contain—and no man is more oblivious of their contents than I am—they cannot be more fatuous than Beethoven's. I have a modest confidence that at the worst I shall not fall below the standard of punctuation set by that great man in the following:

"My angel, my all, my soul!—a few words only today, and those with pencil (with THINE!). After tomorrow it is uncertain where I shall be, what a wretched waste of time this is—why this deep sorrow when necessity speaks—can our love live except by sacrifices, in not asking for all, is thine the power to change it, that thou art not wholly mine, I not wholly thine—O God, behold the beauty of Nature, and let that calm thy mind concerning the inevitable—love rightly demands all, so it is with *me and thee,* with *thee and me*—but thou forgettest so easily that I must live for *myself* and for *thee*—were we not wholly united in heart the pain of this would affect thee as little as it would me—my journey was fearful—I only arrived here yesterday morning at four o'clock," &c. &c.

This is foolish enough; but it is worth quoting as an attempt to *compose* in letters. All Beethoven's music is an expression of his mood; and here he tries to make words do for him what he was accustomed to make notes and chords do.

I must confess to having read the little book from beginning to end with insurmountable scepticism. Not that I doubt the good faith of Frau Tenger; but the fact is, she has such a fifty-Ophelia power of turning everything to favor and to prettiness that to accept everything she says *au pied de la lettre* would amount to an abdication of reason. Here, for instance, is a passage of rapt sweetness which will make the hardiest reader shiver:

"Countess Theresa died in the year 1861. In the place where she loved most to live, and where she had been most deeply beloved, there, *in a cool vault,* she was buried."

A lady whose imagination can set a family vault to the tune of As In Cool Grot is to be envied; but I positively decline to accept her statements at par. Even when she tries to report Cornelius, Baron Spaun, and the Countess herself verbatim, there is a suspicious resemblance in their styles. The following specimen is from the Baron:

"I once went to see Beethoven at an unusual hour. He could not hear me, nor could he see me this time, for he was seated with his back towards me. The light from the window fell on the picture which he held in his hands and was kissing tearfully. He was talking to himself, as he often did when he was alone. I did not wish to be an unbidden listener, and drew back at the words: 'Thou wast too great—too like an angel.' When after a time I returned, I found him at the piano, extemporizing gloriously."

I am willing to believe that the Countess was engaged to Beethoven for four years, and that they then had sense enough not to bring the romance to the test of a marriage. Also, that when the Countess had turned fifty, and it was becoming apparent that to have been Beethoven's *Geliebte* was going to be a very big thing, not lightly to be left altogether to frivolous Guicciardi-Gallenbergs and the like, she may, on coming across such a very sympathetic listener as Frau Tenger, have—shall I say played up? However that may be, Frau Tenger's Theresa and Beethoven are clearly ideal figures, and not portraits. Real people are not made that way.

The speech in the book that carries most conviction

is Guicciardi's "I do so long to throw over Gallenberg* and marry that beautiful, horrible Beethoven—if only it were not such a comedown." The authoress is, apparently, not a musician; but nothing worse comes of this than a confusion between Beethoven's two Masses. The book is easy to read, and the facts stated come out clearly enough through the sentimentalizing, which need not impose on any ordinarily hardheaded reader.

Another book which is in evidence just now is Wagner's famous Opera and Drama. Mr Ashton Ellis has doubled the pace of his translation of Wagner's prose works, which is now coming out in sixtyfour-page two-shilling parts, so as to complete a volume every year. The last few parts have been occupied with the translation of the book which did more than any other writing of Wagner's to change people's minds on the subject of opera.

Like all the books which have this mind-changing property—Buckle's History of Civilization, Marx's Capital, and Ruskin's Modern Painters are the first instances that occur to me—it professes to be an extraordinarily erudite criticism of contemporary institutions, and is really a work of pure imagination, in which a great mass of facts is so arranged as to reflect vividly the historical and philosophical generalizations of the author, the said generalizations being nothing more than an eminently thinkable arrangement of his own way of looking at things, having no objective validity at all, and owing its subjective validity and apparent persuasiveness to the fact that the rest of the world is coming round by mere natural growth to the author's feeling, and therefore wants "proof," historical,

* Giulietta Guicciardi was a Viennese pianist who studied under Beethoven and became his lover. In 1803 she married Count Wenzel Robert von Gallenberg, a composer of ballets.

philosophical, moral, and so on, that it is "right" in its new view. People who are still in a state of perfect satisfaction with Faust and Les Huguenots, and perfectly bored by Tristan and puzzled by Parsifal, will never be persuaded by Opera and Drama that opera is a flimsy sham, standing as an inevitable refuse product at the end of a historic evolution in which the rise of Christianity is but an incident.

Wagner's *aperçus* of the whole history of human thought and aspiration, culminating in the double world-catastrophe of Meyerbeer being mistaken for a great composer and Mendelssohn for a model conductor of Beethoven's symphonies, are enormously suggestive to me, clearing my perception of the whole situation as regards modern music, and entertaining me beyond measure by the author's display of transcendent inventiveness and intellectual power. But I can shift my point of view back to that of the elderly gentlemen who still ask for nothing better than another Mario to sing *Spirto gentil* or *Di pescatore* for them, or a quartet of Italian singers capable of doing justice to *A te, O cara.* To recommend them to join the ranks of Mr Ashton Ellis's subscribers would be to mock them.

I can remember when I was a boy being introduced to Wagner's music for the first time by hearing a second-rate military band play an arrangement of the Tannhäuser march. And do you suppose that it was a revelation to me? Not a bit of it: I thought it a rather commonplace plagiarism from the famous theme in Der Freischütz; and this boyish impression was exactly the same as that recorded by the mature Berlioz, who was to me then the merest shadow of a name which I had read once or twice. At that time I was in a continual state of disappointment because the operatic music which had so delighted and stirred me as a child seemed no longer to inspire singers.

I will hardly be believed now when I say that Donizetti's Lucrezia was once really tragic and romantic, and the Inflammatus in Rossini's Stabat Mater really grand; but it was so. What is now known only as the spavined *cheval de bataille* of obsolete Italian *prima donnas* and *parvenu* Italian tenors was formerly a true Pegasus, which carried fine artists aloft as Gounod's music carries Jean de Reszke—or did until it was superseded in his worship by the music of Wagner (I see by the latest interviews that Jean now declares that Siegfried is his favorite part. I have hardly recovered my breath since).

I have no doubt that if Rossini had had Wagner's brains, he too would have produced magnificent generalizations and proved his William Tell the heir of all the ages; but as he would also in that case have written much better music, I, for one, should not have objected. He would have been quoted with the utmost reverence in the days when people could not hear any melody in Die Meistersinger, and when the Philharmonic Society used to think Spohr's Power of Sound, as it was called, one of the greatest of instrumental masterpieces. Nowadays everybody under forty sees that all the composers that have lived since Beethoven would not, if rolled into one, make a single Wagner; and I am obliged to conceal the fact that I know every bar of Lucrezia as well as I know Pop Goes the Weasel, lest I should be stripped of my critical authority as a hopeless old fogey. Let me then rather pose as a cynical survivor of reputations. It was only last Saturday, at the Popular Concert, that I was compelled to confess that some of the first movement of Haydn's quartet in G minor (Op. 76, No. 2)* shewed

* Shaw was in error here. Haydn's string quartet, Op. 76, No. 2, is in D minor. The Brahms quartet mentioned four lines later is Op. 25, in G minor.

signs of infirmity, one or two passages being positively decrepit. Perhaps in a few years more the whole movement will sound very nearly as old as the next new comic opera. And yet Haydn was all but an immortal once. Brahms's quartet in the same key was quite clearly far in advance of it in harmonic structure and richness of color. That does not seem half so odd as the fact that the newer work is already thirty years old, dating, happily, from those early days when the composer eschewed the intellectual, and did not feel called on to write Requiems. As to Chopin's Funeral March sonata, played very well by Mr Borwick on a magnificent Steinway, nothing was clearer about it than that it beat Haydn's work in point of form. Yes, I quite mean it: it was as if Haydn had put his bricks into a hod in a set pattern, whilst Chopin had built something with his.

Miss Wietrowetz led the quartet admirably. The gentlemen who declare that she plays out of tune do not know the difference between German intonation and Spanish. She is in every way a worthy successor of Neruda. I have been a great admirer of Lady Hallé in her day, and am so still; but she missed the highest excellence as a quartet player by depending too much on her genius and too little on the devotion which expresses itself in careful rehearsal. On that point I think Fräulein Wietrowetz will beat her, as it is fit that the younger artist, standing on the older one's shoulders, should.

A SULPHUROUS SUBLIMITY

The World, 8 November 1893

When the fierce strain put by my critical work on my powers of attention makes it necessary for me to allow my mind to ramble a little by way of relief, I like to go to the Albert Hall to hear one of the performances of the Royal Choral Society. I know nothing more interesting in its way than to wake up occasionally from a nap in the amphitheatre stalls, or to come out of a train of political or philosophic speculation, to listen for a few moments to an adaptation of some masterpiece of music to the tastes of what is called "the oratorio public." Berlioz's Faust is a particularly stiff subject for Albert Hall treatment. To comb that wild composer's hair, stuff him into a frock-coat and tall hat, stick a hymn book in his hand, and obtain reverent applause for his ribald burlesque of an Amen chorus as if it were a genuine Handelian solemnity, is really a remarkable feat, and one which few conductors except Sir Joseph Barnby could achieve. Instead of the brimstonish orgy in Auerbach's cellar we have a *soirée* of the Young Men's Christian Association; the drunken blackguardism of Brander is replaced by the decorous conviviality of a respectable young bank clerk obliging with a display of his baritone voice (pronounced by the local pianoforte tuner equal to Hayden Coffin's); Faust reminds one of the gentleman in Sullivan's Sweethearts; the whiskered pandoors and the fierce hussars on the banks of the Danube become a Volunteer corps on the banks of the Serpentine; and all Brixton votes Berlioz a great composer, and finds a sulphurous sublimity in the whistles on the piccolo and clashes of the cymbals which bring Mr Henschel, as Mephistopheles, out of his chair. This does not mean that Berlioz has converted Brixton: it means that Brixton has converted Berlioz. Such conversions are always going on. The African heathen "embrace" the Christian religion by singing a Te Deum instead of dancing a war-dance after "wetting their spears" in the blood of the tribe next door; the English heathen (a much more numerous body) take to reading the Bible when it is edited for them by Miss Marie Corelli*; the masses, sceptical as to Scott and Dumas, are converted to an appreciation of romantic literature by Mr Rider Haggard; Shakespear and Goethe become world famous on the strength of "acting versions" that must have set them fairly spinning in their graves; and there is a general appearance of tempering the wind to the shorn lamb, which turns out, on closer examination, to be really effected by building a badly ventilated suburban villa round the silly animal, and telling him that the frowsy warmth he begins to feel is that of the sunbeam playing on Parnassus, or the peace of mind that passeth all understanding, according to circumstances. When I was young, I was like all immature critics: I used to throw stones at the windows of the villa, and thrust in my head and bawl at the lamb that he was a fool, and that the villa builders—honest people enough, according to their lights—were swindlers and hypocrites, and nincompoops and sixth-raters. But the lamb got on better with them than with me; and at last it struck me that he was happier and more civilized in his villa than shivering in the keen Parnassian winds that delighted my hardier bones; so that now I have become quite fond of him, and love to lead him out when the

* Miss Corelli, a novelist with a propensity for religious subjects, had just published a successful novel, Barabbas (1893).

weather is exceptionally mild (the wind being in the Festival cantata quarter perhaps), and talk to him a bit without letting him see too plainly what a deplorable muttonhead he is. Dropping the metaphor, which is becoming unmanageable, let me point out that the title of Berlioz's work is The Damnation of Faust, and that the most natural abbreviation would be, not Berlioz's Faust, but Berlioz's Damnation. Now the Albert Hall audience would certainly not feel easy with such a phrase in their mouths. I have even noticed a certain reluctance on the part of mixed assemblies of ladies and gentlemen unfamiliar with the German language to tolerate discussions of Wagner's Götterdämmerung, unless it were mentioned only as The Dusk of the Gods. Well, the sole criticism I have to make of the Albert Hall performance is that the damnation has been lifted from the work. It has been "saved," so to speak, and jogs along in a most respectable manner. The march, which suggests household troops cheered by enthusiastic nursemaids, is encored; and so is the dance of sylphs, which squeaks like a tune on the hurdy-gurdy. The students' Jam nox stellata sounds as though middle-aged commercial travelers were having a turn at it. On the whole the performance, though all the materials and forces for a good one are at the conductor's disposal, is dull and suburban. The fact is, Berlioz is not Sir Joseph Barnby's affair. On Thursday last (note that the concert night is changed back again from Wednesday to Thursday) Gounod's Religious March was played, as at the Crystal Palace. A printed slip was circulated asking the audience to stand up. What value a demonstration manufactured in this way can have I do not see, especially when the performance of the march at the Crystal Palace had proved that it would not have occurred spontaneously. It jarred on me as a forced and flunkeyish maneuvre; and I took no part in it. I have sufficient feeling about Gounod not to permit myself to be instructed in the matter by impertinent persons communicating with me by anonymous slips of paper. Besides, I object to confer on a trumpery *pièce d'occasion* the distinction which is the traditional English appanage of Handel's Hallelujah Chorus

My great difficulty in describing Mr Cowen's Norwich Festival cantata The Water Lily is to find a point of view sufficiently remote from commonsense to enable me to keep my countenance during the process. The most ordinary decencies of professional etiquet bind me to accept with enthusiasm the lines of my distinguished fellow-critic. For instance:

> Though I know not where thou art,
> Well I know thou hast my heart.
>
> . . .
>
> Nor so long be coyly hiding,
> In my arms is thy abiding.
>
> . . .
>
> He is thine, and oer the tide
> Thou shalt go to be his bride,
> Yield thee to love's soft allure,
> Never lived a knight so pure.

If I am ever paid to write a libretto in this style, I will simply buy a bushel of Christmas cards and fall to with scissors and paste. But then I have not the true poetic gift. The worst of it is that Mr Cowen evidently has not got it either; for he has found no inspiration in Mr Bennett's numbers. Perhaps he did not want it: it may be that as long as Mr Cowen has any sort of *locus standi* for his orchestrating and modulating he is happy. But in that case I beg to say emphatically that I am not. The English horn is a very pretty instrument; and when it has some real work to do, as in the third act of Tristan,

I am delighted to hear it. But when, having nothing to do, it insists on shewing itself off to me instead of holding its tongue, I find it an impertinent bore. Similarly, that pet transition from one major common chord to another lying a semitone higher, is magical in the first scene of the third act of Siegfried, where it has some very momentous business to transact; but a mere row of samples of it does not seem to me a fair equivalent for a piece of original composition.

Mr Cowen is too old now to be allowed to play with chords as children do with scraps of colored paper, or even as Mozart and Rossini, in their nonage, played with the ordinary dominant cadence. Some of Mr Cowen's little harmonic sweetmeats are by no means to my taste. It seems a hopelessly obsolete thing to quarrel with a composer for "false relations" nowadays; but still there is reason in everything. Take the case of a phrase in the key of A flat major stepping off C to B flat in order to spring up immediately to E flat, and accompanied in simple two-part harmony by A flat, G, C. Is it good sense, or rather good sound, to make the G flat, unless you want to shew that old prohibition of false relations and consecutive major intervals had something in it after all?

What matter if the G natural would make the phrase remind everyone of the love duet in Gounod's Faust? Better that than the suggestion of a wrong note. However, I suppose Mr Cowen likes it. I can only repeat doggedly, bigotedly, irreconcilably, that I dont. Why should I? If it were expressive of the accompanying words I should accept it without question—without consciousness, probably. But it is set to the words "Sleep and dream." Who on earth dreams of "false relations"?

For the honor of the cloth I must point out how faithfully Mr Bennett gives his composer the full regulation set of chances—the vision, the pastoral, the storm, the tournament, the funeral march, and the love duet all complete. The introduction of the storm is particularly ingenious. Merlin, taking a walk on the sands, sees Ina's ship in full sail, and falls in love with it. After various rapturous compliments, he continues:

Hither, my bird, that I may view thy crest,
Which now appears as though a flower
Had opened that a goddess might emerge.
What! Dost pass me by contemptuously,
With mock obeisance? Thou my power shalt know
In loss of all thy beauty and thy pride,
So soon love turns to hate when love is scorned.
  Spirits of storm, awake, &c. &c.

A fearful tempest then rages in the orchestra, and the ship is annihilated. Merlin's conscience at once begins to act, and he says, with irresistible bathos:

The earth contains so much of beauty less,
And I despise myself.

Perhaps it will be better for me to say now, without further circumlocution, that the whole entertainment bored me. No doubt a great poet, writing at a period when fairy romances had for the moment fascinated the imagination of the world, might have made a real poem of The Water Lily, and inspired a composer to set it to music. But as that period is passed, and Mr Bennett is (as far as I can judge) no more a poet than I am, he has produced nothing that has any beauty in its own versification or any vitality in its matter for the composer to work on.

Mr Cowen has just managed, by an elaboration of his drawing-room ballad style, to produce one or two really pretty and live bits for the soprano; but the rest is the merest playing with chords and instruments. This sort of trifling, in the hands of men in whom professorial pedantry has extinguished all musical susceptibility, sometimes produces a technical experiment or two of a certain mechanical interest to experts. But Mr Cowen, being still a musician, trifles only with effects that have charmed his ear in the music of Wagner and Gounod. For instance, Norma's boat-song, Swiftest birds that ever flew (need I add that the next line is To your mission be ye true?), is a very pretty bit of harmonic change-ringing; but Mr Cowen can hardly expect anyone who has heard those changes in the original compositions from which he has taken them to be much interested.

No doubt plenty of simple people who have never heard these original compositions will be charmed with The Water Lily. The same people will, as likely as not, find Mr Bennett's verses as poetic as Mr Stopford Brooke* finds Wordsworth's. I do not quarrel with their opinion. I simply record my own. The Water Lily, like St John's Eve, Jubal's Dream, and all the other works which have been manufactured by the same process, altogether fail to please me. I do not say they are bad; I do not attempt to prove that they are "wrong"; I do not deny that choral societies sing them, and that audiences pay at least once to hear them sung; I do not question the genius of the composers or the impartiality of the librettist-analyst-critic; I do not assert, suggest, imply, or hint anything about anybody but myself; and of myself I only say—fully admitting that the fact may be entirely discreditable to me—that, if the whole collection of these works were in my power, I would unhesitatingly commit them to the nearest County Council "destructor."

* The Rev. Stopford Brooke, an Irish-born cleric, wrote several studies of English literature. Shaw may have been alluding to his Dove Cottage (1890).

IRISH PATRIOTISM AND ITALIAN OPERA

The World, 15 November 1893

Mr Henschel opened his London Symphony campaign on Wednesday last. When I arrived at half-past eight I found the concert in full swing, and a bevy of belated persons shut out on the stairs and arguing that the concert did not and could not begin at eight because the time printed on their tickets was half-past—much in the vein of the lawyer who proved to the man in the stocks that he could not have been put there because his offence was not legally punishable in that way. You find ladies, in particular, disposed to treat a misunderstanding of this kind as a personal matter between themselves and the gentleman who takes their tickets at the door, and who is, of course, obviously quite innocent and quite helpless. For my part, I magnanimously made no fuss, feeling quite well able to put up with the loss of Tchaikovsky's elegy and of the first two movements of Max Bruch's violin concerto. I will take it for granted that Miss Frida Scotta played those two movements better than the third, which she attacked with a sort of muscular passion that seemed to make her insensible to every consideration except breaking the record for speed. She afterwards re-established herself in some degree by playing Svendsen's Romance with expression and even with refinement; but then Svendsen's Romance is not a very abstruse work. Probably as time goes on Miss Frida Scotta will begin to study her concertos poetically as well as physically, and to assert the feeling of the composition as earnestly as she now asserts her own execution of its technical difficulties. At present her concerto playing, though sometimes astonishing, is prosaic, and often insensitive and inelegant in decorative passages.

Professor Villiers Stanford has broken out again with a very Irish song, Prince Madoc's Farewell, sung so patriotically by Mr Plunket Greene that he once or twice almost burst into the next key. Patriotism is, fundamentally, a conviction that a particular country is the best in the world because you were born in it; and it is therefore as well to keep it strictly in tune when you happen to be in some other country for the moment. Irish patriotism is a particularly trying variety, especially to the Englishman. It is intensely melancholy, for no reason whatever; wheras English patriotism, though equally unreasonable, is convivial.

Again, Irish patriotism has the subjectivity of pure feeling: it expresses itself in wailing melody, and, when forced to associate words with that melody, declines to pronounce them distinctly. But the patriotic Englishman, when sober, is highly articulate, and always knows his words—Britons never, never, &c., We always are ready: steady, boys, steady, We dont want to fight; *but*, &c., Who's afraid? Never say die, and so on—though he frequently breaks down most ingloriously when he tries to remember the tune. Now, in Ireland, nobody ever knows the words of anything; though a native who does not know the tune of everything may safely be put down as having no musical faculty whatever.

It is for this reason that Italian opera is so much more genuinely popular in Ireland than in England, and why librettos sell so badly there. The Irishman is absolutely satisfied with the melody of *Il balen*, and *encores* it for the hundredth time without dreaming of asking what the words mean. If they were English words he would be equally ignorant; for he would never take the trouble to attach any ideas to them. Ask him the English for *Il balen*, and he will pull himself together; make a perceptible intellectual effort; and observe that his Italian is rather rusty, but that he supposes it means a piece of whalebone, or something of that sort. When he turns back to the music, his intellect will go to sleep again, and he will not think for a moment of the absurdity of the Count di Luna passionately apostrophizing a piece of whalebone. Mr Plunket Greene, in spite of all his English experience and training, no sooner got steeped in Stanford's Irish melody than his words began to lose all sharpness of definition, and at last, in one poignant moment, trailed off into an inarticulate cry.

If he would like to learn how that affects an Englishman, he should read Chorley's criticism on Catherine Hayes,* with its complaint that all Irish singers deliver their words indistinctly and without meaning, and are monotonous and uninteresting in spite of their musical facility and charm of voice. It is the old English grievance against us: we are emotionally too barbarously excitable, and intellectually never in earnest. No doubt Mr Plunket Greene, as an Irishman, holds as I do that the real truth of the matter is that the English brain is so dense that it is only by a strenuous and most desperately serious effort that the Englishman can set his intellect in action, a feat so easy to the Irishman that he is constantly doing it merely to amuse himself, and so acquires a playful intellectual manner as naturally as the Englishman acquires a ponderous and solemn one.

It has taken me nearly twenty years of studied self-restraint, aided by the natural decay of my faculties, to make myself dull enough to be accepted as a serious

* Irish soprano (1825–61), student of Garcia, who performed on every continent of the world. She made her London *dèbut* at Covent Garden in Donizetti's Linda di Chamounix, 1849.

person by the British public; and I am not sure that I am not still regarded as a suspicious character in some quarters. But what I would put to Mr Greene is that since we are here, and dependent for our livelihoods on the sixpences and shillings of the British public, we must give them what they like and not what we like. And so, when next Prince Madoc's Farewell is in the program, let the words be delivered with an air of careful and persuasive intelligence, and never mind the melody. Above all, no patriotism.

Professor Stanford is naturally at his best in a piece of folk-music, since it is the one indulgence a professor is allowed by the etiquet of his profession. All the rest of the time the academic musician must write oratorios; search for some form of the plagal cadence that has not been anticipated by Dr Parry; compose canons nineteen-in-twenty-six *al rovescio*; teach students that the theme of the *finale* of Mozart's E flat symphony is "better avoided," because the quaver F, being a passing note, should not skip down to B flat; and generally waste his time, blaspheme against his art, abdicate his manhood, and dishonor his reason. Only, he is allowed occasionally to practise as he pleases on a little folk-music, lest he should commit suicide. And Professor Stanford does it with infinite yearning and relief which enters into his music and gives it a searching pathos. He seems to cry out through all the instruments "I have been starving on Festival fare for years: now at last I may have some music." Mr Joseph Bennett, strange to say, has entirely missed this aspect of Professor Stanford's composition; for not a word is said of it in the analytic program.

To make amends, however, there is a surprisingly eloquent description of Brahms's first symphony, not in inverted commas, and therefore presumably original. This symphony is a wonderful feat of the young Brahms—a mere heap of lumps of absolute music; but then, such magnificent lumps! such color! such richness of substance! one is amazed to find the man who dug them out half smothering them with mere slag, and quite unable to construct anything with them. Mr Henschel, though neither he nor the band were at their best, brought off a vigorous performance which roused much enthusiasm. We also had an orchestral arrangement of the flower-maiden scene from Parsifal. It was rough and hurried, and must have sounded very glum without the girls' voices to those who did not know the work.

But the Bayreuth pilgrims no doubt enjoyed it, and saw in imagination all the *naïve* enchantments of the Festspielhaus—the pantomimic flowers, the damsels running away and returning decorated with monstrous tufts of red and blue paper, and the magical apparition of Kundry, in an antique ball-dress with ruchings, alluringly disposed on a sofa, and pulled out from the wing by a cable, presumably hauled by a pair of horses, the weight being not less than seventeen stone.

I must say I do not clearly see why we should be put off with these "arrangements" of Wagner. Mr Henschel has a choir with plenty of young ladies in it. He can find a tenor and soprano for Parsifal and Kundry just as easily as for Walther and Eva. Why not give us the music as it was written, instead of treating us to the accompaniments alone, with Kundry's call touched in on the cornet-à-piston? What would Mr Henschel say if Richter, instead of engaging him to sing Pogner's address and Wotan's farewell and summons to Loki, were to have them economically performed on the euphonium?

Madame Favart has been revived at the Criterion Theatre. Although it is one of Offenbach's late works, quite mild and domestic in comparison with La Belle Hélène or La Grande Duchesse, it is far less like itself at the Criterion than the works of Planquette, or even Lecocq. Of the true Offenbachianismus—the restless movement, the witty abandonment, the swift, light, wicked touch, the inimitable sly *élan* stealing into concerted pieces as light as puff paste—there is not a trace left in Mr Wyndham's revival. The effervescent orchestration, with its Bohemian economy in the woodwind, and its devilish grace and swagger to make up for its poverty, no longer puts any sort of face on its own shorthandedness. Even the rowdy big drum, which always marked Offenbach out as a musical blackguard in spite of his cleverness, thumps away without any of the old enjoyment.

Of late years we have accustomed ourselves to a ponderous style of execution, sentimental or inane as the case may be, and to thicker scoring, heavier *finales*, and a larger assortment of discords—especially tonic discords—than would have been tolerated in Offenbach's time; and it says a great deal for the grace, gaiety, and intelligence of his work that it should hold its own still even when performed, as it most ruthlessly is at the Criterion, without any of the piquancies of style which he and his librettists had in contemplation. Occasionally, however, it gains by the change; for it is hardly necessary to remark that the old style had its vicious side. It was not only smart, lively, and cynical, but it was abjectly afraid to be anything else; and this cowardice made it irritating and contemptible as soon as it began to get a little stale. Since then a course of Dorothy and her imitators has made us infinitely tolerant of sentimental melodies and witless words; and now that we are turning back to Offenbach, our musical handling of him, though very clumsy, is not so heartless as it used to be, whilst the books of his operas appear quite intellectual to us.

As an operatic manager Mr Wyndham cannot be counted among the moderns. Since he has resorted to comic opera more or less as a stopgap, and is not counting on very long runs, or on the Criterion acquiring an operatic reputation, he is naturally content to fit up his revivals on ready-made lines. Still, there is one matter in which he seems needlessly old-fashioned. Nothing marks off Mr D'Oyly Carte from his rivals more effectually and favorably than the fact that on the Savoy stage the women appear as women, and the men as men. The old rule was that the women should appear as men, and the men be hidden as much as possible behind the women. Every regiment of soldiers was a row of mincing, plump, self-conscious young women in satin uniforms, pinched at the waist and toes, and bulbous in the unpinched regions.

The founders of this tradition must have conceived it to be a seductive one; but I, who have seen whole armies of these female warriors from my credulous boyhood onward, am prepared to have my feelings towards them from first to last tested by the austerest canons of propriety. When I first saw them I thought them comically revolting; and what I now think of them is exactly what the Criterion audience thought last Thursday when two of them crossed the stage to reply to a question from Miss St John. As they marched off in the true *opéra-bouffe* army manner Miss St John contemplated them for a moment with an inimitably dubious gravity, and then, in one of her favorite relapses into *gaminerie*, said slowly: "Thanks, gall'nt orficers." The whole house screamed with merriment; and if Mr Wyndham were wise, he would take the female man as laughed off the stage altogether in that outburst.

Madame Favart has, fortunately, a reasonably good book, though, like most of the books of its period, its merits do not hold out to the third act. Mr Wallace Brownlow plays with plenty of fun and spirit as Favart; and the part, however obviously planned for a more mercurial actor, adapts itself to him fairly well. Mr James can neither sing nor even plausibly pretend to sing, not from lack of ear, but because his trick of speech has made his voice useless for lyric purposes; but he manages to pull Pontsablé cleverly through. Mr Emney is perfectly fitted with the part of Biscotin, who is persistently called "Biscotemps" by the others. Miss St John, of course, carries the whole opera on her shoulders, and is not at all overburdened by it, though the music does not lie so easily for her voice in its present phase, and cannot be so conveniently transposed, as that of The Mascotte. Miss Ellis Jeffreys, who in Madame Angot shewed a certain talent which she might take a little more seriously, plays one or two passages in Suzanne very well; but her performance, on the whole, is still a little crude. The book, by the way, would be the better for an overhauling. The late H. B. Farnie was for an age, but not for all time.

GOETZ ÜBER ALLES

The World, 22 November 1893

I continue to be amazed at the way in which the younger generation plays the fiddle. Formerly there were only two sorts of violinists: the Paganinis or Sivoris, and the bad amateurs whose highest flight was an execrable attempt to scrape through a variation or two on The Carnival of Venice. The orchestral players I leave out altogether; for the trade knack they picked up under stress of breadwinning had nothing to do with violin-playing, as one found out when they got promoted to the leader's desk, and had to play an *obbligato* occasionally. Nowadays all that is changed in the most bewildering manner. Europe appears to be full of young ladies between twenty and thirty who can play all the regulation concertos—Beethoven, Mendelssohn, Brahms, Bruch, and Saint-Saëns—and throw in Bach's chaconne in D minor as a solo piece at the end of the concert.

And yet they are not geniuses, though they do with apparent ease the things that only geniuses used to do. I should be tempted to put it all down to the terrific determination with which women are qualifying themselves in all branches for an independent career, were it not that the improvement is discoverable in the young men also—though, of course, no male can hope for such chances of shewing his mettle as are offered readily enough to young women. The fact is, people do not like concertos for their own sake. A concerto must have a hero or a heroine; and every plucky and passably pretty feminine violinist under thirty is a heroine in the imagination of the male audience; wheras a callow young man is not anybody's hero, having no touch of that art of personal beauty and dignity at which every woman with grit enough to face the public at all is at least a passable amateur. He can only play the hero if he is a real genius, wheras his female rival will be heroine enough for the public if she has worked hard enough to be able to play the concerto as her master tells her to play it. Hence we have half a dozen young ladies getting first-rate chances every season, whilst young men who can play as well, or better, languish for years unheard.

Take the case of Mr August Manns, for instance. His generosity to young gentlemen with unperformed orchestral scores is the theme of all our praises at present; and he is a second father to Miss Mary Cardew, Miss Frida Scotta, Miss Beatrice Langley, and the rest of our young lady violinists. But may I suggest to him that as all young gentlemen compose very much alike, and all young ladies play very much alike, it would be a relief if he were to transpose the sexes next season, and treat us to a series of compositions by young women and violin concerto performances by young men.

The fact is, I am getting tired of ladylike versions of Bruch's concerto in G minor—very agreeable and skilful, certainly, but utterly unmemorable. I was greatly pleased with Miss Beatrice Langley's playing of it at the Crystal Palace the other day: her youth, her dexterity, and her quick and delicate musical feeling would have earned her a handsome tribute of praise and encouragement from me a few years ago; but today, somehow, my mind keeps going back to that note at the end of the program: "This concerto was last played at the Saturday Concerts on February 25th, 1893, by Miss Mary Cardew." I was at that concert; and I remember being "greatly pleased" by Miss Mary Cardew's performance—quite astonished, in fact, by her execution of the Bach chaconne.

But I had completely forgotten the concerto when the paragraph re-informed—not reminded—me of it. That may be my own fault, or Max Bruch's; and yet I do not forget Ysaÿe's performances of Bruch. Anyhow, I plead for a chance for the young male fiddler. However unattractive his sex might be, it must at least produce some small percentage of the beginners who deserve a chance with a concerto at our leading orchestral concerts.

The concert at which Miss Langley made her success, and, let me add, shewed some spirit and commonsense by giving the eternal Saint-Saëns a rest, and introducing a welcome novelty in the shape of a capriccio for violin and orchestra by Niels Gade, also gave a lift to Mr Granville Bantock, whose Caedmar, produced by Signor Lago, made us all curious about his overture, The Fire Worshippers. Unluckily, The Fire Worshippers turned out to be an earlier work than Caedmar, mainly occupied with a six-eight movement which was as pure Mendelssohn as Caedmar was pure Wagner. It explained why Mr Bantock got the Macfarren Scholarship at the R.A.M.; but it threw no new light on his development. The Mendelssohn Worshippers was followed by a performance of the Lohengrin prelude in A, finely executed by the wind, and very poorly indeed by the strings. The gem of the concert was Goetz's symphony, which has fallen into neglect because, I suppose, it is the only real symphony that has been composed since Beethoven died. Beside it Mendelssohn's Scotch symphony is no symphony at all, but only an enchanting *suite de pièces*; Schubert's symphonies seem mere debauches of exquisitely musical thoughtlessness; and Schumann's, though genuinely symphonic in ambition, fall short in actual composition. Goetz alone among the modern symphonists is easily and unaffectedly successful from beginning to end.

He has the charm of Schubert without his brainlessness, the refinement and inspiration of Mendelssohn without his limitation and timid gentility, Schumann's sense of harmonic expression without his laboriousness, shortcoming, and dependence on external poetic stimulus; while as to unembarrassed mastery of the material of music, shewing itself in the Mozartian grace and responsiveness of his polyphony, he leaves all three of them simply nowhere. Brahms, who alone touches him in mere brute musical faculty, is a dolt in comparison to him.

You have to go to Mozart's finest quartets and quintets on the one hand, and to Die Meistersinger on the other, for work of the quality we find, not here and there, but continuously, in the symphony in F and in The Taming of the Shrew, two masterpieces which place Goetz securely above all other German composers of the last hundred years, save only Mozart and Beethoven, Weber and Wagner. Of course, if Goetz were alive this would be an excellent reason for opposing him tooth and nail, for the same reasons that moved Salieri to oppose Mozart. A very little Goetz would certainly spoil the market for Festival symphonies; but now that the man is dead, why may we not have the symphony made a stock-piece at the London Symphony and Richter concerts, and performed oftener than once in four years at the Crystal Palace?

There is that beautiful Spring Overture, too, which the lamented Macfarren denounced as containing unlawful consecutive sevenths. Are we never to hear those consecutive sevenths again? Is it to be always Brahms and Bruch and Liszt, until our rising generation loses all sense of the subtle but immense difference between first-rate and second-rate in contemporary symphonic music?

From Goetz's symphony to the second edition of Morocco Bound is one of those violent transitions which steel the critic to all reverses of fortune. Morocco Bound is not bad fun: its success, as I shall presently shew, is by no means undeserved. But it has certain defects which must be as objectionable to nine out of ten of the people in the theatre as they are to me. Take the orchestration, for example. Does anybody really enjoy music of which every alternate four bars or so is played *fortissimo* on two cornets in unison, one trombone supplying a bass, two horns filling in the middle parts, and a side-drum rolling all the time *con tutta la forza.* The stridency and frequency of this exasperating noise at the Shaftesbury would try the endurance of an agricultural laborer, much less a nervous Londoner. I am prepared to put up with it at a circus or a second-rate music hall; but in a West End theatre, where a stall costs half a guinea, I protest against the marrowbones and cleaver. I find the same kind of fault in the performance of Mr Charles Danby as Higgins. He has plenty of fun in him; and he works hard and successfully to keep the piece going; but he makes an intolerable noise with that brazen voice of his, which at last begins to jar worse than the cornets, horns, trombone, and side-drum all together. Mr Danby may imagine that since he represents a retired costermonger he must bawl through his part as if he were crying the contents of a barrow; but I can assure him, as a critic with a wide and catholic circle of acquaintances, that costermongers do not talk like that, even when they are crying their wares. Persuasiveness is the note of the coster in private conversation; and though in addressing the public he may be stentorian, he is not necessarily unmusical even then. If Mr Danby were a real coster, and were to rasp his customers' ears as he rasped mine nearly all the evening except when he was singing the plantation song, he would go home a bankrupt. Mr Shine, with an equally prominent part, makes fun quietly and with a certain grace and handsomeness which, even in the thinnest parts of the play, protect the audience from being worried. Mr Danby should take the edge off his voice, and provide his grotesque humor with a background of human feeling and expression, however superficial. At present he discounts his fun and amusing feats of activity by that callousness to gratuitously harsh sounds and ugly sights which makes all the difference between the style of an opera comedian like Mr Rutland Barrington, for instance, and that of a music hall "comic."

There is another feature common to Morocco Bound and most entertainments of its class against which I venture to protest. The authors of these works are nothing if not preternaturally smart. It is their boast that there is nothing heavy or Shakespearean about them. Why, then, are they licensed to bore us with elaborate plots and "expositions" thereof which would not be tolerated for a moment from Shakespear or

Goethe? In Morocco Bound there is a plot involving the most complicated family relationships. It is of no use, of no interest: it is tedious, inept, unpardonable; and yet the characters stand there fruitlessly trying to explain it for five minutes at a time as if it were the most succulent dramatic poetry, or the most incandescent comedy. Even if the explanation were successful, and left me in complete command of the fictitious reasons for the presence of Miss Agnes Hewitt, Miss Jennie McNulty, and the rest, I could quite well dispense with them, as I am perfectly willing to accept the company of those ladies without asking any questions. But when the explanation is totally unintelligible, the last excuse for pestering me with it vanishes. If the management must have an "exposition," they had better employ Ibsen or some other reasonably lively person to contrive it for them.

The success of Morocco Bound centres round a single artist—Miss Letty Lind. Sarasate's playing is not more exquisite than her dancing: it is a delight to see her simply march across the stage in time to the music. She is no mere skirt-dancer: if she were invisible from the waist downwards, the motion of her head and wrists would still persuade me to give her anybody's head on a charger—and this is the test of the perfect dancer as distinguished from the mere step-dancer. She gives us all the grace of classical dancing without its insufferable pedantry and its worn-out forms. Her caricatures of academic dancing and amateur dancing are most delicately touched; even the wrestling trick by which Mr Danby throws her heels over head does not disturb her grace and simplicity one jot.

I can quite understand that people go again and again to Morocco Bound to see her; and as she manages to sing very prettily and ingeniously without the formality of a voice, and acts humorously to boot, I do not think

I need hesitate to credit her with practically the entire success of the piece, though I must duly allow that young Mr Grossmith, Mr Colin Coop, and the others kept matters at a very lively pitch between whiles, with Mr Templar Saxe and Miss Maggie Roberts to throw in an occasional drawing-room ballad as a concession to the claims of high art.

THE BARREL-ORGAN QUESTION

The Morning Leader, 27 November 1893, signed "C. di B."

[U] I have been asked for my views on the barrel-organ question. I reply, there is no barrel-organ question. Some years ago I came upon a barrel-organ in the streets of Haarlem; and it was so long since I had heard one before that I stopped to listen to it for the sake of old times. I did not stop long, because I did not know enough of Dutch law to feel sure of a verdict of justifiable homicide in case I impulsively killed the performer; but I could not pass by without dwelling for a moment on the archaic thing that had once been so familiar and so accursed. I will not say that I have not seen one since; but happily I have not heard one. Those which remain are so old and wheezy that the din of the thoroughfare quite drowns their querulous attempts to oblige. There are hundreds of thousands of children in London today who have never heard a barrel-organ. That is a tremendous fact.

When I was a child every respectable house guarded its privacy from the pryings of the people over the way by fitting its parlor window with a perforated wire blind. If you take a magnifying glass and examine the nose of any middle-aged middle-class man you will discover a minute roseate ring pattern printed all over the tip. You can see it on my nose, for instance; and it will go with me to my grave. It is the mark of the perforated wire blind through which I used to peer at the barrel-organs when they ground out their tunes at the area railings. When I look back it seems to me that my whole childhood was passed with my nose pressed against that chilling blind and my eyes riveted either upon an organ-grinder or upon a ton of coals being emptied out of grimy bags through the cellar-plate. The spectacle was not exactly a liberal education; but it enables me to tell the children of today what they have lost through the disappearance of the barrel-organ. There were four varieties of the instrument; the upright, or cottage model, with an effeminate tone intended to be birdlike or fairylike, and perhaps a set of dancing dolls with cymbals; the ordinary square model, usually covered with green baize on which a monkey sat enthroned; the trombone model, which was simply the square one with a trombone bell mounted on it like a maxim gun; and finally the organ on wheels, with a sort of dickey behind in which sat a baby who never grew up. All these, except the last, hung round the performer's neck by a strap, and were supported, when in action, by a stick hooked on underneath. They did not weigh more than half a hundredweight, being made of such light materials that the strain of a single string from a modern street piano would have pulled them to pieces. As to the tone, I will speak as moderately as I can. There were two stops, one consisting of flue pipes, which produced a sort of bronchial cooing, and the other of reed pipes, which snarled self assertively. Both had the property of not standing in tune when exposed to the vicissitudes of our climate. The barrel-organ began its career as an adjunct to divine worship in churches. After about a century of this it took to the streets, and had to be excommunicated.

Twenty years ago it was driven out of the streets by the street piano. It then attached itself to the hobby horse merry-go-round, in connexion with which its peculiar musical qualities, intensified to positive hellishness by steam power, can be sampled by the curious. Any person convicted or even suspected of possessing a steam barrel-organ should have a price placed on his head, to be paid on its delivery, separately from his body, at the nearest Coroner's.

Occasionally I come across a hybrid instrument, half street piano, half barrel-organ, giving forth pianoforte music with wind accompaniments. But Nature has inconsiderately arranged matters so that the change of weather which makes a street pianoforte flat, makes a barrel-organ sharp; and the result is that after a day or two the parts of the combination get into different keys, with an effect so excruciating that even the British Philistine withholds his coppers and hastily takes himself off or orders the executant to move on, as the case may be. So the street piano remains in undisputed possession of the pavement; and I have no doubt that this so-called barrel-organ question on which I am asked, as a musical critic, to give my views, is really the street piano question. Now precisely because I am a musical critic trained by my profession to feats of superhuman endurance of all sorts of musical tortures, I am better able than a layman to bear the street piano. On the other hand, I am accustomed to be paid for my ordeals; and when the street pianist not only refuses to pay me for listening to him, but actually expects me to pay him, I cannot but feel somewhat indignant. Still, I do not allow my temper to get the better of me. When the hat comes round I simply refuse to give on the ground that the tone of the piano is coarse, the variations hackneyed in form, and the performer's undeniable accuracy of execution counterbalanced by his unsympathetic touch.

Unfortunately, I am not backed up in this policy by the citizens of London. They like street pianos. The little girls, too—who seem all nowadays to graduate at Madame Katti Lanner's dancing academy—improvize ballets at the street corners; and this enables people who have grace enough to be ashamed of their vulgar tastes to pretend that they encourage the pianos because they give harmless pleasure to thousands of little ones whose lives sorely need some brightening. Whenever a man begins that story you may safely sit down at once and play him the latest music hall tune 16 times over without stopping. He will *encore* you enthusiastically.

The worst of it is that people with uneducated tastes are in so huge a majority that there is no pressure on the street pianist to improve his performance—that is, to get a better instrument. It must be remembered that instruments with barrels are by no means necessarily coarse or offensive in tone. Messrs Imhof and Mukle will furnish you with a barrel-organ which will turn its own handle and play you all the classical overtures and symphonies with an attention to the composers' marks of expression, *rallentandos, ritardandos,* &c., far more exact and delicate than you would be likely to achieve for yourself with a keyboard. I went into a shop in Regent-street the other day, and was shewn a charming piano-shaped barrel-organ which plays the right notes for you whilst you manipulate the stops so as to produce the orchestral effects, or which you can play in the ordinary way if you please. Elsewhere you can buy a keyboard attachment which, on your simply turning a handle, will play sonatas for you on any pianoforte keyboard, whether it belongs to a £20 cottage terror or a grand by Erard or Steinway. In short, the street piano is only one of a series of automatic musical instruments ranging from the half-crown musical box to the fifteen hundred guinea "orchestrion"; and as street pianos are let out by big capitalist proprietors to the actual players just as hansoms are let out to the drivers, the substitution of a higher class of street instrument for the present model is just as feasible as the introduction of the rubber-tyred cab. The problem is how to bring the demand of the small minority who are educated musicians to bear effectively on the capitalist.

All that is necessary to this end is, I submit, to fall back on the old custom of outlawry. Let a short Act of Parliament be passed, placing all street musicians outside the protection of the law; so that any citizen may assail them with stones, sticks, knives, pistols, or bombs without incurring any penalties—except, of course, in the case of the instrument itself being injured; for Heaven forbid that I should advocate any disregard of the sacredness of property, especially in the form of industrial capital! The effect of this would be that no man would dare play in the streets unless he were sure of being as universally attractive as Orpheus with his lute. He would strive to literally disarm criticism by using a high-class instrument; and his civility and anxious readiness to oblige everybody would be an excellent example to his juvenile admirers. And as the best barrel-organs are far sweeter and less aggressive than the pianos, we should probably get the organ back again, purified and ennobled, but still essentially its old dear self. The plan seems to me to be a practical and reasonable one; and the loss of life would be trifling—nothing to that which has already taken place in the construction of the Manchester Ship Canal, a comparatively insignificant project.

II

Text of a resolution by Shaw, adopted at a meeting of the Betterment of London Association. Musical America, 11 April 1908

Moved: That the attention of the Home Secretary be again directed by the Street Noise Abatement Committee to the inconsiderateness of allowing mechanical pianos, and "musical" instruments generally, to be played in public thoroughfares to the annoyance and disturbance of private life and the serious hindrance of the work of the professional classes. The present plan of first suffering the interruption, and then sending a servant into the street to order the perpetrator of the nuisance to move away (a disagreeable piece of police duty, which should not be required of a domestic servant, and therefore has often to be done by professional men in person) is in itself a nuisance, even when it is efficacious—which it seldom is, as the offender rarely goes out of earshot. It is clearly desirable that the police should, upon their own initiative, put a stop to street "music" as they now put a stop to the far more bearable nuisance of street games.[U]

PADEREWSKI AS COMPOSER

The World, 29 November 1893

Paderewski's Polish Fantasia for pianoforte and orchestra, which he introduced to London at Mr Henschel's second Symphony Concert last Wednesday, shews a considerable advance in his power of composition.

Formerly he was too young to be a good host to his own ideas: he used to contrive an orchestral reception room to assemble them in; but neither in his invitations nor his introductions did he consider how they would get on together, so they for the most part took oneanother into dinner under protest, and the entertainment was more or less a failure, in spite of the prime attraction of his own playing. He arranges things better now: in his latest fantasia there is harmony, congruity, reciprocity—in short, the wholeness which shews the hand of the master composer.

It is greatly to be desired, however, that some skilful surgeon should dexterously split Paderewski into two separate persons—Paderewski the composer and Paderewski the pianist. At present they interfere with one another constantly. The pianist no sooner gets excited by the orchestra than he says to the composer "I understand, I'll do it for you. Leave it all to me," and takes the matter into his own itching fingers. At such moments the composer, if he were split off as I suggest, could say "Do hold your noise. Do you suppose I am going to reduce my grand passages to a mere paroxysm of banging and clattering on your box of wires merely because you cant keep your hands quiet?"

The fact is, Paderewski, though he writes for the orchestra with excellent judgment, shews the deafest partiality when he comes to write for the pianoforte. He cannot deny it a lion's share in all the good things, whether they suit it or not; and the result is that in most of the big climaxes he is making such a thundering noise that he cannot hear the orchestra, whilst the orchestra is making such a thundering noise that the audience cannot hear him, and can only gaze raptly at the inspiring spectacle of his fists flying in the air as he trounces the keyboard. He had much better use a big drum for such emergencies: the sensation of playing it would be equally exhilarating; the fingering would be easier; and everybody would hear it. There is another technical consideration which I must urge if I am to concede the desirability of developing the capacity of the pianoforte as an orchestral instrument to the utmost.

In that case, I submit that one pianoforte is not enough to cover the ground. When Paderewski writes horn parts in his scores he not only employs four instruments, so as to be able to sound four horn-notes simultaneously if necessary: he also divides the four into two pairs, each of diverse range and quality of tone, so that his first horn-player can produce one set of notes and effects, and his fourth another. Now the pianoforte, as used by Paderewski, is an instrument highly specialized for his use so as to produce the utmost lightness, swiftness, and precision of action; and it so happens that an excess of these qualities can only be gained at the cost of richness and softness of tone-color. Paderewski's pianos are made by Erard; but the ordinary Erard grands used by people who are not Paderewskis are much more delightful instruments, though the mechanical difference is probably only a matter of a layer of felt on the hammer.

I suggest, then, that if Paderewski wishes to combine the orchestral effect of the piano as a very brilliant, steel-hard, and transcendently facile and florid instrument of percussion, with that of its richer and more majestic qualities, he should write his fantasias for two pianofortes, a virtuoso's hair-trigger Erard and a normal Erard. If the difference in tone-color between a clarinet in C and one in A, or between a horn in D and one in B flat basso, is worth considering in composition, I do not see why the equally remarkable difference between a Pleyel and a Steinway piano should be ignored. It would add a new sensation to the performance of that Polish Fantasia if there were two pianos on the platform, with the pianist rushing from one to the other according to the character of the passage he was about to play. I do not say that the effect of the multiplication of pianos would be worth what it would cost: what I do say is, that in Paderewski's fantasia not all his power of modifying the tone of the instrument by his touch conceals the fact that the supreme qualifications of the instrument for certain passages act as disqualifications for certain others, and that this could be got over by using two pianos.

At the same time, I had rather see Paderewski, in his next composition for orchestra, drop the piano altogether. It is the one instrument that he does not understand as a composer, exactly because he understands it so well as an executant. The fantasia was very well received, though the audience most certainly did not mean to *encore* the *finale.* What they were after was a solo; and Paderewski, in accepting their persistent acclamations as an *encore* of a full third of his fantasia, took a diabolical revenge on them, consciously or unconsciously, for their shameless mendicity. His performance of Schumann's concerto was enormously satisfactory. If the band had only been able to follow his gradations of tone and to make the little orchestral rejoinders to the pianoforte a little less stolidly, as much might be said for the whole performance. It was impossible not to rejoice in his complete comprehension of the work, and the certainty with which he found the right *tempo,* handling, and expression for every phrase, so that it came out as a living utterance and not as a mere finger trait committed to memory. I cannot speak with any confidence of the orchestral numbers in the program; for my seat was, except as to the piano, almost useless for critical purposes. As far as I could judge, the band was very rough, especially in the Kaisermarsch. As to the new overture by Emmanuel Moor, I could make nothing of it as a whole. One moment it was obviously decorative music: the next it seemed to be following some imaginative subject, as to which the program offered no clue. It was as if a number of bars from Das Rheingold had got mixed up with a Haydn allegro. This slipping from one kind of music to another is common enough with composers who merely echo the sound of the great masters, and are as likely as not to make their symphonies out of scraps of opera, and their operas out of scraps of symphony. Now Mr Moor is not a mere echo: his talent is a fairly strong and self-reliant one; but as far as I could judge from a first hearing under somewhat unfavorable conditions, his overture had been put together without any definite inspiration or intention; and so, having no point to keep to, it turned out neither flesh, fowl, nor good red herring.

At the Albert Hall on Thursday last the Royal Choral Society was much more at home with Handel than it had been at the previous concert with Berlioz. The crisp and vigorous stroke of Handel, and the strength and audacity of his style, were of course lacking, partly because these huge lumbering choirs of which we are so proud always seem to oppress conductors with a sense of their unwieldiness, partly because Sir Joseph Barnby's style is so measured and complacent. He evidently enjoys Handel's high spirits; but as he invariably stops to dwell on them, and, what is more, stops longer as the movement gathers momentum on the paper before him, its qualities remain hidden in his own imagination, and the actual performance gets slower and heavier.

But if the choir is not impetuously led it is certainly well trained. There is a certain vulgarity of speech about it, especially on the part of the men; but the tone is remarkably good and free from incidental noises; the soft passages are pretty and effective; and the execution is careful and precise. If only some spontaneity and forward spring could be substituted for the perpetual leaning back of both the conductor and the choir, the oratorio performances at the Albert Hall would become about as good as it is in the nature of such things to be. Israel in Egypt is an extraordinary example of the way in which a musical giant can carry off an enterprise which is in its own nature a monumental bore, consisting as it does, to a great extent, of passages of cold narrative which not only do not yearn for the intensity of musical expression, but positively make it impossible.

How can any composer set to music the statement that Egypt was glad when they departed? If the fact were exhibited dramatically, and the actual exclamations of gladness uttered by the Egyptians given, something might be done with them; but the mere bald narrative statement is musically out of the question. Handel therefore falls back here on a purely formal display of his professional skill in fugue writing, and in that sort of experimenting with the old modes which consists in writing in the key of E minor and leaving the sharp out of the signature and occasionally out of the music. The result is extremely interesting to deaf persons whose hobby is counterpoint and the ecclesiastical modes; but to the unsophisticated ear it is deadly dull; and it is hard to refrain from laughing outright at the thousands of people sitting decorously at the Albert Hall listening to the choir trudging through And believe-ed the Lord and his ser-vant Mo-oh-zez, and then through And! I! will exaw-aw-aw-aw-alt Him, as if the gross absurdity of these highly scholastic choruses, considered as an expression of the text, were any the less ridiculous because they were perpetrated by a great musician who could not do even an unmusical thing quite unmusically.

The situation was heightened on Thursday by the recollection that at the last concert the joke of the evening was a parody of just such choral writing. Indeed,

Berlioz's burlesque Amen is far less laughable than He led them through the deep as through a wilderness, the insane contrapuntal vagaries of the last four words surpassing in irreverent grotesqueness anything that the boldest buffoon dare offer as professedly comic composition.

While the world lasts these choruses will make a complete performance of Israel a very mixed joy indeed, to be endured only for the sake of the moments in which Handel made a chance for his genius by forcing a vividly descriptive character on the narrative. He could do little with the frogs and flies, and nothing with the blotches and blains, the rinderpest, and the lice; but the thick darkness that might be felt, the hailstones and the fire mingled with the hail running along the ground, the waters overwhelming the enemy, the floods standing upright as a heap, and the depths congealed in the heart of the sea—these he worked up into tone-pictures that make it impossible to leave Israel unperformed, and that bribe us to sit out in patience the obsolete pedantries in which he took refuge when the narrative beat him. One likes, too, to be heartened with the indomitable affirmation that "there was not one—*not one* feeble person among their tribes," and to exult over the "chosen captains" drowned in the Red Sea.

I wish, by the bye, it were possible for Sir Joseph Barnby to find two singers capable of dealing with those chosen captains, instead of falling back on his four hundred tenors and basses, whom at such moments I am guilty of wishing in the Red Sea themselves, so prosaically do they let the great war-song down. On Thursday they broke my spirit so that I went home forthwith, and so heard hardly anything of the soloists except Miss Butt, who sang Their land brought forth frogs, with some little awkwardnesses and nervousnesses and misplaced breaths which she will some day learn to avoid. All the same, she sang it magnificently. The last fourteen bars came with the true musical and dramatic passion which reduces all purely technical criticism to a mere matter of detail—such detail, however, as Miss Butt would do well not to neglect. All those long phrases on single words *can* be sung in one breath if only you know how to do it.

A LECTURE RECITAL

The World, 6 December 1893

Everybody knows the story of "Have a piano, Thack"; although I believe Atlas [Edmund Yates] alone ever tells it correctly. I prophesy that it will presently be grafted on to the biography of Paderewski, in the form of "Have a lecture, Paddy." For it is actually coming to this, that people are demanding lectures at recitals, to save them the trouble of reading analytic programs, and to relieve the tedium of the music. The plan, after all, has its advantages. In St James's Hall, where you get not only trained pianists, but—what is quite as necessary to a first-class recital—a trained audience, I doubt whether the lecturer would be tolerated; but for smaller semi-private recitals, where the little audience is not trained, but is quite willing to be if only someone will take it in hand, the musical lecture can be made a useful institution enough. I came to this conclusion at a "recital-lecture" given by Mrs Liebich, the subject being Chopin. It was clearly better for the audience, assuming them to have come in a quite uninstructed condition, to be told something about Chopin than to hear a string of his compositions played straight off without a notion of their bearings. At the same time, the arrangement created certain difficulties. For instance, Mrs Liebich delivered the lecture; and Mr Liebich played the "illustrations." Now Mr Liebich, though a perfectly presentable player, is not a Paderewski or a Rubinstein; therefore he was entitled to a certain forbearance on the lecturer's part in the matter of raising expectations. I regret to say that his claims in this direction were not deferred to by Mrs Liebich. She seemed to revel in prefacing each performance with a description which might conceivably have been realized by Paderewski, Rubinstein, Liszt, and Chopin himself all rolled into one, especially if powerfully aided by the electric atmosphere of a vast hall crowded with imaginative enthusiasts, but which was out of the question for the unaided skill of Mr Liebich in the select afternoon quietude of Mrs Richards's drawing room in Stanley Crescent.

One passage struck me as particularly inconsiderate. A man may be a very solid musician and skilful pianist, and yet not be able to play a mazurka. That, as it happened, was Mr Liebich's predicament. In the heroic measure of the polonaise he was at his ease; but the mazurka eluded him: he could not make it dance a step. Yet Mrs Liebich, who must have known this, positively expatiated on the rarity of successful mazurka-playing among pianists, and the necessity of judging Chopin's mazurkas in particular only by the performances of those who catch the true genius of the dance. Then, instead of frankly adding "As my husband is one of those players who cannot manage a mazurka, we had better pass on to those broader, stronger rhythms which appeal to his robust Germanic temperament," she sat down, leaving the audience under the impression that he was about to give an exhibition of the most highly specialized aptitude for the mazurka. What made it more cruel was that Mr Liebich seemed a perfectly quiet, well-bred, unostentatious musician—one who would never by himself dream of making such pretensions. But of course Mrs Liebich did not intend this: it arose out of her conscientious endeavor to say the correct thing about Chopin. What she does not see is that this correct thing is an uninteresting abstraction, only to be resorted to on occasions when it happens to be convenient to say nothing at all in a few well-chosen words. Her lecture was carefully prepared and carefully delivered; but the care was the effect of a modesty as to the value of her own opinion which made her shrink from the audacity of sincerity. She did not presume to give us her personal view of Chopin, or to express the conventional view in the language she habitually uses herself in social intercourse. She has not yet discovered that in literature the ambition of the novice is to acquire the literary language: the struggle of the adept is to get rid of it. Though I would not dissuade her from cultivating the literary language until she has brought its logic and its economy to the utmost attainable perfection, she may take my word for it that her meaning will never be seized instantly in all its fullness by the instinct and feeling of her audience, unless she expresses it in vernacular language. In several passages her lecture was quite artificial: it did not rise above a carefully compiled biographical statement, interlined with an auctioneer's catalog of Chopin's work, her own individuality being suppressed throughout in a thoroughly ladylike way.

Now it is one thing to be a lady and quite another thing to be a lecturer. Lecturing is in its own nature a hopelessly unladylike pursuit. It is not ladylike to monopolize the whole conversation for an hour. I greatly doubt whether it is strictly ladylike to appear even remotely conscious of the existence of such a person as Madame Sand, much less of her relations with Chopin. Now, since it is impossible to lecture at all without committing such crimes as these, and since you may as well be hung for a sheep as a lamb, why hesitate to perpetrate the final outrage of letting loose your individuality, and saying just what you think in your own way as agreeably and frankly as you can? Of course you may have no opinion; but in that case, how much easier it would be to simply read aloud the article on Chopin from Grove's Dictionary, or some other standard work, instead of taking weary pains to produce a bad paraphrase of it?

I must apologize to Mrs Liebich for making her lecture the text of so ponderous a discourse on lecturing, for her discourse was far more entertaining than the ordinary private concert; but if the musical lecture is going to become an institution, it is my business to pounce on its weak points, with a view to its improvement, and, finally, to such perfection as it is capable of. By the way, I was reminded that it is not quite a new thing by a lecture in the same week at the London Institution by Mr Karl Armbruster, who has for a long time past been using the lecture platform as a means of propaganda for that great art development of modern times which may be described comprehensively as German music. He is, in fact, a Bayreuth Extension lecturer: that is, he does for Bayreuth what our University Extension lecturers do for Oxford and Cambridge. And I think he has solved the true educational use of the drawing room, as far as music is concerned, by holding classes there from which you can get turned out ready for a trip to Bayreuth, fully equipped with a knowledge of the motifs and their subjects in the dramas to be performed. At the London Institution he was lecturing, not on Wagner, but on Loewe, and on an admirable contemporary German song-composer, Hans Sommer, of whom we shall hear considerably more presently, though he is as yet but a youth of sixty or thereabouts. Miss Pauline Cramer sang the only song of Loewe that ever sends a real shiver down my spine, the grisly Edward; also The Goldsmith's Daughter, the most charming of all his cheerful songs, as far as my knowledge of them goes. Miss Cramer sang them both so well that I wondered for the fiftieth time why she has chosen to hide her talent in a country where her artistic seriousness simply makes the natives uncomfortable. Loewe, being by this time long enough dead, is coming into fashion, though the vogue of his songs will always be restricted by his disregard of the normal limits of the human voice. His own range seems to have been greater than that of any recorded vocalist, except, perhaps, Mr Corney Grain, who, I believe, does not sing his music. Archibald Douglas, which is not open to this reproach, was finely sung at a recent Monday Popular Concert by Mr David Bispham, accompanied by Mr Henry Bird. It was tremendously applauded, partly on its own account, partly because the public has at last discovered that the striking difference between Mr Bispham and most other concert singers is altogether to his advantage. At the same concert I heard for the first time this season Lady Hallé, who gave an astonishingly able performance of Tartini's Trillo—quite equal in all essential qualities to Norman-Neruda's best. Piatti was there too, unimpaired. At this and the next concert I heard two novelties: a pianoforte quintet by Goldmark, and a string quartet by Villiers Stanford. Goldmark is evidently a man of weak academic fibre: he aimed at nothing higher with his fiddles and piano than the production of some extremely pretty music. And he certainly hit his mark. Only for a moment did he awake to a sense of what was due to himself as a scientific musician, and that was in the last movement, when he indulged in a *fugato.* The sound was ludicrous; but artists and audience sat tight, without daring to look at oneanother, and it was soon over. The Stanford quartet was exceedingly clever: this I say in its praise; for if I am to have scientific music, I had rather have it cleverly scientific than stupidly so. And I maintain that Professor Tyndall himself could not have written a quartet more creditable to the Irish intellect. Still, there are blemishes in it. For example, though the *scherzo,* with its recurring trio, is, like the rest of the work, unquestionable in form—respectable precedents being discoverable in Beethoven and elsewhere—it condescends to be enjoyable. And the elaborately invented harmonies of the slow movement, by their very aloofness from the vulgarities of poetic purpose or voluptuous tone-weaving, accidentally acquire an unexpectedness of arrival and a vagueness of destination which might suggest to an ignorant and imaginative hearer that the composer was portraying the wanderings of a blind heroine in an Irish waste. It is in the first and last movements that the professor is most completely himself, though even here there is an escapade or two. I must reserve my final judgment, however, until I have *seen* the quartet. Merely to hear music of this sort is to miss half its qualities.

GENOVEVA

The World, 13 December 1893

The chief musical event of last week was the performance of Schumann's Genoveva for the first time on the English stage by the students of the Royal College of Music. The pit and galleries of Drury Lane (handsomely lent for the occasion) were crammed with students. Parents and uncles and aunts of students were everywhere, interrupting the performance in the wrongest possible places by untimely applause, and feeling that such incomprehensible and solemn music as Schumann's must be excellent training for young people. The stalls and boxes were full of critics and other distinguished persons. Speaking as one of them, may I suggest that when we are so numerous, and consequently so tightly packed, the management should have a steam crane on the site of the prompter's box between the acts, so that any critic desiring to leave his place during the intervals could hook himself by the waistband to the end of the chain and be hoisted out of his seat, swung round, and dropped at the door nearest the refreshment bar?

The orchestra, being nearly eighty strong, was responsible for some of the packing. It was quite the most brilliant part of the house, as thirtyfour out of fifty of the strings were young women, most of them so attractive that for once the average of personal beauty was higher in the band than on the stage. The swarming and chattering when they assembled, and the irreverent waving of bows to friends in the house, put everybody into a good humor—even those critics who were furious at having to begin their afternoon's work as early as half-past one.

Genoveva was an excellent selection for the College to make. Since it is commercially valueless as an opera, we should never have heard it at all if it had not been taken in hand by a purely academic institution; and yet, being by Schumann, it was certain that some interesting music lay buried in it. For Schumann had at least one gift which we have now come to rank very highly among the qualifications of a composer for the stage: to wit, a strong feeling for harmony as a means of emotional expression. There are passages in Genoveva which are in this respect genuinely Wagnerian—and I am not one of those incorrigible people who cry out Wagner whenever they hear an unprepared major "tonic discord."

Unfortunately, in the other qualifications of the music-dramatist, Schumann is as far behind Beethoven as Beethoven was behind Mozart and Wagner. To begin with, he gives away all pretension to seriousness in his enterprise by providing as its subject a book which is nakedly silly. He may have persuaded himself—such a folly would have been just like him—that he could make his heroine do for his opera what Beethoven made Leonore do for Fidelio. But Fidelio, though commonplace and homely, is not silly. Its few harmless stage conventions do not prevent it from being credible and human from beginning to end; wheras Genoveva, from the moment when the witch enters in the first act, degenerates into pure bosh, and remains mostly at that level to the end. The witch's music is frivolous and seriocomic, the orchestration sprouting at the top into an outrageous piccolo part which would hardly be let off with mere indulgent laughter if it came from any less well-beloved composer.

In one place, the villain being left with the heroine, who has fainted, he exclaims "We are alone." Immediately—the witch being round the corner—the piccolo utters a prolonged and derisive squawk, as if a cockatoo were reminding him that it had its eye on him. Instrumentation, as we all know, was not Schumann's strong point; and there is plenty of his characteristic orchestral muddling in Genoveva; but I can remember no other instance of his scoring being foolish in its intention. The witch is perhaps not much worse in the early scenes than Sir Arthur Sullivan's Ulrica in Ivanhoe, or in the incantation scene than Verdi's Ulrica in Un Ballo; but one has only to think of Ortrud in Lohengrin to realize the distance that separates Schumann's second-hand ideas from those of a really creative genius.

Another of the failures of Genoveva is Golo, the villain. As he is, unfortunately, a sentimental villain, it would require a Mozartian subtlety of characterization to differentiate him from the other sentimental people in the opera—the hero and the heroine, for instance. This subtlety Schumann did not possess: accordingly, Siegfried or Genoveva might sing every bar of Golo's music without the smallest incongruity. Imagine the effect of Don Giovanni singing Leporello's music, Elvira Zerlina's, Wotan Loki's, or Alberich Mime's!

Even Beethoven, whose powers in this respect were so blunt that, like a veritable Procrustes, he leveled four different characters in his Fidelio by writing a quarter in canon for them (conceive *Non ti fidar* or *Un di, se ben* in canon!), not to mention that his prison porter and gaoler's daughter are absolutely indistinguishable in kind from his Florestan and Leonore—even Beethoven made Pizarro an unmistakable scoundrel. He could not, like Wagner or Mozart, have given us half a dozen scoundrels, each as distinct from the other as Tartuffe from Harpagon* or Rogue Riderhood from Silas Wegg†; but he could at least distinguish an amiable person from an unamiable one. But this moderate feat has baffled Schumann in Genoveva.

It is obvious, then, that we must fall back on the symphonic, descriptive, and lyrical pages of the score for such merits as it possesses. In none of these can anything be found that need be heard by anyone who knows Schumann's songs, pianoforte pieces, and symphonies. In the nonsensical magic mirror and ghost scenes of the third act, and the demented business in the ravine in the fourth, Schumann, for the most part, leaves the stage to get on as best it can, and retires into pure symphony, with an effect which is only tolerable on condition of dismissing as so much superfluous rubbish all of the actual drama shewn on the boards,

* Molière's hypocrite (Tartuffe, 1664) and miser (The Miser, 1668).

† Characters in Dickens's Our Mutual Friend.

except, perhaps, what may be barely necessary to motivate in the vaguest manner the emotions of Genoveva and her husband.

The opera is at its best when Genoveva is on the stage; and it is never absolutely vulgar and trivial except in the witch music. The departure of the troops in the first act is an effective piece of composition for the stage; and there are one or two episodes in the second act, when Genoveva is alone in her chamber, which are by no means unsuccessful. But the work, as a whole, is a failure; and glad as I am that I have heard it, I cannot blame the world for dropping its acquaintance, though it has left a good many less worthy names on its operatic visiting list.

The performance, conducted by Professor Stanford, went without a hitch. It had been faithfully and thoroughly rehearsed; and the performers, unpaid, and unspoiled by popularity or practical experience of the credulity of that harmless monster, the public, did their very best anxiously and eagerly, the result being, in spite of a hundred comical little accidents due to the nervousness and ineptitude of the performers, a certain satisfactoriness and even a degree of illusion which is the rarest thing in the world at regular professional performances.

The most obtrusively academic part of the affair was the posing, walking, and gesticulation. The unhappy students had been taught "plastique" until they dared not call their arms and legs their own. The plastique professor, with his principles of beauty, and his set of regulations for the attainment of absolute grace of attitude, is almost as fatal a person as the harmony professor with *his* set of regulations for the attainment of "correct" part writing. No attitude, unfortunately for professordom, is unconditionally beautiful. Apollo, eight heads high, and with his shoulders broader than his waist, may look like a god in an attitude in which Smith, seven heads high, and with his waist perhaps broader than his champagne-bottle shoulders, may look absurd.

It is all very well to compile principles of beauty from Greek statuary; but the sculptor can shape his man to suit his attitude, wheras the actor has to make the attitude suit the real human shape, which varies so infinitely from one person to another that methods of identifying criminals by their physical proportions are said to be infallible. As an alteration of an inch in the relation between the size of the body and legs or head may make all the difference in the world in the grace of a pose, it is not to be wondered at that people who copy the attitudes and gestures of others—especially of those famous for their grace—at once make themselves ridiculous. There are, in fact, no standard attitudes; and the utmost a teacher can do is to rouse the pupil's conscience on the subject of personal grace, and leave him, under the guidance of that conscience, to grow his own plastique.

This, of course, is not the view taken at the Royal College. The characters in Genoveva were always defying commonsense, and even the law of gravitation, in standard attitudes. Golo, in particular, was most conscientious: his profile when he placed his right foot on the castle steps in the first act would have delighted Mr Wopsle's* dresser. Later on, however, his efforts to fulfil the precept "Stand always on one leg" wore him out; and he repeatedly supported himself, in mere exhaustion, on two, very unclassically. Genoveva repulsing him with her right arm stretched out and the hand prettily pronated was also an elegant spectacle. But the attitudes, on the whole, lacked conviction.

* Character in Dickens's Great Expectations, who becomes a London actor under the stage name of Mr Waldengarver.

The one or two which came off successfully were abstractly beautiful, perhaps; but they would have been the same in any other drama or with any other individuals. I confidently recommend the youthful posers of the College, whilst cultivating strength, grace, and a fine bodily tone to their heart's content, to carefully forget all the attitudes and rules they have been taught. A graceful attitude is an attitude taken spontaneously by a graceful person; and nothing is more hopeless than to attempt to begin with the attitude and work backwards to the person.

The singing was decidedly better than might have been expected. There was no great success like that of Miss Clara Butt last year in Orfeo, though the audience made a sort of attempt to manufacture one by making a heroine of the witch, who was clever, spirited, fluent, and ready, but whose voice and style were rather shallow. Mr Archdeacon (Siegfried) and Miss Bruckshaw (Genoveva) are to be heartily congratulated on the condition in which they have come out of the destructive process of being taught to sing. We shall certainly hear more of Mr Archdeacon, who has an agreeable baritone voice.

Mr Charles Green, unmercifully victimized by academic principles, both in singing and attitudinizing, did his best as Golo. His voice is stronger than it was; but he is still hampered by the bleating method with which he began. If he will earnestly set himself during the forthcoming year to do exactly the reverse of everything he is told, the favorable results of the new departure can be judged at next year's performance.

There was a great crowd at the Crystal Palace on Saturday to hear Paderewski. A young lady ventured on *O zittre nicht (Non paventar)* from Die Zauberflöte, leading us to expect either the noblest powers of dramatic expression in the *larghetto*, or else the extreme range up to F needed for the florid *allegro*—if not both qualifications. As it turned out, she had neither, her singing of the *larghetto* being exceedingly commonplace, whilst at the crucial point of the *allegro* she sang B C D instead of B D F, thus falling a minor third short of the range required. Under these circumstances what does the lady expect me to say about her choice? Her second selection, the well-worn song of Solveig, from Grieg's Peer Gynt music, was much more sensible, and won her an *encore*, though the hour was late and Paderewski next in the program.

MRS TANQUERAY PLAYS THE PIANO

The World, 20 December 1893

Like all intelligent people, I greatly dislike Christmas. It revolts me to see a whole nation refrain from music for weeks together in order that every man may rifle his neighbor's pockets under cover of a ghastly general pretence of festivity. It is really an atrocious institution, this Christmas. We must be gluttonous because it is Christmas. We must be drunken because it is Christmas. We must be insincerely generous; we must buy things that nobody wants, and give them to people we dont like; we must go to absurd entertainments that make even our little children satirical; we must writhe under venal officiousness from legions of freebooters, all because it is Christmas—that is, because the mass of the population, including the all-powerful middle-class tradesman, depends on a week of license and brigandage, waste and intemperance, to clear off its outstanding liabilities at the end of the year. As for me, I shall fly from it all tomorrow or next day to some remote spot miles from a shop, where nothing worse can befall me than a serenade from a few peasants, or some equally harmless survival of medieval mummery, shyly proffered, not advertized, moderate in its expectations, and soon over. In town there is, for the moment, nothing for me or any honest man to do. There will be no London Symphony Concert until January 11th, no Crystal Palace Saturday Concert until February 17th, no Popular Concert until January 6th, and no new comic opera, I trust, until I am dead.

Mention of the London Symphony Concerts reminds me that I said nothing at the time about the last one, at which Mr Henschel revived Rubinstein's Ramsgate Symphony, sometimes described as The Ocean. In judging this work it should be borne in mind that Rubinstein is a Russian, and that in no country in Europe is it possible to keep so far away from the ocean as in Russia. Also that Rubinstein's rating as a composer is not high. He is only oceanic in respect of not being fresh, and of being drenchingly copious. His songs, duets, and pianoforte pieces are sincerely sentimental and sometimes pretty, though they are all compiled from the works of great composers; but an ocean symphony—no, thank you.

If I cannot have Wagner's sea music, I can content myself with Mendelssohn's Hebrides, or even Grieg's scrap of storm music in Peer Gynt, or, if no better may be, with Strauss's North Sea waltz played in the true Strauss manner. I only draw the line at Rubinstein's attempt to stuff out the chords of C and G major with musical chaff to something like the bigness of the round pond in Kensington Gardens. It is no use: the thing, oceanically considered, is a failure. Leave the ocean out of the question, and you have a commonplace but bustling and passable third-hand Schubert symphony. Mr Henschel mercifully cut two movements out of it; and when he proceeds to cut out the other four my enjoyment of the work will be complete. By way of putting Rubinstein entirely out of countenance, his work was prefaced by Weber's Ocean, thou mighty monster, sung by Mrs Eaton, a lady of formidable physical powers, which she used with due discretion and artistic feeling.

Miss Beatrice Langley played Spohr's ninth concerto. She might have played its arabesques better; but then, in the modern school, which turns out such an amazing quantity of virtuosos, "better is the enemy of well." That principle is a good working one; and I am far from contending that Miss Langley should not play Spohr at all because she cannot play his allegros with ideal elegance: still, I must not imply that she has yet attained the combination of swiftness with perfect pitch and measure required by purely decorative passages which, having no dramatic interest whatever, are nothing if not exquisitely graceful. In the rondo the snapping of a string compelled her to borrow Mr Hollander's fiddle to finish with. I have seen that happen before; but I cannot recollect any other violinist whose first proceeding on borrowing a violin from the band was to hastily alter its tuning. Mr Hollander's chanterelle no doubt sounded flat to Miss Langley's sharp ear, though his and mine were satisfied; but it seemed ungrateful to criticize the tuning of the leader's fiddle before the audience. The performance of the concerto, on the whole, made a brilliant impression; but the famous *adagio* was the only movement which was as nearly up to the mark as the audience thought. The concert wound up with the Meistersinger overture, which was, perhaps, the most successful moment in Mr Henschel's winter campaign so far. The truth is that some such moment was rather badly wanted; for the recent London Symphony Concerts have fallen perceptibly short of the very high standard of excellence attained by them at the beginning of the year.

A miscellaneous concert of considerable pretension was given on Tuesday last week by Mr Fred Fawcett, a gentleman whose singing I had occasion to notice last season at Mr Maud Crament's concert. Such old stories as Madame Belle Cole's singing of *Sognai*, Mr Norman Salmond's of The Wanderer, and Mr Ben Davies's of Deeper and deeper still, need not here be re-told. Fresher in interest was the appearance of Miss Ella Russell, who has, I imagine, been triumphing exceedingly in the provinces. She has evidently discovered that it is not enough to sing well to a public which does not know good singing from bad. It is necessary to assert your qualities, throw your emotions at their heads, wake them up with strenuous tone-vibrations, and keep things going at a lively pace generally, as our music hall artists are trained to do. Miss Russell has developed her style vigorously in this direction; and the audience was encoring her enthusiastically when I came away. This I did not do without hearing The Ladies' Amateur Harp, Mandolin, and Guitar Band, consisting of thirtytwo damsels, of whom three played the harp, four the violin, six the guitar, and nineteen the mandolin. It is disquieting to find that there are nineteen people in England who can play the mandolin; and I sincerely hope the number may not increase. I know nothing more maddening than the *sostenuto* produced from a string by rapid repercussion or replectration (if there is such a word). Pianoforte makers from time to time take out patents for diabolical contrivances to keep something whirring against the string whilst you hold the key down and work a treadle; and the effect of the mandolin band is not unlike that of a monster pianoforte with some such appliance in full blast. The effect is pretty at first; and certainly the band is thoroughly drilled, and makes the best of itself.

No doubt, if there were dancing and singing to divide

one's attention a little, it might go on for a whole evening without turning anyone's hair white; but I confess that ten unrelieved minutes of it left me more than satiated. By the way, I am credibly informed that Chelmsford is happy in the possession of an amateur body called The English Ladies' Orchestral Society, in which the wind and percussion instruments are played by ladies as well as the strings. This is good news for ladies with undeveloped lungs. After all, the chief objection to playing wind instruments is that it prolongs the life of the player beyond all reasonable limits. If you want to become phthisis-proof, drink-proof, cholera-proof, and, in short, immortal, play the trombone well and play it constantly. I hope the Chelmsford ladies will visit London and shew how very unnecessary it is for their sex to waste itself on the mandolin.

The other evening I came upon an extraordinary instance of public insensibility to music. I seldom go to the theatre, partly because my evenings are otherwise engaged, partly because my theatrical sense is so blunt that in spite of my most earnest efforts to improve myself I hardly ever can see any difference between one modern play and another. On Monday last week I went, as I supposed, to a certain concert at Prince's Hall; but though my ticket was not challenged, I found myself, when I got inside, at quite another concert—an amateur orchestral one—to which I had not been invited. I had come a week too soon.

To remain, an unbidden guest, and listen to an amateur band, would have been an act of wantonness; so I hastily retreated by way of King Street, St James's. Here, glancing at the bills on the St James's Theatre, I found that they were performing a play which has attained extraordinary celebrity, and which I had been strongly urged to see as a masterpiece of modern drama. So in I went, and conscientiously applied myself to my usual task of trying to persuade myself that I had never seen anything like it before. I was late, and only saw a scrap of the first act; but when the curtain rose on the second it revealed a pianoforte, at which the chief lady in the piece*—a very attractive person—presently sat down and began to play. To my surprise, she played not only with sufficient skill, but with such convincingly right expression and feeling and so sympathetic a hand that I immediately forgot all about the comedy, and prepared to enjoy Schubert.

Will it be believed that the wretched people on the stage interrupted her after a few bars? The same thing happened at a subsequent and equally promising attempt. After that she never succeeded in even sitting down to the piano; and at last, worn out by repeated interruptions, she left the stage abruptly, and we were presently given to understand that she had committed suicide. No wonder! Now, is it not an extraordinary thing that though her performance has attracted more attention and been more written about than that of any other artist in London this year, nobody seems to have noticed the difference between her playing and the ordinary leading lady's stage strum over the half-dozen easiest bars of some half-forgotten relic of the schoolroom?

Everybody can act more or less—all the world's a stage, unfortunately. But all the world is not a pianoforte; and yet when the dramatic critics for once in their misspent lives hear someone who can touch a piano with a musician's hand, they can talk about nothing but her *acting*—as if she only pretended to play. If the St James's management will give a special performance for the musical critics, with the second act extended so as to

* Mrs Patrick Campbell, in Arthur W. Pinero's The Second Mrs Tanqueray.

allow of a recital of the lady's entire repertory, and the fourth act left out (the motive for the catastrophe being gone), then I think we musical critics, with all our faults, will rise to the occasion.

Everybody, I presume, knows Chappell's Popular Music of the Olden Time, issued in 1859. Perhaps some of my readers have a copy of the original 1840 Collection of National English Airs. A new edition has just been issued called Old English Popular Music, in two volumes, bound bravely in blue buckram, and edited by Mr H. Ellis Wooldridge. The first volume, as may be imagined by anyone who knows how much our eyes have been opened in historical matters during the last thirty years, is a vast improvement on the old edition. Macfarren, the former editor, never really succeeded in conceiving musical ideas as expressible otherwise than in terms of our modern major or minor mode. He believed in his heart that the old musicians, although they omitted the sharps and flats in writing music, modified the notes in performance, except when they simply blundered in their unconscious striving towards modern tonality. The result was, of course, that his editing of those works which date from before the triumph of the two modern modes is now quite unpresentable.

Mr Wooldridge has accordingly rejected the Macfarren versions and arrangements up to 1650; and though he himself is not altogether emancipated from Macfarrenism—for he offers King Henry VIII. an occasional leading note or flattened sixth which would, I strongly suspect, have horribly offended that virtuous Prince's scruples as to our "lascivious" modern musical ways—and though, further, he fits the very oldest tunes with XIX century imitations of late XVI century harmonies which he admits to be anachronisms, yet, as he also gives the original descants, and makes the exact extent of his interference quite clear, no harm is done: indeed, the general public will be glad of such harmonizations of the tunes as are needed to make them acceptable and even intelligible to—shall I say the mob? Anyhow, there are the two volumes, full of tunes, invaluable to the musician, and highly interesting to anyone with the least historical instinct.

THE PIPER OF HAMELIN

The World, 27 December 1893

We seem never to get finally rid of the relics of the autumn festivals. The "specially composed" oratorio, cantata, or symphony, having been duly proclaimed a masterpiece, is set down for its first performance in London later on; and these first performances keep dropping in all the winter and stirring up our worst passions. The latest arrival in this department is the symphony composed by Mr Edward German for the Norwich Festival. It was played at the Crystal Palace on the 16th, and conducted, like the rest of the concert, by the composer, Mr Manns being absent at Glasgow, as he always is for the last concert of the year. One advantage of this arrangement was that we got a more exciting performance of Mendelssohn's Ruy Blas overture than Mr Manns would have indulged us with now that he is waxing grave in his *tempi*, and takes even a Beethoven *scherzo* at ninetysix bars per minute instead of the old hundred and ten or fifteen. Mr German raced the overture; and as Mendelssohn's *allegros* are built for speed, comparing with Beethoven's much as a yacht does with a three-decker, the result was brilliantly satisfactory.

The Norwich symphony struck me as a mass of clever composition wasted. It is dramatic music without any subject, emotional music without any mood, formal music without conspicuous beauty and symmetry of design, externally a symphony, really a fulfilment of a commission or seizure of a professional opportunity, otherwise purposeless. It is much as if the Festival committee had invited Mr Pinero to write an ode, arguing that since odes are literature, and plays literature, and since Mr Pinero, as a producer of plays, is a producer of literature, he must be the right man to produce odes. And no doubt Mr Pinero could string sentences into the form of an ode, just as Mr German has strung themes into the form of a symphony. But compare the symphony with the incidental music to Henry VIII. by the same hand, which was played at the end of the concert; and note how Mr German, when he gets on his own ground, with definite dramatic business in hand, suddenly becomes intelligible, interesting, purposeful, and individual.

The fact is, symphony is no more Mr German's business than epic poetry is mine. Some years ago, when he composed his Richard III. overture for Mr Mansfield, he wavered between descriptive and absolute music, the latter rather getting the better of Richard III. At that time he would probably have written a very creditable Mendelssohn student's symphony. Since then he has developed his descriptive and dramatic powers; and now Fate, maladroit as usual, offers him an opportunity of distinguishing himself in exactly the opposite direction. However, the Festival being happily over, and the first performance in London duly achieved, he can easily break up the symphony, and use the scraps—which are valuable—as material for future work in his own line.

Both the vocalist and the pianist failed to appear at this concert. We accordingly had Rubinstein's concerto in D minor from Herr Schönberger, an artist whose technical instinct would place him in the front rank if his artistic instincts were equally keen and delicate.

On Monday last week the students of Trinity College gave a concert at Prince's Hall. In the band they were helped out by experienced hands and by the careful conducting of Mr F. Corder to an extent which took the full orchestral responsibility off their shoulders; but so far as their share went, it was creditably discharged. In looking through the list of the College professors on the back of the program, I could not help being struck by the fact that the orchestral departments were in the hands of men like Radcliffe and Barrett, Lazarus and Clinton, Malsch, Mann, &c., all known as capable performers on the instruments they teach.

Not for a moment do I question that the gentlemen who teach singing are equally distinguished in private as vocalists; but I am certainly not so familiar with their triumphs; and, as a mere matter of taste, I do not like the results of their teaching so well. I heard a young lady with a contralto voice, the condition of which was a perfect example of the results of the method of teaching singing which has grown up in our musical academies; and I am therefore able to certify that this method seems to be thoroughly understood and carried out in Trinity College. To those who like the academic style of singing this should prove a high recommendation. The most interesting and important item in the program was Ferdinand Hiller's pianoforte concerto in F minor, played by Mr Arthur Lestrange. The selection was not a wise one. The concerto, which is very difficult, very able, very handsome, and quite heartless, requires a certain serene elegance of handling and mundane self-possession on the part of the player, as well as faultless dexterity of finger; wheras Mr Lestrange is, above all things, a feverish player—one who cannot play even a scale without a crisis in it somewhere: in short, just the wrong man for Hiller, and likely to become still more incompatible with him the more he develops his own style as a player; for the modest, conscientious formalism of his youth and pupilage trimmed him closer to the symmetrical propriety of Hiller's style than he will ever be trimmed again, probably. If Mr Lestrange could manage a run abroad—say, in Vienna—for a year or so, his return would be awaited with some interest, as he is well endowed musically, and has initiative and individuality.

Mr Robert Buchanan's opera, The Piper of Hamelin, produced last Wednesday afternoon at the Comedy, was a happy thought in every way. I have been for years wondering why Browning's poem was not snapped up by some English musician: in fact, I once planned a choral symphony on the Pied Piper myself, and the world has lost an interesting work through my lack of leisure to carry out my design. Mr Comyns Carr has shewn himself the right manager for a work of this sort. He knows what no other manager seems yet to have found out—that it is quite possible to fill up the stage with pleasant young people who can dance a little, act a little, sing a little, look educated and presentable, and wear pretty dresses naturally, if only you are sufficiently in touch with general society to know where to look for them, and if you can at the same time make them and their friends feel sure that your theatre is a nice place to be employed in.

I am not here hinting at the current objections to the morals of the rank and file of the comic opera stage. Morals, in that sense, have not half so much to do with the question as manners. Young women of sensibility and refinement, natural or cultivated, know too little of stage morals to care much about them; but they object nonetheless to throw in their lot with a regiment of girls who are studiedly and purposely slangy of speech and brazen of bearing, absurdly conscious of being alluringly dressed and much stared at, and quite incapable of comprehending their artistic function and respecting themselves for discharging it. Now at the Comedy Theatre not only do the principals look like cultivated, decent people, but when they stand among the chorus they seem to be moving in their own set. This is a managerial feat to be proud of: it raises the standard of respectability for comic opera in the very department where the want of it is most odious and most rampant. If Mr Carr's experiment meets with the success it deserves, he and Mr D'Oyly Carte between them will have done much to put the rowdiness of the ordinary comic opera chorus out of countenance and out of fashion.

The stage is the most exclusive profession in the world; and that being so, and necessarily so, there is no reason why we should hesitate to insist on a high standard of manners there. The merest novice in the chorus expects twentyfive shillings a week as a minimum wage; and a man expects thirty. Considering the degree of address and appearance exacted from young women in shops and restaurants who get much worse paid and have to work abominably long hours, I cannot see why so much less social amenity should be expected from a lady of the chorus than from a parlormaid.

On the whole, Mr Carr has reason to congratulate himself. The subject of the opera is an ideal one for his purpose; and his company, his dresses, and his scenery illustrate it in a highly artistic way, the stage spectacle having the quality of a good picture book. Mr Buchanan has gone to play rather than to work in making an opera book of the legend; but Mr Buchanan's imagination never fails him: no matter what he writes, or even how he writes, he can always put the storyteller's spell on us. There was not a prosaic moment in the performance;

and some of the moments were quite affecting—I do not think that is too strong a description of the sensation produced by the close of the first act with the departure of the children after the Piper. The atmosphere of romantic illusion was proof against even the stage rats.

The principals, too, were all competent and interesting. Miss Lena Ashwell would have made a greater hit by her grace and good looks, and by the sincerity of her acting as Liza, if she had not apparently had the misfortune to have derived her ideas of voice production from some particularly conscientious professor of the academic art of How Not to Do It; but even with this drawback she came off very well. As to the Piper, Mr Wyatt, decidedly "fluffy" at times as to his words and music, and not by any means emancipated from the ridiculous Mephistophelean tradition in his grotesque attitudes, yet rose successfully to the occasion at the end of the first act, and was once or twice really striking. The tenor, Mr Leonard Russell, was not a bit insufferable—quite the contrary, in fact; and little Gladys Doree, as the lame child Hans, was so intensely rapt in her part that she made an exceptional impression.

But—for I am loth to have to add that all this is only leading up to a great BUT—why did not Mr Buchanan, Wagner-like, compose the music to his own play? Mr F. W. Allwood, the composer who relieved him of that task, is a gentleman with a very great knowledge of Italian opera and English drawing-room ballad music, from Mercadante down to Mr Cowen; and he has used his knowledge unsparingly. Unfortunately, his memory is not note perfect. He repeatedly tried to make the Piper play It was a dream; but not even at the end, when he brought the whole orchestra to aid him in two heroic final attempts, did he succeed in getting it right. Only for this unlucky infirmity Mr Allwood would have produced a passable *pot-pourri*.

As it was, from the opening reminiscence of the exordium to Mendelssohn's Ruy Blas, and the bold resurrection of *Regnava nel silenzio*, which immediately follows, down to the curiously unsuccessful shot at God Save the Queen, which closes the opera, I heard hardly a theme which did not differ from the authentic version by several notes, and differ for the worse, too. No doubt the truth is that Mr Allwood honestly mistook his memory for his invention; but I do not see how I could have mistaken his invention for my memory; and therefore I am reluctantly compelled to except his score from my otherwise favorable verdict on The Piper of Hamelin.

After the Piper came a burlesque of Sandford and Merton, by Messrs Burnand and Solomon, with Mr Lionel Brough as Barlow. Frankly, I did not like it. That sort of burlesque never entertained me even when it was in the heyday of its popularity; and what is more, I have never seen an audience shew any convincing signs of differing from me in this respect except when some exceedingly droll performer was providing the fun from his own personal resources. However, Sandford and Merton is not, as far as I can judge, worse than other burlesques of its kind; and possibly the peashooters, squirts, squibs, and birchings will amuse the grownup people among the audience. Need I add that none of the more questionable enchantments of burlesque are permitted: hence, probably, the term operetta instead of burlesque in the playbill.

The book of The Piper, well printed by the Chiswick Press and capitally illustrated by Mr Hugh Thomson, is sold in the theatre for eighteenpence. This is, perhaps, the most startling of all Mr Carr's reforms. I never saw anything that a respectable printer would call a book sold in a theatre before.

IN THE WEST COUNTRY

The World, 10 January 1894

I am, I suppose, in the west country, by which I mean generally any place for which you start from Paddington. To be precise, I am nowhere in particular, though there are ascertained localities within easy reach of me. For instance, if I were to lie down and let myself roll over the dip at the foot of the lawn, I should go like an avalanche into the valley of the Wye. I could walk to Monmouth in half an hour or so. At the end of the avenue there is a paper nailed to a tree with a stencilled announcement that The Penallt Musical Society will give a concert last Friday week (I was at it, as shall presently appear); and it may be, therefore, that I am in the parish of Penallt, if there is such a place. But as I have definitely ascertained that I am not in England either ecclesiastically or for the purposes of the Sunday Closing Act; as, nevertheless, Wales is on the other side of the Wye; and as I am clearly not in Ireland or Scotland, it seems to follow that I am, as I have honestly admitted, nowhere. And I assure you it is a very desirable place—a land of quietly beautiful hills, enchanting valleys, and an indescribable sober richness of winter coloring. This being so, need I add that the natives are flying from it as from the plague? Its lonely lanes, where, after your day's work, you can wander amid ghosts and shadows under the starry firmament, stopping often to hush your footsteps and listen to a wonderful still music of night and nature, are eagerly exchanged for sooty streets and gaslamps and mechanical pianos playing the last comic song but two. The fact is, wages in the district do not reflect the sufficiency of the scenery: hence ambitious young men forsake their birthplace to begrime themselves in "the tinworks," symbolic of the great manufacturing industries of the nation, which have all, figuratively speaking, the production of tin as their final cause. I cannot walk far without coming upon the ruins of a deserted cottage or farmhouse. The frequency of these, and the prevalence of loosely piled stone walls instead of hedges, gives me a sensation of being in Ireland which is only dispelled by the appearance of children with whole garments and fresh faces acquainted with soap. But even children are scarce, the population being, as far as I can judge, about one-sixth of a human being per square mile. The only fit pleasures of the place are those of contemplation. Yet one day, as I was coasting a neighboring valley, the sylvan echoes were wakened by an abjectly monotonous Too Too too-too-too-too, Too Too too too-tooting on a poor sort of horn; and presently a huntsman appeared jogging along, followed by a pack of hounds full of eager excitement, which they had to waste, for want of anything else to do, in a restless wagging of their multitudinous tails which quite hid their bodies from me, exactly as the swordsman in the German tale kept himself dry in a shower of rain by waving his sword above his head. Then came some young gentlemen, their bored human instincts struggling with those which they shared with the pack. With them were many older men, of whom a few, if my observation is to be trusted, eke out their incomes by selling horses to the younger ones. Usually, when the hunt is up, my sympathies are with the fox, and I have nothing but contemptuous indignation for its pursuers; but on this occasion the foxless cortège, as it clattered slowly along, comforting itself with flasks and sandwiches, was such a hopeless failure that I pitied it, and would have even provided it with a quarry had I possessed a spirited young tiger or other carnivorous animal able to bring out the manly qualities which are the pride of the sportsman. Had these hunters been wise, they would have satiated their destructive instincts by criticizing musical performances in town, and devoted their country holidays to benevolence and poetry.

There is a band in this place. Two little cornets, four baritone saxhorns, and a euphonium, all rather wasted for want of a competent person to score a few airs specially for them; for the four saxhorns all play the same part in unison instead of spreading themselves polyphonically over the desert between the cornets and the tuba. When their strains burst unexpectedly on my ear on Christmas Day, I supposed, until I went cautiously to the window to reconnoitre, that there were only three instruments instead of seven. With a parish organist to set this matter right for them, and a parish bandmaster to teach them a few simple rules of thumb as to the manipulation of their tuning-slides, the seven musicians would have discoursed excellent music. I submit that, pending the creation of a Ministry of Music, the Local Government Board should appoint District Surveyors of Brass Bands to look after these things. There are also carol singers; but of them I have nothing to say except that the first set, consisting of a few children, sang with great spirit a capital tune which I shall certainly steal when I turn my attention seriously to composition. The second set came very late, and had been so hospitably entertained at their previous performances that they had lost that clearness of intention and crispness of execution which no doubt distinguished their earlier efforts.

But the great event of the Penallt season was the concert. It was taken for granted that I, as an eminent London critic, would hold it in ineffable scorn; and it was even suggested that I should have the condescension to stay away. But, as it happened, I enjoyed it more than any native did, and that, too, not at all derisively, but because the concert was not only refreshingly different from the ordinary London miscellaneous article, but much better. The difference began with the adventurousness of the attempt to get there. There were no cabs, no omnibuses, no lamps, no policemen, no pavement, and, as it happened, no moon or stars. Fortunately, I have a delicate sense of touch in my bootsoles, and this enabled me to discriminate between road and common in the intervals of dashing myself against the gates which I knew I had to pass. At last I saw a glow in the darkness, and an elderly countryman sitting in it with an air of being indoors. He turned out to be the bureau, so to speak; and I was presently in the concert room, which was much more interesting than St James's Hall, where there is nothing to look at except the pictures of mountain and glacier accidentally made—like faces in the fire—by the soot and dust in the ventilating lunettes in the windows. Even these are only visible at afternoon concerts. Here there was much to occupy and elevate the mind pending the appearance of the musicians: for instance, there was St Paul preaching at Athens after Raphael, and the death of General Wolfe after West, with a masonic-looking document which turned out to be the school timetable, an extensive display of flags and paraffin lamps, and an ingenious machine on the window-blind principle for teaching the children to add up sums of money of which the very least represented about eleven centuries of work and wages at current local rates. It presently appeared that the Penallt Musical Society had adopted one of the most advanced suggestions in Wagner's famous Dresden plan for the reformation of the theatre: to wit, the constitution of a Concert and Theatre department under the Minister of Public Worship. In Penallt, accordingly, the music was under the supreme control of the clergyman. He was conductor, he was accompanist, he was *entrepreneur*, he was (in emergencies) leader of the choir, he was chairman, he was master of the ceremonies, and he had written and composed all the comic songs and *trios* on local topics. He even mingled the politician and sociologist with the composer—again reminding one of Wagner in Dresden; for one of his compositions dealt with the Parish Councils Bill, and another with the recent coal difficulties. Furthermore, he had rehearsed the concert thoroughly; and this is the beginning and the end of true righteousness.

The program shewed how varied are the resources of a country parish compared to the helplessness of a town choked by the density and squalor of its own population. We had glees—Hail, Smiling Morn, The Belfry Tower, &c.—by no means ill sung. We had feats of transcendent execution on the pianoforte, in the course of which the Men of Harlech took arms against a sea of variations, and, by opposing, ended them to the general satisfaction. But it was from the performances of the individual vocalists that I received the strongest sense that here, on the Welsh border, we were among a naturally musical and artistic folk. From the young lady of ten who sang When you and I were young, to the robust farmer-comedians who gave the facetious and topical interludes with frank enjoyment and humor, and without a trace of the vulgarity which is the heavy price we have to pay for professionalism in music, the entertainment was a genuine and spontaneous outcome of the natural talent of the people. The artists cost nothing: the pianoforte-tuner, the printer, and the carpenter who fixed the platform can have cost only a few shillings. Comparing the result with certain "grand concerts" at St James's Hall, which have cost hundreds of pounds, and left me in a condition of the blankest pessimism as to the present and future of music in England, I am bound to pronounce the Penallt concert one of the most successful and encouraging of the year.

If I dared, I should proceed to criticize the singers in detail. But only an experienced critic knows the frightful dangers of doing this. Everywhere alike, in the most outlandish village and the greatest capital, amateur singers are the same—one incautious word of appreciation and they are off to study for the operatic stage, abandoning all their real opportunities in life for a doubtful chance of reaching that mirage which looks like the Albert Hall and the Opera, but which is really a huge casual ward of vagabonds and humbugs, whose punishment for having attempted to make Art their catspaw in snatching at riches and fame is perpetual envy and disappointment. Let me, therefore, explicitly forewarn all concerned that when I confess to having been touched and charmed by some of the songs—nay, to having caught a gleam of that "sacred fire" of which we used to talk long ago in the performance of He thinks I do not love him, and of Mr Blockley's old-fashioned setting of Tennyson's O swallow, swallow, I do not mean that if the singers had been transferred from the little schoolroom and the mild cottage piano to the stage of Covent Garden or the platform of St James's Hall, with a full orchestra thundering round them, they could have produced the same effect. Suffice it that they did produce it in Penallt, and gave me thereby greater pleasure than I often get from singers with far greater pretensions. And in one respect their superiority was absolute as well as relative. All their voices were unspoiled. They sang in low keys and used their chest registers a good deal; but the moment the music went above the natural range of that register they unaffectedly quitted it for the comparatively light and unassertive, but sweet and pure falsetto. Need I add that they were untaught, though they probably do not know how heartily they are to be congratulated on that fact. One lady, who sang modern drawing-room ballads by Stephen Adams and Weatherly, rather alarmed me at first by a very effective use of her lower notes, as if she were determined to rival Miss McKenzie. Not that I objected to her using them effectively, but I feared that she would presently try to force that rich quality of tone all over her voice. But no: she was content to have that quality only where Nature gave it to her; and when the concert was over and we all plunged again into the black void without, where we jostled oneanother absurdly in our efforts to find the way home, I had quite made up my mind to advise all our fashionable teachers of singing to go to the singers of Penallt, consider their ways, and be wise.

WAGNER'S THEORIES

The World, 17 January 1894

It is not often that one comes across a reasonable book about music, much less an entertaining one. Still, I confess to having held out with satisfaction to the end of M. Georges Noufflard's Richard Wagner d'après lui-même (Paris, Fischbacher, 2 vols., at 3·50 fr. apiece). Noufflard is so exceedingly French a Frenchman that he writes a preface to explain that though he admires Wagner, still Alsace and Lorraine must be given back; and when he records an experiment of his hero's in teetotalism, he naïvely adds "What is still more surprising is that this unnatural régime, instead of making Wagner ill, operated exactly as he had expected." More Parisian than this an author can hardly be; and yet Noufflard always understands the Prussian composer's position, and generally agrees with him, though, being racially out of sympathy with him, he never entirely comprehends him. He is remarkably free from the stock vulgarities of French operatic culture: for instance, he washes his hands of Meyerbeer most fastidiously; and he puts Gluck, the hero of French musical classicism, most accurately in his true place.

And here let me give a piece of advice to readers of books about Wagner. Whenever you come to a statement that Wagner was an operatic reformer, and that in this capacity he was merely following in the footsteps of Gluck, who had anticipated some of his most important proposals, you may put your book in the wastepaper basket, as far as Wagner is concerned, with absolute confidence. Gluck was an opera composer who said to his contemporaries "Gentlemen, let us compose our operas more rationally. An opera is not a stage concert, as most of you seem to think. Let us give up our habit of sacrificing our commonsense to the vanity of our singers, and let us compose and orchestrate our airs, our duets, our *recitatives*, and our sinfonias in such a way that they shall always be appropriate to the dramatic situation given to us by the librettist." And having given this excellent advice, he proceeded to shew how it could be followed. How well he did this we can judge, in spite of our scandalous ignorance of Gluck, from Orfeo, with which Giulia Ravogli has made us familiar lately.

When Wagner came on the scene, exactly a hundred years later, he found that the reform movement begun by Gluck had been carried to the utmost limits of possibility by Spontini, who told him flatly that after La Vestale, &c., there was nothing operatic left to be done. Wagner quite agreed with him, and never had the smallest intention of beginning the reform of opera over again at the very moment when it had just been finished. On the contrary, he took the fully reformed opera, with all its improvements, and asked the XIX century to look calmly at it and say whether all this patchwork of stage effects on a purely musical form had really done anything for it but expose the absurd unreality of its pretence to be a form of drama, and whether, in fact, Rossini had not shewn sound commonsense in virtually throwing over that pretence and, like Gluck's Italian contemporaries, treating an opera as a stage concert. The XIX century took a long time to make up its mind on the question, which it was at first perfectly incapable of understanding. Verdi and Gounod kept on trying to get beyond Spontini on operatic lines, without the least success, except on the purely musical side; and Gounod never gave up the attempt, though Verdi did.

Meanwhile, however, Wagner, to shew what he meant, abandoned operatic composition altogether, and took to writing dramatic poems, and using all the resources of orchestral harmony and vocal tone to give them the utmost reality and intensity of expression, thereby producing the new art form which he called "music-drama," which is no more "reformed opera" than a cathedral is a reformed stone quarry. The whole secret of the amazing futility of the first attempts at Wagner criticism is the mistaking of this new form for an improved pattern of the old one. Once you conceive Wagner as the patentee of certain novel features in operas and librettos, you can demolish him point by point with impeccable logic, and without the least misgiving that you are publicly making a ludicrous exhibition of yourself.

The process is fatally easy, and consists mainly in shewing that the pretended novelties of reformed opera are no novelties at all. The "leading motives," regarded as operatic melodies recurring in connexion with the entry of a certain character, are as old as opera itself; the instrumentation, regarded merely as instrumentation, is no better than Mozart's and much more expensive;

wheras of those features that really tax the invention of the operatic composer, the airs, the duos, the quartets, the *cabalettas* to display the virtuosity of the trained Italian singer, the dances, the marches, the choruses, and so on, there is a deadly dearth, their place being taken by—of all things—an interminably dull recitative.

The plain conclusion follows that Wagner was a barren rascal whose whole reputation rested on a shop-ballad, O star of eve, and a march which he accidentally squeezed out when composing his interminable Tannhäuser. And so you go on, wading with fatuous self-satisfaction deeper and deeper into a morass of elaborately reasoned and highly conscientious error. You need fear nothing of this sort from Noufflard. He knows perfectly well the difference between music-drama and opera; and the result is that he not only does not tumble into blind hero worship of Wagner, but is able to criticize him—a thing the blunderers never could do. Some of his criticisms: for example, his observation that in Wagner's earlier work the melody is by no means so original as Weber's, are indisputable—indeed he might have said Meyerbeer or anybody else; for Wagner's melody was never original at all in that sense, any more than Giotto's figures are picturesque or Shakespear's lines elegant.

But I entirely—though quite respectfully—dissent from Noufflard's suggestion that in composing Tristan Wagner turned his back on the theoretic basis of Siegfried, and returned to "absolute music." It is true, as Noufflard points out, that in Tristan, and even in Der Ring itself, Wagner sometimes got so rapt from the objective drama that he got away from the words too, and in Tristan came to writing music without coherent words at all. But wordless music is not absolute music. Absolute music is the purely decorative sound pattern: tone-poetry is the musical expression of poetic feeling.

When Tristan gives musical expression to an excess of feeling for which he can find no coherent words, he is no more uttering absolute music than the shepherd who carries on the drama at one of its most deeply felt passages by playing on his pipe.

Wagner regarded all Beethoven's important instrumental works as tone-poems; and he himself, though he wrote so much for the orchestra alone in the course of his music-dramas, never wrote, or could write, a note of absolute music. The fact is, there is a great deal of feeling, highly poetic and highly dramatic, which cannot be expressed by mere words—because words are the counters of thinking, not of feeling—but which can be supremely expressed by music. The poet tries to make words serve his purpose by arranging them musically, but is hampered by the certainty of becoming absurd if he does not make his musically arranged words mean something to the intellect as well as to the feeling.

For example, the unfortunate Shakespear could not make Juliet say:

> O Romeo, Romeo, Romeo, Romeo, Romeo;

and so on for twenty lines. He had to make her, in an extremity of unnaturalness, begin to argue the case in a sort of amatory legal fashion, thus:

> O Romeo, Romeo, wherefore art thou Romeo?
> Deny thy father and refuse thy name,
> Or, if thou wilt not, &c. &c. &c.

It is verbally decorative; but it is not love. And again:

> Parting is such sweet sorrow
> That I shall say goodnight till it be morrow;

which is a most ingenious conceit, but one which a woman would no more utter at such a moment than she would prove the rope ladder to be the shortest way out because any two sides of a triangle are together greater than the third.

Now these difficulties do not exist for the tone-poet. He can make Isolde say nothing but "Tristan, Tristan, Tristan, Tristan, Tristan," and Tristan nothing but "Isolde, Isolde, Isolde, Isolde, Isolde," to their hearts' content without creating the smallest demand for more definite explanations; and as for the number of times a tenor and soprano can repeat "Addio, addio, addio," there is no limit to it. There is a great deal of this reduction of speech to mere ejaculation in Wagner; and it is a reduction directly pointed to in those very pages of Opera and Drama which seem to make the words all-important by putting the poem in the first place as the seed of the whole music-drama, and yet make a clean sweep of nine-tenths of the dictionary by insisting that it is only the language of feeling that craves for musical expression, or even is susceptible of it.

Nay, you may not only reduce the words to pure ejaculation, you may substitute mere *roulade* vocalization, or even balderdash, for them, provided the music sustains the feeling which is the real subject of the drama, as has been proved by many pages of genuinely dramatic music, both in opera and elsewhere, which either have no words at all, or else belie them. It is only when a thought interpenetrated with intense feeling has to be expressed, as in the Ode to Joy in the Ninth Symphony, that coherent words must come with the music. You have such words in Tristan; you have also ejaculations void of thought, though full of feeling; and you have plenty of instrumental music with no words at all. But you have no "absolute" music, and no "opera."

Nothing in the world convinces you more of the fact that a dramatic poem cannot possibly take the form of an opera libretto than listening to Tristan and comparing it with, say, Gounod's Romeo and Juliet. I submit, then, to Noufflard (whose two volumes I none the less cordially recommend to all amateurs who can appreciate a thinker) that the contradictions into which Wagner has fallen in this matter are merely such verbal ones as are inevitable from the imperfection of language as an instrument for conveying ideas; and that the progress from Der Fliegende Holländer to Parsifal takes a perfectly straight line ahead in theory as well as in artistic execution.

The above observations on the perfect consistency of Wagner's theories with the dramatic validity of music without words must not be taken as an endorsement of the Wagner selections given at the London Symphony Concert last Thursday. Not that it was a bad concert: on the contrary, it brought Mr Henschel's enterprise back again to the first-rate standard which it attained last spring, and from which it fell off a little on the resumption of business towards the end of last year. The performance of Schubert's unfinished symphony was admirable, not so much for its technical execution—though that left nothing to be reasonably desired—as for the significant interpretation of several passages which are generally passed over as part of the mere routine of the symphonic form. If all our conductors could "read music" in this fashion we should not hear so much of the tedium of classical music, which certainly is the very dullest infliction in the world when it is served out mechanically from the band parts under the *bâton* of a gentleman to whom conducting a symphony presents itself as a feat exactly analogous to driving eighty trained and perfectly willing horses round a circus ring. But my enjoyment of the symphony did not soften me towards the "arrangements" from Wagner. They may be very well for promenade concerts and provincial tours; but in London there is no reason why we should accept such makeshifts. The procession of the gods into Valhalla with the gods left out does not satisfy me. You may give me the Rhine daughters or not, as you please; but you are not entitled to tantalize me with a ridiculous squeaking oboe imitation of them; and if you are not prepared to build the rainbow-bridge for me with the full complement of harps, then leave the gulf unspanned, and do not make the scene ridiculous by a little thread of a bridge that would not support a sparrow, much less a procession of thunderers. The fact is, these arrangements, except as regards certain string effects, are paltry and misleading. They are allowable when nothing better is attainable; but in a capital city, where plenty of singers, wind players, and harpists are available, as well as halls big enough to cover their cost, the Nibelungen music ought to be performed as Wagner scored it, and not as "arranged" to suit everybody's purse by Messrs Zumpe, Humperdinck & Co. By this time it ought to be possible to repeat the 1877 experiment of an Albert Hall recital of The Ring with a fair chance of success.

The part of the concert which most excited the audience was the appearance of M. César Thomson, a violinist bearing a certain resemblance to the Chandos portrait of Shakespear, with perhaps—I think I may say so without offence to an artist who evidently cultivates the Paganini tradition of unearthliness—a dash of the Wandering Jew. His tone is remarkably sensitive, and not less so on the fourth string than on the chanterelle; whilst his skill extends to the most morbid impossibilities of trick fiddling. His metrical sense is by no means acute: it is difficult to keep the orchestra with him, as Mr Henschel found in Goldmark's concerto, which the band stumbled through in a state which I can only describe as one of utter botheration.

As to his rank as an artist, I altogether decline to give an opinion on the strength of Paganini's contemptible variations on *Non più mesta*, to which I listened with the haughtiest indignation, though they of course produced the usual hysterical effect on those connoisseurs of the marvelous to whom great violinists are only sideshows in a world of fat ladies and children with two heads. As to the concerto by Goldmark, most unwisely substituted at the last moment for that of Brahms, it contained no music good enough to test the higher qualities of the player. It will be remembered chiefly for a gratuitous explosion of scholarship in the shape of an irresistibly ludicrous *fugato* on the theme of Wagner's Kaiser-marsch, and a *cadenza* so difficult that its execution gave the artist the air of a conjurer, and so disagreeable that it gave me a pain the scientific name of which I cannot at this moment recall. M. César Thomson, however, will be listened to with considerable interest as soon as he has taken the measure of London sufficiently to choose his program properly. He may take my word for it that a first-rate violinist no more dreams of playing Paganini's variations on Rossini at St James's Hall than Paderewski does of dropping Beethoven and Chopin out of his repertory, and replacing them by Thalberg and Gottschalk.

BALLET AT THE ALHAMBRA

The World, 24 January 1894

The other evening, feeling rather in want of a headache, I bethought me that I had not been to a music hall for a long time. One of the horrors of a critic's life is his almost nightly suffering from lack of ventilation. Now when to the ordinary products of respiration are added the smoke of hundreds of cigarets and of the hundreds of holes which the discarded ends of them are burning in the rather stale carpets, the effect on a professionally sensitive person who does not smoke is indescribably noxious.

The privilege of smoking and burning the carpets is supposed to make the music hall more comfortable than the theatre. Also, no doubt, the rousing explosions of cornet, trombone, and sidedrum every twenty seconds or so help to reassure the audience as to the suspension of all usages based on a recognition of the fact that some superfine people are almost as particular about the sounds they hear and the air they breathe as about the opinion of their next-door neighbors as to their respectability.

I foresee the day when our habit of sitting for two and a half hours at a stretch in St James's Hall or in a theatre, breathing air that is utterly unfit for human consumption, and that becomes steadily worse and worse as the evening wears on, will seem as sluttish—there is really no other adequate expression—as we now consider those habits of the spacious times of great Elizabeth which startle us in Much Ado About Nothing, when Claudio remarks of Benedick "And when [before he fell in love] was he wont to wash his face?"

Well, I went to a music hall, where I got a comfortable seat at a reasonable price as compared with theatre accommodation, and where I also got my headache, a thoroughly satisfactory one, which lasted all the next day, and was worth the money by itself alone. For once I resisted the attraction of Cavallazzi and Vincenti at the Empire, and went to the Alhambra instead, curious as to whether that institution still maintained its ancient glories as a temple of the ballet.

I found it much the same as ever. The veteran Jacobi was still there, monarchical as *chef d'orchestre*, bold, ingenious, and amazingly copious as composer of dance music. The *danseuses* were still trying to give some freshness to the half-dozen *pas* of which every possible combination and permutation has been worn to death any time these hundred years, still calling each hopeless attempt a "variation," and still finishing up with the teetotum spin which is to the dancer what the high note at the end of a dull song is to a second-rate singer. I wonder is there anything on earth as stupid as what I may call, in the Wagnerian terminology, "absolute dancing"! Sisyphus trying to get uphill with the stone that always rolls down again must have a fairly enjoyable life compared with a ballet master.

Surely it is clear by this time that if the ballet is to live, it must live through dramatic dancing and pantomime. In vain did La Salmoiraghi smile at me and walk about on the points of her toes: she did it very well; but I have seen it done as well as it can be done over and over again until I am heartily tired of it. La Salmoiraghi is a handsome and self-possessed person, rather suggestive of Mrs Merdle*; but she is not dramatic; and her head and neck are not those of the perfect dancer: she hardly moves them. Miss Seale, a less accomplished gymnast, dances with much more feeling. Mr Fred Storey, a clever comedian dancer, with *le diable au corps,* divided with Miss Seale the only grain of imagination in the ballet, the subject of which, as far as it had a subject, was Don Quixote—Doré's, not Cervantes'.†

On the whole, it might easily have been made much more amusing. Unfortunately, when you get thoroughly "popular" audiences, you may always expect to have to endure a mass of academic pedantry which no really cultivated audience would tolerate for a moment. Your ordinary Englishman is scandalized by anything that interests or amuses him: his criterion of a first-rate entertainment, after he is satisfied as to the splendor of

* Character in Dickens's Little Dorrit.

† Paul Gustave Doré's Don Quichotte, a fantastically illustrated edition of the Cervantes novel, appeared in 1863.

its appearance, is that he shall not understand it and that it shall bore him. His recompense for the tedium of the artistic or *inside* of it is the intense unreality of its outside. For it must not be supposed that the poets and artists are the romantic people, and their readers and audiences the matter-of-fact people. On the contrary, it is the poets and artists who spend their lives in trying to make the unreal real; wheras the ordinary man's life struggle is to escape from reality, to avoid all avoidable facts and deceive himself as to the real nature of those which he cannot avoid.

No fact is ever attended to by the average citizen until the neglect of it has killed enough of his neighbors to thoroughly frighten him. He does not believe that happiness exists except in dreams; and when by chance he dreams of his real life, he feels defrauded, as if he had been cheated into night work by his employer or his clients. Hence the more unnatural, impossible, unreasonable, and morally fraudulent a theatrical entertainment is, the better he likes it. He abhors the play with a purpose, because it says to him "Here, sir, is a fact which you ought to attend to." This, however, produces the happy result that the great dramatic poets, who are all incorrigible moralists and preachers, are forced to produce plays of extraordinary interest in order to induce our audiences of shirkers and dreamers to swallow the pill.

Another result, with which I am more immediately concerned, is that the ballet, being the acme of unreality in stage plays, is by no means unpopular on that account—quite the reverse, in fact. Unfortunately, it is so remote from life that it is absolutely unmoral, and therefore incapable of sentiment or hypocrisy. I therefore suggest that by getting rid of the dreary academic dancing, the "variations," and the stereotyped *divertissement* at the end, and making the ballet sufficiently dramatic throughout to add the fascination of moral unreality to that of physical impossibility, it might attain a new lease of life.

The vocal part of the performance interested me specially because of the frequency nowadays of police cases in which young ladies charge professors with obtaining fees from them under pretence of teaching them the art of music hall singing, without the smallest qualification for that task. And yet these young ladies have only lost a pound or two and a few weeks' time. I wonder how many ambitious young people have paid eminent professors hundreds of pounds, and taken lessons for many years, only to find themselves hopelessly bankrupt in voice, chance of success, purse, and sometimes health at the end of the process. There you have the justice of this foolish world. The New Cut professor gets three months' hard labor for a venial exaggeration of his own powers; whilst his rival at the West End, who richly deserves to be transported to Saghalien, gets half a dozen new pupils, all guaranteed to be manufactured into Pattis in the course of five years or so. The most distinguished singer at the Alhambra was Miss Katie Lawrence, who, in addition to the staple music hall qualifications of a fine ear for pitch and the power of making a well-marked refrain go with a perfect swing, has the unusual accomplishment of a pretty *mezza voce*, which derives additional charm from its contrast with the heartily strident tone which she produces, in the received music hall manner, by vigorously extending her chest register all over the middle of her voice. After Miss Lawrence had sung Keep your nose out of my bonnet, with that thoroughness of style which always marks the successful artist, Jacobi, by the sheer majesty of his personality, rebuked an uneasy audience into silence whilst the band played the overture to Fra Diavolo.

The musical side of Mr Daly's revival of Twelfth Night is a curious example of the theatrical tradition that any song written by Shakespear is appropriate to any play written by him, except, perhaps, the play in which it occurs. The first thing that happens in the Daly version is the entry of all the lodging-house keepers (as I presume) on the seacoast of Illyria to sing Ariel's song from The Tempest, Come unto these yellow sands. After this absurdity I was rather disappointed that the sea captain did not strike up Full fathom five thy brother lies, in the course of his conversation with Viola.

Since no protest has been made, may I lift up my voice against the notion that the moment music is in question all commonsense may be suspended, and managers may take liberties which would not be allowed to pass if they affected the purely literary part of the play. Come unto these yellow sands is no doubt very pretty; but so is the speech made by Ferdinand when he escapes, like Viola, from shipwreck. Yet if Mr Daly had interpolated that speech in the first act of Twelfth Night, the leading dramatic critics would have denounced the proceeding as a literary outrage, wheras the exactly parallel case of the interpolation of the song is regarded as a happy thought, wholly unobjectionable.

Later on in the play Shakespear has given the clown two songs: one, Come away, Death, to sing to the melancholy Orsino, and the other, O mistress mine, quite different in character, to sing to his boon companions. Here is another chance of shewing the innate superiority of the modern American manager to Shakespear; and Mr Daly jumps at it accordingly. Come away, Death, is discarded altogether; and in its place we have O mistress mine, whilst, for a climax of perverse disorder, the wrong ballad is sung, not to its delightful old tune, unrivaled in humorous tenderness, but to one which is so far appropriate to Come away, Death, that it has no humor at all. On the other hand, the introduction of the serenade from Cymbeline at the end of the third act, with Who is Sylvia? altered to Who's Olivia? seems to me to be quite permissible, as it is neither an interpolation nor an alteration, but a pure interlude, and a very seductive one, thanks to Schubert and to the conductor, Mr Henry Widmer, who has handled the music in such a fashion as to get the last drop of honey out of it.

I see that Mr Schulz-Curtius has had all his doubts removed concerning the success of a Wagner concert conducted by Mottl, which will accordingly come off on April 17 at Queen's Hall. As I have never stopped at Karlsruhe I do not know much about Mottl; but quite the most perfect performance I ever heard in my life in point of that precision and refinement of execution which can only be secured by a conductor who is master of his band and of his score, was one of Tristan at Bayreuth under his *bâton.* His visit will be the more interesting as in temperament he is not at all like Richter, who is the only first-rate German conductor of whom we know anything in this country.

SNUBBED BY THE BACH CHOIR

The World, 31 January 1894

It was too bad of the Bach Choir to give me the slip on such an occasion as the performance of a Mass by Professor Villiers Stanford. Some years ago I enjoyed the favor of the Bach Choir, and could rely on the customary intimations of their concerts without troubling myself to look out for the announcements. One evening, unfortunately, I was invited to Prince's Hall to hear what the Choir could do in pure part-singing, an art exceedingly difficult, but so beautiful within its own rather narrow limits that it has never become extinct in England, where it has been kept up by various societies for glee and madrigal singing here and there throughout the country.

For instance, some time ago, happening to be caught in a pelting shower in St Martin's Lane on a gloomy evening, I took refuge in the entry to a narrow court, where I was presently joined by three men of prosaic appearance, apparently repectable artisans. To my surprise, instead of beginning to talk horses they began to talk music—pure vocal music, and to recall old feats of their own in that department, illustrating their conversation by singing passages in which certain pet singers of theirs had come out wonderfully. This led to a discussion as to whether they could remember some work which had been an old favorite of theirs. Finally one of them pulled out a pitchpipe; the three sang a chord; and away they went, *sotto voce*, but very prettily, into a three-part song, raising their voices a little when they found that the passers-by were too preoccupied by the deluge to notice them. They were wholly untroubled by any consciousness of the distinguished critic lurking in the shadow a few feet off, greatly pleased with the performance, but withal sufficiently master of his business not to be surprised at this survival.

We all know from our books that England was anciently famous for this sort of music; but to know also what the singing of it sounds like when it is well done is a qualification which a London critic may very well lack if his experience is limited to the fashionable round of concerts and operas. But I, alas! knew well enough; and when the Bach Choristers confidently exhibited their accomplishments as gleemen to me, I at once perceived that they were not within fifty rehearsals of any sort of real proficiency—in short, that they were making an execrable noise under the impression that they were singing a Bach motet.

In discharge of my duty, I explained this and analyzed the noise, in which I found only a mere trace of vocal tone. The Choir was unable to face such critical chemistry: it fled as the Faubourg St Antoine did from Napoleon's whiff of grapeshot; and since that day I have only heard of its concerts by chance. This time, as I have said, chance was unpropitious; and, to my sincere regret, I missed Professor Stanford's Mass. I am not fond of modern settings of the Mass as a rule; but this particular one, as an example of the artistic catholicity of an Irish Protestant (and if you have never been in Ireland you do not know what Protestantism is), especially interests me.

Nothing is more tempting to a keen critic than an opportunity of comparing that religious music into the spirit of which the composer has entered through his dramatic faculty alone, with that which is the immediate expression of his own religious faith. And of such an opportunity I have been deprived because it fell to my lot to give the Bach Choir its first taste of really stimulating criticism. Must I, at this age, come down to studying advertisement columns for concerts like any common mortal?

On Monday last week I looked in at the Popular Concert, where I found myself in so insusceptible a mood that half an hour passed before I could fix my attention on anything. During that half-hour I think a Schumann quartet was played—at least I ascribed a passage or two that broke through my apathy to that composer. Miss Liza Lehmann sang also; but it seemed to me that her tone was dry and thin, her style mannered, and her intonation imperfect even from the German standpoint. This seemed strange; for five years ago Miss Lehmann was a charming singer. I prefer to believe that she is so still, and that my ill-humor was to blame for my unfavorable impression. But for the moment I could not help thinking that we had somehow managed to starve a very promising artistic talent in our drawing rooms just at the point in its development when it most needed nourishment. I saw in Miss Lehmann a ladylike singer with agreeable manners and an amiable personality; but my ears were no longer charmed, my heart no longer touched.

The only part of the concert I enjoyed was Miss Eibenschütz's playing of a couple of new sets of pianoforte pieces by Brahms. In them we had Brahms at his best, overflowing with purely musical impulses and letting them run into their own shapes and not into any academic mould. The music gushes and babbles delightfully; there is no attempt to engineer channels for it; and nobody would suppose for a moment that so charming and wittily brief a composer could be, in that domain where acute and original intellectual power must be brought to bear on musical inspiration, the most stupendous bore in all the realms of sound.

There was something of a crowd at this concert. The attraction, as it turned out, was one of the annual routine performances of Beethoven's septet, with the string quartet reinforced by Mr Reynolds's double bass, and Messrs Egerton, Wotton, and Paersch playing the clarinet, bassoon, and horn parts. It was soon evident, however, that this early work of Beethoven's has lost all power over Lady Hallé. Her effort to play it carefully only led to her playing it slowly. She took the first movement at about two-thirds of the lowest speed needed to sustain life; and the others followed her from note to note, and thought of other things. Poor old septuor! Whether the later movements went any better I cannot say. At the last chord of the *allegro* I hastily avaunted.

THE RELIGION OF THE PIANOFORTE

The Fortnightly Review, February 1894

The other day somebody went to Rubinstein and said "Is the pianoforte a musical instrument?" That is just the sort of question people put nowadays. You call on the Prince of Wales to ask "Is England a republic?" or on the Lord Mayor with "Is London a city?" or on Madame Calvé to take her opinion, as an expert, on "Is Cavalleria Rusticana an opera?" In treating such questions as open ones you have already achieved a paradox; and even if the Prince of Wales should have the presence of mind to simply say No, and the Lord Mayor and Madame Calvé, Yes, and have you immediately shewn out, still you are in a position to fill the contents bill of one of our weekly scrap papers with "Is England a republic?—What the Prince of Wales says"; and so sell off an edition to people who cannot bring themselves to think that the plain explanation of the mystery is that you are a foolish person.

Yet it will not do to reply to "Is the pianoforte a musical instrument?" by a simple Yes. That would be an understatement of a quite extraordinary case. The pianoforte is the most important of all musical instruments: its invention was to music what the invention of printing was to poetry. Just consider the analogy for a moment. What is it that keeps Shakespear alive among us? Is it the stage, the great actors, the occasional revivals with new music and scenery, and agreeably mendacious accounts of the proceedings in the newspapers after the first night? Not a bit of it. Those who know their Shakespear at all know him before they are twentyfive: after that there is no time—one has to live instead of to read; and how many Shakespearean revivals, pray, has an Englishman the chance of seeing before he is twentyfive, even if he lives in a city and not in the untheatred country, or in a family which regards the pit of the theatre as the antechamber to that pit which has no bottom? I myself, born of profane stock, and with a quarter-century of play-going, juvenile and manly, behind me, have not seen as many as a full half of Shakespear's plays acted; and if my impressions of his genius were based solely on these representations I should be in darkness indeed.

For what is it that I have seen on such occasions? Take the solitary play of Shakespear's which is revived more than twice in a generation! Well, I have seen Mr Barry Sullivan's Hamlet, Mr Daniel Bandmann's Hamlet, Miss Marriott's Hamlet, Mr Irving's Hamlet, Signor Salvini's Hamlet, Mr Wilson Barrett's Hamlet, Mr Benson's Hamlet, Mr Beerbohm Tree's Hamlet, and perhaps others which I forget. But to none of these artists do I owe my acquaintance with Shakespear's play of Hamlet. In proof whereof, let me announce that, for all my Hamlet-going, were I to perish this day, I should go to my account without having seen Fortinbras, save in my mind's eye, or watched the ghostly twilight march (as I conceive it) of those soldiers who went to their graves like beds to dispute with him a territory that was not tomb enough and continent to hide the slain. When first I saw Hamlet I innocently expected Fortinbras to dash in, as in Sir John Gilbert's picture, with shield and helmet, like a medieval Charles XII., and, by right of his sword and his will, take the throne which the fencing foil and the speculative intellect had let slip, thereby pointing the play's most characteristically English moral.

But what was my first Hamlet to my first Romeo and Juliet, in which Romeo, instead of dying forthwith when he took the poison, was interrupted by Juliet, who sat up and made him carry her down to the footlights, where she complained of being very cold, and had to be warmed by a love scene, in the middle of which Romeo, who had forgotten all about the poison, was taken ill and died? Or my first Richard III., which turned out to be a wild *pot-pourri* of all the historical plays, with a studied debasement of all the best word music in the lines, and an original domestic scene in which Richard, after feebly bullying his wife, observed "If this dont kill her, she's immortal"? Cibber's Richard III. was, to my youthful judgment, superior to Shakespear's play on one point only, and that was the omission of the stage direction, "Exeunt fighting," whereby Richmond and the tyrant were enabled to have it out to the bitter end full in my view. Need I add that it was not through this sort of thing, with five out of every six parts pitiably ill acted and ill uttered, that I came to know Shakespear?

Later on, when it was no longer Mr Blank's Hamlet and Miss Dash's Juliet that was in question, but "the Lyceum revival," the stage brought me but little nearer to the drama. For the terrible cutting involved by modern hours of performance; the foredoomed futility of the attempt to take a work originally conceived mainly as a long story told on the stage, with plenty of casual adventures and unlimited changes of scene, and to tightlace it into something like a modern play consisting of a single situation in three acts; and the commercial relations which led the salaried players to make the most abject artistic sacrifices to their professional consciousness that the performance is the actor-manager's "show," and by no means their own or Shakespear's: all these and many other violently anti-artistic conditions of modern theatrical enterprise still stood inexorably between the stage and the real Shakespear.

The case of Shakespear is not, of course, the whole case against the theatre: it is, indeed, the weakest part of it, because the stage certainly does more for Shakespear than for any other dramatic poet. The English drama, from Marlowe to Browning, would practically not exist if it were not printed. To extend the argument to literature in general it is only necessary to imagine the nation depending for its knowledge of poetry and romance on the recitations of elocutionists and the readings with which some of our sects replace the "lessons" of the Church of England. Such a conception dies of its own absurdity. Clearly, the literature which the private student cannot buy or borrow to take home and puzzle out by himself may be regarded as, at best, in a state of suspended animation.

But what has all this to do with the pianoforte? Well, can anything be more obvious? I decline to insult the intelligence of the public by explaining.

Let me, however, do an unsolicited service to thousands of fellow creatures who are huddling round the fire trying to kill time with such sensations as they can extract from novels, not suspecting a far more potent instrument stands dumb by the wall, unthought of save as one of those expensive and useless pieces of show furniture without which no gentleman's drawing room is complete. Take a case by way of illustration. You are a youth, let us suppose, poring over The Three Musketeers, or some romance of Scott's. Now, in the name of all that is real, how much satisfaction do you get out of mere *descriptions* of duels, and escapes, and defiances, and raptures of passion? A good deal, you think (being young); but how if you could find a sort of book that would give you not merely a description of these thrilling sensations, but the sensations themselves—the stirring of the blood, the bristling of the fibres, the transcendent, fearless fury which makes romance so delightful, and realizes that ideal which Mr Gilbert has aptly summed up in the phrase "heroism without risk"*? Such a book is within your reach. Pitch your Three Musketeers into the wastepaper basket, and get a vocal score of Meyerbeer's Huguenots. Then to the piano, and pound away. In the music you will find the body and reality of that feeling which the mere novelist could only describe to you; there will come home to your senses something in which you can actually experience the candor and gallant impulse of the hero, the grace and trouble of the heroine, and the extracted emotional quintessence of their love.

As to duels, what wretched printed list of the thrusts in *carte* and *tierce* delivered by D'Artagnan or Bussy d'Amboise† can interest the man who knows Don Giovanni's duel in the dark with the Commandant, or Romeo's annihilation of Tybalt (not Shakespear's, but Gounod's Romeo), or Raoul's explosion of courage on the brink of the fight in the *Pré-aux-Clercs.* And mark, it is only at the piano that that *Pré-aux-Clercs* fight is really fought out—that Maurevert comes out of the darkness with his assassins to back San Bris, and that Marcel, in extremity, thunders his *Ein' feste Burg* at the door of the inn, and brings all the Huguenot soldiers tumbling out to the rescue with their rataplan. Go to the theatre for that scene, and there is no sense in what passes: Maurevert is cut; Marcel is cut; everything that makes the scene grow and live is cut, because the opera is so long that even with the fourth act omitted it is

* In The Mountebanks. See II, 508.

† Characters in novels by Alexandre Dumas *père.* D'Artagnan is the fictional protagonist of Les Trois Mousquetaires (1844). Louis de Bussy-d'Amboise (1549–79) was a French nobleman, who appears in La Dame de Monsoreau (1846).

impossible to present it unmutilated without an ungentlemanly curtailment of the waits between the acts. Besides, it is a curious circumstance that operatic stage managers never read operas, perhaps because, since they never conceive cause and effect as operating in the normal way, the composer's instructions would only lead them astray. At all events, we have Meyerbeer at the same disadvantage on the stage as Shakespear.

Here I can conceive our Musketeer-loving youth interrupting me with some impatience to explain that he cannot play the piano. No doubt he cannot: what of that? Berlioz could not play the piano; Wagner could not play the piano; nay, I myself, a musical critic of European reputation, *I* cannot play. But is any man prevented from reading Othello by the fact that he cannot act or recite? You need not be able to play your Huguenots: if you can read the notes and bungle over them, that is sufficient. This only leads our youth to put his difficulty more precisely: he cannot even read the notes. Of course not; but why? Because he has never discovered that they are worth learning. Pianism has been presented to him as a polite accomplishment, the object of which is to give pleasure to others—an object which has not been attained, he has observed, in the case of his sisters. To him, therefore, I seem to propose that he shall, in pure and probably unsuccessful altruism, spend so many hours a day for a year over Czerny's, Plaidy's, or Cramer's exercises in order that he may be able to play Beethoven's Pathetic Sonata slowly and awkwardly, but note-accurately, to the manifest discomfort and disturbance of all within earshot.

Now, he does not care two straws about the Pathetic Sonata, and would not spend twelve hours, much less twelve months, over Czerny to save all Beethoven's works from destruction, much less to oblige me. Therefore, though he will learn to smoke, to skate, to play billiards, to ride, to shoot, to do half a dozen things much more difficult than reading music, he will no more learn his notes than a sailor will learn ploughing. Why should he, since no pleasure can come of it for himself? As to giving pleasure to others, even sisterless youths know, first, that there are not ten men in Europe among the most gifted and arduously-trained professionals whose playing gives pleasure to enough people to fill St James's Hall; and second, that the effect of ordinary amateur playing on other people is to drive them almost mad. I learnt my notes at the age of sixteen or thereabouts; and since that time I have inflicted untold suffering on my neighbors without having on a single occasion given the smallest pleasure to any human being except myself. Then, it will be asked, Why did I begin? Well, the motive arose from my previous knowledge of music. I had been accustomed all my life to hear it in sufficing quantities; and the melodies I heard I could at least sing; so that I neither had nor desired any technical knowledge. But it happened one day that my circumstances changed, so that I heard no more music.* It was in vain now to sing: my native woodnotes wild—just then breaking frightfully—could not satisfy my intense craving for the harmony which is the emotional substance of music, and for the rhythmic figures of accompaniment which are its action and movement. I had only a single splintering voice; and I wanted an orchestra.

This musical starvation it was that drove me to disregard the rights of my fellow lodgers and go to the piano. I learnt the alphabet of musical notation from a primer, and the keyboard from a diagram. Then, without troubling Czerny or Plaidy, I opened Don

* The reference here is to the departure from Dublin of Shaw's mother and two sisters for London in 1873.

Giovanni and began. It took ten minutes to get my fingers arranged on the chord of D minor with which the overture commences; but when it sounded right at last, it was worth all the trouble it cost. At the end of some months I had acquired a technique of my own, as a sample of which I may offer my fingering of the scale of C major. Instead of shifting my hand by turning the thumb under and fingering $\frac{C\ D\ E\ F\ G\ A\ B\ C}{1\ 2\ 3\ 1\ 2\ 3\ 4\ 5}$, I passed my fourth finger over my fifth and played $\frac{C\ D\ E\ F\ G\ A\ B\ C}{1\ 2\ 3\ 4\ 5\ 4\ 5\ 4}$. This method had the advantage of being applicable to all scales, diatonic or chromatic; and to this day I often fall back on it. Liszt and Chopin hit on it too; but they never used it to the extent that I did. I soon acquired a terrible power of stumbling through pianoforte arrangements and vocal scores; and my reward was that I gained penetrating experiences of Victor Hugo and Schiller from Donizetti, Verdi, and Beethoven; of the Bible from Handel; of Goethe from Schumann; of Beaumarchais and Molière from Mozart; and of Mérimée from Bizet, besides finding in Berlioz an unconscious interpreter of Edgar Allan Poe. When I was in the schoolboy-adventure vein, I could range from Vincent Wallace to Meyerbeer; and if I felt piously and genteelly sentimental, I, who could not stand the pictures of Ary Scheffer or the genteel suburban sentiment of Tennyson and Longfellow, could become quite maudlin over Mendelssohn and Gounod.

And, as I searched all the music I came across for the sake of its poetic or dramatic content, and played the pages in which I found drama or poetry over and over again, whilst I never returned to those in which the music was trying to exist ornamentally for its own sake and had no real content at all, it followed that when I came across the consciously perfect art work in the music dramas of Wagner, I ran no risk of hopelessly misunderstanding it as the academic musicians did. Indeed, I soon found that they equally misunderstood Mozart and Beethoven, though, having come to like their tunes and harmonies, and to understand their mere carpentry, they pointed out what they supposed to be their merits with an erroneousness far more fatal to their unfortunate pupils than the volley of half-bricks with which they greeted Wagner (who, it must be confessed, retaliated with a volley of whole ones fearfully well aimed).

Now, in this fragment of autobiography, what is it that stands as the one indispensable external condition of my musical culture? Obviously, the pianoforte. Without it, no harmony, no interweaving of rhythms and motives, no musical structure, and consequently no opera or music-drama. But on the other hand, with it nothing else was needed, except the printed score and a foreknowledge of the power of music to bring romance and poetry to an enchanting intimacy of realization. Let a man once taste of the fruit that brings that knowledge, and no want of technical instruction will prevent him from doing what I did, if only he can get access to a piano and ten shillings' worth of cheap editions of operas and oratorios. I had not the key to the instrument, but I picked the lock by passing my ring finger over my little finger, driven as I was to that burglarious process by my craving for the booty within. It was easier than learning to read French; and how many of us learn to read French merely to satisfy our craving for a less reticent sort of novel than England produces! It is worth anyone's while to do likewise for the sake of Meyerbeer, Gounod, and Verdi alone—nay, for the sake of Offenbach and the Savoy operas. For one must not affright people of moderate capacity by promising them communion with the greatest men, whom they are apt to find dry.

On the other hand, let me not lead those older and

abler souls to whom the heroics of Verdi, the seraphic philanderings of Gounod, and the pseudo-historical effect-mongering of Meyerbeer are but children's entertainments, to suppose that there is no music at their level. Music is not always serenading Jessica and Lorenzo*: it has higher business than that. As one of those swaggering bronzes from the furniture shops—two cavaliers drawing their swords at oneanother from opposite ends of the mantelpiece—is to a statue by Praxiteles, so is an opera by Meyerbeer to one by Mozart. However you may despise romantic novels, however loftily you may be absorbed in the future destiny of what is highest in humanity, so that for mere light literature you turn from Dante to Goethe, or from Schopenhauer to Comte, or from Ruskin to Ibsen—still, if you do not know Die Zauberflöte, if you have never soared into the heaven where they sing the choral ending of the Ninth Symphony, if Der Ring des Nibelungen is nothing to you but a newspaper phrase, then you are an ignoramus, however eagerly you may pore in your darkened library over the mere printed labels of those wonders that can only be communicated by the transubstantiation of pure feeling for musical tone. The greatest of the great among poets, from Eschylus to Wagner, have been poet-musicians: how then can any man disdain music or pretend to have completed his culture without it?

Thus to the whole range of imaginative letters, from the [W. S. Gilbert] Bab Ballads to [Shelley's] Prometheus Unbound, you have a parallel range of music from Trial by Jury to Tristan und Isolde, conveying to your very senses what the other could only suggest to your imagination. Only, to travel along this higher range rather than along the lesser one, you must use your

* Shakespear's The Merchant of Venice, V, I.

piano. This is the mission of the pianoforte, to assert which adequately is such an answer to "Is the pianoforte a musical instrument?" as will send the questioner away an abashed idiot.

Now let us consider the drawbacks to culture by pianoforte as opposed to culture by ordinary reading. To begin with, people do not read aloud; consequently half a dozen persons can sit in the same room and enjoy six different books by the light of the same lamp. Imagine these people going to six pianos and simultaneously striking up The Mikado, Dinorah, Faust, Aïda, Fidelio, and Götterdämmerung. Nay, imagine them doing it, not in the same room, but even in the same house, or in the same square, with the windows open in summer! In German towns they have a music curfew, and will not let you play after a stated hour in the evening. When Liszt was teaching at Weimar, playing the pianoforte with the window open was a public misdemeanor punishable by fine. The only wonder is that the piano is permitted at all except in lighthouses and other detached residences. At present unmusical people get used to the noise of a piano just as they get used to the noise of cabs clattering past; but in the end the pianos will make most people musical; and then there will be an end of the present anarchic toleration. For just in proportion as you like bungling on a piano yourself does the bungling of others offend and disturb you. In truth, just as the face a man sees when he looks in the glass is not his face as his neighbor sees it, so the music we hear when we play is not what our neighbors hear.

I know no way out of this difficulty just at present. We cannot go back to the clavichord unless we listen to it through a microphone; for though you can play Bach fugues on a clavichord, you cannot play *Suoni la tromba*, or *Di quella pira*, or the Rákóczy March, or the Ride of the Valkyries—at least, not to your heart's content. Even good playing and good pianos are eternally impossible. For the laws of nature forbid good playing with our keyboard, which defies the human hand and only gives us the run of the twelve keys on condition that they are all perceptibly out of tune. And the laws of nature equally seem, so far, to decree that the pianoforte string which gives the most beautiful tone and the pianoforte action which gives the most perfect touch will not last; so that if you get an ideal piano at a cost of some hundreds of pounds, in five years you will want a new one. But you are far more likely, as the income-tax returns prove, to be compelled to put up with a twentyfive pound piano on the three years' system; and though excellent French pianets (considering) are to be had at that price, the ordinary British householder prefers a full-sized walnut piano of the sort that justifies the use of dynamite.

Thus we appear to be driven to this lamentable alternative: either to give up the best part of our culture or else make it a curse to the people downstairs or next door. We seem hardly to have the right to hesitate; for now that the moral basis of pianism as a means of giving pleasure to others is exploded, and shewn to correspond to the exact opposite of the facts of the case, it appears to be our plain duty to forbid amateur music altogether, and to insist on romance and poetry being restricted to their silent, incomplete, merely literary expression.

But this, I submit, we dare not do. Without music we shall surely perish of drink, morphia, and all sorts of artificial exaggerations of the cruder delights of the senses. Asceticism will not save us, for the conclusive reason that we are not ascetics. Man, as he develops, seeks constantly a keener pleasure, in the pursuit of which he either destroys himself or develops new faculties of enjoyment. He either strives to intensify the satisfaction of resting, eating, and drinking, the excitement and exercise of hunting, and the ardor of courtship, by "refining" them into idleness, gluttony, dipsomania, hideous cruelty, and ridiculous vice, or else he develops his feeling until it becomes poetic feeling, and sets him thinking with pleasure of nobler things. Observe, if you please, the order of development here: it is all-important, as I shall shew, even at the cost of a digression. It is feeling that sets a man thinking, and not thought that sets him feeling. The secret of the absurd failure of our universities and academic institutions in general to produce any real change in the students who are constantly passing through them is that their method is invariably to attempt to lead their pupils to feeling by way of thought.

For example, a musical student is expected to gradually acquire a sense of the poetry of the Ninth Symphony by accumulating information as to the date of Beethoven's birth, the compass of the *contra fagotto*, the number of sharps in the key of D major, and so on, exactly analogous processes being applied in order to produce an appreciation of painting, Greek poetry, or what not. Result: the average sensual boy comes out the average sensual man, with his tastes in no discoverable way different from those of the young gentleman who has preferred an articled clerkship in a solicitor's office to Oxford or Cambridge. All education, as distinct from technical instruction, must be education of the feeling; and such education must consist in the appeal of actual experiences to the senses, without which literary descriptions addressed to the imagination cannot be rightly interpreted. Marriage, for instance, is admittedly an indispensable factor in the education of the complete man or woman. But in educational institutions appeals to the senses can only take the form of performances of works of art; and the bringing of such performances to the highest perfection is the true business of our universities.

This statement will surprise nobody but a university man. Fortunately there is no such thing as an absolutely pure specimen of that order. If it were possible to shut off from a boy all the influence of home, and to confine him absolutely to public-school life and university life, the resultant pure product of what we call "education" would be such a barbarous cub or insufferable prig as we can only conceive by carefully observing the approaches to these types which are occasionally produced at present. But such a complete specialization is not possible. You cannot wholly shut art out now, even with the assistance of modern architects. Though my name is to be found on the books of no Oxford college, I have enjoyed all the real education which the university has to offer by simply walking through the university and looking at its beautiful old quadrangles. I know fairly-educated Oxford men—though, to be sure, they are all truants and smugglers, connoisseurs of the London theatres and galleries, with pictures, pianofortes, and beautiful things of one kind or another in their rooms, and shelves upon shelves of books that are never used as textbooks.

I remember conversing once with the late Master of Balliol [Benjamin Jowett], an amiable gentleman, stupendously ignorant probably, but with a certain flirtatious, old-maidish frivolity about him that had, and was meant to have, the charm of a condescension from so learned a man.* In Oxford he was regarded as a master educator. I would ask what right he had to that distinction in a country where Hallé had made, and was conducting, the Manchester band; where August

* Shaw's diary indicates he had "dined with Jowett and the rest of the dons" at Balliol on 21 March 1892.

Manns, with Sir George Grove, had created the Crystal Palace orchestra; and where Richter was teaching us what Wagner taught him? Sir Frederick Burton, as master of the National Gallery, Sir Augustus Harris, as master of the Royal Italian Opera, were and are worth to England, educationally, forty thousand Masters of Balliol. Which is the greater educator, pray—your tutor when he coaches you for the Ireland scholarship or Miss Janet Achurch when she plays Nora for you? You cannot witness A Doll's House without *feeling*, and, as an inevitable consequence, thinking; but it is evident that the Ireland scholarship would break up Oxford unless it could be won without either feeling or thinking. I might give a thousand illustrations, if space permitted, or if criticism of the university system were my main purpose instead of my digression.

Taking it, then, as established that life is a curse to us unless it operates as pleasurable activity, and that as it becomes more intense with the upward evolution of the race it requires a degree of pleasure which cannot be extracted from the alimentary, predatory, and amatory instincts without ruinous perversions of them; seeing, also, that the alternative of "high thinking" is impossible until it is started by "high feeling," to which we can only come through the education of the senses—are we to deliberately reverse our Puritan traditions and aim at becoming a nation of skilled voluptuaries? Certainly. It may require some reflection to see that high feeling brings high thinking; but we already know, without reflection, that high thinking brings what is called plain living. In this century the world has produced two men—Shelley and Wagner—in whom intense poetic feeling was the permanent state of their consciousness, and who were certainly not restrained by any religious, conventional, or prudential considerations from indulging themselves to the utmost of their opportunities. Far from being gluttonous, drunken, cruel, or debauched, they were apostles of vegetarianism and water-drinking; had an utter horror of violence and "sport"; were notable champions of the independence of women; and were, in short, driven into open revolution against the social evils which the average sensual man finds extremely suitable to him. So much is this the case that the practical doctrine of these two arch-voluptuaries always presents itself to ordinary persons as a saint-like asceticism.

If, now, relieved of all apprehensions as to the social safety of allowing the world to make itself happy, we come to consider which of the arts is the most potent to this end, we must concede that eminence to music, because it alone requires for its enjoyment an artistic act on the part of its reader, which act, in its perfection, becomes such an act of re-creation as Wagner found in Liszt's playing of Beethoven's sonatas. There is no need in this account to set up the musician above the painter, the masterbuilder, or the sculptor. There are points at which all rivalry between the arts vanishes. When you are looking at the Turner watercolors in the National Gallery, the poetic feeling which they so exquisitely and sufficingly express completely delivers you from that plane on which mere hero worshipers squabble as to whether the painter or the composer of music is the better man. Nonetheless, in the National Gallery the feeling is expressed by the painter and not by you, although your feeling, too, struggles for expression, sometimes almost painfully. You stand dumb, or at best you turn to your neighbor and say "Pretty, aint it?" of which remark most art criticism is but an elaboration.

Now suppose the feeling were aroused, not by a picture, but by a song! At once your tongue is loosed: you sing the song, and thereby relieve one of your deepest needs—strange as that may sound to people who sing songs solely to gain the applause of others. Further, you gain by practice the power of expressing feeling, and with that power the courage to express it, for want of which power and courage we all go miserably about today, shrinking and pretending, misunderstanding and misunderstood, making remarks on the weather to people whose most nourishing sympathy or most salutary opposition we might enjoy if only we and they could become fully known to each other by a complete self-expression. Music, then, is the most fecund of the arts, propagating itself by its power of forcing those whom it influences to express it and themselves by a method which is the easiest and most universal of all art methods, because it is the art form of that communication by speech which is common to all the race.

This music wisdom has been urged on the world in set terms by Plato, by Goethe, by Schopenhauer, by Wagner, and by myself. As a rule, when, in order to obtain concreteness, I couple my teachings with the name of any individual who enjoys opportunities of carrying out my ideas, he threatens me with legal proceedings, on the ground that I have taken him seriously. And indeed the commonsense of the country under present circumstances feels that to take music as seriously as religion, morals, or politics is clear evidence of malicious insanity, unless the music belongs to an oratorio. The causes of this darkness are economic. What is the matter with us is that the mass of the people cannot afford to go to good concerts or to the opera. Therefore they remain ignorant of the very existence of a dramatic or poetic content in what they call "classical" or "good" music, which they always conceive as a web of learnedly and heavily decorative sound patterns, and never as containing a delicious kernel of feeling, like their favorite Annie Laurie. Consequently they do not crave for pianos; and if they did they could not afford to buy them, and would perforce fall back on the poor man's piano—the German concertina or accordion.

At the same time, our most gifted singers, instead of getting ten or fifteen pounds a week and a pension, have to be paid more than Cabinet Ministers, whose work turns them prematurely grey, or officers in the field, or musical critics. All this must be altered before any serious advance in culture can be effected. The necessity for change in the social structure is so pressing that it drives the musician into the political arena in spite of his own nature. You have Wagner going out in '48 with the revolutionists because the State declined to reform the theatre, just as I am compelled, by a similar obtuseness on the part of our own Governments, to join the Fabian Society, and wildly masquerade as a politician so that I may agitate for a better distribution of piano-purchasing power.

If I were now to string all these points in their logical order on the thread of a complete argument, to prove that the future of humanity depends at present on the pianoforte, I should render my case repugnant to the British mind, which sensibly objects to be bothered with logic. But let me, in allowing the British mind to jump at its conclusion, plead for a large construction for the word pianoforte. An organ, an harmonium, a vocalion, an eolion, an orchestrion, or any instrument upon which the full polyphony of an opera or symphony can be given, may obviously replace the pianoforte; and so far as the playing can be done, wholly or partly, by perforated cards, barrels, or other mechanical means of execution, by all means let it be so done. A fingering mechanism so contrived as to be well under the *artistic* control of the operator would be an unspeakable boon. Supply me with such a thing and I will make an end of Paderewski.

Finally, let no one suppose that because private

readings and performances are better than nothing, they are therefore an efficient substitute for complete dramatic and orchestral representations. Far from it; they are makeshifts, and very miserable makeshifts too. In Italy, when you go from the picture gallery to the photograph shop, you are revolted by the inadequacy of the "reproductions" which turn Carpaccio's golden glow into sooty grime. At Bayreuth when, on your way back of an evening from the Festival Playhouse, you hear someone strumming a pianoforte arrangement of the overture to Die Meistersinger, you wonder how the wretch can bear to listen to himself. Yet, after a few months in England, when you pull out your photograph, or sit down to the pianoforte score of Die Meistersinger, you are very pleasantly and vividly reminded of Carpaccio or Wagner. Also, however diligently you may read your Shakespear or your Ibsen, you must date your full acquaintance with any work of theirs from the time when you see it fully performed on the stage as they meant you to. The day will come when every citizen will find within his reach and means adequate artistic representations to recreate him whenever he feels disposed for them. Until then the pianoforte will be the savior of society. But when that golden age comes, everybody will see at last what an execrable, jangling, banging, mistuned nuisance our domestic music machine is, and the maddening sound of it will thenceforth be no more heard in our streets.

BRAHMS: MUSIC WITHOUT MIND

The World, 7 February 1894

In order to save myself from having to cry Music, Music, when there is no music—for there is nothing beyond the barest routine going on—I diligently attend the Popular Concerts and saturate myself with Brahms. I have been accused of indifference to, and even of aversion from, that composer; but there never was a greater mistake: I can sit with infinite satisfaction for three-quarters of an hour listening to his quintets or sestets—four instruments cannot produce effects rich enough for him—in which he wanders with his eyes shut from barcarolle to pastoral, and from pastoral to elegy, these definite forms appearing for a moment on the surface of the rich harmony like figures in the fire or in the passing clouds. But such works are not the successors of the quintets of Mozart or the quartets of Beethoven. They are the direct and greatly enriched descendants of what the XVIII century masters used to call serenades—things to delight the senses, not to be thought about.

When a German Brahmsite critic proclaims them the latest products of the great school in chamber music, I feel exactly as if a gorgeous Oriental carpet were being nailed up on the wall at South Kensington as a continuation of the Raphael cartoons for the Sistine tapestry. It seems to me that anyone who can see the difference between Monticelli and Mantegna, or between Mr Swinburne and Shakespear, should also be able to perceive the absurdity of classing one of these big serenades of Brahms's with Mozart's quartets. Brahms, feeling his way from one sensuous moment to another, turning from every obstacle and embracing every amenity, produces a whole that has no more form than a mountain brook has, though every successive nook and corner as you wander along its brink may be as charming as possible.

Mozart never follows his inspiration in this manner: he leads it, makes its course for it, removes obstacles, holds it in from gadding erratically after this or that passing fancy, thinks for it, and finally produces with it an admirable whole, the full appreciation of which keeps every faculty on the alert from beginning to end. And though Haydn was a much commoner man than Mozart, and Beethoven a much less clearheaded one, both of them were, on the whole, also masters of their genius, and were able to think and sing at the same time, and so to produce chamber music which no one would dream of describing as merely sensuous. Brahms is built quite otherwise.

Nature inexorably offers him the alternative of Music without Mind, or Mind without Music; and even this hard alternative is not fairly presented, since the mind is of very ordinary quality, wheras the music is as good as mindless music can be. Sometimes Brahms submits to Nature, and, declaring for Music without Mind, produces the charming serenades which Lady Hallé and Piatti, with Messrs Ries, Gibson, Hobday, and Whitehouse, have been playing at recent Monday Popular Concerts, to the unbounded delight of the audiences, including myself. Sometimes he rebels, and proceeds to shew his mental mastery, in which case we have Requiems and general yawning.

It was at one of these recent Brahmsian Populars that Mr Oswald sang some vocal pieces, and Lady Hallé a new Highland Ballad, by the distinguished principal of the Royal Academy of Music. We received them with deep veneration, and called the composer to the platform with three times three. What they meant I do not know: all I can say is that they consisted of elegant musical sentences put together with a practised hand. The Highland Ballad was hardly an instrumental "ballade" of the Chopin type: it was apparently conceived as a piece of Highland ballad music in the ordinary sense. Had I or any other lay person been taken that way, I should have given my melody with words to a human singer. The P. R. A. M., unable to find words worthy of his strains, frankly accepted the consequences of his own ineffability, and made a violin solo of his ballad.

This procedure must be right: otherwise Dr Mackenzie would not adopt it; but as I do not follow its rationale I will not expose my ignorance by an attempt at criticism. Last Saturday Lady Hallé bade us farewell for the season with some Irish airs by Professor Stanford which made excellent fiddling, and gave us at their best points a sense of the thatched roof, the clay floor, the potcheen, and the entire absence of the professorial spirit proper to genuine Irish violinism. The pianist at these two concerts was Mr Leonard Borwick. When he played Schumann for us his slow *tempi* were much too slow; and though he was warmly applauded by the ladies, who all play Schumann worse themselves, I was not particularly interested: Mr Borwick seemed to me to have been dreaming about the pieces instead of thinking about them. Over a sonata by Schubert he—well, I suppose I must not say that he moodled, or maundered, or anything of that sort. But I may at least beg Mr Borwick to recollect what happened to Stavenhagen's reputation a few years ago when he gave up strenuous playing and took to elegant trifling.

There has been a general clearing out from the hall of Barnard's Inn, the Art Workers' Guild betaking themselves to Clifford's Inn, and their whilom tenant, Mr Arnold Dolmetsch, falling back with his viols and virginals on Dowland, his own house at Dulwich. Here he opened his spring campaign on Tuesday last week with a concert of English XVI century music, including a couple of pieces by Henry VIII. which did more to rehabilitate that monarch in my estimation than all the arguments of Mr Froude.* Sheryngam's dialogue, Ah, Gentill Jhesu, set for four voices, four viols, and organ, belongs to XV century art: it has all the *naïveté*, the conscientious workmanship, the deep expression, and the devout beauty of that period. The dialogue is between the Gentill Jhesu and a sinner.

From the Renascence right down to the last provincial Festival, the distinction made between two such persons would have exactly reflected the distinction between a university graduate with a handsome independent income, and a poor tradesman or other comparatively unpresentable person. The essentially medieval character of Sheryngam's work comes out in its entire freedom from this very vulgar convention. His art is as void of the gentility and intellectual ambition of the Renascence as Van Eyck's pictures are. Later on in the concert we got into the atmosphere of the XVI and XVII centuries.

The pieces by Byrd and Morley, played upon the virginals by Mr Fuller Maitland, differed, after all, only in fashion from airs by Rossini with variations by Thalberg. Some of the variations which made the greatest demands on Mr Maitland's dexterity and swiftness of hand did not contain from beginning to end as much feeling as a single progression of Schumann's. Others were pretty and lively; and the airs were tender enough. But when the corner is turned and the middle ages left behind, that charm that is akin to the charm of

* James Anthony Froude was the author of a *History of England*... (1856–70).

childhood or old age is left behind too; and thenceforth only the man of genius has any power. Once my bare historical curiosity has been satisfied, I do not value the commonplaces of *circa* 1600 a bit more than the commonplaces of *circa* 1900.

I hope, therefore, that Mr Dolmetsch will dig up plenty of genuine medieval music for us. The post-Renascence part of his scheme (which will deal mainly with great individuals like Locke, Purcell, Handel, and Bach) is unexceptionable. There will be eight concerts altogether, including some devoted to Italian and French music. The quality of the performances, which has always been surprisingly good, considering the strangeness of the instruments, continues to improve. The vocal music is still the main difficulty. The singers, with their heads full of modern "effects," shew but a feeble sense of the accuracy of intonation and tenderness of expression required by the pure vocal harmonies of the old school. Without a piano to knock their songs into them they seem at a loss; and the only vocalist whom I felt inclined to congratulate was a countertenor, the peculiarity of whose voice had saved him from the lot of the drawing-room songster.

Mr Dolmetsch himself seems to have increased his command of the lute, a villainously difficult instrument. None of the concerted pieces were so well executed as the two "fantazies" for treble and tenor viols which he played with Miss Hélène Dolmetsch; but the three other violists, Messrs Boxall and Milne and Miss Milne, acquitted themselves creditably.

I was able to hear only a couple of acts of Mr Harold Moore's Magic Fountain, produced on Thursday last at St George's Hall. It is practically a ballad opera with the connecting links of dialogue treated as fully accompanied recitative, and certain choral episodes and concerted pieces. The book is a boyish affair—an enchanted fountain, a maiden, a sorcerer, an absent lover, and so forth: one can conceive Scott writing it at eight years old. The seriousness with which Mr Moore has tackled it is boyish too; but it is just this element of nonsensically imaginative youth in the work that pleases. The music, as perhaps need hardly be said under these circumstances, is not novel, nor does it shew any power of characterization or—in connexion with the romantic sylvan scenery—much feeling for Nature; but it flows freely, and is melodious and vigorous. I am informed that the score stands exactly as it was originally written before the author began to study composition. If that is so, then I strongly recommend Mr Moore not to study composition, but to go on scoring. As far as I could judge with the harp part played on a pianoforte, and most of the wind parts put in by an organ, Mr Moore, when he first set to work, found out all he wanted for himself. A professor of composition will no doubt put a good many things into his head that he does not want; but I fail to see how that is likely to improve him as a composer. I am sure literary composition is infinitely more difficult than musical composition; yet I never thought of going to a professor to learn it.

DISPOSAL OF THE DEAD

The World, 14 February 1894

An important point in the translation into English of Wagner's prose works is marked this week by the appearance of the second volume (Kegan Paul, Trübner & Co., 12s. 6d.), in which Opera and Drama is at last placed complete in the hands of the English public. The qualifications which this task required from Mr Ashton Ellis may be mildly estimated at about five or six hundred times those which go to the making of our fashionable books of original art criticism—the Renascence in this or the other place, Leonardo da Vinci as he really wasnt, and so on. If anyone doubts this, he can verify it by turning to the Musical World for 1855–56, where he will find a serial output of almost inconceivable balderdash, purporting to be a translation of this same Opera and Drama, no doubt published expressly to make Wagner ridiculous, but nonetheless made in the sincere belief that Wagner *was* ridiculous, and that it was only necessary to turn what he said into English to prove that fact.

Unfortunately for the poor old Musical World, which lived to be nursed by a Wagnerian on its deathbed*, in order to turn what an author says into English it is necessary to understand what he says. In Wagner's case, that understanding can only be attained through a strong sympathy with the man, producing an eager susceptibility to his extraordinary power of making converts for the religion of Art as he held it. Sympathy alone, however, is not enough: a man may be a very devout Wagnerian and a disorderly or feeble thinker, in which case he will be about as able to reproduce the Wagnerian web of thought in another language as a gouty-fingered old gentleman would be to earn his living as piecer in a cotton mill.

Unless you can think with Wagner as well as feel with Wagner—unless, that is, you can cope with a philosophic intellect of first-rate force and dexterity, and fill up for yourself those large ellipses which are always unconsciously left by geniuses who think with all the impetuosity which a vivid imagination gives—translating him is not your affair. The difficulty of the task culminates in the third part of Opera and Drama, partly

* Edgar F. Jacques edited it until its demise in 1891.

because, as Mr Ashton Ellis shews, the author did not give it his usual careful revision, and partly, as I venture to suggest on my own account, because it was written before Wagner had firmly gripped that distinction between the reasoning faculty and the will which is all-important in his analysis of the work of the artist.

To illustrate: if I am in love with a lady living at Holloway, that feeling sets me thinking whether I shall take a bus or a Great Northern train to see her. It is clear that my desire to see her is pure feeling, and therefore a subject for musical expression, wheras the calculation of the relative expediency of buses and trains utterly defies artistic expression of any sort, though Meyerbeer might perhaps have been foolish enough to attempt it. The distinction here crudely indicated is that which is in Wagner's mind during the first two parts of Opera and Drama, where he speaks of the understanding and the feeling; but later on he begins to identify the two under the name of "thought," which, within the last few pages of the third part, he suddenly defines as recollected feeling, adding that "a thought is the bond between an absent and a present emotion, each struggling for enouncement." He works out this new scheme very suggestively; but it turns the symphony into a fantasia, so to speak.

This is why Mr Ellis's modest doubt as to whether he has succeeded in finding the final and accurate expression of all Wagner's terms seems to me to arise from the fact that Wagner did not on this occasion find the final expression of all of them himself.

My ignorance of the German language is so stupendous that I can claim no weight for my opinion that Mr Ellis's version is a masterpiece of translation; but I think I could point out a sentence or two in which it is clearer than the original. For Mr Ellis, having mastered Wagner's meaning, has been able to check and emphasize the expression of it. His volumes are, of course, not exactly light reading (though they are remarkably amusing and suggestive); but there can hardly be any place in England where a present of a set to the local public library would not considerably fertilize at least a choice few of the inhabitants.

No doubt some time must elapse before the sale of so fine a piece of work will have produced enough to pay Mr Ellis as much as the wages of a dock laborer for the time he has devoted to it; but as all such enterprises must at present be disinterested—more shame for us, by the bye—he will probably esteem himself happy if he escapes being actually out of pocket by his printer's bills.

Wagner's music, nevertheless, is paying its way merrily. Mr Henschel's Wagner Memorial London Symphony Concert on Thursday last was crammed; and the enthusiasts in the gallery took to cheering towards the end as if they were at a political meeting. This was a notable success, considering that the sole attraction was the band; for no soloist, vocal or instrumental, took any part in the proceedings. The remarkable improvement apparent at the last concert was carried much further on this occasion. There had evidently been very careful preparation; and an altogether exceptional pitch of force and refinement was the result. Even in the Parsifal prelude, in that extraordinary rustling of wings during the sacramental motive, the violins, if they fell short of the full effect, were at least not ridiculous, as they usually are at our concert performances of this prelude.

And in the Good Friday music—that happy inspiration from the Lohengrin period set forth with the wonderful workmanship of the Parsifal period—one could hardly believe that the woodwind was the same that had been so often rough and false during the first half of the winter season. Of the Valkyrie Ride we had an original and very effective reading. Everyone knows how Richter charges headlong through the whole piece from beginning to end, aiming solely at a *succès de fou hullaballou*, with the result that the tone, strained to the utmost from the first, cannot be reinforced at the climax, which gets marked by a mere increase of noise, and that the middle wind parts lose their individuality, the wood and horns jumbling together into an odd, dry sound which strikes the ear like a compound of bugle and bass clarinet. Mr Henschel avoided this perfectly. He began with plenty of force and emphasis, but with complete self-command, enabling the band to get the last inch of effect out without excitement and without muddle; and the advantage was soon apparent, not only in the greater play of orchestral color, but in the splendid power and brilliancy of the *fortissimo* when it came.

In thus certifying that Mr Henschel was fully equal to an important occasion, I feel impelled to confess that I cannot say as much for myself. The fact is, I am not always fortunate enough to arrive at these specially solemn concerts in the frame of mind proper to the occasion. The funeral march in the Eroica symphony, for instance, is extremely impressive to a man susceptible to the funereal emotions. Unluckily, my early training in this respect was not what it should have been. To begin with, I was born with an unreasonably large stock of relations, who have increased and multiplied ever since. My aunts and uncles were legion, and my cousins as the sands of the sea without number. Consequently, even a low death-rate meant, in the course of mere natural decay, a tolerably steady supply of funerals for a by no means affectionate but exceedingly clannish family to go to. Add to this that the town we lived in, being divided in religious opinion, buried its dead in two great cemeteries, each of which was held by the opposite faction to be the antechamber of perdition, and by its own patrons to be the gate of paradise. These two cemeteries lay a mile or two outside the town; and this circumstance, insignificant as it appears, had a marked effect on the funerals, because a considerable portion of the journey to the tomb, especially when the deceased had lived in the suburbs, was made along country roads.

Now the sorest bereavement does not cause men to forget wholly that time is money. Hence, though we used to proceed slowly and sadly enough through the streets or terraces at the early stages of our progress, when we got into the open a change came over the spirit in which the coachmen drove. Encouraging words were addressed to the horses; whips were flicked; a jerk all along the line warned us to slip our arms through the broad elbow-straps of the mourning-coaches, which were balanced on longitudinal poles by enormous and totally inelastic springs; and then the funeral began in earnest. Many a clinking run have I had through that bit of country at the heels of some deceased uncle who had himself many a time enjoyed the same sport. But in the immediate neighborhood of the cemetery the houses recommenced; and at that point our grief returned upon us with overwhelming force: we were able barely to crawl along to the great iron gates where a demoniacal black pony was waiting with a sort of primitive gun-carriage and a pall to convey our burden up the avenue to the mortuary chapel, looking as if he might be expected at every step to snort fire, spread a pair of gigantic bat's wings, and vanish, coffin and all, in thunder and brimstone. Such were the scenes which have disqualified me for life from feeling the march in the Eroica symphony as others do. It is that fatal episode where the oboe carries the march into the major key and the whole composition brightens and steps out, so to speak, that ruins me. The moment it begins, I instinctively look beside me for an elbow-strap; and the voices of the orchestra are lost in those of three men, all holding on tight as we jolt and swing madly to and fro, the youngest, a cousin, telling me a romantic tale of an encounter with the Lord Lieutenant's beautiful consort in the hunting field (an entirely imaginary incident); the eldest, an uncle, giving my father an interminable account of an old verge watch which cost five shillings and kept perfect time for forty years subsequently; and my father speculating as to how far the deceased was cut short by his wife's temper, how far by alcohol, and how far by what might be called natural causes. When the sudden and somewhat unprepared relapse of the movement into the minor key takes place, then I imagine that we have come to the houses again. Finally I wake up completely, and realize that for the last page or two of the score I have not been listening critically to a note of the performance. I do not defend my conduct, present or past: I merely describe it so that my infirmities may be duly taken into account in weighing my critical verdicts. Boyhood takes its fun where it finds it, without looking beneath the surface; and, since society chose to dispose of its dead with a grotesque pageant out of which farcical incidents sprang naturally and inevitably at every turn, it is not to be wondered at that funerals made me laugh when I was a boy nearly as much as they disgust me now that I am older, and have had glimpses from behind the scenes of the horrors of what a sentimental public likes to hear described as "God's acre."

I will even go further and confess that this was not the only ritual as to which my faculty of reverence was permanently disabled at an early age by the scandalous ugliness and insincerity with which I always saw it performed. And for this reason I do not in my inmost soul care for that large part of Parsifal which consists spectacularly of pure ritual, and musically of the feeling which ritual inspires in the genuine ritualist. With Siegfried lying under his tree listening to the sounds of the forest I can utterly sympathize; but Parsifal gazing motionless on the ceremony of the Grail with nothing but an open door between him and the free air makes me feel that he is served right when Gurnemanz calls him a goose and pitches him out. And here let me urge upon pious parents, in the interests of thousands of unfortunate children of whom I once was one, that if you take a child and imprison it in a church under strict injunctions not to talk or fidget, at an age when the sole consciousness that the place can produce is the consciousness of imprisonment and consequently of longing for freedom, you are laying the foundation, not of a lifetime of exemplary church-going, but of an ineradicable antipathy to all temples built with hands, and to all rituals whatsoever. That certainly was the effect on me; and one of the secondary consequences was that at this London Symphony Concert, being in a very active and objective state of mind, I became so preoccupied with the ritualistic aspect of the Parsifal music and of the slow movement of the Eroica that I could get into no sort of true communion with the composers, and so cannot say whether Mr Henschel did them justice at these points or not.

RIDE A COCK HORSE

The World, 21 February 1894

I have been unspeakably taken back by a letter from a gentleman who complains of the programs of the last London Symphony Concert as "a curious caricature of what Mr Henschel might be supposed to have imagined the poor Britisher with struggling musical tastes might enjoy." "First," goes on my correspondent, "he must be allowed to hear the Parsifal prelude and another extract [the Good Friday music] very much out of place in St James's Hall; and thereupon, to efface the unavowable and un-British etherealization of temper produced, in spite of surroundings, *he must be relieved by Ride a Cock Horse to Banbury Cross with variations.*" The italicized sentence quite prostrated me. What on earth does he mean by Ride a Cock Horse with variations? I asked myself. The answer was soon only too obvious. The words of the nursery rhyme automatically brought back the only tune I ever heard them sung to, which happened to be that in Mr John Farmer's singing quadrilles. To my dismay I had no sooner thought of the first four notes than I perceived that they were identical with the third bar of the theme of the opening *allegro* of the Eroica. It has come to this, then, that men are growing up around us to whom this *allegro*, the heroism of which never in my life seemed to me any less obvious than the shining of the sun in the heavens, is merely Ride a Cock Horse with variations. I am so disconcerted that for the life of me I cannot tell whether I was always of the gentleman's opinion without knowing it, or whether, like Bunyan's pilgrim, I have been wounded in my faith, my hope, and my understanding by a fiend. I must take time to think it over. He may be right: anyhow, the temptation to be relieved of another old conviction is great.

I have my own moments of impatience over Beethoven; and an excellent way to produce them is to send me to a Popular Concert without any dinner, and treat me to a Rasoumowsky quartet led by Joachim on the first night of his season here, when, bothered by the change of diapason from Germany to England, and finding that his violin is dragging at the pitch somehow, he begins to worry the movement with a notion that perhaps it will come right if it is only driven hard enough. A tendency to drive is an old fault of Joachim as a quartet leader, though of late years he has so far got over it that when he is quite calm and reconciled to the high pitch, his fine tone and sleeplessly thoughtful style (if we could only get it combined with Sarasate's sleeplessly sensitive and steady hand, what a violinist we should have!) are better worth hearing than ever. But when anything flurries him, you find the critics next day full of that dismally deep respect which bewrays the man who has not liked something he thinks he ought to like.

As for me, I said with my usual irreverence "Joachim is flat; and the quartet is not going to be good: I will go and recapture the missing dinner: next week probably he will play splendidly." The next chamber music concert I was at, however, was not a Monday Popular, but one given by Mr Gompertz, who unearthed a very good quartet in A minor, by Professor Villiers Stanford, which for some reason had not been performed in public before in London. It is a genuine piece of absolute music, alive with feeling from beginning to end, and free from those Stanfordian aberrations into pure cleverness which remind one so of Brahms's aberrations into pure stupidity.

It is true that the composer has done one or two things for no other reason that I can discover except that Beethoven did something like them; but a professor is bound, I suppose, to shew himself a man of taste; and at all events the passages in question have borrowed some of the fire, as well as the form, of the master. Unfortunately, the quartet is very difficult; and I cannot honestly say that Messrs Gompertz, Inwards, Kreuz, and Ould were quite equal to it. The performance lacked delicacy and precision. Mr Gompertz is a courageous player who affects a certain rough warmth and vigor of style which occasionally finds its opportunity; but he is not fastidious, and Professor Stanford is; so the quartet was not made the most of.

The great attraction for me at this concert was Beethoven's posthumous quartet in C sharp minor. Why should I be asked to listen to the intentional intellectualities, profundities, theatrical fits and starts, and wayward caprices of self-conscious genius which make up those features of the middle period Beethovenism of which we all have to speak so very seriously, when I much prefer these beautiful, simple, straightforward, unpretentious, perfectly intelligible posthumous quartets? Are they to be always avoided because the professors once pronounced them obscure and impossible? Surely the disapproval of these infatuated persons must by this time prejudice all intelligent persons in favor of the works objected to.

The performance, though the opening *adagio* was taken at a tolerably active *andante*, was an enjoyable one—another proof, by the way, that the difficulties of these later works of Beethoven are superstitiously exaggerated. As a matter of fact, they fail much seldomer in performance nowadays than the works of his middle age.

Between the quartets Mr Shakespeare obliged us with some songs in his wellknown manner. Mr Shakespeare's tone always suggests to me that some very sentimental drawing-room cornet player has dissolved the tone of his instrument in sugar and water, and so transmuted it into a human voice. His singing is pretty; but it is not very difficult—is it? And it is certainly not very majestic. He sang, of all songs, that unfortunate setting of By Celia's Arbor in which Mendelssohn harps on the two lines

> Then if upon her bosom bright
> Some drops of dew should fall from thee

in such a way as to obliterate all recollection of the fact that the poet is addressing a "humid wreath" and not Celia's lover.

Mr Dolmetsch devoted his second viol concert to the music of Henry and William Lawes; and very charming music it is too, inferior to that of Purcell and Handel only because Purcell and Handel happened to be much abler men than the Lawes brothers, and not at all on account of any inferiority of the art of music in their time—rather the contrary, perhaps.

The Crystal Palace concerts recommenced last Saturday, the newest thing in the program being a Symphonic Fantasy for orchestra by R. Burmeister, entitled The Chase after Fortune, suggested by a picture of Henneberg's.* Henneberg has certainly much to answer for. The symphonic fantasy has as little fantasy about it as the most prosaic person could desire. Ambitious, intelligent, utterly commonplace, without a redeeming moment even of weakness, it is the sort of music that will one day be ordered from Whiteley's at so much a pound by our conductors. The first movement is sixth-rate Rienzi, the rest sixth-rate Raff. The audience took it in high dudgeon, as it prolonged the concert until nearly half-past five. Lady Hallé, in one of her happiest hours, played Beethoven's violin concerto with an intimate knowledge and affection which made the performance a triumph for Beethoven and for herself; and Miss Evangeline Florence, who not so long ago came over here a mere singer, and a rather provincial one at that, sang Schubert's *Der Hirt auf dem Felsen* to Mr Clinton's *obbligato* like a cultivated artist, and afterwards gave us the waltz from Mireille, ending in

* Rudolf Friedrich Henneberg (1826–76) was a German historical painter. His painting The Chase after Fortune hung in the Berlin State Museum.

the skies on the upper octave of the keynote with one of those incredible harmonics of hers.

As to the new comic opera at the Vaudeville—Wapping Old Stairs to wit—I condescended to it as hard as I possibly could. I was in the best of humors, ready to be amused by anything. And yet I fear my mirth got hollower and hollower as the evening went on. Miss Jessie Bond, by the most whimsical pursings of her lips and twinklings of her eyelashes and the tip of her nose, "worked loyally," as the dramatic critics say, to secure a success.

But is there no loyalty due to the audience and to art in these matters? Was Kemble disloyal or loyal when he damned Ireland's Vortigern and that play of Godwin's chronicled by Lamb?* Suppose Miss Bond and Messrs Temple, Avon Saxon, Sparling, Bourchier, and the rest make Wapping Old Stairs a success, is that to be counted to them for righteousness or the reverse? I will not undertake to settle the point: all I can say is that the composer, Mr Howard Talbot, has a reasonable talent for the composition of shop ballads, in singing which Miss Mary Turner made an immediate and solid hit; and that the author, Mr Stuart Robertson, has arranged his play with consummate art so that any ten minutes of it is exactly like any other ten minutes of it, neither the scene, nor the story, nor the characters suffering any change, or advance, or development from the rising of the curtain to within a page of the end.

The scenepainter, by the way, has moved Wapping across the river to Rotherhithe in order to bring in St Paul's with a background of the northern heights. All

* William Henry Ireland's pseudo-Shakespearean drama *Vortigern* was produced at Drury Lane in 1799. William Godwin's tragedy Antonio; or, The Soldier's Return was performed at Drury Lane in 1800.

that I can say in praise of the opera is that if it is not very clever, it is at least not deliberately base, as many would-be smart comic operas are: its fun, as far as it goes—and there is some fun in it here and there—is entirely light-hearted and decent. The sailors are men, and not rowdy young women; and altogether, though the author might be more comic and the composer more operatic with advantage, their work is a genuine attempt at what it professes to be, and not a quite different sort of exhibition in disguise.

NO RULES

The World, 28 February 1894

An interesting book has just come into my hands—Mr Arthur Hervey's Masters of French Music (published by Messrs Osgood, McIlvaine and Co.). Mr Hervey is just the man for the work: he loves France and French music; he is an enthusiast and a composer; and I know nothing against him except that he is a musical critic, which, as Mr Riderhood remarked of his three months imprisonment, might happen to any man. I will not say that Mr Hervey expresses my own feelings about French music; for no book could be abusive enough for that and at the same time be entirely fit for publication. But then I should write a very bad book on the subject. To my mind, the French would be a very tolerable nation if only they would let art alone. It is the one thing for which they have no sort of capacity; and their perpetual affectation of it is in them what hypocrisy is in the English, an all-pervading falsehood which puts one out of patience with them in spite of their realities and efficiencies.

Mr Hervey has certain engaging qualities of kindliness and modesty which prevent him from forming these violent opinions. He takes a warm interest in the French school, and, if the score of a grand opera has only as much as a pretty waltz in it, will relent over that instead of throwing the score at the composer's head. In sketching the men themselves he is wonderfully lively and sympathetic considering their superficiality and barrenness from that deeper artistic point of view which he takes when expressing his own feelings, whether as writer or composer. For instance, his sixtyfive pages about Saint-Saëns give the pleasantest impression of that composer's cleverness, his technical ingenuity, his elegant and fanciful handling of the orchestra, his facility, his wit, his wide knowledge of modern music, his charming execution as pianist and organist, and his triumphs at the Opéra and elsewhere as a "master of French music"—observe, not a French master of music: Mr Hervey, instinctively or intentionally, has guarded himself well in turning that phrase. Mr Hervey even declares that Samson et Dalila, with its one heartless, fashionably sensuous love duet, and its whistling Abimelech in the vilest Meyerbeerian manner, ought to be imported to these shores.

Altogether, you would never guess from him that if you take away from Saint-Saëns' music what he has borrowed from Meyerbeer, Gounod, and Bach, or rather from that poetically ornamental vein of Bach which is best sampled in the prelude to the organ fugue in A minor, you will find nothing left but graceful nicknacks—barcarolles, serenades, ballets, and the like, with, of course, the regulation *crescendos*, aspiring modulations, and instrumental climaxes ending with a crash of the cymbals, which do duty for "symphonic poetry" when Phaëton has to be hurled from his car or some other sublimity taken in hand.

But Mr Hervey, all the same, allows him to sum himself up in these significant words: "I admire the works of Richard Wagner profoundly, in spite of their *bizarrerie.* They are superior and powerful, *which suffices for me.* But I have never belonged, I do not belong, and I never shall belong, to the Wagnerian religion." Here you have the French composer all over. To be "superior and powerful": that is enough for him. Accordingly, he imitates Meyerbeer, who deliberately cultivated *bizarrerie* in order to impress the French with the idea that he was "superior and powerful" (and succeeded); he complains of the *bizarrerie* of Wagner, the most sincere and straightforward of composers, whose hatred of *bizarrerie* amounted to loathing; and he then solemnly disclaims "the Wagnerian religion," as if, in any other country in the world except France, he could be suspected for a moment of even knowing what it means.

Bruneau himself, a far abler composer, who is really a tone-poet in his way, is quoted as saying "Owing to Wagner's prodigious genius, the musical drama has entered into a new era—an era of true reason, of vigorous good sense, and of perfect logic." Imagine a man admiring Die Walküre for its good sense and its logic! What Bruneau catches is not the poetry and philosophy of Die Walküre, but the *system* of its composition—the system of representative themes, which he finds perfectly intelligible and reasonable, therefore admirable. Not that he stops here: on the contrary, he goes on to discourse very feelingly on the difference between music-drama and opera; but I cannot help suspecting that he thinks the superiority of the Wagnerian drama is the result instead of the cause of the superior logic of the Wagnerian system.

The most notable saying of Massenet's in the book is his avowal that it was at Rome that he felt his first stirrings of admiration for Nature and for Art. The point of this lies in the fact that he ran away from home at fourteen to be a musician, and played the drums at the Théâtre Lyrique for six years at two pounds fifteen a month before he won the *prix de Rome.* Therefore he recognizes in the above avowal the fact that musical propensity and faculty is one thing and artistic feeling another. Should Massenet require any instances to prove this proposition, England can supply him with several eminent professors who have been musicians by irresistible vocation all their lives, without ever having been artists for five minutes.

One of Mr Hervey's stories about Massenet is too characteristically French to be passed over. When he had to give a "reading" of his Werther to the artists and officials of the Imperial Opera House in Vienna, they all looked so imposing as they sat in a magnificent room round the piano, that when he came in, an unfortunate stranger with a reputation to live up to, and was received with appalling solemnity by the director, he naturally wanted to sit down and cry, just like an Englishman. But an Englishman would have died rather than have expressed his feelings: he would have chilled the assembly by an air of stiff unconcern, and played badly until he had recovered his nerve. Massenet, with a frankness entirely honorable to him, promptly sat down and cried away to his heart's content, whereby throwing his audience into the most sympathetic condition. Another anecdote tells us that "the impression made upon Vincent d'Indy by Brahms's Requiem in 1873 was such that he forthwith started for Germany in order to become acquainted with the master." I had a precisely similar impulse when I first heard that unspeakable work; but I restrained myself, wheras Vincent appears to have actually accomplished his fell purpose. "The result" says Mr Hervey *naïvely* "does not seem to have been so satisfactory as it might have been, the German composer receiving the young enthusiast with a certain amount of reserve."

Finally, I cannot take leave of Mr Hervey without asking him to reconsider his remarks about "rules" of composition on pages 231–233. After shewing conclusively, in defence of Bruneau's Le Rêve, that there are no valid "rules" whatsoever, he adds "Undoubtedly there must be rules of some kind" and proceeds to quote some delusively openminded remarks from the preface to Mr Ebenezer Prout's work on harmony. Now, insofar as Mr Prout's preface means that his own rules are all nonsense, I agree with him. But I submit to Mr Hervey that he must either give up Mr Prout's treatise and its rules unreservedly, or else give up, not only Bruneau, but Mozart, whose conduct in making "a passing note" jump down a whole fifth in his E flat symphony is treated by Mr Prout as a regrettable impropriety which the student must on no account permit himself to imitate.

The fact is, there are no rules, and there never were any rules, and there never will be any rules of musical composition except rules of thumb; and thumbs vary in length, like ears. Doubtless it is bold of me to differ from such great musicians as Albrechtsberger, Marpurg, Kiel, Richter, Ouseley, and Macfarren as against such notoriously licentious musical anarchists as Bach, Handel, Haydn, Mozart, Beethoven, and Wagner; but the fact is, I prefer the music of these insubordinate persons; and I strongly suspect that Mr Prout does too, in spite of his scruples about "passing notes."

Joachim, quite up to English pitch, and in his finest vein, made the Monday Popular Concert last week a memorably enjoyable one. The older I grow, the more I appreciate Joachim's excellences as an artist. His skill as a violinist I knew all about long ago—and, indeed, as far as the mere fiddling goes, he seems to be able to teach young ladies to do that as well as himself. The singer was

Miss Gwladys Wood, a talented young lady, in whose appearance there is latent tragedy, which is suggested still more forcibly by the coldness of her voice. She brought the tragedy into action so cleverly and intensely in a song from Handel's Susannah that the Monday Popular audience, which likes to be musically coddled by its favorites, was not half pleased.

These Monday Popular people sometimes put me out of temper. One of their special pets, Miss Ilona Eibenschütz, who played very well when she first came over here, fresh from Madame Schumann's hands, gave us, on this occasion, a trashy suite by Moszkowski, in which the hypnotic persons present at once found a charming antique flavor, especially in one movement, which was boldly compounded of those wellknown archaic fragments, the prelude to the last act of Il Trovatore and the first subject in Schubert's unfinished symphony. Miss Eibenschütz scrambled through them just as she scrambles through everything now, as if all music were nothing but one huge toccata to shew how fast she can play. The result was a volley of applause which would have flattered Paderewski, and which was only stopped by a hackneyed *encore* piece, which Miss Eibenschütz played as well as the audience deserved—that is, rather worse than before.

I can only hope that Miss Eibenschütz is under no illusion as to the value of that applause. Her playing of the great Beethoven concerto in E flat at the London Symphony Concert on Thursday last did not mend matters. I could discover no other idea in her performance except the intention of making the most of the technical difficulties by playing as fast as possible. In the slow movement, where this was out of the question, and where, during the second half, the sole function of the pianist is to accompany the orchestra sympathetically, she refused even to listen to it, and went on her own way so egotistically and capriciously that the piano became simply an annoyance. Nothing would induce me to go and hear the concerto played in that way again; and yet Miss Eibenschütz has great talent and skill, and was playing quite lately well enough to give us all the greatest pleasure. I live in hope, therefore, that what I am now forced to complain of is only an aberration which will presently pass away and replace her in the honorable artistic position which her first performances won for her.

A noteworthy event at this concert was a performance of a very effective setting of some verses from Goethe's Harzreise im Winter for contralto solo and male chorus, in which, though Brahms has almost totally dehumanized Goethe, his musical power sounded godlike immediately after our pilgrimage through that hopeless failure, Schumann's symphony in D minor, which is barely tolerable for the sake of the introduction and one or two other beautiful scraps. Miss Brema sang the solo in the Harzreise without twopenn'orth of feeling, but with a thousand pounds' worth of intelligence and dramatic resolution. She has of late made a remarkable conquest of the art of singing.

When I first heard Miss Brema, I said "It is magnificent; but she will grind her voice to pieces in five years." But she sang the Harzreise in such a manner as to compel me to extend the five years to fifty. All signs of wear and tear had vanished; and the sustained note at the end was a model of vocal management. In any reasonably artistic country Miss Brema would be pursuing a remarkable career on the lyric stage instead of wasting her qualities on the concert platform.

WANTED: A FLUTE THAT IS A FLUTE

The World, 7 March 1894

Mr Schulz-Curtius announces that the orchestra at the Mottl Wagner Concert at Queen's Hall on April 17 will tune to French pitch. So much the better. I am a confirmed sceptic as to the reality of those poetic differences which musicians imagine they find between one key and another; for I have never known two persons agree as to the alleged characteristics of the keys. Besides, scientific men have explained the differences, and have thereby confirmed my opinion that they do not exist. Accordingly, I do not believe that when the change from Continental to English pitch virtually transposes Beethoven's C minor Symphony into something nearer to C sharp minor, the character and feeling of the composition are totally altered. But neither do I believe anything so foolish as that the difference in absolute pitch does not matter. The difference between the effect of Pop Goes the Weasel played on an oboe and played on a double bassoon is only a matter of absolute pitch; but nobody will deny the difference in the effect on the listener's spirits. And if you take the Funeral March from Götterdämmerung, and play it half a tone higher, you also play it half a tone merrier. Hence the importance of the change announced by Mr Schulz-Curtius.

Another piece of artistic conscientiousness on his part is his promise to provide the four tenor tubas and the bass trumpet for the Nibelungen music. Doubtless the bass trumpet will be a great joy to us; but oh, if we could only get some decent instrument to play the ordinary trumpet parts on! I declare, in all sincerity, to Messrs Ellis, Morrow, and Jaeger that all their skill leaves the cornet as objectionable as ever. I know very well that the slide trumpet of the textbooks is an impracticable nuisance; but cannot something be done with more modern inventions? Has not a gentleman—a Mr Wyatt, if I recollect aright—invented a practicable slide trumpet by making the slide a double one and so halving the length of the shifts?

And what about those so-called Bach trumpets and Handel trumpets that Kosleck, of Berlin, introduced to us here at the Bach bicentenary, and that Mr Morrow occasionally plays? Or, if all these are impossible, are there not at least compensating pistons to correct those notes which come so diabolically out of tune with the ordinary three valves? Instrument-makers like Besson, for instance, solemnly invite the critics and Lord Chelmsford and a few amateurs from time to time to hear such improvements. They seem satisfactory, but are never heard of again. It is just like the experiments which used to take place on the Thames Embankment, when an inventor would build a wooden house, soak it in petroleum, sit down on a heap of shavings in the parlor, set fire to the house, and be found after the conflagration perfectly comfortable and unsinged, thanks to his patent extinguisher or fireproof overcoat, applicable to every household. And yet people go on getting burnt as if such patents had never been heard of.

The fact is, we want some genuine artist to take up the work of producing fine instruments, just as Mr William Morris has taken up the work of producing beautiful printed books. The instrument-makers will never do it, because all their efforts are aimed at better intonation, greater facility of execution, and perfect smoothness of tone. Now smoothness of tone is all very well in its way; but the question remains, what sort of tone? The instrument-makers care only for that one variety, dear to Kneller Hall,* which is the true characteristic tone of the saxhorn or euphonium, but which robs the trumpet, the trombone, and the horn of their individuality.

I verily believe that the instrument-makers would like nothing better than to make all the brass in the orchestra sound as if it consisted of a happy family of saxhorns, from the bombardon to the cornet. Their ideal orchestra would consist of the string quartet with a cavalry band for the brass, and a set of English concertinas, bass, tenor, alto, and treble, for the woodwind. That is why I want an artist-craftsman to take the matter up, with the object, not of inventing some new instrument like the saxophone or sarrusophone which nobody wants, but of giving us back the old instruments which everybody wants, with their individuality developed to the utmost.

In short, we want a maker of instruments for the classical orchestra; and we shall certainly not get him on strictly commercial lines at present, because the great bulk of the instrument business lies with military bands, and with the innumerable bands on the military model which exist throughout the country, from those of the Salvation Army to the amateur bands of the industrial counties, which compete as eagerly for prizes as rival football teams do, and which spend considerable sums out of those prizes in perfecting their instrumental equipment.

The extent to which the evolution of the mechanism of the orchestra is altering its artistic character was impressed on me at a recent Crystal Palace Concert, where we had a flute concerto played by Mr Albert Fransella, an excellent artist who has only recently

* Royal Military School of Music.

joined Mr Manns' band. Like Sivori the violinist, who died only the other day, and who, by the way, greatly astonished my small boyhood—he was the first virtuoso I ever heard—Mr Fransella sacrifices boldness of style to delicacy of tone and perfection of execution. He takes his instrument as it is, and does not enlarge the holes to get a big tone, or otherwise spoil it for all ordinary players, and trust to his power of lip to make it practicable for himself. What we got from him therefore was the normal modern orchestral flute, very well played.

But I should like to have met the ghost of Mozart at that concert in order to ask him whether Mr Fransella's instrument was what he would call a flute. I am convinced that he would have declared it a quite new instrument. He would, no doubt, have been delighted with the accurate intonation and the fascinating peculiarity and beauty of the lower octave; but I think he would have repudiated the higher notes as having absolutely no flute quality at all, the quality aimed at by the manufacturer being apparently that of the harmonica, though really, no doubt, that of the clarinet. These harmonica-like sounds got on my nerves after a while; and I am not at all sure that I should not have enjoyed Mr Fransella's skill and taste more if he had played a fantasia by Kuhlau or some other XVIII century master on an old-fashioned flute. And yet I was so far from being in an old-fashioned humor at this concert that I went home halfway through Schubert's charming symphony in C in a fit of exasperation at its childishness.

Mind, I do not object to the existence and use of these practically new instruments; but I wish they had not usurped the old names; and I still call for the artist-craftsman to give us once more a flute that is a flute, and a trumpet that is a trumpet. When he has done that he may adapt the inventions of Gordon, Sax, and the rest to his masterpieces as much as he pleases; for naturally I do not want the old defects back—the primitive mechanism and the faulty, weak, or missing notes. The intonation of the wind is quite bad enough still, without our turning back to the methods of the old days when it was worse.

Talking of instruments reminds me that the Philharmonic band has only fourteen first and twelve second violins. It ought to have had fifteen of both twenty years ago; and today it ought to employ a hundred men for a fully scored modern work. I did not raise this question while the Society remained in St James's Hall; for one cannot make demands for fresh expenditure without some reference to the size of the hall and the prices charged.

But now that a move has been made to the comparatively huge Queen's Hall, there is no further reason for tolerating a shorthandedness that makes a really effective performance of the works of Berlioz and Liszt impossible. Some of the scores on which Berlioz wrote the words "at least fifteen" before the two violin parts are half a century old now; so it will be seen that I am not unduly hurrying up the venerable directors. They will, I hope, not permit themselves to be beaten in artistic conscientiousness by Mr Schulz-Curtius. And yet I suppose they will disappoint me, as usual. I have no opinion of the Philharmonic directors from the artistic point of view, and never had. Only I think it hard that Art should not have its share of the profit of their move to a larger hall.

For all that, the opening concert of the season on Wednesday last was a great success, thanks to Tchaikovsky's last symphony, which was very interesting, and far too novel and difficult to leave the band any middle course between playing it well and not playing it at all. Tchaikovsky had a thoroughly Byronic power of being tragic, momentous, romantic about nothing at all. Like

Childe Harold*, who was more tragic when there was nothing whatever the matter with him than an ordinary Englishman is when he is going to be executed, Tchaikovsky could set the fateful drum rolling and make the trombones utter the sepulchral voice of destiny without any conceivable provocation.

This last symphony of his is a veritable Castle of Otranto†, with no real depth of mood anywhere in it, but full of tragic and supernatural episodes which, though unmotived, and produced by a glaringly obvious machinery, are nevertheless impressive and entertaining. There are, besides, abundant passages of romance and revelry, with the usual Tchaikovskian allowance of orchestral effects which are so purely that and nothing else that they have absolutely no sense if played on a pianoforte. Take, for instance, the *basso ostinato* at the end of the first movement, and the rushing scale passages for strings and wind in the march. These are, from the symphonic point of view, simple humbug. There is no separate slow movement, its place being taken by the second subject of the opening *allegro,* which appears as an *andante,* fully developed as such. The innovation is so successful in its effect that I shall not be surprised if it be generally adopted.

By way of *scherzo,* there is a charming movement in five-four time, which brought the house down. Most musicians, if asked to note it by ear offhand, would have written the first eight bars of five-four time as twenty bars of two-four, taking the second note as the beginning of the first bar, and dividing the theme into strains of five bars instead of the usual four. No doubt such a scoring would produce a number of accents which

* Byron's Childe Harold's Pilgrimage (1812-18), "a romaunt" in four cantos, became one of his most popular poems.

† Gothic horror novel (1765) by Horace Walpole.

Tchaikovsky did not intend; but our sense of this five-in-a-bar rhythm is still so undeveloped that as I listened I found myself repeatedly breaking the movement into two-four and three-four bars; and, what is more, the band was doing exactly the same thing. After this five-four movement comes a very elaborate and brilliant march, with, it must be confessed, a good deal of nonsense about it. The *finale* brings us back to the Castle of Otranto, and ends in a sufficiently melancholy manner to enable us critics (Tchaikovsky having opportunely died) to give our "swan song" stereo an airing. That reminds me that the list of members in the Philharmonic programs of this year contains no fewer than five black borders, round the names of Cusins, Elvey, Gounod, Tchaikovsky, and Hans von Bülow. As everybody has said something of Bülow, let me add my stone to the cairn by confessing that I contracted an early prejudice against him because his editing of Bach seemed to me to be impudent, and his playing of Beethoven vulgar. Perhaps I was wrong; but I dont believe it: I cannot imagine how anybody could ever have mistaken his odious familiarity with the later pianoforte sonatas of Beethoven for insight into them. His contrapuntal playing was exceedingly clear and intelligent; but his memory would not now be counted a good one; when he was at a loss he used to improvize Schubertian basses in pieces by Handel with an unscrupulousness that ran through all his performances. Of his conducting I know nothing.

To finish the record of this Philharmonic concert, Mr Borwick played Beethoven's E flat concerto blamelessly but unmemorably; and Miss Ella Russell took advantage of her knowledge of how to use her voice by giving us a concert aria—Mendelssohn's Infelice to wit. The audience was large and enthusiastic.

ENGLISH MUSIC

The World, 14 March 1894

In a recent magazine article by a musical critic of whose ability I entertain a high opinion, he described the result of his unaided efforts to acquire the art of pianoforte playing*. The description gained a certain historical significance from the fact that as his plight was that in which the whole world once was, he did exactly what the whole world once did. Mr Arnold Dolmetsch, at his last concert, made some comments on the article before playing a suite of pieces for the harpsichord by Matthew Lock. Mr Dolmetsch had been lucky enough to get hold of an old copy with the fingering marked; and he improved the occasion by describing the XVII century keyboard technique, which was virtually the same as that rediscovered by the above-mentioned critic, and which produced what Mr Dolmetsch happily described as the "winglike" action of the player's hand as we see it painted in old pictures of St Cecilia and other celestial musicians.

Hereupon I desire to add a word or two, because, for a reason which I will presently give, I am by no means sure that pianoforte teaching has yet completely disentangled the new system from the old. Without going into all the detail of the subject, which will be found in a very clear and sufficient article by Franklin Taylor in Grove's Dictionary, I want to invite attention to the main difference between the two methods. If you put your hand on the keyboard, there is no particular

* This, of course, is Shaw's The Religion of the Pianoforte, published a month earlier in the Fortnightly Review.

difficulty in playing the notes that lie under your fingers. You simply strike the key with the finger that happens to be over it, and there you are. But the keyboard is about four feet long; and the question of method comes in the moment you have to make your hand travel without interrupting the music, as in running up a scale.

The old plan was to make the hand *walk* along from note to note on two fingers by passing one over (or sometimes under) the other. The critic quoted by Mr Dolmetsch, for instance, made his right hand walk up the keyboard by making his ring finger step over his little finger. If he had been learning at an old organ keyboard, with the old-fashioned very low seat, he would have found himself compelled to depend altogether on his long fingers, and so would have passed his middle finger over his ring finger. That, however, is only a difference as to the couple of fingers walked on, not as to the walking method. The modern method is to make your hand *spring* along like a pole-jumper by turning the thumb under the two or three next fingers, and so shifting the whole hand along by half or three-quarters its breadth at a time.

Now if you run up a scale on the pianoforte by these two methods alternately in the way that comes most naturally to you, you will find that the old method turns your hand out so much that when you strike the highest note on the keyboard your finger is nearly at right angles to the key, wheras on the modern method the action of turning the thumb under naturally tends to turn the hand in. Now for my reason for going into all this. My mother had the misfortune to be born at the height of the reputation of the once famous teacher, J. B. Logier. From 1839 to his death in 1846 he taught her how *not* to play the pianoforte with such entire success that she has never been able to play it since with any freedom or skill. It is a great testimony to his ability as a teacher that she has been no more able to get rid of his destructive teaching in pianoforte playing than of his instructive teaching in what was then called "thoroughbass," which also remains with her to this day. The secret of her disablement was his insistence on playing with the hands turned out, the wrists lower than the keys, and the body bolt upright.

Now I do not believe Logier simply acted on the general assumption, common enough then and by no means extinct now, that any way of doing things that is unnatural, laborious, and painful is virtuous, and particularly good for children. Granted that Logier, like all pigheadedly and violently wrong people, was to some extent a fool, still, that was not the exact sort of fool he was. I submit that his three notions were superstitions from the days of the old fingering and the low organ seat. Tradition had placed him in possession of a jumble of generalizations made from the attitudes of players in the past, which defeated the fingering of the present so completely that his pupils played worse than if they had been allowed to pick up the art in their own fashion. It may be said, what does all this matter now that Logier is nearly half a century dead? Well, it matters just this, that superstitions die hard.

What Logier was doing fifty years ago, other people are probably doing today, especially those who, having failed as players, have taken to the resource of all musical failures and turned teachers. I have seen many highly skilled pianists in my time, but never two whose action and attitude were the same. The pianist who can sit like Sophie Menter and Madame Schumann at once, or like Rubinstein and Paderewski, has not yet been born, and never will be. If any student thinks that he can make the music sound as it ought to by sitting on top of the instrument and playing with his boots, by all means let him try it. I have heard organists play much better with their feet than some expensively instructed young ladies with their hands. There are three classes of teachers of the pianoforte in this country: those who help their pupils to become players, those who hinder their pupils from becoming players, and those who do neither one nor the other. I recommend the first to the student, the third to the benevolent rich, and the second to the author of all evil.

Mr Dolmetsch's concert interested me especially because it gave us a chance of hearing the chamber music of Matthew Lock, the last English musician who composed for the viols, and the founder of my school of musical criticism. His denunciation of the academic professors of his day is quite in my best manner. Lock's Macbeth used to be known to everybody: whether it is so now I cannot say; but nothing was more firmly hammered into my head when I was a child than the certainty that Macbeth would spill much more blood, and become worse to make his title good. Later on I learnt that Lock had not composed the Macbeth music, a manuscript score of it in the handwriting of Purcell (aged fourteen) having turned up.

Presently, when someone unearths the copies made of Beethoven's symphonies and posthumous quartets by Wagner in his boyhood, we shall all agree that Wagner was the real composer of these works. As a matter of fact, Lock's temperament was about as like Purcell's as Bach's was like Mozart's, or Michael Angelo's like Raphael's. If Purcell had lived to be seventy he would have been younger at that age than Lock was at twenty. If I had a good orchestra and choir at my disposal, as Mr Henschel has, I would give a concert consisting of Purcell's Yorkshire Feast and the last act of Die Meistersinger. Then the public could judge whether Purcell was really a great composer or not, as some people (including myself) assert that he was.

Mr Dolmetsch has taken up an altogether un-English position in this matter. He says "Purcell was a great composer: let us perform some of his works." The English musicians say "Purcell was a great composer: let us go and do Mendelssohn's Elijah over again and make the lord-lieutenant of the county chairman of the committee"—an even more intolerable conclusion than Christopher Sly's "Tis a very excellent piece of work: would twere over," which I am afraid is exactly what most of us say to ourselves at performances of the Ninth Symphony. Mr Dolmetsch gave us the Golden Sonata, some harpsichord lessons, and several songs, one of which, Winter, created quite a burst of enthusiasm by the beauty of its harmony, which Brahms himself, in his very different way, could not have surpassed for richness, much less for eloquence.

The concert wound up with Let the dreadful engines, the finest humorous bass air I know, excepting only *Madamina,* and not excepting Osmin's songs from Die Entführung aus dem Serail, or even O ruddier than the cherry. It was sung with much spirit and success by Mr Albert Fairbairn, who only needs a somewhat lighter and freer vocal touch to make him a valuable bass singer. So good a voice as his does not need to be ground out as he is apt to grind it. The first part of the program was perhaps the more important, as the quality of Purcell's genius is so much better known than that of Lock's. Lock came at a time when musicians had neither given up counterpoint nor taken to the endless repetitions, sequences, and *rosalias,* the *crescendos,* doubles and redoubles, of the operatic instrumental style, the absurdity of which culminated in that immortal composition, the overture to Zampa.

In the pieces selected by Mr Dolmetsch, Lock steers equally clear of the hackneyed imitative entries of the old school and the overdoing of the *rosalias* of the new.

He had not, it seems to me, the delicate poetic sense or dramatic vivacity of Purcell and Mozart, nor the deep feeling of Bach: indeed, I rather doubt whether he was much more "passion's slave" than the elegant Ferdinand Hiller; but he had a depth of musical sense, and a certain force of intelligence and character which enabled him to compose in a genuinely masterly way. The organ fugue which Mr Dolmetsch played had not the gigantic energy and mass of a Bach fugue; but its inferiority was much more one of dimension only than one would have expected: its difference, as distinguished from its inferiority, lay in its intention, which was less exalted than Bach's, but also more captivating to people in search of musical pastime. Its decorative passages were fresh, ingenious, original, and, to my ear, very pretty.

I should perhaps apologize for having devoted so much space to a concert of English music given by a foreigner, when I have on hand plenty of concerts of foreign music given by Englishmen. But if anyone, however unpatriotic, will face the fact that up to the time of Purcell nobody ever supposed that the English were less musical than other people, and that since then they have been blotted out of the music-map of Europe, he cannot but feel curious as to whether any change occurred in the construction of the English ear at the end of the XVII century. But that was not what happened; for there were a few later Englishmen—Pearsall, for instance—who took the old school for their starting point, and shewed that the musical powers of the nation were still as robust as ever.

What broke up English music was opera. The Englishman is musical, but he is not operatic; and since during the last two centuries music has been so confounded with opera that even instrumental music has been either opera without words or else the expression in tone of a sort of poetry which the English express with great mastery in spoken verse, our composers have been able to do nothing but abjectly imitate foreign models: for instance, Sterndale Bennett and Mendelssohn, Bishop and Mozart, Crotch and Handel. It seemed on the point of ending in our being able to compose nothing but analytic programs of foreign masterpieces, when opera, providentially, began to die of its own absurdity, and music at once shewed signs of reviving. Now I am convinced that in this revival the old music must serve as a starting point, just as XIII century work has served, and is serving, in modern revivals of the other arts. That is why I attach such importance to these concerts of Mr Dolmetsch, which are, besides, highly enjoyable both to experts in music and to the ordinary Englishman who, with every respect for "classical music," has deep down in his breast a rooted belief (which I rather share) that three-quarters of an hour is too long for any one instrumental composition to last.

In this connexion let me hail three times three the proposal of Mr Fuller Maitland and Mr Barclay Squire to republish in modern notation, but otherwise without addition or omission, that treasure of the Fitzwilliam Museum at Cambridge, Queen Elizabeth's Virginal Book, so called because, as it contains several pieces which were not composed until after Queen Elizabeth's death, it could not possibly have belonged to her. The editors, who are, as far as I know, the two most competent men in England for the work, will issue it as The Fitzwilliam Virginal Book. It contains nearly three hundred pieces, many of them of great beauty, and all, at this time of day, of some interest. The publication, through Messrs Breitkopf & Härtel, will be by thirtysix monthly parts, costing, by subscription, thirty shillings a year, or, separately, three shillings apiece. As the enterprise is one of enthusiasm and not of commerce, and the editors will probably wish they had never been born before it is completed, I recommend it confidently to the support, not only of musicians, but of those who are in the habit of buying three new waltzes every month, and are consequently beginning to feel the want of some music that they have never heard before.

ON CHARITY

The World, 21 March 1894

I am not prepared just now to deliver my full mind as to charity concerts. Like all persons in sound mental health, I hate charity, whether as giver or receiver, asker or asked. Those who occasionally try to warp my critical integrity by pleading that their concerts are for a "deserving object" little know that they are stirring up my fiercest instinctive antipathies. I have no patience with the people who think that social evils can be cured by a little gush of sympathy and a dip of their hand into all the pockets within their reach. But there is one point upon which I am prepared to commit myself. If you are an artist, and have promised to sing at a charity concert for nothing, then keep your engagement in all respects as if it were an ordinary professional one, and be in your place when your turn comes.

I looked in at a charity concert at Queen's Hall last week, and found the band of the Coldstream Guards desperately playing one selection after another to keep the audience amused until the arrival of the artists who were first on the program, which had at last to be taken anyhow, Miss Evangeline Florence, Mr Charles Warner, and Mr Watkin Mills throwing themselves into the breach and keeping things going, much out of their turn, with the help of Mr Orlando Harley and Mr Leo

Stern, until the missing philanthropists turned up. And now let me venture to sweeten this admonition to charitably disposed artists with a valuable piece of advice concerning the professional services which they throw away every year under the impression that they are giving them to charitable institutions. In nine cases out of ten, probably, the unfortunate charitable institutions only get what little there is left after a committee has wasted all that it can on its own unpunctualities, blunderings, forgettings, and other characteristics of amateur beggars and busybodies.

But even a good committee—and I speak as an experienced committee-man—cannot help having half the steam taken out of it by the consciousness that if it clears a ten-pound note for the charity nobody can find fault with it, and that if it gets a dozen popular artists to perform for nothing, a very moderate exertion in the way of selling tickets and booming the concert will secure that modest minimum. Now suppose it were met by a flat refusal on the part of the artists to abate one farthing of their full terms for the occasion. What would happen? The committee would have to bestir itself in earnest to make the concert successful enough to bring in the artists' salaries as well as the desiderated ten-pound note.

The concert would therefore be handled in a business-like way; the audience would be a paying audience, and not a horde of deadheads entertaining themselves at the expense of the singers and of the purchasers of a few rows of empty stalls; and as the artists would be present on business terms there would be no disappointments, changes of program, apologies, complimentary applause, and squabbles in the green-room as to who should sing first and get away. Then—and this is the cream of my advice from the charitable point of view—the artists could go home and send their cheques straight on to the treasurer of the charity in question, thereby securing to it the full value of their services without the deduction or waste of a single farthing.

I suggest that this might with great advantage be made the professional rule, both for the stage and the concert room. The present system is a nuisance to everybody, from the artists who feel that they are wasting their time and yet do not like to refuse, to the persons who are pestered to buy tickets for an entertainment which they know will be a slovenly affair, with a disappointment and an apology at every third item. If your services have any real value, have that value coined; and then, if you really believe Mr Clement Scott* when he says:

> How can we gladden grim misery's features?
> The answer is evident—GIVE! GIVE! GIVE!

(and Mr Clement Scott never, I can assure him, made a greater mistake in his life), why, you can hand over the coin and feel that you have really given something instead of merely indulged yourself in a public appearance, a round of applause, and an advertisement, which, to be frank, is the true substance of most of the effusive and thoroughly loose-minded "charity" with which our artists are so open-handed.

* Dramatic critic for the *Daily Telegraph*, playwright, and versifier. He is best remembered for his lyric O Promise Me, in Reginald de Koven's Maid Marian (1890), subsequently retitled Robin Hood.

THE BACH CHOIR PERFORMANCE

To The Pall Mall Gazette, 21 March 1894

[U] Sir,—Will you allow me to point out to the five signatories of the protest which appears in your issue of today,* that there is great danger of their letter being taken, both on the Continent and at home, to mean not only that your musical critic is an inept, fatuous, contemptible, mendacious, wilfully malicious, and profoundly ignorant reporter, all of which they no doubt believe, but also that the performance of the St Matthew Passion by the Bach Choir was a good one, which they cannot possibly believe. It was a very bad one indeed—so bad that I had to leave the hall after the end of the first part, unable to bear any more. My own criticism, which I wrote with sincere regret, was so severe that it must be withheld until it has been submitted to those who will be legally responsible for its publication.† I shall not anticipate any detail of that criticism here further than to say, in justice to the five soloists, that the fault was not theirs.

I should not have written this letter but for the appearance of the names of Sir George Grove and Dr Hubert Parry at the end of a letter which I feel certain they did not write, not because I have any private

* The letter of 20 March attacking the Pall Mall Gazette's music critic, Vernon Blackburn, was signed by Sir George Grove, C. Hubert H. Parry, Otto Goldschmidt, A. C. Mackenzie, and Walter Parratt, Master of Music in Ordinary to the Queen.

† Shaw's review was not published. Its suppression was a major factor in his decision to resign from The World at the end of the season.

information on the subject, but because it is a hot-headed and ungenerous attempt to ruin a critic whose verdicts are obviously quite sincere and original, and who has everything to lose and nothing to gain by incurring their displeasure. I knew that Sir George and Dr Parry loved Mr Villiers Stanford well, but I thought they loved Bach more. If you, Mr Editor, will ask them to let you have, for publication, their separate opinions over their separate signatures, I venture to predict that they will be received with a respect which is by no means due to a document which is no more than the greatest common measure of themselves and three other gentlemen, of whom two, as middling conductors, have a direct professional interest in silencing any critic who knows the difference between middling and good conducting. As to the third gentleman, I do not know whether the censorship of musical criticism is included in the duties of the Queen's Master of Musick; but I warn him that if he attempts to exercise such a censorship from any other vantage ground than that of an earned reputation for disinterested artistic enthusiasm, no critic will be a penny the worse for him.

May I, in conclusion, and in all possible good humor, ask gentlemen who may hereafter rush into this controversy, not to mount high horses or write "in the name of English music"? The question at issue is whether a masterpiece of German music was or was not well conducted by an Irishman last Thursday. In settling it I do not ask to be allowed more votes than Dr Mackenzie on the ground that I am a skilled critic and he is not; but neither am I prepared to allow him more votes than I have myself. Each of us has a right to consider himself somebody in particular; but none of us can pretend to be every one in general.—I am, Sir, &c.

G. BERNARD SHAW. [U]

LEARNING FROM DR PARRY

The World, 4 April 1894

On my way down to the country for the Easter holidays I disbursed the respectable sum of twelve shillings to Messrs Kegan Paul & Co. for a copy of The Art of Music, by C. Hubert H. Parry, Master of Arts at Oxford; Doctor of Music at Oxford, Cambridge, and Dublin; and composer of—among other works—those two famous oratorios, Judith and Job. Dr Parry occupies a position in the history of English art not unlike that occupied by Charles I. in English politics. Any objection to his public compositions is immediately met by a reference to the extraordinary amiability of his private character. It is my firm belief that Hampden himself would have paid any assessment of ship money rather than sit out Judith a second time; and the attempt to arrest the five members seems to me a trifle in comparison with Job.* But the defence is always the same—that Dr Parry sums up in his person every excellence that the best type of private gentleman can pretend to.

* John Hampden (1594–1643), wealthy landowner and Puritan M.P., became a political leader in the movement against Charles I. that led ultimately to the English Civil War. In 1635 he rebelled against the king's extension of the "ship money" levy to include inland towns; he lost the case, but his opposition earned him a reputation as a defender of liberty and of property. In 1642 Charles attempted illegally to arrest the parliamentary leader John Pym, Hampden, and three other rebellious M.P.'s, on charges of treason, on the floor of the House of Commons, but they received warning and escaped before the king could carry out his attempt.

Now it should be remembered that long before people began to get tired of Judith they got tired of hearing Aristides called the Just; and if Dr Parry is not to end his days in St Helena, somebody must act as devil's advocate in his case. Out of pure friendliness, therefore, let me try to find fault a little with his book. If I do not do this, nobody else will; for, I may blurt out the truth for once, without regard to the feelings of my colleagues, those musical critics who have sufficient culture and scholarship to grapple with Dr Parry's learning have been driven by mere isolation to associate themselves with the more scholarly of our musicians and artists on terms of personal intimacy which practically involve mutual admiration and logrolling.

These are not the objects of the intimacy, which is perfectly natural and honest, and in some ways beneficial to the public as well as to the principal parties; but they are among its inevitable consequences; and, frankly, I would not give a rap more for any public utterance of our best critics concerning Professor Stanford, Dr Parry, and the rest of their musical friends, than I would advise them to give for any public utterance that I could be persuaded to make concerning those friends of mine with whom I have been closely and specially allied for years past in political matters.

In reading Dr Parry's book I began at the end (my invariable custom with histories of music); and I have not yet quite reached the beginning. However, that does not matter, since it is not with the remoter history of the art that I am now concerned. In the later chapters I find, along with a great deal of criticism with which I agree, and a mass of information which my position as a critic obliges me to pretend that I knew all along, certain observations which smack, to me, of the commoner sort of analytic concert program. Most of these are due to the disturbance of Dr Parry's judgment by his love for Beethoven, which sets him pointing out as choice merits of that composer such features as "insisting on his key," and "often casting his leading idea in terms of the common chord."

If this be the mark of genius, let us not ignore it in Donizetti's choruses, in our comic songs and army trumpet-calls, and in such pretentious platitudes as the first movement of Rubinstein's Ocean symphony. But as it most certainly is not a mark of genius at all, I suggest that Dr Parry should cut all such special pleading out of his second edition, and replace it by a few words as to the manner in which melody follows the development of harmony. When I was a boy, an overture beginning emphatically with an unprepared discord made me expect something tremendous, provided the discord was not more extreme than a third inversion of the dominant seventh (play the common chord, C, E, G, C with your right hand, dear lady, and hit B flat as hard as you can in octaves with your left: that's the effect I mean), which I was familiar with from the overture to Prometheus and *Trema, trema* in Don Giovanni. Later on, the crashing major ninths in the prelude to the second act of Tannhäuser sounded extraordinary to me; and Schumann imposed on me as an enigmatical genius of unfathomable depth, simply because his chords, being strange, were mysterious.

At present nothing surprises me: you may begin the next act of your opera with the sixth inversion of a full chord of the major thirteenth without making me turn a hair. Now the moment I get sufficiently used to a discord to tolerate it unprepared, and to recognize its key and destination, I am ready to accept a figuration of that discord and its resolution as a "popular" melody. When other lips, which everybody recognizes as popular, begins, practically, with a figuration of the resolution of the dominant seventh. Now that the *finale* of the first act of Lohengrin has educated the common ear to the extension of that familiar discord by another major third, any modern Balfe can manufacture an equally acceptable melody by substituting a figuration of the ninth for the seventh, though I doubt whether Dr Parry will compliment him on his "insistence on the key."

The fact is, it is the enormous part which figuration and rum-tum play in modern music—harmonic music, as Dr Parry calls it—that makes it wear so badly in comparison with the old contrapuntal music. I had rather hear the most conventional, fashionable overture that Handel ever wrote than the once brilliant and novel overture to Zampa, with its "insistence on the key"; and I here prophesy that the extent to which Wagner, like all the composers of the harmonic school, resorted to figuration of chords that are daily becoming more familiar and even platitudinous, will one day make many pages of his mere *mélodrame* sound stale and obvious when Bach's polyphony will be as fresh as when it first came from his hand. Why, then, should we hold up this "insistence on the key," which is really nothing but reliance on the chord, as a merit, and, for example, praise the *finale* to Beethoven's symphony in C minor for the features in which it so strongly resembles Cheer, boys, cheer?*

It seems to me that all this part of the book wants restating. The very interesting contrast made in it between Beethoven's first pianoforte sonata and the *finale* to Mozart's G minor symphony is spoiled by an attempt to represent the difference as a superiority on Beethoven's part. Similarly, some very suggestive passages on Bach's refusal to join the harmonic movement are weakened by an assumption that the harmonic

* A song composed and performed by the popular entertainer Henry Russell.

school was a higher development than the contrapuntal one. Surely the truth is that the so-called "development" was really the birth of the modern "tone-poetry" or "music-drama" with which the old music had long been pregnant. The separation was concealed by the extraordinary genius of Mozart, who could produce a piece of music which at once presented to the theatre-goer the most perfect musical reflection of the vagaries of a scene from a farce, and to the professor a "movement" in strict form; but Mozart, nonetheless, made a European revolution in music with the statue scene in Don Giovanni, unmentioned by Dr Parry, which represents the most sensational manifestation of the only side of his work which was followed up.

Beethoven could not touch Mozart as an "absolute musician": a comparison of his attempts at contrapuntal writing with such examples as the minuets in Mozart's quintets or the Recordare in the Requiem seems to me to shew a striking falling off in this respect. Finally we come to Wagner, who, like Weber, could not write absolute music at all—not even an overture; for the Tannhäuser overture is no more an overture than old friend William Tell; and the Faust is simply a horrible reduction to absurdity of the attempt to combine the new art with the old, the beginnings of the said reduction being already plain in the first allegro of no less respectable a classic than Mozart's Hafner symphony. But before Wagner died, "absolute music" was reviving in the hands of men who were musicians alone, and not wits, dramatists, poets, or romancers, seizing on music as the most intense expression of their genius.

Mozart, Beethoven, and Wagner, with all the "program-music" men, practised a delightful and highly compound art which can be understood without any musicianship at all, and which so fascinated the world that it swept genuine absolute music out of existence for nearly a century. But now absolute music has been revived with enormous power by Brahms, and is being followed up in this country by Dr Parry himself, and by Professor Stanford. Unfortunately, neither of them sees this as clearly as I, the critic, see it. Dr Parry knocks the end of an admirable book to pieces by following up the technical development of music, which is, of course, continuous from generation to generation, instead of the development and differentiation of the purposes of the men who composed music. Thus, he treats Mozart as the successor of Bach, and Brahms as the successor of Wagner.

The truth is that Brahms is the son of Bach and only Wagner's second-cousin. Not understanding this, Brahms feels bound to try to be great in the way of Beethoven and Wagner. But for an absolute musician without dramatic genius to write for the theatre is to court instant detection and failure, besides facing a horribly irksome job. Therefore he falls back on a form of art which enables absolute music of the driest mechanical kind to be tacked on to a literary composition and performed under circumstances where boredom is expected, tolerated, and even piously relished. That is to say, he writes requiems or oratorios. Hence Brahms's requiem, Job, and Eden! Eden is evidently the work alluded to in this volume as "one of the finest of recent oratorios, in which the choruses of angels and of devils sing passages which express the characteristic impulses of angelic and diabolic natures to a nicety." O those mixo-Ionian, hypo-Phrygian angels, and those honest major and minor devils! shall I ever forget them?

The future is bright, however: Dr Parry's latest composition is an "overture to an *unwritten* drama"—precisely the right sort of drama for an absolute musician to write an overture to. In process of time he will see that his particular "art of music," though a very noble art, has nothing to do with tragedies, written or unwritten, or with Jobs, or Judiths, or Hypatias, or anything else of the kind. In the meantime I must acknowledge my deep obligation to him for having written a book from which I have learned much. No critic can afford to leave it unread.

STANFORD'S BECKET

The World, 11 April 1894

The audience at the Crystal Palace Saturday Concerts lately had a much better opportunity of judging Professor Villiers Stanford's Becket music than ever Mr Irving enjoyed. Technically, it is a very good piece of work—it has qualities that may almost be described as moral excellences. For instance, the handling of the orchestra is first rate: by which I do not mean, if you please, that there are sensational *tremolandos*, or voluptuous murmurs for the wind, or delicate embroideries for the flute, or solos for the English horn, or scintillations for the triangle, or, generally speaking, any of that rouging of the cheeks of the music and underlining of its eyes which is so cheap nowadays: I mean that the composer knows how and where to get his tone of the right shade and of the best quality, how to balance it, how to vary it otherwise than by crudely obvious contrast, and how to get from the full band that clear, smooth, solid effect for which one has to go to Brahms, or even back to Cherubini, for satisfactory examples.

Add to this a complete intellectual mastery of harmony, and you have an equipment which enables the composer to do anything he wants to do within the known limits of musical composition. As to what he wants, I approach that subject with less than my usual confidence. Something is happening to my attitude towards absolute music. Perhaps I am fossilizing, perhaps I am merely beginning to acquire at last some elementary knowledge of my business as a critic: I cannot say. I am not sure that I did not think at one time that absolute music was dead: that Mozart had been faithless to it; that Beethoven had definitely deserted it; and that Wagner had finally knocked it on the head and buried it at the bottom of the Red Sea. And certainly, whenever an attempt was made to galvanize it by attaching it to an oratorio libretto, or festival cantata, or mayhap to the Requiem Mass, its appearance was sufficiently ghastly and ridiculous to make me regard it as a product, not of composition, but of decomposition; so I reviled its professors for not burying it decently, and devoting themselves with frank singleness of purpose to tone-poems and music-dramas.

For example, it seemed to me that Professor Stanford would have done better to follow up his Cavalier Romances and write for the stage than to hammer away at absolute music. Unfortunately, he did neither the one nor the other: he tried to combine the two in such hybrid works as Eden and The Revenge, concerning which I remain impenitent, more convinced than ever that they are hopeless mistakes. The only opening for critical error concerning them lay in the doubt as to whether the case was one of an absolute musician hampered by a libretto, or a dramatic musician hampered by the traditions of absolute music.

Naturally I was sure to decide in the latter sense when once I had assumed beforehand that absolute music was dead. This decision of mine proves—what it concerns every reader of these columns to bear constantly in mind—that I can be incredibly prejudiced and stupid on occasion, considering that I am in many ways rather an intelligent man. For could anything have been more obvious than that the disturbing element in all these oratorios and cantatas is the libretto—that it is in his efforts to be a poet and dramatist that the composer is an ineffectual amateur, while in his counterpoint he often shews ten times the skill and knowledge of an opera composer? The man who roused me into commonsense on this subject was no other than our friend Brahms.

The truth in his case was too clear to be overlooked. The moment he tried to use music for the purpose of expressing or describing anything in the least degree extraneous to itself he became commonplace and tedious, there being nothing distinguished either in his own or in his view of other men's ideas. On the other hand, when he made music purely for the sake of music, designing sound patterns without any reference to literary subjects or specific emotions, he became one of the wonders of the world: I found myself able to sit listening to him for fortyfive minutes at a stretch without being bored. Absolute music was in him abundant, fresh, hopeful, joyous, powerful, and characterized by a certain virile seriousness and loftiness of taste which gave great relief after the Byzantine corruption of the latest developments of operatic music. It was only when he touched a literary subject of any dimensions that he became, by overpowering contrast with his other self, a positive blockhead. Even his songs are remarkably deficient in vividness after those of Gounod or Schubert.

In other men the ascendant movement of absolute music was less apparent; but the *dégringolade* of dramatic music was obvious. Test it by the operas of European popularity—Don Juan a century ago, Carmen today. Or take program music, with Beethoven's Pastoral Symphony to begin with, and Moszkowski's Joan of Arc and Benoît's Charlotte Corday to finish with. Or compare Mozart's Requiem and Rossini's Stabat Mater with Dvořák's. Surely we have along these lines the most frightful degeneration, which has only been masked from us by the irresistible power with which Wagner drew our attention to himself alone while he was crowning the dramatic movement by his combination of all the arts into the Bayreuth music-drama, just as Bach crowned the contrapuntal movement at the moment when it was worn out and tumbling to pieces in all directions.

Even with Wagner the wearing out of the purely musical material is patent to all unsympathetic critics. If you take Parsifal, and set aside that large part of the score (the best part) which is senseless apart from the poem, and consider the rest from the point of view of absolute music, you find that a good deal of it will not bear comparison for a moment with the musical material of the Leonore overture or the Ninth Symphony.

Music, in fact, is now in revolt against the union of all the arts, since it has meant to her a ruthless exploitation not only by the poet and higher dramatist, but by the sensation-monger and pander. She is now, like our revolting daughters and Doll's House Noras, insisting on being once more considered as an end in herself; and so the union of all the arts falls to pieces before Wagner's cement is dry, and his Art Work of the Future is already the art work of the past.

Of late this view has been pressed home on me in another way. One of the unsolved problems which all critics have been conscious of for a long time has been the collapse of English music in the XVIII century. So long as our knowledge of the old music was confined to the madrigals and other vocal pieces—that is, to the least absolutely musical specimens—the problem remained inert at the back of our minds.

Some of us, of course, had a paper knowledge of the old instrumental music; but I am so deeply sceptical as to the value of such paper knowledge that whenever a musician tells me that reading a score is to him the same as hearing it performed, I either give him credit for deceiving himself, or else accept the statement exactly as I would accept it from a deaf man. Those who make it usually contradict themselves, whenever they get the chance, by taking the trouble to attend performances of the very scores which are on the shelves of their libraries.

Now, for some time past Mr Arnold Dolmetsch has been bringing the old instrumental music to actual performance under conditions as closely as possible resembling those contemplated by the composers; and under this stimulus the unsolved problem has suddenly become active and begun to struggle after its solution as a discord struggles after its resolution. And the explanation appears to be the very simple one that the English gained their great musical reputation up to the XVIII century in absolute music. In the XVIII century the world left off writing absolute music and took to operatic music, for which the English—to the great credit of their national character—had no sort of aptitude. And if they wish to regain their old fame, they must begin where they left off.

While I was still in my teens, the verbal horrors of "opera in English," by the Carl Rosa and other companies, convinced me that if the English language is to be musically treated at all it must be done in the style of Purcell, and not in that of Verdi. This was my first superficial formulation of the solution which completed itself quite lately in my mind at the viol concerts at Mr Dolmetsch's house at Dulwich. Here the music, completely free from all operatic and literary aims, ought, one might have supposed, to have sounded quaintly archaic.

But not a bit of it. It made operatic music sound positively wizened in comparison. Its richness of detail, especially in the beauty and interest of the harmony, made one think of modern "English" music of the Bohemian Girl school as one thinks of a jerry-built suburban square after walking through a medieval quadrangle at Oxford. The operatic charms that were once irresistible—the freedom of melody, the determinateness of form and harmonic movement, the intelligibility of treatment gained by the establishment of a single popular scale and its relative minor as the mode for all music—these seemed for the moment almost as contemptible as the cheapness of workmanship and the theatrical vulgarity and superficiality of aim which they had brought with them.

But the most significant feature of the old English music was its identity in kind with the best music of Brahms, and with all that is hopeful and vital in the efforts of Parry, Stanford, and our latest composers. So that I had no sooner reached the conviction that English music must come to life again by resuming its old exclusive aims, than I began to see that this was what it was actually doing. Consequently the whole problem for the critics at present is how to make Professor Stanford and the rest see their own destiny clearly, and save themselves from the fate of Lot's wife, which will most assuredly overtake them if they look back to the librettos, operatic and "sacred" (save the mark!), which are superstitions from the age of England's musical impotence. Let them leave the theatrical exploitation of music to Kistler, Mascagni, and the rest of the brood of young lions: they themselves, the absolute musicians, will only succeed by sticking to absolute music, wherein their strength lies.

Having thus, I hope, made my critical position clear, I may say of Professor Stanford's Becket music that, together with those excellences which I have already indicated, it marks an advance in the only direction along which he now can advance, and that is the intensification of his grip of his thematic material. He no longer resorts to clever technical trifling to conceal his want of interest in his own work: he now keeps to the point; only the grip is not yet so earnest or the vision so penetrating as—shall I say Beethoven's, since he has reminded me of that mighty man by unconsciously transferring one of the most striking phrases in the *finale* of the Eighth Symphony to the Becket overture. The mills of the gods have not yet ground his cleverness small enough nor his inner purpose fine enough to make it wise to claim for him the place among European composers which he is probably capable of reaching, for he is in some ways a tough, incorrigible subject; but I confess I am more than commonly curious to hear what his next symphony will be like.

CONSTRUCTING AN ORATORIO

The World, 18 April 1894

Last Thursday England came into possession of another oratorio, called Bethlehem, music by Dr Mackenzie, P.R.A.M.; poetry and analytic program by Mr Joseph Bennett. I was duly present at the performance at the Albert Hall, with its thousand choristers, its lavish orchestra, its gigantic organ, and above all its huge audience applauding the composer to the echo—or rather to the two or three echoes which the building harbors—with evident enthusiasm and enjoyment. But I am somehow deficient in the sense to which Bethlehem appeals; and I am so conscious of this that I shall make no attempt to criticize the work seriously.

The music of Bethlehem is noteworthy as a popular development. When Gounod took to writing oratorio, the obvious identity of his devotional music with his love music did not cause any particular scandal, perhaps because Dr Henry Maudsley's essays had convinced the public that a great deal of what passes as religious ecstasy is really only a fantastic manifestation of quite another instinct, perhaps because the love music had been so seraphically refined. At any rate, Gounod met with no remonstrances as he proceeded to build up his oratorios out of the most exquisitely sensuous elements of his operatic music. The only fault found with them was that their sweetness made them cloy after half an hour or so, full-length performances being all but insufferable.

Dr Mackenzie has followed Gounod's example. He is determined that nobody shall accuse him, because he is a Scotchman, of asceticism or Calvinism. His score is crammed with all the luxuries of the musical confectioner. His ultra-sentimental *cantabiles* for the violins, his chimes of bells, his *pianissimo* shakes on the cymbals, his glittering touches with the triangle and pretty breathings on the cornet, make up an abandonedly voluptuous orchestration; and his actual use of the wellknown figure from the Tannhäuser Venusberg music, altered as to the notes, but unmistakable in its rhythm (Mr Bennett calls it "the Shepherds' Terror"), comes in quite naturally in the instrumental saturnalia.

But, as Dr Mackenzie is a hardheaded, vigorous man, proof against an excess of any sort of ecstasy, devotional or romantic, the effect he produces is entirely his own; and instead of suggesting Gounod, he rather suggests a morally reformed Offenbach. There is a Christmas carol at the end of the first part of Bethlehem which is Offenbach all over (minus, of course, the Bohemianism). It is in six-eight time, treated in the most popular fashion, with the orchestra marking the swing of the two divisions of the bar like a huge accordion, and making it like a pious cousin of the pastoral in the first act of Orphée aux Enfers. Another point of resemblance to Offenbach is in the way in which the imposing effects are produced.

Offenbach was no master of harmony: he could write an accompaniment to a tune; but the moment he wanted to produce any harmonic effect he had to modulate, and trust to the gay effect of jumping from one key to another to conceal the fact that when he got into the new key he could do nothing but repeat the rum-tum he had just been exploiting in the old one. When this resource was exhausted, he whipped up the score by making the tunes move more busily and increasing the speed. Finally, there was the big drum to fall back on, and the mere piling up of brute sound.

A great musician, capable of noble part writing, and provided with a patient and serious audience, need not fall back on such cheap expedients. Within the limits of a single key he commands a range of harmonic progressions of sufficient variety of effect and expression to enable him to give a thoughtful inside to his work instead of a popular outside. Now I cannot say that I found Dr Mackenzie's part writing interesting. I even inferred that he did not find it so himself, not alone from the extreme orchestral bedizenment which I have already described, but from the more conclusive fact that whenever he wished to intensify the emotional effect, he immediately began to emphasize the rhythms, to make his melodies stump about more vigorously, and to pile Pelion on Ossa with organ, chorus, and instruments of percussion.

This, with the obviousness and popularity of the rhythms employed, was what suggested to me the apparently incongruous idea that Offenbach, if he had suppressed his humor, and become a respectable British P.R.A.M., might have given us just such a work as Bethlehem. I do not, however, allege this against Dr Mackenzie as a grievance. I only wish to define the artistic rank of his work. If it is once clearly understood that oratorios like Bethlehem stand in the same relation to the works of the great masters as modern blank verse melodramas to the masterpieces of dramatic poetry, then let us by all means applaud it as a well-knit work of its kind.

But I am not convinced that any such understanding has been established. I rather suspect that the public, when it reads the eulogies which we critics lavish on these works, thinks that our words mean exactly the same thing as when we apply them in a cooler, more perfunctory way, to Bach and Handel. Therefore I am forced to be ungraciously explicit as to the distinction I make between Dr Mackenzie and Handel and between Mr Bennett and Milton.

I should explain that Bethlehem is constructed on the system of representative themes. The second part opens with a chorus entitled Cometh a heavenly legion to guard the New Born King. The representative theme employed here is the first strain of the old tune Fare you well, my own Mary Ann, familiar to play-goers who remember Mrs Barney Williams. Probably Dr Mackenzie never heard that lady sing; but to me, who remember her very well, the way in which the cornet would every now and then cap the rhetoric about shining ranks and lofty crests and glittering spears, with a sly, soft echo of A lobstere in a lobstere-pot, had something derisive in it, as if the player were having a little joke in disparagement of the enthusiasm of the cherubim.

Were there no artistic moral to be drawn from this ridiculous reminiscence of mine, my mention of it would be a mere impertinence. But it brings to light one of the limiting conditions of the use of representative themes. Since their effect depends altogether on the intimacy and vividness of their association with the idea they represent, it is important that they should not have pre-established associations with other ideas. It is, therefore, dangerous to give them the form of a tune, or of a fragment of a tune, especially when they are introduced, as in the case of the Mary Ann theme, without a strongly characteristic harmony.

Further—and this condition goes deeper—they should only be attached to leading ideas. Now suppose there are no leading ideas in a poem—suppose it is not a poem at all, but only the contents of a bag of tricks emptied out on a sheet of paper, without any intellectual design, for the use of a composer in search of a libretto! Under such circumstances the wisest thing for the composer to do is not to set the libretto at all. But if he must meddle with it, then let him treat it in the old-fashioned way, as a mere excuse for writing set pieces of music—choruses, marches, songs, duets, and so on, without making a pretence of intellectual architectonicity by dragging in the system of representative themes, which was called into existence for the purposes of a musician who was not only a poetic dramatist, but a psychologist and philosopher.

The notion that the Wagnerian method consists simply in picking out stray ideas and ticketing them with a tune opens up in the path of the oratorio composer abysses of absurdity before which I must really try to place a board marked "Danger." Let me illustrate. Suppose some composer, inferring from the case of Mr Joseph Bennett that a musical critic is the proper person to write a libretto, asks me to provide him with words for a cantata, and resolves beforehand to employ "the system of representative themes" because that is the fashion now.

Let us further suppose that the following is a section of my libretto, designed to combine the pious with the popular:

Recit.—Let us eat and drink; for tomorrow we die.
Chorus.—We wont go home til morning,
We wont go home til morning,
We wont go home til morning,
Til daylight doth appear.

In the above there is one leading idea and one only—an idea which plays a huge and significant part in every world drama, from the plague described by Thucydides to the London of our day. No composer of Wagnerian capacity would miss the central thought, or confuse it by introducing themes representing the inessential ideas mentioned.

But your composer who should set to work merely to imitate the Wagner fashion would regard this as a very feeble and barren view of the case. He would say, with relish, "Aha, here we have plenty of material! In the phrase 'Let us eat and drink,' we shall require a food theme and a drink theme, with orchestration to suggest the clatter of knives and forks and the clinking of glasses. In the following phrase we have a death motive, just as in Tristan, as well as the first hint of a morning theme, which can be fully developed on the word 'morning,' in the following chorus, and raised to its utmost musical splendor at the phrase 'daylight doth appear.'" Naturally a man occupied with the elaboration of such brilliant opportunities would entirely overlook the central thought which is the real substance of the passage.

And the audience, occupied solely with that central thought, would entirely overlook the food and drink and death and morning themes unless there were an elaborate analytic program to point out the ingenuities of the work. Mr Bennett has saved Dr Mackenzie from such oversights by providing him with a book in which there are no central thoughts or leading ideas. Nevertheless, the analytic program quotes a dozen or two of representative themes from the score. I can only say that without Mr Bennett's assistance I should not have identified one of them, save only Fare you well, my own Mary Ann.

HERR MOTTL'S INSIGHT

The World, 25 April 1894

I must entirely applaud Mr Henschel's spirited cutting-in between Herr Felix Mottl and the expectant public with a Wagner program identical, save as to one item (the Flying Dutchman overture), with that announced for Herr Mottl's first appearance in England. I have heard people say that such a challenge was in bad taste; but in this case, as in ninetynine out of a hundred others in which the same complaint is made, good taste would have meant simply moral cowardice, a quality in which we in England are always anxious to be kept in countenance. Mr Henschel was quite right, in the face of the flourish of trumpets which heralded Mottl's arrival, to decline to admit the pretensions of the stranger to give us lessons in Wagner conducting; and he could only protest effectively by at once offering a performance by his own band as a sample of what London can do, thus tacitly daring Herr Mottl to beat him.

Nothing could be fairer; nothing could be bolder; nothing could be more entirely creditable to the challenger. If I could add that the invader had been put to shame—that he had done nothing that Mr Henschel had not done as well, or better, then indeed it would be a proud day for London. But to that length I must not go. Mr Henschel, in the heat of his spirit, underrated his adversary. He was not bad; but Mottl bettered him in every bar. Before the Rienzi overture was half through it was evident that London was going to have a most exemplary beating from Karlsruhe. One after another the blemishes and stupidities to which we have become so inured here that we have ceased to record them against our conductors vanished under Mottl's hand.

Let me, before speaking of his highest qualities, give an illustration or two of his resources as a manager of the orchestra. We all know the overture to Tannhäuser by heart by this time. Well, have we not often shrunk from the coarse and unsatisfactory effect of the three trombones at the climax of the pilgrims' march in the first section of the overture? With Richter it is rather worse than with the others, since he insists on the full power of the fortissimo. Mottl effected a magical transformation. The chant was as powerful as Richter could have desired; and yet it was beautiful, broad, easy, with a *portamento* which an Italian singer might have envied.

How was this brought about? In the simplest way in the world. Instead of keeping strict Procrustean time for the florid work of the violins, thus forcing the trombones to chop their phrases so as to fit the accompaniment, Mottl gave the trombones a free hand, allowing them to give the time to the whole band, and making the violins wait, when necessary, between the bars, so to speak, until the slow-speaking brass instruments had turned their phrases with unembarrassed majesty. The effect was magnificent. In exactly the same way, and with still more splendid effect, he gave us the great passage at the end of Die Walküre, where the trombones reaffirm the last words of Wotan.

Again, take the Flying Dutchman overture. In the second half of this, the contrast between the furious raging of the storm on the one hand, and the consolation of the salvation theme on the other, should be so obvious, one would think, to any ordinarily imaginative conductor, that Wagner thought it sufficient to indicate the necessary changes of tempo by such hints as *ritenuto*, *stringendo*, and the like, depending on their apparent inevitability for their full comprehension. Yet we are accustomed to hear our bands dragged tearing through the salvation theme at almost the same speed as through the storm, some attempt being made to strike a balance by taking the one too slow and the other too fast. Mottl varied his speed from *allegro* to *adagio*, managing the transitions with perfect address, and producing the full effect which everybody except our conductors knows to be what Wagner intended.

His *allegro*, too, was a true *allegro con brio*, as marked, and not the customary *allegro pomposo*. His treatment of those batteries of chords which lead up to the first *forte* in the quick movement reminded me of Wagner himself, whom I once saw stamping to them with his foot, and, I am afraid, swearing at the band between his teeth because they would not hit them out tremendously enough for him. He would certainly have been satisfied with the cannonade which Mottl got from the drums in this passage. It is one of Mottl's salient characteristics as a conductor that he seizes on the accents of the music with immense energy, always using them to obtain force of expression, and never merely to set people dancing, in the manner of an Austrian band.

This distinction came out strikingly in the instrumental version of Tannhäuser's pæan to Venus in the overture, commonly played as if it were something between a march and a galop, under which treatment the two trumpet blasts with which the opening notes are emphasized sound like a rather boyish bit of decoration, as if someone had tipped two out of a row of iron railings with gilding for no particular purpose, except to see the gold glitter. In Mottl's hands these two trumpet notes explained themselves at once as necessary reinforcements to two all-important accents; and the effect was not to make the movement still more march-like, but, on the contrary, to entirely prevent any such suggestion, and to produce the true accent of oratorical passion, the intensive impulses of which are no more like the merely go-ahead lilt of a march or dance than a furnace is like a skyrocket.

In short, though Mottl is a very forcible conductor, and, in spite of all that has been said about his slowness, a very fast conductor when the right tempo happens to be very fast, he is not in the least an impetuous one: his self-possession is completed instead of destroyed by excitement; and his speed and energy are those of a strong man on level ground, and not those of an ordinary one going downhill. It must not be supposed that this intensive, concentric force, characteristic of the true art passion, is always manifesting itself in the energetic way in him.

For example, his conducting of the Lohengrin prelude was quite a study in physical expression of just the opposite mode of musical feeling. Needless to say, the band fell considerably short of the ethereal perfection of sound at which the composer aimed. Mottl's face and gesture, entreating, imploring, remonstrating, deprecating, pleading, would have softened hearts of stone; and the violins made it as easy for him as they could, which was perhaps not very easy, especially in the first section.

In the Tannhäuser, too, the fine tone and expressive phrasing of the violoncellos at their first entry in the pilgrims' march was something to be for ever grateful for; while the perfect freedom allowed to the clarinet to develop all the sweetness of the Venus strain (which I heard then, for the first time in my life, as it was meant to be heard) produced an effect only surpassed when, at the end of the Tristan prelude, the Liebestod, usually murdered by being taken too fast, came stealing in, with the conductor doing exactly what Wagner declared to be the whole duty of a conductor, "giving the right time to the band." Is it vain to hope that nobody will ever take it too fast again?

Perhaps the most convincing instance of Mottl's delicacy of touch was the way in which he managed to veil the cheapness and Rossinian tum-tum of the Rienzi overture, which Mr Henschel had stripped naked with a ruthless hand. But it is unnecessary to multiply illustrations. Those which I have given will serve to shew that I am not merely turning an empty phrase in compliment to a Bayreuth reputation when I say that Mottl is a conductor of the very first rank, with, to boot, immense physical energy and personal influence. I was filled with admiration by his efficiency and insight; and I imagine my feelings were shared by all present who were capable of discriminating between one conductor and another. It is greatly to be desired that Mr Schulz-Curtius should follow up the great success of his enterprise (the room was crammed, and the seats had all been sold months in advance) by establishing an annual series of concerts under Mottl. A second concert is already announced for May 22; but the program will have to be changed in one particular. As it stands at present, Beethoven is represented by the overture to Egmont only. This—with due respect to the authors of the program—is all nonsense. Mottl must conduct the C minor symphony: that is the sample of Beethoven for which all his qualities mark him out. By all means, however, let us have Egmont as well, and sacrifice one of the Wagner selections.

And this brings me to the question of that recent artistic phenomenon, the Wagner program, which, as we are assured by the directors of the Crystal Palace, is the most attractive program nowadays. It may be so;

but it is an artistic misdemeanor all the same. In satisfying our craving for the sound of Wagner's music, the concert room is, against its own nature, doing the work of quite another social organ—to wit, the theatre.

We have, unfortunately, no Wagner theatre here; and we must either leave Wagner unheard, or else stuff our concert programs with selections arranged for orchestra alone, as in the second part of a Covent Garden promenade concert. For an arrangement of the Liebestod for a band is really not a bit more defensible at a first-rate concert than an arrangement of the Miserere scene from Il Trovatore or a Pinafore *pot-pourri*. It is better to hear the Bayreuth music done in this way than not to hear it at all, perhaps; but it need not on that account be allowed to squeeze concert music proper out of our concerts. I confess that towards the end of Mr Henschel's program my attention began to wander; and if I had seen Mottl conducting as often as I have seen Mr Henschel, I doubt whether even his concentrated power could hold me with the Parsifal prelude played as postlude to ninety minutes' music.

Indeed, to make the confession complete, I may as well add that my attention to the last piece at the Mottl concert cost me a distinct effort. Something comparatively cheap and violently self-assertive, like the Walkürenritt (which Mottl very properly left out of his scheme) is needed to end long concerts, if long concerts must be inflicted on us. Indeed it would be far more reasonable to take these chronological-order programs backwards, so that we could give our unwearied attention to the best pieces first, and reserve the Rienzi overture to waken us up and demoralize the band when our edge has been well dulled.

I have one other strong reason for desiring to see Mottl established here as a conductor. His greatest rival, Richter, is so far above the heads of the public that he has no external stimulus to do his best in London. Only a very few people can perceive the difference between his best and his second best; but the difference between his second best and Mottl's best would be felt at once by a considerable body of amateurs. Now I do not suggest that Richter ever consciously does less than his best; but I am materialist enough in these matters to believe that even the best man does more work under pressure than in a vacuum. Mr Henschel, for instance, whose concert was not up to his own standard, much less to Mottl's, will be quite able, now that he is put on his mettle, to surpass himself.

It is so long since I have mentioned the pianoforte in this column that I must add, before concluding, that Sophie Menter and Sapellnikoff are in London. I was unable to attend the Philharmonic when Sapellnikoff played there on Thursday last; but I heard Madame Menter at the Crystal Palace on Saturday. She is still irresistible; but there were signs of wear and tear on her playing of the two transcriptions from Schubert. Probably she has played them too often; at all events, there was more of her old power and audacity in her playing of the concerto (Liszt in E flat).

Mr Frederick Dawson has given a recital. He is a pleasant, frank-looking, somewhat irresponsible young gentleman with a technique which enables him to rattle off Beethoven's sonatas quite cheerfully. His best effort, as far as I heard, was Mendelssohn's Variations Sérieuses, in which he seemed to be quite in his depth. With Beethoven and Schumann he was just a little too light-hearted.

RUSKIN ON MUSIC

The World, 2 May 1894

I have been indulging in five shillings' worth of Ruskin on Music, in a volume just published by Mr George Allen. As it happened, the first sentence I lighted on when I opened the book was "the oratorio, withering the life of religion into dead bones on the Syren sands." Immediately I woke up; for the fact that modern oratorio is mostly a combination of frivolity and sensuality with hypocrisy and the most oppressive dulness is still sufficiently a trade secret to make its discovery by an outsider interesting. A few pages off I found Mr Ruskin describing the singing he heard south of the Alps. Usually the Englishman in Italy, carefully primed beforehand with literary raptures concerning a nation of born musicians speaking the most vocal language in the world, is sufficiently careful of his own credit as a man of taste to discover a Giuglini in every gondolier and St Cecilia's lute in every accordion.

Mr Ruskin innovated so far as to use his own judgment; and here is the result: "Of bestial howling, and entirely frantic vomiting up of damned souls through their still carnal throats, I have heard more than, please God, I will ever endure the hearing of again, in one of His summers." I take the liberty of squeezing Mr Ruskin's hand in mute sympathy with the spirit of this passage. In Italy, where the chance of being picked up off the streets and brought out as *primo tenore* at the Opera occupies the same space in the imagination of the men as the chance of selecting a Derby winner does in England, you cannot get away from the ignoble bawling which Mr Ruskin describes so forcibly—and yet not too forcibly, or forcibly enough; for language will not hold the full pretentiousness and cupidity of the thing, let alone the unpleasantness of the noise it makes.

It is at once the strength and weakness of Mr Ruskin in dealing with music that he is in love with it. There is always a certain comedy in the contrast between people as they appear transfigured in the eyes of those who love them, and as they appear to those who are under no such inspiration—or, for the matter of that, as they appear to themselves. And the tragi-comedy of the love of men and women for oneanother is reproduced in their love for art.

Mr Ruskin is head and ears in love with Music; and so am I; but I am married to her, so to speak, as a professional critic, wheras he is still a wooer, and has the illusions of imperfect knowledge as well as the illuminations of perfect love. Listen to this, for example:

"True music is the natural expression of a lofty passion for a right cause. In proportion to the kingliness and force of any personality, the expression either of its joy or suffering becomes measured, chastened, calm, and capable of interpretation only by the majesty of ordered, beautiful, and worded sound. Exactly in proportion to the degree in which we become narrow in the cause and conception of our passions, incontinent in the utterance of them, feeble of perseverance in them, sullied or shameful in the indulgence of them, their expression by musical means becomes broken, mean, fatuitous, and at last impossible: the measured waves of heaven will not lend themselves to the expression of ultimate vice: it must be for ever sunk in discordance or silence."

I entirely agree with Mr Ruskin in this; but it will not hold water, for all that. "The measured waves of heaven" are not so particular as he thinks. Music will express any emotion, base or lofty. She is absolutely unmoral: we find her in Verdi's last work heightening to the utmost the expression of Falstaff's carnal gloating over a cup of sack, just as willingly as she heightened the expression of "a lofty passion for a right cause" for Beethoven in the Ninth Symphony. She mocked and prostituted the Orpheus legend for Offenbach just as keenly and effectively as she ennobled it for Gluck. Mr Ruskin himself has given an instance of this—a signally wrong instance, by the way; but let that pass for a moment:

"And yonder musician, who used the greatest power which (in the art he knew) the Father of Spirits ever yet breathed into the clay of this world; who used it, I say, to follow and fit with perfect sound the words of the Zauberflöte and of Don Giovanni—foolishest and most monstrous of conceivable human words and subjects of thought—for the future amusement of his race! No such spectacle of unconscious (and in that unconsciousness all the more fearful) moral degradation of the highest faculty to the lowest purpose can be found in history."

This is a capital instance of Mr Ruskin's besetting sin—virtuous indignation. If these two operas are examples of "foolishest and most monstrous" words fitted and followed with perfect sound—that is, with true music—what becomes of the definition which limits true music to "the natural expression of a lofty passion for a right cause"? Clearly, that will not do.

And now may I beg Mr Ruskin to mend his illustration, if not his argument? The generation which could see nothing in Die Zauberflöte but a silly extravaganza was one which Mr Ruskin certainly belonged to in point of time; and he has for once sunk to the average level of its thought in this shallow criticism of the work which Mozart deliberately devoted to the expression of his moral sympathies. Everything that is true and vital in his worship of music would be shattered if it were a fact—happily it is not—that the music of Sarastro came from a silly and trivial mood. If I were to assure Mr Ruskin that Bellini's Madonna with St Ursula, in Venice, was originally knocked off as a sign for a tavern by the painter, Mr Ruskin would simply refuse to entertain the story, no matter what the evidence might be, knowing that the thing was eternally impossible. Since he sees no such impossibility in the case of Die Zauberflöte, I must conclude that he does not know the masterpieces of music as he knows those of painting.

As to Don Giovanni, otherwise The Dissolute One Punished, the only immoral feature of it is its supernatural retributive morality. Gentlemen who break through the ordinary categories of good and evil, and come out at the other side singing *Finch' han dal vino* and *Là ci darem*, do not, as a matter of fact, get called on by statues, and taken straight down through the floor to eternal torments; and to pretend that they do is to shirk the social problem they present. Nor is it yet by any means an established fact that the world owes more to its Don Ottavios than to its Don Juans.

It is, of course, impossible to make a serious stand on a libretto which is such an odd mixture of the old Punch tradition with the highly emancipated modern philosophy of Molière; but whether you apply Mr Ruskin's hasty criticism to Punch and Judy or to Le Festin de Pierre, you will, I think, see that it is fundamentally nothing but an explosion of pious horror of the best Denmark Hill brand. The hard fact is that Don Giovanni is eminent in virtue of its uncommon share of wisdom, beauty, and humor; and if any theory of morals leads to the conclusion that it is foolish and monstrous, so much the worse for the theory.

I must, further, remonstrate with Mr Ruskin about his advice to the girls of England. First, like a veritable serpent in the garden, he tempts the young English lady, already predisposed to self-righteousness, with the following wicked words: "From the beginning consider all your accomplishments as means of assistance to others." This is Denmark Hill with a vengeance. But the artist in Mr Ruskin is always getting the better of Denmark Hill; and on the very next page he says "Think only of accuracy; never of effect or expression."

Now, will anyone kindly tell me how a young lady is to consider all her accomplishments "as means of assistance to others"—that is, to think of nothing but effect and expression, and consequently to cultivate self-consciousness and its attendant personal susceptibility up to the highest point—and at the same time not to think of effect or expression at all, but only of accuracy. Speaking as a rival sage—as one who, in musical matters at least, considers himself fitted to play Codlin to Mr Ruskin's Short*—I earnestly advise the young ladies of England, whether enrolled in the Guild of St George or not, to cultivate music solely for the love and need of it, and to do it in all humility of spirit, never forgetting that they are most likely inflicting all-but-unbearable annoyance on every musician within earshot, instead of rendering "assistance to others."

The greatest assistance the average young lady musician can render to others is to stop. Mind, I speak of life as it is. Some day, perhaps, when it is like a page out of [Goethe's] Wilhelm Meister or [Ruskin's] Sesame and Lilies, when the piano is dead and our maidens go up into the mountains to practise their first exercises on the harp, Mr Ruskin's exhortations as to the sinfulness of doing anything merely because you like it may gain some sort of plausibility. At present they will not wash.

"It is I believe" says Mr Ruskin "as certain that in the last twenty years we have learnt to better understand

* Codlin and Short were itinerant showmen in Dickens's The Old Curiosity Shop.

good music, and to love it more, as that in the same time our knowledge and love of pictures have not increased. The reason is easily found. Our music has been chosen for us by masters; and our pictures have been chosen by ourselves."

Alas! how easy it is to find a reason for the thing that is not! Not that there is not here, as usual, a hundred times more insight in Mr Ruskin's mistake than in most other men's accuracies. It is quite true that the favorite works at our good concerts are of a much higher class than the favorite works at the Royal Academy, and that the difference is due to the fact that Beethoven and Wagner are still in a position to dictate to the public what is good for them. But the public is not really conscious of that part of Beethoven's work which raises it above the level of popular painting. It finds a great deal of Beethoven incomprehensible, and therefore dull, putting up with it only because the alternative is either no music at all or something a good deal duller. But will it put up with it when vulgar musicians have completely mastered the trade of producing symphonies and operas containing all the cheap, popular, obvious, carnal luxuries of the Beethovenian music, without its troublesome nobilities, depths, and spiritual grandeurs?

I doubt it. Wagner accused Meyerbeer of following the great masters as a starling follows the plough, picking up the titbits which their force unearthed, and serving them up to Paris unmixed with noble matter. That process, which has been going on in music for less than a century, has been going on in painting for three or four hundred years, so that our contemporary popular painters have rid themselves far more completely of what was greatest in the great masters of Florence, Rome, and Venice, than our contemporary composers of what was greatest in Mozart, Beethoven, and Wagner; but the process is going on all the same under the influence of popular demand; and we shall soon have the field held by vulgar music as much as by vulgar painting, as is right and proper in a country with a vulgar population.

I need hardly add that Mr Ruskin himself, true to his method of never collating his utterances, but taking his inspiration as it comes, so that on every possible subject he says the right thing and the wrong thing with equal eloquence within the same ten minutes, does not really believe any such nonsense as that people can be kept on high ground by having their music chosen for them by masters. For instance:

"You cannot paint or sing yourselves into being good men. You must be good men before you can either paint or sing; and then the color and the sound will complete all in you that is best."

Neither can people appreciate good music, whether chosen for them by masters or not, except to the extent to which they are "good" themselves. You can chain a terrier to Richter's desk, and force it to listen to all the symphonies of Beethoven, without changing its opinion one jot as to the relative delights of rathunting and classical music; and the same thing is true in its degree of mankind. The real point is, that most of us, far from being chained to the desk, never get the chance of finding out whether we can appreciate great music or not.

Mr Ruskin is probably right in anticipating that a change in the tone of public feeling would be produced "if, having been accustomed only to hear black Christy's,* blind fiddlers, and hoarse beggars scrape and howl about their streets, the people were permitted daily audience of faithful and gentle orchestral rendering of the work of the highest classical masters."

* Blackfaced street entertainers emulating the famed Christy Minstrels.

Here I must leave an infinitely suggestive and provocative book, the publication of which no musical critic can very well ignore. To finish, I will give, without comment, one more quotation as a sample of what Mr Ruskin's musical criticism would, perhaps, have been like if he had taken to my branch of the trade instead of to his own:

"Grisi and Malibran sang at least one-third slower than any modern *cantatrice*; and Patti, the last time I heard her, massacred Zerlina's part in *Là ci darem*, as if the audience and she had but the one object of getting Mozart's air done with as soon as possible. . . . Afterwards I was brought to the point of trying to learn to sing, in which, though never even getting so far as to read with ease, I nevertheless, between my fine rhythmic ear and true-lover's sentiment, got to understand some principles of musical art, which I shall perhaps be able to enforce, with benefit on the musical public mind, even today."

THAT POLISH FANTASIA AGAIN

The World, 9 May 1894

I have again had the privilege of hearing Paderewski play that Polish Fantasia of his, this time by special request of the Philharmonic directors, who were probably afraid that he might otherwise have played Beethoven or some other tedious classical composer. I have now heard that Fantasia three times; and though Paderewski seems to be entirely of Macbeth's opinion as to crying "Hold, enough!" I confess I do not want to hear it again, at least not for another week or so. The fact is, he can play much better music than he has yet composed; and it offends all my notions of artistic economy to see Paderewski the first-rate player thrown away on Paderewski the second-rate composer.

That Fantasia does not contain a bar of pianoforte music of the highest class: it is brilliant, violent, ingenious, here and there romantic; but what do I care for all that at my age? Now that I have worn out the somewhat obvious charms of the themes, I care for little more than the careful and intelligent workmanship. As for those flashy rapid traits, played on a piano which has been spoiled to make them practicable, they are lost on me: Liszt, and even Tausig, in spite of his vulgar vandalism, were more amusing in this department. People who challenge musical criticism in a double capacity put me in a difficulty.

Take Rubinstein, for instance. He was a player of stupendous manual dexterity, with immense power, passion, and spontaneity. Had his intellect been as keen as his will was energetic he would have been unsurpassable: as it was, he stood, after the retirement of Liszt, the foremost player of his time. But he insisted on composing profusely, strenuously, earnestly, loading up Europe with big instrumental compositions which it was most painful, in view of one's regard for him as a pianist, to have to set down as huge trumperies, intolerably diffuse considering their commonness, and containing no qualities that were not far more suitably employed on his songs, duets, pianoforte pieces, and other domestic ware.

Rubinstein's place has now been taken by Paderewski, intellectually his superior, and made of steel where he was made of iron, consequently rather less ready to glow and melt. And now Paderewski, too, is beginning to compose, with the same earnestness and the same ambition. The result is very different: the Russian pitted against the Pole comes out as childishly in intellectual and critical power as an ancient Roman or modern

Bulgarian against a Greek; but the old difficulty none-theless reproduces itself: Paderewski stands higher as a player than he does as a composer; and consequently his playing of his own works is a waste of his finest powers.

Were I he, I should not condescend to play that Polish Fantasia at a Philharmonic concert: I should say to the directors "No, gentlemen: at your classical concerts I play Beethoven, or Bach, or Chopin, or some other great composer, instead of that deserving but not as yet exactly first-rate young aspirant Paderewski, on whose behalf I must, however, thank you for your kind encouragement." We so rarely hear Paderewski with an orchestra behind him that the choice between a Beethoven concerto and one of his own works is forced upon us rather sharply; and I should belittle him as a player if I hesitated to say that I now want to hear him play Beethoven in G for the first time, or Beethoven in E flat for the second time, much more than I want to hear him play that Fantasia for the fourth time.

Now that the Crystal Palace Saturday Concert season is over, the recitals at Queen's Hall will perhaps come in for a larger share of attention. I have been present at two, and found them enjoyable enough. Mr Cowen has a first-rate band; and he conducts with more freedom than he used to. I cannot say that his curious freak of taking the Walkürenritt in the slow tempo proper to the Lohengrin prelude, and the Lohengrin prelude in the lively tempo proper to the Walkürenritt, revealed any new beauties in these works: rather the contrary, in fact; but still it was interesting—for once. The recital of an act of Lohengrin, without the usual stage cuts, is artistically valuable in this unhappy town, where everything is mutilated to fit the dinner hour.

And it is a mistake to suppose that you can "cut" Lohengrin as you can cut an Italian opera. The first (and last) time I ever caught a lizard by the tail, it disconcerted me extremely by breaking itself into three pieces, and making off with the piece in which its head happened to be. This power is one of the privileges of low organization: if a man were to elude a police constable in that manner he would die; and possibly the policeman would die too, of the shock. Now there is almost as great a difference in complexity of organization between an Italian opera and a Wagnerian music-drama as between a reptile and a man. The degree of mutilation which is only inconvenient to the opera is fatal to the music-drama.

Those who heard at Queen's Hall the transition from the first to the second scene of the third act of Lohengrin given without the usual opera house butchery must have been astonished at the effect of all that gathering of legions and clangor of trumpets which makes the opening of the final scene so exciting and impressive. Last Saturday we had the third act of Tannhäuser, less of a novelty, and perhaps for that reason more of a favorite on the concert platform. Mr Edward Lloyd fills the tenor parts at these entertainments, occasionally playing a little to the gallery by style of declamation not precisely classic, though sufficiently sincere and effective; and Miss Ella Russell, a very capable artist, of whom we have rather failed hitherto to make any adequate use, is the leading soprano.

There are the materials for excellent performances at Queen's Hall; and all Mr Cowen need do to realize them is, not to conduct like Mottl, since he is not built that way, but simply to faithfully carry out Wagner's instructions; insist on accurate reading of the notes and nuances; and get from his band at least five gradations of tone, *pianissimo*, *piano*, *mezzo forte*, *forte*, and *fortissimo*, over and above those mechanically produced by the increase or decrease of the number of instruments employed, instead of slopping along with a lazy *piano* and *mezzo forte* only. I do not mean to imply that Mr Cowen is consciously careless: far from it, the activity of his conscience is visible to all; but there are a good many indications in the score which he either overlooks or fails to value adequately.

Mention of Mottl reminds me that my feeling that he should break ground as a Beethoven conductor here by the C minor symphony is evidently shared by Mr Schulz-Curtius and himself; for the program for the 22nd now includes that work, along with six pieces by Wagner and two by Berlioz. As we never hear Berlioz handled successfully in London, except on one of the scarce visits of the Manchester Band, it will be interesting to hear what Mottl, whose appreciation of Berlioz carried him to the length of producing Les Troyens at Karlsruhe, will be able to do with him.

It is impossible not to admire the vigorous individuality and irrepressible musical talent of Signor Scuderi, who gave a concert the other day at Steinway Hall; and I am indebted to him for letting me hear the *obbligato* to the serenade in Don Giovanni played on the instrument for which it was written, that is, the mandolin, though I do not believe in the least that Mozart meant it to be "double-tongued," if I may borrow that expression to describe the effect of turning each semiquaver into a rapidly repeated demisemiquaver. But much as I admire the way in which Signor Scuderi can adapt himself to any instrument, I protest against his readiness to adapt any instrument to any piece of music. The very quality which makes the mandolin the ideal instrument to accompany *Deh vieni alla finestra* puts it quite out of the question for Wolfram's apostrophe to the evening star in Tannhäuser; yet Signor Scuderi plucked out the harp part to that song on his mandolin, whilst Mr Oscar Noyes sang the foolish Italian arrangement of it for concert use in two verses. I can only describe the instrumental effect as blasphemous. Mr Noyes, who is by no means an unpromising singer, might get more effect out of the serenade by singing it exactly as Mozart wrote it, instead of muddling away the effect of the low D at the end by a rather clumsy *gruppetto*.

The Crystal Palace Saturday Concerts are now over for the season. I have still to complain of the excessive length of the concerts. I admit that my desire to shorten my work operates in the contrary direction to the desire of the public to get as much value as possible for its money; but if anyone will compare a modern Philharmonic program with an ancient one, or a playbill of the palmy days with Mr Irving's of last night, he will see that the march of evolution involves shortening. It is not that people are less tolerant of music than they were: on the contrary it is because they listen with an intensity formerly undreamt of.

We do not all realize how modern an institution the silent audience is. Even in the dreariest moments of a bad concert nowadays we do not talk, or go in and out noisily, or beat time with our boots, unless, indeed, we are country cousins, unfamiliar with concert room usages, in which case our neighbors generally make us aware very soon that we are misbehaving. Critics have had to eliminate from their stereo such phrases as "the vast audience was hushed," &c., because audiences always are hushed. Even "the Bayreuth hush" has acquired its eminence solely through its being quite the noisiest thing of the kind, owing to the way in which the older English ladies, confused by the darkness, and not realizing the solemnity of the moment, will ask questions of their daughters and provoke angry "Sh-sh-es" from incontinent foreigners and fanatic Wagner worshipers.

But things were not always on this footing. An audience in a concert room or playhouse formerly kept up a continual buzz of conversation, nobody having any notion that he should not talk if he wanted to, and, what is more surprising nowadays, nobody listening to the performance with any such strain on their attention as is necessary to make the buzz of conversation unendurable. The relics of this state of things are to be seen in the Crystal Palace concert room in the shape of notices requesting people not to talk, and informing them, as something that they are not likely to know, that any noise made by them will interfere with the enjoyment of their neighbors. These hints on good behavior have long been out of date as far as the Saturday audiences are concerned; and my contention is that this change involves the supersession of the long program half listened to by the short program thoroughly listened to.

The fatigue of thorough listening is so great that when the concentration is carried to the utmost, as at Bayreuth, where the fact that nothing is visible except the stage produces great intensity of observation, you come out from a two hours' shift, such as the last act of Die Meistersinger, in a state of exhaustion not to be described. I suggest, therefore, that an hour and three-quarters should be fixed as the extreme outside limit for a concert of high-class music, and that the addition of any item whatsoever to a program containing the Ninth Symphony should be punished by imprisonment without option. When this work was done a few Saturdays ago at the Crystal Palace the concert was almost spoiled by the unnecessary addition of three or four songs which, with the honorable exception of one by Miss Fillunger, were so abominably sung that I cannot believe that the singers themselves would dispute the point with me, especially the gentleman who had forgotten Adelaide and had to fall back on improvization once or twice. But this leads me to a consideration of the music we have had at the Palace; and I must postpone that matter for the present for want of space.

YVETTE GUILBERT

The World, 16 May 1894

Another great artist has come. I suppose I ought to have been quite familiar with her performances already when I went to her reception of the English Press (musical critics *not* included) at the Savoy Hotel last week*; but as a matter of fact I had never heard her before. The fact is I am a very bad Parisian. I have never been to the Chat Noir: I have looked at its advertisements on the Boulevards time after time without the least conviction that my sense of being in the fastest forefront of the life of my age would culminate there. To me, going to Paris means going back fifty years in civilization, spending an uncomfortable night, and getting away next morning as soon as possible. I know, of course, that there must be places and circles in Paris which are not hopelessly out of date; but I have never found them out; and if I did, what figure could I make in them with my one weapon, language, broken in my hand?

Hence it is that I had never seen Mlle Yvette Guilbert when Monsieur Johnson, of the Figaro, introduced her to a carefully selected audience of the wrong people (mostly) at the Savoy Hotel as aforesaid. Monsieur Johnson, as a veteran, will not feel hurt at any comment which only goes to prove that "the power of beauty he remembers yet"†; therefore I need have no delicacy in saying that the remarks which he addressed to the

* Miss Guilbert made her first London theatre appearance at the Empire on 9 May 1894, singing *La Promise, A La Villette, Sur le scène*, and *La Femme à Narcisse.*

† Variant of the opening lines of John Dryden's poem Cymon and Iphigenia, in his Fables, Ancient and Modern (1700).

audience by way of introducing Mlle Guilbert were entirely fatuous when his emotion permitted them to be heard. When the young lady appeared, it needed only one glance to see that here was no mere music hall star, but one of the half-dozen ablest persons in the room. It is worth remarking here that in any society whatever of men and women there is always a woman among the six cleverest; and this is why I, who have a somewhat extensive experience of work on the committees of mixed societies, have been trained to recognize the fact that the Efficient Person in this world is occasionally female, though she must not on that account be confounded with the ordinary woman—or the ordinary man, for that matter—whom one does not privately regard as a full-grown responsible individual at all.

You do not waste "homage" on the female Efficient Person; you regard her, favorably or unfavorably, much as you regard the male of the Efficient species, except that you have a certain special fear of her, based on her freedom from that sickliness of conscience, so much deprecated by Ibsen, which makes the male the prey of unreal scruples; and you have at times to defend yourself against her, or, when she is an ally, to assume her fitness for active service of the roughest kinds, in a way which horrifies the chivalrous gentlemen of your acquaintance who will not suffer the winds of heaven to breathe on a woman's face too harshly lest they should disable her in her mission of sewing on buttons.

In short, your chivalry and gallantry are left useless on your hands, unless for small-talk with the feminine rank and file, who must be answered according to their folly, just like the male rank and file. But then you get on much better with the female masterspirits, who will not stand chivalry, or gallantry, or any other form of manly patronage. Therefore let others, who have not been educated as I have been, pay Mlle Guilbert gallant compliments: as for me, no sooner had the lady mounted the platform with that unmistakable familiarity with the situation and command of it which shews itself chiefly by the absence of all the petty affectations of the favorite who has merely caught the fancy of the public without knowing how or why, than I was on the alert to see what an evidently very efficient person was going to do.

And I was not at all deceived in my expectancy. It amuses her to tell interviewers that she cannot sing, and has no gestures; but I need not say that there would be very little fun for her in that if she were not one of the best singers and pantomimists in Europe. She divided her program into three parts: Ironic songs, Dramatic songs, and—but perhaps I had better use the French heading here, and say *Chansons légères.* For though Mlle Guilbert sings the hymns of a very ancient faith, profusely endowed and sincerely upheld among us, we deny it a name and an establishment. Its *Chansons ironiques* are delivered by her with a fine intensity of mordant expression that would not be possible without profound conviction beneath it; and if there is anything that I am certain of after hearing her sing *Les Vierges*, it is the perfect integrity of her self-respect in an attitude towards life which is distinctly not that of the British matron.

To kindle art to the whitest heat there must always be some fanaticism behind it; and the songs in which Mlle Guilbert expresses her immense irony are the veil of a propaganda which is not the propaganda of asceticism. It is not my business here to defend that propaganda against the numerous and highly respectable British class which conceives life as presenting no alternative to asceticism but licentiousness: I merely describe the situation to save people of this way of thinking from going to hear Mlle Yvette, and proposing to treat her as their forefathers treated Joan of Arc.

Perhaps, however, they would only laugh the innocent laugh of the British lady who, not understanding French, and unwilling to let that fact appear, laughs with the rest at the points which prevented Mlle Guilbert from inviting the episcopal bench as well as the Press to her reception. In spite of her superb diction, I did not understand half her lines myself. Part of what I did understand would have surprised me exceedingly if it had occurred in a drawing-room ballad by Mr Cowen or Sir Arthur Sullivan; but I am bound to add that I was not in the least shocked or disgusted, though my unlimited recognition of an artist's right to take any side of life whatsoever as subject matter for artistic treatment makes me most indignantly resentful of any attempt to abuse my tolerance by coarse jesting.

The fact is, Mlle Guilbert's performance was for the most part much more serious at its base than an average Italian opera *scena.* I am not now alluding to the avowedly dramatic songs like *Le Conscrit* and *Morphinée*, which any ordinary actress could deliver in an equally effective, if somewhat less distinguished, manner. I am thinking of *Les Vierges*, *Sur la scène*, and the almost frightful *La Pierreuse.* A *pierreuse*, it appears, is a garroter's decoy. In the song she describes how she prowls about the fortifications of Paris at night, and entraps some belated bourgeois into conversation. Then she summons her principal with a weird street cry; he pounces on his prey; and the subsequent operations are described in a perfect war dance of a refrain.

Not so very horrible, perhaps; but the last verse describes not a robbery, but the guillotining of the robber; and so hideously exquisite is the singing of this verse that you see the woman in the crowd at La Roquette; you hear the half-choked repetition of the familiar signal with which she salutes the wretch as he is hurried out; you positively see his head flying off;

above all, you feel with a shudder how the creature's impulses of terror and grief are overcome by the bestial excitement of seeing the great State show of killing a man in the most sensational way.

Just as people would not flog children if they could realize the true effect of the ceremony on the child's pet playmates, to whom it is supposed to be a wholesome warning, so the French Government would certainly abolish public executions *sans phrase* (and perhaps private ones too) if only they would go and hear Mlle Guilbert sing *La Pierreuse.*

Technically, Mlle Guilbert is a highly accomplished artist. She makes all her effects in the simplest way, and with perfect judgment. Like the ancient Greeks, not to mention the modern music hall artists, she relies on the middle and low registers of her voice, they being the best suited for perfectly well-controlled declamation; but her *cantabile* is charming, thanks to a fine ear and a delicate rhythmic faculty. Her command of every form of expression is very remarkable, her tones ranging from the purest and sweetest pathos to the cockiest Parisian cynicism.

There is not a trace of the rowdy restlessness and forced "go" of the English music hall singer about her; and I suggest to those members of the London County Council who aim at the elevation of the music hall that they could not do better than offer Mlle Guilbert handsome terms to follow up her reception of *la Presse anglaise* by a series of receptions of Miss Marie Lloyd, Miss Katie Lawrence, and other eminent English *prima donnas*, in order that they might be encouraged to believe that there is room in music hall singing for art of classic self-possession and delicacy without any loss of gaiety, and that the author of a music hall song may not be the worse for being a wit, or even a poet.

Some time ago Mr Bonawitz invited me to an invisible

concert. I did not go, because I felt that I had been entirely misunderstood. I do not at all object to seeing the performers at a concert: it is hearing them that upsets me. If Mr Bonawitz will try an inaudible concert, he may rely on my eager support: meanwhile, I actually did, one day last week, succeed for the first time in my life in going to a concert without hearing a note of music. It was given by Mrs Clarinda Webster, and was called a Mendelssohn concert. When I arrived, some gentleman who had evidently covered himself with glory was retiring, violin in hand, amid thunders of applause. I had settled myself down comfortably to enjoy the next item, when Mrs Webster, observing that a Mendelssohn concert would be incomplete without a sketch of the life of Mendelssohn (which seemed no more than reasonable), proceeded to read a biography of the master. This was all very well for the ignorant multitude; but it was very poor fun for me, who know all about Mendelssohn. However, I reflected that as he died young, the biography could not last very long; and I held on until Mrs Webster began to read a letter from the composer descriptive of his reception at Buckingham Palace. I regret to say that my loyalty broke down under this strain. I stole out as quietly as I could, hoping Mrs Webster would not look up from her manuscript and catch me in the act. And so, though I have no doubt the concert was a capital one, I heard none of it. It was rather an unlucky day in this way; for in the evening I repaired to the same place (Queen's Hall, the concert room at the top of the building) to hear Mr Charles Fry recite Eugene Aram* to an accompaniment composed by Dr Mackenzie. I arrived just in time to have the door

* XVIII century schoolmaster and murderer, subject of a poem by Thomas Hood, a novel by Edward Bulwer-Lytton, and a play by W. G. Wills.

closed in my face, under the very proper rule which forbids people to come in during the performance of a piece. And here I discovered the value of Mr Bonawitz's invention of the invisible concert; for the spectacle of Mr Fry, apparently making faces at me through the glass door (which cut off all sound) in derision of my baffled plight outside, was more than I could bear; and I again retreated musicless.

Mr Max Laistner's choir distinguished itself at St James's Hall last week by an excellent performance of Max Bruch's setting of Schiller's Lay of the Bell. Mr Laistner is a capital choirmaster; and it is a pity that his concerts are not more frequent, in view of the dearth at the West End of good choral concerts with choirs of reasonable size and manageableness. But why on earth did Mr Laistner play Schumann's pianoforte concerto in public? Surely he must know that his hands, musicianly as they are, have not the trained strength of the pianoforte athlete's. I did not hear half the notes. Besides, it made the concert absurdly long. Bruch's work, passionate and grandiose at best, and lively and interesting at worst, is so very superior to the sort of thing we turn out here that I cannot, for very shame, insist on its limitations in an English paper. It might well be heard oftener.

I see that Mr Daniel de Lange has again brought his choir over from Amsterdam. He did so ten years ago, when I vainly tried to draw public attention to the extraordinary merit of his performances of the old choral music of the great Netherlandish school. I came upon one of his concerts at the Inventions Exhibition at South Kensington, quite accidentally; and I shall never forget the effect produced on me, or the stupendous insensibility of most of the other droppers-in to the fact that they were listening to one of the very finest and rarest performances they had ever heard in their lives.

I have not heard the choir since, and so do not know whether it maintains its former excellence; but it gives me great pleasure to acknowledge my old debt to Mr de Lange by urging all lovers of the pure choral counterpoint of the XV and XVI centuries (than which, in its way, there is no more beautiful music in the world) not to lose this opportunity as that of 1885 was lost.

BORN-AGAIN ITALIAN OPERA

The World, 23 May 1894

I have been to the Opera six times; and I still live. What is more, I am positively interested and hopeful. Hitherto I have had only one aim as regards Italian opera: not, as some have supposed, to kill it, for it was dead already, but to lay its ghost. It was a troublesome phantom enough. When one felt sure that it had been effectually squeezed out at last by French opera, or Hebraic opera, or what may be called operatic music-drama—Lohengrin, for instance—it would turn up again trying to sing *Spirto gentil* in the manner of Mario, raving through the mad scene in Lucia amid childish orchestral tootlings, devastating Il Trovatore with a totally obsolete style of representation, or in some way gustily rattling its unburied bones and wasting the manager's money and my patience.

The difficulty was to convince those who had been brought up to believe in it (as I was myself) that it was all over with it: they *would* go on believing that it only needed four first-rate Italian singers to bring the good old times back again and make the rum-tum rhythms, the big guitar orchestration, the florid cabalettas, the cavatinas in regular four-bar lines, the choruses in thirds and sixths, and all the rest of it swell out to their former grandeur and sweep Wagner off the boards. I have no doubt they believe it as devoutly as ever, and that if Mr Mapleson were to start again tomorrow, he would announce Lucia and Il Barbiere and Semiramide with unshaken confidence in their freshness and adequacy, perhaps adding, as a concession to the public demand for novelty, a promise of Ponchielli's La Gioconda.

But now an unlooked-for thing has happened. Italian opera has been born again. The extirpation of the Rossinian dynasty, which neither Mozart nor Wagner could effect, since what they offered in its place was too far above the heads of both the public and the artists, is now being accomplished with ease by Mascagni, Leoncavallo, Puccini, and Verdi. Nobody has ever greeted a performance of Tristan und Isolde by such a remark as "We shall never be able to go back to L'Elisir d'Amore after this," or declare that Lucrezia was impossible after Brynhild. The things were too far apart to affect oneanother: as well might it be supposed that Ibsen's plays could be accepted as a substitute for popular melodrama, or Shakespear wean people from the circus. It is only by an advance in melodrama itself or in circuses themselves that the melodrama or circus of today can become unpresentable to the audiences of ten years hence.

The same thing is true of Italian opera. The improvement of higher forms of art, or the introduction of new forms at a different level, cannot affect it at all; and that is why Tristan has no more killed L'Elisir than Brahms's symphonies have killed Jullien's British Army Quadrilles. But the moment you hear Pagliacci, you feel that it is all up with L'Elisir. It is true that Leoncavallo has shewn as yet nothing comparable to the melodic inspiration of Donizetti; but the advance in serious workmanship, in elaboration of detail, in variety of interest, and in capital expenditure on the orchestra and the stage, is enormous. There is more work in the composition of Cavalleria than in La Favorita, Lucrezia, and Lucia put together, though I cannot think—perhaps this is only my own old-fashionedness—that any part of it will live as long or move the world as much as the best half-dozen numbers in those three obsolete masterpieces,

And when you come to Puccini, the composer of the latest Manon Lescaut, then indeed the ground is so transformed that you could almost think yourself in a new country. In Cavalleria and Pagliacci I can find nothing but Donizettian opera rationalized, condensed, filled in, and thoroughly brought up to date; but in Manon Lescaut the domain of Italian opera is enlarged by an annexation of German territory. The first act, which is as gay and effective and romantic as the opening of any version of Manon need be, is also unmistakably symphonic in its treatment. There is genuine symphonic modification, development, and occasionally combination of the thematic material, all in a dramatic way, but also in a musically homogeneous way, so that the act is really a single movement with episodes instead of being a succession of separate numbers, linked together, to conform to the modern fashion, by substituting interrupted cadences for full closes and parading a Leitmotif occasionally.

Further, the experiments in harmony and syncopation, reminding one often of the intellectual curiosities which abound in Schumann's less popular pianoforte works, shew a strong technical interest which is, in Italian music, a most refreshing symptom of mental vigor, even when it is not strictly to the real artistic point. The less studied harmonies are of the most modern and stimulating kind. When one thinks of the old school, in which a dominant seventh, or at most a minor ninth, was the extreme of permissible discord, only to be tolerated in the harsher inversions when there was a murder or a ghost on hand, one gets a rousing sense of getting along from hearing young Italy beginning its most light-hearted melodies to the chord of the thirteenth on the tonic.

Puccini is particularly fond of this chord; and it may be taken as a general technical criticism of the young Italian school that its free use of tonic discords, and its reckless prodigality of orchestral resources, give its music a robustness and variety that reduce the limited tonic and dominant harmonic technique of Donizetti and Bellini, by contrast, to mere Christy minstrelsy. No doubt this very poverty of the older masters made them so utterly dependent on the invention of tunes that they invented them better than the new men, who, with a good drama to work on, can turn out vigorous, imposing, and even enthralling operas without a bar that is their own in the sense in which *Casta Diva* is Bellini's own; but Puccini, at least, shews no signs of atrophy of the melodic faculty: he breaks out into catching melodies quite in the vein of Verdi: for example, *Tra voi, belle,* in the first act of Manon, has all the charm of the tunes beloved by the old operatic guard.

On that and other accounts, Puccini looks to me more like the heir of Verdi than any of his rivals. He has arranged his own libretto from Prévost d'Exiles' novel; and though the miserable end of poor Manon has compelled him to fall back on a rather conventional operatic death scene in which the *prima donna* at Covent Garden failed to make anyone believe, his third act, with the roll-call of the female convicts and the embarkation, is admirably contrived and carried out: he has served himself in this as well as Scribe ever served Meyerbeer, or Boïto Verdi.

If now it is considered that this opening week at Covent Garden began with Manon, and ended with

Falstaff; Cavalleria and Pagliacci coming in between, with nothing older than Faust and Carmen to fill up except the immortal Orfeo, it will be understood how I find myself with the startling new idea that Italian opera has a future as well as a past, and that perhaps Sir Augustus Harris, in keeping a house open for it, has not been acting altogether as an enemy of the human race, as I used sometimes to declare in my agony when, in a moment of relenting towards that dreary past, he would let loose some stout matron to disport herself once more as Favorita, or spend untold gold in indulging Jean de Reszke with a revival of that concentrated bore and outrage, Le Prophète, when I wanted to see the prince of tenors and procrastinators as Siegfried or Tristan.

Falstaff drew an enormous house on Saturday, and was received with an enthusiasm which was quite unforced up to the end of the clothes-basket scene. After that the opera suffered for a while from the play outlasting the freshness of the subject, a fate that invariably overtakes The Merry Wives of Windsor, except when the actor who plays Falstaff has an extraordinary power of inventing humorous and varied character traits.

The first scene of the third act was undeniably a little dull. The merry wives cackled wearisomely; Pessina's comic stock was exhausted, so that he could do nothing but repeat the business of the earlier scenes; and Mrs Quickly, who had been charming for the first ten minutes in the novel character of the youthful and charming Signorina Ravogli, gave the final blow to the dramatic interest of the scene by not being her detestable old self.

Fortunately, the excitement revived in the forest scene at the end, which is full of life and charm. It ends with a sort of musical practical joke in the shape of a fugue which is everything that a fugue ought not to be, and which, failing more rehearsal than it is worth, has to be execrably sung in order to get the parts picked up. It was listened to with deep reverence, as if Verdi, in his old age, had clasped hands with Sebastian Bach. Always excepting the first scene of the third act, the opera went like wildfire.

Boïto's libretto is excellent as far as it is a condensation of Shakespear, except that he has not appreciated the great stage effectiveness of Falstaff's description to Ford of his misadventure in the basket, with its climaxes, dear to old Shakespearean actors, of "Think of that, Master Brook." His alterations, notably the screen business in the basket scene, make some fun; but they also make the scene in Ford's house quite outrageously impossible. As far as acting is concerned, the weight of the whole opera lies in the scene between Ford and Falstaff at the Garter Inn; and here Pessina played with considerable humor and vigor, though without any particular subtlety.

Pini-Corsi's acting was better than operatic acting generally is; but it hardly satisfied those of us who have seen anything like an adequate impersonation of Ford on the English stage. The women were rather unintelligently and monotonously merry; and on the whole the success was, past all question, a success of the musical setting, which is immensely vivacious and interesting. The medieval scenery is attractive, especially the garden and the room in Ford's house. The interior of the inn is not sunny enough: modern painting, with its repudiation of the studio light, and its insistence on work in the open air, has made the traditional stage interior look old-fashioned in this respect.

The company at Covent Garden is a very strong one. The representations of Cavalleria and Pagliacci derive an altogether exceptional dramatic force from the acting of De Lucia and Ancona in parts which are in constant danger of being handed over to a second-rate tenor and baritone. Beduschi, who plays Des Grieux in Manon with success, is another tenor of the Gayarré school, without the goat bleat and *tremolo* of its extreme disciples. He is a capable actor, small in figure, with a face which will probably be described as dark and ugly by a good many people, nevertheless by no means an unprepossessing face. Cossira, a tenor of heavier build than Beduschi, made some effect by his passion and sincerity in the love scene in the second act of Carmen. Albers, a baritone, made his first appearances as Valentin in Faust and the Toreador in Carmen. His treatment of Bizet's daintily written scene between José and Escamillo before the fight in the third act gave me an extremely unfavorable impression of the delicacy of his musical sense; but the rougher part of his work was presentably done. Bonnard, a French *tenorino*, made a satisfactory Philémon in Philémon et Baucis, in which, however, the honors went to Plançon for a splendid appearance as Jupiter.

Philémon brought back Mlle Simonnet, whose voice is somewhat thicker and richer, especially in the middle, than when she charmed us first in Bruneau's Le Rêve. I am not sure that the same remark does not apply, in a slight degree, to Mlle Simonnet's figure, though she was certainly as trim and youthful as could be desired as Micaela in Carmen. She also played Marguerite in Faust, of which I saw only the last act and a half. Her Micaela was not good: she slipped through the music in a pointless way, apparently finding the part trivial and uninteresting, and certainly making it so. Her Marguerite—what I saw of it—was clever and pretty, but prosaic. It was only as Baucis that she fully justified the admiration excited by her first performances in this country, though none of her three appearances passed without a burst of applause for some happily sung passage. The leading parts in the two new operas were taken by Olga Olghina, a clever Russian lady with chiseled features and a somewhat courtly fastidiousness of manner, just a little too ladylike for Manon and a little too mundane for Anne Page, but able to make a distinct mark in both by her acting in the embarkation scene of the one opera and her singing in the forest scene of the other. Mlle Pauline Joran played Siebel and Lola in Cavalleria, the latter cleverly. Of Bauermeister the invaluable, the inevitable, I need not speak; and of Signorine Zilli and Kitzu I shall perhaps speak later on, when my impressions of them are more definite. Of the two great dramatic artists of the company, Giulia Ravogli struck me as suffering from underwork; and as to the incomparable Calvé, at least a week must elapse before I can trust myself to speak of her Carmen and her Santuzza, or, indeed, of herself, with a decent pretence of critical coolness.

The Amsterdam Choir, after a brief spell at St Martin's Hall, is singing this week at Queen's Hall. The expectations I expressed last week have been far surpassed. The choir now consists of twentytwo singers, each of them a singer in a thousand. In England we should set the whole thousand bawling together, and then brag all over Europe about our supremacy in choral music.

Mr Daniel de Lange eliminates the worst nine hundred and ninetynine from each thousand, and produces with the remainder a choir the *fortissimo* of which would drown the biggest of our feebly monstrous choral societies, and the *pianissimo* of which almost embraces perfect silence. I wish I had space to do justice to the extraordinary excellence of their execution and the surpassing interest and beauty of the music, sacred and secular, of Josquin, Orlando, Sweelinck, and the rest of the heros of the old Netherlandish school.

TWENTY YEARS TOO LATE

The World, 30 May 1894

We live in an age of progress. Patti has been singing a song by Wagner. Never shall I forget the sensation among the critics at the Albert Hall when, on turning over the pages of their programs, they saw among the names there that of The Master, cropping up like a modest crocus among those of Mozart, Rossini, and other contemporaries of Madame Patti's grandmother. There is now no denying the fact that Madame Patti—Adelina Patti—*the* Patti—the lady who used to appear and reappear as Rosina in Il Barbiere at Covent Garden until the old *régime* died of it, actually did, on the afternoon of Saturday, May 19, 1894, sing the study on Tristan und Isolde, No. 5 of the Five Poems composed by Richard Wagner, late of Bayreuth, in 1862. What is more, she sang it extremely well, and, when the inevitable *encore* came, repeated it instead of singing Home, Sweet Home or Within a Mile.

And yet there was something exasperating in the thought that this demonstration by a fine singer that Wagner's music is as singable as Mozart's came just twenty years after it was most needed. Nobody now supposes that in Wagner's works the women must shriek and the men howl, and that no human voice can stand the wear and tear for more than a year or two. But that was once a very common opinion, most devoutly acted on by many operatic artists, with, of course, fully corroborative results as far as the prophesied wear and tear was concerned. What was Madame Patti doing in those dark days, when she might have rescued Tannhäuser from the horrors of its first performance at

Covent Garden in the decline and fall of the seventies? Alas! in those days she sang *Bel raggio* in the key of A, and did not sing Wagner at all.

It was left to Jean de Reszke, by his Walther in Die Meistersinger, to give the final proof that Wagner requires and repays the most delicate lyrical treatment; and now Madame Patti, with the ground made safe for her, comes forward and, having first propitiated the first quarter of the expiring century by singing *Bel raggio* in the key of G, at last ventures on this simple little *Träume*, and is perhaps surprised to find that the thrill is deeper and the applause more sincere than that which follows Rossini's shallow *bravura*. For my part, I regard Patti's brilliancy as a singer of florid decorative music as one of her greatest misfortunes. In the first place, she has never done it superlatively well: it has always been a little jerky and tricky in comparison with the finest execution of such a perfect singer of *roulade* as Marimon, for instance, not to mention others.

I never fully appreciated Patti until one night at Covent Garden when I heard her sing, not *Una Voce* or anything of that sort, but God save the Queen. The wonderful even soundness of the middle of her voice, its beauty and delicacy of surface, and her exquisite touch and diction, all qualify her to be great in expressive melody, and to occupy a position in the republic of art high above the pretty flummery of newspaper puffs, flowers, recalls, *encores*, and so forth which makes it so difficult for people who take art seriously to do justice to the talent and the artistic pains with which she condescends to bid for such recognition.

I am so far from regretting that Time has stolen some of the five or six notes above the high B flat which she once possessed, and has made the rest hardly safe for everyday use, that I shall heartily congratulate her when the day comes when *Bel raggio* and *Ah, non giunge*, in any key whatsoever, must be dropped, and replaced in her repertory by more such songs as *Träume*; for it is my firm belief that Patti is capable of becoming a great singer, though the world has been at such pains and expense to spoil her for the last thirtyfive years. At her concert on the 19th, her voice was better than at last year's concerts; and altogether she was brighter, more efficient, more successful—if there can be said to be degrees in Patti's success—than when I last heard her.

The difference between the old order in opera and the new suggests to my imagination such a vast period of time that it seems odd to me that I should have witnessed Patti's latest triumph on the morrow of Calvé's appearance at Covent Garden as Carmen. It is only fair that I should warn the public against attaching too much importance to anything I may say about Madame Calvé. As I have often explained, it is one of the conditions of that high susceptibility which is my chief qualification as a critic that good or bad art becomes a personal matter between me and the artist.

I *hate* performers who debase great works of art: I long for their annihilation: if my criticisms were flaming thunderbolts, no prudent Life or Fire Insurance Company would entertain a proposal from any singer within my range, or from the lessee of any opera house or concert room within my circuit. But I am necessarily no less extreme in my admiration of artists who realize the full value of great works for me, or who transfigure ordinary ones. Calvé is such an artist; and she is also a woman whose strange personal appearance recalls Titian's wonderful Virgin of the Assumption at Venice, and who has, in addition to that beauty of aspect, a beauty of action—especially of that sort of action which is the thought or conception of the artist made visible—such as one might expect from Titian's Virgin if the picture were made alive. This description will perhaps sufficiently shew the need for a little discount off such eulogies as I may presently be moved to in speaking of her performances in detail.

But I have no eulogies for her Carmen, which shocked me beyond measure. I pointed out on a previous occasion, when dealing with a very remarkable impersonation of that character by Giulia Ravogli, that the success of Bizet's opera is altogether due to the attraction, such as it is, of seeing a pretty and respectable middle-class young lady, expensively dressed, harmlessly pretending to be a wicked person, and that anything like a successful attempt to play the part realistically by a powerful actress must not only at once betray the thinness and unreality of Prosper Mérimée's romance, but must leave anything but a pleasant taste on the palate of the audience. This was proved by the fact that Giulia Ravogli's Carmen, the most powerful that had then been seen in England, was received with a good deal of grumbling, and was shelved to make way for that pretty little imposition, the Carmen of Miss de Lussan, who was, as everybody could see, a perfect young lady innocently playing at being naughty.

And yet Giulia Ravogli flattered Carmen by exhibiting her as a woman of courage and strength of character. Calvé makes no such concession. Her Carmen is a superstitious, pleasure-loving good-for-nothing, caught by the outside of anything glittering, with no power but the power of seduction, which she exercises without sense or decency. There is no suggestion of any fine quality about her, not a spark of honesty, courage, or even of the sort of honor supposed to prevail among thieves. All this is conveyed by Calvé with a positively frightful artistic power of divesting her beauty and grace of the nobility—I had almost written the sanctity—which seems inseparable from them in other parts. Nobody else dare venture on the indescribable allurements which she practises on the officers in the first act, or such touches as the attempt to get a comprehensive view of her figure in Lillas Pastia's rather small looking-glass, or her jealously critical inspection of Micaela from the same point of view in the third act.

Her death scene, too, is horribly real. The young lady Carmen is never so effectively alive as when she falls, stage dead, beneath José's cruel knife. But to see Calvé's Carmen changing from a live creature, with properly coordinated movements, into a reeling, staggering, flopping, disorganized thing, and finally tumble down a mere heap of carrion, is to get much the same sensation as might be given by the reality of a brutal murder. It is perhaps just as well that a great artist should, once in a way, give our opera-goers a glimpse of the truth about the things they play with so lightheartedly. In spite of the applause and the curtain calls, it was quite evident that the audience was by no means as comfortable after the performance as Miss de Lussan would have left them.

But nothing would induce me to go again. To me it was a desecration of a great talent. I felt furious with Calvé, as if I had been shewn some terrible caricature by Hogarth of the Titian. That, however, may have been a personal sentiment. What I am perfectly sure was a legitimate critical sentiment was my objection to Carmen carrying her abandonment to the point of being incapable of paying the smallest attention to the score. I have never seen, at Bayreuth or anywhere else, an operatic actress fit her action more perfectly and punctually to its indication in the orchestra than Giulia Ravogli did as Carmen. And I have never seen, even at Covent Garden, the same artistic duty so completely disregarded as it was by Calvé. She acted out of time the whole evening; and I do not see why artists should act out of time any more than sing out of time.

I go back with relief from Carmen to Cavalleria, in which her Santuzza was irresistibly moving and beautiful, and fully capable of sustaining the inevitable comparison with Duse's impersonation of the same part.*

But Duse makes the play more credible, not because an opera is less credible than a spoken play—for though that can be proved logically, the facts are just the other way, the superior intensity of musical expression making the opera far more real than the play—but because Duse makes the woman not only intensely pitiable, but hopelessly unattractive, so that Turiddu's preference for Lola seems natural, wheras in the opera his desertion of Calvé is not to be tolerated as the act of a sane man: one cannot take any interest in such an ass.

The desolating Arctic wind which parched the liver of London last week swept blightingly through the ranks of Mottl's band at his second concert, and laid the program waste. Himself in something less than his highest spirits, he nevertheless made a brave effort to rally his prostrated forces. But he got nothing like the response they made to him at the previous concert. The effect of this general indisposition was unfortunately emphasized by the change from Wagner to Berlioz and Beethoven. Beethoven did not know how to get his effects with the orchestra as Wagner did: some of the most powerful traits in his musical designs are disappointing in orchestral execution. Berlioz, of whom this cannot be said, is a Frenchman; and though Mottl's freedom from anything like German heaviness makes him as good a Berlioz conductor as it is in the nature of

* The celebrated Italian actress Eleonora Duse had performed Giovanni Verga's one-act drama, Cavalleria Rusticana, during her first repertory season in London in May–June 1893.

any German who lives and works in his own country to be, yet he simply sent me asleep with the extracts from Roméo et Juliette; for his fine reflective handling took all the passion and pathos out of Romeo's brainless reveries, and his splendid self-possession equally took all the brimstone out of the dance music, which makes but a poor show in the vein of Die Meistersinger. With all these deductions, and the slackness of the band, the hateful wind, and the somewhat injudicious order and excessive length of the program into the bargain, Mottl made a strong impression on those who had not been present at his first appearance as a conductor in England; and I have nothing to retract or modify in the opinion I then expressed of his ability.

STALENESSES OF THE OPERA SEASON

The World, 6 June 1894

After the freshness of the opera season, come in inevitable course the stalenesses of it. I sat out Les Huguenots the other evening; and I cannot quite pass it over without asking whether something cannot be done to recover the original flavor of what is, after all, an interesting and effective piece of stage work. Would it not be possible for the chorus and Bevignani to be born again with certain modifications, and for someone to compile Tales from Meyerbeer in the style of Lamb's Tales from Shakespear, and make a present of a copy to the stage manager? I am a person of strong economic instincts, cultivated by circumstances as well as by study; and when I calculate the appalling sum it must cost to send the curtain up at Covent Garden, it infuriates me to see the minimum instead of the maximum of value given to the manager and the public for all that gigantic expenditure.

Nobody who does not know the score can have any idea of the mutilated state of the work as performed at Covent Garden, or how completely obsolete is the phase of public taste which influenced the mutilators in their choice of cuts. A couple of years ago Maurel restored a page in the first act for the sake of a *bravura* passage which he wanted to sing. This year Plançon has done the same in the third act in order to get one more turn at his chorale. Nothing is gained by this, except to make the original cut rather more ridiculous than it was before; and, to counterbalance it, there is a new cut in the first act, from the beginning of the scene where Nevers and the rest begin to vie with oneanother in flattering Raoul, up to the exclamation "Tous," which is the cue for the last movement of the *finale.*

The third act is too silly for description. The duel in which, after the most heroic preliminaries, the parties no sooner cross swords than they bolt, every man of them, without any apparent reason except their conviction that he who fights and runs away may live to fight another day, is only an example of the insensate way in which the work was cut fifty years ago; but even in the earlier parts of the act, which stand much as they were written, all pretence of knowing or caring what the scene is about has been dropped by everyone except the principals. When the Catholics remonstrate with Marcel for not taking off his hat during the Ave Maria, they keep their own hats tightly on; and though, for once in a way, the Huguenot soldiers who back Marcel did not last Thursday take their helmets off or kneel down, I can only regard that as a lazy neglect on their parts of what they doubtless still believe to be their duty.

The whole stage business of the act is like blindman's buff from beginning to end, the crowd caring for nothing but to get out of the way of the principals; and the choral singing matches it exactly. Just as a railway porter who has been told to call out the name of his station soon allows the words he pronounces to muddle themselves away into a cry which conveys no import and renders no service to any human traveler, so, at Covent Garden, the choristers have come in the course of long years to gabble over something that was once the Rataplan Chorus or the Vesper Hymn, but which is now nothing but a public indulgence of an intolerably slovenly habit. I cannot understand why Sir Augustus Harris allows himself to be so badly served in these matters as he is.

I am quite well aware of the impossibility of rehearsing every opera adequately; and though it is my business as a critic to put all that aside and proceed on the plain assumption that things that cannot be done reasonably well should not be done at all, I am nevertheless anxious to make every possible allowance for the difficulties of the situation. But I will only do so on condition that the difficulties are struggled with to the utmost. The moment they are made an excuse for letting things slide, then all tolerance is out of the question. If the supreme authority is goodnatured enough to accept from his stage manager and conductor an assurance that the third act of Les Huguenots cannot be done any better than that under the circumstances, then I am not; and if Sir Augustus, as *impresario*, will not make himself unpleasant, I, as critic, will. Rehearsal or no rehearsal, I expect at Covent Garden to see the stage full of people who are punctual, alert, in earnest, under the eye of a conductor who is not to be trifled with.

If we cannot have, at what professes to be the leading opera house in Europe, a great conductor, before whom everyone will be ashamed not to do his or her best, let us at least have a martinet before whom they will be afraid to risk a mistake. There are few persons whom I have less desire to see alive again than Costa; but there are moments when Bevignani makes me miss him. I do not wish to do Bevignani an injustice: I admire the obligingness and adroitness with which he accompanies the principal singers through all their extremely *ad libitum* readings, and the determination and briskness with which he thwacks the choruses along so as to get the opera over early and leave plenty of time for very long waits between the acts, so that the critics may have ample opportunities for saying to oneanother in the foyer what they never say to the public in print.

The more *blasé* I grow the more the performance of an opera becomes to me a piece of routine which has to be got through somehow every night in the season with as little friction as possible, the more do I feel inclined to stand by Bevignani. But sometimes the thought will come unbidden that I have heard Richter conduct Die Meistersinger, Mottl Tristan, and Faccio Otello; and that not only was the music much more effective, but the whole character of the performance, from the attitudes and tone of the chorus down to the frequency with which they were willing to shave, changed under the eye of these strong men. In short, to be quite frank, though I appreciate the way in which the Covent Garden conductors pull things through under difficulties, none of them is such a Napoleon of the orchestra as is needed to establish himself as ruler by divine right in the prevailing anarchy of a London opera house.

Pending the re-cutting and consequent re-rehearsal of Les Huguenots, I need only record what is necessary of the performance last week. The Valentine was a Madame Adiny, a tall, powerfully built lady with a serviceable high C, and plenty of feeling of a not uncommon kind, but without invention as an actress, even in the matter of stage business. Cossira has not the range for Raoul—who has? Instead of transposing the duel septuor, and driving the basses into their boots as De Reszke does, he sang it in the original key and replaced the C sharp by a B natural. I cannot say that it did as well; but it was the frankest and wisest thing to do under the circumstances. He sang the duet with the queen very well. Plançon carried off the honors of the performance for his Marcel, which, as he happens to have that first important requisite for the part, a true bass voice, was a relief after the attempts of Edouard de Reszke to squeeze it into the compass of a somewhat limited *basso cantante.*

Mlle Olitska, who played Urbain, should have omitted the song in the second act, since she was unable to execute the volley of little runs down half the scale, which are a leading feature in it. She is a clever and ambitious artist; but her method, artificially throaty and naturally rather nasal, runs counter to my prejudices as to what is desirable in vocal tone. Madame Adiny did not make any serious pretence of giving us the double chromatic scale in the duet with Raoul; but nobody seems to mind these little licenses nowadays; and indeed I cannot say that I think an artist should be disqualified from attempting a part like Valentine merely by the difficulties of a trait of this sort. The Nevers of Albers was a great improvement on his bullfighter in Carmen.

On Saturday last we had Faust, with Melba as Margaret. De Lucia accosted her in the second act in Italian; she snubbed him in French; Bauermeister kept her in countenance by conversing with her in French in the garden; and Mephistopheles, at home in all countries, tempted Faust in Italian and Marta in French. And, to give the devil his due, his French was the best in the collection: Margaret's, in particular, being occasionally rather like mine. De Lucia's dramatic instinct helped him well through a part in which he seemed likely to be overweighted. Several times in the garden scene he found the right musical treatment with exceptional success.

Ancona's Valentin is the best we have had for a long time. His *Dio possente*, sung in the original key with great expression and with a magnificent high G, was one of the features of the representation. But he should go over the part with the book some morning; for he has forgotten the exact notation of one or two passages. I am not, of course, alluding to his intentional taking of the first line of the *reprise* in *Dio possente* right up the scale to the high E flat. Melba, with her unspoiled, beautiful voice, and, above all, her perfect intonation—you never realize how wide a gap there is between the ordinary singer who simply avoids the fault of singing obviously out of tune and the singer who sings really and truly in tune, except when Melba is singing—received boundless welcome, and, with the usual mysterious luck of American and colonial *prima donnas*, received flowers across the footlights in those large baskets which English ladies and gentlemen invariably carry with them in the theatre, and which they present to singers in moments of uncontrolable admiration. Melba has commanded Sir Augustus to put on that favorite Donizettian *chef-d'œuvre* Lucia di Lammermoor, for the better display of her *roulades*; and Sir Augustus has gallantly consented. Having heard the work rather frequently in the course of my early career, I do not look forward to the occasion with much curiosity.

The second Patti concert at the Albert Hall ended with a recital of a "lyric drama, in one act, entitled Gabriella, specially composed for, and dedicated to, Madame Adelina Patti, by Emilio Pizzi." I came rather late: in fact, if the honest truth must be told, I did not get to the Albert Hall until a quarter of an hour before the close of the concert, by which time all the characters were in their death agonies, struggling with a tempestuous orchestration, and uttering ejaculations like "Madre infelice," "alla morte," "Ohime! perduto," and so on. There was nothing whatever to take exception to in what I heard of the music. Of the tenor, Mr Robert Kaufmann, I must say a word. This gentleman made his first appearance here lately at a concert which was declared by some high musical authorities to be England's absolutely finest musical achievement, and by others, including myself, to be one of the severest afflictions of the century. I did not hear Mr Kaufmann again until he sang the other day at Mlle Kleeberg's pianoforte recital at St James's Hall, when he proved himself a singer of exceptionally fine artistic sensibility and intelligence, doing a great deal with a by no means extraordinary voice. On this occasion Miss Kleeberg who, if not so perfectly neat and even-handed as she used to be, has gained in freedom of expression, began solemnly by playing Beethoven, that being the proper thing to do in St James's Hall. I bore it like a man, and even enjoyed one variation in the sonata Op. 110, which gave Mlle Kleeberg an opportunity in the style of playing in which she excels. I have also heard M. Sevadjian, in appearance at least a pianist to the last few inches of his hair. His reading of Beethoven's Funeral March sonata was entirely original; but it did not carry conviction to me as the reading intended by the composer. M. Sevadjian, too, though an accurate player, has a peculiar way of scrutinizing the keyboard as if he did not quite know where he would find the note he wanted, which gives him an odd resemblance to a person trying to write a word on a typewriter for the first time. These peculiarities of manner perhaps handicapped him a little unfairly with the audience. My apologies to the givers of many other concerts and recitals, notice of which must stand over for the present.

ON MUSICAL CRITICISM

The World, 13 June 1894

Dr Villiers Stanford has been favoring us with his views on Some Aspects of Musical Criticism in England in the shape of a magazine article. I am very strongly tempted to quote it here at full length; for it is the best article I ever saw on the subject, unexceptionally judicious and accurate, and much better written than most musical criticisms are. I shall at least quote his exposition of his main point, as I cannot paraphrase it to any advantage:

"A new opera, which has been, perhaps, the work of years, and the outcome of the daily thought and labor of composer and librettist, is produced on a Monday night; and by 2 A.M. on Tuesday morning a critic, who has just made his first acquaintance with the composition, is expected to have completed a full and just chronicle of its merits and faults, its workmanship and its effect, fit to be put into print, and intended to instruct the public before breakfast as to what attitude they should be prepared to take when they find themselves in the audience. I say, as one who is, from much experience in the musician's craft, perhaps exceptionally quick in seizing the points of a new work at first hearing, that to expect the best possible criticism, or indeed criticism of any lasting value at all under such circumstances is grotesque; and the insistence upon such hot haste production is a hardship to the writer, an injury to the producer, and a mischief to the public."

True as this is, and deeply as I am touched by the tribute here implied, and elsewhere explicitly rendered, to the superiority of those weekly articles of which my own may be taken as examples, I am not sure that the opinion elaborated in a week is always so much more valuable than the impression made in a moment. The only musical compositions which will bear thinking of for more than half an hour are those which require an intimate acquaintance of at least ten years for their critical mastery. As to the weekly article being any more "just" than the daily one, I do not see how that can be sustained for a moment. Let us try to vivify our ideas on the subject by getting away from the abstraction "criticism" to the reality from which it is abstracted: that is, the living, breathing, erring, human, nameable and addressable individual who writes criticism.

To avoid getting into trouble I shall not cite any musical critics. The dramatic and parliamentary ones will serve my turn as well. Two of the best dramatic critics in London, Mr Clement Scott and Mr Walkley, write both weekly essays and two-o'clock-in-the-morning notices of new plays. Both write the immediate notice as impressionists. Mr Scott writes his deferred notice also as an impressionist, rubbing in his first impression, and as often as not spoiling it. Mr Walkley is an acute analyst; and in his case the gain in intellectual elaboration in the deferred notice is immense. But has anyone ever observed any gain in either case in the matter of justice? I certainly never have.

Take another case in point. I have for years urged upon editors the necessity of sending a fine critic into the House of Commons to write notices of the sittings of the House exactly as they send a critic to the Opera. The result of giving such a critic a brief for Lord Rosebery against Lord Salisbury is as absurd as it would be to give me a brief for Calvé as against Melba, or my colleague William Archer a brief for Mr Irving as against Mr Tree. Of late years the custom of prefacing the verbatim reports of the sittings of the House by a descriptive report has been developing parliamentary criticism on my lines.

For example, Mr Massingham, a typical parliamentary critic of the new kind, will, in criticizing a debate, praise the performances of Mr Balfour and Mr John Burns, and slate Sir William Harcourt and Mr Chamberlain, or *vice versa*, as if there were no such thing as party politics in the world. This sounds impartial; but does anybody find Mr Massingham "just"; or is it likely that he would be any the juster if his extraordinary small-hour performances were replaced by weekly ones? The fact is, justice is not the critic's business; and there is no more dishonest and insufferable affectation in criticism than that impersonal, abstract, judicially authoritative air which, since it is so easy to assume, and so well adapted to rapid phrase stringing, is directly encouraged by the haste which Dr Stanford deprecates.

In Dr Stanford's article which is a masterpiece in the way of tact, no individual critic now alive and working on the English press is talked either of or at. Instead, we have "the critic," "the musical correspondent," and so on. Now "the critic" is a very fine character. One can quite believe that if only the noble creature is given time to consider his utterances, he will hold the scales balanced to a hair's breadth. But just substitute for "the critic" the initials G.B.S. Instantly the realities of the case leap to light; and you see without any argument that the lapse of a few days between the performance and the notice, far from obliterating the writer's partialities and prejudices, his personal likes and dislikes, his bias, his temperament, his local traditions, his nationality—in a word, himself, only enables him to express them the more insidiously when he wishes to conceal their influence.

No man sensitive enough to be worth his salt as a critic could for years wield a pen which, from the nature of his occupation, is scratching somebody's nerves at every stroke, without becoming conscious of how monstrously indefensible the superhuman attitude of impartiality is for him. If the countless injustices which I have done in these columns had been perpetrated in that attitude I should deserve hanging. I therefore add to Dr Stanford's plea for the more considerate utterance of the weekly feuilleton, a further plea for sincerity of expression, not only of the critic's opinion, but of the mood in which that opinion was formed.

We cannot get away from the critic's tempers, his impatiences, his sorenesses, his friendships, his spite, his enthusiasms (amatory and other), nay, his very politics and religion if they are touched by what he criticizes. They are all there hard at work; and it should be his point of honor—as it is certainly his interest if he wishes to avoid being dull—not to attempt to conceal them or to offer their product as the dispassionate dictum of infallible omniscience. If the public were to receive such a self exhibition by coldly saying "We dont want to know the sort of person you are: we want to know whether such a work or artist or performance is good or bad," then the critic could unanswerably retort "How on earth can you tell how much my opinion on that point is worth unless you know the sort of person I am?" As a matter of fact the public never does meet a good critic with any such rebuff. The critic who cannot interest the public in his real self has mistaken his trade: that is all.

Dr Stanford touches a painful point when he speaks of "the danger that editors who happen themselves to be ignorant of music, should engage the services of writers almost equally ignorant merely because they possess the gift of literary style." Here, for almost the only moment in his article, Dr Stanford speaks without inside knowledge of journalism. Editors, by some law of Nature which still baffles science, are *always* ignorant of music, and consequently always abjectly superstitious on the subject. Instead of looking the more keenly to the critic's subject. Instead of looking the more keenly to the critic's other qualifications because they cannot judge of his musical ones, they regard him with an awe which makes them incapable of exercising any judgment at all about him.

Find me an editor who can tell at a glance whether a review, a leading article, a London letter, or a news paragraph is the work of a skilled hand or not, and who has even some power of recognizing what is money's worth and what is not in the way of a criticism of the Royal Academy or the last new play; and I, by simply writing that "the second subject, a graceful and flowing theme contrasting happily with the rugged vigor of its predecessor, appears unexpectedly in the key of the dominant," will reduce that able editor to a condition so abject that he will let me inundate his columns with pompous platitude, with the dullest plagiarisms from analytic programs, with shameless puffery, with bad grammar, bad logic, wrong dates, wrong names, with every conceivable blunder and misdemeanor that a journalist can commit, provided I do it in the capacity of his musical critic.

Not that my stuff will not bore and worry him as much as it will bore and worry other people; but what with his reluctance to risk a dispute with me on a subject he does not understand and his habit of considering music as a department of lunacy, practised and read about by people who are not normally sane and healthy human beings, he will find it easiest to "suppose it is all right" and to console himself with the reflection that it does not matter anyhow. Dr Stanford says "If editors appoint an incompetent person, public opinion is pretty sure, sooner or later, to find out and expose the ignoramus." This expectation is so entirely and desperately unwarranted by experience that I may take it that Dr Stanford only offers it rather than leave the difficulty without at least a pretence of a solution.

But why not form a Vigilance Committee of musicians for the exposure of incompetent critics? The other day, as we all remember, five eminent musicians published a protest against a certain musical critic. [See III, 166.] Being new to their work, they did not do it well; and the critic got the best of it; but I sincerely hope the five will not be discouraged. After a few trials, a Vigilance Committee would learn to attack cautiously and effectively, and to avoid the professional weakness of exaggerating the importance of those blunders as to historic facts and musical technicalities which sometimes give a ludicrous air to really shrewd and essentially sound criticism.

Musical criticisms, like sermons, are of low average quality simply because they are never discussed or contradicted; and I should rejoice were such a committee to be formed, especially if Dr Stanford were to be chairman, and would undertake the drafting of such public protests as it might be deemed advisable to issue.

The Philharmonic orchestra has been distinguishing itself at the last two concerts in the hands of Grieg and Saint-Saëns. Grieg is so successful in getting fine work out of the band that if the directors were wise they would make him a handsome offer to take it in hand permanently.

Saint-Saëns also persuaded it to give him a very smooth and fine-drawn performance of his symphony for orchestra with pianoforte and organ, a model of elegant instrumentation, in which the effect of the adoption of what I may call the Lohengrin orchestra, with three woodwind instruments of each kind instead of two, is to my ear conclusive as to the advisability of its general employment in symphony. It is a pity that this particular work of Saint-Saëns degenerates so frightfully at the end. All that barren *coda* stuff, with its mechanical piling of instruments, its whipping of rhythms, and its ridiculous scraps of *fugato*, should be ruthlessly excised: it has no real theme, and only spoils the rest. Grieg's suite of *entr'actes* and incidental music is, for a composer of his pretension, trumpery stuff enough, except for a fanciful and delicate movement for muted violins *pianissimo*, with starts and shudders on the drum, representing somebody's uneasy dreams. Whether Grieg was clever enough to get all the rehearsal to himself I do not know; but a rather abject performance of Beethoven's eighth symphony suggested that he had not left much time to Dr Mackenzie, who, by the way, was exceptionally successful with Wagner's Faust overture at the next concert.

Mr Ben Davies self-sacrificingly added his name to the long list of tenors who have failed in Beethoven's Adelaide, which is virtually a sonatina for tenor voice, and should be treated accordingly. This was rather a drop after the clever singing of Mlle Landi on the previous occasion.

Mr Bispham's Schumann concert last week was so prodigiously successful that I had to retreat unwillingly into the fresh air before it was quite over. Mr Bispham's artistic judgment served him well in his choice of Mrs Henschel and Miss Marguerite Hall as colleagues no less than in his own fine singing, which is getting almost too gentle in its touch for large popular audiences, and will probably be all the better for the greater sharpness of definition and vigor of stroke which Drury Lane will demand from him in the forthcoming German Opera season there.

Mr Henry Bird, in the very important position of Schumann accompanist, divided the honors with the singers, his only failure being in the scene from Faust, which requires a broad orchestral handling altogether different from that of the songs. However, I rejoice to find Mr Bispham turning his attention to this undeservedly neglected piece of Schumann's work; and I take the opportunity to repeat my old suggestion that he should be invited by the Philharmonic or Crystal Palace directors, or by Richter or Mottl, to take part in a performance of the whole of the middle section of the work, from the sunrise scene to the death of Faust.

MISS EAMES SELF-POSSESSED

The World, 20 June 1894

Whoever has not seen Miss Eames as Charlotte has not realized the full force of Thackeray's picture of the young lady who, when she saw the remains of her lover

> Borne before her on a shutter,
> Like a well-conducted person,
> Went on cutting bread and butter.*

I never saw such a well-conducted person as Miss Eames. She casts her propriety like a Sunday frock over the whole stage, and gives Mr Stedman's choirboys, as she cuts the bread and butter for them, a soapy nosed, plastery haired, respectable-aged-mothered appearance which they totally lack in Carmen under the influence of Calvé. Like Goldsmith's hero in She Stoops to Conquer, I am ill at ease in the company of ladylike women; and during the first act of Werther at Covent Garden I grew shyer and more awkward in my stall, until, upon Charlotte informing Werther that she was another's, I felt ready to sink into the earth with confusion. In the third act, when Werther, breaking down under the strain of a whole year's unintermitted well-behavedness, desperately resolved to have a kiss,

* Sorrows of Werther, in W. M. Thackeray's Ballads (1855).

and to that end offered the young lady violence, the whole audience shared the chills with which he was visibly struggling. Never, since Miss Mary Anderson* shed a cold radiance on the rebuked stage, have virtue and comeliness seemed more awful than they do at Covent Garden on Werther nights. How I envy Miss Eames her self-possession, her quiet consciousness of being founded on a rock, her good looks (oh, those calmly regular eyebrows!), and, above all, that splendid middle to her voice, enabling her to fill the huge theatre without an effort!

Werther is a more congenial subject for Massenet than even Manon was. When he gets away from the artificial and rhetorical into the regions of candid sentiment and the childlike sincerities of love and grief he is charming. Des Grieux, a hero whom we forgive even for cheating at cards, suited him well: Werther suits him still better. The surroundings suit him too. The constant hum and murmur of the country evening, and the pleasant noisiness of the children when they are not rehearsing their carol or munching the bread and butter, make the first act quite delightful to a jaded critic sitting in a well-situated and comfortable stall.

In the rococo of the following scenes the modishness is made interesting by a certain frank naturalness which never deserts Massenet as long as he is treating subjects that give it a chance—that is, as long as he steers clear of the traditions of Parisian grand opera. On his own ground he has an engaging force and charm of expression; and though he is not exactly a creator in harmony or orchestration, yet in both he has a lively individual style. At all events, he has succeeded in

* American actress of great beauty and haughty mien but limited talent. She retired from the stage after her marriage in 1889.

keeping up the interest of a libretto consisting of four acts of a lovelorn tenor who has only two active moments, one when he tries to ravish a kiss from the fair as aforesaid, and the other when he shoots himself behind the scenes.

Naturally, the success of the work in performance depends a great deal on the artist who plays Werther; and Massenet is certainly fortunate in Jean de Reszke, whose performances as Werther and Romeo last week were masterly. His grip of these two parts is now extraordinarily firm and intimate: he is in the heart of them from the first note to the last. Not a tone nor gesture has a touch of anything common or cheap in it: the parts are elaborately studied and the execution sensitively beautiful throughout, the result, aided by his natural grace and distinction, being in both operas an impersonation not only unflaggingly interesting, but exquisitely attractive. His voice leaves nothing to be desired: at the beginning of the evening there is the slightest possible fur on the first two or three notes; but it wears off at once, and leaves him in the most confident possession of all his forces.

In Werther there are several formidable declamatory passages, accompanied by the full power of the orchestra. He attacks these with triumphant force, and next moment is singing quietly with his voice as unstrained, as responsive, as rich in quality as if it had been wrapped in cotton wool for a week, instead of clashing against Massenet's most strenuous orchestration with a vehemence that would put most tenors practically *hors de combat* for several minutes. He seems to me to be at the height of his physical powers, and at the same time to have perfected his artistic integrity, if I may so express myself, my meaning being that he is now magnificently in earnest about his work and undivided in his attention to it.

The effect of this on his colleagues is excellent: Melba especially surpasses herself when playing with him. I must admit reluctantly that these performances of Werther and Romeo seem sure of a place in the front rank of my operatic recollections. I say reluctantly, because, after all, Romeo is *vieux jeu* and Werther is hardly to be counted a great part; therefore it still rankles in me that we have to send for Herr Alvary to play Tristan and Siegfried.

Edouard de Reszke made his re-entry for the season as Frère Laurent. In that matter of artistic integrity he lags behind his brother. The old Adam is strong within him, and tempts him to bawl occasionally. When he yields, he invariably adds an apologetic attempt at a *piano* passage, which gets out of tune from the after effects of the bawling, and leaves him abashed. When he sings with a dignified reticence, content with the normal strength of his abnormally powerful voice, he is hugely satisfying from the musical, if not from the severely intellectual, point of view. Bonnard was not precisely the man for Tybalt, a part which requires before all things a swordsman.

If Jean de Reszke had gone for him as he used to go for the condescending Montariol, he would infallibly have stained the Covent Garden boards with his gore. On the whole, the duels were made failures by the extreme caution needed to prevent their becoming mortally realistic successes. Miss Lucile Hill, who ought to have played Romeo's page very well, missed her chance, apparently for want of a few hours' scale practice. Her voice was in very indifferent order; her French diction was hardly presentable after De Reszke's; and the effect of certain passages— for instance, the skip of an octave in *Que fais-tu*—was quite unworthy of her former performances. She got through the part on the strength of her appearance and reputation, instead of doing justice to it. I invite her to retrieve this shortcoming: she can do it easily enough if she likes. Of Albers as Mercutio I cannot speak, as I was prevented by a concert from hearing the first act.

In Rigoletto the final duet was restored. As far as I know, it has never been done on the stage since its excision immediately after the opera was first produced. Its orchestration is celestially pretty, so much so that, as I have not a full score within my reach, I will not undertake to swear that it has not been touched up by Mancinelli, or someone with all the latest discoveries at his fingers' ends.

Ancona's Rigoletto was a disappointment. Considering that he has shewn considerable dramatic feeling, and that he has exactly the voice for which the part was written—that is, a rich baritone of such range as to enable him not only to sing with ease up to G, but to keep singing for pages together above the bass stave, as if that were the middle of his voice—great things were expected of him; and I am almost compelled to admire the ingenuity with which he avoided doing them.

In all the less important moments he was tremendous, or looked as if he was going to be; but when the crises arrived, and one expected those terrible explosions of ferocity or paroxysms of abasement which are the great opportunities of the part, he somehow slipped round them with an entirely gentlemanlike aversion to anything like making a scene.

He sang the music with consummate ease, always excepting his consistent failure from beginning to end to seize and strike the right dramatic accent; but after Maurel, who only gets through the music by an occasionally almost painful exercise of vocal ingenuity, he made no mark; and the honors of the performance went to Giulia Ravogli for a very clever piece of playing as Maddalena; to De Lucia, who, over-parted as he was, got through with the Duke's music adroitly and pluckily; and, of course, to Melba, whose acting, if conventional, was earnest and careful, and whose long shake at her exit after *Caro nome* was as beautiful as ever.

Monterone was impersonated by that versatile artist De Vaschetti, who has played, since the season commenced, more parts than most of the leading artists have ventured upon in all their lives. Innkeeper, nobleman, courtier, ghost, bandit, soldier, statesman, chemist, buffoon: nothing comes amiss to De Vaschetti, whose brazen voice rings throughout all operas, and whose old weakness for singing the most unexpected and startling wrong notes—he once, as the statue in Don Giovanni, planted one of these unearthly intervals on me with such deadly effect that, before I could think, I had bounded out of my stall with a shriek, to the great terror of my neighbors—has now yielded to experience and, presumably, study. He has gained a firm hold on the affection of the subscribers, and will, I doubt not, flourish usefully at the Royal Italian Opera for the next thirty or forty years, outliving as many reputations as that veteran tenor Rinaldini.

I am glad that Mr Leonard Borwick's recital on Tuesday last week gave me an opportunity of renewing the regard for him as a pianist which has of late been almost destroyed by the frequency with which I have come upon him when he has been dealing with Beethoven. He cannot play Beethoven: his attempts to sentimentalize and prettify that virile master's work are quite beyond my patience. But his playing of Chopin's sonata in B flat minor is really worth hearing, and was deservedly received with enthusiasm. In Mendelssohn's fine prelude and foolish fugue in E minor, Saint-Saëns' Alceste caprice, and some pieces by Schumann, he gave the concourse of young ladies who filled St James's Hall further excellent value for their money. The Don Juan fantasia he had better, perhaps, have let alone.

At Mr Isidor Cohn's recital a trio by Dvořák in E minor, called Dumky for some reason, was played for the first time by Mr Cohn, Mr Whitehouse, and Lady Hallé. What I heard of it—I missed the first movement—was mere rhapsody, with more or less pretence of sonata form about it, pretty enough, but not getting much higher than that. Miss Lydia Müller sang some German songs very competently.

LA NAVARRAISE

The World, 27 June 1894

On Wednesday last week, at about half-past ten at night or thereabout, the inhabitants of Covent Garden and the neighborhood were startled by a most tremendous cannonade. It was the beginning of La Navarraise; and it did heavy execution among the ladies and gentlemen who cultivate their nerves on tea and alcohol. As one who has relieved the serious work of musical criticism by the amusement of dramatic authorship, I can testify to the great difficulty of getting artillery and musketry fire of really good tone for stage purposes; and I can compliment Sir Augustus Harris unreservedly on the thundering amplitude of sound and vigorous attack of his almost smokeless explosives.

They gave the piece a magnificent send-off: Calvé had no need to shake a ladder behind the scenes, according to the old receipt, in order "to strike twelve at once"; for before the curtain had been up thirty seconds, during which little more than half a ton of gunpowder can have been consumed, she was a living volcano, wild with anxiety, to be presently mad with joy, ecstatic with love, desperate with disappointment, and so on in ever culminating transitions through mortification, despair, fury, terror, and finally—the mainspring breaking at the worst of the strain—silly maniacal laughter. The opera, which lasts less than an hour, went like lightning; and when the curtain came down there was something like a riot both on the stage and off. All sorts of ridiculous incidents crowded upon oneanother. Plançon, fetching bouquets for Calvé, turned to present them to her with stately courtesy, and found himself bowing elaborately to the curtain, which had just descended behind him and cut him off from the main body of the stage army. When it went up—and stayed up, there being no prospect of the applause stopping—it became evident that Massenet was bashfully concealed in the wing. Calvé rushed off to fetch him, but returned empty-handed, breathless, and conveying to the audience by speaking gestures that the composer had wrestled with her victoriously. Then the stalls, forgetting the decorum proper to indispensable evening dress, positively yelled for Massenet. Calvé made another attempt, and again returned defeated. The tumult thereupon redoubled; and she, resolving in her desperation to have somebody out, made a fresh plunge, and came up with Flon of Brussels, the conductor. But the house would not be satisfied with Flon; and finally Sir Augustus himself had to appear. As he stepped forward to the footlights a deep hush fell on the assembled multitude. He looked for a moment at some person behind the scenes; and immediately I was reminded of Captain Cuttle's last appeal to Bunsby when that unfortunate mariner was allowing himself to be married to Mrs Macstinger for mere want of resolution enough to run away. Everyone remembers the formula "Jack Bunsby, will you once?" "Jack Bunsby, will you twice?" and so on.* If Sir

* Scene in Dickens's Dombey and Son.

Augustus had actually uttered the words "Jules Massenet, will you once?" the situation could not have been more patent. But, like the fated Bunsby, Jules Massenet wouldnt once; and Sir Augustus, looking the audience in the face with that steadfastness to which the mere truth can never nerve a mortal man, explained that M. Massenet had left the theatre to smoke a cigaret, and that the gratifying news of the success of his work should be communicated to him, by telegraph, or otherwise, as soon as possible. I immediately withdrew, feeling that I could no longer lend the moral sanction of my presence to the proceedings; and for all I know, the audience may be there calling for Jules still.

As to the work itself, there is hardly anything to be said in face of the frankness with which Massenet has modeled it on Cavalleria. He has not composed an opera: he has made up a prescription; and his justification is that it has been perfectly efficacious. The drama is simple and powerful, the events actually represented being credible and touching, and the assumptions, explanations, and pretexts on which they are brought about so simple and convenient that nobody minds their being impossible. Alvarez, in the tenor part, seconded Calvé with almost brutal force and vividness, dividing the honors with her in the final scene: that is to say, making a remarkable success as an actor.

But no triumph of the genius of an individual artist has half the significance in operatic history of the fact that in La Navarraise we had the management at last in full artistic activity. La Navarraise has not been shoveled on to the stage: it has been really *produced.* It was no mere matter of extravagance in gunpowder: the whole staging of the piece was excellent. The scenery was not ordered from the painter and exhibited anyhow: it was lighted, placed, and considered in the exits and entrances of the troops in such a manner as to secure the utmost illusion and make the audience imagine much more than it was possible to make them actually see. The change from night to morning during the intermezzo, with the mountain summit brightening in the sun while the town below was still in darkness, and the stealing down of the light, were capitally represented.

The couple of bells sounding the F sharp and G an octave below the bass stave (which means that they were huge and expensive pieces of bell-founding) must have been cast expressly for the occasion. In short, when Sir Augustus came on the stage at the end, he was, as manager, in his place as an artist who had taken a leading and highly successful part in the performance.

But in criticism there is no such thing as gratitude. I have got, in La Navarraise, what I have been clamoring for all these years; and now I want more. The newly born operas are splendid; but when are the old operas going to be born over again? I have spoken of shoveling operas on to the stage, and trusting to the genius of the principal artists to pull them through; and I know quite well that, with such a repertory as the London one, shoveling is forced on the management by the mere limits of time, space, and skilled labor. But even shoveling can be carefully or carelessly done; and what I have said in praise of the way in which La Navarraise has been handled would carry no weight if I did not couple it with a most vehement protest against the way in which Die Walküre was shoveled on at Drury Lane on Tuesday last week, when the German opera season opened.

Take the second act, for example, which is supposed to take place in a mountain gorge. Now I am not going to be unreasonable. I do not ask for a new scene. I do not object to the mountains being provided with flights of stairs and galleries exactly like the hall of an old manor house; for however seldom these freaks of natural architecture may be met with by the chamois, they are undoubtedly convenient for opera singers who have to bound up four thousand feet or so and cross from one range to another whilst the orchestra is playing a dozen bars. Neither do I complain of the venerable smuggler's cave which provides a useful entrance on the ground floor of the valley. To bring these things into some remote harmony with nature would involve a revolution; and you cannot, let it be fairly admitted, make revolutions at Drury Lane and produce La Navarraise at Covent Garden on successive evenings.

But there are some things that you can do, or at least blow up the responsible official for not doing; and one of them is lighting the stage properly. When a rock in the foreground, supposed to be illuminated by the sun overhead, throws a strong black shadow *upwards* on a rock behind which is higher than itself; and when this system of black shadows is carried out through the whole scene, destroying all effects of distance, and making the stage look like a mere store room for dingy canvases, then you can go round and speak burning words to the person whose business it was to have seen that there were sufficient lights placed on the floor between each set of rocks to overcome the shadow from the footlights and to make the back of the stage look five miles away from the front.

The fact is, the music of Die Walküre so enthrals the imagination of both Sir Augustus and most of the audience that they are unconscious of things that would instantly leap to their apprehension in Faust or Carmen. I am under no such spell, the music being as familiar to me as God save the Queen, and the work as capable of boring me as any old-fashioned opera when it is not finely executed.

There is another reform in the staging of these Nibelung dramas upon which I must appeal to the leading artists. Why is it that Brynhild always looks ridiculous and ugly, no matter how attractive the artist impersonating her may be? And why, on the night in question, did Fräulein Klafsky, in bounding up the mountain staircase, trip, tumble, and have a narrow escape of adding to the year's list of Alpine casualties? Simply because she would go mountaineering, according to German etiquet, in a trailing white skirt. Imagine a helmeted, breastplated, spear-armed war-maiden dashing through battles and scaling crags in a skirt in which no sensible woman would walk down Regent-street! I do not suggest gaiters and a tailor-made skirt, nor yet bicycling knickerbockers, though either would be better than the present Valkyrie fashion; but I do urge the claims of a tunic.

Surely the antique Diana is more beautiful and more decent than the late Hablot Browne's picture of Mrs Leo Hunter as Minerva in a gown,* which is exactly the model followed by the Valkyries. The modern lyric drama owes to the German nation three leading features. First, the works of Wagner. Second, tenors who never sing in tune. Third, *prima donnas* who dress badly. I plead earnestly with Sir Augustus for a strenuous resistance to the two last, combined with a hearty welcome to the first. It must never be forgotten that on De Reszke nights, when Covent Garden is at its best, there are moments when Bayreuth is left positively nowhere in point of vocal beauty and dramatic grace; and in bringing the other moments—which are certainly rather numerous—up to a corresponding level, it cannot be too patriotically believed that we have nothing to learn from the Germans, tolerant as they are of uglinesses

* Hablot Knight Browne, prolific book illustrator, provided the illustrations, under the pseudonym Phiz, for Dickens's Pickwick Papers (1836–7).

and stupidities, that we cannot teach ourselves much better for our own purposes.

The performance of Die Walküre improved as it went on. The first act was bad—very bad. Sieglinde was a cipher. Alvary began by singing out of the key. Later on he found the key, and merely sang out of tune. He posed with remarkable grace and dramatic eloquence: I can imagine no finer Siegmund from the point of view of a deaf man; but he may take my word for it—the word of a critic who has highly appreciated some of his performances—that he will have to get much nearer the mark in point of pitch, and assimilate his vocal phrasing much more to his admirable pantomime in point of grace, if he intends to hold his own within two minutes' walk of Jean de Reszke.

The white-armed Klafsky herself, in spite of her dramatic passion, which produced all its old effect in the more tempestuous passages, often betrayed the influence of a low standard of accuracy in intonation and distinction in phrasing. In the more violent passages she sang in tune or out of tune just as it came; and throughout the performance her "in tune" only meant commonly—seldom or never exquisitely—in tune. The only one of the principals who was free from the touch of provincialism given by this sort of laxness was Mr Bispham.

Wiegand was a rather inert Wotan, grumbling, crusty, and distinctly lazy; but he woke up at the end and finished well. He made a few inessential alterations here and there to avoid the highest notes; but happily he did not, like Theodore Reichmann, for whom the part lies too low, ruin the second act by cutting out the first half of the narrative to Brynhild. This, one of the finest passages in the drama, was powerfully supported by Klafsky, who, having nothing to do but listen, did so with a dramatic intensity that helped Wiegand out very materially.

Sieglinde, a part which requires an artist of the first rank, did not have one on this occasion, to the great detriment of the first act. Fricka was more fortunate in the hands of Olitska, who played very well, and could easily have sustained the interest of the pages which were cut. Herr Lohse, the conductor, was energetic; but he failed to get really fine work out of the band, partly, perhaps, because the men were overworked with the Richter concerts and the Handel Festival, and partly, I venture to guess, because they were sulky about the low pitch.

One circumstance struck me as curious in connexion with the stress laid on the fact that Drury Lane is "the National Theatre." One at least of the Valkyries was an English lady, Mrs Lee. But the playbill of the National Theatre drew the line at "Mrs." In Klafsky's case it wavered between Frau and Fräulein; Pauline Joran was Miss one day and Mlle the next; "Mr" was tolerated in the case of Mr Bispham; but Mrs Lee was always Madame Lee. May I suggest in a friendly way that it is time to drop this old-fashioned nonsense?

A MULTIPLICATION OF NOBODIES

The World, 4 July 1894

In this oppressive weather, with the season advanced to a point at which each successive concert brings a heavier burden of fatigue than the one before, it is hard to have a Handel Festival hurled at one like the stone of Polyphemus.* Like all our national institutions, the Handel Festival has a great deal of nonsense about it, and is applauded for its nonsense much more than for its sense. As, for example, the size of the thing, though, after all, it is only about quarter as large as the London

* The blinded Cyclops in Homer's The Odyssey.

police force, about which nobody makes any fuss. Mr Manns is much praised for the Napoleonic feat of conducting nearly four thousand performers, as if that were fifty times as difficult as conducting the seventyfive or eighty who constitute his band at an ordinary Saturday concert.

Of course such a calculation is pure folly: you cannot get artistic magnitude by the multiplication of nobodies, although you can get, on any given note in the performance, enough suburban amateur choristers singing right, and enough country parsons, surgeon-majors, and young ladies playing their fiddles right, to extinguish the irresolute and unconcerted efforts of the minority who are singing and playing wrong. This advantage apart, the bigness of the affair is a heavy drawback except insofar as the vastness of the audience impresses the principal singers, and stimulates them to rise to what they conceive to be a great occasion. The multitudinous choristers, singing what is to them the easiest and most familiar music in the world, taken so slowly that there is plenty of time for them to consider what they are about, have only to observe the simplest mechanical conditions of their art: that is, accuracy as to the notes, clearness of pronunciation, and an occasional reduction of their chronic *forte* to *piano*.

The number of effects they can produce could be counted on the fingers of one hand even by an average worker at a circular saw; so that in half an hour the interest of their performance is quite exhausted. There remains, of course, the interest of Handel's work, as far as it can be realized under such circumstances; but this limitation is so serious that I do not hesitate to say that whoever has heard an oratorio of Handel's at the Handel Festival only has never heard it at all.

The other day Mr de Lange's Amsterdam choir of thirty-odd singers had to leave London abruptly because they were not inclined to allow the British public the customary ten years or so which it takes to find out a superlatively good thing. That choir was worth ten Handel Festival choirs piled one on top of the other. Even in mere volume and penetrating force of sound it was superior: its imposing *fortissimo* struck home in a way unknown at the Crystal Palace, where the attempt to produce gigantic explosion at such points as Wonderful! Counselor! in the Messiah invariably fails, exactly as the simultaneous discharge of four thousand muskets would fail to produce the boom of a single cannon. In range and delicacy of gradation, in power and subtlety of expression, in short, in artistic capacity, it differed from the Handel choir as a living creature differs from a machine.

If the sole useful function of a choral performance were the perfect execution of the masterpieces of choral music, then I should unhesitatingly recommend the dispersion of the Handel choir by armed force, with or without a preliminary reading of the Riot Act. But in England it has another function—a social one. Choral singing with us is not an artistic pursuit: it is a game of skill which we play just as our athletic friends play cricket or football; and as a game of skill we understand it, on the whole, very well. The degree of connoisseurship which such entirely popular assemblages as Festival choirs and audiences display in the recognized points of the game often puts the professed musical critic to shame.

Take an example from the present year's Festival. The hero of the occasion among the soloists was Mr Santley. The roar of applause which followed each of his songs was stupendous. Now this was not by any means a mere ignorant hero-worship of Mr Santley. He is a popular favorite, no doubt; but Mr Lloyd, Madame Albani, Mr Ben Davies, Madame Melba, and the rest are also popular favorites; and yet none of them got quite the same cheer that followed Honor and Arms and *Nasce al bosco.* It was not the loveliness of the songs either: *Nasce al bosco* cannot touch an audience like *Ombra mai fù*, which Albani gave us, nor charm them like Love in her eyes sits playing, which Mr Lloyd sang to perfection.

As to the hackneyed Honor and Arms, it is, from any point of view that includes commonsense as a factor in human utterance, an obsolete absurdity. In a modern opera it would be received with shouts of laughter. And there is something else to be explained. Mr Santley, in spite of all the applause he wins—in spite of the fact that, as I shall presently shew, he wins it by a genuine objective superiority which is intelligently appreciated by the audience—has told us in one of the most sincere and unaffected autobiographical sketches we possess that the English public never supported him in his efforts to complete his artistic activity and develop his powers to the highest degree as a dramatic singer. The only encouragement he got was at the Italian Opera under the old *régime*, where "artistic activity" consisted in playing Don Giovanni for the first time after one rehearsal, at which the tenor (the illustrious Mario) did not take the trouble to appear until it was half over.

All this is inexplicable to the Wagnerian amateur who judges all music as tone-poetry, and all singing by its expressiveness. But the Handel Festival enthusiasts care nothing for poetry or its expression: they are absolute materialists in music. They know the points of a good voice, and the rarities of vocal execution; and they like familiar music that shews off those points and demands those rarities. In Honor and Arms the phrase Though I could end thee at a blow is set sensibly to eight notes in a way to which neither Gluck nor Wagner could take the smallest exception; but it is not at all preferred to the single word "glory," set to a "division" consisting of no less than thirtysix notes.

Santley's singing of the division of Selection Day was, humanly speaking, perfect. It tested the middle of his voice from C to C exhaustively; and that octave came out of the test hallmarked: there was not a scrape on its fine surface, not a break or a weak link in the chain anywhere; while the vocal touch was impeccably light and steady, and the florid execution accurate as clockwork. The phrase Though I could end thee at a blow was admired, not for its rational setting, but for the irrationality of the repetition of the eight notes a sixth higher, compelling the singer to sing up the scale from his low G to the G above, and immediately afterwards from E flat to E flat, thereby exhibiting his whole compass (barring the top E natural and F, which were repeatedly in evidence under more difficult conditions in *Nasce al bosco*) in such a way as made it impossible for him to conceal any blemish, if there had been one.

Everyone else broke down under these Handelian tests except Mr Lloyd, whose voice, homogeneous as it is from top to bottom, and charming as its color is, has not quite the beautiful firmness and purity of tone which the public has learnt the value of from Patti and Sims Reeves as well as from Santley. Madame Melba might perhaps have held her own on this point had she risen to the immense care and vocal conscientiousness of those three artists; but she underrated her task, and all but came to grief in the (for her) only really difficult "division" in Let the bright Seraphim, which she seemed to me to be reading at first sight. Albani's voice, wonderful enough, in spite of its obvious pulsation, from E to B natural at the top, is conspicuously deficient in the middle.

Mr Ben Davies, when remorselessly compelled in Waft Her, Angels, to walk his voice slowly up from A to

A so deliberately as to allow every step to be scrutinized, had to confess to a marked "break" on F sharp, or thereabouts; and this was promptly scored against him, according to the rules of the game, though it is only fair to him to add that a strong contrast of registers often produces very charming effects, which Handel, however, certainly did not lay his music out for.

And so, though all the artists I have named were hugely applauded, Santley, having scored the most points, was the hero of the day, all the more popular because his method, which many of our young baritones carefully avoid (rather an easy thing to do, by the way), has stood the wear and tear of forty years' work; for Santley began to sing in public at about the date when I began to cry in private, and more than twenty years before Albani was heard of in this country. That is a remarkable record; and a noteworthy feature of it is that he sang at this Festival better than he did at the one three years ago, and must therefore be considered to be still improving.

The fact that the British public understands the game of singing so well as its appreciation of Santley, Patti, and Sims Reeves proves, shews that we are a musical and sporting nation, not in the least that we are an artistic one. Santley might have perpetrated almost any conceivable artistic atrocity at that Festival without losing the most infinitesimal part of his popularity. He might have interpolated the vulgarest claptrap *cadenzas*, or achieved the finest strokes of poetic insight, without rebuke in the one case or encouragement in the other.

To the Briton with a turn for music he is just what Dr Grace* is to the Briton with a turn for cricket; and when

* Dr W. G. Grace, a Bristol surgeon, became a supreme cricketer, in his 43 years' career making 126 centuries, scoring 54,896 runs, and taking 2876 wickets in first-class cricket.

he gives us more than is implied in that, he gives it for its own sake, knowing that its existence will be a secret between himself and a very few people, and that this great lumping oratorio public, with all its apparently unerring discrimination and enlightened loyalty to old favorites, is really a people walking in exceeding darkness. And that is all I need to say about the Handel Festival, except just to note that the sopranos were the weak point in an otherwise very fine chorus, and that the Festival was at all points as good as the Palace authorities could possibly have made it.

The real musical problem of the day, however, is not the multiplication of the sound-producing power of the musical individual by five thousand. He already makes noise enough, with his iron-framed piano, to bring him under stringent police regulation in Germany, and to make him an almost impossible neighbor in London. Why is it that the closer we get crowded together and piled up, in flats costing from two hundred to two thousand a year, the louder we make our musical instruments? In older times, when space was so cheap that no man was tempted to knock down his house and cut up his grounds into building lots, we played the viol instead of the violin, and the lute or the virginals instead of the piano. We played "fantasies" and "consorts" instead of transcriptions of the Tannhäuser overture and the Walkürenritt. When we got in a good new instrument it did not cost us from £80 to £250 net, nor did it take several strong men to get it upstairs, leaving marks, as of a discharge of grape, at every corner and on every doorframe, and finally causing an extensive settlement of the floor. A virginal or a clavichord is more portable than a housemaid's dressing-table, and takes up no more room.

A first-rate clavichord from the hands of an artist-craftsman who, always learning something, makes no two instruments exactly alike, and turns out each as an individual work of art, marked with his name and stamped with his style, can be made and sold for £40 or less, the price of a fourth-rate piano (No. 5768 from Messrs So-and-so's factory), which you can hardly sell for £15 the day after you have bought it. Above all, you can play Bach's two famous sets of fugues and preludes, not to mention the rest of a great mass of beautiful old music, on your clavichord, which you cannot do without great alteration of character and loss of charm on the piano.

These observations have been provoked by the startlingly successful result of an experiment made by the students of the Royal College of Music. They, on having their ears and minds opened by Mr Arnold Dolmetsch's demonstrations to the beauty of our old instruments and our old music, took the very practical step of asking him to make them a clavichord. It was rather a staggering request to a collector and connoisseur; but Mr Dolmetsch, in the spirit of the Irishman who was invited to play the fiddle, had a try; and after some months' work he has actually turned out a little masterpiece, excellent as a musical instrument and pleasant to look at, which seems to me likely to begin such a revolution in domestic musical instruments as William Morris's work made in domestic furniture and decoration, or Philip Webb's domestic architecture.* I therefore estimate the birth of this little clavichord as, on a moderate computation, about forty thousand times as important as the Handel Festival, or even the production at Covent Garden on Saturday last of Mr Cowen's Signa, of which I hope to treat at befitting length in my next article.

* Webb was a wellknown architect, who designed more than sixty homes in London and the provinces, and supplied decorative designs for Morris's firm.

THREE NEW OPERAS

The World, 11 July 1894

This is certainly an amazingly prolific opera season. Last Wednesday Sir Augustus Harris produced his sixth new opera, L'Attaque du Moulin, and shewed that his resources were still unexhausted by promising yet another by no less a composer than Bach. I presume this means the celebrated Bach, the composer of Irmengarde,* and not the poor old Leipzig cantor, John Sebastian of that ilk, who used to pass current as "Bach" pure and simple. L'Attaque du Moulin followed hard upon Signa, separated from it only by Mirette at the Savoy. Mirette was interesting enough from the critical point of view. I have made a careful analysis of it, and have formed the following opinion as to the process by which it was produced. First, it was decided, in view of the essentially English character of the Savoy enterprise, to engage a French librettist and a French composer. Then came the appalling difficulty that Frenchmen are often clever, and are consequently in danger of writing above the heads of the British public. Consequently Messager was selected as having learnt by the financial failure of his Basoche at the Royal English Opera (now a music hall) how very stupid the English nation is. Carré was warned to ascertain the exact British gauge by a careful preliminary study of the works of Mr Weatherly, the most popular of English providers of words for music. Both composer and poet followed their

* Chevalier Emil Bach, whose one-act opera The Lady of Longford, with a libretto by Sir Augustus Harris and Frederic Weatherly, was performed at Covent Garden on 21 July.

instructions conscientiously and adroitly. Never has the spirit of Mr Weatherly, never has the depth of his poetic passion, the breadth of his view of life, and the peculiar amenity of his literary touch been more exactly reproduced than by Carré. As to Messager, he has hit off Sir Arthur Sullivan, in Sir Arthur's worldliest moods, with a quite exquisite felicity. The only drawback to this double success is that the result, however curious to experts in theatrical manufacture, is not particularly delectable as an opera. In fact, if I were a private individual, and could escape from the public responsibility which forbids a critic to tell the truth, I should say flatly that Mirette goes, in pointlessness and tediousness, to the extreme limits compatible with production at the Savoy Theatre. I have the less hesitation in allowing the acute reader to guess this private conviction of mine since Mr D'Oyly Carte, apparently realizing that the opera was open to misconstruction, circulated on the first night a managerial note explaining that it was not on Gilbert-Sullivan lines, but was rather like Il Barbiere, L'Étoile du Nord, Carmen, and Basoche. Also that the book dealt with a subject which has interested the world for some thousands of years. It gave me quite an uncanny sense that the order of nature was being suspended and even reversed without a word of warning when I found the subject which had enjoyed this prolonged popularity falling perfectly flat on me. And for the life of me I could not see where the resemblance to L'Étoile du Nord came in. Further, Mr Carte is anxious lest the comic man should stamp the opera as a comic opera in the English sense. "This personage" says the managerial manifesto "falls into a pond and gets wet [as a matter of fact he adhered closely to stage tradition by falling into a pond and *not* getting wet], displays cowardice, and dances: actions which may possibly be laughed at again as they have been since plays were first written. He also gives utterance to certain anachronisms." I wonder what the anachronisms were. The gentleman sang in a duet about Noah, and gave us a song about special editions; but neither of these seemed at all out of place, perhaps because of the extreme difficulty of referring the events or personages of the opera to any conceivable period of human history. Surely the plain fact of the matter (unless I dreamt that special-edition song and other cognate features) is that an attempt was made in manufacturing Mirette to repeat the Haddon Hall experiment of combining sentimental opera in the style of Balfe with topical extravaganza in the style of Mr Gilbert. I can quite well understand how Mr Carte, when he saw the result, felt impelled to urge that the work should not be criticized from that point of view; but he can hardly suppose that it would mend matters if I were to criticize Mirette as an attempt at a work of the class of Carmen. I cannot even wholly endorse his modest plea that "it is a very simple love story, not too exciting or absorbing, but which may please." The story, briefly told, is as follows: Mirette, who is adored by Picorin, adores Gerard, who adores her, but is adored by Bianca. This is disagreeable for Picorin and Bianca, and not particularly pleasant for Gerard and Mirette, who are separated by a considerable difference in social position. Finally, Mirette very sensibly concludes that it would save no end of trouble if she were to marry Picorin and Gerard to marry Bianca. Gerard falls in with the suggestion at once; and down comes the curtain. I do not deny that this is "a very simple love story": my only doubt is whether it is not rather too simple to give even that mild degree of pleasure which Mr Carte hopes for. Perhaps, in view of my scepticism and in justice to M. Michel Carré, I should state that the exact account of the authorship given in the program is "The book by Michel Carré; English lyrics by Fred E.

Weatherly; English dialogue by Harry Greenbank." This may mean either that Mr Greenbank has supplied dialogue to M. Carré's scenario, or that he has translated M. Carré's dialogue. But I am afraid it does not greatly matter.

Of the music I need only say that at the very outset Messager announced, *fortissimo*, that he was going to be as commonplace as he possibly could; and he kept his word in the main, though he could not help once or twice lapsing into habits of distinction and refinement formed in his own unhappy country. Miss Maud Ellicott, as a Bohemian girl who dwells in marble halls in the second act, and so does not need to dream about them, proved herself a very capable young lady, with a ready fund of dramatic feeling and musical talent, backed by a voice which, if not particularly remarkable for richness of color or purity of tone, is vigorous and serviceable, and has in the middle and lower registers a not unattractive peculiarity which answers perhaps to a touch of swarthy color in her complexion. The other parts are in the hands of old friends, none of whom have any opportunity of adding to their reputations: indeed Mr Scott Fishe has to exert all his tact to keep Prince Gerard from having an unintended success as a wild burlesque of Lucia di Lammermoor. The opera is staged with all the taste and thoroughness that distinguish the Savoy: nothing is missing except Mr Rutland Barrington and a good work for him to appear in.

Mr Cowen's Signa can hardly, I think, be said to have a fair chance either of success or failure at Covent Garden. When a four-act opera is cut down to two acts, the composer is entitled to claim suspension of judgment as to the merit of his work as a whole. I have seldom been so taken aback as when the three leading persons in the opera, whose acquaintance we had barely made on quite amiable terms, suddenly pulled out daggers and ended oneanother's existences on no discernible provocation.

I can understand that Ancona, in stabbing Madame de Nuovina, may have yielded simply to an irresistible impulse to finish the opera and go home; but why on earth did Mr Ben Davies, regardless of his growing portliness, not only stab himself, but immediately afterwards gather himself together and launch himself on all fours into the air, exactly as an inexperienced bather goes off a springboard for the first time, descending on the prostrate form of the lady with a crash that overpowered the full force of the orchestra? When the curtain went up to enable him to acknowledge the tempest of applause evoked by this singular feat, he, taken unawares, was discovered apparently picking portions of the stage out of his knees; whilst, amazing to relate, Madame de Nuovina, erect and apparently without a single broken bone, smiled and bowed with Spartan fortitude.

On the whole, the opera rather missed its chance—such as that chance was. A pretty tune with guitar accompaniment was sung villainously out of tune by a handful of tenors from the chorus, these gentlemen, like all thoroughly bad singers, being able to hit a note accurately only on condition of being allowed to bawl it at the utmost stretch of their throats. Madame de Nuovina, a lady with genuine talent for the stage, has unluckily contracted a habit of sending her voice on edge through the house with a recklessness equally destructive to itself and to the peace of mind of the audience. This does not do for Mr Cowen's music, nor, indeed, for any composer's music; and if Madame de Nuovina wishes to establish her reputation in London, and to realize the full value of her striking appearance and personal force, she must resolutely face the fact that the expression of dramatic passion by music and its expression by physical violence are incompatible. She must touch our ears and hearts, not tear them. Ancona, in the part of a homicidal elderly farmer, displayed his fine voice at great length.

Mr Ben Davies made almost the only hit of the opera by his singing of a song in the first act, which was the most effective number in the work as it stood; but his success would have been greater if a somewhat smarter physical training had made him less obviously a popular and liberally fed London concert singer. The music of Signa, judging by the samples presented, suffers from Mr Cowen's old fault of presenting themes which are nothing if not flowing and popular, and then checking them, just as they are getting into full career, by some rather pettily selfconscious interval or progression from which they never recover. After half a dozen such disappointments, one is apt to lose interest in a work, if not to lose patience.

Nevertheless, Signa is freer from these checks than Mr Cowen's previous works; and in one instance, that of the tenor song in the first act, he has succeeded in bringing off a fairly big climax without a hitch. The only respect in which there is no improvement is in the orchestration. This is pretty enough within the limits of the old-fashioned symphony orchestra; but the trombone and percussion parts are stuck on in a flagrantly inorganic fashion. With the exception of Ancona, none of the performers, either in the rank and file or among the principals, can be said to have done their best for the work.

L'Attaque du Moulin was a good deal better supported. Madame de Nuovina had more scope for her power of acting, and had perhaps been warned to use her voice more mercifully. At all events, she rent the air only once or twice, in pressing emergencies. There had been great talk of Madame Delna's Marcelline; but, frankly, it was not a bit good, Madame Delna being a lady of an essentially urbane charm, much more likely to have two daughters well married in society than two sons as rankers in the Army, and quite out of the question as nurse and housekeeper to a country miller. Her voice, a bright mezzo-soprano, is a little the worse for violent wear at the top.

Bouvet would have been very good if he had not forced his voice so furiously in the more exciting passages. It was clearly Bruneau's intention that at these points I, as audience, should be excited, and Bouvet, as actor, cool and efficient. As a matter of fact, it was the other way about. The music is like all Bruneau's music: that is, it has every sort of originality except musical originality. It is impossible not to admire the composer's freedom from technical superstitions. In his perfect readiness to play two tunes at once without exacting any harmonic coincidences or even community of key, and the almost Mozartian *sans-gêne* with which he makes the music go where he wants it, even if he has to step over all sorts of professional fences and disregard all sorts of academic notice-boards in doing so, he shews himself not only a man of strong character, but a keen musical observer of what the ear will tolerate. He will combine a few hackneyed fanfares, or a rum-tum pedal bass with a few commonplace progressions and snatches of tunes, in such a way as to make people talk as if he had conquered a new musical domain.

But, for all that, his musical stock-in-trade is very limited, and entirely borrowed. Like Boïto, he is ever so much abler and more interesting than some of the poor musical bees and silkworms whose honey and silk he manufactures; but he is himself barren: he invents novel combinations, but does not discover new harmonies—can keep an opera cast singing the whole evening, but could not, for the life of him, produce one of Sir Arthur Sullivan's ballads—stands, as artificer compared with creative artists, in the same relation to Gounod as Boïto to Verdi, or as Berlioz to the whole romantic movement in music, from Gluck to the Eroica symphony and the operas of Meyerbeer and Spontini. I am very curious to see what rank these literary exploiters of music—these Delaroches and Kaulbachs* of the orchestra—will take finally in the republic of art; for I have noticed that they generally make their living as musical critics; and I am not sure that I could not compose a little in their style myself. Will any *impresario* with a commission to give take the hint?

GERMAN OPERA AT DRURY LANE

The World, 18 July 1894

The production of Der Freischütz and Fidelio at the German Opera momentarily transferred the centre of operatic interest, for me at least, from Covent Garden to Drury Lane. It was amusing to find these two masterpieces arousing quite a patronizing interest as old-fashioned curiosities, somewhat dowdy perhaps, but still deserving of indulgence for the sake of tradition. As to the Freischütz, hardly anyone could remember its last performance in London; and I was astonished when the questions addressed to me on this point made me conscious that although the work is as familiar to me as the most familiar of Shakespear's plays, and counts, indeed, as a permanent factor in my consciousness, I could only clearly recollect two actual representations of it, one in Munich, and the other in my native town,

* Paul Delaroche (1797–1856), founder of the Eclectic school of painting, and Wilhelm von Kaulbach (1805–74) were historical painters and muralists.

which is not in England. I will not swear that I have not seen it oftener; for I have long since given free play to my inestimable gift of forgetting, and have lost count of the performances I have witnessed almost as completely as I have lost count of my headaches, but still, even in my case, it is somewhat significant that I should be unable to recall a representation of Der Freischütz in London. Such a doubt as to the abysmally inferior Carmen would be a ridiculous affectation.

Perhaps, therefore, the first question to answer is "How has Der Freischütz worn?" To which I am happy to be able to reply that its freshness and charm delighted everyone as much as its unaffected sincerity of sentiment impressed them. I will not, of course, pretend that the hermit strikes the popular imagination as he did in the days when hermits habitually trod the stage, and were deferred to, at sight of their brown gowns, rope girdles, and white beards, by all the civil and military authorities, exactly as if they were modern French deputies exhibiting their scarves to the police in *émeutes*.

And it would be vain to conceal the fact that the terrors of the Wolf's Gulch and the casting of the magic bullets were received with audible chuckling, although Sir Augustus Harris had made a supreme effort to ensure the unearthliness of the incantation by making the stage a sort of museum of all the effects of magic and devilry known in the modern theatre. He had illuminated steam clouds from Bayreuth, and fiery rain from the Lyceum Faust; he had red fire, glowing hell-mouth caverns, apparitions, skeletons, vampire bats, explosions, conflagrations, besides the traditional wheels, the skulls, the owl, and the charmed circle.

And yet nobody could help laughing, least of all, I should imagine, Sir Augustus himself. The owl alone would have sufficed to set me off, because, though its eyes were not red like those of previous stage owls, and it was therefore not so irresistibly suggestive of a railway signal as I had expected, one of its eyes was much larger than the other, so that it seemed to contemplate the house derisively through a single eyeglass. This quaint monocle notwithstanding, the scene produced some effect until the other phenomena supervened. If they had been omitted—if the apparitions had been left to our imaginations and to Weber's music, the effect would have been enormously heightened. Owls, bats, ravens, and skeletons have no supernatural associations for our rising generations: the only function an owl or a bat can now fulfil in such a scene is to heighten that sense of night in a forest which is one of Nature's most wonderful effects.

But this change in public susceptibility makes it necessary to take much greater pains with stage illusions than formerly. When the bat was a mere bogy to terrify an audience of grown-up children, it was, no doubt, sufficient to dangle something like a stuffed bustard with huge moth's wings at the end of a string from the flies to make the pit's flesh creep. Nowadays, unless a manager can devize some sort of aërial top that will imitate the peculiar flitting of the real flittermouse he must forgo bats altogether.

To appeal to our extinct sense of the supernatural by means that outrage our heightened sense of the natural is to court ridicule. Pasteboard pies and paper flowers are being banished from the stage by the growth of that power of accurate observation which is commonly called cynicism by those who have not got it; and impossible bats and owls must be banished with them. Der Freischütz may be depended on to suggest plenty of phantasmagoria without help from out-of-date stage machinists and property masters.

Except during the absurdities of the Wolf's Gulch, the performance appeared to me to be an exceptionally successful one. The orchestra has improved greatly since the first week; and though Lohse has one trick which I greatly dislike—that of hurrying at every *crescendo*—he is equal to his weighty duties as Wagner and Beethoven conductor. His handling of Fidelio was at many points admirable. Beethoven had not any bats or skeletons to contend with; but he had what was quite as bad in its way: to wit, an execrable chorus of prisoners who, on catching sight of the sentinels, would break in on the German text with mistuned howls of "Silenzio, silenzio." In both operas there were moments when the singing was beyond all apology.

Alvary's Florestan, vocally considered, was an atrocious performance; and Klafsky did not finish the aria in the first act without perceptible effort. Weber's music was, of course, far more singable; and even Alvary, saving a few intervals the corruption of which must, I suppose, be put up with from him as part of his mannerism, sang fairly in tune according to his German scale, which, let me point out, not for the first time, is not precisely the southern scale dear to our ears.

But Wiegand, as Caspar, dropped all pretence of singing before he came to the *coda* of the Revenge song. He simply shouted the words hoarsely through the orchestration, and left the audience to infer that Weber meant it to be done that way—a notion of which I beg somewhat indignantly to disabuse them. Yet in spite of all this and more, these three artists, Klafsky, Alvary, and Wiegand, with Mr Bispham and Rodemund to help them, made Fidelio and Der Freischütz live again. Their sincerity, their affectionate intimacy with the works, their complete absorption in their parts, enable them to achieve most interesting and satisfactory performances, and to elicit demonstrations of respect and enthusiasm from the audience, which, nevertheless, if it has any ears, must know perfectly well that the singing has been at best second-rate, and at worst quite outside the category of music.

Klafsky is the best German leading soprano we have accepted here since Titiens; and though Klafsky has in her favor the enormous superiority of the era of Brynhild and Isolde to the era of Semiramide and Lucrezia, Titiens would certainly have been greatly disconcerted, if not actually terrified, had she, at Klafsky's age, been overtaken by as many vocal disasters in the course of an opera as Klafsky seems to take as a matter of course. It is a great mistake to assume, as these German artists evidently do, that their rough, violent, and inaccurate singing does not matter.

A very striking proof of this was forthcoming at the last concert at the Albert Hall, where Patti continued her new departure into Wagnerland by singing Elisabeth's prayer from Tannhäuser. Now, if I express some scepticism as to whether Patti cares a snap of her fingers for Elisabeth or Wagner, I may, after all these years of *Una voce* and *Bel raggio*, very well be pardoned. But it is beyond all doubt that Patti cares most intensely for the beauty of her own voice and the perfection of her singing. What is the result? She attacks the prayer with the single aim of making it sound as beautiful as possible; and this being precisely what Wagner's own musical aim was, she goes straight to the right phrasing, the right vocal touch, and the right turn of every musical figure, thus making her German rivals not only appear in comparison clumsy as singers, but actually obtuse as to Wagner's meaning.

At the first performance of Tristan at Drury Lane this season Klafsky, by sheer dramatic power, was really great in the death song which is the climax of the opera; but she did not sing it half as well as Nordica, who carries much lighter guns as a dramatic artist, has sung it here; and what is more, she completely perverted the music by making it express the most poignant grief for the loss of Tristan—the very sort of stage commonplace to which Isolde's sacred joy in the death towards which the whole work is an aspiration, ought to be the most complete rebuke.

If the song were beautifully sung, it simply could not take the wrong expression; and if Patti were to return to the stage and play Isolde, though she might very possibly stop the drama half a dozen times in each act to acknowledge applause and work in an *encore*—though she might introduce Home, Sweet Home, in the ship scene, and The Last Rose in the garden scene—though nobody would be in the least surprised to see her jump up out of her trance in the last act to run to the footlights for a basket of flowers, yet the public might learn a good deal about Isolde from her which they will never learn from any of the illustrious band of German Wagner heroines who are queens at Bayreuth, but who cannot sing a *gruppetto* for all that.

In offering these disparagements to the German artists, I am not for a moment forgetting that to them we owe the fact that we have any lyric stage left at all. When I turn from Klafsky playing Leonore, Agathe, Brynhild, and Isolde at Drury Lane, to Melba trying to revive Lucia at Covent Garden, or even to Calvé playing Carmen and scoring cheap triumphs with trashy one-act melodramas; and when I go on the same night from witnessing the discordant but heroic struggles of Alvary with Florestan to see Jean de Reszke gravely airing his latest achievement—nothing less than getting up the tenor part in Mr Bemberg's inanely pretty Elaine (Mr Bemberg being, as I am told, and can well believe, a rich young gentleman much better worth obliging than Beethoven or Wagner)—when I see all this, remembering what I do of the miserable decay and extinction of the old operatic *régime* under the sway of the two-hundred-a-night *prima donnas*, I am in no danger of losing sight of the fact that when singers sing so well that it no longer matters what they sing, they keep the theatre stagnant with all their might, the stagnation, of course, presently producing putrescence; whilst, on the other hand, the ambition of lyric artists who could not by mere charm of vocalization raise the receipts at any concert or theatre bureau by £5 makes strongly for dramatic activity and for the reinforcement of the attractions of the individual artist by those of the masterpieces of musical composition.

It is because Alvary is a much less attractive singer than Jean de Reszke that he has to summon Wagner to his aid, and play Siegfried or Tristan with infinite pains while de Reszke is giving his thousandth impersonation of such comparatively cheap and easy characters as Gounod's Faust or Romeo. This is not altogether creditable to Monsieur Jean: it makes him appear too little the chivalrous hero and devoted artist, and too much "the economic man" (sometimes supposed to be a figment of Adam Smith's, but actually one of the most real of ancient and modern types of humanity). I have appealed so often and so utterly in vain to de Reszke in these columns to do for the sake of art what Alvary does because he must, that I do not propose to waste any more ink on the matter.

To the Germans I would point out that their apparent devotion to the poetic and dramatic side of their art can claim no credit as long as it is forced upon them by the fact that they sing so badly that nobody would listen to them for their own sakes alone. The standard of beauty of execution in vocal music has fallen so low on their stage that we find an artist like Rodemund going through the music of Mime without taking the trouble to sing a single note in tune, and thereby losing all the elfin charm and doting pathos which Lieban's fine musical instinct enabled him to get from it. Yet Rodemund can distinguish the pitch of a note accurately enough, as he shewed in Beethoven's music and Weber's. In Wagner's he evidently believes it does not matter.

What the Germans have to learn from us is that it does matter. Wagner meant his music to be sung with the most exquisite sensitiveness in point of quality of tone and precision of pitch, exactly as Mozart did. In a day or two I shall be within the walls of the temple at Bayreuth, laying in a stock of observations for the further enforcement of this moral; for I am really tired of going to the theatre to hear the best music associated with the worst singing, and the best singing with the worst music.

BASSETTO AT THE WAGNER FESTIVAL

The Star, 21, 23–26 July 1894

19 July, 5.45.

[U] The first act of the opening performance of Parsifal is over. It is against all my principles to rush out of a theatre and write criticism under the influence of what in an ordinary man might be called temper. Let me, therefore, be scrupulously calm. Only, as I know Parsifal very well, I must earnestly beg those who have been present with me in the theatre to believe me when I say that the music is beautiful. For instance, a more exquisite page of music, even in the quite popular sense, than that of Amfortas when he is carried in on his litter on his way to the bath could not be desired. I know it did not sound so; but that, believe me, was because Theodore Reichmann did not sing a note of it in tune. As to the execrable, damnable, abominable—but no:

these singers have their living to get, and might take an action.

Let me say then, briefly, that there was one really good vocal artist in the act, and that was Fenten, the Titurel, who sang his two or three phrases admirably. All the rest, as far as the principals were concerned, was bad: Parsifal and Gurnemanz being the worst—Gurnemanz worse than Parsifal chiefly because he had much more to sing. His reproof to Parsifal over the murdered swan could hardly have been coarser in conception or commoner in vocal execution. Judgment on Parsifal must be suspended until the end of the second act. There is the usual excellence in everything that depends on careful rehearsal and the best intentions on the part of everybody concerned. Everything, on the other hand, that depends on individual delicacy of musical perception on the part of the leading artists has made me wish I had never been born, or at least that I had been born into some other profession. If matters do not improve in the next act I shall do something desperate.

The next act is over. I was wrong in fearing that it might be worse than the first. A man should not fear impossibilities. As a matter of fact, it was better. There was no Gurnemanz and no Amfortas. The flower maidens sang prettily, and their waltz came quite up to the standard of execution of our Savoy operas. Parsifal, a brawny young man named Birrenkoven, went at his part like a blacksmith, and was so sincere, honest, and strong, so much better than a more cultivated gentleman might have been, that I am loth to deal ungenerously with him; but the fact is that if Madame Wagner cannot get artists of greater experience and voices of greater beauty to play Parsifal, she had better hand the performing rights over to people who can. Rosa Sucher did her best with Kundry, and her best, as everyone knows, is not to be lightly disparaged, but this part she cannot touch. Klingsor managed to make his scene stupid somehow—a very clever thing to do, though I wish he had not done it.

I write this in desperate haste to catch the last post to England. My Wagnerite friends have begged me to sleep over it; but I prefer to serve up my opinion red hot. I paid a pound for my seat; and I have a right to express myself as to the value I got for it. I shall try to be more prudent later on: at present the truth is bursting out of me at every pore.

20 July.

Owing to the postal arrangements here I had to leave the record of the first Parsifal unfinished at the end of the second act. The third consists so largely of what may be called ritual that its effect, which is extremely impressive, depends comparatively little on the individual powers of the leading artists. For instance, Kundry, who is on the stage throughout, and seems to take—and indeed, from the spectator's point of view, *does* take—a large part in the proceedings, only utters two words, or rather one word repeated. For the rest, the actress, having dressed appropriately, has only to surrender herself, in an almost passive attitude of humility and adoration, to the feelings suggested by the religious character of the scene, and to do a little stage business in which anybody could be "coached" in a few rehearsals, in order to make her effect, not as an actress or singer, but as an acolyte. To so competent a woman as Sucher this was mere child's play, and the audience was deeply touched by her for the first time during the evening. But any other presentable *prima donna* could have done the same, or, rather, been used by Wagner to as good purpose. Parsifal in his black armor praying before his spear; Parsifal in his white robes being anointed by Gurnemanz and having his feet washed by Kundry and dried with her long black hair; Gurnemanz celebrating what is to all intents and purposes a beautiful Good Friday service: all this, as I have said, is ritual, and requires, not acting, but simple earnestness and beauty of delivery.

The earnestness was unstinted, the beauty, alas! missing. The more solemn Gurnemanz felt, the more he howled; the more fervent Parsifal became, the more he bawled. In one or two passages which he had been persuaded to sing softly, he shewed that even in Germany bad singers are made, not born, and that in any other country he might have been taught that a singer's first duty is his duty to satisfy the craving of the musician's ear for a nobly beautiful sound, and not to gratify that half literary, half German-national zeal for Wagnerism which seems to be the ruling spirit here. Reichmann, in whose makeup the pallor of the tortured custodian of the Grail was contrasted with a fascinating beard and moustache of the cut popularized by Victor Capoul, was better in the last scene, his invitation to the knights to plunge their swords in his bosom being better adapted to his operatic style than the earlier scenes. His acting was graceful and effective, if not particularly sincere, throughout, offering an interesting contrast to that of Birrenkoven, who was desperately sincere, but raw and even boorish.

On the whole, leaving Plank (Klingsor) out of the question as a mere cipher, Grengg (Gurnemanz), who lately played Wotan in London with the Hamburg company for Sir Augustus Harris, was the least efficient member of the cast. He succeeded in making the first scene of the first act all but unendurable; and his efforts to force his voice to its very noisiest at the end of every passage that had any resemblance to an operatic solo suggested that nothing would have pleased him better than to have been able to finish with a Rossinian *cabaletta* and an *encore*. In spite of all these drawbacks the work produced a great effect—an effect in some cases of disgust and repulsion, in others of awe and even of ecstasy; but in all cases a powerful effect. The perfect smoothness with which the panoramic changes of scenery in the first and third acts worked, the clever changes from dusk to full light, the beauty of the temple of the Grail, the smooth and thoroughly rehearsed choral singing, the magic of the orchestra, and above all, of course, that prodigious *coup de théâtre*, the celebration of the rite of Holy Communion on the stage, with the sacred chalice glowing with ruby light, and the Holy Ghost descending in the form of a dove in dazzling celestial radiance, could not fail to affect very deeply an audience of the somewhat cathedrally class (if I may use the expression) which alone can afford to go to Bayreuth. There was an English bishop present yesterday. I shall not mention his see lest I should get him into trouble.

But Corno di Bassetto is not to be consoled for the absence of the highest artistic work by any amount of carefully planned ritual and smoothly worked mechanism. I heard every note that was rough and violent, every phrase that was coarsely turned, as distinctly and as pitilessly as I saw the wire that produced the electric light inside the grail chalice. And smooth as the orchestra was, I felt to the marrow of my bones the vulgarity that no care on the part of the players could conceal in the tone of the instruments, most of which, in the brass especially, were the usual military band articles, turned out for the trade by the hundred like Tottenham Court Road furniture, and having not a trace of that individuality and delicacy of tone which would distinguish an instrument separately designed and made by a true artist craftsman. That is, of course, not at present a remediable fault: Madame Wagner, like other theatrical managers, must take the orchestra as it exists and make the best of it. But it is just as well that we should have no more hyperbole about the exquisite beauty of the Bayreuth orchestra, especially from Londoners, who have often heard fragments of Wagner's work better done in St James's Hall, and who, at the Crystal Palace, have heard incomparably finer tone from the wind under Mr Manns' conductorship than one hears at Bayreuth. If we could only get the thorough rehearsal and the consequent intimate familiarity with the score that the Germans enjoy (to their great credit and our corresponding disgrace) we should easily leave Bayreuth nowhere; for our instruments are better, and our standard of execution higher.

It will be highly interesting, after this ultra-German Parsifal to note the effect of Lohengrin today with Van Dyck (a Belgian) as Lohengrin, Nordica (an American) as Elsa, and Marie Brema (an Englishwoman) as Ortrud. You shall hear all about it from me tomorrow.

The elevated tone of this communication is due to the fact that it has been written on the highest point in Bayreuth: that is, at the top of the "war tower" on the summit of the hill on which the Wagner Theatre stands. The tower was erected to the memory of those soldiers who met "hero death" in the war of 1870–71. I wonder how much a day this grateful Fatherland gave the said heros whilst they were alive.

P.S. I rejoice to be able to get in a postscript before the mail leaves to announce that the curtain has just fallen on the first act of Lohengrin amid a roar of enthusiasm, in which everybody, the bishop included, *must* have joined in order to swell it to such thundering volume. This triumph is due primarily, of course, to Wagner, whose stage instructions have been exactly carried out for the first time with quite terrific success (kindly send a copy of The Star containing this to Covent Garden with Bassetto's compliments); but a great deal is due to

Nordica. The moment she began, the sound of real singing so enchanted the Germans that it set them all singing too; we all shouted for joy; and I have no doubt the morning star would have joined in if that had been possible at a quarter past six in the evening.

21 July.

It is an odd sensation, this of seeing Lohengrin for the first time after having gone to see it so often during the last twenty years. From Nilsson and Campanini to Melba and de Reszke I have seen many Elsas and many Lohengrins, with certain large bits of Wagner's work sticking to them; but the work as produced here in Bayreuth is as new to me as a complete representation of Mozart's Don Giovanni will no doubt be if ever such a thing is achieved within my lifetime. It must not be concluded that the restoration of the omitted portions tends to make the work less operatic than the ordinary acting version. On the contrary, I was struck with the ultra-operatic effect of the restored choruses and *ensembles*, and could not help seeing that the managers agreed to cut them out, not in the least because they were specially Wagnerian even in the old days when that word meant something, but because they were specially troublesome. Further, the Bayreuth performance, lasting about four hours without counting the intervals, and therefore much longer than the Covent Garden version, did not seem to be so long. A great deal of the action is carried on here by the chorus, which gives immense vivacity and interest to several of the scenes by means of quite simple business which might be adopted at Covent Garden tomorrow without any very extraordinary trouble.

When I say that the retention of the scene of the assembly of the tribes at the beginning of the last act involved four separate entries of chieftains on horseback,

I am sure that Sir Augustus Harris will make it a point of honor to put it on at once at Covent Garden with eight horses. All such details as the keeping of the Saxons and Brabantines in two separate bodies, rushing forward and clashing their swords and shields severally, and observing such distinctions of custom as the Saxons sticking their swords into the earth, whilst the Brabantines throw them flat on the ground, also the business of the men in the second act interlacing their arms by threes, and improvizing a tramp round to the vigorous marching measure of the chorus in honor of the herald's proclamation—all these matters helped the work amazingly. Stage management of this kind made the scene of Lohengrin's arrival in the boat drawn by the swan irresistibly exciting. As to the effect of the restorations on the principal personages, the only one much concerned was Telramund, who, from being the feebly obstructive shadow of a conventional villain as we know him, became an important and powerful character. Ortrud shared his gain to some extent; and it is noteworthy that the scene between the two at the beginning of the second act, which has always been cut down as impossibly tedious and rather bears out that complaint in its mutilated state, was not at all tedious at full length.

The tumultuous interest produced by the first act was not maintained at full pitch all the evening. It must never be forgotten, in judging the Lohengrin drama, that Wagner himself was perplexed about the ending, tried more than one version of it, and finally, after the work was out of his hands for good, saw that the real flaw in the story is that Elsa was perfectly right in refusing to keep the monstrous condition imposed on her by Lohengrin, and that the drama, in representing her more or less as a weak woman who breaks her word and fails in her duty, is perfectly wrong. All Wagner's later heroines, Brynhild, Isolde, Sieglinde, and Eva, are treated in a very different spirit: they are true woman heroines, and not dolls for men's imaginations to play with. This vital weakness in the work has always to be reckoned with, especially during the latter half of the opera, except when a Lohengrin of altogether exceptional nobility of appearance and charm of utterance so rivets the worship of the audience that they do not trouble themselves about the merits of his case against Elsa.

A good deal was expected from Van Dyck in the part; but at the last moment some transient affection of the throat decided him to put off his appearance and leave the first performance to Gerhäuser. Gerhäuser is a highly sympathetic Lohengrin—too sympathetic, in fact; for in the last scene his emotion interfered somewhat with his vocal efficiency. Personally he presents his most exact resemblance to Mr Brandon Thomas,* who, if he ever tries the operatic stage, will probably take the same kindly and dignified view of the part. Gerhäuser's efforts to sing are pathetic: he does not know how to do it; but at least he does not shout except when some formidable high note—say G—is impossible on any other terms. Grengg, who appears to be a little overcome, no doubt by nervousness and the excitement of the festival, roared through the music of the King, and made it a worthy pendant to his impersonation of Gurnemanz. Popovici, as Telramund, was good. At first the chopped-up *brusquerie* of his declamation, and his apparently conscientious resolution to avoid anything like a *cantabile* phrase, was rather alarming; but his dramatic force and intelligence carried him well through, and his singing, though apparently rough and

* A popular actor and playwright, who had written, and appeared as Colonel Chesney in, the farce Charley's Aunt (1892).

fierce, was not out of tune, and not wanting in pathos on occasion, especially in the scene with Ortrud. The Herald, Bachmann, was brisk and vigorous, just what a herald should be who is resolved to be neither a nonentity nor a bore.

So much for the men in the cast. The English section of the audience, and perhaps the German section too, waited with far more curiosity for the American Elsa and the English Ortrud. Those who have seen Nordica as Elsa in London, and who have perhaps been struck with the characteristically American shallowness and limpidity in her of the sort of sentiment of which German women possess such turbid oceanic depths, and with a certain want of color and variety of tone in the voice which she produces so skilfully, will hardly realize the effect she made here, especially at her first entrance and in the balcony scene in the second act. The unspeakable delight, after all that crude shouting and screaming in Parsifal, of hearing a perfectly formed voice, responding to the lightest touch, and able to caress a phrase in turning it, was as manna in the desert to starving men. That was the whole secret of it.

For the rest, Nordica is built in the American way, not in the Germanic Elsa way. She was graceful, skilful, clever, at times excitable; but she was not sentimental, not *naïve*; and she was charming with the active charm of a capable, intelligent woman rather than with the passive appeal of the freshness and helplessness of youth. Her stage business was too well done for the age of the part: and from the latter half of the second act onward she frankly made Elsa a highly civilized modern woman of not less than twentyseven, marrying a comparatively green Lohengrin.

Miss Brema, with her uncontrolable energy, made, as might have been expected, a biting Ortrud. She was cruelly, hatefully derisive, absolutely without tenderness in love or majesty in misfortune, simply fiercely wilful and impatient. Any less extraordinarily energetic person would have shattered herself with such dramatic violence as that with which she hurled herself into her invocation of Odin and the ancient gods: as it was, the effect was less than she could have produced by simple singing without a movement. She rescued herself from the consequences of this resort to main force by still more main force, and finally came off as one of the most remarkable Ortruds we have seen, odious, but frightfully strong. She sang with great power. One likes grit in an artist; but Miss Brema is all grit. I think she would be improved by being passed half a dozen times through a particularly heavy pair of millstones. I venture to advise her, by the way, not to submit to the stage management which condemns her to stand like Lot's wife all through the first act, moving only to strike a very artificial attitude at the end. Madame Wagner is a clever stage manager; but one of the faults of her qualities is to conceive a dramatic representation as a series of *tableaux vivants*, and to invent attitudes for people instead of continuous and natural action, the result being that artists get stuck for ten minutes at a time into poses that become ridiculous after ten seconds.

I cannot complain of the orchestra, which gave a first-rate exhibition of the Bayreuth speciality of producing a perfectly unbroken flow of tone. But the leveling process which this involves was overdone in the preludes: the climax of the first one missed fire somehow. And I wish some of the woodwind players would come to England and learn how to cut their reeds. No doubt our reeds are harder to blow; but they do not squeak in the cheap way that the oboe does here. As a set-off I must add that the accompaniments were quite exquisitely played, and many points made which have never been noticed in England.

The curtain has just fallen on the first act of Tannhäuser. Never have I witnessed a more desperate effort on the part of a respectable establishment to be improper on a fine Sunday afternoon than this exhibition of the allurements of the Venusberg on the Bayreuth stage. Shall I ever forget those three plain Graces in long white skirts, for all the world like three respectable dairymaids on an archbishop's estate, or Venus herself, defying even the boldest admirer to see her ankles, or those mænads with whom I would have trusted Don Juan as implicitly as St Anthony. And the Cupids!—oh, the Cupids, poor little things, dangling helplessly at the ends of long wires in mid air, making terrified little pretences of drawing their toy bows, and looking so horribly frightened that no respectable factory inspector would have tolerated the spectacle for a moment. Anything more futile, more feebly scandalous, more cowardly in its attitude towards Mrs Grundy cannot be imagined. The effect, however, was highly moral: at no period of my life have I felt so disposed to enter a monastery as I do now. When it was all over, and the main business of the opera began, the relief was immense. The overture was smooth but pointless, not to be compared with dozens of London performances. The trumpets sound: I must hurry into the theatre.

22 July.

Bayreuth may bless the hour that inspired Wagner with the third act of Tannhäuser; for up to the end of the second act on Sunday evening we all felt that our burden was almost greater than we could bear. [Richard] Strauss, the new conductor, seemed a hopeless failure; he kept the band as smooth, but also as inane, as a linen collar; and his *tempi*, except for an occasional gallop in the wrong place, were for the most part insufferably slow. After Mottl's handling of Lohengrin this sort of thing would not bite on us at all; and we all sat wishing that we had not come, and that Strauss had never been born. The singing, too, was exasperating even for Bayreuth. Reichmann, as Wolfram, was determined to shew us that a German singer could be a bit of a *virtuoso*. He therefore turned on a rather wheezy *mezza voce*, often sinking to an ineffable *pianissimo*, and always flat enough to drive a sensitive musician beside himself. Grüning evidently regarded Tannhäuser as a disgraceful character; for he played him in an unexpectedly hangdog fashion, without an atom of knightly nobility or charm. The two women, though neither of them could sing without great effort and expenditure of wind, were better that the men. Mailhac, as Venus, succeeded for a few minutes in the first act in gripping the audience by her dramatic vigor; and Wiborg, the Elisabeth, sympathetic and a little quaint, like a medieval painter's Virgin, was moderately interesting. But they could not redeem the prevalent unsatisfactoriness; and when the march missed fire in consequence of Strauss thwacking it along exactly in the style of Bevignani, I resigned myself to apathetic endurance, and counted the slow minutes to the end of the act much as I shall soon count them from Ostend to Dover if it is at all rough.

During the interval I met with no apologist for the performance; my energetic expressions of disappointment seemed to please instead of, as usual, provoking mild remonstrance. But the third act changed the situation. The curtain fell amid just such a roar of applause as followed the first act of Lohengrin, and even after the tableau had been again exhibited, many of the English visitors were still so impressed that they persisted in calling for somebody—probably for Sir Augustus Harris. The intense sentiment, the dramatic force, and the powerful pictorial appeal of the act had proved irresistible. Grüning, uneasy as he had been as knight and minstrel, woke up when he found himself a moribund vagrant and outcast, and quite came out in telling the story of his pilgrimage. The Venusberg vision was well managed and highly effective; and on its disappearance, with the arrival of the bearers of Elisabeth's bier, the pathos of Tannhäuser's death, with the exclamation "Pray for me, St Elisabeth," got quite home to the audience, and blotted out all the shortcomings of the preceding acts. Wiborg sang Elisabeth's prayer better than she sang anything else during the evening; and though she did not make as much of the vain search for Tannhäuser in the ranks of the returning pilgrims as we have seen Albani do at much greater disadvantage in the way of stage mounting, she at least did nothing to hinder or spoil the effect which the scene and music can always make by themselves if let alone. And so the evening ended successfully after all.

The moral of the performance was the impossibility of failure with Tannhäuser when any sort of fair play is given to the last act. Unfortunately, when it was first produced in England at Covent Garden under Mr Gye's management, it was treated in a manner which common politeness forbids me to describe candidly; and it has never since recovered from that bad start. It is true that the grotto of Venus in the first act no longer consists of a "front scene" with a few vague clouds daubed on it, and a cheap imitation of a First Empire sofa for Venus to lie on; but the last act is as ridiculous as ever. If it were not so, the opera would be as popular as Faust or Carmen. As there is nothing in the way in which this act is managed in Bayreuth that would not be child's play to Sir Augustus Harris, I see no reason why Tannhäuser should in future fare worse in London than it does here. The greatest difficulty would be the restoration of the cuts in the second act, which greatly injure the effect of Elisabeth's interference to save Tannhäuser; but as the performance here, though a very slow one, lasted less than four hours (not counting the intervals), and included Leda and the Swan and all the voluptuosities of the Parisian edition of the Venusberg, most of which comes out on the stage as vulgar, indecent, and unnecessary rubbish, it seems to me that the work might be played with very little cutting at one of our half-past seven London opera nights.

Parsifal will be repeated tomorrow with Van Dyck and Miss Brema instead of Birrenkoven and Sucher. After that the glories of the season will be considerably shorn by the departure for England of Corno di Bassetto.

P.S. Monday evening. Swindled! Sold! Done! The same cast for Parsifal as before! Birrenkoven again instead of Van Dyck, who is reported to have left the town, tenor-like, in a rage, but who is really here safely enough, and will play Lohengrin on Friday! Sucher again, instead of Miss Brema, whom I and all the critics from England came expressly to see! Grengg again, Plank again: Potztausend! Donnerwetter!*

23 July.

The disappointment of the repetition of Parsifal with the same cast as before was due to two causes: first, Van Dyck's throat getting out of order, which was nobody's fault; and second, Sucher's demand, backed by a threat of withdrawal, that she should play Kundry at the first three representations of Parsifal. The effect of this ultimatum, and probably its object, is to prevent the critics, who naturally make for the early performances,

* Beneath this was an editor's note: "The editor of The Star, whilst straining to the utmost the extra latitude always allowed to so esteemed a correspondent as Di Bassetto, is obliged to suppress the remainder of this postscript. It is quite unfit for publication. It conveys towards the end, however, that the second performance of Parsifal was a great improvement on the first."

from seeing Miss Brema in the part. This is hardly generous of Frau Sucher; but she is probably right from her own point of view in refusing to contrast her rather stale and in no way remarkable impersonation of Kundry with that of a much younger and fresher rival, who has shewn the most striking talent, and whose faults, arising as they do from almost uncontrolable energy, do not render her any the less formidable.

Under the circumstances I should be more than an angel if I took much trouble to conceal the fact that Frau Sucher's Kundry does not improve on acquaintance. In her effort to be savage and derisive she becomes coarse, and sings as much out of tune as Rodemund in Mime, at Drury Lane; and in the more fascinating passages she is handicapped by the fact that her voice has no brightness left except when she is using it with the utmost vigor. It is only in the pathetic dumb show of the last act that she is really effective; and, as I have already pointed out, this is success where failure is hardly possible. But if Sucher's Kundry does not gain on a second hearing, Birrenkoven's Parsifal certainly does. Birrenkoven is not a handsome man. His blunt head, his squat frame, his brawny chest and arms, his bull neck, his comfortable but muscular paunch, and his short, powerful legs, apparently set at right angles to the normal position, make up a figure which might with very few touches be made into a Quasimodo*: yet he has genuine dignity, plenty of force, and sufficient likeableness and manhood in him to enable him to dispense with conventional elegance and charm. In short, now that he has got over his first embarrassment, and the audience over the first shock of his appearance, he is by no means an unacceptable or uninteresting Parsifal.

No doubt the whole performance gained by the fact that the first one had taught us the worst, and so was

* Victor Hugo's hunchback of Notre Dame.

able to save us from the disappointment which added so much bitterness to the opening afternoon; also that we were more used to the bad intonation; but the work was really better done, too. Grengg moderated his roaring and plunging, and gave his voice—the best bass voice in Germany, Levi assured me—some chance. Kaschmann, who replaced Reichmann as Amfortas, was comparatively weak in voice and limited in acting; but he spared us Reichmann's exhibitions of the art of singing flat. Plank, as Klingsor, woke up amazingly, and would have been quite lively had his tublike outline been compatible with the requisite activity. The result of the improvement was that the work gave us something like the true Bayreuth sensation, which is by no means confined to the mechanical marvels and ritualistic celebrations.

The leading poetic theme is that of the innocent greenhorn (I really cannot give a more becoming translation of *der reine Thor*) who, guided only by his instinct of compassion for suffering, finds the way of salvation. As to Kundry, I am afraid the audience does not care to see too clearly the point of her passionate love of and longing for purity and holiness in somebody else in order that she may use them as luxuries for her own gratification. We are all familiar with the fact that the more thorough a blackguard a man is, the more severely particular he is about the perfect correctness of the lady he deigns to marry, and how anxious he sometimes is that she should dedicate her purity to the task of reclaiming him. That is precisely what Kundry proposes to do with *der reine Thor* in the scene of the enchanted garden, and precisely what Parsifal, even without having studied the works of Sarah Grand,* flatly refuses

* Sarah Grand, novelist and ardent feminist, had recently published a highly successful novel The Heavenly Twins (1893), which won Shaw's admiration for its sensible treatment of the sex question.

to lend himself to. But there is another bearing of the case. What about the people who go to Bayreuth to enjoy the luxury of an hour with Wagner—just that hour that Kundry asks from Parsifal—but who have not the remotest intention of themselves producing any of that purity and holiness which they relish so much when they purchase it at a pound per performance at the bar where Wagner has left it on tap? One would like to know, without becoming offensively moral, whether the Holy Grail cast its supernatural radiance on any of the shareholders' meetings where the spoils were divided which fill the till at Bayreuth. I suspect a good deal of the Parsifallic devotion current in the Wagner Theatre is much like poor Kundry's devotion on the cheap and on the make. Need I add that I am suffering from a tedious and filthily dusty railway journey across Germany, and that my temper's the worse for it?[U]

A CROWD OF CONCERTS

The World, 25 July 1894

The time has come when I must leave Handel Festivals, operas, and the more highly organized musical species generally, to glance for a moment over the crowd of concerts and recitals which have been devastating my afternoons for weeks past. Fortunately for myself I have not been to everything of the kind that has been given during this rather busy season. There are concerts which I shirk, and concerts which shirk me. There are concerts the promoters of which send me invitations without sending me programs, as if, at my age, I were likely to run the risk of walking into a public hall and finding myself at the same old miscellaneous concert that has been in stock for years—Popper's Papillons, *Sognai*, *La mia Piccirella*—no, thank you! Then there are the concerts fixed for the first night of some new opera, or on the afternoon of Selection Day at the Handel Festival, given by enthusiasts who write begging me to be present, and expressing a hope that I have no other engagement. There are concerts which I am too lazy to go to, or too busy to go to, or which I would rather die than go to, not to mention the concerts which are in the hands of sensitive souls who smart under injustices perpetrated in this column, and who mercifully lighten my season's work by not inviting me to their entertainments. But with all these deductions I lead a dog's life from May to July inclusive.

One new feature of the present season is the variety of concert rooms. Instead of the old unvaried round of Steinway Hall, Prince's Hall, and St James's Hall, we have the large Queen's Hall, which is a happy success acoustically, and the smaller room at the top of the building, now much the most comfortable of our small concert rooms, though, as I am unfortunately a bad sailor, its cigar shape and the windows in the ceiling suggest a steamer saloon so strongly that I have hardly yet got over the qualmishness which attacked me when I first entered it. Messrs Brinsmead, too, have set apart a room "in cellar cool," outside which the belated critic can sit cosily on the warm stairs and enjoy an excellent view of the platform through the banisters. The room in the basement of the Grafton Gallery has not been in evidence this season, as far as I know; but Messrs Érard have just opened a London "Salle Érard" in Great Marlborough-street, which is by a very great deal the best-looking room of the kind our great pianoforte houses have yet given us.

This Érard room was opened the other day with a reception at which Paderewski was the chief attraction. I was unable to go and be received on that occasion: but

I seized an opportunity to see the new room at a concert given there next day by Clément, the tenor from the Paris Opéra Comique, and Léon Delafosse, of whom I had not previously heard, though I am not likely soon to forget him. He is a vigorous and nimble-fingered young gentleman with remarkably high animal spirits, in the ebullition of which he fell on Beethoven's Moonlight Sonata and left it for dead in the shortest time on record. The Érard room has two defects: excessive resonance, and painted windows which would pass very well in a restaurant, but which are not at all up to the artistic standard set by the handsome proportions of the room and its plain but elegant wainscoting. Everything in such a room ought to be the best of its kind; and I strongly urge Messrs Érard either to call in Morris and Burne-Jones and make the stained glass in the room one of the sights to be starred in Baedeker, or else, if that would cost too much, or if the light is too scanty for good stained glass, to substitute plain lattice windows like those in the halls of Barnard's or Clifford's Inn. It is a pity to spoil a good room by a single conspicuous touch of Philistinism; and I suggest to Messrs Érard that it would be a prudent as well as a gracious act to present the windows to some free library or municipal school of music, so that those dreadful medallion portraits of great composers, which are neither fine drawings nor good likenesses, might smile, in perfect harmony with their surroundings, on some gamboge-tiled staircase, with a bust of the mayor on the landing. Having already heard Clément at St James's Hall, I had great hopes that he would break the windows with one of those strident notes of which he is so proud. I must own that he did his best; but the glass was too thick; and finally it was I who was sent flying into the street. I would ask Clément seriously whether he thinks that the English people have built up their nation through all these centuries only to sit down now and hear a young man yell at the top of his voice. That may do very well for the gallery at the Opéra Comique, for the suburbs, for the provinces, for Australia, for South Africa, for City dinners, for smoking concerts, and other barbarous places; but in the true artistic centre of London "people dont do such things," as Judge Brack has it.* I have no doubt that Clément could sing very nicely if he wanted to; but, like most tenors, he doesnt want to. That is why great tenors are so rare, although good voices are so plentiful. Clément's concert at St James's Hall was a fashionable affair, because Plançon and Melba sang and Réjane recited. This was a very necessary diversion, since all the music was selected from the compositions of Mr Bemberg, who does not seem sufficiently alive to the fact that it is possible to have too much of a good thing. As far as I can judge, Mr Bemberg's ambition is to succeed to the business so long carried on in first-rate style by Gounod. It therefore concerns him to know that in this country we have found by our experiments with Mors et Vita and The Redemption that a whole concert of Gounod is insufferable. No doubt that is due to the imperfection of our own natures; but the fact, creditable to us or not, is indisputable; and if Mr Bemberg is wise he will in future be content with half an hour or so, and give Beethoven or some other composer a chance.

Another notable concert at St James's Hall was Miss Liza Lehmann's farewell to the concert platform. As Miss Lehmann's only reason for retiring is that she is getting married, I question whether her renunciation of the lucrative activity of public singing will be permanent. Though a bachelor, I venture to doubt whether matrimony is so absorbing a pursuit as she thinks at

* This is the last line in Ibsen's Hedda Gabler.

present; and I look forward to the time when Miss Lehmann will reappear as Madame, and once more sing Love may go hang rather more appropriately than she did on this occasion.

At all events, I decline to treat the farewell as a particularly solemn one; and when I say that Miss Lehmann sang very well, and seemed to have quite recovered the freshness and charm which at one time seemed to be wearing off under the influence of a trying course of sentimental popularity at the Monday Popular Concerts, I trust that my opinion may derive authority from the certainty that, if she unhappily had not sung well, I should have said so without the smallest remorse, farewell or no farewell. Madame Alice Gomez, who also sang, rather confirmed an impression which she gave me at the last Patti concert, that she is singing with somewhat less refinement than before, and that her voice is a little roughened in consequence.

Mr J. Robertson sang a couple of songs, in gratitude for which I will tell him exactly why his singing, in spite of the care he takes of his voice, and his sensitive and entirely praiseworthy repudiation of violent methods, is unsatisfactory. He sings out of time—that is the whole secret. You never once feel the swing and form of the melody, never get rocked or lilted by it: he pulls it to pieces as thoughtlessly as a child pulls the legs out of a fly. A week at the music halls would teach Mr Robertson a good deal in this respect. If Miss Marie Lloyd, or Miss Katie Lawrence, or Mr Dan Leno were to spoil a tune in such a fashion, their popularity would be gone in one turn.

Among the concerts which more particularly interested me was one at the Chelsea Town Hall, where I found Sir John Stainer gravely conducting a setting of Rossetti's Blessed Damozel by Lady Ramsay of Banff. It was very pretty; and it was quite original in the sense of having evidently been composed by Lady Ramsay entirely and sincerely on her own impulse and in her own way. But if Lady Ramsay were to ask me how much she knows of composition, I should reply "Just enough to write a barcarolle."

The Blessed Damozel consists of that barcarolle, with reminiscences (quite unconscious) of Mendelssohn's I waited for the Lord and Molloy's Dresden Shepherdess, and a few pages of occasionally quite irreparable part-writing. The barcarolle is the vital part; and it is no worse than any other barcarolle, and much more refined in feeling than some. But a barcarolle, if Lady Ramsay will only consider it attentively, is nothing more than the seesaw of two chords, like an improvisation on the accordion. Lady Ramsay varies and prettifies her seesaw by shifting it from key to key with sugary little modulations, and occasionally seesawing from the tonic to some sentimental old chromatic chord—Neapolitan sixth or the like—instead of from tonic to dominant; but from the harmonist's point of view she is always like a child in a swing: the motion is delightful and becoming, and enables the child to pretend to itself that it is flying; but it is really only an exploitation of the force of gravitation, and the child can only go where the swing takes it, and back, over and over again.

The harmonization of a chorale by Bach or Wagner (*Wach' auf!* in Die Meistersinger, for example) is, in comparison, like the march of an army round a province. These master harmonists can, without once repeating themselves or leaving the key, move freely through a circle of dozens of progressions back to their starting-point; while Lady Ramsay—or, not to confine the lesson invidiously to her, Auber or Offenbach—can make but one oscillation across and back. And that is why The Blessed Damozel is not what Sir John Stainer would call a great cantata; though whether Sir John has had the artistic probity to say as much to a lady who sings so very well, and is otherwise so attractive as Lady Ramsay, is best known to himself.

I have been at some excellent concerts of good chamber music given by Miss Emily Shinner, Miss Fillunger, and Mr Leonard Borwick, and by Miss Amina Goodwin, Madame Lilian Griffiths, and Mr Paul Ludwig at Queen's Hall—two independent sets of high-class concerts which were well worth the subscription. Herr Zeldenrust's pianoforte recital proved him to be very neat, smart, and vigorous with his fingers, and gifted with a high degree of musical intelligence; but he failed to convince me that his evident enjoyment of his skill in playing was accompanied by much love of what he played; and so the impression he left was not very deep. Miss Douste de Fortis and her sister, Miss Jeanne Douste, who has now become an accomplished concert singer, have been active as usual: I heard them at a *matinée* given at Brinsmeads' by Miss Edith Nalborough, whose pianoforte playing I am not able to judge from the little I heard of it—though that was satisfactory as far as it went. One gentleman, Mr Sidney Dark, invited me to a vocal and dramatic recital at which he alternated various bass songs, from *Qui sdegno* to A Friar of Orders Grey,* with recitations from standard authors, from Marlowe to Rudyard Kipling. I heard Mandalay, Fuzzy Wuzzy, and the Friar, and am bound to say that Mr Dark acquitted himself, both as elocutionist and singer, very handsomely, and with a certain personal ability not too common in his profession. A different sort of combination of the orator with the musician was that effected by Miss d'Esterre Keeling in her lectures on great composers. As a rule I detest lady-lecturers on

* Title song of "a drawing room operetta" (1872) by William Mason, with lyric ascribed to E. Legge.

music, because they never even pretend to say what they think; but Miss d'Esterre Keeling relied on her mother-wit, and made it go as far as a ton of clergy. I disagreed with some of her observations, and gathered from a certain severity of style on her part towards her audience that she had a low opinion of our intelligence, which was doubtless justified; but I was not bored; and the playing was adequate. Probably Mr Isidore de Lara started a Parisian fashion in opening his recital on the 17th by a lecture from Paul Milliet, the editor of Le Monde Artiste. I say probably, since my pilgrimage to Bayreuth, of which I shall presently have plenty to say, prevents me from answering for anything that happened last week.

BAYREUTH'S INDIFFERENCE TO BEAUTY

The World, 1 August 1894

When I ran across to Bayreuth the other day I was fully aware that the cost of my trip would have been better spent in bringing a German critic to England. And I greatly regret that this article is not written in German, and for a German paper, since it is now evident that, as far as any musical awakening and impulse can come from one country to another, it must come for the present from England to Bayreuth, and not from Bayreuth to England.

First, as to the wonderful Bayreuth orchestra, to the glories of which we have been taught to look with envious despair. I beg to observe here, in the most uncompromising manner, that the Bayreuth orchestra, judged by London standards, is not a first-rate orchestra, but a very carefully worked up second-rate one. The results of the careful working up are admirable; the smoothness, the perfect *sostenuto*, the unbroken flow of tone testify to an almost perfect orchestral execution in passages which lend themselves to such treatment. But there are two factors in the effect produced by an orchestra: the quality of the execution, and the quality of the instruments on which the execution is done. How much this may vary may be judged by the wide range of prices for musical instruments, even leaving out of account the scarcity values reached by certain exceptionally desirable old fiddles and bassoons.

Take, for example, the cheapest and most popular wind instrument in the orchestra—the cornet. Heaven knows how low the prices of the vilest specimens of cornet may run! but between the cheapest orchestrally presentable cornet and a first-rate one by Courtois or a good English maker the variation in price, without counting anything for electroplating or decoration of any sort, is from about thirtyfive shillings to eight or ten pounds. Fiddles range from a few shillings to the largest sums any orchestral player can afford to give for them; and the scale of prices for woodwind instruments varies from one to three figures.

Now, if there were such a thing as an international musical parliament, I should certainly agitate for a return of the prices of the instruments used in the Bayreuth and Crystal Palace orchestras respectively; and I should be surprised if the German total came to as much as half the English one. In the brass especially, the peculiar dull rattle of inferior thin metal at once strikes an ear accustomed to the smooth, firm tone of the more expensive instruments used in England. There is a difference in brightness too; but that I leave out of the question, as possibly due to the difference between Continental and English pitch, a difference which is all to the bad for us.

In judging the woodwind I am on less certain ground, since the tone is so greatly affected by the way in which the reed is cut. I have heard in the street what I supposed to be an execrable cracked cornet, and on coming round the corner have found an old man playing a clarinet with an old slack reed as easy for his feeble jaws as the reed one cuts for a child in a cornfield. The tone produced by such ancient men and that produced by Lazarus in his best days (which was, I think, purer, if less rich, than Mühlfeld's) mark the two poles of my experience of clarinet-playing; and I have always found that in German orchestras the standard tone leans more to the man in the street than to Lazarus.

Unfortunately, I am not expert enough to discriminate confidently between the difference due to the cutting of the reed and that due to the quality of the instrument; but except in the case of unusually fine players, who generally take the first chance of coming to England and settling here, the German woodwind player is content with a cheaper tone than the English one; and Bayreuth is no exception to this rule. The oboe there is as reedy as the *cor anglais* is here. The strings, as compared with ours, are deficient in power and richness; and even in the case of the horns, which we somehow or other cannot play, whilst the Germans can, the tone is much rougher and more nearly allied to that of the Alpine cowhorn than what may be called the standard tone here.

I rather harp on the word standard, because the facts that so many of our best orchestral players are Germans, and that Mr August Manns, the conductor whose band, in the wind section, puts the Germans most completely to shame in point of fineness of tone, is himself not merely a German, but a Prussian, conclusively prove that the inferiority of the German orchestra to the English is not an inferiority in natural capacity, but an inferiority in the current national standard of musical beauty—that is, an inferiority in the higher physical culture, and consequently in the quality of the demand to which the orchestral supply is a response.

That this inferiority is no new thing, and was well weighed by Wagner himself, is clear from the stress which he laid on the superiority of the instruments used by our Philharmonic band, and also by the fact that he always cited the Conservatoire concerts in Paris as the source of what he had learned from actual experience as to fineness of orchestral execution. All the other points he so strenuously urged on conductors have been mastered at Bayreuth; and the superficialities of the Mendelssohnian system have disappeared.

But the material of it all—the brute physical sound of the instruments which are so ably handled—still remains comparatively cheap and ugly; and the worst of it is that no German seems to care. As far as I can make out, the payment of an extra five pounds to an instrument maker for the sake of a finer tone would strike both conductor and player as an unreasonable waste of money.

And yet this German indifference to the final degrees of excellence in instrumental tone is conscientiousness itself compared to their atrocious insensibility to the beauty of the human voice and the graces of a fine vocal touch. The opening performance of Parsifal this season was, from the purely musical point of view, as far as the principal singers were concerned, simply an abomination. The bass howled, the tenor bawled, the baritone sang flat, and the soprano, when she condescended to sing at all, and did not merely shout her words, screamed, except in the one unscreamable song of Herzeleide's death, in which she subsided into commonplaceness.

The bass, who was rather flustered, perhaps from nervousness, was especially brutal in his treatment of the music of Gurnemanz; and it struck me that if he had been a trombone player in the band, instead of a singer, the conductor, Levi of Munich, would have remonstrated. Indeed, I presently heard a trombone player, who was helping with the fanfares outside the theatre between the acts, pulled up by the sub-conductor for being "a little too strong." Accordingly, having the opportunity of exchanging a few words with Levi afterwards, I expressed my opinion about the bass in question. Levi appeared surprised, and, declaring that the singer had the best bass voice in Germany, challenged me to find him anyone who would sing the part better, to which I could only respond with sufficient emphasis by offering to sing it better myself, upon which he gave me up as a lunatic.

It had to be explained to him that I was accustomed to the "smooth" singing popular in England. That settled the question for the Bayreuth conductor. Good singing there is merely "glatt," obviously an effeminate, silly, superficial quality, unsuited to the utterances of primeval heros. The notion that this particular sort of smoothness is one of the consequences of aiming at beauty of tone and singing in tune is apparently as strange in Germany as the notion that it is more truly virile to sing like a man than like a bullock.

If I had passed the whole season listening to Alvary, Klafsky, and Wiegand at Drury Lane, no doubt I should not have noticed any great deficiency in Grengg or Rosa Sucher. Even as it was, after the first three performances my ear became so corrupted that the second performance of Parsifal did not infuriate me as the first one did. I had become accustomed to second-rate intonation, especially after Tannhäuser, in which from beginning to end there was not a vocal note placed, I will not say as Melba or Miss Eames or the de Reszkes would have placed it, but as any tolerable English concert singer would have placed it.

This inveterate carelessness of intonation is only partly due to bad method. It is true that German singers at Bayreuth do not know how to sing: they shout; and you can see them make a vigorous stoop and lift with their shoulders, like coalheavers, when they have a difficult note to tackle, a *pianissimo* on any note above the stave being impossible to them.

But this system is nothing like so injurious to them as that of many of the operatic singers to whom we are accustomed. Their voices, it is true, get stale and rough; but they last astonishingly in that condition; the singers themselves are as robust as dray horses; and sixty appears to be about the prime of their shouting life. The thin, worn, shattered voice, with its goat-bleat or tremolo, and its sound as if it had taken to drink and wrecked its nerves and constitution, all shockingly common here, even among quite young singers, is not to be heard, as a rule, at Bayreuth. Singing there, in fact, is exactly like public speaking in England—not a fine art, but a means of placing certain ideas intelligibly and emphatically before the public without any preoccupation as to beauty of voice or grace of manner.

The music-dramas, are, so to speak, effectively debated; and the exposition of the poetic theme has all the qualities of a good Budget speech; but there is just about as much charm of voice and style as there is at a conference of the National Liberal Federation. The English political speaker learns his business by practice, and has neither the vices of the artificial elocutionist nor the fascinations of the cultivated artist. Nobody will listen to his voice for its own sake; but he does not break it: it lasts him until he is old enough to retire; and his general health is improved by the vigorous exercise of his lungs.

And that is just exactly the case of the German singer. Unfortunately, this disqualifies him from presenting the works of Wagner as completely as Sir William Harcourt is disqualified from playing Hamlet—a matter which will appear more fully when I come to describe the fate of Parsifal and Tannhäuser in the hands of German singers as compared with that of Lohengrin as performed by Belgian, Roumanian, American, and English singers. For I shall require more than one article to make myself sufficiently unpleasant to help those German lovers of music who are in revolt against the coarseness and laxity of German taste in this matter, and who are struggling to awaken the national conscience to the impossibility of a school of art in which the first lesson is one of callous indifference to beauty.

THE BAYREUTH FESTIVAL

Pall Mall Budget, 2, 9, and 16 August 1894

I.—ITS IMPROPRIETIES

[U] I begin with the improprieties of Bayreuth mainly because everybody else is likely to begin at the other end. There is something unbecoming in my plan, I know; for the journey to Bayreuth is essentially a pilgrimage, and should be described altogether in that spirit. But I have a constitutional inaptitude for solemn occasions which makes me the worst pilgrim in the world. It is not, believe me, that I am deficient in depth of feeling or seriousness of character. Rather, on that very account, the spectacle of people deliberately appointing a day and hour for a solemn mood, and making elaborate and costly mechanical preparations without the least misgiving as to their being able to live up to them when the hour strikes, is one which brings out the Mephistophelean side of me at once. In my youth, belonging, as I did, to a clan so numerous that in the mere course of senile decay and death funerals were pretty frequent, I soon disqualified myself from attending them by the unseasonable mirth which they always excited in me. And yet I could have written Gray's Elegy when there was no hearse in sight. Hamlet himself could not have improved the occasion more than I have done on a chance stroll like his among the tombs; and I rather insist on its being remembered that the moment Hamlet was interrupted at Yorick's grave by a funeral, he began to misbehave, even though the funeral was that of the woman he loved. I should have done exactly the same thing myself. It is ridiculous to have your hour of emotion fixed for you by an undertaker as your hour of catching a train is fixed by Bradshaw. This is what disables me at Bayreuth. Pecksniff* saying "Let us be merry" and taking a captain's biscuit was spontaneity itself compared to Wagner saying "Let us be solemn" and taking a theatre—building one, in fact. I know, of course, that he could not have effected his purpose in any other way, and also that I am not like other people in this respect, since most of them seem able to reserve their seriousness for fixed occasions as easily as they reserve their piety for Sunday. But I have no such power over myself. Like Kundry in Parsifal, I am the victim of an impulse to laugh at inappropriate moments. In the enchanted garden scene of that work, when the piccolo gives a derisive shriek, and the lady points, by a descent of a diminished double octave from B natural above the stave to a C sharp below it, the enormity of her confession, "Ich lachte" ("I laughed"), I always feel inclined to say "Dont take on about it, *gnädige Frau*: so have I, often, at equally unsuitable crises." In fact, I am

* Character in Dickens's Martin Chuzzlewit.

worse than Kundry, for I never feel the slightest remorse for my misconduct, if misconduct it be to laugh at Wagner in Bayreuth and to uphold him everywhere else. And so I shall begin, as aforesaid, with the improprieties.

By the improprieties of Bayreuth, please let it be understood that I mean the worst that the phrase suggests. Further, that the improprieties are conscious and intentional. Not that there is anything very dreadful coming—continue reading, young lady: I am not going to shock you—at least not much. But still there certainly are improprieties; and this is how they arose. In 1861, Wagner went to Paris, when the tide of Offenbach's popularity was coming in rapidly there, and succeeded in "passioning" Paris, including the Princess Metternich, with his music. The Princess asked Napoleon III. to command a performance of Tannhäuser at the Opéra; and it is alleged that the knightly Emperor offered to do so if the Princess succeeded in dislodging his hat by a high kick of the kind made fashionable by the Offenbachian vogue of the *can-can*. The story, which need not be believed, but which gives a valid hint as to the artistic situation in Paris at that time, goes on to declare that the Princess, rising to the emergency, succeeded in uncovering the Emperor in the desiderated manner. At all events, the performance was duly ordained. But no *grand opéra* can be performed in Paris without a ballet. A ballet without an opera might be feasible, but not the reverse. Wagner accordingly "wrote up" the opening scene—that of the Venusberg—for the occasion. He cut out the closing section of the overture, and made the middle, or bacchanalian, section lead straight into a wild orgy of fauns and satyrs, nymphs and mænads, naiads and sirens, with the Three Graces presiding, cupids flying through the air and darting their arrows at the frenzied throng, and *tableaux* of the stories of Europa and Leda. The motives of the management in spending a huge sum on all this were probably unworthy enough; but Wagner, always craving to give the intensest expression to his work, was perfectly willing to give them not only the Venusberg on an ordinary scale of theatrical expenditure, but the Venusberg with a vengeance, since they were willing to pay for it.

There was a terrible difficulty in the way of this new version. When Wagner described to the Paris ballet master the wild ebullition of *la joie de vivre* which he had planned, that functionary promptly declined to explain the situation to his dancers. He dared not. With a company consisting exclusively of first-rate artists the thing might have been done; but to invite ordinary ladies and gentlemen of the ballet in the year 1861 to indulge in an orgy on the stage was to run the risk of being taken at one's word with scandalous literalness. So there were no explanations. What the result was nobody exactly knows. The members of the Jockey Club came to the stalls fortified with horns, whistles and other instruments not provided for in the score, and for reasons quite beside the merits of the work made it impossible for the representations to be continued after the third night.

It is this Parisian version of Tannhäuser which has come down to Bayreuth as an artistic bequest burdened with a sort of legacy duty of impropriety. The first performance this year took place on the 22nd July: that is to say, on a Sunday afternoon, the Venusberg ballet thus breaking upon a morning spent, presumably, in religious contemplation by an audience composed largely of the most respectable English ladies and gentlemen, with the President of the Royal Academy and a bishop to give a firm social tone to the assembly. Now, if Sir Frederic Leighton or Bouguereau had painted a picture of the Three Graces, he would have painted them with nothing on; and the bishop would have acquiesced in this treatment as classically correct and artistically delightful. And the painting would have been reproduced as a "living picture" at the Palace Theatre without surprising anyone. How different are the Three Graces of Bayreuth. Look at them!*

This, for a deliberate attempt at a terrible example of impropriety, intended to warn all future Tannhäusers, is not very terrible—it it? The operation of the old rule for making a statue wicked—"Put a garter on it"—has been quite defeated by draping these three excellent young ladies so copiously that, but for that ravishing glimpse of their alabaster shoulders which is a received incident of evening dress for ladies, they only require veils and gloves to be totally invisible. And as to their dancing, I pledge my word for its freedom from the feats attributed in the fable to the Princess Metternich. A minuet would have appeared quite bacchanalian in contrast with their demure and unspeakably uninteresting movements.

And now, for who do you take this lady in the veil and coronet, who refuses to wear even a low-bodied dress, and whose respectability puts the Graces to shame, particular as they are?

She is the Venus of Bayreuth, Mlle Mailhac. Like all the great German *prima donnas*, she has fine arms and a powerful hard-worn voice. You will observe that she holds her arms up according to the strictest rules of graceful deportment as taught by Miss Pinkerton,† reminding me rather of an aunt of mine who played several instruments, but always insisted on playing the

* Here and elsewhere Shaw offers illustrations of Bayreuth performers and their ludicrous costumes and physical shapes.

† It is from Miss Jemima Pinkerton's academy for young ladies that Becky Sharp and Amelia Sedley depart in the first chapter of W.M. Thackeray's Vanity Fair (1847–8).

tambourine at specially dazzling parties, because it shewed off her hands, which were very beautiful. As to the costume, I challenge England to produce a schoolmistress more decorously draped. And yet Bayreuth, bless its innocence! offers her as a warning to all females of an abandoned turn, and surrounds her with rosy clouds and voluptuous orchestration, amid which she moves to all appearance the very personification of virtuous indignation. Only once, in the last act, was Mlle Mailhac at all forward in her manners; and then she shocked me, as she was the last person in the world from whom I should have expected anything of the sort.

I am strongly tempted to insert here a picture of one of the wicked flower maidens in Parsifal, whose dresses, made of huge dock-leaves, come down very little below their knees; but I doubt if the editor would allow it. Besides, I have lost it somehow on my journey back. I only mention it lest any lady should bring her daughters to Bayreuth, and be confronted with a crowd of young persons shewing almost as much of their ankles as if they were Englishwomen mountaineering in tailor-made dresses. What makes it worse is that these flower maidens really do make downright bold advances to Parsifal, who very properly gives them no encouragement.

On the whole, perhaps, the tone of the Venusberg is a little lower than that of the Enchanted Garden where the flower maidens grow. In spite of the well-draped seemliness of Venus and the Graces, in which they are scrupulously imitated by Leda, the fauns and nymphs play a sort of lumpish kiss-in-the-ring game, with occasionally rather trying indications of an attempt to carry out those intentions of Wagner's which the Parisian *maître de ballet* thought had better not be explained. Meanwhile a cluster of tiny Cupids sit bunched on top of the rock which serves Venus for a reclining-board to maintain her admirable straightness of shoulders and ladylikeness of carriage. It presently appears that these poor little creatures are trussed-up in that posture, and attached to long wires reaching to the flies; for they are presently swung off and made to hover over the rompers below, whom they pretend to shoot as best they can when their hearts are obviously in their mouths, and every moment threatens to overbalance them as they hang. I shall, of course, be told that they like it; and I have no doubt they do, but not that part of it. If I had been trussed-up and dangled in the air like that I should have screamed to be taken down; and I have not the slightest doubt that these children would do the same were they not afraid of being sent away, and deprived for ever of their pretty dresses and toy wings and bows and arrows. These Cupids are by far the worst of the Bayreuth improprieties.

II.—ITS INCONGRUITIES

Incongruity at Bayreuth arises partly from the inaptitude of modern German civilization for producing figures of the primitive heroic type, and partly from the fact that life is short and art long. It is an old complaint that an actress cannot learn enough of her business to play Juliet until she is too old to look the part. This, however, is largely a question of eating and drinking—especially drinking. Taking Talma's estimate of twenty years as the necessary period of apprenticeship for a fully qualified stage artist,* and assuming that a physically well-preserved person can produce on the stage an acceptable illusion of youth up to the verge of fifty, it seems possible that at all times there should be a

* François-Joseph Talma (1763–1826), the supreme tragedian of his age, was a founding member of the Théâtre Français de la Rue Richelieu. He wrote an illuminating preface, Reflexions sur Lekain et l'art théâtral, to the memoirs (1801) of the actor Henri-Louis Lekain.

supply of Romeos and Juliets able to look their parts as well as act them. Substitute Tristan and Isolde for Shakespear's pair, and the argument applies equally to Wagnerian music drama. Unhappily, the preservation of figure and freshness up to fifty is not compatible with the main factor of German culture. That factor is beer. If you wish to make an impression of the most unexampled singularity and eccentricity in Germany, you have only to reply to the universal inquiry "Pilsener or Münchener?" with a statement that you do not drink beer at all. You may not surprise the waiter, because a waiter is too thoroughly cosmopolitan to be surprised at anything; but your untraveled neighbors will at once begin to watch you furtively to see how you manage to sustain life in a condition of such unnatural abstinence. As a rule, of course, you do not abstain: on the contrary, you praise German beer for its wonderful lightness, by which you mean the immoderate quantity you can venture to drink without seeing double. You generally end by urging its general use in England as a sort of temperance drink. Never was there a more pernicious delusion. If men must have a given quantity of alcohol, why compel them to water-log their tissues with gallons of fluid, when a single glass, made in the English way, will leave them equally happy without making them half so puffy and tub-like? You seldom meet a well-to-do German who does not carry an excess weight of a stone or two of solidified swill overlying what is real of him in the way of bone and muscle. It is not fat: there is not the making of half-a-pound of candles in the whole superfluity of the man. Probably it is mostly water and sugar. And it accumulates, not on the biceps, but beneath the belt. An average German, with an average middle-class income—that is to say, one to whom the price of a fifth or sixth mug of beer is a matter of some concern—is too fleshy to play Romeo or Tristan gracefully when he is twentytwo. Make him an opera singer, with comparatively unlimited pocket money; and what will he be by the time he becomes ripe for leading business at Bayreuth?

Can you conceive the Klingsor of the Parsifal poem, the adroit spearman, the untiring intriguer, the personification of unrest, eagerly weaving his enchantments, and sardonically chucking over the rout of his own despised slaves, otherwise than as an intensely active man, lean, nervous, with perhaps a dash of the serpent, the fox, the tiger in him, but certainly without a trace of the hippopotamus? Well, here is the Klingsor of Bayreuth—Herr Fritz Plank, of Karlsruhe.

I submit that at least two-thirds of Fritz's bulk, whether he accumulated it himself or inherited it, must consist of the national beverage, and only one-third of genuine Klingsor stuff. Plank is celebrated at Karlsruhe for his impersonation of Wotan; but then Wotan, if I recollect aright, had to empty a drinking-horn, the end of which was secretly connected with the sea; so that one can conceive him as running a little to flabbiness. But I really do not think Plank should have undertaken Klingsor without getting into better physical training. And the fact that the matter is mainly one of training is my justification for positively refusing to accept the old plea that criticism should not be "personal." Criticism of artists who offer their own persons as the material of their art cannot be other than personal. If a hunchbacked, one-eyed artist, with a very beautiful voice and great dramatic talent, were to appear on the stage, no doubt the critics, having once decided that the deformity and the blemish were tolerable for the sake of the voice and talent, would not betray any consciousness of them. But if an artist spoils a part by refusing to train for it, then I do not see why that artist's feelings should be spared any more than those of a gymnast, a prizefighter, a jockey, a dancer, or any of the other persons who, knowing that they *must* regulate their weight if they are to maintain their position, succeed in doing so by the simple expedient of not eating and drinking too much. I have seen a very eminent and gifted *prima donna* die prematurely, after making all the operas she appeared in ridiculous for several years, simply because the critics shrank from holding her responsible for her own weight. And I have in mind another *prima donna*, with a much more marked natural tendency to bodily exuberance, who, coming twenty years later, kept herself not only alive, but eminently presentable. The first was a German: the second is a Canadian.*

The new Parsifal, a young Rhinelander named Birrenkoven, has, at twentynine, symptoms of stoutness which would set a Londoner of forty banting at once. The ideal Parsifal does not need to be described: such scenes as that in which the repentant Kundry anoints his feet and dries them with her hair, or in which the dove descends above his head in a flood of heavenly light as he uplifts the glorified Grail, at once suggest the appropriate figure. Birrenkoven, being a sort of rough diamond, is not a bad Parsifal when once you are used to him; but even when you are more used to Von Uhde's pictures than to Ary Scheffer's, the first shock of his appearance can only be compared to that which young ladies receive when a perusal of Browning's Paracelsus drives them to hunt up the wellknown portrait of that philosopher. I append on the preceding page the most flattering photograph of Birrenkoven I have been able to procure.

An incongruity of quite another kind arises in the case of Madame Nordica, an American *prima donna*, wellknown to us as a bright, clever artist, and a very

* Therese Tietjens, who died in 1877, and Emma Albani.

skilful singer. Frau Wagner has entrusted her with the part of Elsa in Lohengrin, the production of which for the first time at Bayreuth is the great event there this year. We all know the Elsa of the poem, the *naïve* medieval maiden who firmly believes that the fairy knight of her dreams will actually appear to defend her in the ordeal of trial by battle. Now Madame Nordica is, for stage purposes, quite as young as Elsa; her figure is entirely guiltless of the incongruities of Klingsor's and Parsifal's; her voice, in comparison with the German voices, is divinely fresh and pure; and yet——

You must admit, I think, that this essentially mundane modern lady of the most brilliant type is possible as Elsa of New York, but not possible as Elsa of Brabant. And the worst of it is that her first Bayreuth Lohengrin, Emil Gerhäuser, a young German of the amiable, studious type, had an air of being so much less able to take care of himself in the world than she, that whilst one could not but congratulate him on his bride, one felt, all the same, that she was too much the superior force to leave him much choice in the matter. He went to the altar like a lamb.

These are the types of incongruity which are most destructive to the stage illusion at the Wagner Theatre.

III.—IS IT WORTH GOING TO?

This is not exactly the sort of question that can be answered offhand. It is an economic question; and there are no absolute "yes or no" answers to economic questions. It all depends on where you live and how much you have to live on. To the Bayreuther the cost is the price of admission to the Wagner Theatre—£1 per performance, prohibitive to the vast majority of the population, but a trifle compared to what must be paid by the Londoner, who has to travel to Bayreuth and back again. The cost of the journey varies according to the route and length of sea voyage. By Dover, Ostend (four hours' sea), Brussels, Cologne, and Nuremberg, which is on the whole the most expeditious route, the price of a return ticket, second-class, with first-class on the boat, is £6. 11*s.* 6*d.* A room in Bayreuth, which can be easily engaged by writing to the Wohnungs Comité, and simply calling for the address at their room in the railway station when you step out of the train, costs two or three marks a night, with an extra mark for breakfast. As three works are being performed this year, Parsifal, Tannhäuser, and Lohengrin, and it is customary and advisable to see Parsifal twice, beginning and ending with it, the expenditure for tickets amounts to £4. It is a mistake to spend the night in Bayreuth after the last performance you attend: the wise thing to do is to leave your luggage in the cloak-room in the course of the day, and go from the theatre to the station, making for Nuremberg by the eleven train. Consequently you need only pay for four nights' lodging in the town, allowing for one day on which there is no performance. It is, therefore, possible to limit your absence from London to seven days; but in that case all you will remember of your first Parsifal is the darkening of the theatre, the hush, the strains of the prelude stealing drowsily up from the hidden orchestra, and then a sleep deeper than that of Kundry. Better take nine or ten days, and allow £5 for expenses, since it is a poor heart that never rejoices. Here, then, for the modest solitary traveler, we have the following bill: theatre tickets £4, traveling expenses £6. 11*s.* 6*d.*, other expenses, including lodging at Bayreuth, £5: total, over £15, which is perhaps the smallest sum with which anyone not absolutely a fanatic can be reasonably recommended to undertake the pilgrimage, and which can be exceeded with the greatest possible facility by persons whose Wagnerian program does not include plain living as well as high thinking.

In fairness one must include in the value received for this sum, not only the performances at Bayreuth and the pleasant mornings in the scented pine woods on the hills there, but a trip along the most popular reaches of the Rhine, the Holbein Madonna at Darmstadt, the pictures in the Städel Institute at Frankfurt, the sights of Nuremberg, and a glimpse of Cologne and Brussels. The effect of this is to make Bayreuth much better worth visiting to those who have never been over this ground before than to seasoned tourists, who are apt to regard the run from London to the longitude of Nuremberg as only a tedious preliminary to getting to any place worth mentioning in Central Europe. But for this very reason the seasoned tourist can easily take Bayreuth on his way elsewhither. On the whole I should say that for persons who are accustomed to spend £20 or upwards every autumn on a continental trip, Bayreuth is well worth a visit in Festival time. I am speaking, of course, of people with an ordinary fondness for the theatre and the opera: the thorough-going Philistine should not go at all; and the thorough-going Wagnerite should go at all hazards. Indeed the out-and-out fanatic, if he can afford it, sees the whole five sets of performances right through, and then goes on to Munich to have some more.

For my own part, I have never found it worth my while to see any work performed more than once at Bayreuth except Parsifal, which cannot be seen elsewhere. To the English professional critic, who goes to Bayreuth at the close of a season during which he had heard the best that London can offer, and whose ear has been made irritably sensitive by overwork, Bayreuth is by no means an unmixed treat. To hear Tannhäuser there within a fortnight of having heard Patti sing Elisabeth's prayer, to plunge straight out of earshot of tenors like Jean de Reszke and Edward Lloyd, basses and baritones like Plançon, Edouard de Reszke and

Santley, sopranos like Melba, Miss Eames, and Calvé, contraltos like Giulia Ravogli and Clara Butt, into the realms of Birrenkoven and Grüning, Grengg and Reichmann, Wiborg and Sucher, is to receive a cruelly harsh lesson in the inferiority of German singing—if it can be called singing—to that which we, ignorant of our happiness, grumble at in England. It was all very well for Wagner to urge the tenors and *prima donnas* of his day to consider in their singing a little more the What, and a little less the How; but if he were alive now he would change his note. Here is one of the most famous German *prima donnas*, Rosa Sucher, a lady with a powerful voice, a fine person, and strong dramatic feeling. Her Isolde is famous throughout Germany; and it is not so long since we saw her rather too soldier-like, but still bright and powerful Brynhild in London. But as she considers the What entirely to the neglect of the finer shades of the How, I had almost rather not hear her sing at all, so entirely common—apart from the mere physical vigor which it displays—is her work as a vocalist. She is eclipsed in this department, not only by the American Lilian Nordica—whose portrait I gave last week—but by the English Marie Brema, who, as Ortrud in Lohengrin, was fortunate enough to be associated with a Telramund with an ear as well as good dramatic gifts. But then Popovici is not a German, but a Roumanian.

Germany beats us, however, very handsomely in the matter of conductors. The Bayreuth orchestra, though not to be compared to what may be called the London orchestra or Sir Charles Hallé's Manchester band in the excellence of its instruments and, probably, the readiness and steadiness of its members, is so ably handled and thoroughly drilled that our London work sounds quite haphazard by contrast. The conductors best known in Bayreuth are Hans Richter—our Richter—Felix Mottl, and Hermann Levi. This year Richter does not conduct at Bayreuth, his place being filled by a young composer named Richard Strauss, who is fastidious enough as to smoothness of execution, but who fails, on the whole, in energy and breadth of style, especially in immediate comparison with Mottl, whose handling of Lohengrin was masterly in its combination of strength, precision, dramatic insight, and delicacy of execution, as those who heard him conduct the Wagner concert at the Queen's Hall last spring can well believe.

When Mottl returns in the forthcoming season, he will be associated with another conductor, no less interesting a person than the son of "The Master." I have not seen him conduct, and have no idea of how far he may be able to contend against the fate of Mozart's son, who, though reported on good authority to have been an excellent pianist, found it impossible to live up to the expectations which his name created. To be named Wagner is to start heavily handicapped enough in all conscience; but this unlucky young man is identified with his father up to the hilt by being called Siegfried Wagner. Here they are, father and son together. Siegfried has a good brow and plenty of head above his ears (this is the point by which you measure the distance which separates a man from a donkey); but he has not quite his father's fighting chin, has he?—that chin that went through Europe like a ploughshare through a clod. [U]

THE FIRST BAYREUTH LOHENGRIN

The World, 8 August 1894

Sitting, as I am today, in a Surrey farmhouse with the sky overcast, and a big fire burning to keep me from shivering, it seems to me that it must be at least four or five months since I was breathing balmy airs in the scented pine-woods on the hills round Bayreuth. If I could only see the sun for five minutes I could better recall what I have to write about. As it is, I seem to have left it all far behind with the other vanities of the season. I no longer feel any impulse to describe Lohengrin and Tannhäuser as I promised, or to draw morals for Frau Wagner on the one hand, or Sir Augustus Harris on the other. For months I have held the whole subject of musical art in an intense grip, which never slackened even when I was asleep; but now the natural periodicity of my function asserts itself, and compels me to drop the subject in August and September, just as hens moult in November (so they tell me here in the farmhouse).

What I feel bound to record concerning the Bayreuth Lohengrin—remember that this is the first time the work has been done there, and probably the first time it has ever been thoroughly done at all, if we except the earliest attempt under Liszt at Weimar—is that its stage framework is immensely more entertaining, convincing, and natural than it has ever seemed before. This is mainly because the stage management is so good, especially with regard to the chorus. In Lohengrin there are only two comparatively short scenes in which the chorus is not present and in constant action.

The opera therefore suffers fearfully on ordinary occasions from the surprising power of the average Italian chorister to destroy all stage illusion the moment he shambles on the scene with his blue jaws, his reach-me-down costume, his foolish single gesture, his embarrassed eye on the prompter, and his general air of being in an opera chorus because he is fit for nothing better. At Covent Garden he is, in addition, generally an old acquaintance: it is not only that he is destroying the illusion of the opera you are looking at, but that he has destroyed the illusion of nearly all the operas you have ever seen; so that the conflict of his claim upon you as one of "the old familiar faces" with the claims of the art which he outrages finally weakens your mind and disturbs your conscience until you lose the power of making any serious effort to get rid of him. As to the ladies of our opera chorus, they have to be led by competent, sensible women; and as women at present can only acquire these qualities by a long experience as mothers of large families, our front row hardly helps the romance of the thing more than the men do.

Now I am not going to pretend that at Bayreuth the choristers produce an overwhelming impression of beauty and chivalry, or even to conceal the fact that the economic, social, and personal conditions which make the Covent Garden chorus what it is in spite of the earnest desire of everybody concerned that it should be something quite different, dominate Frau Wagner just as they dominate Sir Augustus Harris, and compel her to allot to Elsa a bevy of maidens, and to Henry the Fowler a band of warriors, about whose charms and prowess a good deal of make-believe is necessary. The stouter build of the men, the prevalence of a Teutonic cast among them, and their reinforcement by a physically and artistically superior class of singers who regard it as an honor to sing at Bayreuth, even in the chorus, certainly help the illusion as far as the Saxon and Brabantine warriors in Lohengrin are concerned; but this difference in raw material is as nothing compared with the difference made by the intelligent activity of the stage manager.

One example of this will suffice. Those who know the score of Lohengrin are aware that in the *finale* to the first act there is a section, usually omitted in performance, in which the whole movement is somewhat unexpectedly repeated in a strongly contrasted key, the modulation being unaccountable from the point of view of the absolute musician, as it is not at all needed as a relief to the principal key. At Bayreuth its purpose is made clear. After the combat with Telramund and the solo for Elsa which serves musically as the exposition of the theme of the *finale*, the men, greatly excited and enthusiastic over the victory of the strange knight, range themselves in a sort of wheel formation, of which Lohengrin is the centre, and march round him as they take up the *finale* from Elsa in the principal key. When the modulation comes, the women, in their white robes, break into this triumphal circle, displace the men, and march round Elsa in the same way, the striking change of key being thus accompanied by a correspondingly striking change on the stage, one of the incidents of which is a particularly remarkable kaleidoscoping of the scheme of color produced by the dresses.

Here you have a piece of stage management of the true Wagnerian kind, combining into one stroke a dramatic effect, a scenic effect, and a musical effect, the total result being a popular effect the value of which was proved by the roar of excitement which burst forth as the curtains closed in. A more complex example of the same combination was afforded by the last act of Tannhäuser, which produced the same outburst from the audience, and which was all the more conclusive because none of the enthusiasm could be credited to the principal artists, who had, in the first two acts, effectually cleared themselves of all suspicion of being able to produce any effect except one of portentous boredom.

Here, then, we have the point at which Bayreuth beats Drury Lane and Covent Garden in staging Wagner and every other composer whose works have been for some years in our repertory. I have over and over again pointed out the way in which the heroic expenditure of Sir Augustus Harris gets wasted for want of a stage manager who not only studies the stage picture as it is studied, for instance, at the Savoy Theatre, or at any of our music halls where ballets form part of the entertainment, but who studies the score as well, and orders the stage so that the spectator's eye, ear, and dramatic sense shall be appealed to simultaneously.

I have sometimes had to point out, in the case of old stock operas, that there is often reason to suspect that the stage manager either does not even know the story of the opera he has in hand, or has become cynically convinced that an opera is in itself such a piece of nonsense that an extra absurdity or two cannot matter much. This is of course quite a tenable view argumentatively; but it is not the understanding upon which the public pays for its seats. The moment you take a guinea, or half-a-crown, or whatever it may be, from an individual for a performance of an opera, you are bound to treat the performance as a serious matter, whatever your private philosophic convictions may be.

At Bayreuth they do take the performance seriously in all its details: the heroine does not die in the middle of the street on a lodging-house sofa, nor does the tenor step out of a window with a rope ladder attached to it, and openly walk off at the level of the chamber floor. The rank and file are carefully instructed as to what they are supposed to be doing; and nobody dreams of taking any liberties with the work or with the public. It is quite a mistake to suppose that the makeshifts which circumstances force upon Covent Garden are unknown at Bayreuth, or that the stock works are as well rehearsed and prepared as the new works; but there is, at any rate, always the habit of discipline; and though things may be left undone for want of time or ill done for want of rehearsal, nothing is let slide on the assumption that it is not worth doing. I have been tortured there by bad singing, and bored by solemnly prosaic acting; but I have never been offended by wanton trifling.

I have sufficiently explained in my last article how Bayreuth's scrupulous artistic morality is heavily counterbalanced by the callousness of its musical sensibility. The cure for this, however, is not the writing of homilies about it, but the cultivation of the German ear by actual experience of something better than the singing they are accustomed to tolerate. Already the popularity of Van Dyck, a Belgian singer with none of the German bluntness about him, whose charm of voice and style was sufficient, when he appeared as Des Grieux at Covent Garden, to produce on Jean de Reszke, who was at that time taking his supremacy for granted somewhat too lazily, the effect popularly known as "making him sit up," is rendering the Bayreuth stage more accessible to foreigners, who will finally, if the Germans do not realize their own deficiencies, make it difficult for a German singer to get an engagement there. This year we have Nordica and Miss Brema as well as Van Dyck; and it is probable that Frau Wagner will look for more help in the same direction—across the frontier, that is—on future occasions.

I am not quite done with the subject even yet; but as this farmhouse is beyond the sphere of the Post Office, I must conclude, in order to allow three or four days for the journey of thirty miles or so which my communication must make before it reaches London.

POSTSCRIPT 1931.—As it happened I *was* done with the subject. I had already resigned my post as musical critic to The World on the death of its editor Edmund Yates on the 19th May 1894. But his successor [Major Arthur Griffiths] pleaded that it would seem a personal slight to himself if I did not go on under his editorship until the end of the season; and this, to save appearances, I consented to do. After the autumn recess my vacant place was filled by Mr Robert Smythe Hichens, who had trained himself as a musician, not knowing that he was destined to be a famous novelist.

I never again undertook regular duties as a critic of music.

THE MUSICAL REVOLUTION

The Musical Courier, September 1894

[U] Not long ago I was at a concert in the Albert Hall in London. The Albert Hall accommodates an audience of about 8000 people: that is to say, it is nearly three times as large as the next largest concert hall in London. Its extraordinary dimensions make it impossible for me to say whether it is a good hall for music, since I should have to attend at least a hundred concerts and sit in a different place every time, to qualify myself for an exhaustive opinion; but I can vouch at least for the fact that fine musical tone, however delicate, can be heard perfectly at the remotest points in the building, and that, on the other hand, base musical tones of any sort, including certain organ mixture stops, are either not distinctly heard at all, or else betray themselves at once as abominable. There is a story of an Irish fiddler who played so well at a fair, that Ole Bull, who happened to be present, asked him whether he played by note or by ear. The man replied that he played neither by note nor by ear, but "by main strength." This is an exceedingly common plan with both players and singers; and the temptation to try to overcome the vastness of the Albert Hall by it is only natural. But the Albert Hall revenges itself by letting loose a whole pack of echoes, which respond to all attempts at shouting with a volley of derisive barks. I have heard Henry Irving recite in the hall, also Sarah Bernhardt and Beerbohm Tree. Tree selected a piece which required a vigorous and rather explosive style of declamation, with the result that he was followed by a double echo all through. Irving read a rhymed address with quiet, precise delivery, and very carefully formed tone. I was at a considerable distance from him, and heard him as if he were speaking very quietly close to me. Sarah Bernhardt's voice was perfectly audible; but the handicap of a foreign language was too much for her intelligibility; and at the end, on receiving a somewhat bewildered and obviously formal round of applause, she conveyed to us very plainly by the manner of her withdrawal that she considered us a parcel of imbeciles.

On the whole, the hall is not suitable for speakers; but the experiments that have been made by speakers there confirm my opinion that monster concerts, like those in the Albert Hall and of the Handel Orchestra in the Crystal Palace, tend to encourage good singing and playing by selecting as fittest those artists who have the finest sense of beauty and firmness of tone, and by making rough and violent work suicidal and impossible. Thus a violinist who in a small room makes such a noise that you look curiously at his instrument to see whether it is not made of corrugated zinc roofing, a tenor or soprano whose voice seems to rip up the upholstery of your drawing room, or a bass who makes the whole house buzz and rattle when he practises, can hardly be heard four rows off in the Albert Hall; whilst Sarasate playing his favorite Chopin nocturne in a tone that would not sound excessive in a sentry box—which might even be criticized there by a soldier of robust tastes as perhaps a little thin; Sims Reeves singing Watchman, will the night soon pass? with that lackadaisical mannerism which led ignorant people, years before his retirement, to declare that he had no voice left and that nobody could hear him at a distance; Patti singing phrases in Home, Sweet Home or Within a mile in a pianissimo that is almost a whisper, and Santley singing anything you please without doing the smallest violence to his voice, can all be heard in these great spaces apparently more intimately than when they are at your elbow in a private house. Therefore, if you want to test the purely musical value of an instrument or of an artist's method, listen to it in an auditorium big enough to accommodate 8000 people.

When I was receiving my musical education, which, as far as it was real, consisted in hearing music and not in reading foolish books about Mozart and Beethoven (though I did that, too, so as to get plenty of practice in the invaluable art of unlearning) I was led to believe that a modern iron-framed pianoforte was enormously superior to the miserable harpsichords and clavichords with which Bach and Handel had to be content. In particular I was taught that the sound of the clavichord was so tiny that it could only be heard at very close quarters. I did not question this alleged fact, which struck me as having advantages for the people next door. At last, in the course of time, I heard a clavichord played by Mr Hipkins, a noted expert in old instruments and an admirable performer upon them, though, perhaps, to the part of the world that knows nothing about clavichords, he is better known by his connexion with Broadwoods. His clavichord was certainly not a loud instrument any more than Patti is a loud singer; but though the performance took place in a room large enough to hold a few hundred persons, yet when you went to the end farthest from the clavichord, it seemed just as audible as when you were close to it. On examining the instrument I found that it could not be played violently, and that it has absolutely no "action"—nothing but a stick on a pivot, which went up and hit the string at one end when you pressed down the other. In short, there was nothing to save the player from simply making a foolish noise except the skill of his own hand; so that the clavichord came into line with the violin or the human larynx in respect of being an absurd and offensive instrument when badly handled and a beautiful one only when well handled.

Now I come to the concert at the Albert Hall with which I started this disquisition. At that concert Patti sang, and Santley sang, with the satisfactory effect which I have already described. But something else happened. A lady played the piano. It was a first-rate piano, fitted with the most perfect "action" known, by a maker whose instruments have been special favorites with the greatest pianists. But in the Albert Hall it sounded mechanical, uninteresting, and futile. And that, I presume, is why Paderewski does not, in spite of his immense popularity in London, take his instrument to the Albert Hall, though he has exactly the same pecuniary interest as Patti in bringing it to the largest hall in which it can be used to good purpose. The pianoforte cannot be played effectively in a large space; and recent concerts at which the experiment has been tried of playing dozens of grand pianos simultaneously have proved that nothing can be gained even in magnitude of effect by this means. Paderewski's own criticism of the pianoforte is implied in the fact that he insists on having the hammers of the instruments he uses hardened to such an extent that though a feathery lightness and swiftness of execution is made possible, the tone, especially at the top, is spoiled beyond all power of correction even by the most tender touch. I have never heard a pianist of the first rank who so definitely gave up perfect beauty of sound as a bad job, and concentrated himself on thoughtfulness of interpretation, astonishing manipulation and eloquence of style. He is a wonderful player on a brilliantly detestable instrument. That his judgment is sound in making this choice appears to be proved by the experience of players equal if not superior to him in technical attainments—Sapellnikoff, for instance—who face heavier finger work for the sake of greater richness of tone, and yet do not seem to gain as much as they lose.

Now what is the moral of this discourse? First, that the enormous popularity of singers who produce the most perfectly musical and accurately pitched tone shews that the public, which in the mass is so utterly unintellectual in its view of music that it makes no categorical distinction between The Bohemian Girl and Tristan, has really far sounder ears than those enthusiasts who, in their preoccupation with the dramatic and poetic content of modern music, lose all concern for the beauty of the sounds, vocal and instrumental, by which this content is conveyed to them. Thus at monster ballad concerts you hear beautiful singing; and at Bayreuth, before audiences which would consider themselves intellectually compromised if they were seen at a ballad concert, you hear singing which may be indulgently described as damnable, accompanied by instruments which have no more individual artistic character than the furniture in a steamer saloon has.

Second, that this callousness of ear and alertness of intellect among cultivated musicians is largely due to their domestic use of such a very ugly instrument as the pianoforte. A man who can tolerate Bach and Scarlatti on a modern piano can tolerate anything.

Third, that there is going to be a great awakening of the purely musical conscience by men like Arnold Dolmetsch, who sits down with a beautiful old clavichord before him, and makes a still more beautiful new one with his own hands instead of reading books by Wolzogen on Wagner. That clavichord will start just such a reform in musical instruments as William Morris started in domestic furniture. It is noteworthy, by the way, that Morris, whose ear, as I can testify from personal observation, is as good as any musician's, and whose powers as poet, artist and craftsman have made him famous, hates the pianoforte, and is evidently affected by modern music much as he is affected by early Victorian furniture. He will not go to an ordinary concert; but he will confess to a strong temptation to try his hand at making fiddles; and he has been seen at one of Dolmetsch's viol concerts apparently enjoying himself. Probably he will not make the fiddles; but Dolmetsch will make more clavichords; and as the movement gains ground, other men will rebel against the military bandmaster's ideal which governs the instrument manufacturing trade today, and will make trumpets, flutes and horns (to mention only the three most militarized victims) which will be really worth listening to for their own sound.

Fourth, you will have, concurrently with the movement in instrument-making and interacting powerfully with it, a revival of the best of the beautiful music composed before the opera came in the XVIII century and turned musicians aside from the single-hearted pursuit of beauty in their art. In a few years the musical taste of this century will strike us exactly as we are now struck by the literary taste of the century which thought Pope a greater poet than Chaucer.

Fifth, the movement will have the capacity for becoming a popular movement, a thing eternally impossible to the music of the pianistic era. [U]

SIEGFRIED'S TOD

The Pall Mall Budget, 15 November 1894

I do not wish to hurt your feelings, O respectable reader; but do you really think a man of genius would feel much more at home in your company than you would in the galleys? Your objection to a galley slave, after all, is only that he is a coarser fellow than yourself, insensible to the extremes of your points of honor in decency and morality; tolerant of sights, sounds, and deeds that are horrible to you; and callously reckless, even to bodily violence, of the delicacies and amenities which are to you the indispensable conditions of bearable human intercourse. Among such creatures, shrinking and constant apprehension would be your lot; and yet it would not be safe to shew your fear any more than if you were in a den of hyenas and jackals. I submit to you, then, as politely as such a thing may be submitted, that since Plato, Dante, Shakespear, Goethe, and men of that kind are esteemed great only because they exceed us average persons exactly as we exceed the galley slave, it follows that they must walk through our world much as through a strange country full of dangerous beasts. It must, therefore, take something like a liontamer's nerve to be a man of genius; and when the man of genius is timid—and fear is the beginning of wisdom—he must suffer much more than the ordinary coward, who can, at any rate, choose a safer pursuit than liontaming, wheras your hapless man of genius is born into the den and must stay there until he is carried out in his coffin.

Obviously, I have never seen Goethe or Shakespear or Plato: they were before my time. But I have seen Richard Wagner, who was so vehemently specialized by

Nature as a man of genius that he was totally incapable of anything ordinary. He fought with the wild beasts all his life; and when you saw him coming through a crowded cage, even when they all felt about him as the lions felt about Daniel, he had an air of having his life in his hand, as it were, and of wandering in search of his right place and his own people, if any such there might be. When he had nothing else to do he would wander away to the walls and corners, apparently in search of some door or stairway or other exit from the world, not finding which he would return disconcerted, and either sit down in desperation for a moment before starting off on a fresh exploration, or else—being a most humane man—pet one of the animals with a little conversation.

In 1883 Wagner wandered to Venice, and there at last stumbled upon that long-sought exit, since when he has not been seen by mortal man. You may well believe, then, how ghostly a sensation I had when, at Queen's Hall in London ten years later, I saw, making its guarded way through the crowd on the platform, a phantom Wagner, again, in Bunyan's phrase, "walking through the wilderness of this world." Of course I knew perfectly well that it was really Siegfried Wagner, son of Richard, and grandson of Liszt; for had I not come there expressly to see him? But, for all that, what appeared to me was the father in his habit as he lived, the old face with immortal youth in it, the set expression of endurance, the apprehensive step, and the unmistakable feeling of supernaturalness among the wild beasts.

This illusion did not wear off so soon as I expected: it came back again and again whilst Siegfried was conducting. It only broke up completely when, in response to the applause, he turned round smiling; made a series of boyish bows which had all the pleasant qualities of friendly nods; and became quite a young fellow in his earliest manhood. When he got to work again, the old look came back: there was something of the quaint gravity of an old-fashioned child: one remembered, in trying to account for it, that his father was over fifty when he was born, and his mother, though much younger than that, still a mature woman. His handling of the music, too, was very Wagnerian, more so even than that of Wagner himself; for Wagner had roots in the past which have been pulled up since before Siegfried's time. No man born in 1813, as Richard Wagner was, could have conducted Les Preludes or the Siegfried Idyll with such a complete detachment from the mechanical swing of the old dance and march measures from which their forms are descended.

We are certainly all old fogies compared to this young man, who shews not only a perfect comprehension of the poetic side of his father's and grandfather's music—a much less troubled and turbid comprehension at certain points than the composers themselves had—but an instinctive gentleness and strong patience of handling of the finest masculine quality, complemented by a sensitiveness of feeling of the finest feminine quality. He gave us the Mephisto Waltzes without a whiff of brimstone, the Flying Dutchman overture without a touch of violence. He treated the overture's atmosphere of curse and storm, its shrieking tempest and scurrying damnation, with scrupulous artistic care and seriousness, albeit with a certain youthful share in the excitement which was perhaps not far remote from amusement; but it was with the theme of love and salvation that he opened the music to its very depths. And this is the clue to him as a conductor, and to those complaints of sentimentality which have been made against him by critics who were in an unregenerate mood and missed the violence and the brimstone—missed the bitterness of death in his beatific version of Isolde's Liebestod—found heaven, in short, rather dull after London. For my part, I was touched, charmed, more than satisfied. I can appreciate Richter's grandeur of tone and breadth of style. I like the thunder of Mottl's drums, the splendid energy of his accents, and the fastidious polish and refinement of his manner. But there is a place left—and a very high one—for this old-young conductor, with his rare combination of insight and innocence, and his purity and delicacy of sentiment, not to mention complete technical knowledge of his business and a first-rate standard of orchestral execution. It is of course as impossible for him as it was for Mottl to make the immense impression here as a conductor that Richter made, not because Richter is a greater conductor than either Mottl or Siegfried, but because they have had to follow Richter, wheras Richter had only to follow Cusins, Costa, Carl Rosa, and Vianesi, by comparison with whom the pupil of Wagner could not help appearing a demi-god. Except Mr August Manns at the Crystal Palace, nobody in London at Richter's advent could possibly have known what modern orchestra handling meant. Siegfried Wagner is, at a moderate computation, about six hundred times as great a conductor as Cusins, Costa, Carl Rosa, and Vianesi rolled into one, with Dr Mackenzie, Dr Villiers Stanford, Mr Cowen, Sir Arthur Sullivan, Mr Randegger, and Signor Bevignani thrown in as makeweights; but he would certainly make no greater claim as against Richter than Michael Angelo made against Brunelleschi: "Different, but not better."

There is little more to be said. The penetrating musical criticism of our day, which nothing escapes, has pointed out already that Siegfried conducts with his left hand, and that he uses a score. I can add nothing except to say that the concert, though it left Siegfried's ability as a symphony conductor unsettled, there being nothing in sonata form in the program, placed his talent as an interpreter of tone-poetry beyond all doubt. He comprehended everything; and it was gratifying to find that though he did not take command of the army like Richter, nor head the charge like Mottl, but simply gave the band plenty of time to turn in, and trusted without misgiving or embarrassment to the rightness of his own reading, he got their very best work out of the players. They surpassed the Bayreuth orchestra not only in volume of tone—a sort of superiority which is a foregone conclusion in London, our instruments being better—but ran Bayreuth hard in point of smoothness of combination, delicacy, and precision in the execution of what may be called the stage effects of the Wagner scores. It seems to me—though in this I may be wrong, since I am only guessing by the general effect, and not by any particular instance that I can put my finger on—that more trouble has been taken at these concerts to secure accuracy in the band parts than has ever been taken before.

POSTSCRIPT, 1937. I grieve to have to add that the magic of Siegfried's first concert was not maintained at the second. The orchestra had thrown itself wholeheartedly into making a success of his first appearance; but he must have got on the wrong side of his players after this; for at the second concert they were not helpful; and the evening fell rather flat. Siegfried, it appeared, was the sort of conductor his father most abhorred: a gentleman conductor, meaning a conductor who is a gentleman first and a conductor afterwards, an order of things which ends in his not being a conductor at all. In short, a snob conductor. Our universities produced a succession of them which made the advent in London of Richter with Wagner in 1877 a revelation and a revolution. It was many many years before Siegfried came to London again to conduct a concert at the Albert Hall. He was then an elderly person, still extremely gentlemanly. His conducting was too depressing to be describable as maddening; but it made us all feel as if we were at a garden party in a cathedral town being welcomed by a highly connected curate who failed to find any tea for us. There was in the program a harmless little piece by himself: the elegant diversion of a superior person who dabbled in light composition. The farewell and fire music from Die Walküre was handled as it had never within our experience been handled before, and will, I trust, never be handled again. The trombones echoing Wotan's final *Wer meines Speeres Spitze fürchtet* sounded like an evening hymn, slow and sweet, all but *sotto voce.* The critics, I think (I was no longer one of them) got up and left after this; for the man seemed hopeless; and the politeness of the applause was deadlier than silence.

Then an incredible thing happened. The last item in the program was the overture to Die Meistersinger. The last, and, as it at once promised, the worst. Its slowness, its genteelness, made me doubt whether I was not dreaming. I felt that the overture would certainly peter out and stop from sheer inertia if he did not speed up the final section. Instead, to my amazement, he achieved the apparently impossible feat of slowing it down. And the effect was magical. The music broadened out with an effect that is beyond description. It was immense, magnificent. At the end the audience, which ten minutes before would have murdered him but for the police, was frantically recalling him to the platform again and again and again and yet again. The next we heard of him was that he was dead. It was his swan song.

HOW TO BECOME A MUSICAL CRITIC

The Scottish Musical Monthly, December 1894; reprinted in The New Music Review, October 1912

My own plan was a simple one. I joined the staff of a new daily paper as a leader writer. My exploits in this department spread such terror and confusion that my proposal to turn my attention to musical criticism was hailed with inexpressible relief, the subject being one in which lunacy is privileged. I was given a column to myself precisely as I might have been given a padded room in an asylum; and from that time up to the other day—a period of nearly seven years—I wrote every week, in that paper or another, an article under the general heading "Music," the first condition of which was, as a matter of good journalism, that it should be as attractive to the general reader, musician or non-musician, as any other section of the paper in which it appeared. Most editors do not believe that this can be done. But then most editors do not know how to edit. The late Edmund Yates, who did, believed in a good musical column as an important reinforcement to a journal. He placed a whole page of The World at the disposal of his musical critic. And the success of this page proved that in the hands of a capable writer music is quite as good a subject from the purely journalistic point of view as either painting or the drama, whilst the interest taken in it is much more general than in party politics, the stock exchange, or even the police intelligence. Let me add that Edmund Yates had no more special interest in music than he had in chemistry; for young musical critics should be warned that of all editors for their purposes, the musical-amateur editor is the very worst. Only, let me in justice add, too, that the critic who is a musical amateur and nothing else is equally objectionable.

It is quite clear that if musical criticism is to win from all papers the space and consideration allowed it in The World, the critics must be persons of considerable accomplishment. There are three main qualifications for a musical critic, besides the general qualification of good sense and knowledge of the world. He must have a cultivated taste for music; he must be a skilled writer; and he must be a practiced critic. Any of these three may be found without the others; but the complete combination is indispensable to good work. Take up any of our musical papers—those which are taken in by the organist as The Lancet is taken in by the doctor—and you will find plenty of articles written by men of unquestionable competence and even eminence as musicians. These gentlemen may write without charm because they have not served their apprenticeship to literature; but they can at all events express themselves at their comparative leisure as well as most journalists do in their feverish haste; and they can depend on the interest which can be commanded by any intelligent man who has ordinary powers of expression, and who is dealing with a subject he understands. Why, then, are they so utterly impossible as musical critics? Because they cannot criticize. They set to work like schoolmasters to prove that this is "right" and that "wrong"; they refer disputed points to school authorities who have no more authority in the republic of art than the head master of Eton has in the House of Commons; they jealously defend their pet compositions and composers against rival claims like ladies at a musical at-home; they shew no sense of the difference between a professor teaching his class how to resolve the chord of the dominant seventh and a critic standing in the presence of the whole world and its art, and submitting his analysis of the work of an artist whose authority is at least equal to his own. A man may have counterpoint at his finger ends; but if, being no more than a second-rate music teacher, he petulantly treats composers of European reputation as intrusive and ignorant pretenders who ought to be suppressed—a very different thing from genuine criticism, however unfavorable, of their works—he obviously puts himself out of the question as a member of the staff of any general newspaper or magazine.

It is not so easy to cite instances of writers who fail because, being critics, they have neither literary skill nor musical culture. A man cannot become an expert in criticism without practicing on art of some kind; and if that art is not music, then he naturally confines himself to the art he is accustomed to handle, writing about it if he has the requisite literary faculty, and if not, teaching it. As to the literary artist who is neither musician nor critic, he has every inducement to devote himself to pure literature, like Mr Stevenson or Mr Rudyard Kipling, and no temptation whatever to eke out his income by sham musical criticism. But since, for the purposes of journalism, the literary qualification is the main one—since no editor who is supplied with entertaining "copy" ever asks whether it is criticism or gossip, or cares whether its technology is a bit sounder than the sham sailing directions given in Gulliver's ship, cases are not lacking of journalists taking the post of musical critic merely because it is the only opening that presents itself, and concealing their deficiencies by plenty of descriptive reporting and scraps of news about music and musicians. If such a critic has critical and musical faculty latent in him, he will learn his business after some years; but some writers of this sort have not the faculty, and never learn.

It is worth remarking here—at least I cannot resist mentioning it—that the experienced editor has usually found the mere musician critic so useless on a paper, and the mere journalist critic so sufficient for all purposes, that the critic whose articles are at all readable by people who only read to be amused is usually suspected by his fellow journalists of being a musical impostor, a suspicion which reaches absolute certainty in the mind of his editor. When my own articles on music first began to attract some attention, the cream of the joke was supposed by many persons to be the fact that I knew nothing whatever about music. Several times it happened to me to be introduced to admirers who, on discovering from my reply to the question, "What put it into your head to write about music?" that I did so because it happened to be the art I knew most about, have turned away cruelly disappointed and disillusioned by this prosaic explanation, which seemed to rob my exploits of all their merit. Even when the hypothesis of my total ignorance became untenable, I still used occasionally to encounter people who appealed to me to candidly admit that my knowledge of music did not extend to its technicalities. They missed, I imagine, the Mesopotamianism of the sort of musical writing which parades silly little musical parsing exercises to impress the laity exactly as the performances of the learned pig impress the rustics at a fair.

A critic who does not know his business has two advantages. First, if he writes for a daily paper he can evade the point, and yet make himself useful and interesting, by collecting the latest news about forthcoming events, and the most amusing scandal about past ones. Second, his incompetence can be proved only by comparing his notice of a month ago with his notice of today, which nobody will take the trouble to do. Any man can write an imposing description of Madame Calvé, or of Slivinski, but if you turn back to his description of Miss Eames or of Sapellnikoff, you will find, if he is no critic, that the same description did duty for them also, just as it did duty, before he was born, for Catalani and Pasta, Cramer and Czerny. When he attempts to particularize the special qualities of the artists he criticizes, you will find him praising Sarasate and Paderewski for exactly those feats which their pupils, Miss Nettie Carpenter and Miss Szumowska, are able to copy to the life. Whether he is praising or blaming, he always dwells on some of the hundred points that all players and executants have in common, and misses the final ones that make all the difference between mediocrity and genius, and between one artist and another.

I know this by my own experience. Nearly twenty years ago a musician who wished to help me accepted a post as musical critic to a London paper. I wrote the criticisms; and he handed the emoluments over to me without deduction, contenting himself with the consciousness of doing generously by a young and forlorn literary adventurer, and with the honor and glory accruing from the reputed authorship of my articles. To them I owe all my knowledge of the characteristics of bad criticism. I cannot here convey an adequate impression of their demerits without overstepping the bounds of decorum. They made me miserable at the time; but I did not know even enough to understand that what was torturing me was the guilt and shame which attend ignorance and incompetence. The paper, with my assistance, died, and my sins are buried with it; but I still keep, in a safe hiding place, a set of the critical crimes I contributed to it, much as a murderer keeps the bloodstained knife under which his victim fell.* Whenever I feel that I am getting too conceited, or am conscious of crediting myself with a natural superiority to some younger brother of the craft, I take myself down by reading some of that old stuff—though indeed the bare thought of it is generally sufficient. And yet neither in literary ability nor musical knowledge was I unpardonably deficient at that time. I should have been a very decent critic for my age, if only I had known how to criticize. Not knowing that, however, my musical knowledge and power of literary expression made me much more noxious than if I had been a mere newsman in music and a phrasemonger in journalism. When I broke out again, about ten years later, I had graduated as a critic, as a writer, and as a citizen (a most important item) by constant work as an author, a critic of books, pictures, and politics, a public speaker, and a social reformer, including the function of the wirepuller and committee man, as well as of the theorist and Utopian. All this had nothing to do with music; yet, in my musical criticism, it made all the difference between an execrable amateur and a reasonably competent workman. I was enormously helped as a critic by my economical studies and my political practice, which gave me an invaluable comprehension of the commercial conditions to which art is subject. It is an important part of a critic's business to agitate for musical reforms; and unless he knows what the reforms will cost, and whether they are worth that cost, and who will have to pay the bill, and a dozen other cognate matters not usually included in treatises on harmony, he will not make any effective impression on

* It is from this set of "critical crimes," carefully preserved by Shaw for three-quarters of a century, and now in his archive in the British Library, that The Hornet materials reprinted in the present edition are drawn.

the people with whom the initiative rests—indeed he will not know who they are. Even his artistic verdicts will often be aimed at the wrong person. A manager or an artist cannot be judged fairly by any critic who does not understand the economic bearings of profits and salaries. It is one thing to set up an ideal of perfection and complain as long as it is not reached; but to blame individuals for not reaching it when it is economically unattainable, instead of blaming the conditions which make it unattainable; or to blame the wrong person—for instance, to blame the artist when the fault is the manager's, or the manager when the fault is the public's—is to destroy half your influence as a critic. All the counterpoint or literary brilliancy in the world will not save a critic from blunders of this kind, unless he understands the economics of art.

I need say no more as to the accomplishments of a musical critic, because I have already brought myself face to face with an economic difficulty in my own path. The emoluments of a musical critic are not large. Newspaper proprietors offer men from a pound a week to five pounds a week for musical criticism, the latter figure being very exceptional, and involving the delivery of a couple of thousand words of extra brilliant copy every week. And, except in the dead season, the critic must spend most of his afternoons and evenings, from three to midnight, in concert rooms or in the opera house. I need hardly say that it is about as feasible to obtain the services of a fully-qualified musical critic on these terms as it would be to obtain a pound of fresh strawberries every day from January to December for five shillings a week. Consequently, to all the qualifications I have already suggested, I must insist on this further one—an independent income, and sufficient belief in the value of musical criticism to sustain you in doing it for its own sake whilst its pecuniary profits are enjoyed by others. And since this condition is so improbable in any given case as to take my subject completely out of the range of the practicable, I may as well stop preaching, since my sermon ends, as all such sermons do, in a demonstration that our economic system fails miserably to provide the requisite incentive to the production of first-rate work.

HERMANN LEVI

Unsigned sub-leader in The Daily Chronicle, 29 April 1895

[U] The exploits of Herr Levi, the famous Munich orchestral conductor, are not reassuring to English concert-goers, accustomed as they are to take our native conducting on trust as a first-rate article. Herr Levi is one of the Bayreuth conductors. If there is one thing that the humble outsider, gleaning his notions from common rumor and from the musical critics, has hitherto supposed better established than another, it is that the Bayreuth orchestra is a wonder far beyond English resources, the inference being that if our conductors could only get such an instrument to play on, the result would cause the esthetic sense of our nation to reel with ecstasy. But how is it, then, that the Bayreuth conductors, when they come to England and feel the London orchestra under their hands for the first time, exhibit a sort of intoxication like that of a pianist who, after having had to make the best of poor and cheap instruments all his life, is suddenly set down to a Steinway or Erard concert grand? Even Richter, whose first experiences here came at a time when things, orchestrally speaking, were admittedly very bad with us, appears to have felt this; for Herr Levi, who has expressed his astonishment and delight freely to his interviewers, lets out the little secret that Richter prepared him for a rare treat; and Herr Felix Mottl certainly owed some of the magnificent efficiency which he shewed at his first concert here to the excitement of having under his command an orchestra for the splendor of which his Bayreuth experience had not in the least prepared him.

Still, neither Richter nor Mottl has confessed himself so openly and so oddly as Herr Levi. He evidently felt that his remarks to the interviewers would not carry conviction, since a stranger in a foreign land will say anything to an interviewer. So he reserved the real compliment to our resources for the moment of action on the concert platform. The announcement of Beethoven's Seventh Symphony as the chief item in the program was not at first very tempting, because Richter, who is rather addicted to endless repetitions of his old successes, has worn that work threadbare. But the performance under Levi proved full of surprises. The *coda* of the first movement, the magic which has eluded so many conductors, almost took away the breath of the audience by its sudden and surprising realization, apparently without the slightest preoccupation or effort; and whilst the Beethoven devotees were still staring reverently at the conductor who had wrought the miracle, he coolly stopped beating, and comfortably contemplated the band doing it *by themselves*, with the air of a modest amateur in the half-crown seats. In the last movement, the exhilarating gallop of which has been urged along by all the other Wagnerian conductors with the excitement of chariot racers, Herr Levi got the movement into its stride in two bars, and then, putting down his stick, proceeded to blow his nose, rub his hands, and otherwise convey to the audience that he was only the fly on the wheel of the English band. Of course, the English band, knowing its master all the better for his consummate knowledge of when he was wanted and when he was not, obeyed the *bâton* when it came into play again, as if every nerve in the orchestra were in direct communication with his brain. Even the Tannhäuser overture, so hackneyed by this time that one almost longs for William Tell by way of novelty, was a revelation; the cadence to the song of Venus, and the final section of The Pilgrims' March, with the new reading for the drums, produced an effect never heard here before.

These repeated triumphs of the Bayreuth conductors give fresh point to Wagner's own definition of the conductor's function, simple as Columbus's solution of the egg problem. He says nothing about parsing scores, or doing without them, or being able to play every instrument in the orchestra, or giving every man his cue (and letting everyone in the room see you do it): according to him, the whole duty of the conductor is simply "to give the right time to the band." Herr Levi, it appears, knows so perfectly where this function stops, that when the band has got the right time from him, he puts down his stick until the next modification of speed is due. It seems simple; but our own conductors do not seem to find it so. Levi bids fair, in some ways, to become the most popular of all the famous conductors brought out by Mr Schulz-Curtius. Richter's bulk and grandeur, Mottl's concentrated force and finesse, and Siegfried Wagner's poetic charm were all fascinating, but they have not in any way forestalled the dry enthusiasm, the unerring artistic cunning, the wiry activity, the humorous sanity and tough, healthy, workmanlike delight in doing the thing with a sure hand as well as it can be done, of this amiably crafty old gentleman, who, after two rehearsals, plays with our rather stiff-necked London orchestra as a potter plays with his clay.

But now comes the home question, to which all these compliments to foreign conductors are only by way of preamble. If we admittedly produce the best band in the world, why in the name of British patriotism do we produce the worst conductors in the world? Why have we to send to Vienna, to Karlsruhe, to Munich, for men able to shew us the value of the orchestra we have produced; and why is it that when they come, the first effect of their achievements is to convict all our own conductors of being mere amateurs, and appallingly bad amateurs at their worst? No one with any commonsense will accept the crude solution that the Englishman is a worse musician or a less resolute and resourceful leader than the German or the Jew. There is no evidence to shew that any of the Wagnerian conductors is as highly gifted musically as Professor Stanford; and Sir Alexander Mackenzie is clearly not inferior to, say, Siegfried Wagner, in nerve and physical energy. The real difference, of course, is the difference of education. The German musician gets soaked in music from his childhood—not street-piano music, nor Margate Pier music, nor Jackson in F, but in the masterpieces of Beethoven and the music dramas of Wagner; whilst the musical Englishman can only thumb out "arrangements" on a cheap piano, and save his shillings, if he is within reach of London, Manchester, or Glasgow, to go once or twice a year and hear a symphony conducted either by a German expert or an English novice, or perhaps to the Royal Italian Opera to hear Gounod's Faust conducted by Signor Bevignani. Occasionally the provinces are regaled with a "Festival," the proceeds of which, instead of being devoted to the establishment of permanent artistic activities in our wretchedly dull and philistine provincial towns, are coolly appropriated by the hospitals on the ground that the Festival was originally only a "charity sermon" with a special anthem.

Mottl says of the art of conducting that it cannot be learnt—that you step to the desk, and if you can do it, you do it. But when the Englishman steps to the desk he does *not* do it—cannot do it. How could he when the whole *technique* and tradition of the orchestra is as strange to him, no matter how splendid his musical endowment may be, as [ice] skating is to a South Sea Islander? There are plenty of competent men to be found in the orchestras of our theatres and music halls, accompanying comic singers, arranging music for pantomimes and melodramas, pulling through comic operas in the provinces with bands of from two to ten incompetent performers, or presiding proudly during the *entr'acte* in a London theatre over a waltz or Reminiscences of Sullivan. But they are only competent at the work to which they have served their apprenticeship. Give them the same practice and training in the symphonies of Beethoven and the music dramas of Wagner, and there will be no need to import conductors. The whole subject is one which should be taken into consideration by local authorities. Why we should have so deep a sense of the duty of shewing the people casts from the antique, and putting bookshelves loaded with poetry within their reach, and yet never dream of giving them an opportunity of hearing the masterpieces of music, is not apparent. The brass band for the parks, though an excellent institution, no more meets the difficulty than the shop windows of the Haymarket and Bond-street supply the need of a National Gallery. Every town corporation of any importance in the country ought to negotiate with Mr Schulz-Curtius, or Herr Richter, or Mr Henschel, or Sir Charles Hallé, or Mr August Manns for one or two first-rate symphony concerts in each year, to serve as a standard of excellence to a local orchestra, which should be founded as part of the municipal school of art, and supplied with instruments at the public expense. We should then very soon begin to grow our own conductors, instead of having to go up the Rhine for them.[U]

BEETHOVEN'S EIGHTH SYMPHONY

Unsigned sub-leader in The Daily Chronicle, 6 November 1895

In the last instalment of Mr Ashton Ellis's translation of the prose works of Richard Wagner occurs a well-known story about the third movement of Beethoven's Eighth Symphony. Says Wagner:

> I once was in Mendelssohn's company at a performance of this symphony in Dresden, conducted by the now deceased Kapellmeister Reissiger, and told him how I had—as I believed—arranged for its right performance by Reissiger, since he had promised open-eyed to take the trio of the minuet slower than of wont. Mendelssohn quite agreed with me. We listened. The third movement began, and I was horrified to hear the old familiar Laendler tempo once again. Before I could express my wrath, Mendelssohn was rocking his head in pleased approval, and smiling to me: "Thats capital! Bravo!" So I fell from horror into stupefaction. Mendelssohn's callousness towards this curious artistic *contretemps* inspired me with very natural doubts as to whether the thing presented any difference at all to him. I fancied I was peering into a veritable abyss of superficiality—an utter void.

A quarter of a century ago, when this was written, and for long enough after it, every conductor in England used to murder the Eighth Symphony exactly as Reissiger murdered it; and every violoncellist in the

Philharmonic orchestra used to dread the trio of the third movement. It was not likely that we were going to alter our ways at the suggestion of a man blasphemous enough to consider the composer of Elijah superficial, [and] who produced abominably cacophonous music like that of Tannhäuser. For we little thought then that before the century was over the man who thought Mendelssohn superior to Wagner would enjoy about as much authority in musical criticism as a literary critic who should assume that Longfellow was obviously greater than Shakespear, still less that on the wettest day in winter, with the stalls at 15s., St James's Hall could be sold out on the announcement of an orchestral program three-fifths Wagner and the rest Beethoven and Berlioz, without even an allusion to Mendelssohn's Italian Symphony or Spohr's Consecration of Sound, which we used to call The Power of Sound because consecration was too metaphysical to seem good sense to us. That happened last Monday, and was by no means a remarkable or unprecedented event. It is mentioned here solely because the concert began with that very Eighth Symphony whereby the Mendelssohn tale hangs.

Last year, it will be remembered, Siegfried Wagner visited us for the first time, and was handsomely received. But on his second visit he conducted the Eighth Symphony and the overture to Der Freischütz—also much mentioned in the Essay on Conducting quoted above—and conducted them, of course, "*à la* Wagner" as best he could. Unhappily this time the band was in a bad temper; and the youthful conductor, staggering under the weight of a great name, yet had the hardihood to introduce himself as a composer by a symphonic poem which, though certainly a good deal better than his father used to turn out at his age, might have been replaced with great advantage by the Italian Symphony. The result was that, though Richter sat in the front row and applauded demonstratively, especially after the *allegretto* of the Eighth Symphony, the press turned and rent poor Siegfried; so that for a moment it seemed as though he would share the fate of the son of Mozart, and be crushed by a name to which no mere mortal could live up. The fact is, however, that Siegfried scored many charming points both in the symphony and the overture, and seems to need nothing but the tact and authority which a very young man necessarily lacks to hold his own in London, where, to confess the truth, we have not only put up with, *faute de mieux*, but wantonly glorified and bragged of much worse conductors than the one who stands in Siegfried's shoes.

We are still, with all our crowding to hear Richter and Mottl, a horribly unmusical city. You can tell this by our Gargantuan musical digestion. When a Theatre Royal performs nightly a favorite *comédietta*, a celebrated sensational drama, a Shakespearean tragedy, a grand Christmas pantomime, and a screaming farce to wind up with, you do not conclude that the taste for dramatic literature is in a flourishing condition in that town: quite the contrary. But what then must we say of the program of the last Richter concert? Let us premise that a single Beethoven symphony is quite as full a meal as any real musician can digest at one sitting. Now for the horrible particulars. The Eighth Symphony, Berlioz's King Lear overture, the Tannhäuser overture with the Venusberg bacchanal, the first act of Die Walküre from the exit of Hunding to the end, and, by way of a liqueur at the end, the Ride of the Valkyries. Will future ages be able to credit such monstrous, undiscriminating gorging and gormandizing? Even the Ninth Symphony is not enough for one concert—an overture and a concerto, or perhaps Schubert's Unfinished Symphony, with Adelaide sandwiched between, must be thrown in to give the audience value for its money. This means, of course, that the British amateur does not follow the development of a symphony at all: he only listens for a pretty bit here and there, like a child picking raisins out of a stodgy cake. How schoolboyish he is can be seen by his love of the Ride of the Valkyries and the Venusberg orgy, which have no business in a concert room at all. Indeed, the popularity of the Seventh Symphony, which Richter repeats *ad nauseam*, is evidently due to the galloping rhythm of the first movement, and the stamping, racing vigor of the last, not to mention the simple hymn-tune form of the pretty *allegretto*. In all subtler respects the Eighth is better, with its immense cheerfulness and exquisite playfulness, its perfect candor and naturalness, its filaments of heavenly melody suddenly streaming up from the mass of sound, and flying away cloudlike, and the cunning harmonic coquetry with which the irresistibly high-spirited themes, after innumerable feints and tantalizing invitations and promises, suddenly come at you round the most unexpected corners, and sweep you away with a delightful burst of joyous energy. The man who, being accessible to all this, asks for more—and such a lot more—or even supposes himself capable of entertaining it, is an inconceivable person.

Richter, by his handling of the Eighth Symphony, again shewed himself a consummate Beethoven conductor. There was no Reissiger-Mendelssohn mistake about the trio, no confusion of the movement "in the time of a minuet" (as danced) with the old brisk Haydn Symphony minuet, which is such a very different thing. It goes without saying that the unforgetable second theme of the last movement—perhaps the most ravishing of those aforesaid filaments of melody—was divine; but what unhappily does not go without saying in this unhappy country was the masterly phrasing of the chain of passages which follows it. It is at such points that the connoisseur in finely intelligent execution recognizes the master. Yet it now turns out, as was perhaps inevitable, that the perfect Beethoven conductor, even when taught by Wagner—though, depend on it, a conductor like Richter is nobody's pupil but his own—cannot also be the perfect Wagner conductor. Anyone who has heard Mottl conduct Wagner has found out that Richter conducts him like a drill sergeant. The discipline is perfect, and the tone fine in quality and majestic in volume; but listen to the ruthless rigidity of the *tempo* and the stiffening of the melodies! What clarinet player, giving us the song of Venus in the Tannhäuser overture, would care to be pulled up short in his cadence by Richter after being coaxed into caressing the audience with it by Mottl? And in Die Walküre, when the woe-devoted Siegmund sits by the fire crooning dreamily to the warm glow, until, as it dies out, he compares it to the fire without light in his own heart, would Mottl be capable of going straight on from the light to the darkness without the faintest inflection of the *tempo*, even under the influence of the paralyzing Philistinism of Mr Edward Lloyd, who, finding the deep gloom of the low notes to which the words *Tief in des Busens Berge* are set uncomfortably for his voice, cheerfully sings them an octave higher, a proceeding to which the attention of the Recording Angel has probably been very seriously called by Wagner? And yet Mottl can do comparatively nothing with Beethoven: there Richter has his revenge. Levi, who was good at both, has paid for his ambidexterity with his reason, like Faccio. Let us wish him a speedy recovery and a trip to England to confirm it. The only wonder is that our inhumanly long programs have not by this time driven us all mad, as they would if we really knew how to listen to them.

A STATE CONCERT—NEW STYLE

The Daily Chronicle, 14 November 1895

[U] The seventh annual musical display by the London Board Schools, at Queen's Hall yesterday afternoon, would have been altogether commendable but for the element of competition introduced by the Challenge Medallion. Only six school choirs had been selected to compete; but a glance at the addresses of the schools and at the dress and physique of the children was sufficient to shew that nothing but an elaborate and odious system of handicapping could have made the competition even approximately fair. It soon became apparent that the medallion must go either to the Fleet Road School in Hampstead, or the Lyndhurst Grove School in Camberwell, both of them starting with considerable advantages in the way of home polish on their raw material. As between these two schools no satisfactory decision was possible. Both choirs were wonderfully steady and accurate, vanquishing the sightreading test with just one moment of uncertainty apiece. The Lyndhurst Grove choir was larger, better balanced in voices and luckier in having in its ranks one or two of those exceptionally gifted children whose sense of pitch enables them to read music from almost any notation without doubt or hesitation, and who are, therefore, invaluable to a choirmaster as leaders in the part-singing. Their teacher, Mr A. Everett, very cleverly chose for his showpiece Schubert's The Lord is my Shepherd, a composition calculated to make the most of the fine tone which was the strong point of his choir; for, being very slow, it could easily be sung with great care and without flurry; and being very beautiful, it was sure to bias the judges—Sir John Stainer and Mr McNaught—who are musicians but not critics.

The Fleet Road choir, smaller and less fortunately constituted, was a little inferior in mass and balance of tone, though not in quality, but, on the other hand, it was more spontaneous and expressive; it shewed much greater variety of excellence; its showpiece was not all on one string; in the test piece—Webbe's When winds breathe soft—it greatly surpassed its competitor in crispness of pronunciation and vivacity of execution; above all, its artistic spirit was wonderful; every individual child in it was swaying with enthusiasm as it sang. But the musician-examiners of course gave the medallion to the choir which had sung Schubert's The Lord is my Shepherd for them; and Mr Harris, the Fleet Road master, evidently an excellent teacher and a genuine artist, had to be content with second place. The audience felt, and felt rightly, that this was an injustice; but the injustice would only have been shifted by slighting Mr Everett instead.

Even if both choirs had been declared equally entitled to the medallion, there would have been something ungenerous in the implied disparagement to the other choirmasters, some of whom had done wonders with rather rough material. For example, Mr T. H. Griffiths brought from the Ancona Road School, at Plumstead, a little band of child singers, who were obviously very happy over their work. They got through the reading test well; they sang the vigorous second section of When winds breathe soft much more spiritedly and smartly than any of the rest; and they were the only competitors who produced a really stimulating *fortissimo*, Mr Griffiths evidently thinking—and justifying his opinion by excellent results—that it is possible to sacrifice too much to an ideal delicacy and purity of tone which is certainly not natural to young Plumstead, however dear it may be to Sir John Stainer.

Mr R. McIvor, who cultivates the native woodnotes wild of the children of Buckingham Terrace, North Kensington, has also rather stubborn material to work up, the alto voice of that region being astonishingly strong and not a little coarse. North Kensington was nimble and impetuous at the florid passages, and gave a good account of a hunting song which was in many ways more difficult than The Lord is my Shepherd. Again, Mr Bishop, with a choir of boys from the Tower Hamlets division (why do the girls not sing there?), had no chance of the medallion; but his work was good enough to make one feel what a pity it was that there was any medallion to humiliate his boys with. The same remark applies to Mr H. Smith's choir from Highbury Vale, though it must be confessed that Mr Smith's phrasing of The Minstrel Boy was elaborately unnatural.

On the whole, it was impossible not to feel how thoroughly Sir John Stainer would have had the public with him if, instead of delivering the expected award, he had risen and said: "Gentlemen of the London School Board, the annual concert of your and our children is not a football match; and the applause of the audience will serve better than any score that Mr McNaught and I can keep." It is time, by the way, that the applause of the audience—unusually discriminating applause, be it noted—should be supplemented by careful criticism from the Press. Why should newspapers send their musical critics to write useless notices of the five thousandth repetition of Home, Sweet Home, by Madame Patti, at a purely commercial concert, whilst ignoring the music that is paid for daily by public money, and only submitted to public judgment once a twelvemonth?

This year for the first time the program included a

feat which shewed real technical knowledge on the part of the children. An exercise in three-part harmony was played on the organ note by note: the bass first, then the alto, then the treble; and the children wrote the notes down as they were sounded in the Tonic Sol-fa notation. They then sang the exercise from their notation report with perfect success. Beethoven-street School rose to its title to the extent of sending a string band, and, though the violins used were not exactly Strads, the peculiar vigor and fulness of tone which characterize the strings in an English orchestra were embryonically but unmistakably recognizable in the performance.

Of the chin music which followed the performance of the children it is eminently possible to speak too highly. If the Board cannot see the advisability of selecting the mouthpieces of their musical enthusiasm from among those members who are not opposed to the provision of pianofortes in Board Schools, they might at least put forward their best platform speakers. Of these Lord Londonderry can hardly be considered a first-rate sample. His statement that everything had been rendered that day "with the greatest possible perfection," and his allusion to competitions "whereby the public are capable of judging the results," were neither critically nor oratorically happy. Mr Roston Bourke, not content with having composed a sightreading test so abominably and unscannably unsymmetrical that all the children whose metrical sense was intact stumbled at the fourth bar—for which it is to be hoped that Sir John Stainer gave them a good mark—proceeded to deliver a speech in which he portentously announced that Mr McNaught had been "painted in oils." The effect of this having fallen short of that expected by the orator, he paused, and added—"and framed, of course," which naturally brought down the house.

Mr Diggle, in the character of a man profoundly

moved by the concord of sweet sounds, rescued the proceedings from the adult fatuity which had followed the silencing of the children; but the audience did not recover their spirits until they were roused by Sir John Gorst. His brief but significant speech, evidently a carefully premeditated declaration of the educational policy of the most Progressive supporters of the Government, made a startling impression, and was received with resignation by Mr Diggle, and with exultant shouts by Mr Diggle's foes. But Sir John Gorst and his policy are not to the present purpose, which is a purely musical one. Nobody who was present at the competition will ever vote for the anti-piano party at a School Board election again—except perhaps out of resentment against the fourth bar of the sightreading test by Mr Roston Bourke, who is unhappily a progressive. The Board should really insist on the elected representative being kept as distinct from the technical expert, in music as in other matters. Next year the competition should be, not a competition, but a concert; the sightreading test should be composed by a musician, and its difficulties should be metrical ingenuities and not metrical blunders; and whilst Sir John Stainer and Mr McNaught should still carefully watch the performance and discuss it with the teachers afterwards, anything in the nature of an award of merit should be left to the audience and to the Press.[U]

BASSETTO AT BAYREUTH

The Star, 22–25 July 1896; signed "C. di B."

I

19 July.—There are moments when Providence takes a joke seriously by way of restraining our sense of humor.

We all know (or ought to know) the moment near the close of Das Rheingold, when, the ring being disposed of to the giants, and Freia and her apples of eternal youth restored to the gods, Donner, mounting the rock, calls the clouds to him, and, when their black legions, crowding about him, have hidden him in their mists, swings his hammer, splits them with a thousand blinding ribbons of lightning, and reveals the skiey towers of Valhall, with Froh's rainbow bridge spanning the valley to the gate of the wonderful castle—the home of the gods. The effect of this on the stage of the Wagner Theatre is magnificent, but the management, not content to wait for this, took advantage of the Bayreuth custom of summoning the audience by sound of trumpet, to blare out Donner's call to the real heavens before the performance began. What was the result? No sooner was the call sent echoing from hill to hill than the cloudless sky darkened, and the trombones were answered by a distant roll of thunder. I was up in the pine woods at the time, discussing high themes with the brilliant editor* of a paper which I will disguise as the D***y Chr*****e. He had persisted in whistling I dreamt that I dwelt in marble halls all the way from Victoria to Nuremberg (the turbulent part of the Channel excepted), and I was trying to get him off that subject when I heard the brazen voices sending forth their

He da! He da!
Duftig Gedünst
Donner ruft euch zu Heer.

The thunder—the real thunder—answered, and we sprang up from our carpet of scented pine needles and made for the theatre precipitately. Just as we reached it

* H. W. Massingham, of the Daily Chronicle.

the rain came down in torrents. Consequently the entry of the audience to the first performance, usually a gay, busy, eager, hopeful function, was this time a damp scuttle. Nearly every seat in the house was filled a quarter of an hour before the performance began.

Das Rheingold, being only the prologue to the colossal music-drama of The Niblung's Ring, which takes three nights to perform, is not divided into acts, and therefore compels the audience to sit for about two hours and a half without a rest. I sat it out without turning a hair; and my companion did not whistle a single bar during the hundred and fifty minutes; but some of the audience found their powers of endurance somewhat strained. One lady fainted, and her removal, with the curious flash of bright daylight into the dark theatre and across the lurid picture of Nibelheim as the door was opened to let her out, made an unwelcome disturbance.

The performance was, on the whole, an excellent one. Its weakest point was Perron's Wotan, a futile impersonation. The orchestra, although it was too good, as orchestras go, to be complained of, was very far from being up to the superlative standard of perfect preparedness, smoothness, and accuracy of execution expected at Bayreuth. We in London have taught Richter to depend too much on his reputation, and on his power of pulling a performance through on the inspiration of the moment. The result of our instruction is now apparent. The effect of the Das Rheingold score was not the Bayreuth effect, but the London effect: that is, it sounded like a clever reading of the band parts at sight by very smart players, instead of an utterance by a corps of devotees, saturated with the spirit of the work, and in complete possession of its details. The strings were poor; the effects were not always well calculated—for instance, the theme of the magic helmet was hardly heard at first; and in the prelude, the great booming pedal note—the mighty ground tone of the Rhine—was surreptitiously helped out, certainly with excellent effect, by the organ.

The stage management is—I can no longer conceal it—radically bad at all the points where ordinary amateur intelligence, devotedly exercised, is not sufficient to find out the right way. The plain truth is that Madame Wagner does not know what acting can and cannot do, or how much the imagination of the audience will do when the situation goes beyond the resources of acting. Over and over again, when overwhelming crises of emotion are reached—crises which occur in the minds of the spectators as they follow the drama, and which, though they are supported with the most powerful sympathy by the orchestra, are not provoked by any particular action of the figures on the stage, and are utterly beyond expression by any such means—we find the Bayreuth artists making the most violent demonstrations, striking the most overcharged attitudes, and attempting to look ineffable things at the very moment, in short, when the slightest betrayal of any share on their part in the excitement of the audience must mar the whole effect—the moment, consequently, when a skilled actor allows the play itself, helped by the imagination of the spectators, to do all the work. This is the whole secret of the amateurishness of Bayreuth. Madame Wagner is beyond question a very clever lady, and a most able woman of business; but she knows so little how dramatic effects are produced technically that at the very points where her husband's genius and the emotions to which it appealed are producing their most searching effects she assumes that no effect will be produced at all if the *prima donna* does not exhibit the most demonstrative consciousness of it. I call this amateurish, but from the Bayreuth point of view it is even worse than amateurish: it is heretical, being the most foolish characteristic of Italian operatic acting. I do not say that Wagner himself was free from it. Though his tendency always seemed to me to be to err in the direction of taking too much of the work for the music—that is, for himself—and leaving too little to the actor, who is often instructed to stand motionless for long periods whilst the orchestra conveys, often with the most extraordinary vividness, not only how he feels, but what he is thinking about, yet it may be that the vehemence of Wagner's imagination, and the success with which he had himself enlarged the limits of forcible expression by mechanical means in the orchestra, may have led him occasionally to demand superhuman demonstrations from his actors. But I rather doubt this in view of the care with which his scores, with all their wealth of instrumentation, are contrived so as not to overwhelm the singer. He was perhaps the most practical of all the great composers, and the last man in the world, apparently, to demand impossibilities. At all events, whether the fault lies with the Wagner tradition or Madame Wagner's present supervision, there can be no doubt of the fact that a stage manager who understands acting—if the world can produce so unusual a phenomenon—is badly wanted at Bayreuth.

There is a good deal to be done, too, in the way of getting rid of mere old-fashionedness. Probably it is not possible at present to convince a German *prima donna* that Mrs Leo Hunter was not thoroughly right and ladylike in wearing a modish gown along with her helmet when she impersonated Minerva. I do not for one moment dare to suggest that the Rhine maidens should take a hint from our "living pictures," and dress like Rhine maidens. The world is not decent enough for that yet. But is it necessary for the three ladies to go to the other extreme and swim about in muslin *fichus* and teagowns? They gave me a strong impression that they had forgotten their gloves and hats; and even a parasol to save their complexions when the sunlight came shimmering down through the water on the Rhinegold would hardly have been out of keeping with their costumes. Happily, their movements were fairly mermaidenly. The old fire escape machinery of 1876 has been discarded; and the three are now suspended from above, like Mlle Enea,* or Miss Kate Rorke in Mr Buchanan's last play,† with plausible and graceful results.

Another antiquated stage trick which Bayreuth clings to is that of attitudinizing on the stage with a corner of your mantle held between your fingers, in the manner of the antique Niobe. But wheras Niobe held up her mantle to screen herself and her children from the arrows of Apollo, the Bayreuth *prima donna* does it solely to display her drapery in the German historico-classical manner, with unspeakably ridiculous and dowdy effect.

One more disparagement. In 1876 the use of jets and clouds of steam for stage effects was a novelty. We all remember how it was transferred from the Bayreuth stage to the Lyceum by Sir Henry Irving in the late W. G. Wills's version of Faust. But it cannot be denied that from the very first it carried with it a prosaic flavor of washing day, totally irreconcilable with the magical strangeness of the wishing cap or *tarnhelm.* It is effective only for one purpose—that of producing an illusion of a cloud of fire when a powerful light is turned upon it; and to that use, I suggest, it cannot be too strictly limited.

For the rest, I have nothing but praise, although there certainly was a Rhinedaughter whose top note was

* An equestrienne in variety and pantomime billed as The Flying Fairy.

† The Wanderer from Venus; or, Twenty-four Hours with an Angel, by Robert Buchanan and Charles Marlowe, which Shaw had reviewed in the Saturday Review on 13 June 1896.

distressingly flat. The singing, on the whole, was much better than I expected it to be. The Germans are evidently becoming conscious that there are in the world de Reszkes and other people who have demonstrated that Wagner's music can be sung beautifully, and that even a basso should not deliver himself as if the Bayreuth audience were a Hyde Park demonstration. I admit, of course, that Friedrichs, as Alberich, occasionally howled and shouted in the old Wagnerian style; but he also sang at times—even at most times—and sang not badly either. The veteran Vogl, who played Loge at Bayreuth twenty years ago, played it again last Sunday with a vocal charm which surpassed the most sanguine expectations. Both he and Friedrichs acted with great spirit and intelligence. Burgstaller, who is to play Siegfried presently, took the small part of Froh, and made his mark in it by a certain radiant sensitiveness and enthusiasm which became him very well. Frau Schumann-Heink, who will be remembered in London as the contralto of the Munich company brought over by the late Sir Augustus Harris, was magnificent as Erda. Calvé herself could not have surpassed her in dramatic power and beauty, and her voice was at its best. Marie Brema, the only English member of the cast, was Fricka, never a very popular goddess, her modern name being Mrs Grundy. Miss Brema sang very well and shewed no diminution of her old energy; but she devotedly does (and occasionally overdoes) what she is told to do by Madame Wagner, besides wearing what she is told to wear. No human *prima donna* could make a perfect success under these conditions, and I urge Miss Brema, whose ability is of a very high order, to take her fate into her own hands for the future. Acting is her own business: it is not Madame Wagner's; and the sooner that is realized, the better for Bayreuth. The rest of the cast was adequate—Breuer as Mime perhaps a trifle more than that.

You shall hear further from me presently. My friend the editor has now got I dreamt that I dwelt mixed up with the Rhinedaughters' *trio.* The combination of Balfe and Wagner is novel, and somewhat trying at first, but it grows upon one with use.

P.S.—The first act of Die Walküre has just been rescued from a *succès de sommeil* by the perennial and passionate Sucher, who suddenly broke into one of her triumphs as Sieglinde. Gerhäuser, as Siegmund, made up as a stout middleaged gentleman in sheepskins and a red beard, has been as null and wooden as anybody could desire. With the assistance of Wachter as Hunding, he all but put us asleep in the first half of the scene. In pulling the sword from the tree he was much less exciting than an English vestryman taking his hat from a peg. But Sucher carried everything before her. She could not transfigure Gerhäuser, but she made us forget him and remember only the Siegmund of Wagner's poem—that poor devil of a hero to whose moment of happiness our hearts all go out. Bravo Rosa!

II

20 JULY.—Die Walküre is endured by the average man because it contains four scenes for which he would sit out a Scotch sermon, or even a House of Commons debate. These are the love duet in the first act, Brynhild's announcement to Siegmund of his approaching death in the second, the ride of the Valkyries and the fire charm in the third. For them the ordinary play-goer endures hours of Wotan, with Christopher Sly's prayer in his heart—"Would twere over!"* Now I am one of those elect souls who are deeply moved by Wotan. I grant you that as a longwinded, one-eyed gentleman

* Shakespear's The Taming of the Shrew, Act I, Scene 1 (Would 'twere done.)

backing a certain champion in a fight, and letting himself be henpecked out of his fancy because his wife objects to the moral character of the champion, he is a dreary person indeed, and most ungodlike. But to those who have seen on the greater stage of the world how Religion has fortified itself by an alliance with Law and Order and Morals and Propriety; how it has gained temporal power at the cost of that eye which is not the eye to the main chance; how it has become so entangled in these alliances and bargains that when new and higher forces are born of its holiest wisdom it is driven first to use its authority over them to make them war against Truth as dangerous, and Love as an unnatural vice, and then when they defy its authority, in spite of that filial love, to silence them in sleep (since they cannot be killed), and surround their couch with juggling fires to scare away mankind from waking them—to those who have seen all that, there is nothing trivial, nothing tedious in Die Walküre.

Wotan's one eye is not ridiculous; his spear, the symbol of his temporal power, with the runes and bargains engraved on its shaft, is no mere stage property; his wife Fricka, shuddering with horror and wrath at her broken moral laws, and forcing him to abandon his love-child to the "justice" of her worshiper, is no mere henpecking Mrs Caudle*; and when Brynhild, the child of his wisdom, rebels against the command which Fricka has forced from him, and is put to sleep on the mountain peak, surrounded by the fires of Loge, there is more in it than the somewhat fifth-of-Novembery pyrotechnics—mostly squibs and steam—of the Bayreuth stage machinist. You, Mr Star Editor, familiar as you are with the tragedy of Religion married (for money) to the State; with a people frightened away from truth and knowledge

* Douglas Jerrold's Mrs Caudle's Curtain Lectures (1846).

by a display of brimstone that can scorch no hand that is fearlessly thrust into it; and with other matters which are no doubt mentioned in your political columns—you would understand Die Walküre well enough. And in a dim way, many of the people who have no general ideas, and who yawn and fidget when Wotan is at the seven hundred and seventyseventh bar of one of his disquisitions, with no sign of any intention of stopping, do perceive that something of public importance is going on and must be put up with. They may not exactly see how or why the god finds that all the power he has built up has only enslaved himself—still less do they understand the apparent contradiction of his secret hope and longing for his own downfall and destruction even whilst he is working with all his might to defend himself and make Valhall impregnable and eternal; but they see his trouble; and, after all, it is trouble that moves us to sympathy, and not the explanation of the trouble.

At the same time let me confess that Die Walküre at full length, beginning at four and ending at half-past nine, and involving three hours and a half of concentrated attention, is hard work for a critic, and a considerable test of the endurance of an amateur, except when the performers are sufficiently gifted to make you forget everything but the drama. The Bayreuth artists cannot all do this; in fact, some of them rather excel in the art of making five minutes seem like twenty. In Die Walküre the all-important performer is Wotan; and, as I hinted in my last communication, Perron is not the ideal Wotan. He is a tall but awkward and straddling person, and is perhaps as clever in private life as many other people who appear stupid on the stage. His acting consists of striking a graceless attitude and holding on to it until the fear of cramp obliges him to let go. Why then, you will ask, was he selected for such a part on such an occasion? Well, simply because he has an excellent voice, of which he takes commendable care. From its low G to its top F it comes without effort, is clear, resonant, powerful without noisiness or roughness, and agreeable in quality. At the end of Die Walküre he shewed no sign of fatigue. And that is why he takes the place which so many keener artists, without this physical endowment of his, must deeply envy him. Gerhäuser's voice has matured since he sang the part of Lohengrin here a couple of years ago; but as Siegmund the Unlucky he was quite overparted—conscientious, but slow, dull, and resourceless almost beyond bearing. Wagner has provided such formidable lengths of dumb show in this work that, unless an actor is inventive, highly accomplished in pantomime, and able to make himself personally fascinating, he must inevitably be left again and again helplessly staring at the conductor and waiting for his cue. And that is just what Siegmund and Hunding were doing most of the time. Of Sucher's great success as Sieglinde I told you in the hurried postscript which I dispatched after the first act. The second act began with a very fine performance of Fricka's scene by Miss Marie Brema, whose performance entitles us to say in England that we have produced one of the very best living Wagnerian artists. It was a first-rate piece of work, having the vocal qualities that the Germans neglect as well as the dramatic qualities they value, with, to boot, the excellent quality of Miss Brema's own individuality, which happily got completely the better of the Bayreuth tradition this time. Miss Lilli Lehmann, now Frau Lehmann-Kalisch, played her old part of Brynhild; but she was ill, and had to be helped by both prompter and conductor in passages which she had had at her fingers' ends for many years.

Die Walküre has the advantage over Das Rheingold of being much more frequently performed. Probably everybody concerned, from the stage carpenters to the *prima donna*, knew it better. The difference was very noticeable in the orchestra. Richter was in his best form, interpreting the score convincingly, and getting some fine work from the band. In the scene of the apparition of the Valkyrie in the second act, the effect of the wind instruments was quite magically beautiful. The deep impression made, in spite of the fact that none of the men could cope with their parts, and that Brynhild, though capably played, was not altogether suitably impersonated, was due very largely to the force with which Richter, through his handling of the orchestra, imposed Wagner's conception on the audience.

The weather here is excellent; and we all wish that the old plan of giving the audience one day's holiday were in force. Parsifal also is badly missed. But Der Ring is Der Ring, and there is an end. Among the visitors the Germans seem to be in a large majority this year, but no doubt the American and English tourists will turn up and assert themselves later on.

P.S., 6.15 p.m.—The first act of Siegfried has been the worst disappointment so far. Grüning, as Siegfried, is hardly to be described without malice. Imagine an XVIII century bank clerk living in a cave, with fashionable sandals and cross garters, an elegant modern classic tunic, a Regent-street bearskin, and a deportment only to be learnt in quadrilles. Or, rather, do not imagine it; but pray that I, who have seen the reality, may not be haunted by it in my dreams. He only needed a tinder-box instead of a furnace, and a patent knife-cleaning machine instead of an anvil, to make him complete. I really cannot conscientiously advise Englishmen to come to Bayreuth until Grüning comes to England. Fortunately there was some relief. Breuer was excellent as Mime; and Perron, in the Wanderer Scene, where voice alone can do almost everything, and the costume makes awkwardness impossible, was at his best. And the orchestra is keeping up to its Walküre standard.

III

22 JULY.—With all possible goodwill towards the Bayreuth management, I cannot bring myself to congratulate it on Siegfried. If the performance had been given at an ordinary German theatre, with ordinary German prices, I should have been delighted with the orchestra and the mounting; but I should have roundly denounced the choice of the principal artist. And since Siegfried is a drama which depends as much on the actor who plays the title part as Hamlet does, my condemnation of Herr Grüning practically gives away the whole performance. I must add that Madame Wagner—who is understood to be responsible for the casting of Der Ring—is not in this case the victim of an unexpected collapse. Herr Grüning is no novice. I have never yet succeeded in visiting Bayreuth without hearing him sing. He has played Parsifal and Tannhäuser, and Madame Wagner knows to a hair's breadth, as well as I do, what he can do and what he cannot do. Consequently the people who have made tedious and costly pilgrimages from the ends of the earth to Bayreuth, as the one place in the world where Wagner's music-dramas can be witnessed in their utmost attainable excellence and fidelity of representation, have every right to remonstrate indignantly at being deliberately put off with a third-rate Siegfried. As far as I can judge, there can have been no attempt even to make the best of him by careful rehearsal. We have seen Alvary manage the business of the Wagnerian stage with the precision of a French pantomimist, at a scratch performance in London, with everything behind the scenes at sixes and sevens and only enough interval between the acts to clear away one scene and tumble

another on. Why cannot the same result be obtained here, where the intervals are an hour long, and the simple-minded pilgrims are fed all day with stories of the months of rehearsal, the scrupulous observance of the Master's wishes, the inexorable conscientiousness of Madame Wagner? The truth is that all these devout professions are borne out by the carpenters, machinists, and gasmen, and by them alone. The changes of scene, the wonderful atmospheric effects, the jets of steam, and so on are worked with a smoothness and punctuality that are beyond praise. Once only, in the change of scene from the depths of the Rhine to Valhall, did I hear something tumble with a thud behind the gauzes, accompanied by a strenuous whispering of instructions. That was no doubt an accident—a very trifling one to me, who have so often sat in Covent Garden during the change from the second to the third scene of Boïto's Mefistofele, listening to the mysterious strains of the orchestra, whilst dim figures of stage carpenters stumbled and rushed wildly about in the stage twilight, stimulating and exhorting oneanother in language which owed its frantic force to profanity rather than to grammar. At Bayreuth the clouds move, night follows day, and calm follows storm apparently without human agency. But it is one thing to drill a staff of workmen, and quite another to drill a tenor. If any of the men at work in the flies had botched his work last night as Grüning several times botched his, he would be an unemployed man this morning.

Yet, on the whole, the tenor was more conscientious than the *prima donna*. Frau Lilli Lehmann-Kalisch is famous for her Brynhild—famous in America. She has a bright soprano voice, brilliant at the top, but not particularly interesting in the middle—just the wrong sort of voice for Wagner. When dressed as the war-maiden, she is plump, pretty, very feminine, and not at all unlike our clever comedienne, Miss Kate Phillips—therefore just the wrong sort of person for Brynhild. She is clearly conscious that her golden hair is hanging down her back, and since she refuses, as she lies asleep on the mountain top, to allow her face to be covered by the vizor of her helmet, she is, in that attitude, so unmistakably and indeed aggressively a conventionally pretty woman, emphasizing a well-developed bust with a toy cuirass, that Siegfried's assumption that she is a man, and the emotional shock with which he subsequently discovers that the supposed sleeping warrior is a young woman, are made incredible and ridiculous. And this, if you please, is Bayreuthian fidelity to "The Meister."

However, I quite admit that Frau Lehmann-Kalisch is an artist of considerable qualifications; and I should like to see her as Marguerite in Gounod's Faust. Her singing is open to exception in the matter of phrasing: in fact, she absolutely destroys one of the most characteristic turns in that section of the great duet (excuse the word; but it *is* a duet, and actually has a concerted *cadenza* in it) with which the familiar Siegfried Idyll begins. But her offences in this respect were as nothing beside Grüning's. Even in the sword-forging scene, when he was comparatively cool, the swinging triplets which occur in the bellows music were too much for his powers of execution; and at the end, when he was wrecked with emotion over which he had not an artist's mastery, the manner in which he gasped his way from note to note, producing effects which had exactly the same relation to Wagner's shapely phrases as a heap of broken glass has to a crystal goblet, is not to be described.

In justice to Herr Grüning, let me add that he has some agreeable points. He is handsome and, in a pleasant, robust, very German way, elegant in the manner of the last century. In a periwig, as a sympathetic young man of sensibility, with a not too exacting vocal part, he would pass as a tenor who ought to be doing better things. Apparently he loves Wagner, and is anxious to do him justice; and when he fails, he fails honestly. But I must not insult him by an open attempt to spare his feelings on this occasion; and I have no desire to spare the feelings of the managers. He was overparted in Siegfried; and I repeat that they knew beforehand that it would be so. The guarantee of a first-rate performance—that guarantee which is the basis of the authority and prosperity of the Wagner Theatre—has been broken, and broken deliberately, not for the first time.

Let me now forget Marguerite-Brynhild and her young man, and recall the moments when neither were on the stage. Then, I grant you, the representation was splendid. Perron, with his straddling legs, knock knees, and unhappy expression hidden by the gown, the beard, and the wide hat of the Wanderer, and with his fine voice in full play, did nothing to contradict the majesty of the Wotan music. He missed the humor of the passages with the dwarf and with Siegfried at the foot of the mountain; but that was only a small deduction from the satisfaction of the general effect. Breuer, as Mime, repeated himself a good deal; but his play was so clever that it was worth repeating. Frau Schumann-Heink as Erda, and Friedrichs as Alberich, sustained the impression they made in Das Rheingold; and the orchestra was again very fine, especially in Mime's nightmare after Wotan's visit, and in the tragic thunderclouds of music in the first scene of the third act. Die Götterdämmerung tonight will probably redeem all that was lost last night, since it depends so much less on Siegfried. At all events, we are full of hope.

P.S.—There is joy over Die Götterdämmerung: Grüning has vanished, and Burgstaller, the alternative

Siegfried, reigns in his stead. So far, the improvement is due more to the faults of Grüning than the qualities of Burgstaller, but he promises well. We are all somewhat exhausted after a first act lasting two hours, yet most of us are ready to go through it again. The scene between Brynhild and Waltraute has affected us beyond all my adjectives: not even Frau Schumann-Heink's combination of black-blue Valkyrie armor and shield with a summer gown and fashionable sleeves could spoil its sublimity. I shall start for London after the performance (unless it kills me). The interval is too short [to write] more.

IV

23 JULY.—The completion of the first cycle of the Nibelungen tetralogy at Bayreuth has been celebrated by applause lasting for seven minutes, the object being to bring Richter and the principal artists before the curtain. But at Bayreuth nobody takes a curtain call, except the—well, the dove in Parsifal. Nevertheless the audience hammered and bravoed very lustily, the English taking an unmistakable lead in the noisier part of the demonstration, but failing to keep the Germans up to the standard of perseverance set by the first night of The Rogue's Comedy at the Garrick, when a vain attempt to call out Mr Henry Arthur Jones was kept up for twentyfive minutes. The enthusiasm was certainly justified by the performance. The new Siegfried, Burgstaller, a product of Bayreuth and its Wagner school, won the audience over completely in the second and third acts. In the first act he was a little handicapped by a certain novelty (after the Germanically handsome Grüning) in his aspect, and by a helmet which had to be rescued from falling off whenever he ventured on an impulsive advance to Brynhild.

He is a young man, of the build and features which

we associate rather with Syria and Maida Vale than with the primeval Rhineland, and in his makeup he aimed only partly at Siegfried, and chiefly at—say, Parsifal. But he has none of the pretentiousness and lack of simplicity which sometimes distinguish the clever Oriental from the stupid Saxon. On the contrary, his chief personal charm lies in a certain combination of courageous shyness and a touch of the unformedness of youth in his movements, with impulsive enthusiasm and an artistic judgment very remarkable at his age. In the third act, when he came to tell that story of the ring and the helmet, the sword and the dragon, which everybody in the tetralogy tells at full length whenever the smallest opening for it is perceptible, he quite charmed us by his bright delivery. In narrating the incident of the woodbird, he was far more interesting than the woodbird itself had been; and this result was largely due to clever and skilful singing. Not only did he give us some very pretty contrasts of tone, but he made the rhythms dance in a way that was quite delightful after the trudging and trampling of those who had been over the same ground before him. He has, too, qualities of joyousness and humor in his temperament that are invaluable in relieving the heavy earnestness which occasionally oppresses Bayreuth. In the first act he accidentally slipped into his head register on a high note, the effect being by no means unhappy; and immediately the foolish people whose ears are just sharp enough to distinguish the note of a piccolo from that of a trombone began to wonder whether his voice would stand the strain of the performance. They might have spared their anxiety; his voice was never in the slightest danger. His success was complete and legitimate; and I hope that Mr Schulz-Curtius will some day induce him to make a trip to London and tell his Götterdämmerung story for us at a Mottl concert.

Nobody who is acquainted with Der Ring will need to be told by me that The Dusk of the Gods brought the sensation of the tetralogy to a climax. The truth is—I may dare to say so now that I am clear of Bayreuth in full flight for London—Das Rheingold, Die Walküre, and the first two acts of Siegfried are music-drama in the fullest possible integrity of that genre; but Die Götterdämmerung, like the end of Siegfried, is opera. In it we have choruses and *finales*; we have a great *scena* for the *prima donna* with the chorus looking on very much as they used to do when Semiramide was singing *Bel raggio*; above all, we have the tenor stabbed to death and then coming to life to sing pretty things about his love before he finally expires, just like Edgardo in Lucia di Lammermoor. The resemblance is not shirked at Bayreuth. When two stalwart members of the chorus picked up the slain Siegfried, and pretended to support him whilst he stood up and had a few more bars about Brynhild, it was impossible not to see that we had come round again to Valentin in Gounod's Faust. It is true that we had come round, like the Hegelian spiral, on a higher plane—a prodigiously higher plane; but the fact remains that Wagner, instead of abandoning opera for ever after Lohengrin, only abandoned it for a time to invent and create the music-drama, since his great world-poem could not find its musical expression otherwise. But the powers which he acquired in creating Das Rheingold, Die Walküre, and most of Siegfried—powers so gigantic in comparison with those which Meyerbeer, Gounod, and others acquired by practice in mere opera-composing on the old scale that it is hardly possible now to conceive Meyerbeer and Wagner as beings of the same order and species—completely changed the situation for him. It gave him a technical command over dramatic music which made him as complete a master of the opera as Beethoven was of the symphony, Bach of the fugue, or Mozart of the decorative forms into which he poured his apparently spontaneous and unconditioned dramatic music. Die Götterdämmerung, Die Meistersinger, and Tristan are just as much operas as anything else: the fact that they are dramatic poems, and that Il Barbiere and Fra Diavolo are not, is no more an objection to the inclusion of the four under the same general heading of opera than the fact that Beethoven's Ninth Symphony is a dramatic poem is an objection to its being called by the same technical name as Haydn's Surprise Symphony. On the other hand, I should hesitate to call Das Rheingold an opera, since it deliberately excludes all operatic features, wheras Die Götterdämmerung excludes nothing, the composer like a true past-master of his art availing himself of all forms and methods with entire freedom, even when they led him, as they sometimes did, to all the outward and visible signs of Italian opera.

No doubt this is the explanation of the popularity of those works of Wagner which followed his relapse, as music-drama doctrinaires should call it, into opera in the last scene of Siegfried. Certainly the effect of Die Götterdämmerung was very rich and splendid on Wednesday. The music is from beginning to end the very luxury of sound woven into a gorgeous tissue by a consummately skilful master. I shall make no attempt to describe it: those who know the music will understand when I say that the conductor and the band understood their work, and that Waltraute's description of Wotan waiting in Valhall for his doom surpassed expectation in its beauty of sound, majesty of movement, and psychological luck in producing the golden moment of the first act. And to those poor barbarians who do not know the work, why should I address myself at all, since they would not understand me?

In point of technical execution, perhaps, the worst feature of the performance was the Hagen of Grengg. His voice, once described to me by Levi as "the best bass voice in Germany," is coarsened and shaken by abuse. He breaks his phrases in the worst pseudo-Wagnerian style, pumping out almost every note with a separate effort, and seldom conveying more than the roughest broken outline of the phrase. His acting is heavy and undistinguished. They are possibly proud of him at Bayreuth; but I am prepared to back Mr Bispham to drain a tankard of laudanum and then play Hagen twice as smartly and ten times more artistically. The English singer, Miss Marie Brema, had been announced as one of the Norns, but she did not appear, to my great disappointment, as her Fricka in Die Walküre proved her to be, by temperament, physical qualifications, voice, and skill, one of the most powerful and accomplished Wagnerian heroines Madame Wagner has yet discovered. Her place was filled by the somewhat provincial expedient of doubling the part of the first Norn with that of Waltraute. Madame Schumann-Heink has thus played three parts in the tetralogy, the third being Erda, and in all of them she has made a deep impression by her fine contralto voice and the passion and power of her delivery.

The contrast, vocally, was a little hard on the other Norns, one of whom was no less an artist than Sucher. In the river scene, the Rhinemaidens, no longer suspended by ropes, but still clinging to their *fichus*, rose out of the river with their hair elaborately dressed like three wax heads in a Bond-street shop window, and would have been exceedingly ridiculous if the music and the drama and Siegfried had not swept away all such considerations. Frau Lilli Lehmann-Kalisch's high notes, bright and true, and her saturation with the feeling of a part so magnificent that no woman with a heart and brain could possibly play it without rising far out of her ordinary self, achieved a triumph which makes it ungracious to qualify a very warm commendation of her performance. I must not, however, call her a great Brynhild. She acts intelligently, sings effectively and in tune, and is attractive enough, attaining in all these respects a degree of excellence that makes it impossible to call her commonplace; but for all that she is conventional, and takes the fullest advantage of the fact that plenty of ideas suggested by Wagner will attach themselves to her if only she stands her ground impressively. Gunther and Gutrune did their work without distinguishing themselves remarkably one way or the other; and the chorus bellowed with a will, substituting real primeval roughness for an artistic representation of roughness, which is a very different and more difficult thing.

But these criticisms of executive details, though they are important inasmuch as it is only by the most vigilant and unsparing activity in making them that Bayreuth can be kept conscious of the fact that it must conquer fresh prestige from performance to performance, and never for a moment rest on its reputation and the Master's laurels, must yet seem trivial and impertinent to those who can feel nothing but the tremendous impression made on them by a representation, complete in every word, note, and picture, of the mightiest art work our century has produced. I exhort all those who have lazily made up their minds that Bayreuth is too far, or that they cannot spare the money for the trip, to reconsider their decision and insist on the ever-resourceful Mr Schulz-Curtius finding them tickets for one of the remaining cycles. If even I, to whom Bayreuth has no novelty, and who can detect faults at the rate of about three in each bar, can say that I have been more than overpaid for the trouble and expense of my trip, how much more will not a visit be worth to those who can add the enchantments of a fool's paradise to the genuine recreation—I use the word in its highest sense—to be gained from the prodigious sum of really successful artistic effort which each performance represents? Therefore hesitate no longer, but buy your tickets, pack up your traps, and away with you. Only, if you value a cordial welcome, perhaps you had better not mention that you come on my recommendation.

SIR GEORGE GROVE

Review of Sir George Grove's Beethoven and His Nine Symphonies. The Saturday Review, 14 November 1896. Reprinted in Pen Portraits and Reviews and in Our Theatres in the Nineties (as Beethoven's Symphonies), London, 1931

On cold Saturday afternoons in winter, as I sit in the theatrical desert, making my bread with great bitterness by chronicling insignificant plays and criticizing incompetent players, it sometimes comes upon me that I have forgotten something—omitted something—missed some all-important appointment. This is a legacy from my old occupation of musical critic. All my old occupations leave me such legacies. When I was in my teens I had certain official duties to perform, which involved every day the very strict and punctual discharge of certain annual payments, which were set down in a perpetual diary. I sometimes dream now that I am back at those duties again, but with an amazed consciousness of having allowed them to fall into ruinous arrear for a long time past. My Saturday afternoon misgivings are just like that. They mean that for several years I passed those afternoons in that section of the gallery of the Crystal Palace concert room which is sacred to Sir

George Grove and to the Press. There were two people there who never grew older—Beethoven and Sir George. August Manns' hair changed from raven black to swan white as the years passed; young critics grew middle-aged and middle-aged critics grew old; Rossini lost caste and was shouldered into the promenade; the fire-new overture to Tannhäuser began to wear as threadbare as William Tell; Arabella Goddard went and Sophie Menter came; Joachim, Hallé, Norman-Neruda, and Santley no longer struck the rising generations with the old sense of belonging to tomorrow, like Ysaÿe, Paderewski, and Bispham; the men whom I had shocked as an iconoclastic upstart Wagnerian, braying derisively when they observed that "the second subject, appearing in the key of the dominant, contrasts effectively with its predecessor, not only in tonality, but by its suave, melodious character," lived to see me shocked and wounded in my turn by the audacities of J. F. Runciman; new evening papers launched into musical criticism, and were read publicly by Mr Smith, the eminent drummer, whenever he had fifty bars rest; a hundred trifles marked the flight of time; but Sir George Grove fed on Beethoven's symphonies as the gods in Das Rheingold fed on the apples of Freia, and grew no older. Sometimes, when Mendelssohn's Scotch symphony, or Schubert's Ninth in C, were in the program, he got positively younger, clearing ten years backward in as many minutes when Manns and the band were at their best. I remonstrated with him more than once on this unnatural conduct; and he was always extremely apologetic, assuring me that he was getting on as fast as he could. He even succeeded in producing a wrinkle or two under stress of Berlioz and Raff, Liszt and Wagner; but presently some pianist would come along with the concerto in E flat;* and then, if I sat next him, strangers

* No. 5 (Emperor), Op. 73.

would say to me "Your son, sir, appears to be a very enthusiastic musician." And I could not very well explain that the real bond between us was the fact that Beethoven never ceased to grow on us. In my personality, my views, and my style of criticism there was so much to forgive that many highly amiable persons never quite succeeded in doing it. To Sir George I must have been a positively obnoxious person, not in the least because I was on the extreme left in politics and other matters, but because I openly declared that the *finale* of Schubert's symphony in C could have been done at half the length and with twice the effect by Rossini. But I knew Beethoven's symphonies from the opening bar of the first to the final chord of the ninth, and yet made new discoveries about them at every fresh performance. And I am convinced that "G" regarded this as evidence of a fundamental rectitude in me which would bear any quantity of superficial aberrations. Which is quite my own opinion too.

It may be asked why I have just permitted myself to write of so eminent a man as Sir George Grove by his initial. That question would not have been asked thirty years ago, when "G," the rhapsodist who wrote the Crystal Palace programs, was one of the best ridiculed men in London. At that time the average programist would unblushingly write "Here the composer, by one of those licenses which are, perhaps, permissible under exceptional circumstances to men of genius, but which cannot be too carefully avoided by students desirous of forming a legitimate style, has abruptly introduced the dominant seventh of the key of C major into the key of A flat, in order to recover, by a forced modulation, the key relationship proper to the second subject of a movement in F: an awkward device which he might have spared himself by simply introducing his second subject in its true key of C." "G," who was "no musician," cultivated this style in vain. His most conscientious attempts at it never brought him any nearer than "The lovely melody then passes, by a transition of remarkable beauty, into the key of C major, in which it seems to go straight up to heaven." Naturally the average Englishman was profoundly impressed by the inscrutable learning of the first style (which I could teach to a poodle in two hours), and thought "G's" obvious sentimentality idiotic. It did not occur to the average Englishman that perhaps Beethoven's symphonies were an affair of sentiment and nothing else. This, of course, was the whole secret of them. Beethoven was the first man who used music with absolute integrity as the expression of his own emotional life. Others had shewn how it could be done—had done it themselves as a curiosity of their art in rare, self-indulgent, *unprofessional* moments—but Beethoven made this, and nothing else, his business. Stupendous as the resultant difference was between his music and any other ever heard in the world before his time, the distinction is not clearly apprehended to this day, because there was nothing new in the musical expression of emotion: every progression in Bach is sanctified by emotion; and Mozart's subtlety, delicacy, and exquisite tender touch and noble feeling were the despair of all the musical world. But Bach's theme was not himself, but his religion; and Mozart was always the dramatist and storyteller, making the men and women of his imagination speak, and dramatizing even the instruments in his orchestra, so that you know their very sex the moment their voices reach you. Haydn really came nearer to Beethoven, for he is neither the praiser of God nor the dramatist, but, always within the limits of good manners and of his primary function as a purveyor of formal decorative music, a man of moods. This is how he created the symphony and put it readymade into Beethoven's hand. The revolutionary giant at once seized it, and throwing supernatural religion, conventional good manners, dramatic fiction, and all external standards and objects into the lumber room, took his own humanity as the material of his music, and expressed it all without compromise, from his roughest jocularity to his holiest aspiration after that purely human reign of intense life—of Freude—when

Alle Menschen werden Brüder,
Wo dein sanfter Flügel weilt.*

In thus fearlessly expressing himself, he has, by his common humanity, expressed us as well, and shewn us how beautifully, how strongly, how trustworthily we can build with our own real selves. This is what is proved by the immense superiority of the Beethoven symphony to any oratorio or opera.

In this light all Beethoven's work becomes clear and simple; and the old nonsense about his obscurity and eccentricity and stage sublimity and so on explains itself as pure misunderstanding. His criticisms, too, become quite consistent and inevitable: for instance, one is no longer tempted to resent his declaration that Mozart wrote nothing worth considering but parts of Die Zauberflöte (those parts, perhaps, in which the beat of *dein sanfter Flügel* is heard), and to retort upon him by silly comparisons of his tunes with *Non più andrai* and *Deh vieni alla finestra.* The man who wrote the Eighth symphony has a right to rebuke the man who put his raptures of elation, tenderness, and nobility into the mouths of a drunken libertine, a silly peasant girl, and a conventional fine lady, instead of confessing them to himself, glorying in them, and uttering them without motley as the universal inheritance.

I must not make "G" responsible for my own opinions;

* Choral Finale on Schiller's Ode to Joy, Symphony No. 9 in D minor, Op. 125.

but I leave it to his old readers whether his huge success as a program writer was not due to the perfect simplicity with which he seized and followed up this clue to the intention of Beethoven's symphonies. He seeks always for the mood, and is not only delighted at every step by the result of his search, but escapes quite easily and unconsciously from the boggling and blundering of the men who are always wondering why Beethoven did not do what any professor would have done. He is always joyous, always successful, always busy and interesting, never tedious even when he is superfluous (not that the adepts ever found him so), and always as pleased as Punch when he is not too deeply touched. Sometimes, of course, I do not agree with him. Where he detects anger in the Eighth Symphony, I find nothing but boundless, thundering elation. In his right insistence on the jocular element in the symphonies, I think he is occasionally led by his personal sense that octave skips on the bassoon and drum are funny to conclude too hastily that Beethoven was always joking when he used them. And I will fight with him to the death on the trio of the Eighth symphony, maintaining passionately against him and against all creation that those cello *arpeggios* which steal on tiptoe round the theme so as not to disturb its beauty are only "fidgety" when they are played "*à la* Mendelssohn," and that they are perfectly tender and inevitable when they are played "*à la* Wagner." The passage on this point in Wagner's essay on Conducting is really not half strong enough; and when "G" puts it down to "personal bias" and Wagner's "poor opinion of Mendelssohn," it is almost as if someone had accounted in the same way for Beethoven's opinion of Mozart. Wagner was almost as fond of Mendelssohn's music as "G" is; but he had suffered unbearably, as we all have, from the tradition established by Mendelssohn's conducting of Beethoven's symphonies. Mendelssohn's music is all *nervous* music: his *allegros*, expressing only excitement and impetuosity without any ground, have fire and motion without substance. Therefore the conductor must, above all things, *keep them going*; if he breaks their lambent flight to dwell on any moment of them, he is lost. With Beethoven the longer you dwell on any moment the more you will find in it. Provided only you do not sacrifice his splendid energetic rhythm and masterly self-possessed emphasis to a maudlin preoccupation with his feeling, you cannot possibly play him too sentimentally; for Beethoven is no reserved gentleman, but a man proclaiming the realities of life. Consequently, when for generations they played Beethoven's *allegros* exactly as it is necessary to play the overture to Ruy Blas, or Stone him to death—a practice which went on until Wagner's righteous ragings stopped it—our performances of the symphonies simply spoiled the tempers of those who really understood them. For the sake of redeeming that lovely trio from "fidgetiness," "G" must let us face this fact even at the cost of admitting that Wagner was right where Mendelssohn was wrong.

But though it is possible thus to differ here and there from "G," he is never on the wrong lines. He is always the true musician: that is, the man the professors call "no musician"—just what they called Beethoven himself. It is delightful to have all the old programs bound into a volume, with the quotations from the score all complete, and the information brought up to date, and largely supplemented. It is altogether the right sort of book about the symphonies, made for practical use in the concert room under the stimulus of a heartfelt need for bringing the public to Beethoven. I hope it will be followed by another volume or two dealing with the pianoforte concertos—or say with the G, the E flat, the choral fantasia, and the three classical violin concertos: Beethoven, Mendelssohn, and Brahms. And then a

Schubert-Mendelssohn-Schumann volume. Why, dear "G," should these things be hidden away in old concert programs which never circulate beyond Sydenham?

WHAT IT FEELS LIKE TO BE SUCCESSFUL

The Star, 16 January 1897; signed "Corno di Bassetto"

Well, how do I know? I am amazed—overwhelmed—at having such a question put to me, of all living men. Who says I am successful? Everybody knows I am brilliant, paradoxical, eccentric, witty, and all the rest of it. But *how* do they know it? Simply because I have told London so every week at two or three thousand words' length during the whole of the nine years of The Star's existence.* Englishmen dont find out these things for themselves: they require to be told what to say and think about me just as much as about Shakespear.

And, pray, when did I ever say I was successful? Would you call the Ancient Mariner a successful man merely because people could not help listening to him, even when they heard the loud bassoon? Did anybody believe him? Did anybody consider him an agreeable character? Was he in a position to entertain people at Metropole banquets like the late Colonel North, or to get knighted like the late Sir Augustus Harris? No. Very well, then, am I better off than the Ancient Mariner? Have I any money? Am I respectably dressed? Do people read me except to laugh at me and at the victims

* Shaw does not imply here that he has written weekly feuilletons for The Star for nine years, but merely that he has been so employed throughout this period by various London journals and newspapers.

of what they call my sarcasm? Why, the first time a journalist saw me draw a cheque, the fact was considered so extraordinary that it was mentioned in half a dozen papers. Success! What use have I for success, what time for it? Can you eat success without losing your wind, or drink it without hobnailing your liver, or wear it without bagging it at the knees, or feel it without secretly knowing yourself to be a humbug?

And will you tell me this? What tribunal now existing has the right to decide whether I am successful or not? Public opinion, perhaps! You forget that it is my function, as critic, to judge for the public, not theirs to judge for themselves. What do they know about it? Or posterity! If I did not hope that posterity will soon have grown out of all possibility of ever understanding what any creature of this rascally century could write, should I take the trouble to be a Socialist, do you think? And what a nice successful thing it is to be a Socialist, isnt it?

Besides, Mr Star Editor, have you reflected that success is death? What is the summit? The last step before the descent. I thank my stars that the crags still tower above me. If you think I have yet succeeded, I hope you underrate my destiny.

What made the success of The Star? I reply, emphatically, the articles of Corno di Bassetto. You habitually misprinted him; and you sometimes felt that your good fortune in discovering him was almost more than you could bear. But you *did* discover him; and that was success, beyond a doubt. What does it feel like?

COMPOSERS AND PROFESSORS IN THE COMING CENTURY

The Musician, 19 May 1897

[U] The composers of the XX century! What an easy time they will have, compared with their predecessors in the XIX! There lies the whole material of music before them to do just what they like with. No more forbidden progressions; no more prescribed forms; any chord or discord or no-chord you please, without preparation or resolution; modulation unnecessary, even between G treble sharp major and B major; false relations at a premium, lest any two simultaneous parts should seem to be insipidly in the same key; complete chromatic scales on all the wind instruments; executants to whom the *bravuras* of the old soloists are but quaint commonplaces; audiences trained to wait for a full close for two hours without turning a hair; and all this open not only to the master whose genius defies all rules, but to the journeyman who cannot work without them! Does it not seem as if we should be flooded with music—as if symphonic poems and music-dramas will be extemporized at every street corner under such conditions?

Alas! the master is bound, and the slave is free. Is literature any the easier now that every man may write in his mother tongue, without verse, rhyme, canto, or description of the shield of Achilles? Is sculpture easier now that the sculptor is no longer forbidden to produce anything but a copy of a crude image or symbol of some ancient God? Are good illustrated Bibles easier to get than they were when even Holbein obediently redrew the old conventional drawings, and Doré and Tissot would have been burnt for blasphemy? The truth is, the abolition of the rules only clears the way to the real difficulties of musical composition. It brings the composer straight to the point, and denies him all credit for compliances with conditions which nobody makes outside the classroom. Now that the rules are gone; now that professordom's foolish plea for a livelihood, "Learn how to write a fugue, and then—dont do it," has lost its charm; now that every intelligent student knows that he must learn what *has* been done direct from the great composers, and find out what *can* be done for himself; now that the way is open to the sciolist and the amateur as freely as to the diplomaed baccalaureus, the very works which have established this musical freedom of speech have raised the standard of attainment necessary for greatness to an appalling height.

If you doubt this, take whichever oratorio of Handel's you think the greatest, and consider how childishly simple and mechanical a business it is compared to what would be expected from Handel nowadays. The Messiah, we are told (as if it were something to be proud of) was finished in twentyfour days. A modern composer might well say "If you will let me do it that way, I'll finish it in twenty." I do not say that the boast could be made good, except, perhaps, in the matter of ingenious counterpoint, in which Handel has been left behind by comparatively commonplace men, much as Raphael was outdone by Pietro da Cortona in anatomy and perspective; but I do say that if what Handel did in twentyfour days be compared with what Wagner took twentyfour years to do, it will be evident that Handel won his laurels far more cheaply than Wagner. Again, Don Giovanni is one of the miracles of art; but consider it merely as an undertaking, and what a trifle it is compared to Tristan or Die Meistersinger! It is, of course, arguable that we have lost more than we have gained; for the law of the Conservation of Energy so far holds good in this matter that in putting heavier conditions on our composers we have reduced the number of works which it is possible for them to execute in a lifetime. Der Ring des Nibelungen, the central masterpiece of religious music in our times, is a work compared to which half a dozen Messiahs or Zauberflötes, or even Choral Symphonies ending in odes to Joy, seem the merest child's play. A whole century of industrial evolution, ending in actual warfare and exile for the composer, went to the making of Alberich and his Nibelheim. A second Reformation—that of the XIX and XX centuries—is in Wotan, with his Valhalla, his false fire to protect the Church against the Truth, and his final conversion to his own doom. In a work pregnant with this mighty burthen, Alberich cannot express himself in the "divisions" of Honor and Arms, nor Siegfried woo Brynhild in the couplets of *Là ci darem.* But then Handel and Mozart did not waste the time saved by the greater simplicity of their work. There must be a considerable number of amateurs who know familiarly every bar of music Wagner wrote; but where is the man who knows half the output of Handel, or of Mozart, who had only 38 years of life as against Wagner's 70? Besides, Handel and Mozart practised in every department of their art. Wagner was a specialist in musical composition, though his labors as politician, philosopher, critic, poet, conductor, organizer and manager made him, humanly speaking, much less a specialist than either of them.

And here we come to another difference between the past and the future. Just as literature began with poetry, music began with dancing and lyrical declamation. Literature has now developed until poetry forms only an infinitesimally small portion of it. The vast majority of our authors and dramatists never write a line of verse;

and the English dramatist is puzzled at first, and amused afterwards, by the German habit of calling the dramatic author "the poet." The same development is going on in music. Already it is not necessary that a dramatic composer should be able to write a ballad or a minuet: a Christy Minstrel tune orchestrally elaborated into an intermezzo or prelude supplies all the "absolute music" he needs. We shall soon have operas announced as music-dramas by A. W. Pinero, composed by A. B. C., with lyrics by Adrian Ross, composed (as well as the dances) by X. Y. Z.

This specialization would already have gone further if it had not been for the unfortunate versatility of Mozart. If Mozart had been a journalist, he would have retarded the advance of the Press for a century by establishing the practice of writing leading articles in heroic verse, and the police intelligence in a string of delicate sonnets. If he had not had the facility which enabled him to make one and the same musical "number" a perfect bit of musical comedy, a charming symmetrical decoration in sound, and sometimes an ingenious contrapuntal device into the bargain, he might not have been so wonderful a man; but Meyerbeer would assuredly have been a far more efficient opera maker; for it was this superhuman Mozartian tradition of doing two things at the same time that maimed Meyerbeer, who really had a very remarkable and original dramatic talent; only, coming after Mozart and before Wagner, what could he do with it, since he was no Luther to break up the established order of his craft? He could only cobble up his fine dramatic phrases into childish couplets, quatrains and quadrilles by such means as an able prose writer might employ to turn a straightforward love letter into a bad valentine, or a bit of nervous dialogue into mechanical blank verse. Now that Wagner has cleared all that away, making it intolerably trivial and ridiculous, there is a musical career open for men like Meyerbeer—nay, for men much less musicians in the old sense than he was—men who could no more compose *Nobil donna* or *Ombra leggiera* than he could have composed *La donna e mobile.*

This is a good thing for some people and a bad thing for others. It is a good thing for THE MUSICIAN, which is now as interesting to people who are "no musicians" (among whom, be it remembered, Handel quite logically included Gluck) as to adepts. On the other hand, it is a bad thing for the old-fashioned professors of composition, who are becoming more ridiculous to composers than professors of literature are to authors and journalists. An art in which nothing is any longer forbidden defies pedagogy. The ancient and illpaid practice of telling students that they must not do what all the great masters of the present do, and what all the great masters of the past either did or limited their achievements by not doing, cannot survive the unprecedented publicity now given to really authoritative views as to the aims and methods of artistic creation. When the student had nothing in his hand but Mozart's Succinct Thoroughbass he took a very different view of his teacher from that of the student of today, who has explicit and vehement communications from Liszt and Wagner to guide him, whose very pedants are men as eminent as Berlioz and Schumann, and who can buy a better musical library of XVIII century scores for a pound than Cherubini's pupils could for twenty, not to mention his familiarity with a mass of XIX century music and a growing number of Bayreuth-inspired performances.

But the professors need not despair. Beethoven found Haydn a nuisance to him, and Albrechtsberger a help. I cannot say that the bad attacks of *fugato* to which Beethoven was subject all his life suggest to me that Albrechtsberger did him much good; but I can understand the desire of a beginner to have the opinion of a sensible expert friend *who is also a first-rate critic.* And that is the moral of the whole business for the professors: what they must learn now is not counterpoint but criticism. It is not so easy; but it is more useful.[U]

WAGNER ON RICHMOND HILL

To The Saturday Review, 27 August 1898

[U] Sir,—Why this outburst of autumnal fury at the expense of Mr Schulz-Curtius? If no Englishman is intelligent or enterprising enough to give us the particular sort of summer theatre that has been so prodigiously successful at Bayreuth, are we therefore to refuse our support to a German entrepreneur? Had Mr Schulz-Curtius rushed greedily in to grab a popular English investment, there might be some ground for waving him aside, and patriotically reserving the opportunity for (say) Sir Thomas Lipton. But as it has been offering itself to British enterprise for the last ten years in vain, British enterprise need not grudge Mr Schulz-Curtius the opening it has not had the gumption to jump into.

It is quite true, as you say, that we want an English opera, manned by English composers. But if an unpatriotic providence will persist in making its Handels and Wagners in Germany, is that the fault of Mr Schulz-Curtius? And how many English composers of dramatic music are we likely to produce if our students are forbidden to hear the best that has been done in that department except by taking a trip to Bayreuth at a cost of fifteen or twenty pounds poured into the pockets of German innkeepers, German railway companies, and German musicians? What is Bayreuth, from the patriotic-commercial point of view, but a means of securing to these wicked Germans thousands of pounds of English and American money that Mr Schulz-Curtius's proposed theatre will intercept at Richmond for the benefit of the country of his adoption?

Finally, as to the German bandsman. Why does the German bandsman supplant the English bandsman? Not because he is better (except perhaps in the case of horn players), but because he is cheaper. There are two remedies. One is for the English player to lower his terms to the German level, and use a cheaper and worse instrument. The other is to insert a fair-wages clause in the constitution of the Wagner Memorial Theatre, and so put a stop to pecuniary competition in a matter which should be decided by artistic merit. Let there be a fixed standard of remuneration for the band on the highest English scale; and the management, unable to save money by importing cheap players, will turn its attention to getting the best artistic value attainable for its fair wage, without respect to nationality. Under such circumstances the appointments will go to the best players, which is exactly where they ought to go.

I am quite prepared to pitch Mr Schulz-Curtius's circular into the wastepaper basket if any better scheme presents itself. But to declare against it in favor of doing nothing is to play the dog in the manger. As to Mr Schulz-Curtius himself, let us by all means throw him over, if some Englishman of equal experience and credit will put his hand to the work, and prove his superiority by obtaining more support than he. Failing the appearance of that enthusiastic islander, I, for one, shall take my good where I find it, and subscribe a modest morsel of the capital of the Wagner Memorial Theatre, Limited, of Richmond Hill.—Yours truly,

G. BERNARD SHAW.[U]

THE HINDHEAD HALL CONCERTS

The Farnham, Haslemere and Hindhead Herald, 12 and 19 November, 3 and 17 December 1898, signed "G.B.S."

I

[U] The first of a series of four subscription concerts of chamber music took place last Monday afternoon at Hindhead Hall. The conditions of the enterprise are all that could be desired. The acoustical properties of the hall are excellent: and the country in which it stands is the most beautiful in Surrey. Possibly the dwellers on Hindhead are so accustomed to fresh air, plenty of elbow room, and enchanting scenery that they hardly realize how much a concert gains under such circumstances. But to the critic who has had to spend years in stuffy London concert rooms on muddy nights and gloomy afternoons, Hindhead Hall is an ideal place for fine music. Indeed, as far as its surroundings are concerned, it has all the natural advantages which contribute so much to the success of the Wagner Theatre at Bayreuth.

The program of the first concert began with Beethoven's A major quartet, Op. 18, No. 5, and ended with Haydn's quartet in G major, Op. 7. These two works are masterpieces of their kind, written with perfect skill for the four instruments, and full of musical invention, fresh, unstrained, copious. It was probably in order to instruct Haslemere in the value of these qualities that Messrs Elderhorst, Kornfeld, Hobday, and Whitehouse played Schumann's quartet in F major, Op. 41, in the middle of the concert. But the lesson recoiled on their own heads, for a good many of the audience probably mistook the effect of Schumann's unskilful scoring for confused and ineffective playing. Yet the four artists were not at fault in point of execution. No doubt a smoother execution and better balanced tone might have done something to help Schumann through his uneasiest moments, especially in the middle sections of the quick movements; but that would have involved more rehearsal than the work is worth. In truth, the kindest and most artistic way to treat Schumann is never to present his chamber music in immediate contrast with the works of the true masters of this most difficult art. The F major quartet, taken by itself, will always be forgiven its shortcomings for the sake of its occasional strains of imaginative melody, and a fanciful sally or two. In the slow movement the harping on points affectionately reproduced from Beethoven is tolerable so long as Beethoven himself is not in the neighborhood. But coming as it did at Hindhead Hall immediately after a Beethoven quartet, it inevitably seemed a poor and scrappy affair in point of invention, whilst as to the handling of the instruments, it is not too much to say that when the Haydn quartet followed, it seemed as if two or three fiddles in difficulties had suddenly changed into an orchestra, so marked was the accession in power, clearness and beauty of tone; the explanation being, of course, that Haydn thoroughly understood how to write for strings, wheras Schumann, with all his enthusiasm and imaginativeness, never succeeded in writing well for any instrument except at moments and by accident. And it is just those moments and those accidents which have endeared him to us sufficiently to make us somewhat angry when comparisons are forced on him which he cannot sustain.

The quartet led by Mr Elderhorst is a very competent one, and it has the advantage of being a fairly young one. The constancy of the English public to its prime favorites is, no doubt, creditable to the nation, but it is also responsible for the fact that most of us have gathered our knowledge of chamber music from the performances of quartet players whose united age was seldom less than a couple of centuries. Such veterans for many years held our concert platform to the exclusion of the younger generation, which—however it may compare with its predecessors in other respects—certainly plays the fiddle, on the average, a good deal better, and is on much more genuinely intimate terms with the great masters. The players at Hindhead Hall are either in their prime or on the right side of it. Two of them, MM. Hobday and Whitehouse, succeeded to the viola and cello some years ago at the Popular Concerts at St James's Hall, when Straus and Piatti began at last to seek repose. The reputation of Mr Elderhorst, the leader, is more recent. Mr Kornfeld, the second violin, is a capable and experienced player. They have all worked together sufficiently to form an efficient quartet. In quartet playing this is essential, for the four greatest *virtuosi* in Europe would infallibly spoil a Haydn quartet if they attacked it without long practice together. The players at Hindhead Hall have this qualification, and are, besides, sufficiently accomplished as executants to turn it to satisfactory account.

II

The second of the four concerts of chamber music at Hindhead Hall took place on Monday afternoon last. It was as good of its kind as the first, but it was heavily bowed down under the weight of a grand piano. My experience of English country houses has convinced me that our landed gentry can stand anything that will add to the acreage of walnut and rosewood in their drawing rooms, and produce the sort of tone a primeval savage might delight to strike out of a poker and tongs. In the face of all the pianoforte music written by the great composers, I dare not agitate for the entire abolition of the instrument, but if we must have pianos, why not have quiet ones? Most modern grands are very far inferior as musical instruments to the best surviving specimens of the virginals of Shakespear's time, when England enjoyed the same supremacy in music that she now has in cotton spinning. I am aware that the burning of the *châteaux* which preceded the French revolution, and indeed formed the most practical part of it, had its disadvantages, but if ever anything of the kind happens in this country, we shall at least have the satisfaction of knowing that for every country house that perishes, there will be a grand piano the less in the world.

Under these circumstances I cannot sufficiently express my gratitude to Madame Adeline de Lara for the scrupulously merciful and artistic way in which, so to speak, she steered her ironclad through Monday's program. What the audience wanted from her was a solo between two string quartets, but unfortunately quartets are expensive, and pianists are expensive; so that you cannot have them both at the same concert except in large halls, amid city populations. Consequently the program had to be made up of two pianoforte trios, and a sonata for violin and piano. Madame de Lara was thus hard at work all the time, mitigating the evil effect of the necessarily falsified tuning of the piano on the intonation of the strings and the nicer susceptibilities of the human ear. As I have said, she did it as mercifully as such a thing may be done; but then it should not be done at all for two hours at a stretch.

The trios selected were Beethoven's in D, and Schubert's in B flat. The Beethoven, played when the attention of the audience was quite fresh, and being by far the finest piece of music in the program, was altogether welcome. Then came Brahms's addleheaded but irresistible violin sonata in G major, played by Mr

Elderhorst, who revelled, as all good violinists do, in the plunges into rich two-part melody with which Brahms so repeatedly extricates himself from the ramblings which constitute the connective tissue of the sonata. In works like these Brahms is not dull; the music that wells out of him is delightful; and the difficulties created by his brainlessness are as amusing as the antics of a child playing at being grown up. The Schubert trio was not played, unluckily, until the audience had had quite enough of the combination of string and iron-framed grand. Extremely brilliant and pretty as it is, it came when it was not wanted; and I rather sympathized with the people near the door who bolted at the end of the slow movement. I venture to prophesy that at the next concert, which will be devoted to quartets exclusively, the two hours music will be listened to with far less fatigue; and if I were Miss Fanny Davies, who is to re-introduce the piano at the fourth concert, I should plead strongly for a revision of the program, so as to give the instrument a rest during at least one item. I should have mentioned that the cello was again in the hands of Mr Whitehouse, who, in the Schubert trio, played with apparent ease a very difficult and not particularly grateful part.

III

It will be remembered that at the first concert of this series I was moved to enthusiasm by the situation of the concert hall in the midst of the most beautiful scenery in Surrey. I compared it to Bayreuth: I said the life of a musical critic would be almost happy if all the concerts he attended were on Hindhead. I do not desire to retract these joyful observations; but I am bound to admit that the delights of Hindhead Hall are rather more dependent on the weather than I could wish. Making every possible allowance for last Monday afternoon, I can say no less than that it was abominably cold and detestably wet. When I reached the concert hall I made straight for the grating over the hot water pipes, only to discover that the pipes were so cold that the finger with which I touched them was almost frostbitten. Now I will not pretend that it is any great crime to freeze a critic; but I do say that it is bad economy on the part of the managers of a concert to freeze the fiddlers. When Messrs Elderhorst, Kornfeld, Hobday, and Whitehouse stepped on to the platform, they smiled bravely, as men do when they virtuously get up in winter to take a walk before breakfast, and are resolved to find it a fine, bracing morning, and to congratulate oneanother on not missing the matutinal freshness in bed. But mere force of character will not enable any violinist to feel his strings or his bow when he cannot feel his fingers; and though the four artists plunged into Schubert's quartet in D minor as from a springboard, by the time they came to the variations on Death and the Maiden, I was reconciled to Death and indifferent to the Maiden.

My consolation was that this particular quartet did not greatly matter. The prudent composer uses variations of the Georgian period mainly as a safety valve for his silliness; and though these variations are very pretty (when the players are properly warmed), they are mostly an outrage on the sentiment of the theme. The first movement of the quartet is no more chamber music than a Rossinian overture is; it should be played in a large concert room on a whole orchestra of strings. The *scherzo* has become popular since 1876 by the curious accident that it reminds everyone of Mime the dwarf in Wagner's great Nibelungen tetralogy, whose hammer motif it so spiritedly anticipates. The final *presto*, with its galloping six-eight measure, did a charitable deed. It warmed up the players. When they got within about seventy bars of the final *prestissimo*, Mr Elderhorst's violin suddenly sung out with a tone that proclaimed him a thawed man.

It is hard to understand how Borodin's quartet in D has made its way across the frontiers of its native land. If it were a novel it would not be translated into English. If it were a picture it would not make its way to Bond-street. Not that it is without merit; but every country can produce art of its class for itself. Unfortunately the English nation has lost its self-respect in the matter of music; and though there are dozens of musicians in London—mostly conductors of theatre orchestras—who could produce just as pretty and just as dainty suites as this that Borodin calls a quartet, yet it would not be worth their while to do so, because the substitution of Watkins or Thompson for Borodin would effectually exclude a much better piece of music from any English program of the Hindhead Hall type. This, of course, is not Mr Borodin's fault; and I have nothing to say in disparagement of his elegant little set of pieces. They have no more pretension to be classic than, for example, the dances and interludes which Sir Arthur Sullivan and Mr Edward German compose to order for Sir Henry Irving and Mr George Alexander*; but what they aim at being, they are.

On the whole the audience shewed a good deal of discrimination. The applause for the Schubert quartet was due partly to politeness, and partly to the fact that

* Alexander was the manager of the St James's Theatre, for whose productions of As You Like It (1896) and Much Ado about Nothing (1898), as well as Irving's Lyceum productions of King Henry VIII. (1892) and Romeo and Juliet (1895), Edward German had supplied incidental music. Sir Arthur Sullivan had, as Shaw expressed it in the Saturday Review (19 January 1895), "sweeten[ed] the sentiment here and there" of Irving's production of J. Comyns Carr's King Arthur "by penn'orths of orchestral sugarstick . . ."

our hands, like our teeth, were chattering with cold. But the last item on the program was Mozart's quartet in B flat. Between this work and the two others no comparison can possibly be instituted; in any ten bars of it there is more beauty and more mastery, nobly and frankly displayed, than in the whole of the other two quartets. By this time, fortunately, the room had been warmed by the ancient Russian method of shutting up a number of people in it for a sufficiently long time; and the players were at last in perfect possession of all their resources. The result was a spontaneous and sincere burst of applause which brought the concert to a triumphant conclusion.

IV

The managers of the Hindhead Hall concerts are certainly quick to take a hint as to the comfort of the public. It will be remembered that after the last concert I suggested that the concert room might, with advantage, be made a little warmer. This time I found a tropical atmosphere, in which the newcomers were hastily taking off the Polar furs and wraps with which they had provided themselves. As to the rest, the energetic ones were opening the windows, the quieter spirits languishing uncomplainingly, and the majority, I am afraid, execrating the officiousness of the Herald in bringing this heat wave upon them.

The program, like that of the second concert, was a pianoforte one. And such a piano! When its clangor first burst on my ears, I wondered what new maker had astonished the world. Judge of my surprise when, standing up to look at the instrument, I saw that it bore the familiar name of Broadwood. When I shook the dust of musical criticism from my feet in 1894, I certainly did not think that the world would stand still on that account; time and change, I knew, would pursue their accustomed revolutionary work. But one thing I knew to be impossible, and that was that Broadwoods would ever overstring their pianos. Yet, after four years, here was an overstrung Broadwood, beside which the modest and retiring Steinway grand of the previous concert would have been "banged into dumbness."* They even tell me that this uproarious instrument is not the latest Broadwood achievement, which is barless, and audible for miles in reasonable weather.

Now Hindhead Hall is of a moderate size, but very resonant; and Miss Fanny Davies, being of Celtic stock, is a fiery player; indeed, she is nothing if not fiery, for that quietly noble mood which was so attractive in such great players of her school as Clara Schumann and Agathe Backer-Gröndahl, is not in her temperament. Consequently, she is not at her best when any sort of reticence is imposed on her. May I venture upon a guess, that at the end of the Tchaikovsky trio some of the unfortunate occupants of the front row, stunned by the thunders of the overstrung Broadwood, made an appeal for mercy, which was injudiciously communicated to the pianist? However that may be, it is certain that during the rest of the concert Miss Davies only half used her instrument, with the result that the Mendelssohn trio, in which a brilliant display of execution and leadership might have been expected from her, fell positively flat in the first and last *allegros*. The remedy, in fact, was a mistaken one. The piano should have been taken into the next field, and there handled with unrestricted impulsiveness by Miss Davies. We should then have enjoyed all her unrivaled verve and *maëstria*, whilst distance would have tamed the piano.

I have purposely mentioned leadership among Miss

* An allusion to Shakespear's Twelfth Night, III, 2: You should have banged the youth into dumbness.

Davies's gifts, for she exhibited it to a very marked degree in the Tchaikovsky trio. This work exhibits all the qualities which have made its composer so popular now that he is dead, and we have had plenty of time to think about it. I have seen him conducting his own works in London without receiving any earnest of the enthusiasm now lavished on his Pathetic Symphony (which has the advantage of not being in the least pathetic). The main movements of the trio are full of Byronic romanticism, which is the specific Tchaikovskyan characteristic. His musical restlessness and versatility find vent in the second movement, consisting of a very dainty theme, with variations as ingenious and brilliant as could be desired. Miss Davies's lightning scales in the fourth variation were much applauded. The fifth contains a catching musette or bagpipe freak. The sixth is a waltz. The seventh is full of those eccentric *contra-tempi* in which some composers, notably Schumann and Tchaikovsky, puzzle their executants by writing two-four measures in three-four bars. The eighth variation, insanely described in the program as a fugue, is a very pretty barcarolle, with a charming accompaniment of rippling waves of sound from the violin. The audience accepted it in perfect good faith as a fugue, and, liking it extremely, were much gratified at the improvement in their taste. The tenth variation is a mazurka.

As the trio ends, quite gratuitously, with a tiny funeral march, the people who found nothing to their taste in the trio must have been uncommonly hard to please. It was splendidly played. Miss Davies, using all the power of her instrument without stint, led it with the most inspiriting dash; and Mr Elderhorst quite surpassed himself, playing with greater power and feeling than he has before exhibited. He is a player of the Wilhelmj school, by which I do not mean that he is necessarily a pupil of Wilhelmj, but that he enjoys the passionate floods of melody of the modern school more than the elegant periods of the first half of the century, and consequently plays them more sympathetically.

Between the two trios, Miss Davies and Mr Whitehouse played Brahms's violoncello sonata in E minor, a piece of true chamber music, to which a public performance, even on the Hindhead Hall scale, and especially after such an excitingly public piece of work as the Tchaikovsky trio, does unnecessary violence.

Thus we have reached the conclusion of an excellent series of concerts. They have not been above criticism; no concert given by mortals, under earthly conditions, ever will or can be that. But the residents on Hindhead have no reason to complain of the enterprise. They have been very well served indeed, both by the artists and the managers, and, I may add, very cheaply served too. Compare the subscription of one guinea for four concerts with the subscription rate for St James's or Queen's Hall, plus railway fares! The result of that calculation will, I think, be as satisfactory from the business point of view as the performances have been from the artistic.[U]

THE PERFECT WAGNERITE

A Commentary on the Niblung's Ring

PREFACE TO THE FIRST EDITION
1898

This book is a commentary on The Niblung's Ring, Richard Wagner's chief work. I offer it to those enthusiastic admirers of Wagner who are unable to follow his ideas, and do not in the least understand the dilemma of Wotan, though they are filled with indignation at the irreverence of the Philistines who frankly avow that they find the remarks of the god too often tedious and nonsensical. Now, to be devoted to Wagner merely as a dog is devoted to his master, sharing a few elementary ideas, appetites and emotions with him, and, for the rest, reverencing his superiority without understanding it, is no true Wagnerism. Yet nothing better is possible without a stock of ideas common to master and disciple. Unfortunately, the ideas of the revolutionary Wagner of 1848 are taught neither by the education nor the experience of English and American gentleman-amateurs, who are almost always political mugwumps, and hardly ever associate with revolutionists. The earlier attempts to translate his numerous pamphlets and essays into English resulted in ludicrous mixtures of pure nonsense with the absurdest distortions of his ideas into the ideas of the translators. We now have a translation which is a masterpiece of interpretation and an eminent addition to our literature; but that is not because its author, Mr Ashton Ellis, knows his German dictionary better than his predecessors. He is simply in possession of Wagner's ideas, which were to them inconceivable.

All I pretend to do in this book is to impart the ideas which are most likely to be lacking in the conventional Englishman's equipment. I came by them myself much as Wagner did, having learnt more about music than about anything else in my youth, and sown my political wild oats subsequently in the revolutionary school. This combination is not common in England; and as I seem, so far, to be the only publicly articulate result of it, I venture to add my commentary to what has already been written by musicians who are no revolutionists, and revolutionists who are no musicians. G. B. S.

PITFOLD, HINDHEAD, 1898.

PREFACE TO THE SECOND EDITION

1901

The preparation of a Second Edition of this booklet is quite the most unexpected literary task that has ever been set me. When it first appeared I was ungrateful enough to remonstrate with its publisher for printing, as I thought, more copies than the most sanguine Wagnerite could ever hope to sell.* But the result proved that exactly one person buys a copy on every day of the year, including Sundays; and so, in the process of the suns, a reprint has become necessary.

Save a few verbal slips of no importance, I have found nothing to alter in this edition. As usual, the only protests the book has elicited are protests, not against the opinions it expresses, but against the facts it records. There are people who cannot bear to be told that their hero was associated with a famous Anarchist in a rebellion; that he was proclaimed as "wanted" by the police; that he wrote revolutionary pamphlets; and that his picture of Niblunghome under the reign of Alberic is a poetic vision of unregulated industrial capitalism as it was made known in Germany in the middle of the XIX century by Engels' Condition of the Laboring Classes in England. They frantically deny these facts, and then declare that I have connected them with Wagner in a paroxysm of senseless perversity. I am sorry I have hurt them; and I appeal to charitable publishers to bring out a new life of Wagner, which shall describe him as a court musician of unquestioned fashion and orthodoxy, and a pillar of the most exclusive Dresden circles. Such a work would, I believe, have a large sale,

* The first edition of the book consisted of 1100 copies.

and be read with satisfaction and reassurance by many lovers of Wagner's music.

As to my much demurred-to relegation of Night Falls on The Gods to the category of grand opera, I have nothing to add or withdraw. Such a classification is to me as much a matter of fact as the Dresden rising or the police proclamation; but I shall not pretend that it is a matter of such fact as everybody's judgment can grapple with. People who prefer grand opera to serious music-drama naturally resent my placing a very grand opera below a very serious music-drama. The ordinary lover of Shakespear would equally demur to my placing his popular catchpenny plays, of which As You Like It is an avowed type, below true Shakespearean plays like Measure for Measure. I cannot help that. Popular dramas and operas may have overwhelming merits as enchanting make-believes; but a poet's sincerest vision of the world must always take precedence of his prettiest fool's paradise.

As many English Wagnerites seem to be still under the impression that Wagner composed Rienzi in his youth, Tannhäuser and Lohengrin in his middle age, and The Ring in his later years, may I again remind them that The Ring was the result of a political convulsion which occurred when Wagner was only thirtysix, and that the poem was completed when he was forty, with thirty more years of work before him? It is as much a first essay in political philosophy as Die Feen is a first essay in romantic opera. The attempt to recover its spirit twenty years later, when the music of Night Falls on The Gods was added, was an attempt to revive the barricades of Dresden in the Temple of the Grail. Only those who have never had any political enthusiasms to survive can believe that such an attempt could succeed. G.B.S.

LONDON, 1901.

PREFACE TO THE THIRD EDITION
1913

In 1907 The Perfect Wagnerite was translated into German by my friend Siegfried Trebitsch.* On reading through his version in manuscript I was struck by the inadequacy of the merely negative explanation given by me of the irrelevance of Night Falls on The Gods (Die Götterdämmerung) to the general philosophic scheme of The Ring. That explanation was correct as far as it went; but, put as I had put it, it seemed to me to suggest that the operatic character of Night Falls on The Gods was the result of indifference or forgetfulness produced by the lapse of twentyfive years between the first projection of The Ring and its completion. Now it is clear that in whatever other ways Wagner may have changed, he never became careless and never became indifferent. I therefore inserted in the first German edition a new section in which I shewed how the revolutionary history of Western Europe from the Liberal explosion of 1848 to the confused attempt at a popular and *quasi* Socialist military and municipal administration by the Commune of Paris in 1871 (that is to say, from the literary beginning of The Niblung's Ring by Wagner to the long-delayed musical completion of Night Falls on The Gods) had demonstrated practically that the passing away of the present capitalistic order was going to be a much more complicated business than it appears in Wagner's dramatization.

* Trebitsch (1869–1956), an Austrian, was for half a century Shaw's authorized German translator.

Since 1907, then, the German edition has been more complete than the English one.* I now, after six years' pure procrastination, for which I have no excuse except preoccupation with other work, add the German extension to the English text. Otherwise the book remains as it was.

I have sometimes been asked why anyone should read a philosophic treatise merely to find out the story of The Ring. I take this opportunity to reply publicly that there is, as far as I know, no reason why anyone should take any trouble in the matter at all unless they want to, and that the degree of trouble must be determined by the degree of want, which, again, will be determined by the wanter's capacity. But this I will say. Even for the purposes of the idlest Bayreuth tourist the story of The Ring must be told as Wagner's score tells it if it is to be of any real use to the visitor who cannot understand what the singers are saying. Anyone can, without knowing a bar of the score, string the events narrated in The Ring together in the order of their occurrence on the stage, add the names of the *dramatis personæ* and a description of the scenes, and offer the result as a guide to The Ring. But such a mechanical account of the affair will hinder more than it will help. It will pass over as trivial, or even omit altogether, points to which Wagner has given immense weight and consequence, either by the length or intensity of his direct musical treatment or by the recurrence of themes connected with them; and it will rhetorically emphasize or spread itself descriptively over the more obvious matters which speak for themselves to the spectator and occupy little

* The Brentano edition published in New York in 1909 had, however, contained the original texts of the preface to the first German edition and the added chapter "Why He Changed His Mind." The latter was revised for the 1913 English edition.

space and less depth in the musical fabric. People primed with such accounts sit waiting to see the bear or the dragon or the rainbow, or the transformation of Alberic into a snake and a toad, or the magic fire or the swimming feats of the Rhine daughters, and are bored because these exciting spectacles are so unconscionably delayed whilst Wotan, Fricka, Brynhild, Erda, Alberic, and Loki discuss things of which the "synopsis" gives no hint.

Now the story as it is told in this book has its centres of gravity placed exactly where Wagner has placed them in his score. What Wagner has made much of, I have made much of; and I have explained why he made much of it. What he passed lightly over, I have passed lightly over. There is a good deal in The Ring which is on the surface of the score: nobody with ears and eyes can miss its significance at the performance. But there is also a good deal that was at the back of Wagner's mind, and that determined what I have called the centres of gravity; and this, which is neither in the score nor in the stage action, being assumed by Wagner to be part of the common consciousness of mankind, is what I have chiefly attended to. For this, obvious as it was to Wagner, and as it is to anyone who has reflected on human history and destiny in the light of a competent knowledge of modern capitalistic civilization, is an absolute blank to many persons who are highly susceptible to the musical qualities of Wagner's music and poetry, but have never reflected on human destiny at all, and have been brought up in polite ignorance of the infernal depths our human society descended to in the XIX century. Clearly none of your synopses or popular guides or lists of musical themes would be of the slightest use here. That, I take it, is why this little book remains, after some fifteen years, still in demand, and why I have found it necessary to complete it in this edition by a chapter dealing neither with music nor poetry, but with European history. For it was in that massive material, and not in mere crotchets and quavers, that Wagner found the stuff for his masterpiece. G. B. S.

AYOT ST LAWRENCE, 1913.

PREFACE TO THE FOURTH EDITION 1923

Much water, some of it deeply stained with blood, has passed under the bridges since this book was first published twentyfour years ago. Musically Wagner is now more old-fashioned than Handel and Bach, Mozart and Beethoven, whose fashions have perished though their music remains; whilst his own fashion has been worn to rags by young composers in their first efforts to draw the bow of Ulysses. Finally, it has been discarded as Homerically impossible; and England, after two centuries of imitative negligibility, has suddenly flung into the field a cohort of composers whose methods have made a technical revolution in musical composition so complete that the conductor does not dare to correct the most cacophonous errors in band parts lest the composer should have intended them, and looks in vain for key signatures because young men no longer write in keys but just mark their notes flat or sharp as they come. One can imagine Wagner trying to conduct the latest British tone poem, and exclaiming in desperation "Is this music?" just as his own contemporaries did when they were confronted with the "false relations" in the score of Tristan. It is true that most of the modern developments, as far as they are really developments and not merely experimental eccentricities, are implicit in Parsifal. Indeed, for that matter, they are implicit in Bach: still, the first man to be scandalized by a new departure is usually he that found the path for it; and I cannot feel sure that Wagner would have encouraged Messrs Bax, Ireland, Cyril Scott, Holst, Goossens, Vaughan Williams, Frank Bridge, Boughton, Holbrooke, Howells and the rest (imagine being able to remember offhand so many names of British composers turning out serious music in native styles of their own!!!) any more than Haydn encouraged Beethoven. Wagner, after his 1855 London season as conductor of the Philharmonic, would not have believed that such a thing could happen in England. Had he been told that within two years a British baby Elgar would arrive who would attain classic rank as a European composer, he would hardly have kept his temper. Yet all this has happened very much as it happened before in Shakespear's time; and the English people at large are just as unconcerned about it, and indeed unconscious of it, as they were then.

Also the English have taken, as I said in this book they might, to Wagner singing and acting; and there is now no question of going to Bayreuth or importing German singers when we wish to hear The Ring or Parsifal; for much better performances of both can be heard now from English companies in England than Wagner ever heard at Bayreuth; and even a transpontine theatre like the Old Vic. thinks no more of doing Tannhäuser than it would have thought of doing Black-Eyed Susan* half a century ago.

Another change has outmoded my description of the Bayreuth Festival Playhouse as an ultra modern theatre. Bayreuth has a pictorial stage framed by a proscenium, and the framed picture stage is not now in the latest fashion. When the monarchy and the theatre were restored in England simultaneously on the accession of

* Hugely successful melodrama (1829) by Douglas Jerrold, frequently revived.

Charles II., the representation of Shakespear's plays as he planned them was made impossible by the introduction of pictorial scenery and of the proscenium with its two curtains, the act drop and the final green baize, to divide the plays into acts and hide the stage for intervals during which elaborate scenes were built up on it. His plays had to be chopped into fragments; divided into acts; rewritten and provided with new endings to make effective "curtains," in which condition they were intolerably tedious except as mere pedestals for irresistibly attractive actors and actresses.

Thus the pictorial stage not only murdered Shakespear, and buried the old Athenian Drama, but dictated the form of opera (which grew up with it) and changed the form of the spoken drama. Wagner submitted to it as inevitable; but when he conceived the performances of The Ring, and planned a theatre for them, he made a desperate effort to elaborate its machinery so as to enable complete changes of scene to be made without stopping the performance and keeping the audience staring idly for fifteen minutes at a dropped curtain, or scrambling to and from their seats to fill up the time by smoking cigarets and drinking. One of his devices was to envelop the stage in mists produced by what was called a steam curtain, which looked exactly like what it really was, and made the theatre smell like a laundry. By its aid The Rhine Gold was performed without a break instead of in three acts with long intervals between each.

One had to admit at Bayreuth that here was the utmost perfection of the pictorial stage, and that its machinery could go no further. Nevertheless, having seen it at its best, fresh from Wagner's own influence, I must also admit that my favorite way of enjoying a performance of The Ring is to sit at the back of a box, comfortable on two chairs, feet up, and listen without looking. The truth is, a man whose imagination cannot serve him better than the most costly devices of the imitative scenepainter, should not go to the theatre, and as a matter of fact does not. In planning his Bayreuth theatre, Wagner was elaborating what he had better have scrapped altogether.

But as this did not occur to him, he allowed his technical plan of The Ring to be so governed by pictorial visions that it is as unreasonable to ask Bayreuth to scrap the Wagner tradition as it would be to ask the Théâtre Français to scrap the Molière tradition. Only, I must now treat that tradition as old-fashioned, wheras when this book was first published it was the latest development. What has happened since in England is that an Englishman, Mr Harley Granville-Barker, developing certain experiments made from time to time by Mr William Poel, another Englishman, inaugurated XX century Shakespear by a series of performances in which the plays were given with unprecedented artistic splendor without the omission of a single decently presentable line, undivided into acts, without the old pictorial scenery, and with, as a result, a blessed revelation of Shakespear as the Prince of Entertainers instead of the most dreaded of bores, and a degree of illusion which the pictorial theatre had not only failed to attain, but had sedulously destroyed, nowhere more effectively than (save only in certain scenes of pure ritual in Parsifal) at Bayreuth.

Almost simultaneously with Mr Granville-Barker's revolutionary restoration of Shakespear, the pictorial stage triumphantly announced that at the English Bayreuth, which is the Shakespear Memorial Theatre at Stratford-on-Avon, the play of Coriolanus had been, by climax of Procrustean adaptation, cut down to a performance lasting only one hour, in which state it was humbly hoped that the public would steel itself to bear it just once or twice for the sake of our national playwright. That was too much. Mr Bridges-Adams, who had started with Mr Granville-Barker, took the new method to Stratford, where the former victims of the pictorial stage now find to their amazement that three hours of unabbreviated Shakespear fly faster than one hour of Procrusty Coriolanus. And at the Old Vic. in London, where the reform was adopted by Mr Atkins, Shakespear now draws better than would-be popular melodrama.*

Thus have Englishmen left Wagner behind as to methods, and made obsolete all that part of his book which presents him as a pioneer. I must add that nobody who knows the snobbish contempt in which most Englishmen hold oneanother will be surprised when I mention that in England the exploits of Poel, Granville-Barker, Bridges-Adams, Atkins, and the English designers and painters who have worked for them, are modestly attributed to Herr Reinhardt, their eminent German contemporary. The only Englishman who is given any credit by his countrymen is Mr Gordon Craig, a fascinating propagandist who still loves the stage picture better than the stage play, and, living in the glamor of the Continent, seldom meddles with the actual theatre except to wipe his boots on it and on all the art that grows on its boards.

As to the sociological aspect of The Ring, which is unaffected by the rapid ageing of its technical aspect as a musical composition and a theatrical spectacle, it

* William Bridges-Adams was the founder of the New Shakespeare Company at Stratford-on-Avon in 1919. He staged 29 of Shakespear's plays with this company during the next fifteen years. Robert Atkins, an actor turned director, staged Shakespearean productions, principally at the Old Vic. from 1915 to 1925.

seems to challenge the so-called Great War to invalidate it if it can. Gross as the catastrophe has been, it has not shaken Bayreuth. But postwar contemplation of The Ring must not make us forget that all the progress Wagner saw was from the revolutions of 1848, when he was with the barricaders, to the Imperialist climax of 1871, when he sang:

> Hail, hail, our Cæsar!
> Royal William!
> Rock and ward of German freedom!

What would he have said had he lived to see 1917 in Russia and 1918 in Germany, with England singing "Hang, hang that Kaiser!" and Germany sympathizing to such an extent that the grandson of Wagner's William had to seek safety in Holland? Rhinemaidens walking out with British Tommies, Senegalese negros in Goethe's house, Marx enthroned in Russia, pistolled Romanoffs, fugitive Hapsburgs, exiled Hohenzollerns marking the ruins of empires with no more chance of restoration than the Stuarts and Bourbons: such a Götterdämmerung, in short, as in its craziness can be fitted into no allegory until its upshot becomes plainer than it now is: all this has so changed the political atmosphere in which Wagner lived, and in which this book was written, that it says much for the comprehensiveness of his grasp of things that his allegory should still be valid and important. Indeed the war was more a great tearing off of masks than a change of face: the main difference is that Alberic is richer, and his slaves hungrier and harder worked when they are so lucky as to have any work to do. The Ring ends with everybody dead except three mermaids; and though the war went far enough in that conclusive direction to suggest that the next war may possibly kill even the mermaids with "depth charges," the curtain is not yet down on our drama, and we have to carry on as best we can. If we succeed, this book may have to pass into yet another edition: if not, the world itself will have to be re-edited.

AYOT ST LAWRENCE, 1922.

THE PERFECT WAGNERITE

PRELIMINARY ENCOURAGEMENTS

A few of these will be welcome to the ordinary citizen visiting the theatre to satisfy his curiosity, or his desire to be in the fashion, by witnessing a representation of Richard Wagner's famous tetralogy: The Niblung's Ring.

First, The Ring, with all its gods and giants and dwarfs, its water-maidens and Valkyries, its wishing-cap, magic ring, enchanted sword, and miraculous treasure, is a drama of today, and not of a remote and fabulous antiquity. It could not have been written before the second half of the XIX century, because it deals with events which were only then consummating themselves. Unless the spectator recognizes in it an image of the life he is himself fighting his way through, it must needs appear to him a monstrous development of the Christmas pantomimes, spun out here and there into intolerable lengths of dull conversation by the principal baritone. Fortunately, even from this point of view, The Ring is full of extraordinarily attractive episodes, both orchestral and dramatic. The nature music alone—music of river and rainbow, fire and forest—is enough to bribe people with any love of the country in them to endure the passages of political philosophy in the sure hope of a prettier page to come. Everybody, too, can enjoy the love music, the hammer and anvil music, the clumping of the giants, the tune of the young woodsman's horn, the trilling of the bird, the dragon music and nightmare music and thunder and lightning music, the profusion of simple melody, the sensuous charm of the orchestration: in short, the vast extent of common ground between The Ring and the ordinary music we use for play and pleasure. Hence it is that the four separate music-plays of which it is built have become popular throughout Europe as operas. We shall presently see that one of them, Night Falls on The Gods, actually is an opera.

It is generally understood, however, that there is an inner ring of superior persons to whom the whole work has a most urgent and searching philosophic and social significance. I profess to be such a superior person; and I write this pamphlet for the assistance of those who wish to be introduced to the work on equal terms with that inner circle of adepts.

My second encouragement is addressed to modest citizens who may suppose themselves to be disqualified from enjoying The Ring by their technical ignorance of music. They may dismiss all such misgivings speedily and confidently. If the sound of music has any power to move them, they will find that Wagner exacts nothing further. There is not a single bar of "classical music" in The Ring—not a note in it that has any other point than the single direct point of giving musical expression to the drama. In classical music there are, as the analytical programs tell us, first subjects and second subjects, free fantasias, recapitulations, and *codas*; there are fugues, with counter-subjects, *strettos*, and pedal points; there are passacaglias on ground basses, canons *ad hypodiapente,* and other ingenuities, which have, after all, stood or fallen by their prettiness as much as the simplest folk-tune. Wagner is never driving at anything of this sort any more than Shakespear in his plays is driving at such ingenuities of verse-making as sonnets, triolets, and the like. And this is why he is so easy for the natural musician who has had no academic teaching. The professors, when Wagner's music is played to them, exclaim at once "What is this? Is it aria, or recitative? Is there no *cabaletta* to it—not even a full close? Why was that discord not prepared; and why does he not resolve it correctly? How dare he indulge in those scandalous and illicit transitions into a key that has not one note in common with the key he has just left? Listen to those false relations! What does he want with six drums and eight horns when Mozart worked miracles with two of each? The man is no musician." The layman neither knows nor cares about any of these things. If Wagner were to turn aside from his straightforward dramatic purpose to propitiate the professors with correct exercises in sonata form, his music would at once become unintelligible to the unsophisticated spectator, upon whom the familiar and dreaded "classical" sensation would descend like the influenza. Nothing of the kind need be dreaded. The unskilled, untaught musician may approach Wagner boldly; for there is no possibility of a misunderstanding between them: the Ring music is perfectly single and simple. It is the adept musician of the old school who has everything to unlearn; and him I leave, unpitied, to his fate.

THE NIBLUNG'S RING

The Ring consists of four plays, intended to be performed on four successive evenings, entitled The Rhine Gold (a prologue to the other three), The Valkyrie, Siegfried, and Night Falls on The Gods; or, in the original German, Das Rheingold, Die Walküre, Siegfried, and Die Götterdämmerung.

THE RHINE GOLD

Let me assume for a moment that you are a young and goodlooking woman. Try to imagine yourself in that character at Klondike five years ago. The place is teeming with gold. If you are content to leave the gold alone, as the wise leave flowers without plucking them, enjoying with perfect *naïveté* its color and glitter and preciousness, no human being will ever be the worse for your knowledge of it; and whilst you remain in that frame of mind the golden age will endure.

Now suppose a man comes along: a man who has no sense of the golden age, nor any power of living in the present: a man with common desires, cupidities, ambitions, just like most of the men you know. Suppose you reveal to that man the fact that if he will only pluck this gold up, and turn it into money, millions of men, driven by the invisible whip of hunger, will toil underground and overground night and day to pile up more and more gold for him until he is master of the world! You will find that the prospect will not tempt him so much as you might imagine, because it involves some distasteful trouble to himself to start with, and because there is something else within his reach involving no distasteful toil, which he desires more passionately; and that is yourself. So long as he is preoccupied with love of you, the gold, and all that it implies, will escape him: the golden age will endure. Not until he forswears love will he stretch out his hand to the gold, and found the Plutonic empire for himself. But the choice between love and gold may not rest altogether with him. He may be an ugly, ungracious, unamiable person whose affections may seem merely ludicrous and despicable to you. In that case, you may repulse him, and most bitterly humiliate and disappoint him. What is left to him then but to curse the love he can never win, and turn remorselessly to the gold? With that, he will make short work of your golden age, and leave you lamenting its lost thoughtlessness and sweetness.

In due time the gold of Klondike will find its way to the great cities of the world. But the old dilemma will keep continually reproducing itself. The man who will turn his back on love, and upon all the fruitful, creative, life-pursuing activities into which the loftiest human energy can develop it, and will set himself singleheartedly to gather gold in an exultant dream of wielding its Plutonic powers, will find the treasure yielding quickly to his touch. But few men will make this sacrifice voluntarily. Not until the Plutonic power is so strongly set up that the higher human impulses are suppressed as rebellious, and even the mere appetites are denied, starved, and insulted when they cannot purchase their satisfaction with gold, are the energetic spirits driven to build their lives upon riches. How inevitable that course has become to us is plain enough to those who have the power of understanding what they see as they look at the plutocratic societies of our modern capitals.

FIRST SCENE

Here, then, is the subject of the first scene of The Rhine Gold. As you sit waiting for the curtain to rise, you suddenly catch the booming ground-tone of a mighty river. It becomes plainer, clearer: you get nearer to the surface, and catch the green light and the flights of bubbles. Then the curtain goes up and you see what you heard—the depths of the Rhine, with three strange fairy fishes, half water-maidens, singing and enjoying themselves exuberantly. They are not singing barcarolles or ballads about the Lorely and her fated lovers, but simply trolling any nonsense that comes into their heads in time to the dancing of the water and the rhythm of their swimming. It is the golden age; and the attraction of this spot for the Rhine maidens is a lump of the Rhine gold, which they value, in an entirely uncommercial way, for its bodily beauty and splendor. Just at present it is eclipsed, because the sun is not striking down through the water.

Presently there comes a poor devil of a dwarf stealing along the slippery rocks of the river bed, a creature with energy enough to make him strong of body and fierce of passion, but with a brutish narrowness of intelligence and selfishness of imagination: too stupid to see that his own welfare can only be compassed as part of the welfare of the world, too full of brute force not to grab vigorously at his own gain. Such dwarfs are quite common in London. He comes now with a fruitful impulse in him, in search of what he lacks in himself, beauty, lightness of heart, imagination, music. The Rhine maidens, representing all these to him, fill him with hope and longing; and he never considers that he has nothing to offer that they could possibly desire, being by natural limitation incapable of seeing anything from anyone else's point of view. With perfect simplicity he offers himself as a sweetheart to them. But they are thoughtless, elemental, only half real things, much like modern young ladies. That the poor dwarf is repulsive to their sense of physical beauty and their romantic conception of heroism, that he is ugly and awkward, greedy and ridiculous, disposes for them of his claim to live and love. They mock him atrociously, pretending to fall in love with him at first sight, and then slipping away and making game of him, heaping ridicule and disgust on the poor wretch until he is beside himself with mortification and rage. They forget him when the water begins to glitter in the sun, and the gold to reflect its glory. They break into ecstatic worship of their treasure; and though they know the parable of Klondike quite well, they have no fear that the gold will be wrenched away by the dwarf, since it will yield to no one who has not forsworn love for it, and it is in pursuit of love that he has come to them. They forget that they have poisoned that desire in him by their mockery and denial of it, and that he now knows that life will give him nothing that he cannot wrest from it by the Plutonic power. It is just as if some poor, rough, vulgar, coarse fellow were to offer to take his part in aristocratic society, and be snubbed into the knowledge that only as a millionaire could he ever hope to bring that society to his feet and buy himself a beautiful and refined wife. His choice is forced on him. He forswears love as thousands of us forswear it every day; and in a moment the gold is in his grasp, and he disappears in the depths, leaving the water-fairies vainly screaming "Stop thief!" whilst the river seems to plunge into darkness and sink from us as we rise to the cloud regions above.

And now, what forces are there in the world to assist Alberic, our dwarf, in his new character of sworn plutocrat? He is soon at work wielding the power of the gold. For his gain, hordes of his fellow creatures are thenceforth condemned to slave miserably, overground and underground, lashed to their work by the invisible whip of starvation. They never see him, any more than the victims of our "dangerous trades" ever see the shareholders whose power is nevertheless everywhere, driving them to destruction. The very wealth they create with their labor becomes an additional force to impoverish them; for as fast as they make it it slips from their hands into the hand of their master, and makes him mightier than ever. You can see the process for yourself in every civilized country today, where millions of people toil in want and disease to heap up more wealth for our Alberics, laying up nothing for themselves, except sometimes horrible and agonizing disease and certainty of premature death. All this part of the story is frightfully real, frightfully present, frightfully modern; and its effects on our social life are so ghastly and ruinous that we no longer know enough of happiness to be discomposed by it. It is only the poet, with his vision of what life might be, to whom these things are unendurable. If we were a race of poets we would make an end of them before the end of this miserable century. Being a race of moral dwarfs instead, we think them highly respectable, comfortable and proper, and allow them to breed and multiply their evil in all directions. If there were no higher power in the world to work against Alberic, the end of it would be utter destruction.

Such a force there is, however; and it is called Godhead. The mysterious thing we call life organizes itself into all living shapes, bird, beast, beetle and fish, rising to the human marvel in cunning dwarfs and in laborious muscular giants, capable, these last, of enduring toil, willing to buy love and life, not with suicidal curses and renunciations, but with patient manual drudgery in the service of higher powers. And these higher powers are called into existence by the same self-organization of life still more wonderfully into rare persons who may by comparison be called gods, creatures capable of thought, whose aims extend far beyond the satisfaction of their bodily appetites and personal affections, since they perceive that it is only by the establishment of a social order founded on common bonds of moral faith that the world can rise from mere savagery. But how is this order to be set up by Godhead in a world of stupid giants, since these thoughtless ones pursue only their narrower personal ends and can by no means understand the aims of a god? Godhead, face to face with Stupidity, must compromise. Unable to enforce on the world the pure law of thought, it must resort to a mechanical law of commandments to be enforced by brute punishments and the destruction of the disobedient. And however carefully these laws are framed to represent the highest thoughts of the framers at the moment of their promulgation, before a day has elapsed that thought has grown and widened by the ceaseless evolution of life; and lo! yesterday's law already fallen out with today's thought. Yet if the high givers of that law themselves set the example of breaking it before it is a week old, they destroy all its authority with their subjects, and so break the weapon they have forged to rule them for their own good. They must therefore maintain at all costs the sanctity of the law, even when it has ceased to represent their thought; so that at last they get entangled in a network of ordinances which they no longer believe in, and yet have made so sacred by custom and so terrible by punishment, that they cannot themselves escape from them. Thus Godhead's resort to law finally costs it half its integrity—as if a spiritual king, to gain temporal power, had plucked out one of his eyes—and it finally begins secretly to long for the advent of some power higher than itself which will destroy its artificial empire of law, and establish a true republic of free thought.

This is by no means the only difficulty in the dominion of Law. The brute force for its execution must be purchased; and the mass of its subjects must be persuaded to respect the authority which employs this force. But how is such respect to be implanted in them if they are unable to comprehend the thought of the lawgiver? Clearly, only by associating the legislative power with such displays of splendor and majesty as will impress their senses and awe their imaginations. The god turned lawgiver, in short, must be crowned Pontiff and King. Since he cannot be known to the common folk as their superior in wisdom, he must be known to them as their superior in riches, as the dweller in castles, the wearer of gold and purple, the eater of mighty feasts, the commander of armies, and the wielder of powers of life and death, of salvation and damnation after death. Something may be done in this way without corruption whilst the golden age still endures. Your gods may not prevail with the dwarfs; but they may go to these honest giants who will give a day's work for a day's pay, and induce them to build for Godhead a mighty fortress, complete with hall and chapel, tower and bell, for the sake of the homesteads that will grow up in security round that church-castle. This only, however, whilst the golden age lasts. The moment the Plutonic power is let loose, and the loveless Alberic comes into the field with his corrupting millions, the gods are face to face with destruction; since Alberic, able with invisible hunger-whip to force the labor of the dwarfs and to buy the services of the giants, can outshine all the temporal shows and splendors of the golden age, and make himself master of the world, unless the gods, with their bigger brains, can capture his gold. This, the dilemma of the Church today, is the situation created by the exploit of Alberic in the depths of the Rhine.

SECOND SCENE

From the bed of the river we rise into cloudy regions, and finally come out into the clear in a meadow, where Wotan, the god of gods, and his consort Fricka lie sleeping. Wotan, you will observe, has lost one eye; and you will presently learn that he plucked it out voluntarily as the price to be paid for his alliance with Fricka, who in return has brought to him as her dowry all the powers of Law. The meadow is on the brink of a ravine, beyond which, towering on distant heights, stands Godhome, a mighty castle, newly built as a house of state for the one-eyed god and his all-ruling wife. Wotan has not yet seen this castle except in his dreams: two giants have just built it for him whilst he slept; and the reality is before him for the first time when Fricka wakes him. In that majestic burg he is to rule with her and through her over the humble giants, who have eyes to gape at the glorious castles their own hands have built from his design, but no brains to design castles for themselves, or to comprehend divinity. As a god, he is to be great, secure, and mighty; but he is also to be passionless, affectionless, wholly impartial; for Godhead, if it is to live with Law, must have no weaknesses, no respect for persons. All such sweet littlenesses must be left to the humble stupid giants to make their toil sweet to them; and the god must, after all, pay for Olympian power the same price the dwarf has paid for Plutonic power.

Wotan has forgotten this in his dreams of greatness. Not so Fricka. What she is thinking of is this price that Wotan has consented to pay, in token whereof he has promised this day to hand over to the giants Fricka's sister, the goddess Freia, with her golden love-apples. When Fricka reproaches Wotan with having selfishly forgotten this, she finds that he, like herself, is not prepared to go through with his bargain, and that he is trusting to another great world-force, the Lie (a European Power, as Lassalle said), to help him to trick the giants out of their reward. But this force does not dwell in Wotan himself, but in another, a god over whom he has triumphed, one Loki, the god of Intellect, Argument, Imagination, Illusion, and Reason. Loki has promised to deliver him from his contract, and to cheat the giants for him; but he has not arrived to keep his word: indeed, as Fricka bitterly points out, why should not the Lie fail Wotan, since such failure is the very essence of him?

The giants come soon enough; and Freia flies to Wotan for protection against them. Their purposes are quite honest; and they have no doubt of the god's faith. There stands their part of the contract fulfilled, stone on stone, port and pinnacle all faithfully finished from Wotan's design by their mighty labor. They have come undoubtingly for their agreed wage. Then there happens what is to them an incredible, inconceivable thing. The god begins to shuffle. There are no moments in life more tragic than those in which the humble common man, the manual worker, leaving with implicit trust all high affairs to his betters, and reverencing them wholly as worthy of that trust, even to the extent of accepting as his rightful function the saving of them from all roughening and coarsening drudgeries, first discovers that they are corrupt, greedy, unjust and treacherous. The shock drives a ray of prophetic light into one giant's mind, and gives him a momentary eloquence. In that moment he rises above his stupid gianthood, and earnestly warns the Son of Light that all his power and eminence of priesthood, godhood, and kingship must stand or fall with the unbearable cold greatness of the incorruptible lawgiver. But Wotan, whose assumed character of lawgiver is altogether false to his real passionate nature, despises the rebuke; and the giant's ray of insight is lost in the murk of his virtuous indignation.

In the midst of the wrangle, Loki comes at last, excusing himself for being late on the ground that he has been detained by a matter of importance which he has promised to lay before Wotan. When pressed to give his mind to the business immediately in hand, and to extricate Wotan from his dilemma, he has nothing to say except that the giants are evidently altogether in the right. The castle has been duly built: he has tried every stone of it, and found the work first-rate: there is nothing to be done but pay the price agreed upon by handing over Freia to the giants. The gods are furious; and Wotan passionately declares that he only consented to the bargain on Loki's promise to find a way for him out of it. But Loki says no: he has promised to find a way out if any such way exist, but not to make a way if there is no way. He has wandered over the whole earth in search of some treasure great enough to buy Freia back from the giants; but in all the world he has found nothing for which Man will give up Woman. And this, by the way, reminds him of the matter he had promised to lay before Wotan. The Rhine maidens have complained to him of Alberic's theft of their gold; and he mentions it as a curious exception to his universal law of the unpurchasable preciousness of love, that this gold-robber has forsworn love for the sake of the fabulous riches of the Plutonic empire and the mastery of the world through its power.

No sooner is the tale told than the giants stoop lower than the dwarf. Alberic forswore love only when it was denied to him and made the instrument for cruelly murdering his self-respect. But the giants, with love within their reach, with Freia and her golden apples in their hands, offer to give her up for the treasure of Alberic. Observe, it is the treasure alone that they desire. They have no fierce dreams of dominion over their superiors, or of moulding the world to any conceptions of their own. They are neither clever nor ambitious: they simply covet money. Alberic's gold: that is their demand, or else Freia, as agreed upon, whom they now carry off as hostage, leaving Wotan to consider their ultimatum.

Freia gone, the gods begin to wither and age: her golden apples, which they so lightly bargained away, they now find to be a matter of life and death to them; for not even the gods can live on Law and Godhead alone, be their castles ever so splendid. Loki alone is unaffected: the Lie, with all its cunning wonders, its glistenings and shiftings and mirages, is a mere appearance: it has no body and needs no food. What is Wotan to do? Loki sees the answer clearly enough: he must bluntly rob Alberic. There is nothing to prevent him except moral scruple; for Alberic, after all, is a poor, dim, dwarfed, credulous creature whom a god can outsee and a lie can outwit. Down, then, Wotan and Loki plunge into the mine where Alberic's slaves are piling up wealth for him under the invisible whip.

THIRD SCENE

This gloomy place need not be a mine: it might just as well be a match factory, with yellow phosphorus, phossy jaw, a large dividend, and plenty of clergymen shareholders. Or it might be a whitelead factory, or a chemical works, or a pottery, or a railway shunting yard, or a tailoring shop, or a little gin-sodden laundry, or a bakehouse, or a big shop, or any other of the places where human life and welfare are daily sacrificed in order that some greedy foolish creature may be able to hymn exultantly to his Plutonic idol:

> Thou mak'st me eat whilst others starve,
> And sing while others do lament:
> Such unto me Thy Blessings are,
> As if I were Thine only care.

In the mine, which resounds with the clinking anvils of the dwarfs toiling miserably to heap up treasure for their master, Alberic has set his brother Mime—more familiarly, Mimmy—to make him a helmet. Mimmy dimly sees that there is some magic in this helmet, and tries to keep it; but Alberic wrests it from him, and shews him, to his cost, that it is the veil of the invisible whip, and that he who wears it can appear in what shape he will, or disappear from view altogether. This helmet is a very common article in our streets, where it generally takes the form of a tall hat. It makes a man invisible as a shareholder, and changes him into various shapes, such as a pious Christian, a subscriber to hospitals, a benefactor of the poor, a model husband and father, a shrewd, practical, independent Englishman, and what not, when he is really a pitiful parasite on the commonwealth, consuming a great deal, and producing nothing, feeling nothing, knowing nothing, believing nothing, and doing nothing except what all the rest do, and that only because he is afraid not to do it, or at least pretend to do it.

When Wotan and Loki arrive, Loki claims Alberic as an old acquaintance. But the dwarf has no faith in these civil strangers: Greed instinctively mistrusts Intellect, even in the garb of Poetry and the company of Godhead, whilst envying the brilliancy of the one and the dignity of the other. Alberic breaks out at them with a terrible boast of the power now within his grasp. He paints for them the world as it will be when his dominion over it is complete, when the soft airs and green mosses of its valleys shall be changed into smoke, slag, and filth; when slavery, disease, and squalor, soothed by drunkenness and mastered by the policeman's *bâton*, shall become the foundation of society; and when nothing shall escape ruin except such pretty places and pretty women as he may like to buy for the slaking of his own lusts. In that kingdom of evil he sees that there will be no power but his own. These gods, with their moralities and legalities and intellectual subtlety, will go under and be starved out of existence. He bids Wotan and Loki beware of it; and his "Hab' Acht!" is hoarse, horrible, and sinister. Wotan is revolted to the very depths of his being: he cannot stifle the execration that bursts from him. But Loki is unaffected: he has no moral passion:

indignation is as absurd to him as enthusiasm. He finds it exquisitely amusing—having a touch of the comic spirit in him—that the dwarf, in stirring up the moral fervor of Wotan, has removed his last moral scruple about becoming a thief. Wotan will now rob the dwarf without remorse; for is it not positively his highest duty to take this power out of such evil hands and use it himself in the interests of Godhead? On the loftiest moral grounds, he lets Loki do his worst.

A little cunningly disguised flattery makes short work of Alberic. Loki pretends to be afraid of him; and he swallows that bait unhesitatingly. But how, inquires Loki, is he to guard against the hatred of his million slaves? Will they not steal from him, whilst he sleeps, the magic ring, the symbol of his power, which he has forged from the gold of the Rhine? "You think yourself very clever" sneers Alberic, and then begins to boast of the enchantments of the magic helmet. Loki refuses to believe in such marvels without witnessing them. Alberic, only too glad to shew off his powers, puts on the helmet and transforms himself into a monstrous serpent. Loki gratifies him by pretending to be frightened out of his wits, but ventures to remark that it would be better still if the helmet could transform its owner into some tiny creature that could hide and spy in the smallest cranny. Alberic promptly transforms himself into a toad. In an instant Wotan's foot is on him; Loki tears away the helmet; they pinion him, and drag him away a prisoner up through the earth to the meadow by the castle.

FOURTH SCENE

There, to pay for his freedom, he has to summon his slaves from the depths to place all the treasure they have heaped up for him at the feet of Wotan. Then he demands his liberty; but Wotan must have the ring as well. And here the dwarf, like the giant before him, feels the very foundations of the world shake beneath him at the discovery of his own base cupidity in a higher power. That evil should, in its loveless desperation, create malign powers which Godhead could not create, seems but natural justice to him. But that Godhead should steal those malign powers from evil, and wield them itself, is a monstrous perversion; and his appeal to Wotan to forego it is almost terrible in its conviction of wrong. It is of no avail. Wotan falls back again on virtuous indignation. He reminds Alberic that he stole the gold from the Rhine daughters, and takes the attitude of the just judge compelling a restitution of stolen goods. Alberic, knowing perfectly well that the judge is taking the goods to put them in his own pocket, has the ring torn from his finger, and is once more as poor as he was when he came slipping and stumbling among the slimy rocks in the bed of the Rhine.

This is the way of the world. In older times, when the Christian laborer was drained dry by the knightly spendthrift, and the spendthrift was drained by the Jewish usurer, Church and State, religion and law, seized on the Jew and drained him as a Christian duty. When the forces of lovelessness and greed had built up our own sordid capitalist systems, driven by invisible proprietorship, robbing the poor, defacing the earth, and forcing themselves as a universal curse even on the generous and humane, then religion and law and intellect, which would never themselves have discovered such systems, their natural bent being towards welfare, economy, and life instead of towards corruption, waste, and death, nevertheless did not scruple to seize by fraud and force these powers of evil on pretence of using them for good. And it inevitably happens that when the Church, the Law, and all the Talents have made common cause to rob the people, the Church is far more vitally harmed by that unfaithfulness to itself than its more mechanical confederates; so that finally they turn on their discredited ally and rob the Church, with the cheerful cooperation of Loki, as in France and Italy for instance.

The twin giants come back with their hostage, in whose presence Godhead blooms again. The gold is ready for them; but now that the moment has come for parting with Freia the gold does not seem so tempting; and they are sorely loth to let her go. Not unless there is gold enough to utterly hide her from them—not until the heap has grown so that they can see nothing but gold—until money has come between them and every human feeling, will they part with her. There is not gold enough to accomplish this: however cunningly Loki spreads it, the glint of Freia's hair is still visible to Giant Fafnir, and the magic helmet must go on the heap to shut it out. Even then Fafnir's brother, Fasolt, can catch a beam from her eye through a chink, and is rendered incapable thereby of forswearing her. There is nothing to stop that chink but the ring; and Wotan is as greedily bent on keeping that as Alberic himself was; nor can the other gods persuade him that Freia is worth it, since for the highest god, love is not the highest good, but only the universal delight that bribes all living things to travail with renewed life. Life itself, with its accomplished marvels and its infinite potentialities, is the only force that Godhead can worship. Wotan does not yield until he is reached by the voice of the fruitful earth, that before he or the dwarfs or the giants or the Law or the Lie or any of these things were, had the seed of them all in her bosom, and the seed perhaps of something higher even than himself, that shall one day supersede him and cut the tangles and alliances and compromises that already have cost him one of his eyes. When Erda, the First Mother of life, rises from her sleeping place in the heart of the earth, and warns him to yield the ring, he obeys her; the ring is added to the heap of gold; and all sense of Freia is cut off from the giants.

But now what Law is left to these two poor stupid laborers whereby one shall yield to the other any of the treasure for which they have each paid the whole price in surrendering Freia? They look by mere habit to the god to judge for them; but he, with his heart stirring towards higher forces than himself, turns with disgust from these lower forces. They settle it as two wolves might; and Fafnir batters his brother dead with his staff. It is a horrible thing to see and hear, to anyone who knows how much blood has been shed in the world in just that way by its brutalized toilers, honest fellows enough until their betters betrayed them. Fafnir goes off with his booty. It is quite useless to him. He has neither the cunning nor the ambition to establish the Plutonic empire with it. Merely to prevent others from getting it is the only purpose it brings him. He piles it in a cave; transforms himself into a dragon by the helmet; and devotes his life to guarding it, as much a slave to it as a jailor is to his prisoner. He had much better have thrown it all back into the Rhine and transformed himself into the shortest-lived animal that enjoys at least a brief run in the sunshine. His case, however, is far too common to be surprising. The world is overstocked with persons who sacrifice all their affections, and madly trample and batter down their fellows to obtain riches of which, when they get them, they are unable to make the smallest use, and to which they become the most miserable slaves.

The gods soon forget Fafnir in their rejoicing over Freia. Donner, the Thunder god, springs to a rocky summit and calls the clouds as a shepherd calls his flocks. They come at his summons; and he and the castle are hidden by their black legions. Froh, the Rainbow god, hastens to his side. At the stroke of Donner's hammer the black murk is riven in all directions by darting ribbons of lightning; and as the air clears, the castle is seen in its fullest splendor, accessible now by the rainbow bridge which Froh has cast across the ravine. In the glory of this moment Wotan has a great thought. With all his aspirations to establish a reign of noble thought, of righteousness, order, and justice, he has found that day that there is no race yet in the world that quite spontaneously, naturally, and unconsciously realizes his ideal. He himself has found how far short Godhead falls of the thing it conceives. He, the greatest of gods, has been unable to control his fate: he has been forced against his will to choose between evils, to make disgraceful bargains, to break them still more disgracefully, and even then to see the price of his disgrace slip through his fingers. His consort has cost him half his vision; his castle has cost him his affections; and the attempt to retain both has cost him his honor. On every side he is shackled and bound, dependent on the laws of Fricka and on the lies of Loki, forced to traffic with dwarfs for handicraft and with giants for strength, and to pay them both in false coin. After all, a god is a pitiful thing. But the fertility of the First Mother is not yet exhausted. The life that came from her has ever climbed up to a higher and higher organization. From toad and serpent to dwarf, from bear and elephant to giant, from dwarf and giant to a god with thoughts, with comprehension of the world, with ideals. Why should it stop there? Why should it not rise from the god to the Hero? to the creature in whom the god's unavailing thought shall have become effective will and life, who shall make his way straight to truth and reality over the laws of Fricka and the lies of Loki with a strength that overcomes giants and a cunning that outwits dwarfs? Yes: Erda, the First Mother, must travail again, and breed him a race of heros to deliver the world and himself from his limited powers and disgraceful bargains. This is the vision that flashes on him as he turns to the rainbow bridge and calls his wife to come and dwell with him in Valhalla, the home of the gods.

They are all overcome with Valhalla's glory except Loki. He is behind the scenes of this joint reign of the Divine and the Legal. He despises these gods with their ideals and their golden apples. "I am ashamed" he says "to have dealings with these futile creatures." And so he follows them to the rainbow bridge. But as they set foot on it, from the river below rises the wailing of the Rhine daughters for their lost gold. "You down there in the water" cries Loki with brutal irony "you used to bask in the glitter of your gold: henceforth you shall bask in the splendor of the gods." And they reply that the truth is in the depths and the darkness, and that what blazes on high there is falsehood. And with that the gods pass into their glorious stronghold.

WAGNER AS REVOLUTIONIST

Before leaving this explanation of The Rhine Gold, I must have a word or two about it with the reader.

It is the least popular of the sections of The Ring. The reason is that its dramatic moments lie quite outside the consciousness of people whose joys and sorrows are all domestic and personal, and whose religions and political ideas are purely conventional and superstitious. To them it is a struggle between half a dozen fairytale personages for a ring, involving hours of scolding and cheating, and one long scene in a dark, gruesome mine, with gloomy, ugly music, and not a glimpse of a handsome young man or pretty woman. Only those of wider consciousness can follow it breathlessly, seeing in it the whole tragedy of human history and the whole horror of the dilemmas from which the world is shrinking today. At Bayreuth I have seen a party of English tourists, after enduring agonies of boredom from Alberic, rise in the middle of the third scene, and almost force their way out of the dark theatre into the sunlit pinewood without. And I have seen people who were deeply affected by the scene driven almost beside themselves by this disturbance. But it was a very natural thing for the unfortunate tourists to do, since in this Rhine Gold prologue there is no interval between the acts for escape. Roughly speaking, people who have no general ideas, no touch of the concern of the philosopher and statesman for the race, cannot enjoy The Rhine Gold as a drama. They may find compensations in some exceedingly pretty music, at times even grand and glorious, which will enable them to escape occasionally from the struggle between Alberic and Wotan; but if their capacity for music should be as limited as their comprehension of the world, they had better stay away.

And now, attentive Reader, we have reached the point at which some foolish person is sure to interrupt us by declaring that The Rhine Gold is what they call "a work of art" pure and simple, and that Wagner never dreamt of shareholders, tall hats, whitelead factories, and industrial and political questions looked at from the socialistic and humanitarian points of view. We need not discuss these impertinences: it is easier to silence them with the facts of Wagner's life. In 1843 he obtained the position of conductor of the Opera at Dresden at a salary of £225 a year, with a pension. This was a first-rate permanent appointment in the service of the Saxon State, carrying an assured professional position and livelihood with it. In 1848, the year of revolutions, the discontented middle class, unable to rouse the Church-and-State governments of the day from their bondage to custom, caste, and law by appeals to morality or constitutional agitation for Liberal reforms, made common cause with the starving wage-working class, and resorted to armed rebellion, which reached Dresden in 1849. Had Wagner been the mere musical epicure and political mugwump that the term "artist" seems to suggest to so many critics and amateurs—that is, a creature in their own lazy likeness—he need have taken no more part in the political struggles of his day than Bishop took in the English Reform agitation of 1832, or Sterndale Bennett in the Chartist or Free Trade movements. What he did do was first to make a desperate appeal to the King to cast off his bonds and answer the need of the time by taking true kingship on himself and leading his people to the redress of their intolerable wrongs (fancy the poor monarch's feelings!), and then, when the crash came, to take his side with the right and the poor against the rich and the wrong. When the insurrection was defeated, three leaders of it were especially marked down for vengeance: August Roeckel, an old friend of Wagner's to whom he wrote a well-known series of letters; Michael Bakoonin, afterwards a famous apostle of revolutionary Anarchism; and Wagner himself. Wagner escaped to Switzerland: Roeckel and Bakoonin suffered long terms of imprisonment. Wagner was of course utterly ruined, pecuniarily and socially (to his own intense relief and satisfaction); and his exile lasted twelve years. His first idea was to get his Tannhäuser produced in Paris. With the notion of explaining himself to the Parisians he wrote a pamphlet entitled Art and Revolution, a glance through which will shew how thoroughly the socialistic side of the revolution had his sympathy, and how completely he had got free from the influence of the established Churches of his day. For three years he kept pouring forth pamphlets—some of them elaborate treatises in size and intellectual rank, but still essentially the pamphlets and manifestos of a born agitator—on social evolution, religion, life, art, and the influence of riches. In 1853 the poem of The Ring was privately printed; and in 1854, five years after the Dresden insurrection, The Rhine Gold score was completed to the last drum tap.

These facts are on official record in Germany, where the proclamation summing up Wagner as "a politically dangerous person" may be consulted to this day. The pamphlets are now accessible to English readers in the translation of Mr Ashton Ellis. This being so, any person who, having perhaps heard that I am a Socialist, attempts to persuade you that my interpretation of The Rhine Gold is only "my socialism" read into the works of a dilettantist who borrowed an idle tale from an old saga to make an opera book with, may safely be dismissed from your consideration as an ignoramus.

If you are now satisfied that The Rhine Gold is an allegory, do not forget that an allegory is never quite consistent except when it is written by someone without dramatic faculty, in which case it is unreadable. There is only one way of dramatizing an idea; and that is by putting on the stage a human being possessed by that idea, yet none the less a human being with all the human impulses which make him akin and therefore interesting to us. Bunyan, in his Pilgrim's Progress, does not, like his unread imitators, attempt to personify Christianity and Valor: he dramatizes for you the life of the Christian and the Valiant Man. Just so, though I have shewn that Wotan is Godhead and Kingship, and Loki Logic and Imagination without living Will (Brain without Heart, to put it vulgarly); yet in the drama Wotan is a religiously moral man, and Loki a witty, ingenious, imaginative and cynical one. As to Fricka, who stands for State Law, she does not assume her allegorical character in The Rhine Gold at all, but is simply Wotan's wife and Freia's sister: nay, she contradicts her allegorical self by conniving at all Wotan's rogueries. That, of course, is just what State Law would do; but we must not save the credit of the allegory by a quip. Not until she reappears in the next play (The Valkyrie) does her function in the allegorical scheme become plain.

One preconception will bewilder the spectator hopelessly unless he has been warned against it or is naturally free from it. In the old-fashioned orders of creation, the supernatural personages are invariably conceived as greater than man, for good or evil. In the modern humanitarian order as adopted by Wagner, Man is the highest. In The Rhine Gold, it is pretended that there are as yet no men on the earth. There are dwarfs, giants, and gods. The danger is that you will jump to the conclusion that the gods, at least, are a higher order than the human order. On the contrary, the world is waiting for Man to redeem it from the lame and cramped government of the gods. Once grasp that; and the allegory becomes simple enough. Really, of course, the dwarfs, giants, and gods are dramatizations of the three main orders of men: to wit, the instinctive, predatory, lustful, greedy people; the patient, toiling, stupid, respectful, money-worshipping people; and the intellectual, moral, talented people who devize and administer States and Churches. History shews us only one order higher than the highest of these: namely, the order of Heros.

Now it is quite clear—though you have perhaps never thought of it—that if the next generation of Englishmen consisted wholly of Julius Cæsars, all our political, ecclesiastical, and moral institutions would vanish, and the less perishable of their appurtenances be classed with Stonehenge and the cromlechs and round towers as inexplicable relics of a bygone social order. Julius Cæsars would no more trouble themselves about such contrivances as our codes and churches than a Fellow of the Royal Society will touch his hat to the squire and listen to the village curate's sermons. This is precisely what must happen some day if life continues thrusting towards higher and higher organization as it has hitherto done. As most of our English professional men are to Australian bushmen, so, we must suppose, will the average man of some future day be to Julius Cæsar. Let any man of middle age, pondering this prospect, consider what has happened within a single generation to the articles of faith his father regarded as eternal, nay, to the very scepticisms and blasphemies of his youth (Bishop Colenso's criticism of the Pentateuch, for example!*); and he will begin to realize how much of our barbarous Theology and Law the man of the future will do without. Bakoonin, the Dresden revolutionary leader with whom Wagner went out in 1849, put forward later on a program, often quoted with foolish horror, for the abolition of all institutions, religious, political, juridical, financial, legal, academic, and so on, so as to leave the will of man free to find its own way. All the loftiest spirits of that time were burning to raise Man up, to give him self-respect, to shake him out of his habit of grovelling before the ideals created by his own imagination, of attributing the good that sprang from the ceaseless energy of the life within himself to some superior power in the clouds, and of making a fetish of self-sacrifice to justify his own cowardice.

Further on in The Ring we shall see the Hero arrive and make an end of dwarfs, giants, and gods. Meanwhile,

* John W. Colenso, bishop of Natal, published a Critical Examination of the Pentateuch (1862–79), in which he concluded that the first five books of the Bible were post-exile forgeries.

let us not forget that godhood means to Wagner infirmity and compromise, and manhood strength and integrity. Above all, we must understand—for it is the key to much that we are to see—that the god, since his desire is toward a higher and fuller life, must long in his inmost soul for the advent of that greater power whose first work, though this he does not see as yet, must be his own undoing.

In the midst of all these far-reaching ideas, it is amusing to find Wagner still full of his ingrained theatrical professionalism, and introducing effects which now seem old-fashioned and stagey with as much energy and earnestness as if they were his loftiest inspirations. When Wotan wrests the ring from Alberic, the dwarf delivers a lurid and bloodcurdling stage curse, calling down on its every future possessor care, fear, and death. The musical phrase accompanying this outburst was a veritable harmonic and melodic bogey to mid-century ears, though time has now robbed it of its terrors. It sounds again when Fafnir slays Fasolt, and on every subsequent occasion when the ring brings death to its holder. This episode must justify itself purely as a piece of stage sensationalism. On deeper ground it is superfluous and confusing, as the ruin to which the pursuit of riches leads needs no curse to explain it; nor is there any sense in investing Alberic with providential powers in the matter.

THE VALKYRIE

Before the curtain rises on the Valkyrie, let us see what has happened since it fell on The Rhine Gold. The persons of the drama will tell us presently; but as we probably do not understand German, that may not help us.

Wotan is still ruling the world in glory from his giant-built castle with his wife Fricka. But he has no security for the continuance of his reign, since Alberic may at any moment contrive to recover the ring, the full power of which he can wield because he has forsworn love. Such forswearing is not possible to Wotan: love, though not his highest need, is a higher than gold: otherwise he would be no god. Besides, as we have seen, his power has been established in the world by and as a system of laws enforced by penalties. These he must consent to be bound by himself; for a god who broke his own laws would betray the fact that legality and conformity are not the highest rule of conduct—a discovery fatal to his supremacy as Pontiff and Lawgiver. Hence he may not wrest the ring unlawfully from Fafnir, even if he could bring himself to forswear love.

In this insecurity he has hit on the idea of forming a heroic bodyguard. He has trained his love children as war maidens (Valkyries) whose duty it is to sweep through battlefields and bear away to Valhalla the souls of the bravest who fall there. Thus reinforced by a host of warriors, he has thoroughly indoctrinated them, Loki helping him as dialectician-in-chief, with the conventional system of law and duty, supernatural religion and self-sacrificing idealism, which they believe to be the essence of his godhood, but which is really only the machinery of the love of necessary power which is his mortal weakness. This process secures their fanatical devotion to his system of government; but he knows perfectly well that such systems, in spite of their moral pretensions, serve selfish and ambitious tyrants better than benevolent despots, and that, if once Alberic gets the ring back, he will easily out-Valhalla Valhalla, if not buy it over as a going concern. The only chance of permanent security, then, is the appearance in the world of a hero who, without any illicit prompting from

Wotan, will destroy Alberic and wrest the ring from Fafnir. There will then, he believes, be no further cause for anxiety, since he does not yet conceive Heroism as a force hostile to Godhead. In his longing for a rescuer, it does not occur to him that when the Hero comes, his first exploit must be to sweep the gods and their ordinances from the path of the heroic will.

Indeed, he feels that in his own Godhead is the germ of such Heroism, and that from himself the Hero must spring. He takes to wandering, mostly in search of love, from Fricka and Valhalla. He seeks the First Mother; and through her womb, eternally fertile, the inner true thought that made him first a god is reborn as his daughter, uncorrupted by his ambition, unfettered by his machinery of power and his alliances with Fricka and Loki. This daughter, the Valkyrie Brynhild, is his true will, his real self (as he thinks): to her he may say what he must not say to anyone, since in speaking to her he but speaks to himself. *"Was keinem in Worten ich künde"* he says to her *"unausgesprochen bleib es denn ewig: mit mir nur rat' ich, red' ich zu dir."**

But from Brynhild no hero can spring until there is a man of Wotan's race to breed with her. Wotan wanders further; and a mortal woman bears him twins: a son and a daughter. He separates them by letting the girl fall into the hands of a forest tribe which in due time gives her as wife to a fierce chief, one Hunding. With the son he himself leads the life of a wolf, and teaches him the only power a god can teach, the power of doing without happiness. When he has given him this terrible training, he abandons him, and goes to the bridal feast of his

* Stewart Robb, in The Ring of the Nibelung (New York: Dutton, 1960), translates this: "What never was uttered to any will stay unuttered, now and forever. Myself I speak to, speaking to you."

daughter Sieglinda and Hunding. In the blue cloak of the wanderer, wearing the broad hat that flaps over the socket of his forfeited eye, he appears in Hunding's house, the middle pillar of which is a mighty tree. Into that tree, without a word, he strikes a sword up to the hilt, so that only the might of a hero can withdraw it. Then he goes out as silently as he came, blind to the truth that no weapon from the armory of Godhead can serve the turn of the true Human Hero. Neither Hunding nor any of his guests can move the sword; and there it stays awaiting the destined hand. That is the history of the generations between The Rhine Gold and The Valkyrie.

THE FIRST ACT

This time, as we sit looking expectantly at the curtain, we hear, not the deep booming of the Rhine, but the patter of a forest downpour, accompanied by the mutter of a storm which soon gathers into a roar and culminates in crashing thunderbolts. As it passes off, the curtain rises; and there is no mistaking whose forest habitation we are in; for the central pillar is a mighty tree, and the place fit for the dwelling of a fierce chief. The door opens; and an exhausted man reels in: an adept from the school of unhappiness. Sieglinda finds him lying on the hearth. He explains that he has been in a fight; that his weapons, not being as strong as his arms, were broken; and that he had to fly. He desires some drink and a moment's rest; then he will go; for he is an unlucky person, and does not want to bring his ill-luck on the woman who is succoring him. But she, it appears, is also unhappy; and a strong sympathy springs up between them. When her husband arrives, he observes not only this sympathy, but a resemblance between them, a gleam of the snake in their eyes. They sit down to table; and the stranger tells them his unlucky story. He is the son of Wotan, who is known to him only as Wolfing, of the race of the Volsungs. The earliest thing he remembers is returning from a hunt with his father to find their home destroyed, his mother murdered, and his twin sister carried off. This was the work of a tribe called the Neidings, upon whom he and Wolfing thenceforth waged implacable war until the day when his father disappeared, leaving no trace of himself but an empty wolfskin. The young Volsung was thus cast alone upon the world, finding most hands against him, and bringing no good luck even to his friends. His latest exploit has been the slaying of certain brothers who were forcing their sister to wed against her will. The result has been the slaughter of the woman by her brothers' clansmen, and his own narrow escape by flight.

His luck on this occasion is even worse than he supposes; for Hunding, by whose hearth he has taken refuge, is clansman to the slain brothers and is bound to avenge them. He tells the Volsung that in the morning, weapons or no weapons, he must fight for his life. Then he orders the woman to bed, and follows her himself, taking his spear with him.

The unlucky stranger, left brooding by the hearth, has nothing to console himself with but an old promise of his father's that he shall find a weapon to his hand when he most needs one. The last flicker of the dying fire strikes on the golden hilt of the sword that sticks in the tree; but he does not see it; and the embers sink into blackness. Then the woman returns. Hunding is safely asleep: she has drugged him. She tells the story of the one-eyed man who appeared at her forced marriage, and of the sword. She has always felt, she says, that her miseries will end in the arms of the hero who shall succeed in drawing it forth. The stranger, diffident as he is about his luck, has no misgivings as to his strength and destiny. He gives her his affection at once, and abandons himself to the charm of the night and the season; for it is the beginning of Spring. They soon learn from their confidences that she is his stolen twin sister. He is transported to find that the heroic race of the Volsungs need neither perish nor be corrupted by a lower strain. Hailing the sword by the name of Nothung (or Needed), he plucks it from the tree as her bridegift, and then, crying "Both bride and sister be of thy brother; and blossom the blood of the Volsungs!" clasps her as the mate the Spring has brought him.

THE SECOND ACT

So far, Wotan's plan seems prospering. In the mountains he calls his war maiden Brynhild, the child borne to him by the First Mother, and bids her see to it that Hunding shall fall in the approaching combat. But he is reckoning without his consort, Fricka. What will she, the Law, say to the lawless pair who have heaped incest on adultery? A hero may have defied the law, and put his own will in its place; but can a god hold him guiltless, when the whole power of the gods can enforce itself only by law? Fricka, shuddering with horror, outraged in every instinct, comes clamoring for punishment. Wotan pleads the general necessity of encouraging heroism in order to keep up the Valhalla bodyguard; but his remonstrances only bring upon him torrents of reproaches for his own unfaithfulness to the law in roaming through the world and begetting war maidens, "wolf cubs," and the like. He is hopelessly beaten in the argument. Fricka is absolutely right when she declares that the ending of the gods began when he brought this wolf-hero into the world; and now, to save their very existence, she pitilessly demands his destruction. Wotan has no power to refuse: it is Fricka's mechanical force, and not his thought, that really rules the world. He has to recall Brynhild; take back his former instructions; and ordain that Hunding shall slay the Volsung.

But now comes another difficulty. Brynhild is the inner thought and will of Godhead, the aspiration from the high life to the higher that is its divine element, and only becomes separated from it when its resort to kingship and priestcraft for the sake of temporal power has made it false to itself. Hitherto, Brynhild, as Valkyrie or hero chooser, has obeyed Wotan implicitly, taking her work as the holiest and bravest in his kingdom; and now he tells her what he could not tell Fricka—what indeed he could not tell to Brynhild, were she not, as she says, his own will—the whole story of Alberic and of that inspiration about the raising up of a hero. She thoroughly approves of the inspiration; but when the story ends in the assumption that she too must obey Fricka, and help Fricka's vassal, Hunding, to undo the great work and strike the hero down, she for the first time hesitates to accept his command. In his fury and despair he overawes her by the most terrible threats of his anger; and she submits.

Then comes the Volsung Siegmund, following his sister bride, who has fled into the mountains in a revulsion of horror at having allowed herself to bring her hero to shame. Whilst she is lying exhausted and senseless in his arms, Brynhild appears to him and solemnly warns him that he must presently leave the earth with her. He asks whither he must follow her. To Valhalla, to take his place there among the heros. He asks, shall he find his father there? Yes. Shall he find a wife there? Yes: he will be waited on by beautiful wish-maidens. Shall he meet his sister there? No. Then, says Siegmund, I will not come with you. She tries to make him understand that he cannot help himself. Being a hero, he will not be so persuaded: he has his father's sword, and does not fear Hunding. But when she tells him that she comes from his father, and that the sword of a god will not avail in the hands of a hero, he accepts his fate, but will shape it with his own hand, both for himself and his sister, by slaying her, and then killing himself with the last stroke of the sword. And thereafter he will go to Hell, rather than to Valhalla.

How now can Brynhild, being what she is, choose her side freely in a conflict between this hero and the vassal of Fricka? By instinct she at once throws Wotan's command to the winds, and bids Siegmund nerve himself for the combat with Hunding, in which she pledges him the protection of her shield. The horn of Hunding is soon heard; and Siegmund's spirits rise to fighting pitch at once. The two meet; and the Valkyrie's shield is held before the hero. But when he delivers his sword-stroke at his foe, the weapon shivers on the spear of Wotan, who suddenly appears between them; and the first of the race of heros falls with the weapon of the Law's vassal through his breast. Brynhild snatches the fragments of the broken sword, and flies, carrying off the woman with her on her war horse; and Wotan, in terrible wrath, slays Hunding with a wave of his hand, and starts in pursuit of his disobedient daughter.

THE THIRD ACT

On a rocky peak, four of the Valkyries are waiting for the rest. The absent ones soon arrive, galloping through the air with slain heros, gathered from the battlefield, hanging over their saddles. Only, Brynhild, who comes last, has for her spoil a live woman. When her eight sisters learn that she has defied Wotan, they dare not help her; and Brynhild has to rouse Sieglinda to make an effort to save herself, by reminding her that she bears in her the seed of a hero, and must face everything, endure anything, sooner than let that seed miscarry. Sieglinda, in a transport of exaltation, takes the fragments of the sword and flies into the forest. Then Wotan comes; the sisters fly in terror at his command; and he is left alone with Brynhild.

Here, then, we have the first of the inevitable moments which Wotan did not foresee. Godhead has now established its dominion over the world by a mighty Church, compelling obedience through its ally the Law, with its formidable State organization of force of arms and cunning of brain. It has submitted to this alliance to keep the Plutonic power in check—built up primarily for the sake of that soul in itself which cares only to make the highest better and the best higher; and now here is that very soul separated from it and working for the destruction of its indispensable ally, the lawgiving State. How is the rebel to be disarmed? Slain it cannot be by Godhead, since it is still Godhead's own very dearest soul. But hidden, stifled, silenced it must be; or it will wreck the State and leave the Church defenceless. Not until it passes completely away from Godhead, and is reborn as the soul of the hero, can it work anything but the confusion and destruction of the existing order. How is the world to be protected against it in the meantime? Clearly Loki's help is needed here: it is the Lie that must, on the highest principles, hide the Truth. Let Loki surround this mountain top with the appearance of a consuming fire; and who will dare penetrate to Brynhild? It is true that if any man will walk boldly into that fire, he will discover it at once to be a lie, an illusion, a mirage through which he might carry a sack of gunpowder without being a penny the worse. Therefore let the fire seem so terrible that only the hero, when in the fulness of time he appears upon earth, will venture through it; and the problem is solved. Wotan, with a breaking heart, takes leave of Brynhild; throws her into a deep sleep; covers her with her long warshield; summons Loki, who comes in the shape of a wall of fire surrounding the mountain peak; and turns his back on Brynhild for ever.

The allegory here is happily not so glaringly obvious to the younger generations of our educated classes as it was forty years ago. In those days, any child who expressed a doubt as to the absolute truth of the Church's teaching, even to the extent of asking why Joshua told the sun to stand still instead of telling the earth to cease turning, or of pointing out that a whale's throat would hardly have been large enough to swallow Jonah, was unhesitatingly told that if it harbored such doubts it would spend all eternity after its death in horrible torments in a lake of burning brimstone. It is difficult to write or read this nowadays without laughing; yet no doubt millions of ignorant and credulous people are still teaching their children that. When Wagner himself was a little child, the fact that hell was a fiction devized for the intimidation and subjection of the masses was a wellkept secret of the thinking and governing classes. At that time the fires of Loki were a very real terror to all except persons of exceptional force of character and intrepidity of thought. Even thirty years after Wagner had printed the verses of The Ring for private circulation, we find him excusing himself from perfectly explicit denial of current superstitions, by reminding his readers that it would expose him to prosecution. In England, so many of our respectable voters are still grovelling in a gloomy devil worship, of which the fires of Loki are the main bulwark, that no Government has yet had the conscience or the courage to repeal our monstrous laws against "blasphemy."

Sieglinda, when she flies into the forest with the hero's son unborn in her womb, and the broken pieces of his sword in her hand, finds shelter in the smithy of a dwarf, where she brings forth her child and dies. This dwarf is no other than Mimmy, the brother of Alberic, the same who made for him the magic helmet. His aim in life is to gain possession of the helmet, the ring, and the treasure. and through them to obtain that Plutonic mastery of the world under the beginnings of which he himself writhed during Alberic's brief reign. Mimmy is a blinking, shambling, ancient creature, too weak and timid to dream of taking arms himself to despoil Fafnir, who still, transformed to a monstrous serpent, broods on the gold in a hole in the rocks. Mimmy needs the help of a hero for that; and he has craft enough to know that it is quite possible, and indeed much in the ordinary way of the the world, for senile avarice and craft to set youth and bravery to work to win empire for it. He knows the pedigree of the child left on his hands, and nurses it to manhood with great care.

His pains are too well rewarded for his comfort. The boy Siegfried, having no god to instruct him in the art of unhappiness, inherits none of his father's ill luck, and all his father's hardihood. The fear against which Siegmund set his face like flint, and the woe which he wore down, are unknown to the son. The father was faithful and grateful: the son knows no law but his own humor; detests the ugly dwarf who has nursed him; chafes furiously under his claims for some return for his tender care; and is, in short, a totally unmoral person, a born anarchist, the ideal of Bakoonin, an anticipation of the "overman" of Nietzsche. He is enormously strong, full of life and fun, dangerous and destructive to what he dislikes, and affectionate to what he likes; so that it is fortunate that his likes and dislikes are sane and healthy. Altogether an inspiriting young forester, a son of the morning, in whom the heroic race has come out into the sunshine from the clouds of his grandfather's majestic entanglements with law, and the night of his father's tragic struggle with it.

THE FIRST ACT

Mimmy's smithy is a cave, in which he hides from the light like the eyeless fish of the American caverns. Before the curtain rises the music already tells us that we are groping in darkness. When it does rise Mimmy is in difficulties. He is trying to make a sword for his nursling, who is now big enough to take the field against Fafnir. Mimmy can make mischievous swords; but it is not with dwarfmade weapons that heroic man will hew the way of his own will through religions and governments and plutocracies and all the other devices of the kingdom of the fears of the unheroic. As fast as Mimmy makes swords, Siegfried Bakoonin smashes them, and then takes the poor old swordsmith by the scruff of the neck and chastizes him wrathfully. The particular day on which the curtain rises begins with one of these trying domestic incidents. Mimmy has just done his best with a new sword of surpassing excellence. Siegfried returns home in rare spirits with a wild bear, to the extreme terror of the wretched dwarf. When the bear is dismissed, the new sword is produced. It is promptly smashed, as usual, with, also, the usual effects on the temper of Siegfried, who is quite boundless in his criticisms of the smith's boasted skill, and declares that he would smash the sword's maker too if he were not too disgusting to be handled.

Mimmy falls back on his stock defence: a string of maudlin reminders of the care with which he has nursed the little boy into manhood. Siegfried replies candidly that the strangest thing about all this care is that instead of making him grateful, it inspires him with a lively desire to wring the dwarf's neck. Only, he admits that he always comes back to his Mimmy, though he loathes him more than any living thing in the forest. On this admission the dwarf attempts to build a theory of filial instinct. He explains that he is Siegfried's father, and that this is why Siegfried cannot do without him. But Siegfried has learned from his forest companions, the birds and foxes and wolves, that mothers as well as fathers go to the making of children. Mimmy, on the desperate ground that man is neither bird nor fox, declares that he is Siegfried's father and mother both. He is promptly denounced as a filthy liar, because the birds and foxes are exactly like their parents, wheras Siegfried, having often watched his own image in the water, can testify that he is no more like Mimmy than a toad is like a trout. Then, to place the conversation on a plane of entire frankness, he throttles Mimmy until he is speechless. When the dwarf recovers, he is so daunted that he tells Siegfried the truth about his birth, and for testimony thereof produces the pieces of the sword that broke upon Wotan's spear. Siegfried instantly orders him to repair the sword on pain of an unmerciful thrashing, and rushes off into the forest, rejoicing in the discovery that he is no kin of Mimmy's and need have no more to do with him when the sword is mended

Poor Mimmy is now in a worse plight than ever; for he has long ago found that the sword utterly defies his skill: the steel will yield neither to his hammer nor to his furnace. Just then there walks into his cave a Wanderer, in a blue mantle, spear in hand, with one eye concealed by the brim of his wide hat. Mimmy, not by nature hospitable, tries to drive him away; but the Wanderer announces himself as a wise man, who can tell his host, in emergency, what it most concerns him to know. Mimmy, taking this offer in high dudgeon, because it implies that his visitor's wits are better than his own, offers to tell the wise one something that *he* does not know: to wit, the way to the door. The imperturbable Wanderer's reply is to sit down and challenge the dwarf to a trial of wit. He wagers his head against Mimmy's that he will answer any three questions the dwarf can put to him.

Now here were Mimmy's opportunity, had he only the wit to ask what he wants to know, instead of pretending to know everything already. It is above all things needful to him at this moment to find out how that sword can be mended; and there has just dropped in upon him in his need the one person who can tell him. In such circumstances a wise man would hasten to shew to his visitor his three deepest ignorances, and ask him to dispel them. The dwarf, being a crafty fool, desiring only to detect ignorance in his guest, asks him for information on the three points on which he is proudest of being thoroughly well instructed himself. His three questions are, Who dwell under the earth? Who dwell on the earth? and Who dwell in the cloudy heights above? The Wanderer, in reply, tells him of the dwarfs and of Alberic; of the earth, and the giants Fasolt and Fafnir; of the gods and of Wotan: himself, as Mimmy now recognizes with awe.

Next, it is Mimmy's turn to face three questions. What is that race, dearest to Wotan, against which Wotan has nevertheless done his worst? Mimmy can answer that: he knows the Volsungs, the race of heros born of Wotan's infidelities to Fricka, and can tell the Wanderer the whole story of the twins and their son Siegfried. Wotan compliments him on his knowledge, and asks further with what sword Siegfried will slay Fafnir? Mimmy can answer that too: he has the whole history of the sword at his fingers' ends. Wotan hails him as the knowingest of the knowing, and then hurls at him the question he should himself have asked: Who will mend the sword? Mimmy, his head forfeited, confesses with loud lamentations that he cannot answer. The Wanderer reads him an appropriate little lecture on the folly of being too clever to ask what he wants to know, and informs him that a smith to whom fear is unknown will mend Nothung. To this smith he leaves the forfeited head of his host, and wanders off into the forest. Then Mimmy's nerves give way completely. He shakes like a man in *delirium tremens*, and has a horrible nightmare, in the supreme convulsion of which Siegfried, returning from the forest, presently finds him.

A curious and amusing conversation follows. Siegfried himself does not know fear, and is impatient to acquire it as an accomplishment. Mimmy is all fear: the world for him is a phantasmagoria of terrors. It is not that he is afraid of being eaten by bears in the forest, or of burning his fingers in the forge fire. A lively objection to being destroyed or maimed does not make a man a coward: on the contrary, it is the beginning of a brave man's wisdom. But in Mimmy, fear is not the effect of danger: it is a natural quality of him which no security can allay. He is like many a poor newspaper editor, who dares not print the truth, however simple, even when it is obvious to himself and all his readers. Not that anything unpleasant would happen to him if he did—not, indeed, that he could fail to become a distinguished and influential leader of opinion by fearlessly pursuing such a course, but solely because he lives in a world of imaginary terrors, rooted in a modest and gentlemanly mistrust of his own strength and worth, and consequently of the value of his opinion. Just so is Mimmy afraid of anything that can do him any good, especially of the light and the fresh air. He is also convinced that anybody who is not sufficiently steeped in fear to be constantly on his guard must perish immediately on his first sally into the world. To preserve Siegfried for the enterprise to which he has destined him he makes a grotesque attempt to teach him fear. He appeals to his experience of the terrors of the forest, of its dark places, of its threatening noises, its stealthy ambushes, its sinister flickering lights, its heart-tightening ecstasies of dread.

All this has no other effect than to fill Siegfried with wonder and curiosity; for the forest is a place of delight for him. He is as eager to experience Mimmy's terrors as a schoolboy to feel what an electric shock is like. Then Mimmy has the happy idea of describing Fafnir to him as a likely person to give him an exemplary fright. Siegfried jumps at the idea, and, since Mimmy cannot mend the sword for him, proposes to set to work then and there to mend it for himself. Mimmy shakes his head, and bids him see now how his youthful laziness and frowardness have found him out—how he would not learn the smith's craft from Professor Mimmy, and therefore does not know how even to begin mending the sword. Siegfried Bakoonin's retort is simple and crushing. He points out that the net result of Mimmy's academic skill is that he can neither make a decent sword himself nor even set one to rights when it is damaged. Reckless of the remonstrances of the scandalized professor, he seizes a file, and in a few moments utterly destroys the fragments of the sword by rasping them into a heap of steel filings. Then he puts the filings into a crucible; buries it in the coals; and sets to at the bellows with the shouting exultation of the anarchist who destroys only to clear the ground for creation. When the steel is melted he runs it into a mould; and lo! a sword-blade in the rough. Mimmy, amazed at the success of this violation of all the rules of his craft, hails Siegfried as the mightiest of smiths, professing himself barely worthy to be his cook and scullion; and forthwith proceeds to poison some soup for him so that he may murder him safely when Fafnir is slain. Meanwhile Siegfried forges and tempers and hammers and rivets, uproariously singing the while as nonsensically as the Rhine daughters themselves. Finally he assails the anvil on which Mimmy's swords have been shattered, and cleaves it with a mighty stroke of the newly forged Nothung.

THE SECOND ACT

In the darkest hour before the dawn of that night, we find ourselves before the cave of Fafnir; and there we find Alberic, who can find nothing better to do with himself than to watch the haunt of the dragon, and eat his heart out in vain longing for the gold and the ring. The wretched Fafnir, once an honest giant, can only make himself terrible enough to keep his gold by remaining a venomous reptile. Why he should not become an honest giant again, and clear out of his cavern, leaving the gold and the ring and the rest of it for anyone fool enough to take them at such a price, is the first question that would occur to anyone except a civilized man, who would be too accustomed to that sort of mania to be at all surprised at it.

To Alberic in the night comes the Wanderer, whom the dwarf, recognizing his despoiler of old, abuses as a shameless thief, taunting him with the helpless way in which all his boasted power is tied up with the laws and bargains recorded on the haft of his spear, which, says Alberic truly, would crumble like chaff in his hands if he dared use it for his own real ends. Wotan, having already had to kill his own son with it, knows that very well; but it troubles him no more; for he is now at last rising to abhorrence of his own artificial power, and looking to the coming hero, not for its consolidation but its destruction. When Alberic breaks out again with his still unquenched hope of one day destroying the gods and ruling the world through the ring, Wotan is no longer shocked. He tells Alberic that Brother Mime approaches with a hero whom Godhead can neither help nor hinder. Alberic may try his luck against him without disturbance from Valhalla. Perhaps, he suggests, if Alberic warns Fafnir, and offers to deal with the hero for him, Fafnir may give him the ring. They accordingly wake up the dragon, who condescends to enter into bellowing conversation, but is proof against their proposition, strong in the magic of property. "I have and hold" he says "leave me to sleep." Wotan, with a wise laugh, turns to Alberic. "That shot missed" he says "no use abusing me for it. And now let me tell you one thing. All things happen according to their nature; and *you* cant alter them." And so he leaves him. Alberic, raging with the sense that his old enemy has been laughing at him, and yet prophetically convinced that the last word will not be with the god, hides himself as the day breaks, and his brother approaches with Siegfried.

Mimmy makes a final attempt to frighten Siegfried by discoursing of the dragon's terrible jaws, poisonous breath, corrosive spittle, and deadly, stinging tail. Siegfried is not interested in the tail: he wants to know whether the dragon has a heart, being confident of his ability to stick Nothung into it if it exists. Reassured on this point, he drives Mimmy away, and stretches himself under the trees, listening to the morning chatter of the birds. One of them has a great deal to say to him; but he cannot understand it; and after vainly trying to carry on the conversation with a reed which he cuts, he takes to entertaining the bird with tunes on his horn, asking it to send him a loving mate such as all the other creatures of the forest have. His tunes wake up the dragon; and Siegfried makes merry over the grim mate the bird has sent him. Fafnir is highly scandalized by the irreverence of the young Bakoonin. He loses his temper; fights; and is forthwith slain, to his own great astonishment.

In such conflicts one learns to interpret the messages of Nature a little. When Siegfried, stung by the dragon's vitriolic blood, pops his finger into his mouth and tastes it, he understands what the bird is saying to him, and, instructed by it concerning the treasures within his reach, goes into the cave to secure the gold, the ring and the wishing cap. Then Mimmy returns, and is confronted by Alberic. The two quarrel furiously over the sharing of the booty they have not yet secured, until Siegfried comes from the cave with the ring and the helmet, not much impressed by the heap of gold, and disappointed because he has not yet learned to fear.

He has, however, learnt to read the thoughts of such a creature as poor Mimmy, who, intending to overwhelm him with flattery and fondness, only succeeds in making such a self-revelation of murderous envy that Siegfried smites him with Nothung and slays him, to the keen satisfaction of the hidden Alberic. Caring nothing for the gold, which he leaves to the care of the slain; disappointed in his fancy for learning fear; and longing for a mate, he casts himself wearily down, and again sppeals to his friend the bird, who tells him of a woman sleeping on a mountain peak within a fortress of fire that only the fearless can penetrate. Siegfried is up in a moment with all the tumult of spring in his veins, and follows the flight of the bird as it pilots him to the fiery mountain.

To the foot of the mountain comes also the Wanderer, now nearing his doom. He calls up the First Mother from the depths of the earth, and begs counsel from her. She bids him confer with the Norns (the Fates). But they are of no use to him: what he seeks is some foreknowledge of the way of the Will in its perpetual strife with these helpless Fates who can only spin the net of circumstance and environment round the feet of men. Why not, says Erda then, go to the daughter I bore you, and take counsel with her? He has to explain how he has cut himself off from her, and sets the fires of Loki between the world and her counsel. In that case the First Mother cannot help him: such a separation is part of the bewilderment that is ever the first outcome of her eternal work of thrusting the life energy of the world to higher and higher organization. She can shew him no way of escape from the destruction he foresees. Then from the innermost of him breaks the confession that he rejoices in his doom, and now himself exults in passing away with all his ordinances and alliances, with the spear-sceptre which he has only wielded on condition of slaying his dearest children with it, with the kingdom, the power and the glory which will never again boast themselves as "world without end." And so he dismisses Erda to her sleep in the heart of the earth as the forest bird draws near, piloting the slain son's son to his goal.

Now it is an excellent thing to triumph in the victory of the new order and the passing away of the old; but if you happen to be part of the old order yourself, you must nonetheless fight for your life. It seems hardly possible that the British army at the battle of Waterloo did not include at least one Englishman intelligent enough to hope, for the sake of his country and humanity, that Napoleon might defeat the allied sovereigns; but such an Englishman would kill a French *cuirassier* rather than be killed by him just as energetically as the silliest soldier ever encouraged, by people who ought to know better, to call his ignorance, ferocity and folly, patriotism and duty. Outworn life may have become mere error; but it still claims the right to die a natural death, and will raise its hand against the millennium itself in self defence if it tries to come by the short cut of murder. Wotan finds this out when he comes face to face with Siegfried, who is brought to a standstill at the foot of the mountain by the disappearance of the bird. Meeting the Wanderer there, he asks him the way to the mountain where a woman sleeps surrounded by fire. The Wanderer questions him, and extracts his story from him, breaking into fatherly delight when Siegfried, describing the mending of the sword, remarks that all he knew about the business was that the broken bits of Nothung would be of no use to him unless he made a new sword out of them right over again from the beginning. But the Wanderer's interest is by no means reciprocated by Siegfried. His majesty and elderly dignity are thrown away on the young anarchist, who, unwilling to waste time talking, bluntly bids him either shew him the way to the mountain, or else "shut his muzzle." Wotan is a little hurt. "Patience, my lad" he says "if you were an old man I should treat you with respect." "That would be a precious notion" says Siegfried. "All my life long I was bothered and hampered by an old man until I swept him out of my way. I will sweep you in the same fashion if you dont let me pass. Why do you wear such a big hat; and what has happened to one of your eyes? was it knocked out by somebody whose way you obstructed?" To which Wotan replies allegorically that the eye that is gone—the eye that his marriage with Fricka cost him—is now looking at him out of Siegfried's head. At this, Siegfried gives up the

Wanderer as a lunatic, and renews his threats of personal violence. Then Wotan throws off the mask of the Wanderer; uplifts the world-governing spear; and puts forth all his divine awe and grandeur as the guardian of the mountain, round the crest of which fires of Loki now break into a red background for the majesty of the god. But all this is lost on Siegfried Bakoonin. "Aha!" he cries, as the spear is leveled against his breast: "I have found my father's foe"; and the spear falls in two pieces under the stroke of Nothung. "Up then" says Wotan: "I cannot withhold you," and disappears forever from the eye of man. The fires roll down the mountain; but Siegfried goes at them as exultantly as he went at the forging of the sword or the heart of the dragon, and shoulders his way through them, joyously sounding his horn to the accompaniment of their crackling and seething. And never a hair of his head is singed. Those frightful flames which have scared mankind for centuries from the Truth have not heat enough in them to make a child shut its eyes. They are mere phantasmagoria, highly creditable to Loki's imaginative stage-management; but nothing ever has perished or will perish eternally in them except the Churches which have been so poor and faithless as to trade for their power on the lies of a romancer.

BACK TO OPERA AGAIN

And now, O Nibelungen Spectator, pluck up; for all allegories come to an end somewhere; and the hour of your release from these explanations is at hand. The rest of what you are going to see is opera, and nothing but opera. Before many bars have been played, Siegfried and the wakened Brynhild, newly become tenor and soprano, will sing a concerted *cadenza*; plunge on from that to a magnificent love duet; and end with a precipitous *allegro a capella*, driven headlong to its end by the impetuous semiquaver triplets of the famous *finales* to the first act of Don Giovanni or the *coda* to the Leonore overture, with a specifically contrapuntal theme, *points d' orgue*, and a high C for the soprano all complete.

What is more, the work which follows, entitled Night Falls on The Gods, is a thorough grand opera. In it you shall see what you have so far missed, the opera chorus in full parade on the stage, not presuming to interfere with the *prima donna* as she sings her death song over the footlights. Nay, that chorus will have its own chance when it first appears, with a good roaring strain in C major, not, after all, so very different from, or at all less absurd than the choruses of the courtiers in La Favorita or *Per te immenso giubilo* in Lucia. The harmony is no doubt a little developed, Wagner augmenting his fifths with a G sharp where Donizetti would have put his fingers in his ears and screamed for G natural. But it is an opera chorus all the same; and along with it we have theatrical grandiosities that recall Meyerbeer and Verdi: *pezzi d' insieme* for all the principals in a row, vengeful conjurations for trios of them, romantic death song for the tenor: in short, all manner of operatic conventions.

Now it is probable that some of us will have been so talked by the more superstitious Bayreuth pilgrims into regarding Die Götterdämmerung as the mighty climax to a mighty epic, more Wagnerian than all the other three sections put together, as not to dare notice this startling atavism, especially if we find the trio-conjurations more exhilarating than the metaphysical discourses of Wotan in the three true music dramas of The Ring. There is, however, no real atavism involved. Die Götterdämmerung, though the last of The Ring dramas in order of performance, was the first in order of conception, and was indeed the root from which all the others sprang.

The history of the matter is as follows. All Wagner's works prior to The Ring are operas. The last of them, Lohengrin, is perhaps the best known of modern operas. As performed in its entirety at Bayreuth, it is even more operatic than it appears at Covent Garden, because it happens that its most old-fashioned features, notably some of the big set concerted pieces for principals and chorus (*pezzi d' insieme* as I have called them above), are harder to perform than the more modern and characteristically Wagnerian sections, and for that reason were cut out in preparing the abbreviated fashionable version. Thus Lohengrin came upon the ordinary operatic stage as a more advanced departure from current operatic models than its composer had made it. Still, it is unmistakably an opera, with chorus, concerted pieces, *grand finales*, and a heroine who, if she does not sing florid variations with flute *obbligato*, is nonetheless a very perceptible *prima donna*. In everything but musical technique the change from Lohengrin to The Rhine Gold is quite revolutionary.

The explanation is that Night Falls on The Gods came in between them, although its music was not finished until twenty years after that of The Rhine Gold, and thus belongs to a later and more masterful phase of Wagner's harmonic style. It first came into Wagner's head as an opera to be entitled Siegfried's Death, founded on the old Niblung Sagas, which offered to Wagner the same material for an effective theatrical tragedy as they did to Ibsen. Ibsen's Vikings in Helgeland is, in kind, what Siegfried's Death was originally intended to be: that is, a heroic piece for the theatre, without the metaphysical or allegorical complications of The Ring. Indeed, the ultimate catastrophe of the Saga cannot by any perversion of ingenuity be adapted to the perfectly clear allegorical design of The Rhine Gold, The Valkyrie, and Siegfried.

SIEGFRIED AS PROTESTANT

The philosophically fertile element in the original project of Siegfried's Death was the conception of Siegfried himself as a type of the healthy man raised to perfect confidence in his own impulses by an intense and joyous vitality which is above fear, sickliness of conscience, malice, and the makeshifts and moral crutches of law and order which accompany them. Such a character appears extraordinarily fascinating and exhilarating to our guilty and conscience-ridden generations, however little they may understand him. The world has always delighted in the man who is delivered from conscience. From Punch and Don Juan down to Robert Macaire, Jeremy Diddler* and the pantomime clown, he has always drawn large audiences; but hitherto he has been decorously given to the devil at the end. Indeed eternal punishment is sometimes deemed too high a compliment to his nature. When the late Lord Lytton, in his Strange Story, introduced a character personifying the joyousness of intense vitality, he felt bound to deny him the immortal soul which was at that time conceded even to the humblest characters in fiction, and to accept mischievousness, cruelty, and utter incapacity for sympathy as the inevitable consequence of his magnificent bodily and mental health.

In short, though men felt all the charm of abounding life and abandonment to its impulses, they dared not, in their deep self-mistrust, conceive it otherwise than as a force making for evil—one which must lead to universal

* A confidence man in J. Kenney's play Raising the Wind (1803), whose name gave rise to the verb "to diddle", *i.e.*, to cheat or swindle.

ruin unless checked and literally mortified by self-renunciation in obedience to superhuman guidance, or at least to some reasoned system of morals. When it became apparent to the cleverest of them that no such superhuman guidance existed, and that their secularist systems had all the fictitiousness of "revelation" without its poetry, there was no escaping the conclusion that all the good that man had done must be put down to his arbitrary will as well as all the evil he had done; and it was also obvious that if progress were a reality, his beneficent impulses must be gaining on his destructive ones. It was under the influence of these ideas that we began to hear about the joy of life where we had formerly heard about the grace of God or the Age of Reason, and that the boldest spirits began to raise the question whether churches and laws and the like were not doing a great deal more harm than good by their action in limiting the freedom of the human will. Four hundred years ago, when belief in God and in revelation was general throughout Europe, a similar wave of thought led the strongest-hearted peoples to affirm that every man's private judgment was a more trustworthy interpreter of God and revelation than the Church. This was called Protestantism; and though the Protestants were not strong enough for their creed, and soon set up a Church of their own, yet the movement, on the whole, has justified the direction it took. Nowadays the supernatural element in Protestantism has perished; and if every man's private judgment is still to be justified as the most trustworthy interpreter of the will of Humanity (which is not a more extreme proposition than the old one about the will of God) Protestantism must take a fresh step in advance, and become Anarchism. Which it has accordingly done, Anarchism being one of the notable new creeds of the XVIII and XIX centuries.

The weak place which experience finds out in the Anarchist theory is its reliance on the progress already achieved by "Man." There is no such thing as Man in the world: what we have to deal with is a multitude of men, some of them great rascals, some of them great statesmen, others both, with a vast majority capable of managing their personal affairs, but not of comprehending social organization, or grappling with the problems created by their association in enormous numbers. If "Man" means this majority, then "Man" has made no progress: he has, on the contrary, resisted it. He will not even pay the cost of existing institutions: the requisite money has to be filched from him by "indirect taxation." Such people, like Wagner's giants, must be governed by laws; and their assent to such government must be secured by deliberately filling them with prejudices and practising on their imaginations by pageantry and artificial eminences and dignities. The government is of course established by the few who are capable of government, though, its mechanism once complete, it may be, and generally is, carried on unintelligently by people who are incapable of it, the capable people repairing it from time to time when it gets too far behind the continuous advance or decay of civilization. All these capable people are thus in the position of Wotan, forced to maintain as sacred, and themselves submit to, laws which they privately know to be obsolescent makeshifts, and to affect the deepest veneration for creeds and ideals which they ridicule among themselves with cynical skepticism. No individual Siegfried can rescue them from this bondage and hypocrisy; in fact, the individual Siegfried has come often enough, only to find himself confronted with the alternative of governing those who are not Siegfrieds or risking destruction at their hands. And this dilemma will persist until Wotan's inspiration comes to our governors, and they see that their business is not the devizing of laws and institutions to prop up the weaknesses of mobs and secure the survival of the unfittest, but the breeding of men whose wills and intelligences may be depended on to produce spontaneously the social wellbeing our clumsy laws now aim at and miss. The majority of men at present in Europe have no business to be alive; and no serious progress will be made until we address ourselves earnestly and scientifically to the task of producing trustworthy human material for society. In short, it is necessary to breed a race of men in whom the life-giving impulses predominate, before the New Protestantism becomes politically practicable.*

The most inevitable dramatic conception, then, of the XIX century is that of a perfectly naïve hero upsetting religion, law and order in all directions, and establishing in their place the unfettered action of Humanity doing exactly what it likes, and producing order instead of confusion thereby because it likes to do what is necessary for the good of the race. This conception, already incipient in Adam Smith's Wealth of Nations, was certain at last to reach some great artist, and be embodied by him in a masterpiece. It was also certain that if that master happened to be a German, he should take delight in describing his hero as the Freewiller of Necessity, thereby beyond measure exasperating Englishmen with a congenital incapacity for metaphysics.

* The necessity for breeding the governing class from a selected stock has always been recognized by Aristocrats, however erroneous their methods of selection. We have changed our system from Aristocracy to Democracy without considering that we were at the same time changing, as regards our governing class, from Selection to Promiscuity. Those who have taken a practical part in modern politics best know how farcical the result is. [GBS]

Unfortunately, human enlightenment does not progress by nicer and nicer adjustments, but by violent corrective reactions which invariably send us clean over our saddle and would bring us to the ground on the other side if the next reaction did not send us back again with equally excessive zeal. Ecclesiasticism and Constitutionalism send us one way, Protestantism and Anarchism the other; Order rescues us from confusion and lands us in Tyranny; Liberty then saves the situation and is presently found to be as great a nuisance as Despotism. A scientifically balanced application of these forces, theoretically possible, is practically incompatible with human passion. Besides, we have the same weakness in morals as in medicine: we cannot be cured of running after panaceas, or, as they are called in the sphere of morals, ideals. One generation sets up duty, renunciation, self-sacrifice as a panacea. The next generation, especially the women, wake up at the age of forty or thereabouts to the fact that their lives have been wasted in the worship of this ideal, and, what is still more aggravating, that the elders who imposed it on them did so in a fit of satiety with their own experiments in the other direction. Then that defrauded generation foams at the mouth at the very mention of duty, and sets up the alternative panacea of love, their deprivation of which seems to them to have been the most cruel and mischievous feature of their slavery to duty. It is useless to warn them that this reaction, if prescribed as a panacea, will prove as great a failure as all the other reactions have done; for they do not recognize its identity with any reaction that ever occurred before. Take for instance the hackneyed historic example of the austerity of the Commonwealth being followed by the license of the Restoration. You cannot persuade any moral enthusiast to accept this as a pure oscillation from action to reaction. If he is a Puritan he looks upon the Restoration as a national disaster: if he is an artist he regards it as the salvation of the country from gloom, devil worship, and starvation of the affections. The Puritan is ready to try the Commonwealth again with a few modern improvements: the Amateur is equally ready to try the Restoration with modern enlightenments. And so for the present we must be content to proceed by reactions, hoping that each will establish some permanently practical and beneficial reform or moral habit that will survive the correction of its excesses by the next reaction.

DRAMATIC ORIGIN OF WOTAN

We can now see how a single drama in which Wotan does not appear, and of which Siegfried is the hero, expanded itself into a great fourfold drama of which Wotan is the hero. You cannot dramatize a reaction by personifying the reacting force only, any more than Archimedes could lift the world without a fulcrum for his lever. You must also personify the established power against which the new force is reacting; and in the conflict between them you get your drama, conflict being the essential ingredient in all drama. Siegfried, as the hero of Die Götterdämmerung, is only the *primo tenore robusto* of an opera book, deferring his death, after he has been stabbed in the last act, to sing rapturous love strains to the heroine exactly like Edgardo in Donizetti's Lucia. In order to make him intelligible in the wider significance which his joyous, fearless, conscienceless heroism soon assumed in Wagner's imagination, it was necessary to provide him with a much vaster dramatic antagonist than the operatic villain Hagen. Hence Wagner had to create Wotan as the anvil for Siegfried's hammer; and since there was no room for

Wotan in the original opera book, Wagner had to work back to a preliminary drama reaching primarily to the very beginnings of human society. And since, on this world-embracing scale, it was clear that Siegfried must come into conflict with many baser and stupider forces than those lofty ones of supernatural religion and political constitutionalism typified by Wotan and his wife Fricka, these minor antagonists had to be dramatized also in the persons of Alberic, Mime, Fafnir, Loki, and the rest. None of these appear in Night Falls on The Gods save Alberic, whose weird dream-colloquy with Hagen, effective as it is, is as purely theatrical as the scene of the Ghost in Hamlet, or the statue in Don Giovanni. Cut the conference of the Norns and the visit of Valtrauta to Brynhild out of Night Falls on The Gods, and the drama remains coherent and complete without them. Retain them, and the play becomes connected by conversational references with the three music dramas; but the connexion establishes no philosophic coherence, no real identity between the operatic Brynhild of the Gibichung episode (presently to be related) and the daughter of Wotan and the First Mother.

THE LOVE PANACEA

We shall now find that at the point where The Ring changes from music-drama into opera, it also ceases to be philosophic, and becomes didactic. The philosophic part is a dramatic symbol of the world as Wagner observed it. In the didactic part the philosophy degenerates into the prescription of a romantic nostrum for all human ills. Wagner, only mortal after all, succumbed to the panacea mania when his philosophy was exhausted, like any of the rest of us.

The panacea is by no means an original one. Wagner was anticipated in the year 1819 by a young country gentleman from Sussex named Shelley, in a work of extraordinary artistic power and splendor. Prometheus Unbound is an English attempt at a Ring; and when it is taken into account that the author was only 27, wheras Wagner was 40 when he completed the poem of The Ring, our vulgar patriotism may find an envious satisfaction in insisting upon the comparison. Both works set forth the same conflict between humanity and its gods and governments, issuing in the redemption of man from their tyranny by the growth of his will into perfect strength and self-confidence; and both finish by a lapse into panacea-mongering didacticism by the holding up of Love as the remedy for all evils and the solvent of all social difficulties.

The differences between Prometheus Unbound and The Ring are as interesting as the likenesses. Shelley, caught in the pugnacity of his youth and the first impetuosity of his prodigious artistic power by the first fierce attack of the New Reformation, gave no quarter to the antagonist of his hero. His Wotan, whom he calls Jupiter, is the almighty fiend into whom the Englishman's God had degenerated during two centuries of ignorant Bible worship and shameless commercialism. He is Alberic, Fafnir, Loki and the ambitious side of Wotan all rolled into one melodramatic demon who is finally torn from his throne and hurled shrieking into the abyss by a spirit representing that conception of Eternal Law which has been replaced since by the conception of Evolution. Wagner, an older, more experienced man than the Shelley of 1819, understood Wotan and pardoned him, separating him tenderly from all the compromising alliances to which Shelley fiercely held him; making the truth and heroism which overthrow him the children of his inmost heart; and representing him as finally acquiescing in and working for his own supersession and annihilation. Shelley, in his later works, is seen progressing towards the same tolerance, justice, and humility of spirit, as he advanced towards the middle age he never reached. But there is no progress from Shelley to Wagner as regards the panacea, except that in Wagner there is a certain shadow of night and death come on it: nay, even a clear opinion that the supreme good of love is that it so completely satisfies the desire for life that after it the Will to Live ceases to trouble us, and we are at last content to achieve the highest happiness of death.

This reduction of the panacea to absurdity was not forced upon Shelley, because the love which acts as a universal solvent in his Prometheus Unbound is a sentiment of affectionate benevolence which has nothing to do with sexual passion. It might, and in fact does, exist in the absence of any sexual interest whatever. The words mercy and kindness connote it less ambiguously than the word love. But Wagner sought always for some point of contact between his ideas and the physical senses, so that people might not only think or imagine them in the XVIII century fashion, but see them on the stage, hear them from the orchestra, and feel them through the infection of passionate emotion. Dr Johnson kicking the stone to confute Berkeley* is not more bent on commonsense concreteness than Wagner: on all occasions he insists on the need for sensuous apprehension to give reality to abstract comprehension, maintaining, in fact, that reality has no other meaning. Now he could apply this process to poetic love only by following it back to its alleged origin in sexual passion,

* Discussing Bishop George Berkeley's theory of the non-existence of matter, James Boswell observed that, though we may be satisfied that the doctrine is false, we are powerless to refute it. Dr Samuel Johnson, dramatically kicking a stone, replied that he refuted it thus. (Boswell, Life of Johnson, 6 August 1763.)

the emotional phenomena of which he has expressed in music with a frankness and forcible naturalism which would possibly have scandalized Shelley. The love duet in the first act of The Valkyrie is brought to a point at which the conventions of our society demand the precipitate fall of the curtain; whilst the prelude to Tristan and Isolde is such an astonishingly intense and faithful translation into music of the emotions which accompany the union of a pair of lovers that it is questionable whether the great popularity of this piece at our orchestral concerts really means that our audiences are entirely catholic in their respect for life in all its beneficently creative functions, or whether they simply enjoy the music without understanding it.

But however offensive and inhuman may be the superstition which brands such exaltations of natural passion as shameful and indecorous, there is at least as much commonsense in disparaging love as in setting it up as a panacea. Even the mercy and loving-kindness of Shelley do not hold good as a universal law of conduct: Shelley himself makes extremely short work of Jupiter, just as Siegfried does of Fafnir, Mime, and Wotan; and the fact that Prometheus is saved from doing the destructive part of his work by the intervention of that very nebulous personification of Eternity called Demogorgon does not in the least save the situation, because, flatly, there is no such person as Demogorgon, and if Prometheus does not pull down Jupiter himself, no one else will. It would be exasperating, if it were not so funny, to see these poets leading their heros through blood and destruction to the conclusion that, as Browning's David puts it (David of all people!), "All's Love; yet all's Law."*

* Robert Browning's poem Saul, in Men and Women (1855).

Certainly it is clear enough that such love as that implied by Siegfried's first taste of fear as he cuts through the mailed coat of the sleeping figure on the mountain, and discovers that it is a woman; by her fierce revolt against being touched by him when his terror gives way to ardor; by his manly transports of victory; and by the womanly mixture of rapture and horror with which she abandons herself to the passion which has seized on them both, is an experience which it is much better, like the vast majority of us, never to have passed through, than to allow it to play more than a recreative holiday part in our lives. It did not play a very large part in Wagner's own laborious life, and does not occupy more than two scenes of The Ring. Tristan and Isolde, wholly devoted to it, is a poem of destruction and death. The Mastersingers, a work full of health, fun and happiness, contains not a single bar of love music that can be described as passionate: the hero of it is a widower who cobbles shoes, writes verses, and contents himself with looking on at the sweetheartings of his customers. Parsifal makes an end of it altogether. The truth is that the love panacea in Night Falls on The Gods and in the last act of Siegfried is a survival of the first crude operatic conception of the story, modified by an anticipation of Wagner's later, though not latest, conception of love as the fulfiller of our Will to Live and consequently our reconciler to night and death.

NOT LOVE, BUT LIFE

The only faith which any reasonable disciple can gain from The Ring is not in love, but in life itself as a tireless power which is continually driving onward and upward—not, please observe, being beckoned or drawn by *Das ewig Weibliche* or any other external sentimentality, but growing from within, by its own inexplicable energy, into ever higher and higher forms of organization, the strengths and the needs of which are continually superseding the institutions which were made to fit our former requirements. When your Bakoonins call out for the demolition of all these venerable institutions, there is no need to fly into a panic and lock them up in prison whilst your parliament is bit by bit doing exactly what they advised you to do. When your Siegfrieds melt down the old weapons into new ones, and with disrespectful words chop in twain the antiquated constable's staves in the hands of their elders, the end of the world is no nearer than it was before. If human nature, which is the highest organization of life reached on this planet, is really degenerating, then human society will decay; and no panic-begotten penal measures can possibly save it: we must, like Prometheus, set to work to make new men instead of vainly torturing old ones. On the other hand, if the energy of life is still carrying human nature to higher and higher levels, then the more young people shock their elders and deride and discard their pet institutions the better for the hopes of the world, since the apparent growth of anarchy is only the measure of the rate of improvement. History, as far as we are capable of history (which is not saying much as yet), shews that all changes from crudity of social organization to complexity, and from mechanical agencies in government to living ones, seem anarchic at first sight. No doubt it is natural to a snail to think that any evolution which threatens to do away with shells will result in general death from exposure. Nevertheless, the most elaborately housed beings today are born not only without houses on their backs but without even fur or feathers to clothe them.

ANARCHISM NO PANACEA

One word of warning to those who may find themselves attracted by Siegfried's Anarchism, or, if they prefer a term with more respectable associations, his neo-Protestantism. Anarchism, as a panacea, is just as hopeless as any other panacea, and will still be so even if we breed a race of perfectly benevolent men. It is true that in the sphere of thought Anarchism is an inevitable condition of progressive evolution. A nation without Freethinkers—that is, without intellectual Anarchists—will share the fate of China. It is also true that our criminal law, based on a conception of crime and punishment which is nothing but our vindictiveness and cruelty in a virtuous disguise, is an unmitigated and abominable nuisance, bound to be beaten out of us finally by the mere weight of our experience of its evil and uselessness. But it will not be replaced by anarchy. Applied to the industrial or political machinery of modern society, anarchy must always reduce itself speedily to absurdity. Even the modified form of anarchy on which modern civilization is based: that is, the abandonment of industry, in the name of individual liberty, to the upshot of competition for personal gain between private capitalists, is a disastrous failure, and is, by mere necessities of the case, giving way to ordered Socialism. For the economic rationale of this, I must refer disciples of Siegfried to a tract from my hand published by the Fabian Society and entitled The Impossibilities of Anarchism, which explains why, owing to the physical constitution of our globe, society cannot effectively organize the production of its food, clothes, and housing, nor distribute them fairly and economically on any anarchic plan: nay, that without concerting our social action to a much higher degree than we do at present we can never get rid of the wasteful and iniquitous welter of a little riches and a great deal of poverty which current political humbug calls our prosperity and civilization. Liberty is an excellent thing; but it cannot begin until society has paid its daily debt to Nature by first earning its living. There is no liberty before that except the liberty to live at somebody else's expense, a liberty much sought after nowadays, since it is the criterion of gentility, but not wholesome from the point of view of the common weal.

SIEGFRIED CONCLUDED

In returning now to the adventures of Siegfried there is little more to be described except the *finale* of an opera. Siegfried, having passed unharmed through the fire, wakes Brynhild and goes through all the fancies and ecstasies of love at first sight in a duet which ends with an apostrophe to *Leuchtende Liebe, lachender Tod*!, which has been romantically translated into Love that illumines, laughing at death, wheras it really identifies enlightening love and laughing death as involving each other so closely as to be virtually one and the same thing.

NIGHT FALLS ON THE GODS

PROLOGUE

Die Götterdämmerung begins with an elaborate prologue. The three Norns sit in the night on Brynhild's mountain top spinning their thread of destiny, and telling the story of Wotan's sacrifice of his eye, and of his breaking off a bough from the World Ash to make a haft for his spear, also how the tree withered after suffering that violence. They have also some fresher news to discuss. Wotan, on the breaking of his spear by Siegfried, has called all his heros to cut down the withered World Ash and stack its faggots in a mighty pyre about Valhalla. Then, with his broken spear in his hand, he has seated himself in state in the great hall, with the Gods and Heros assembled about him as if in council, solemnly waiting for the end. All this belongs to the old legendary materials with which Wagner began The Ring.

The tale is broken by the thread snapping in the hands of the third Norn; for the hour has arrived when man has taken his destiny in his own hands to shape it for himself, and no longer bows to circumstance, environment, necessity (which he now freely wills), and all the rest of the inevitables. So the Norns recognize that the world has no further use for them, and sink into the earth to return to the First Mother. Then the day dawns; and Siegfried and Brynhild come, and have another duet. He gives her his ring; and she gives him her horse. Away then he goes in search of more adventures; and she watches him from her crag until he disappears. The curtain falls; but we can still hear the trolling of his horn, and the merry clatter of his horse's shoes trotting gaily down the valley. The sound is lost in the grander rhythm of the Rhine as he reaches its banks. We hear again an echo of the lament of the Rhine maidens for the ravished gold; and then, finally, a new strain, which does not surge like the mighty flood of the river, but has an unmistakable tramp of hardy men and a strong land flavor about it. And on this the opera curtain at last goes up—for please remember that all that has gone before is only the overture.

THE FIRST ACT

We now understand the new tramping strain. We are in the Rhineside hall of the Gibichungs, in the presence of King Gunther, his sister Gutruna, and Gunther's grim half brother Hagen, the villain of the piece. Gunther is a fool, and has for Hagen's intelligence the respect a fool always has for the brains of a scoundrel. Feebly fishing for compliments, he appeals to Hagen to pronounce him a fine fellow and a glory to the race of

Gibich. Hagen declares that it is impossible to contemplate him without envy, but thinks it a pity that he has not yet found a wife glorious enough for him. Gunther doubts whether so extraordinary a person can possibly exist. Hagen then tells him of Brynhild and her rampart of fire; also of Siegfried. Gunther takes this rather in bad part, since not only is he afraid of the fire, but Siegfried, according to Hagen, is not, and will therefore achieve this desirable match himself. But Hagen points out that since Siegfried is riding about in quest of adventures, he will certainly pay an early visit to the renowned chief of the Gibichungs. They can then give him a philtre which will make him fall in love with Gutruna and forget every other woman he has yet seen.

Gunther is transported with admiration of Hagen's cunning when he takes in this plan; and he has hardly assented to it when Siegfried, with operatic opportuneness, drops in just as Hagen expected, and is duly drugged into the heartiest love for Gutruna and total oblivion of Brynhild and his own past. When Gunther declares his longing for the bride who lies inaccessible within a palisade of flame, Siegfried at once offers to undertake the adventure for him. Hagen then explains to both of them that Siegfried can, after braving the fire, appear to Brynhild in the semblance of Gunther through the magic of the wishing cap (or Tarnhelm, as it is called throughout The Ring), the use of which Siegfried now learns for the first time. It is of course part of the bargain that Gunther shall give his sister to Siegfried in marriage. On that they swear blood-brotherhood; and at this opportunity the old operatic leaven breaks out amusingly in Wagner. With tremendous exordium of brass, the tenor and baritone go at it with a will, shewing off the power of their voices, following each other in canonic imitation, singing together in thirds and sixths, and finishing with a lurid unison, quite in the manner of

Ruy Gomez and Ernani, or Otello and Iago. Then without further ado Siegfried departs on his expedition, taking Gunther with him to the foot of the mountain, and leaving Hagen to guard the hall and sing a very fine solo which has often figured in the programs of the Richter concerts, explaining that his interest in the affair is that Siegfried will bring back the Ring, and that he, Hagen, will presently contrive to possess himself of that Ring and become Plutonic master of the world.

And now it will be asked how does Hagen know all about the Plutonic empire; and why was he able to tell Gunther about Brynhild and Siegfried, and to explain to Siegfried the trick of the Tarnhelm. The explanation is that though Hagen's mother was the mother of Gunther, his father was not the illustrious Gibich, but no less a person than our old friend Alberic, who, like Wotan, has begotten a son to do for him what he cannot do for himself.

In the above incidents, those gentle moralizers who find the serious philosophy of the music-dramas too terrifying for them may allegorize pleasingly on the philtre as the maddening chalice of passion which, once tasted, causes the respectable man to forget his lawfully wedded wife and plunge into adventures which eventually lead him headlong to destruction.

We now come upon a last relic of the tragedy of Wotan. Returning to Brynhild's mountain, we find her visited by her sister Valkyrie Valtrauta, who has witnessed Wotan's solemn preparations with terror. She repeats to Brynhild the account already given by the Norns. Clinging in anguish to Wotan's knees, she has heard him mutter that were the ring returned to the daughters of the deep Rhine, both Gods and world would be redeemed from that stage curse of Alberic's in The Rhine Gold. On this she has rushed on her warhorse through the air to beg Brynhild to give the Rhine back its ring. But this is asking Woman to give up love for the sake of Church and State. She declares that she will see them both perish first; and Valtrauta returns to Valhalla in despair. Whilst Brynhild is watching the course of the black thundercloud that marks her sister's flight, the fires of Loki again flame high round the mountain; and the horn of Siegfried is heard as he makes his way through them. But the man who now appears wears the Tarnhelm: his voice is a strange voice: his figure is the unknown one of the king of the Gibichungs. He tears the ring from her finger, and, claiming her as his wife, drives her into the cave without pity for her agony of horror, and sets Nothung between them in token of his loyalty to the friend he is impersonating. No explanation of this highway robbery of the ring is offered. Clearly, this Siegfried is not the Siegfried of the previous drama.

THE SECOND ACT

In the second act we return to the hall of Gibich, where Hagen, in the last hours of that night, still sits, his spear in his hand, and his shield beside him. At his knees crouches a dwarfish spectre, his father Alberic, still full of his old grievances against Wotan, and urging his son in his dreams to win back the ring for him. This Hagen swears to do; and as the apparition of his father vanishes, the sun rises and Siegfried suddenly comes from the river bank tucking into his belt the Tarnhelm, which has transported him from the mountain like the enchanted carpet of the Arabian tales. He describes his adventures to Gutruna until Gunther's boat is seen approaching, when Hagen seizes a cowhorn and calls the tribesmen to welcome their chief and his bride. It is most exhilarating, this colloquy with the startled and hastily armed clan, ending with a thunderous chorus, the drums marking the time with mighty pulses from dominant to tonic, much as Rossini would have made them do if he had been a pupil of Beethoven's.

A terrible scene follows. Gunther leads his captive bride straight into the presence of Siegfried, whom she claims as her husband by the ring, which she is astonished to see on his finger: Gunther, as she supposes, having torn it from her the night before. Turning on Gunther, she says "Since you took that ring from me, and married me with it, tell him of your right to it; and make him give it back to you." Gunther stammers "The ring! I gave him no ring—er—do you know him?" The rejoinder is obvious. "Then where are you hiding the ring that you had from me?" Gunther's confusion enlightens her; and she calls Siegfried trickster and thief to his face. In vain he declares that he got the ring from no woman, but from a dragon whom he slew; for he is manifestly puzzled; and she, seizing her opportunity, accuses him before the clan of having played Gunther false with her.

Hereupon we have another grandiose operatic oath, Siegfried attesting his innocence on Hagen's spear, and Brynhild rushing to the footlights and thrusting him aside to attest his guilt, whilst the clansmen call upon their gods to send down lightnings and silence the perjured. The gods do not respond; and Siegfried, after whispering to Gunther that the Tarnhelm seems to have been only half effectual after all, laughs his way out of the general embarrassment and goes off merrily to prepare for his wedding, with his arm round Gutruna's waist, followed by the clan. Gunther, Hagen and Brynhild are left together to plot operatic vengeance. Brynhild, it appears, has enchanted Siegfried in such a fashion that no weapon can hurt him. She has, however, omitted to protect his back, since it is impossible that he should ever turn that to a foe. They agree accordingly that on the morrow a great hunt shall take place, at which Hagen shall thrust his spear into the hero's vulnerable back. The blame is to be laid on the tusk of a wild boar. Gunther, being a fool, is remorseful about his oath of blood-brotherhood and about his sister's bereavement, without having the strength of mind to prevent the murder. The three burst into a herculean *trio*, similar in conception to that of the three conspirators in Un Ballo in Maschera; and the act concludes with a joyous strain heralding the appearance of Siegfried's wedding procession, with strewing of flowers, sacrificing to the gods, and carrying bride and bridegroom in triumph.

It will be seen that in this act we have lost all connexion with the earlier drama. Brynhild is not only not the Brynhild of The Valkyries, she is the Hiordis of Ibsen, a majestically savage woman, in whom jealousy and revenge are intensified to heroic proportions. That is the inevitable theatrical treatment of the murderous heroine of the Saga. Ibsen's aim in The Vikings was purely theatrical, and not, as in his later dramas, also philosophically symbolic. Wagner's aim in Siegfried's Death was equally theatrical, and not, as it afterwards became in the dramas of which Siegfried's antagonist Wotan is the hero, likewise philosophically symbolic. The two master-dramatists therefore produce practically the same version of Brynhild. Thus on the second evening of The Ring we see Brynhild in the character of the truth-divining instinct in religion, cast into an enchanted slumber and surrounded by the fires of hell lest she should overthrow a Church corrupted by its alliance with government. On the fourth evening, we find her swearing a malicious lie to gratify her personal jealousy, and then plotting a treacherous murder with a fool and a scoundrel. In the original draft of Siegfried's Death, the incongruity is carried still further by the conclusion, at which the dead Brynhild, restored to her godhead by

Wotan, and again a Valkyrie, carries the slain Siegfried to Valhalla to live there happily ever after with its pious heros.

As to Siegfried himself, he talks of women, both in this second act and the next with the air of a man of the world. "Their tantrums" he says "are soon over." Such speeches do not belong to the novice of the preceding drama, but to the original Siegfried's Tod, with its leading characters sketched on the ordinary romantic lines from the old Sagas, and not yet reminted as the original creations of Wagner's genius whose acquaintance we have made on the two previous evenings. The very title Siegfried's Death survives as a strong theatrical point in the following passage. Gunther, in his rage and despair, cries "Save me, Hagen: save my honor and thy mother's who bore us both." "Nothing can save thee" replies Hagen "neither brain nor hand, but *Siegfried's Death.*" And Gunther echoes with a shudder "*Siegfried's Death!*"

A WAGNERIAN NEWSPAPER CONTROVERSY

The devotion which Wagner's work inspires has been illustrated lately in a public correspondence on this very point. A writer in the Daily Telegraph having commented on the falsehood uttered by Brynhild in accusing Siegfried of having betrayed Gunther with her, a correspondence in defence of the beloved heroine was opened in the Daily Chronicle.* The imputation of

* The discussion of "Brünnhilde's 'Deceit'" in the correspondence columns of the Daily Chronicle, 24 June—5 July 1898, included the views of William Ashton Ellis, Shaw, Edward Baughan, and Basil Crump, concerning the operatic character of Die Götterdämmerung and the personal character of Brünnhilde. All of the Shavian arguments in the two letters published on 28 June and 5 July were anticipated in his critiques on Bayreuth or reiterated in The Perfect Wagnerite.

falsehood by Brynhild was strongly resented and combated, in spite of the unanswerable evidence of the text. It was contended that Brynhild's statement must be taken as establishing the fact that she actually was ravished by somebody whom she believed to be Siegfried, and that since this somebody cannot have been Siegfried, he being as incapable of treachery to Gunther as she of falsehood, it must have been Gunther himself after a second exchange of personalities not mentioned in the text. The reply to this—if so obviously desperate a hypothesis needs a reply—is that the text is perfectly explicit as to Siegfried, disguised as Gunther, passing the night with Brynhild with Nothung dividing them, and in the morning bringing her down the mountain *through the fire* (an impassable obstacle to Gunther) and there transporting himself in a single breath, by the Tarnhelm's magic, back to the hall of the Gibichungs, leaving the real Gunther to bring Brynhild down the river after him. One controversialist actually pleaded for the expedition occupying two nights, on the second of which the alleged outrage might have taken place. But the time is accounted for to the last minute: it all takes place during the single night watch of Hagen. There is no possible way out of the plain fact that Brynhild's accusation is to her own knowledge false; and the impossible ways just cited are only interesting as examples of the fanatical worship which Wagner and his creations have been able to inspire in minds of exceptional power and culture.

More plausible was the line taken by those who admitted the falsehood. Their contention was that when Wotan deprived Brynhild of her Godhead, he also deprived her of her former high moral attributes; so that Siegfried's kiss awakened an ordinary mortal jealous woman. But a goddess can become mortal and jealous without plunging at once into perjury and murder.

Besides, this explanation involves the sacrifice of the whole significance of the allegory, and the reduction of The Ring to the plane of a child's conception of The Sleeping Beauty. Whoever does not understand that, in terms of The Ring philosophy, a change from godhead to humanity is a step higher and not a degradation, misses the whole point of The Ring. It is precisely because the truthfulness of Brynhild is proof against Wotan's spells that he has to contrive the fire palisade with Loki, to protect the fictions and conventions of Valhalla against her.

The only tolerable view is the one supported by the known history of The Ring, and also, for musicians of sufficiently fine judgment, by the evidence of the scores; of which more anon. As a matter of fact Wagner began, as I have said, with Siegfried's Death. Then, wanting to develop the idea of Siegfried as neo-Protestant, he went on to The Young Siegfried. As a Protestant cannot be dramatically projected without a pontifical antagonist, The Young Siegfried led to The Valkyrie, and that again to its preface The Rhine Gold (the preface is always written after the book is finished). Finally, of course, the whole was revised. The revision, if carried out strictly, would have involved the cutting out of Siegfried's Death, now become inconsistent and superfluous; and that would have involved, in turn, the facing of the fact that The Ring was no longer a Niblung epic, and really demanded modern costumes, tall hats for Tarnhelms, factories for Nibelheims, villas for Valhallas, and so on—in short, a complete confession of the extent to which the old Niblung epic had become the merest pretext and name directory in the course of Wagner's travail. But, as Wagner's most eminent English interpreter once put it to me at Bayreuth between the acts of Night Falls on The Gods, the master wanted to "Lohengrinize" again after his long abstention from opera; and Siegfried's Death (first sketched in 1848, the year before the rising in Dresden and the subsequent events which so deepened Wagner's sense of life and the seriousness of art) gave him exactly the libretto he required for that outbreak of the old operatic Adam in him. So he changed it into Die Götterdämmerung, retaining the traditional plot of murder and jealousy, and with it, necessarily, his original second act, in spite of the incongruity of its Siegfried and Brynhild with the Siegfried and Brynhild of the allegory. As to the legendary matter about the world-ash and the destruction of Valhalla by Loki, it fitted in well enough; for though, allegorically, the blow by which Siegfried breaks the god's spear is the end of Wotan and of Valhalla, those who do not see the allegory, and take the story literally, like children, are sure to ask what becomes of Wotan after Siegfried gets past him up the mountain; and to this question the old tale told in Night Falls on The Gods is as good an answer as another. The very senselessness of the scenes of the Norns and of Valtrauta in relation to the three foregoing dramas, gives them a highly effective air of mystery; and no one ventures to challenge their consequentiality, because we are all more apt to pretend to understand great works of art than to confess that the meaning (if any) has escaped us. Valtrauta, however, betrays her irrelevance by explaining that the gods can be saved by the restoration of the ring to the Rhine daughters. This, considered as part of the previous allegory, is nonsense; so that even this scene, which has a more plausible air of organic connexion with The Valkyrie than any other in Night Falls on The Gods, is as clearly part of a different and earlier conception as the episode which concludes it, in which Siegfried actually robs Brynhild of her ring, though he has no recollection of having given it to her. Night Falls on The Gods, in fact, was not even revised into any real coherence with the world-poem which sprang from it; and that is the authentic solution of all the controversies which have arisen over it.

THE THIRD ACT

The hunting party comes off duly. Siegfried strays from it and meets the Rhine maidens, who almost succeed in coaxing the ring from him. He pretends to be afraid of his wife; and they chaff him as to her beating him and so forth; but when they add that the ring is accursed and will bring death upon him, he discloses to them, as unconsciously as Julius Cæsar disclosed it long ago, that secret of heroism, never to let your life be shaped by fear of its end.* So he keeps the ring; and they leave him to his fate. The hunting party now finds him; and they all sit down together to make a meal by the river side, Siegfried telling them meanwhile the story of his adventures. When he approaches the subject of Brynhild, as to whom his memory is a blank, Hagen pours an antidote to the love philtre into his drinking horn, whereupon, his memory returning, he proceeds to narrate the incident of the fiery mountain, to Gunther's intense mortification. Hagen then plunges his spear into the back of Siegfried, who falls dead on his shield, but gets up again, after the old operatic custom, to sing about thirty bars to his love before allowing himself to be finally carried off to the strains of the famous Trauermarsch.

* "We must learn to die, and to die in the fullest sense of the word. The fear of the end is the source of all lovelessness; and this fear is generated only when love begins to wane. How came it that this love, the highest blessedness to all things living, was so far lost sight of by the human race that at last it came to this: all that mankind did, ordered, and established, was conceived only in fear of the end? My poem sets this forth."—Wagner to Roeckel, 25 January 1854. [GBS]

The scene then changes to the hall of the Gibichungs by the Rhine. It is night; and Gutruna, unable to sleep, and haunted by all sorts of vague terrors, is waiting for the return of her husband, and wondering whether a ghostly figure she has seen gliding down to the river bank is Brynhild, whose room is empty. Then comes the cry of Hagen, returning with the hunting party to announce the death of Siegfried by the tusk of a wild boar. But Gutruna divines the truth; and Hagen does not deny it. Siegfried's body is brought in; Gunther claims the ring; Hagen will not suffer him to take it; they fight; and Gunther is slain. Hagen then attempts to take it; but the dead man's hand closes on it and raises itself threateningly. Then Brynhild comes; and a funeral pyre is raised whilst she declaims a prolonged *scena*, extremely moving and imposing, but yielding nothing to resolute intellectual criticism except a very powerful and elevated exploitation of theatrical pathos, psychologically identical with the scene of Cleopatra and the dead Antony in Shakespear's tragedy. Finally she flings a torch into the pyre, and rides her warhorse into the flames. The hall of the Gibichungs catches fire, as most halls would were a cremation attempted in the middle of the floor (I permit myself this gibe purposely to emphasize the excessive artificiality of the scene); but the Rhine overflows its banks to allow the three Rhine maidens to take the ring from Siegfried's finger, incidentally extinguishing the conflagration as it does so. Hagen attempts to snatch the ring from the maidens, who promptly drown him; and in the distant heavens the Gods and their castle are seen perishing in the fires of Loki as the curtain falls.

COLLAPSE OF THE ALLEGORY

In all this, it will be observed, there is nothing new. The musical fabric is enormously elaborate and gorgeous; but you cannot say, as you must in witnessing The Rhine Gold, The Valkyries, and the first two acts of Siegfried, that you have never seen anything like it before, and that the inspiration is entirely original. Not only the action, but most of the poetry, might conceivably belong to an Elizabethan drama. The situation of Cleopatra and Antony is unconsciously reproduced without being bettered, or even equaled in point of majesty and musical expression. The loss of all simplicity and dignity, the impossibility of any credible scenic presentation of the incidents, and the extreme staginess of the conventions by which these impossibilities are got over, are no doubt covered from the popular eye by the overwhelming prestige of Die Götterdämmerung as part of so great a work as The Ring, and by the extraordinary storm of emotion and excitement which the music keeps up. But the very qualities that intoxicate the novice in music enlighten the adept. In spite of the fulness of the composer's technical accomplishment, the finished style and effortless mastery of harmony and instrumentation displayed, there is not a bar in the work which moves us as the same themes moved us in The Valkyrie, nor is anything but external splendor added to the life and humor of Siegfried.

In the original poem, Brynhild delays her self-immolation on the pyre of Siegfried to read the assembled choristers a homily on the efficacy of the Love panacea. "My holiest wisdom's hoard" she says "now I make known to the world. I believe not in property, nor money, nor godliness, nor hearth and high place, nor pomp and peerage, nor contract and custom, but in Love. Let that only prevail; and ye shall be blest in weal or woe." Here the repudiations still smack of Bakoonin; but the savior is no longer the volition of the fullgrown spirit of Man, the Free Willer of Necessity, sword in hand, but simply Love, and not even Shelleyan love, but vehement sexual passion. It is highly significant of the extent to which this uxorious commonplace lost its hold of Wagner (after disturbing his conscience, as he confesses to Roeckel, for years) that it disappears in the full score of Night Falls on The Gods, which was not completed until he was on the verge of producing Parsifal, twenty years after the publication of the poem. He cut the homily out, and composed the music of the final scene with a flagrant recklessness of the old intention. The rigorous logic with which representative musical themes are employed in the earlier dramas is here abandoned without scruple; and for the main theme at the conclusion he selects a rapturous passage sung by Sieglinda in the third act of The Valkyrie (**III**, 454, *ante*) when Brynhild inspires her with a sense of her high destiny as the mother of the unborn hero. There is no dramatic logic whatever in the recurrence of this theme to express the transport in which Brynhild immolates herself. There is of course an excuse for it, inasmuch as both women have an impulse of self-sacrifice for the sake of Siegfried; but this is really hardly more than an excuse; since the Valhalla theme might be attached to Alberic on the no worse ground that both he and Wotan are inspired by ambition, and that the ambition has the same object, the possession of the ring. The commonsense of the matter is that the only themes which had fully retained their old hold on Wagner's intellectual conscience when he composed Night Falls on The Gods are those which are mere labels of external features such as the Dragon, the Fire, the Water and so on. This particular theme of Sieglinda's is, in truth, of no great musical merit: it might easily be the pet climax of a popular sentimental ballad: in fact, the gushing effect which is its sole valuable quality is so cheaply attained that it is hardly going too far to call it the most trumpery phrase in the entire tetralogy. Yet, since it undoubtedly does gush very emphatically, Wagner chose, for convenience' sake, to work up this final scene with it rather than with the more distinguished, elaborate and beautiful themes connected with the love of Brynhild and Siegfried.

He would certainly not have thought this a matter of no consequence had he finished the whole work ten years earlier. It must always be borne in mind that the poem of The Ring was complete and printed in 1853, and represents the sociological ideas which, after germinating in the European atmosphere for many years, had been brought home to Wagner, who was intensely susceptible to such ideas, by the crash of 1849 at Dresden. Now, no man whose mind is alive and active, as Wagner's was to the day of his death, can keep his political and spiritual opinions, much less his philosophic consciousness, at a standstill for quarter of a century until he finishes an orchestral score. When Wagner first sketched Night Falls on The Gods he was 35. When he finished the score for the first Bayreuth festival in 1876 he had turned 60. No wonder he had lost his old grip of it and left it behind him. He even tampered with The Rhine Gold for the sake of theatrical effect when stage-managing it, making Wotan pick up and brandish a sword to give visible point to his sudden inspiration as to the raising up of a hero. The sword had first to be discovered by Fafnir among the Niblung treasures and thrown away by him as useless. There is no sense in this device; and its adoption shews the same recklessness as to the original intention which we find in the music of the last act of The Dusk of The Gods.*

*Die Götterdämmerung means literally Godsgloaming. The English versions of the opera are usually called The Dusk of The Gods, or The Twilight of The Gods. I have purposely introduced the ordinary title in the sentence above for the reader's information. [GBS]

Wagner, however, was not the man to allow his grip of a great philosophic theme to slacken, even in twentyfive years, had the theme stood the test of the world's experience. If the history of Germany from 1849 to 1876 had been the history of Siegfried and Wotan transposed into the key of actual life, Night Falls on The Gods would have been the logical consummation of The Rhine Gold and The Valkyrie instead of the operatic anachronism it actually is.

But, as a matter of fact, Siegfried did not arrive and Bismarck did. Roeckel faded into a prisoner whose imprisonment made no difference. Bakoonin broke up, not Valhalla, but The International, which petered out in an undignified quarrel between him and Karl Marx. The Siegfrieds of 1848 were hopeless political failures, wheras the Wotans and Alberics and Lokis were conspicuous political successes. Even the Mimes held their own as against Siegfried. With the single exception of Ferdinand Lassalle, there was no revolutionary leader who was not an obvious Impossibilist in practical politics; and Lassalle got himself killed in a romantic and quite indefensible duel after wrecking his health in a titanic oratorical campaign which convinced him that the great majority of the working classes were not ready to join him, and that the minority who were ready did not understand him. The International, founded in 1864 by Karl Marx in London, and mistaken for several years by nervous newspapers for a red spectre, was really only a turnip ghost. It achieved some beginnings of international Trade Unionism by inducing English workmen to send money to support strikes on the continent, and recalling English workers who had been taken across the

North Sea to defeat such strikes; but on its revolutionary socialistic side it was a romantic figment. The suppression of the Paris Commune, one of the most tragic examples in history of the pitilessness with which capable practical administrators and soldiers are forced by the pressure of facts to destroy romantic amateurs and theatrical dreamers, made an end of melodramatic Socialism. It was as easy for Marx, with his literary talent, to hold up Thiers as the most execrable of living scoundrels, and to put upon Gallifet a brand indelible enough to ostracize him politically for ever, as it was for Victor Hugo to bombard Napoleon III., from his paper battery in Jersey. It was also easy to hold up Félix Pyat and Delescluze as men of much loftier ideals than Thiers and Gallifet*; but the one fact that could not be denied was that when it came to actual shooting, it was Gallifet who got Delescluze shot and not Delescluze who got Gallifet shot, and that when it came to administering affairs of France, Thiers could in one way or another get it done,whilst Pyat could neither do it nor stop talking and allow somebody else to do it. True, the penalty of

* Gaston, Marquis de Gallifet, was a French military leader who, as Minister of War, firmly suppressed the Paris Commune revolts in 1871. Louis-Adolphe Thiers, political leader and historian, negotiated the peace settlement with Bismarck after the Franco-Prussian war and, with German assistance, repressed the Socialist uprising of the Paris Commune. He was elected president of the new republic. Louis-Charles Delescluze, radical republican journalist, led the Paris Commune's attack against the government; he deliberately placed himself fatally in the line of fire in one of the last barricades. Félix Pyat, playwright and political revolutionist who joined the Paris Communard in 1869, later fled to England to escape a death sentence. After the 1880 amnesty he returned to France, where he was elected to the chamber of deputies.

following Thiers was to be exploited by the landlord and capitalist; but then the penalty of following Pyat was to be shot like a mad dog, or at best sent to New Caledonia, quite unnecessarily and uselessly.

To put it in terms of Wagner's allegory, Alberic had got the ring back again, and was marrying into the best Valhalla families with it. He had thought better of his old threat to dethrone Wotan and Loki. He had found that Nibelheim was a very gloomy place, and that if he wanted to live handsomely and safely, he must not only allow Wotan and Loki to organize society for him, but pay them very handsomely for doing it He needed splendor, military glory, loyalty, enthusiasm, and patriotism; and his greed and gluttony were wholly unable to create them, wheras Wotan and Loki carried them all to their most triumphant climax in Germany in 1871, when Wagner himself celebrated the event with his Kaisermarsch, which sounded much more convincing than the Marseillaise or the Carmagnole.*

How, after the Kaisermarsch, could Wagner go back to his idealization of Siegfried in 1853? How could he believe seriously in Siegfried slaying the dragon and charging through the mountain fire, when the immediate foreground was occupied by the Hôtel de Ville with Félix Pyat endlessly discussing the principles of Socialism whilst the shells of Thiers were already battering the Arc de Triomphe and ripping up the pavement of the Champs Elysées? It is not clear that things had taken an altogether unexpected turn; that although The Ring may, like the famous Communist Manifesto of Marx and Engels, be an inspired guess at the historic laws and predestined end of our capitalistic-theocratic epoch, yet Wagner, like Marx, was too

* Song and dance of the French revolutionists, almost invariably performed at the guillotine executions in 1792–3.

inexperienced in technical government and administration and too melodramatic in his hero-contra-villain conception of the class struggle, to foresee the actual process by which his generalization would work out, or the part to be played in it by the classes involved.

Let us go back for a moment to the point at which the Niblung legend first becomes irreconcilable with Wagner's allegory. Fafnir in the real world becomes a capitalist; but Fafnir in the allegory is a mere hoarder. His gold does not bring him any revenue. It does not even support him: he has to go out and forage for food and drink. In fact, he is on the way to his drinking pool when Siegfried kills him. And Siegfried himself has no more use for the gold than Fafnir: the only difference between them in this respect is that Siegfried does not waste his time watching a barren treasure that is useless to him, wheras Fafnir sacrifices his humanity and his life merely to prevent anybody else getting it. This contrast, true to human nature, is not true to modern economic development. The real Fafnir is not a miser: he seeks dividends, a comfortable life, and admission to the circles of Wotan and Loki. His only means of procuring these is to restore the gold to Alberic in exchange for scrip in Alberic's enterprises. Thus fortified with capital, Alberic exploits his fellow dwarfs as before, and also exploits Fafnir's fellow giants who have no capital. What is more, the competitive strategy and large-scaled enterprise the exploitation involves, and the self-respect and social esteem its success wins, effect a development in Alberic's own character which neither Marx nor Wagner appears to have foreseen. He discovers that to be a dull, greedy, narrowminded moneygrubber is not the way to make money on the modern scale; for though greed may suffice to turn tens into hundreds and even hundreds into thousands, to turn thousands into hundreds of thousands requires economic magnanimity and a will to power as well as to pelf. And to turn hundreds of thousands into millions, Alberic must make himself an earthly Providence for masses of workmen, creating towns, and governing markets. In the meantime, Fafnir, wallowing in the dividends he has done nothing to earn, may rot, intellectually and morally, from mere disuse of his energies and lack of incentive to excel; but the more impotent he becomes, the more dependent he is upon Alberic for his income, on Loki for his politics, and on Wotan for his respectability and safety from rebellion: Alberic, as the pursebearer, being, under Destiny, the real master of the situation. Consequently, though Alberic in 1850 may have been merely the vulgar Manchester factory owner portrayed in Friedrich Engels' Condition of the Working Classes, in 1876 he was well on the way towards becoming exoterically a model philanthropic employer and esoterically a financier.

Now, without exaggerating the virtues of such gentlemen, it will be conceded by everybody except perhaps those veteran Social-Democrats who have made a cult of obsolescence under the name of Marxism, that the dominant sort of modern employer is not to be displaced and dismissed so lightly as Alberic in The Ring. Wotan is hardly less dependent on him than Fafnir: the War-Lord visits his works, acclaims them in stirring speeches, and imprisons his enemies; whilst Loki does his political jobs in Parliament, making wars and commercial treaties for him at command. And he owns and controls a new god, called The Press, which manufactures public opinion on his side, and organizes the persecution and suppression of Siegfried.

The end cannot come until Siegfried learns Alberic's trade and shoulders Alberic's burden. Not having as yet done so, he is still completely mastered by Alberic. He does not even rebel against him except when he is too stupid and ignorant, or too romantically impracticable, to see that Alberic's work, like Wotan's work and Loki's work, is necessary work, and that therefore Alberic can never be superseded by a warrior, but only by a capable man of business who is prepared to continue his work without a day's intermission. Even though the proletarians of all lands were to become "class-conscious," and obey the call of Marx by uniting to rush the class struggle to a proletarian victory in which all capital should become common property, and Monarchs, Millionaires, Landlords, and Capitalists become common citizens, the triumphant proletarians would have either to starve in anarchy next day or else do the political and industrial work which now gets itself done somehow under limited monarchs, despotic presidents, irresponsible financiers, and bourgeois parliaments. And in the meantime these magnates must defend their power and property with all their might against the revolutionary forces until these forces become positive, executive, administrative forces, instead of the conspiracies of protesting, moralizing, virtuously indignant amateurs who mistook Marx for a man of affairs and Thiers for a stage villain.

Now all this represents a development of which one gathers no forecast from Wagner or Marx. Both of them prophesied the end of our epoch; and, though in 1913 that epoch seemed so prosperous that the prophecy seemed ridiculously negligible, within ten years the centre had fallen out of Europe; and humane men could only shake their heads and shrug their shoulders when they were asked for another half-crown to help to save another ten million children from starvation. Alberic had prospered so greatly that he had come to believe himself immortal; and his alliances with Wotan had brought his sons and daughters under the influences, dangerous to commerce, of feudal militarist ideals. The abyss in his path had been pointed out to him not only by Wagner and Marx, but by men who, instead of vainly consulting the oracle in the pages of Das Kapital, had sought new and safe paths by the light of contemporary history and practical administrative experience. But Alberic would neither believe that the old path led to the abyss nor explore the new paths; and the masses knew nothing of paths and much of poverty. So he went faster and faster, at last marching sword in hand with his feudal sons-in-law, blasting his way with cyclopean explosives, at which point he crashed into the abyss he had not believed in, bringing down the civilization of Central and Eastern Europe along with him, and leaving the Bolshevists (*ci-devant* Marxists), Social-Democrats, Republicans and amorphous revolutionaries generally to extricate it as best they could, and to learn in the process the truth of these last few pages.

But Wagner did not live to see this reduction of Alberic to absurdity. What he did see was the reduction of Siegfried to absurdity. Siegfried had done nothing that promised success in his struggle with Alberic; and Alberic had not yet outdone Siegfried in ineptitude by committing suicide. Now Wagner was compelled by his profession to be, compared with Siegfried, a practical man. It is possible to learn more of the world by producing a single opera, or even conducting a single orchestral rehearsal, than by ten years reading in the library of the British Museum. Wagner must have learnt between The Rhine Gold and the Kaisermarsch that there are yet several dramas to be interpolated in The Ring after The Valkyrie before the allegory can tell the whole story. If anyone doubts the extent to which Wagner's eyes had been opened to the administrative childishness and romantic conceit of the heros of the revolutionary generation that served its apprenticeship on the barricades of 1848-49, and perished on those of 1871 under Thiers' *mitrailleuses*, let him read Eine Kapitulation, that scandalous burlesque in which the poet and composer of Siegfried, with the levity of a schoolboy, mocked the French republicans who were doing in 1871 what he himself was exiled for doing in 1849. He had set the enthusiasm of the Dresden revolution to his own greatest music; but he set the enthusiasm of twenty years later in derision to the music of Rossini. There is no mistaking the tune he meant to suggest by his doggerel of Republik, Republik, Republik-lik-lik. The Overture to William Tell is there as plainly as if it were noted down in full score.

In the case of such a man as Wagner, you cannot explain this *volte-face* as mere jingoism produced by Germany's overwhelming victory in the Franco-Prussian war, nor as personal spite against the Parisians for the Tannhäuser fiasco. Wagner had more cause for personal spite against his own countrymen than he ever had against the Parisians: he was ten times bitterer against his respectable prosperity in Dresden than against his starvation in Paris. No doubt his outburst gratified the pettier feelings which great men have in common with small ones; but he was not a man to indulge in such gratifications or indeed to feel them as gratifications, if he had not become convinced of the administrative impotence of the agitators who were trying to wield Nothung, and who had done less for Wagner's own art than a single German king, and he, too, a mad one. Wagner had by that time done too much himself not to know that the world is ruled by deeds, not by good intentions, and that one efficient sinner is worth ten futile saints and martyrs.

I need not elaborate the point further in these pages. Like all men of genius, Wagner had exceptional sincerity, exceptional respect for facts, exceptional freedom from the hypnotic influence of sentimental popular movements, exceptional sense of the realities of political power as distinguished from the pretences and idolatries behind which the real masters of modern States pull their wires and train their guns. When he scored Night Falls on The Gods, he had accepted the failure of Siegfried and the triumph of the Wotan-Loki-Alberic trinity as a fact. He had given up dreaming of heros, heroines, and final solutions, and had conceived a new protagonist in Parsifal, whom he announced, not as a hero, but as a fool armed, not with a sword which cut irresistibly, but with a spear which he held only on condition that he did not use it: one who, instead of exulting in the slaughter of a dragon, was ashamed of having shot a swan. The change in the conception of the Deliverer could hardly be more complete. It reflects the change which took place in Wagner's mind between the composition of The Rhine Gold and Night Falls on The Gods; and it explains why he found it so easy to drop the Ring allegory and fall back on Lohengrinizing.

WAGNER'S OWN EXPLANATION

And now, having given my explanation of The Ring, can I give Wagner's explanation of it? If I could (and I can) I should not by any means accept it as conclusive. Nearly half a century has passed since the tetralogy was written; and in that time the purposes of many half instinctive acts of genius have become clearer to the common man than they were to the doers. Some years ago, in the course of an explanation of Ibsen's plays, I pointed out that it was by no means certain or even likely that Ibsen was as definitely conscious of his thesis as I. All the stupid people, and some critics who, though not stupid, had not themselves written what the Germans call "tendency" works, saw nothing in this but a fantastic affectation of the extravagant self-conceit of knowing more about Ibsen than Ibsen himself. Fortunately, in taking exactly the same position now with regard to Wagner, I can claim his own authority to support me. "How" he wrote to Roeckel on the 23rd August 1856 "can an artist expect that what he has felt intuitively should be perfectly realized by others, seeing that he himself feels in the presence of his work, if it is true Art, that he is confronted by a riddle, about which he, too, might have illusions, just as another might?"

The truth is, we are apt to deify men of genius, exactly as we deify the creative force of the universe, by attributing to logical design what is the result of blind instinct. What Wagner meant by "true Art" is the operation of the artist's instinct, which is just as blind as any other instinct. Mozart, asked for an explanation of his works, said frankly "How do I know?" Wagner, being a philosopher and critic as well as a composer, was always looking for moral explanations of what he had created; and he hit on several very striking ones, all different. In the same way one can conceive Henry the Eighth speculating very brilliantly about the circulation of his own blood without getting as near the truth as Harvey did long after his death.

Nonetheless, Wagner's own explanations are of exceptional interest. To begin with, there is a considerable portion of The Ring, especially the portraiture of our capitalistic industrial system from the socialist's point of view in the slavery of the Niblungs and the tyranny of Alberic, which is unmistakable, as it dramatizes that portion of human activity which lies well within the territory covered by our intellectual consciousness. All this is concrete Home Office business, so to speak: its meaning was as clear to Wagner as it is to us. Not so that part of the work which deals with the destiny of Wotan. And here, as it happened, Wagner's recollection of what he had been driving at was completely upset by his discovery, soon after the completion of The Ring poem, of Schopenhauer's famous treatise The World as Will and Representation. So obsessed did he become with this masterpiece of philosophic art that he declared that it contained the intellectual demonstration of the conflict of human forces which he himself had demonstrated artistically in his great poem. "I must confess" he writes to Roeckel "to having arrived at a clear understanding of my own works of art through the help of another, who has provided me with the reasoned conceptions corresponding to my intuitive principles."

Schopenhauer, however, had done nothing of the sort. Wagner's determination to prove that he had been a Schopenhauerite all along without knowing it only shews how completely the fascination of the great treatise on the Will had run away with his memory. It is easy to see how this happened. Wagner says of himself that "seldom has there taken place in the soul of one and the same man so profound a division and estrangement between the intuitive or impulsive part of his nature and his consciously or reasonably formed ideas." And since Schopenhauer's great contribution to modern thought was to educate us into clear consciousness of this distinction—a distinction familiar, in a fanciful way, to the Ages of Faith and Art before the Renascence, but afterwards swamped in the Rationalism of that movement—it was inevitable that Wagner should jump at Schopenhauer's metaphysiology (I use a word less likely to be mistaken than metaphysics) as the very thing for him. But metaphysiology is one thing, political philosophy another. The political philosophy of Siegfried is exactly contrary to the political philosophy of Schopenhauer, although the same clear metaphysiological distinction between the instinctive part of man (his Will) and his reasoning faculty (dramatized in The Ring as Loki) is insisted on in both. The difference is that to Schopenhauer the Will is the universal tormentor of man, the author of that great evil, Life; whilst reason is the divine gift that is finally to overcome this life-creating will and lead, through its abnegation, to cessation and peace, annihilation and Nirvana. This is the doctrine of Pessimism. Now Wagner was, when he wrote The Ring, a most sanguine revolutionary Meliorist, contemptuous of the reasoning faculty, which he typified in the shifty, unreal, delusive Loki, and full of faith in the life-giving Will, which he typified in the glorious Siegfried. Not until he read Schopenhauer did he become bent on proving that he had always been a Pessimist at heart, and that Loki was the most sensible and worthy adviser of Wotan in The Rhine Gold.

Sometimes he faces the change in his opinions frankly enough. "My Niblung drama" he writes to Roeckel "had taken form at a time when I had built up with my reason an optimistic world on Hellenic principles, believing that nothing was necessary for the realization of such a world but that men should wish it. I ingeniously set aside the problem why they did not wish it. I remember that it was with this definite creative purpose that I conceived the personality of Siegfried, with the intention of representing an existence free from pain." But he appeals to his earlier works to shew that behind all these artificial optimistic ideas there was always with him an intuition of "the sublime tragedy of renunciation, the negation of the will." In trying to explain this, he is full of ideas philosophically, and full of the most amusing contradictions personally. Optimism, as an accidental excursion into the barren paths of reason on his own part, he calls "Hellenic." In others he denounces it as rank Judaism, the Jew having at that time become for him the whipping boy for all modern humanity. In a letter from London he expounds Schopenhauer to Roeckel with enthusiasm, preaching the renunciation of the Will to Live as the redemption from all error and vain pursuits: in the next letter he resumes the subject with unabated interest, and finishes by mentioning that on leaving London he went to Geneva and underwent "a most beneficial course of hydropathy." Seven months before this he had written as follows: "Believe me, I too was once possessed by the idea of a country life. In order to become a radically healthy human being, I went two years ago to a Hydropathic Establishment, prepared to give up Art and everything if I could once more become a child of Nature. But, my good friend, I was obliged to laugh at my own naïveté when I found myself almost going mad. None of us will reach the promised land: we shall all die in the wilderness. Intellect is, as some one has said, a sort of disease: it is incurable."

Roeckel knew his man of old, and evidently pressed him for explanations of the inconsistencies of The Ring with Night Falls on The Gods. Wagner defended himself with unfailing cleverness and occasional petulances, ranging from such pleas as "I believe a true instinct has kept me from a too great definiteness; for it has been borne in on me that an absolute disclosure of the intention disturbs true insight," to a volley of explanations and commentaries on the explanations. He gets excited and annoyed because Roeckel will not admire the Brynhild of Night Falls on The Gods; reinvents the Tarnhelm scene; and finally, the case being desperate, exclaims "It is wrong of you to challenge me to explain it in words: you must feel that something is being enacted that is not to be expressed in mere words."

Sometimes he gets very far away from Pessimism indeed, and recommends Roeckel to solace his captivity, not by conquering the will to live at liberty, but by "the inspiring influences of the Beautiful." The next moment he throws over even Art for Life. "Where life ends" he says, very wittily "Art begins. In youth we turn to Art, we know not why; and only when we have gone through with Art and come out on the other side, we learn to our cost that we have missed Life itself." His only comfort is that he is beloved. And on the subject of love he lets himself loose in a manner that would have roused the bitterest scorn in Schopenhauer, though, as we have seen (pp. 479–80), it is highly characteristic of Wagner. "Love in its most perfect reality" he says "is only possible between the sexes: it is only as man and woman that human beings can truly love. Every other manifestation of love can be traced back to that one absorbingly real feeling, of which all other affections are but an emanation, a connexion, or an imitation. It is an error to look on this as only one of the forms in which love is revealed, as if there were other forms coequal with it, or even superior to it. He who after the manner of metaphysicians prefers *unreality* to *reality,* and derives the concrete from the abstract—in short, puts the word before the fact—may be right in esteeming the idea of love as higher than the expression of love, and may affirm that actual love made manifest in feeling is nothing but the outward and visible sign of a pre-existent, non-sensuous, abstract love; and he will do well to despise that sensuous function in general. In any case it were safe to bet that such a man had never loved or been loved as human beings can love, or he would have understood that in despising this feeling, what he condemned was its sensual expression, the outcome of man's animal nature, and not true human love. The highest satisfaction and expression of the individual is only to be found in his complete absorption, and that is only possible through love. Now a human being is both *man* and *woman*: it is only when these two are united that the real human being exists; and thus it is only by love that man and woman attain to the full measure of humanity. But when nowadays we talk of a human being, such heartless blockheads are we that quite involuntarily we only think of man. It is only in the union of man and woman by love (sensuous and supersensuous) that the human being exists; and as the human being cannot rise to the conception of anything higher than his own existence—his own being—so the transcendent act of his life is this consummation of his humanity through love."

It is clear after this utterance from the would-be Schopenhauerian, that Wagner's explanations of his works for the most part explain nothing but the mood in which he happened to be on the day he advanced them, or the train of thought suggested to his very susceptible imagination and active mind by the points raised by his questioner. Especially in his private letters, where his outpourings are modified by his dramatic consciousness of the personality of his correspondent, do we find him taking all manner of positions, and putting forward all sorts of cases which must be taken as clever and suggestive special pleadings, and not as serious and permanent expositions of his works. These works must speak for themselves: if The Ring says one thing, and a letter written afterwards says that it said something else, The Ring must be taken to confute the letter just as conclusively as if the two had been written by different hands. However, nobody fairly well acquainted with Wagner's utterances as a whole will find any unaccountable contradictions in them. As in all men of his type, our manifold nature was so marked in him that he was like several different men rolled into one. When he had exhausted himself in the character of the most pugnacious, aggressive, and sanguine of reformers, he rested himself as a Pessimist and Nirvanist. In The Ring the quietism of Brynhild's "Rest, rest, thou God" is sublime in its deep conviction; but you have only to turn back the pages to find the irrepressible bustle of Siegfried and the revelry of the clansmen expressed with equal zest. Wagner was not a Schopenhauerite every day in the week, nor even a Wagnerite. His mind changes as often as his mood. On Monday nothing will ever induce him to return to quill-driving: on Tuesday he begins a new pamphlet. On Wednesday he is impatient of the misapprehensions of people who cannot see how impossible it is for him to preside as a conductor over platform performances of fragments of his works, which can only be understood when presented strictly according to his intention on the stage: on Thursday he gets up a concert of Wagnerian selections, and when it is over writes to his friends describing how profoundly both bandsmen and audience were impressed. On Friday he exults in the self-assertion of Siegfried's will against all moral ordinances, and is full of a revolutionary sense of "the universal law of change and renewal": on Saturday he has an attack of holiness, and asks "Can you conceive a moral action of which the root idea is not renunciation?" In short, Wagner can be quoted against himself almost without limit, much as Beethoven's adagios could be quoted against his scherzos if a dispute arose between two fools as to whether he was a melancholy man or a merry one.

THE MUSIC OF THE RING

THE REPRESENTATIVE THEMES

To be able to follow the music of The Ring, all that is necessary is to become familiar enough with the brief musical phrases out of which it is built to recognize them and attach a certain definite significance to them, exactly as any ordinary Englishman recognizes and attaches a definite significance to the opening bars of God Save the Queen. There is no difficulty here: every soldier is expected to learn and distinguish between different bugle calls and trumpet calls; and anyone who can do this can learn and distinguish between the representative themes or "leading motives" (Leitmotifs) of The Ring. They are the easier to learn because they are repeated again and again; and the main ones are so emphatically impressed on the ear whilst the spectator is looking for the first time at the objects, or witnessing the first strong dramatic expression of the ideas they denote, that the requisite association is formed unconsciously. The themes are neither long, nor complicated, nor difficult. Whoever can pick up the flourish of a coach-horn, the note of a bird, the rhythm of the postman's knock or of a horse's gallop, will be at no loss in picking up the themes of The Ring. No doubt, when it comes to forming the necessary mental association with the theme, it may happen that the spectator may find his ear conquering the tune more easily than his mind conquers the thought. But for the most part the themes do not denote thoughts at all, but either emotions of a quite simple universal kind, or the sights, sounds and fancies common enough to be familiar to children. Indeed some of them are as frankly childish as any of the funny little orchestral interludes which, in Haydn's Creation, introduce the horse, the deer, or the worm. We have both the horse and the worm in The Ring, treated exactly in Haydn's manner, and with an effect not a whit less ridiculous to superior people who decline to take it goodhumoredly. Even the complaisance of good Wagnerites is occasionally rather overstrained by the way in which Brynhild's allusions to her charger Grani elicit from the band a little rum-ti-tum triplet which by itself is in no way suggestive of a horse, although a continuous rush of such triplets makes a very exciting musical gallop.

Other themes denote objects which cannot be imitatively suggested by music: for instance, music cannot suggest a ring, and cannot suggest gold; yet each of these has a representative theme which pervades the score in all directions. In the case of the gold the association is established by the very salient way in which the orchestra breaks into the pretty theme in the first act of The Rhine Gold at the moment when the sunrays strike down through the water and light up the glittering treasure, hitherto invisible. The reference of the strange little theme of the wishing cap is equally manifest from the first, since the spectator's attention is wholly taken up with the Tarnhelm and its magic when the theme is first pointedly uttered by the orchestra. The sword theme is introduced at the end of The Rhine Gold to express Wotan's hero inspiration; and I have already mentioned that Wagner, unable, when it came to practical stage management, to forego the appeal to the eye as well as to the thought, here made Wotan pick up a sword and brandish it, though no such instruction appears in the printed score. When this sacrifice to Wagner's skepticism as to the reality of any appeal to an audience that is not made through their bodily sense is omitted, the association of the theme with the sword is not formed until that point in the first act of The Valkyrie at which Siegmund is left alone by Hunding's hearth, weaponless, with the assurance that he will have to fight for his life at dawn with his host. He recalls then how his father promised him a sword for his hour of need; and as he does so, a flicker from the dying fire is caught by the golden hilt of the sword in the tree, when the theme immediately begins to gleam through the quiver of sound from the orchestra, and only dies out as the fire sinks and the sword is once more hidden by the darkness. Later on, this theme, which is never silent whilst Sieglinda is dwelling on the story of the sword, leaps out into the most dazzling splendor the band can give it when Siegmund triumphantly draws the weapon from the tree. As it consists of seven notes only, with a very marked measure, and a melody like a simple flourish on a trumpet or post horn, nobody capable of catching a tune can easily miss it.

The Valhalla theme, sounded with solemn grandeur as the home of the gods first appears to us and to Wotan at the beginning of the second scene of The Rhine Gold, also cannot be mistaken. It, too, has a memorable rhythm; and its majestic harmonies, far from presenting those novel or curious problems in polyphony of which Wagner still stands suspected by superstitious people, are just those three simple chords which festive students who vamp accompaniments to comic songs "by ear" soon find sufficient for nearly all the popular tunes in the world.

On the other hand, the ring theme, when it begins to hurtle through the third scene of The Rhine Gold, cannot possibly be referred to any special feature in the general gloom and turmoil of the den of the dwarfs. It is not a melody, but merely the displaced metric accent which musicians call syncopation, rung on the notes of the familiar chord formed by piling three minor thirds on top of oneanother (technically, the chord of the minor ninth, *ci-devant* diminished seventh). One soon picks it up and identifies it; but it does not get introduced in the unequivocally clear fashion of the themes described above, or of that malignant monstrosity, the theme which denotes the curse on the gold. Consequently it cannot be said that the musical design of the work is perfectly clear at the first hearing as regards all the themes; but it is so as regards most of them, the main lines being laid down as emphatically and intelligibly as the dramatic motives in a Shakespearean play. As to the coyer subtleties of the score, their discovery provides fresh interest for repeated hearings, giving The Ring a Beethovenian inexhaustibility and toughness of wear.

The themes associated with the individual characters get stamped on the memory easily by the simple association of the sound of the theme with the appearance of the person indicated. Its appropriateness is generally pretty obvious. Thus, the entry of the giants is made to a vigorous stumping, tramping measure. Mimmy, being a quaint, weird old creature, has a quaint, weird theme of two thin chords that creep down eerily one to the other. Gutruna's theme is pretty and caressing: Gunther's bold, rough, and commonplace. It is a favorite trick of Wagner's, when one of his characters is killed on the stage, to make the theme attached to that character weaken, fail, and fade away with a broken echo into silence.

THE CHARACTERIZATION

All this, however, is the mere child's play of theme work. The more complex characters, instead of having a simple musical label attached to them, have their characteristic ideas and aspirations identified with special representative themes as they come into play in the drama; and the chief merit of the thematic structure of The Ring is the mastery with which the dramatic play of the ideas is reflected in the contrapuntal play of the themes. We do not find Wotan, like the dragon or the horse, or, for the matter of that, like the stage demon in Weber's Freischütz or Meyerbeer's Robert the Devil, with one fixed theme attached to him like a name plate to an umbrella, blaring unaltered from the orchestra whenever he steps on the stage. Sometimes we have the Valhalla theme used to express the greatness of the gods as an idea of Wotan's. Again, we have his spear, the symbol of his power, identified with another theme, on which Wagner finally exercises his favorite device by making it break and fail, cut through, as it were, by the tearing sound of the theme identified with the sword, when Siegfried shivers the spear with the stroke of Nothung. Yet another theme connected with Wotan is the Wanderer music which breaks with such a majestic reassurance on the nightmare terror of Mimmy when Wotan appears at the mouth of his cave in the scene of the three riddles. Thus not only are there several Wotan themes, but each varies in its inflexions and shades of tone color according to its dramatic circumstances. So, too, the merry horn tune of the young Siegfried changes its measure, loads itself with massive harmonies, and becomes an exordium of the most imposing splendor when it heralds his entry as fullfledged hero in the prologue to Night Falls on The Gods. Even Mimmy has his two or three themes: the weird one already described; the little one in triple measure imitating the tap of his hammer, and fiercely mocked in the savage laugh of Alberic at his death; and finally the crooning tune in which he details all his motherly kindnesses to the little foundling Siegfried. Besides this there are all manner of little musical blinkings and shamblings and whinings, the least hint of which from the orchestra at any moment instantly brings Mimmy to mind, whether he is on the stage at the time or not.

In truth, dramatic characterization in music cannot be carried very far by the use of representative themes. Mozart, the greatest of all masters of this art, never dreamt of employing them; and, extensively as they are used in The Ring, they do not enable Wagner to dispense with the Mozartian method. Apart from the themes, Siegfried and Mimmy are still as sharply distinguished from oneanother by the character of their music as Don Giovanni from Leporello, Wotan from Gutruna as Sarastro from Papagena. It is true that the themes attached to the characters have the same musical appropriateness as the rest of the music: for example, neither the Valhalla nor the spear themes could, without the most ludicrous incongruity, be used for the forest bird or the unstable, delusive Loki; but for all that the musical characterization must be regarded as independent of the specific themes, since the entire elimination of the thematic system from the score would leave the characters as well distinguished musically as they are at present.

One more illustration of the way in which the thematic system is worked. There are two themes connected with Loki. One is a rapid, sinuous, twisting, shifty semiquaver figure suggested by the unsubstantial, elusive logic-spinning of the clever one's braincraft. The other is the fire theme. In the first act of Siegfried, Mimmy makes his unavailing attempt to explain fear to Siegfried. With the horror fresh upon him of the sort of nightmare into which he has fallen after the departure of the Wanderer, and which has taken the form, at once fanciful and symbolic, of a delirious dread of light, he asks Siegfried whether he has never, whilst wandering in the forest, had his heart set hammering in frantic dread by the mysterious lights of the gloaming. To this, Siegfried, greatly astonished, replies that on such occasions his heart is altogether healthy and his sensations perfectly normal. Here Mimmy's question is accompanied by the tremulous sounding of the fire theme with its harmonies most oppressively disturbed and troubled; wheras with Siegfried's reply they become quite clear and straightforward, making the theme sound bold, brilliant, and serene. This is a typical instance of the way in which the themes are used.

The thematic system gives symphonic interest, reasonableness and unity to the music, enabling the composer to exhaust every aspect and quality of his melodic material, and, in Beethoven's manner, to work miracles of beauty, expression and significance with the briefest phrases. As a set-off against this, it has led Wagner to indulge in repetitions that would be intolerable in a purely dramatic work. Almost the first thing that a dramatist has to learn in constructing a play is that the persons must not come on the stage in the second act and tell oneanother at great length what the audience has already seen pass before its eyes in the first act. The extent to which Wagner has been seduced into violating this rule by his affection for his themes is startling to a practised playwright. Siegfried inherits from Wotan a mania for autobiography which leads him to inflict on everyone he meets the story of Mimmy and the dragon, although the audience have spent a whole evening witnessing the events he is narrating. Hagen tells the story to Gunther; and that same night Alberic's ghost tells it over again to Hagen, who knows it already as well as the audience. Siegfried tells the Rhine maidens as much of it as they will listen to, and then keeps telling it to his hunting companions until they kill him. Wotan's autobiography on the second evening becomes his biography in the mouths of the Norns on the fourth. The little that the Norns add to it is repeated an hour later by Valtrauta. How far all this repetition is tolerable is a matter of individual taste. A good story will bear repetition; and if it has woven into it such pretty tunes as the Rhine maidens' yodel, Mimmy's tinkling anvil beat, the note of the forest bird, the call of Siegfried's horn, and so on, it will bear a good deal of rehearing. Those who have but newly learnt their way through The Ring will not readily admit that there is a bar too much repetition.

But how if you find some anti-Wagnerite raising the question whether the thematic system does not enable the composer to produce a music-drama with much less musical fertility than was required from his predecessors for the composition of operas under the old system!

Such discussions are not within the scope of this little book. But as the book is now finished (for really nothing more need be said about The Ring), I am quite willing to add a few pages of ordinary musical criticism, partly to please the amateurs who enjoy that sort of reading, and partly for the guidance of those who wish to obtain some hints to help them through such critical small talk about Wagner and Bayreuth as may be forced upon them at the dinner table or between the acts.

THE OLD AND THE NEW MUSIC

In the old-fashioned opera every separate number involved the composition of a fresh melody; but it is quite a mistake to suppose that this creative effort extended continuously throughout the number from the first to the last bar. When a musician composes according to a set metrical pattern, the selection of the pattern and the composition of the first stave (a stave in music corresponds to a line in verse) generally completes the creative effort. All the rest follows more or less mechanically to fill up the pattern, an air being very like a wallpaper design in this respect. Thus the second stave is usually a perfectly obvious consequence of the first; and the third and fourth an exact or very slightly varied repetition of the first and second. For example, given the first line of Pop Goes the Weasel or Yankee Doodle, any musical cobbler could supply the remaining three. There is very little tune-turning of this kind in The Ring; and it is noteworthy that where it does occur, as in Siegmund's spring song and Mimmy's croon *Ein zullendes Kind*, the effect of the symmetrical staves, recurring as a mere matter of form, is perceptibly poor and platitudinous compared with the free flow of melody which prevails elsewhere.

The other and harder way of composing is to take a strain of free melody, and ring every variety of change of mood upon it as if it were a thought that sometimes brought hope, sometimes melancholy, sometimes exultation, sometimes raging despair and so on. To take several themes of this kind, and weave them together into a rich musical fabric passing panoramically before the ear with a continually varying flow of sentiment, is the highest feat of the musician: it is in this way that we get the fugue of Bach and the symphony of Beethoven. The admittedly inferior musician is the one who, like Auber and Offenbach, not to mention our purveyors of drawing-room ballads, can produce an unlimited quantity of symmetrical tunes, but cannot weave themes symphonically.

When this is taken into account, it will be seen that the fact that there is a great deal of repetition in The Ring does not distinguish it from the old-fashioned operas. The real difference is that in them the repetition was used for the mechanical completion of conventional metric patterns, wheras in The Ring the recurrence of the theme is an intelligent and interesting consequence of the recurrence of the dramatic phenomenon which it denotes. It should be remembered also that the substitution of symphonically treated themes for tunes with symmetrical eight-bar staves and the like, has always been the rule in the highest forms of music. To describe it, or be affected by it, as an abandonment of melody, is to confess oneself an ignoramus conversant only with dance tunes and ballads.

The sort of stuff a purely dramatic musician produces when he hampers himself with metric patterns in composition is not unlike what might have resulted in literature if Carlyle (for example) had been compelled by convention to write his historical stories in rhymed stanzas. That is to say, it limits his fertility to an occasional phrase, and three quarters of the time exercises only his barren ingenuity in fitting rhymes and measures to it. In literature the great masters of the art have long emancipated themselves from metric patterns. Nobody claims that the hierarchy of modern impassioned prose writers, from Bunyan to Ruskin, should be placed below the writers of pretty lyrics, from Herrick to Mr Austin Dobson.* Only in dramatic literature do we find the devastating tradition of blank verse still lingering, giving factitious prestige to the platitudes of dullards, and robbing the dramatic style of the genuine poet of its full natural endowment of variety, force, and simplicity.

This state of things, as we have seen, finds its parallel in musical art, since music can be written in prose themes or in versified tunes; only here nobody dreams of disputing the greater difficulty of the prose forms and the comparative triviality of versification. Yet in dramatic music, as in dramatic literature, the tradition of

* English light-verse poet and essayist, a civil servant in the Board of Trade.

versification clings with the same pernicious results; and the opera, like the tragedy, is conventionally made like a wallpaper. The theatre seems doomed to be in all things the last refuge of the hankering after cheap prettiness in art.

Unfortunately this confusion of the decorative with the dramatic element in both literature and music is maintained by the example of great masters in both arts. Very touching dramatic expression can be combined with decorative symmetry of versification when the artist happens to possess both the decorative and dramatic gifts, and to have cultivated both hand in hand. Shakespear and Shelley, for instance, far from being hampered by the conventional obligation to write their dramas in verse, found it much the easiest and cheapest way of producing them. But if Shakespear had been compelled by custom to write entirely in prose, all his ordinary dialogue might have been as good as the first scene of As You Like It; and all his lofty passages as fine as "What a piece of work is Man!"; thus sparing us a great deal of blank verse in which the thought is commonplace, and the expression, though catchingly turned, absurdly pompous. The Cenci might either have been a serious drama or might never have been written at all if Shelley had not been allowed to carry off its unreality by Elizabethan versification. Still, both poets have achieved many passages in which the decorative and dramatic qualities are not only reconciled, but seem to enhance oneanother to a pitch otherwise unattainable.

Just so in music. When we find, as in the case of Mozart, a prodigiously gifted and arduously trained musician who is also, by happy accident, a dramatist comparable to Molière, the obligation to compose operas in versified numbers not only does not embarrass him, but actually saves him trouble and thought. No matter what his dramatic mood may be, he expresses it in exquisite musical verses more easily than a dramatist of ordinary singleness of talent can express it in prose. Accordingly, he too, like Shakespear and Shelley, leaves versified airs, like *Dalla sua pace* or Gluck's *Che farò senza, Euridice*, or Weber's *Leise, leise*, which are as dramatic from the first note to the last as the untrammelled themes of The Ring. In consequence, it used to be professorially demanded that all dramatic music should present the same double aspect. The demand was unreasonable, since symmetrical versification is no merit in dramatic music: one might as well stipulate that a dinner fork should be constructed so as to serve also as a tablecloth. It was an ignorant demand too, because it is not true that the composers of these exceptional examples were always, or even often, able to combine dramatic expression with symmetrical versification. Side by side with *Dalla sua pace* we have *Il mio tesoro* and *Non mi dir*, in which exquisitely expressive opening phrases lead to decorative passages which are as grotesque from the dramatic point of view as the music which Alberic sings when he is slipping and sneezing in the Rhine mud is from the decorative point of view. Further, there is to be considered the mass of shapeless "dry recitative" which separates these symmetrical numbers, and which might have been raised to considerable dramatic and musical importance had it been incorporated into a continous musical fabric by thematic treatment. Finally, Mozart's most dramatic *finales* and concerted numbers are more or less in sonata form, like symphonic movements, and must therefore be classed as musical prose. And sonata form dictates repetitions and recapitulations from which the perfectly unconventional form adopted by Wagner is free. On the whole, there is more scope for both repetition and convention in the old form than in the new; and the poorer a composer's musical gift is, the surer he is to resort to the XVIII century patterns to eke out his invention.

THE NINETEENTH CENTURY

When Wagner was born in 1813, music had newly become the most astonishing, the most fascinating, the most miraculous art in the world. Mozart's Don Giovanni had made all musical Europe conscious of the enchantments of the modern orchestra and of the perfect adaptability of music to the subtlest needs of the dramatist. Beethoven had shewn how those inarticulate mood-poems which surge through men who have, like himself, no exceptional command of words, can be written down in music as symphonies. Not that Mozart and Beethoven invented these applications of their art; but they were the first whose works made it clear that the dramatic and subjective powers of sound were enthralling enough to stand by themselves quite apart from the decorative musical structures of which they had hitherto been a mere feature. After the *finales* in Figaro and Don Giovanni, the possibility of the modern music-drama lay bare. After the symphonies of Beethoven it was certain that the poetry that lies too deep for words does not lie too deep for music, and that the vicissitudes of the soul, from the roughest fun to the loftiest aspiration, can make symphonies without the aid of dance tunes. As much, perhaps, will be claimed for the preludes and fugues of Bach; but Bach's method was unattainable: his compositions were wonderful webs of exquisitely beautiful Gothic traceries in sound, quite beyond all ordinary human talent. Beethoven's far blunter craft was thoroughly popular and practicable: not to save his soul could he have drawn one long Gothic line in sound as Bach could, much less have woven several of them together with so apt a harmony that even when the composer is unmoved its progressions saturate themselves with the emotion which (as modern critics are a little apt to forget) springs as warmly from our delicately touched admiration as from our sympathies, and sometimes makes us give a composer credit for pathetic intentions which he does not entertain, just as a boy imagines a treasure of tenderness and noble wisdom in the beauty of a woman. Besides, Bach set comic dialogue to music exactly as he set the recitatives of the Passion, there being for him, apparently, only one recitative possible, and that the musically best. He reserved the expression of his merry mood for the regular set numbers in which he could make one of his wonderful contrapuntal traceries of pure ornament with the requisite gaiety of line and movement. Beethoven bowed to no ideal of beauty: he only sought the expression for his feeling. To him a joke was a joke; and if it sounded funny in music he was satisfied. Until the old habit of judging all music by its decorative symmetry had worn out, musicians were shocked by his symphonies, and, misunderstanding his integrity, openly questioned his sanity. But to those who were not looking for pretty new sound patterns, but were longing for the expression of their moods in music, he achieved a revelation, because, being single in his aim to express his own moods, he anticipated with revolutionary courage and frankness all the moods of the rising generations of the XIX century.

The result was inevitable. In the XIX century it was no longer necessary to be born a pattern designer in sound to be a composer. One had but to be a dramatist or a poet completely susceptible to the dramatic and descriptive powers of sound. A race of literary and theatrical musicians appeared; and Meyerbeer, the first of them, made an extraordinary impression. The frankly delirious description of his Robert the Devil in Balzac's short story entitled Gambara, and Goethe's astonishingly mistaken notion that he could have composed music for Faust, shew how completely the enchantments of the new dramatic music upset the judgment of artists of eminent discernment. Meyerbeer was, people said (old gentlemen still say so in Paris), the successor of Beethoven: he was, if a less perfect musician than Mozart, a profounder genius. Above all, he was original and daring. Wagner himself raved about the duet in the fourth act of Les Huguenots as wildly as anyone.

Yet all this effect of originality and profundity was produced by a quite limited talent for turning striking phrases, exploiting certain curious and rather catching rhythms and modulations, and devizing suggestive or eccentric instrumentation. On its decorative side, it was the same phenomenon in music as the Baroque school in architecture: an energetic struggle to enliven organic decay by mechanical oddities and novelties. Meyerbeer was no symphonist. He could not apply the thematic system to his striking phrases, and so had to cobble them into metric patterns in the old style; and as he was no "absolute musician" either, he hardly got his metric patterns beyond mere quadrille tunes, which were either wholly undistinguished, or else made remarkable by certain brusqueries which, in the true rococo manner, owed their singularity to their senselessness. He could produce neither a thorough music-drama nor a charming opera. But with all this, and worse, Meyerbeer had some genuine dramatic energy, and even passion; and sometimes rose to the occasion in a manner which, whilst the imagination of his contemporaries remained on fire with the novelties of dramatic music, led them to overrate him with an extravagance which provoked Wagner to conduct a long critical campaign against his supremacy. In the eighteen sixties this was inevitably ascribed to the professional jealousy of a disappointed rival. Nowadays young people cannot understand how anyone could ever have taken Meyerbeer's influence seriously. The few who remember the reputation he built on The Huguenots and The Prophet, and who now realize what a no-thoroughfare the path he opened proved to be, even to himself, know how inevitable and how impersonal Wagner's attack was.

Wagner was the literary musician *par excellence.* He could not, like Mozart and Beethoven, produce decorative tone structures independently of any dramatic or poetic subject matter, because, that craft being no longer necessary for his purpose, he did not cultivate it. As Shakespear, compared with Tennyson, appears to have an exclusively dramatic talent, so exactly does Wagner compared with Mendelssohn. On the other hand, he had not to go to third-rate literary hacks for "librettos" to set to music: he produced his own dramatic poems, thus giving dramatic integrity to opera, and making symphony articulate. A Beethoven symphony (except the articulate part of the ninth) expresses noble feeling, but not thought: it has moods, but no ideas. Wagner added thought and produced the music-drama. Mozart's loftiest opera, his Ring, so to speak, The Magic Flute, has a libretto which, though none the worse for seeming, like The Rhine Gold, the merest Christmas tomfoolery to shallow spectators, is the product of talent immeasurably inferior to Mozart's own. The libretto of Don Giovanni is coarse and trivial: its transfiguration by Mozart's music may be a marvel; but nobody will venture to contend that such transfigurations, however seductive, can be as satisfactory as tone-poetry or drama in which the musician and the poet are at the same level. Here, then, we have the simple secret of Wagner's pre-eminence as a dramatic musician. He wrote the poems as well as composed the music of his "stage festival plays," as he called them.

Up to a certain point in his career Wagner paid the penalty of undertaking two arts instead of one. Mozart had his trade as a musician at his fingers' ends when he was twenty, because he had served an arduous apprenticeship to that trade and no other. Wagner was very far from having attained equal mastery at thirtyfive: indeed he himself has told us that not until he had passed the age at which Mozart died did he compose with that complete spontaneity of musical expression which can only be attained by winning entire freedom from all preoccupation with the difficulties of technical processes. But when that time came, he was not only a consummate musician, like Mozart, but a dramatic poet and a critical and philosophical essayist, exercising a considerable influence on his century. The sign of this consummation was his ability at last to play with his art, and thus to add to his already famous achievements in sentimental drama that lighthearted art of comedy of which the greatest masters, like Molière and Mozart, are so much rarer than the tragedians and sentimentalists. It was then that he composed the first two acts of Siegfried, and later on The Mastersingers, a professedly comedic work, and a quite Mozartian garden of melody, hardly credible as the work of the straining artificer of Tannhäuser. Only, as no man ever learns to do one thing by doing something else, however closely allied the two things may be, Wagner still produced no music independently of his poems. The overture to The Mastersingers is delightful when you know what it is all about; but only those to whom it came as a concert piece without any such clue, and who judged its reckless counterpoint by the standard of Bach and of Mozart's Magic Flute overture, can realize how atrocious it used to sound to musicians of the old school. When I first heard it, with the clear march of the polyphony in Bach's B minor Mass fresh in my memory, I confess I thought that the parts had got dislocated, and that some of the band were half a bar behind the others. Perhaps they were; but now that I am familiar with the work, and with Wagner's harmony, I can still quite understand certain passages producing that effect on an admirer of Bach even when performed with perfect accuracy.

THE MUSIC OF THE FUTURE

The ultimate success of Wagner was so prodigious that to his dazzled disciples it seemed that the age of what he called "absolute" music must be at an end, and the musical future destined to be an exclusively Wagnerian one inaugurated at Bayreuth. All great geniuses produce this illusion. Wagner did not begin a movement: he consummated it. He was the summit of the XIX century school of dramatic music in the same sense as Mozart was the summit (the word is Gounod's) of the XVIII century school. All those who attempted to carry on his Bayreuth tradition have shared the fate of the forgotten purveyors of secondhand Mozart a hundred years ago. As to the expected supersession of absolute music, Wagner's successors in European rank were Brahms, Elgar, and Richard Strauss. The reputation of Brahms rests on his absolute music alone: such works as his German Requiem endear themselves to us as being musically great fun; but to take them quite seriously is to make them oppressively dull. Elgar followed Beethoven and Schumann: he owes nothing essential to Wagner, and secured his niche in the temple by his symphonies and his Enigma Variations, which are as absolutely musical as any modern music can be. Although Strauss produced works for the musical theatre which maintained it at the level to which Wagner had raised it, his new departure was a form of musical drama, comic epic, and soul autobiography in which stage, singers, and all the rest of the theatrical material of Bayreuth save only the orchestra are thrown overboard, and the work effected by instrumental music alone, even Beethoven's final innovation of a chorus being discarded. Just the same thing happened when Elgar took as his theme Shakespear's Henry IV., with Falstaff as its chief figure. He made the band do it all, and with such masterful success that one cannot bear to think of what would have been the result of a mere attempt to turn the play into an opera.

The Russian composers whose vogue succeeded that of Wagner were not in the least Wagnerian: they developed from the romantic school, from Weber and Meyerbeer, from Berlioz and Liszt, much as they might have done had Wagner never existed except as a propagandist of the importance of their art. A disparaging attitude towards Wagner resembling that of Chopin to Beethoven, and a very similar escape from his influence even in technique, was quite common among the composers whose early lives overlapped the last part of his. In England the composers who are the juniors of Elgar, but the seniors of (for example) Bax and Ireland, the most notable of whom are Mr Granville Bantock and Mr Rutland Boughton, were heavily Wagnerized in their youth, and began by Tristanizing and Götterdämmerunging heroically; but when they found themselves their Wagnerism vanished. The younger men do not begin with Wagner nor even with Strauss: they are mostly bent on producing curiosities of absolute music until they settle down into a serious style of their own. All that can be said for the Wagner tradition is that it finally killed the confusion between decorative pattern music and dramatic music which muddled Meyerbeer and imposed absurd repetitions on the heros and heroines of Handel and Mozart. Even in absolute music, the post-Wagnerite sonata form has become so much less mechanical and thoughtless that the fact that it still persists in essentials is hardly worth asserting.

Writing before any of these developments had happened, I said in the first edition of this book that there was no more hope in attempts to out-Wagner Wagner in music drama than there had been in the old attempts to make Handel the starting point of a great school of oratorio. How true this was is now so obvious that my younger readers may wonder why I thought it worth while to say it. But if veterans did not indulge in these day-before-yesterdayisms Music would lose the thread of its history.

BAYREUTH

When the Bayreuth Festival Playhouse was at last completed, and opened in 1876 with the first performance of The Ring, European society was compelled to admit that Wagner was "a success." Royal personages, detesting his music, sat out the performances in the row of boxes set apart for princes. They all complimented him on the astonishing "push" with which, in the teeth of all obstacles, he had turned a fabulous and visionary project into a concrete commercial reality, patronized by the public at a pound a head. It is as well to know that these congratulations had no other effect upon Wagner than to open his eyes to the fact that the Bayreuth experiment, as an attempt to evade the ordinary social and commercial conditions of theatrical enterprise, was a failure. His own account of it contrasts the reality with his intentions in a vein which would be bitter if it were not so humorous. The precautions taken to keep the seats out of the hands of the frivolous public and in the hands of earnest disciples, banded together in little Wagner Societies throughout Europe, had ended in their forestalling by ticket speculators and their sale to just the sort of idle globetrotting tourists against whom the temple was to have been strictly closed. The money, supposed to be contributed by the faithful, was begged by energetic subscription-hunting ladies from people who must have had the most grotesque misconceptions of the composer's aims: among others, the Khedive of Egypt and the Sultan of Turkey!

Since then, subscriptions are no longer needed; for the Festival Playhouse pays its own way now, and is commercially on the same footing as any other theatre. The only qualification required from the visitor is money. A Londoner spends twenty pounds on a visit: a native Bayreuther spends one pound. In either case "the Folk," on whose behalf Wagner turned out in 1849, are effectually excluded; and the Festival Playhouse must therefore be classed as infinitely less Wagnerian in its character than Hampton Court Palace. Nobody knew this better than Wagner; and nothing can be further off the mark than to chatter about Bayreuth as if it had succeeded in escaping from the conditions of our modern civilization any more than the Grand Opera in Paris or London.

Within these conditions, however, it effected a new departure in that excellent German institution, the summer theatre. Unlike the old opera houses, which are constructed so that the audience may present a splendid pageant to the delighted manager, it was designed to secure an uninterrupted view of the stage, and an undisturbed hearing of the music, to the audience. The dramatic purpose of the performances was taken with entire and elaborate seriousness as the sole purpose of them; and the management was jealous for the reputation of Wagner. The sightseeing globetrotter no longer crowds out the genuine disciple: the audiences are now as genuinely devoted as Wagner could have desired: the disconcerted, bewildered, bored followers of fashion have vanished with the sportsman on a holiday: the atmosphere is the right one for the work. There is, apparently, an effective demand for summer theatres of the highest class. There is no reason why the experiment should not be tried in England. If our enthusiasm for Handel can support Handel Festivals, laughably dull, stupid and anti-Handelian as these choral monstrosities are, as well as annual provincial festivals on the same model, there is no likelihood of a Wagner Festival failing. Suppose, for instance, a Wagner theatre were built at Hampton Court or on Richmond Hill, not to say Margate pier, so that we could have a delightful summer evening holiday, Bayreuth fashion, passing the hours between the acts in the park or on the river before sunset, is it seriously contended that there would be any lack of visitors? If a little of the money that is wasted on grandstands, Eiffel towers, and dismal Halls by the Sea, all as much tied to brief annual seasons as Bayreuth, were applied in this way, the profit would be far more certain and the social utility prodigiously greater. Any English enthusiasm for Bayreuth that does not take the form of clamor for a Festival playhouse in England may be set aside as mere pilgrimage mania.

Besides, the early Bayreuth performances were far from delectable. The singing was sometimes tolerable, and sometimes abominable. Some of the singers were mere animated beer casks, too lazy and conceited to practise the self-control and physical training that is expected as a matter of course from an acrobat, a jockey or a pugilist. The women's dresses were prudish and absurd. It is true that after some years Kundry no longer wore an early Victorian ball dress with "ruchings," and that Freia was provided with a quaintly modish copy of the flowered gown of Spring in Botticelli's famous picture; but the mailclad Brynhild still climbed the mountains with her legs carefully hidden in a long white skirt, and looked so exactly like Mrs Leo Hunter as Minerva that it was quite impossible to feel a ray of illusion whilst looking at her. The ideal of womanly beauty aimed at reminded Englishmen of the barmaids of the 'seventies, when the craze for golden hair was at its worst. Further, whilst Wagner's stage directions were sometimes disregarded as unintelligently as at the old opera houses, Wagner's quaintly old-fashioned tradition of half rhetorical, half historical-pictorial attitude and gesture prevailed. The most striking moments of the drama were conceived as *tableaux vivants* with posed models, instead of as passages of action, motion, and life.

I need hardly add that the supernatural powers of control attributed by credulous pilgrims to Wagner's widow, and later on to his son, did not exist. *Prima donnas* and tenors were as unmanageable at Bayreuth as anywhere else. Casts were capriciously changed; stage business was insufficiently rehearsed; the audience was compelled to listen to a Brynhild or Siegfried of fifty when they had carefully arranged to see one of twentyfive, much as in any ordinary opera house. Even the conductors upset the arrangements occasionally. On the other hand, we could always feel assured that in thoroughness of preparation of the chief work of the season, in strenous artistic pretentiousness, in pious conviction that the work was of such enormous importance as to be worth doing well at all costs, the Bayreuth performances would deserve their reputation. Their example raised the quality of operatic performances throughout the world, even in apparently incorrigible centres of fashion and frivolity.

BAYREUTH IN ENGLAND

In 1898 I purposely dwelt on the early shortcomings of Bayreuth to shew that there was no reason in the world why as good and better performances of The Ring should not be given in England, and that neither Wagner's widow nor his son could pretend to handle them with greater authority than any artist who feels the impulse to interpret them. Nobody will ever know what Wagner himself thought of the artists who established the Bayreuth tradition: he was obviously not in a position to criticize them. For instance, had Rubini survived to create Siegmund, Wagner could hardly have written so amusing and vivid a description as he did of his Ottavio in the old Paris days. Wagner was under great obligations to the heros and heroines of 1876; and he naturally said nothing to disparage their triumphs; but there is no reason to believe that all or indeed any of them satisfied him as Schnorr of Karelsfeld satisfied him as Tristan, or Schröder-Devrient as Fidelio.* It was just as likely that the next Schnorr or Schröder would arise in England. Nowadays it seems odd that anyone should need to be told all this. British and American singers have long since replaced the Bayreuth veterans to considerable advantage.

WAGNERIAN SINGERS

No nation need have any difficulty in producing a race of Wagnerian singers. With the single exception of Handel, no composer has written music so well cal-

* Ludwig Schnorr von Karelsfeld (1836-65), brief-lived, legendary tenor, created Tristan at Munich just before his death. Wilhelmine Schröder-Devrient (1804-60), eminent soprano, created Adriano Colonna in Wagner's Rienzi, at Dresden, in 1842, and later sang in Fidelio under his direction as conductor of the Dresden Opera orchestra.

culated to make its singers vocal athletes as Wagner. Abominably as the Germans sang in Wagner's day, it was astonishing how they throve physically on his leading parts. His secret is the Handelian secret. Instead of specializing his vocal parts after the manner of Verdi and Gounod for shrieking sopranos, goat-bleating tenors, and tremulous baritones with an effective compass of about a fifth at the extreme tiptop of their ranges, and for contraltos with chest registers forced all over their compass in the manner of music hall singers, he employs the entire range of the human voice, demanding from everybody nearly two effective octaves. The bulk of the work lies easily in the middle of the voice, which is nevertheless well exercised all over, one part of it relieving the other healthily and continually. He uses the highest notes sparingly, and is ingeniously considerate in the matter of instrumental accompaniment.Even when the singer seems to dominate all the thunders of the full orchestra, a glance at the score will shew that he is well heard, not because of a stentorian voice, but because Wagner meant him to be heard. The old lazy Italian style of orchestral accompaniment as we find it in Rossini's Stabat or Verdi's Trovatore, where the strings play a rum-tum accompaniment whilst the whole wind band blares away, *fortissimo*, in unison with the singer, is somehow not so brutally opaque in practice as it looks on paper; but Wagner never condescends to it. Even in an ordinary opera house, with the orchestra ranged directly between the singers and the audience, his instrumentation is transparent to the human voice.

On every point, then, a Wagner theatre and Wagner festivals are much more generally practicable than the older and more artificial forms of dramatic music. A presentable performance of The Ring is a big undertaking only in the sense in which the construction of a railway is a big undertaking: that is, it requires plenty of work and plenty of professional skill; but it does not, like the old operas and oratorios, require those extraordinary vocal gifts which only a few individuals scattered here and there throughout Europe are born with. Singers who could never execute the *roulades* of Semiramis, Assur, and Arsaces in Rossini's Semiramide, could sing the parts of Brynhild, Wotan, and Erda without missing a note. Any Englishman can understand this if he considers for a moment the difference between a Cathedral service and an Italian opera at Covent Garden. The service is a much more serious matter than the opera. Yet provincial talent is sufficient for it, if the requisite industry and devotion are forthcoming. Even at the Opera I have seen lusty troopers and porters, without art or manners, accepted by fashion as principal tenors during the long interval between Mario and Jean de Reszke; and the two most extraordinary dramatic singers of the XX century, Chaliapin and Vladimir Rosing,* are quite independent of the old metropolitan artificialities. Let us remember that Bayreuth has recruited its Parsifals from the peasantry, and that the artisans of a village in the Bavarian Alps are capable of a famous and elaborate Passion Play, and then consider whether any country is so poor in talent that its amateurs must journey to the centre of Europe to witness a Wagner Festival.

WAGNERISM WITH WAGNER LEFT OUT

In spite of the fact that my old suggestion of a Festival Playhouse on Richmond Hill has now been

* Shaw had heard the celebrated Russian basso Fyodor Chaliapin sing in Prince Igor and Khovantschina at Drury Lane in 1914. Vladimir Rosing was an exciting young Russian tenor, who had first sung in London in 1913. Two years later he created the *rôle* of Herman in Tchaikovsky's The Queen of Spades at the London Opera House.

proved perfectly feasible as far as the availability of the necessary home talent is concerned, only one serious attempt to establish a Bayreuth in England has come to my knowledge; and that one, far from concerning itself with Wagner, owes its success to native British music with some early ultra-classical assistance from Gluck. Mr Rutland Boughton, who began his career as a composer when the influence of Wagner was at its height, has attempted to do in Somerset what Wagner did in Thuringia, with the very material difference that Wagner had the King of Bavaria at his back, and Mr Boughton had nothing material at his back at all. He selected Glastonbury as his Bayreuth; and has established an annual festival there which can already shew a remarkable record of work done. The very desperation of the enterprise has been its salvation. Had Mr Boughton been obsessed, as Wagner was, with the scale to which the Grand Operas of Paris, London, and Berlin work, he would have had to wait for a king to help him: that is, he would have waited forever. Fortunately he remembered that Wagner was not only the highly professionalized royal conductor of Dresden, brought up in the belief that the only success that can hallmark an opera is a Meyerbeerian success at the Paris Opéra: he was also the author of the saying that music is kept alive, not by the triumphs of fashionable commercial professionalism, but on the cottage piano of the amateur. Mr Rutland Boughton began in ordinary village halls in Somerset, with a piano and his own fingers for orchestra, his wife as scenepainter and costumier, and a fit-up for a stage. The singing and acting was done by the villagers and by anyone else who would come; and a surprising number of quite distinguished talents did come. On these terms performances were achieved which in point of atmosphere and intimacy of interest were actually better than the performances at the enormously more pretentious Festival Playhouse in Bayreuth, or its copy the Prince Regent Theatre in Munich. There were friendly subscribers, not enough to prevent each festival from ruining Mr Boughton for six months or so, but enough to enable him to devote the remaining six months to preparation for another financial catastrophe, encouraged by the fact that the crashes were less and less disastrous as his enterprise became better and better known. His festival is now a yearly event in Avalon, once an island, now a city in a plain, Glastonbury, steeped in traditions which make it holy ground. But it still has no theatre, no electric light, no convenience for Wagnerian drama that every village does not possess. Yet it is here that the Wagnerist dream has been best realized in England.

That dream, truly interpreted, did not mean that the English soil should bring forth performances of Wagner's music copied from those at Bayreuth. It meant that the English soil should produce English music and English drama, and that English people should perform them in their own way. It is precisely because Mr Boughton has never performed a work of Wagner's, but, with the scholastic exception of an opera or two by Gluck, has composed his own music and had it and other English music sung in English ways, that he can claim to be a Perfect Wagnerite.

By this time there may be other and cognate experiments less known to me. During the XX century an important social development has transformed that costly and deleterious bore, the British holiday, into a genuinely recreative change. Under the title of Summer Schools, voluntary associations of artistically minded students of sociology, theosophy, science, history, and what not—shall we say people who take life, or some department of life, seriously, and cannot be happy unless they are using their brains and learning something in the intervals of dancing and singing for pure fun?—now appear every autumn in the prettiest country districts. These Schools are open to everybody; they afford intimate glimpses of more or less celebrated people who come and lecture to them for the sake of propaganda; and they are very much jollier, as well as substantially cheaper and more genial, than the so-called pleasure resorts in which irritable and overworked professional entertainers hypnotize credulous Britons into believing that they are enjoying themselves when they are only paying through the nose for being worried and pillaged. Where there were formerly only one or two elderly congresses, like the meetings of the British Association, with no activity but that of elderly lecturers all lecturing at the same time in different rooms, there are now dozens of smaller but more youthful and vital gatherings in which, whatever the main subject to be studied may be, Art is continually breaking in in one form or another.

I myself, after a larger experience of professionally and commercially organized art than most men can afford (for I had to earn my living as a critic of such art in my early days), find that it is at such gatherings and from such voluntary enterprises that I can oftenest recapture something of that magic which music and drama had for me in my childhood, and which it is so utterly impossible to preserve under commercial conditions. Commerce in art can save me from many ridiculous blunders and makeshifts that do not matter; but it seldom achieves the things that do matter, never indeed except when they are forced on it in spite of its teeth by some individual artist, mostly one heavily persecuted by it as Wagner was.

Amateur art is discredited art insofar only as the amateur is known as the ape of commercial art. Persons who go to the theatre and opera house only to be smitten with an infatuate ambition to reproduce in their own untrained persons what they see the great professional artists doing there, are mostly foredoomed to failure and ridicule. Here and there one of them succeeds, only to be absorbed by the commercial profession. But the countryside is full of stout characters with no such folly and no such ambition, who will do as much for any really gifted artistic leader as they have done for Mr Boughton and for the organizers of our provincial choirs and brass bands. If Little Bethel has raised the miners of England in a few generations from troglodyte savagery to pious respectability, Little Bayreuth may as easily raise them from pious respectability to a happy consciousness of and interest in fine art, without which all their piety and respectability will not save their children from resorting to cruel sports and squalid sensualities in their natural need for enjoyment. And so, good luck to Little Bayreuth; and may it be as successful as Little Bethel in demonstrating that the laughter of fools is as the crackling of thorns under a pot!

SOME IMPERFECT WAGNERITES

I

The Critic, Supplement, 28 January 1899

[U] The reception of The Perfect Wagnerite by my colleagues the critics has naturally been extremely polite. Wagner's position is now established: failure to appreciate it convicts the delinquent either of hopeless fogeyism or provincial crudity. My own fitness for the most eminent task that music has presented to criticism during the past half century is, for journalistic purposes, conceded on the strength of my successful career as a professional critic of music—unsatisfactory evidence, perhaps, but enough to ensure me a respectful hearing from reviewers who do not wish to announce themselves as novices or nobodies. With all the prepossessions thus in my favor, I have taken a certain minimum of eulogistic endorsement as a matter of course, and counted only the generosities and enthusiasms or the irrepressible protests which have carried some of my critics away from the safe level of conventional consideration for my publisher.

As to the generosities and enthusiasms, I need say no more than enough to clear myself of any affectation of indifference to them. Though a book written expressly to excite those generosities and enthusiasms would be an abomination, yet as bye-products they are encouraging.

As to the protests, they have shewn me that there is one line of attack against which all books about Wagner should be carefully fortified. I mean the attack which bases itself on the authority, not of Wagner's scores and essays, but of the musical guidebooks with which the stationers' shops in Bayreuth are stocked in festival time. The compilers of these books profess to pick out from the score of The Ring the representative themes, and present them, duly sorted, docketed, and labeled for the instruction of Bayreuth pilgrims, who buy them and read them piously. Of such wares I must speak very guardedly; for though I have opened a few samples of them at random, I have never had patience to read further than the two or three pages in which they reduce themselves to absurdity.

They do this in three principal ways. First, they not only quote the themes, but invent trivially sentimental titles for them, to the confusion of the pilgrim, who finds that the theme and its meaning undergo all sorts of modifications, whilst the spurious label remains woodenly invariable throughout.

Second, they pad their pages by quoting secondary passages which are either not motifs at all, or are only members of motifs, the general effect being that of an entomological museum with the legs and wings pulled out of the insects and exhibited as separate and complete specimens.

Third, they hunt out imaginary cross references between the themes on the strength of the inevitable coincidences which arise between melodies which have all to be constructed from the seven notes of the diatonic scale and their five chromatic modifications. For example, O thou that tellest, in Handel's Messiah, is, note for note up to the tenth note inclusive, identical with God Save the Queen; yet five generations have not produced a single person foolish enough to attach any importance to the coincidence or to assume that Handel was conscious of it.

Let me now give an example of the sort of thing I have to endure when these unauthorized guidebooks are accepted by Ring-struck critics as if they were the inspired revelations of Wagner's purposes. Here is a passage from a recent criticism of The Perfect Wagnerite:

To describe the noble Redemption through Love motive as almost "the most trumpery phrase in the whole tetralogy" is a judgment bordering on the grotesque, revealing, as it does, however, the interesting fact that Mr Shaw has not grasped in the least degree the musical significance of this particular motive. Rightly enough he recalls its first appearance in the mouth of Sieglinde in Die Walküre, but evidently he does not recognize its connection with the beautiful Brynhild theme—the first five of its eight notes are identical with the latter—which occurs all through the Götterdämmerung.

Here the critic takes a theme from The Ring and calls it the Redemption through Love motive without the smallest hint to the uninstructed reader that the title is his own (or, perhaps, the guidebook's) and not Wagner's. It occurs in The Valkyries as the response of a woman to an appeal to her maternal instinct, and does not occur again until the last lover in The Ring is on the brink of the destruction that Love brings to all its mortal heros and heroines.

Now, as to the first five notes. I say the theme is trumpery: my critic says it is noble. Why? Because it stirs memories in him—memories of the sort of music that moved him most deeply in his youth. He was evidently one of the many million admirers of Grandfather's Clock when that melody conquered the world. The clock has now stopped, never to go again; but its first six notes (not five) survive in Sieglinde's maternal cry. My critic may consider Grandfather's Clock a noble melody. I do not. In a popular song it is in its right place: in The Ring it sounds trumpery; and the man who finds it "noble" beside the themes of Siegfried may take my word for it that, in music, he does not know chalk from cheese.

I will now proceed to demonstrate that, on guidebook principles, the theme probably refers to the inconstancy of Siegfried. In Messrs Gilbert and Sullivan's Trial by Jury, the following words are put into the mouth of the hero:

> O gentlemen, listen, I pray:
> Though I own that my heart has been ranging,
> Of nature the laws I obey;
> For nature is constantly changing.

The first five notes of the melody are identical with those of the two Ring themes cited by my critic. Wagner was finishing Die Götterdämmerung when Sir Arthur Sullivan was at work on Trial by Jury. Clearly the two composers, having to find a musical expression for inconstancy, spontaneously uttered the same five notes!

To deal seriously with the absurdity of the cross reference between the Grandfather Clock and Brynhild themes would require music type. I may say, however, that the notes common to both, which form nearly a bar and a half of the Clock theme, are in the Brynhild theme a mere turn or *gruppetto* in the accompaniment, which no musician would dream of treating as an integral part of the melody: in fact, *they do not occur in the voice part*—perhaps because no German *prima donna* can sing a *gruppetto.* Further, as even the most exclusively Wagnerian musician ought to know, the whole phrase in which the turn occurs is a reproduction of a phrase in Rienzi, where the turn is indicated, not by notes, but simply by one of the signs in use for conventional ornaments. Wagner would probably have used the same sign in the Brynhild melody but for his experience of Rienzi, in performing which the violinists invariably misread the sign and reversed the direction of the turn. The *gruppetto* is so familiar and obvious a musical commonplace that it has been used again and again by composers of all ranks, both as ornament and melody. The captivating theme, specially dear to Wagner, which forms the most popular feature of Weber's Freischütz overture, is nothing but a chain of these turns. In it my critic will find his cherished first five notes again, as he will in a dozen other equally familiar compositions. If he leaves the exact notes out of account, and includes in his survey all the melodies in which the passage from the first to the second step is effected by a turn—for instance, Mozart's *Non mi dir* and Way Down upon de Swanee River—he will find them multitudinous and inevitable. And that will teach him why Wagner's fondness for the most hackneyed form of the turn so often produces an unexpected effect of commonness in his more sentimental melodies.

In short, The Ring is a dramatic poem and not a collection of acrostics. It is really too bad, now that the "analytical program" style of musical criticism, with its mock learned parsings of sonata grammar, has been knocked on its hollow head, to find it replaced by the Bayreuth guidebook style. Unfortunately, when the technical mysteries of music are the theme, the public and the Press are alike helpless with the helplessness of ignorance. I will not go so far as to pretend that if a critic were to denounce me as ignorant of the rudiments of music because I have written of "the key" of a symphony in defiance of the fact that a key is an instrument used to open doors with, any editor would let such a blunder pass; but I am quite sure that if, avoiding the too familiar instance of a door, the critic founded himself on the fact that a key is part of the mechanism of the ophicleide, the editor would regard him as a man of no small musical learning. At all events, I have just been denounced by one impostor (if he will excuse the exactitude of that hard word) for using the word "stave" in its original musical sense, as defined in all the dictionaries, instead of in the only sense known to him: to wit, the technical sense in which it is used by sellers of music paper. Another gentleman, the discoverer of the five identical notes, concludes his observations by remarking that "it is unpleasant to have to expose Mr Shaw's blunders in this painful fashion." Imagine poor Mr Shaw's feelings!

The critics who have exasperated me most, however, are those who have spun out their copy by telling the whole story of The Ring over again, in the style of the "argument" prefixed to a Covent Garden "book of the words," and then coolly adding "Somewhat in this manner does Mr Shaw set forth the well-known story of the tetralogy." This is enough to make the most patient man forget himself. To take that story and tell it as Wagner tells it in his score, throwing the emphasis of thought and incident and leading up to the catastrophes exactly as Wagner does by his music, is a piece of skilled professional work, requiring much consideration and an intimate familiarity with the tetralogy as a musical whole. Just think what it feels like when some blundering apprentice does the whole thing over again in his own incoherent, misunderstanding way, even interpolating absolutely spurious incidents which he imagines to be in the original just as many people imagine the Satanic incidents in Paradise Lost to be in the Bible, and then informs the public that this is the kind of stuff they will find in The Perfect Wagnerite. If that book contained a line of such inept reporting, I would eat it and die of shame and indigestion. And yet these well-intentioned duffers mean mostly to be complimentary to me!

As I expected, the magic of art has been proof against my statement of facts as regards Die Götterdämmerung. That statement is fanatically put aside as "a theory." I point out that The Ring began with a sketch of what is now the concluding section of it; that the three earlier sections grew out of this sketch in reverse order; that by this process a sketch for an opera became a drama of universal significance; that the sketch was never re-adjusted to the world-drama, and could not be, because it had, in fact, been superseded by it, so that it retains, in its completed state as Die Götterdämmerung, not only the personages in their superseded operatic character, but speech after speech proper to the 1848 sketch and wholly incongruous with the matured fruit of it; and that the music to Die Götterdämmerung was not finished until more than twenty years had elapsed since its inception, during which time Wagner had left the phase in which he wrote the Ring poem far behind him and been captured by a new philosophy. This is not my theory, nor my opinion, nor my judgment, nor my taste, nor anything that is subjectively mine or me: it is pure history and biography, as easily verifiable as anything in Whitaker's Almanack. Yet a few very Ringstraked lambs of criticism plead to have it all set aside as Shawesque paradox—which usually means some unexpected revelation of a fact which Shaw has divined and verified, and of which his critic is ignorant.

Again, as to "Wagner as Revolutionist," I state the fact that Wagner took part on the revolutionary side in the Dresden rising in 1849 and spent many years in exile for it. I quote the police proclamation against him. I refer to his pamphlet, Art and Revolution, the most explicitly revolutionary document of the '48 period. Does this produce any effect on the Ringstraked ones? Not at all. They explain that Wagner was just such a man as Gounod; that the Ring, like Gounod's Faust, means Redemption through Love; that no great artist ever means anything at all; and that Mr Shaw's "theories" about Wagner, clever and amusing as they are, are, of course, merely his little joke. One gentleman made an effort to cope with the historical evidence. He cited one of the letters in which Wagner urges Liszt to try to get the ban of exile removed on the ground that he was "only an artistic revolutionary." But the Government, with Art and Revolution to refer to, rightly preferred inartistic revolutionaries to artistic ones, as being, on the whole, much less thorough.

I need not say much more. The amateurs who believe that art like Wagner's is a product of the mere beautymaker, and that artists become great in proportion to their success in pandering to voluptuaries, may be left to Tolstoy's essay on art, through which they will find themselves drawn as persuasively as a cat is drawn through a sausage machine. And serve them right!

Finally, in response to many questions as to why I have called the tetralogy The Ring of the Niblungs, instead of, as Wagner did, The Niblung's Ring, I reply that I dont know. The Niblung literature has established in me a plural habit of mind as regards that fabled race, I suppose. And then I know so many Alberics. Probably if Wagner had read my book he would have used the plural too.[U]

II

To The Saturday Review, 11 February 1899

[U] Sir,—Why does J. F. R.* turn from his warfare with the Old Critics to make a parricidal onslaught on me, the father of the New Criticism? His only grievance is that I have, as he puts it, "scalped" the other critics and spared him. But—to pursue the metaphor—why superfluously scalp a man who cannot keep his own hair

* J. F. Runciman, Shaw's friend and fellow Fabian, who had recently resigned as musical critic of the Saturday Review.

on? Besides, I have no quarrel with competent criticism: if I am right, the competent critics will find that out presently without putting me to the trouble of saying my say twice over. The object of my published reply, undertaken at the suggestion and request of the editor of the Critic, was simply, in the interests of musical criticism generally, to warn the beginner, to expose the impostor, and to deprive the ignoramus of the confidence of his deluded editor. J. F. R. does himself an injustice by flying out at me as if I had included him in these categories.

However, if J. F. R. insists on my tomahawking him, I will cheerfully do so for the amusement of the readers of the SATURDAY, to whom we both owe much. I will not go so far as to say that he is wrong about Die Götterdämmerung and Das Rheingold. I will content myself with proving that he cannot possibly be right. Here is the position! I allege that Das Rheingold is an allegory. J. F. R. instantly exclaims "This I emphatically deny: I assert, on the contrary, that while looking at Das Rheingold you can only think of its symbolic and allegorical meaning [the existence of which J. F. R. has just emphatically denied] by abstracting yourself from the play going on before your eyes. And to do this means to turn a mighty and beautiful work of art into an instructive Fabian tract . . . . a work of art stands or falls by itself accordingly as it is good or bad art . . . an artist is greater than a political economist . . . a beautiful thing is better than all the political economy in the world," and so on, through the familiar art cant of Maida Vale, unspeakably unworthy of J. F. R. But the moment I meet him so far as to admit that Die Götterdämmerung is what he means here by "a work of art" and is guiltless of political economy, he rightly feels that I have struck a mortal blow at its credit, and protests that it is "the logical outcome of the problem set in The Rhinegold."

This, if you please, in the very next paragraph to his repudiation of the possibility of there being any "problem" in Das Rheingold! Can I expect J. F. R. to agree with me when he will not hear of agreeing even with himself?

Need I add that when I proceed to shew that Die Götterdämmerung is not an allegory, but a romantic opera, J. F. R. instantly faces right about; throws over Maida Vale and the all-sufficiency of ART; and is resolved to find allegory in every bar of the work. First, however, he accuses me of having thrown over Die Götterdämmerung because it would not fit into my explanation of The Ring. On referring to his own explanation I find (see page 203 of his Old Scores and New Readings) that "The Rhinegold, in spite of its glorious music, is entirely superfluous." So there is not much to be gained, apparently, by shifting from my ground to J. F. R.'s. Now let us see what his attempt to make Die Götterdämmerung an allegory comes to. He says Brynhild is "incarnate love." Then why does she refuse to give up her wedding ring to save her father and all her early friends from destruction? Why does she falsely accuse Siegfried of rape, and call on Gunther to kill him? Why does she make Hagen stab him in the back? Because, explains J. F. R., in Die Götterdämmerung she is "simply a woman. Siegfried treats her treacherously; and she very naturally takes vengeance on him. Mr Shaw speaks as though he wished her to be a bread-and-butter miss,* &c." Very well; but what, then, has become of the allegory of "incarnate love"? The person who is "simply a woman," and revenges herself in that character by committing perjury, murder, and suicide lest anyone should consider her a bread-and-butter miss, is precisely the sort of person I have

* See III, 242.

represented the Brynhild of Die Götterdämmerung to be: to wit, an operatic Lady Macbeth or Cleopatra. Whereupon, of course, J. F. R. comes right-about-face again with a bound, and will have it that she is as allegorical a person as the Valkyrie who is "Wotan's Will," and in speaking to whom Wotan speaks "but to himself." And then, giddy with these gyrations, he gasps out that my book is "illogical and unreasonable"!

"What!" exclaims J. F. R., when his breath comes back, "did Wagner write Siegfried to explain The Dusk of the Gods, The Valkyrie to explain Siegfried, and The Rhinegold to explain The Valkyrie? No, thank you, Mr Shaw." J. F. R. might as well exclaim "What! is Bristol west of Greenwich; and did Beethoven write the ninth symphony after the eighth?" The correct answer is that Wagner *did* write the four poems in that order and in that relation, and could not have written them in any other order or relation. And it is precisely because my commentary is based on this historical fact and its circumstances, instead of on the order in which the four were printed and set to music, that I have escaped the confusion which attends every attempt to trace them forward instead of backwards. For the subject of Das Rheingold is the origin of the conflicts which make social problems so intensely dramatic. Now when you deal with origins, you have to think your way back to them *up* the stream of time, whether you are Darwin or Wagner. But when you publish the results you carry the reader *down* the stream of time, placing the chapter you last arrived at at the beginning of your book or tetralogy, and the chapter from which you started at the end. On the other hand, when you write a Christmas number about love, and death, and jealousy, and ghosts, and all the other things that raise our hack novelists in their own opinion (and apparently in J. F. R.'s whenever anybody happens to affirm the contrary) above Dante,

Bunyan, Goethe, and other "political economists," you omit the thinking process and go straight ahead. J. F. R., by putting The Ring into the romantic category, arrives at the conclusion that Wagner began with Das Rheingold and ended with Die Götterdämmerung—also that Das Rheingold became superfluous in the process. I have shewn that the exact contrary is the case. And in this I am not tomahawking J. F. R. with arguments: I am dissolving his fiery recalcitrance into a cloud of hissing steam by a cold douche of fact.

However, I do not propose to throw over Die Götterdämmerung. We can accept the fact that The Ring is allegorical music-drama up to the beginning of the final scene of Siegfried, and opera from that point to the end, without deploring the existence of the operatic section. When the music to the second act of Siegfried was completed, Wagner put the work aside for more than twelve years, during which he produced Tristan and Die Meistersinger, and reached the phase of his career in which J. F. R., infuriated by Parsifal, describes him as "exhausted," "effete," in "the mood which follows Tristan as certainly as night follows day," producing work, "not only immoral, but also dispiriting and boring, inconsequential and pointless." Now I want J. F. R. to tell me why he believes that this Tristan-Meistersinger period, which, as he contends, placed such a tremendous gap between Siegfried and Parsifal, placed none at all between Die Walküre and the score of Die Götterdämmerung? Again I take refuge from his assault behind the facts. At fortyfive Wagner abandons a colossal task conceived in the comparative leisure, reflection, and reaction of exile in Switzerland. At fiftyseven, worn by twelve years of renewed public activity, he returns to the work, and swiftly finishes it for performance at the Bayreuth inauguration, with technical powers developed to a magnificent pitch of professionalism, but with the old feeling for the revolutionary allegory almost effaced by Schopenhauer, by Tristan, and by hard work, high spirits, money, second marriage, and advancing age. Does J. F. R. seriously contend that these events made no difference?—that there is no gap in The Ring corresponding to the gap they made? Let me appeal to him on his surest side—his musical side. Granted that Die Götterdämmerung is ten times as expertly composed as Die Walküre, does the music of Gunther ever arrest him like that of Hunding? Has he ever for a moment mistaken the mere bandmastership and stage management of the funeral march for the inspiration of the scene between the Valkyrie and Siegmund? is he, of all critics, taken in by the unscrupulous hotch-potch of themes at the end, which I have compared to a fantasia on Grandfather's Clock? I ask in despair, is there no Englishman who can admire a *chef-d'œuvre* without mistaking it for an inspiration—who can be excited and delighted by art without becoming its dupe—who can distinguish between a man of genius and a divinity? Dare J. F. R. tell me publicly that he has sat through the whole Ring cycle at Bayreuth without being as much startled by the complete change in spirit and workmanship which marks the twelve year's interval, as if A Midsummer Night's Dream had suddenly changed into Julius Cæsar?

I lay stress on the musical test, because it is quite possible for an ingenious and witty critic, suppressing the historical facts and ignoring the evidence of the music, to trace a continuation of the allegory through Die Götterdämmerung. Indeed, a Daily Chronicle reviewer has succeeded in doing this as a *jeu d'esprit* without either disturbing my explanation of the earlier dramas or degrading the Ring to the level of a novelette by the usual hackneyed rubbish about love and death and the curse of gold. That writer must be quite clever enough to invent, if he chose, an explanation of Die Götterdämmerung on my lines so apparently serious and consistent that I could not discredit it by any process of argument. I could only appeal against it to the musician's ear and artistic perception. If J. F. R. cannot see the professionalism of a splendid theatrical entertainment blazing out of every augmented fifth in that score; if he has a real unhysterical tear for its theatrical pathos; if he finds anything but exultant, unconscionable, high-spirited revelry in consummate power over music in the part that is new (as distinguished from the old material *réchauffé* with cunning harmonic pepper and orchestral sauce), then I give him up as a prematurely Old Critic, and take to my bosom the able anti-Wagnerite critic of Musical Opinion, who, whilst standing by the ancient notion that the early Ring dramas were deliberate experiments in bald, ugly, unvocal music, yet does clearly perceive that in Die Götterdämmerung their peculiar style is replaced by a "developed operatic style."

At all events, let us have some more musical criticism from J. F. R. on the subject. Let him point out to us the scenes in Die Götterdämmerung in which he finds the characteristic poetic quality of Wagner's work in the Valkyrie period. Let him explain how we are to find such long scenes in Das Rheingold as the wrangle between Wotan and the Giants, the boasting and menaces of Alberic in the mine, the knocking out of Fasolt's brains by Fafnir to an accompaniment of thumps on the drum, interesting and impressive on "gloriously musical" grounds. The fact is, there is not twopenn'orth of "glorious" *dramatic* music in Das Rheingold outside the wellworn concert selections from it. There is breathless horror behind it from the point of view of the revolutionary Socialist and ultra-Protestant of 1849. From any other point of view there is nothing in it, either dramatically or musically; and J. F. R. no sooner abandons that point of view than he outdoes Mr Joseph Bennett by finding Das Rheingold "superfluous"; reproaching Wagner for "shoving old Wotan on to the stage again and again to recapitulate his troubles"; and wildly smiting at me, the innocent founder of his critical dynasty, in his championship of incarnate love against political economy. Far better take counsel with The Perfect Wagnerite, consider its ways, and be wise.

This feeble defence is the best I, being now but a crippled invalid,* can make against an attack as fierce as it is unnatural. G.B.S.[U]

RECENT WAGNER BOOKS

Review of David Irvine's "Parsifal" and Wagner's Christianity, Ernest Newman's A Study of Wagner, Alfred Forman's Wagner's "Parsifal" in English Verse, and Richard Wagner's Prose Works, translated by W. Ashton Ellis, Vol. VII. The Daily Chronicle, 9 June 1899

[U] Seldom do two authors, writing at the same moment on the same subject, offer so neatly fitted a contrast as Messrs Ernest Newman and David Irvine. Mr Newman illumines the darkness of his anti-Wagnerism by a lucidity of style which puts the laziest reader at his ease. Mr Irvine obscures his inner Wagnerian light by a method of exposition which not only shakes the student's reason, but produces a sullen and injurious temper, in which, far from manfully facing the difficulties of the book, he indulges his imagination with gloomy dreams of assaults committed on the author. If it be true that history forgives all faults save want of conviction, then

* Shaw had been incapacitated for several months by an infected foot and a broken arm.

Mr Irvine will assuredly find salvation. But since it is certainly true that reviewers are apt to judge a book by the trouble it gives them to read it, Mr Irvine will probably be less civilly treated than Mr Newman by the few weary journalists who will make any serious attempt to grapple with his book at all.

Mr Newman's position is no doubt to some extent still a representative English one. In the third quarter of this century, when rationalism and the most prosaic "scientific" materialism dominated culture, it would have been *the* representative one on every point concerning Wagner, except the beauty of his music. In those days metaphysics were a folly, while the supremacy of the physicist and reasoner, and the futility of the philosopher, had been demonstrated to the satisfaction of "every schoolboy" by Macaulay's essay on Bacon. Art had nothing to do with doctrine, because it could prove nothing. Religion was the particular branch of metaphysics that obstructed science and opposed the story of Adam and Eve to the theory of Darwin. The only unsettled question as to the constitution of the universe was as to whether it should be regarded as built of bacteria or of magnetic atoms. If any German musician had told Professor Tyndall* then that before the end of the century his "scientific" knowledge of the shape of the earth, the constituents of the atmosphere, the evidence of the spectroscope, and the efficacy of the Listerian carbolic spray in surgery would be added to "the mistakes of Moses," with religion and philosophy meanwhile recovering their medieval vogue, he would have felt as calmly superior to that musician on the intellectual side as Mr Newman now feels towards Wagner. Mr Newman's thorough-going materialism is summed up

* John Tyndall, Irish-born physicist and popularizer of science, who died in 1893.

in his criticism of Mendelssohn's violin concerto, certain effects in which, he says, "*must* delight us as long as our auditory nerves remain what they are." Probably Mr Newman knows that many men, women, and animals with similar auditory nerves are as variously disposed towards Mendelssohn as people with similar optical nerves are towards Mr Whistler; and that the collapse of Beethoven's auditory nerves left him as good a musician as before. But that does not daunt him: anybody who draws a distinction between the senses and consciousness is to him "a dull metaphysician." Causation is the most real and inevitable thing in the world to him: and he will not tolerate the claim that there is "a philosophy" in The Ring, because an opera can prove nothing, and "the premises do not really lead to the conclusion."

He is in a chronic transport of amazement at Wagner's stupidity. He takes the most pathetic pains to prove, by instance after instance, that Wagner saw and felt and interpreted the world quite differently from ordinary people, as if that were the most surprising and unreasonable proceeding on the part of a man of genius; and then he complains repeatedly of his "quite distressing mediocrity." He declares that the philosophy of The Ring has "little interest for anyone but those constructed somewhat upon Wagner's pattern." "To the majority of us" he says "it is merely dull." This is but too true. Mr Newman is not "constructed somewhat upon Wagner's pattern"; and that is precisely why it takes him four hundred pages to "reiterate that Wagner had no more capacity for philosophical speculation than an average curate." The nearest dustman—if presented with Mr Irvine's treatise in lieu of the usual tip—would have said as much for Wagner with a single incarnadined epithet.

Let me give a few samples of Mr Newman's elaborate ratiocinations. He points out that Wagner "blunders" in the use of representative themes in The Mastersingers and Tristan because, at a first hearing, nobody can "spontaneously correlate" a theme developed, say, in the instrumental prelude to the third act to a single rather obscure citation of it in the second act. Mr Newman returns to this impossibility again and again, giving Wagner the *coup de grâce* by a triumphant quotation from Opera and Drama, in which Wagner himself, criticizing the Meyerbeerian operatic prelude on themes from the opera (as distinguished from the old independent overture), says that "every man of commonsense must know that these tone-pieces should have been performed *after* the drama instead of *before* it, if they were meant to be understood."

Mr Newman ironically adds that "it never occurred to Wagner that a *tu quoque* was possible." Mr Newman is wrong: it did. Wagner made virtually the same criticism of his own Tannhäuser overture. The effective reply to the objection will exasperate Mr Newman, because, as it is of a metaphysical nature, he will think it "the merest verbal absurdity." It is that nobody can "spontaneously correlate" either musical motives or anything else until he has found for them a refuge in the memory from the category of time, as Parsifal did in the Grail Temple. For instance, among the latter plays of Ibsen there is not one of which the first act is fully intelligible to anyone who witnesses it without foreknowledge of the last; and this is necessarily true of every work of art which rises in complexity above the "half-price at nine o'clock" level. If Mr Newman cannot spontaneously correlate every thematic reference in Tristan or The Mastersingers on the first night, the moral is, not to call Wagner a blunderer, but simply to go again.

Just as Mr Newman does not seem to know whether he considers Wagner a mediocre thinker or an abnormal one, so does he fluctuate between a conception of himself as a hearty Philistine scoffer at philosophy, and a sage who has gone so deep that Wagner's philosophy is to him "crude and primitive," "confused and amateur rambling," and, indeed, "arrant nonsense." On one page he demands "Who cares for all this vaporing about 'the individual' and 'constituted authority' and 'the immorality of convention'? Who wants the characters of an opera to be a procession of dull abstractions, drawn alternately from anarchistic and socialistic handbooks?" To which I reply conclusively that *I do.* Such questions depend for all their force on the certainty of the reply being "Nobody,"as it would be if Mr Newman were to ask in the ring at Newmarket, Who wants to offer up a prayer?

But on the next page he suddenly changes his ground, and declares solemnly that "the so-called philosophy of The Ring is merely the crude statement of a man incapable of thinking out the great problems he was interested in." So these matters about which nobody cares are "great problems" after all; and Mr Newman, we are led to infer, has thought them out on correct lines, and arrived at conclusions which entitle him to dismiss Schopenhauer with contempt. Will Mr Newman kindly communicate those conclusions to a breathless world?

Mr Newman, I am afraid, puts himself out of court by taking the familiar view of Art as a huge sweetshop, licensed for the sale of stimulants. "Philosophy and politics," he says, are "outside the circle of art. A novel that is a tract is bad enough: a poem that is a tract is infinitely worse; but what shall be said of a musical drama that is a tract?" Farewell, then, Wagner: farewell, too, Moses and the prophets, Dante, Bunyan, Blake, Shelley, Bach, Handel, Mozart, Beethoven, Wordsworth, Tennyson, Browning, Morris, Longfellow,

Ouida, Hall Caine, Miss Marie Corelli, Mrs Humphry Ward, Sarah Grand, Ibsen, Miss Elizabeth Robins, Shakespear, Homer, Wilson Barrett, Junius, La Rochefoucauld, Voltaire, Rousseau, Goethe, Tolstoy, Giotto, Sir William Richmond, Mr G. F. Watts, Plutarch, Mr William Watson, Sir Edwin Arnold, and Plato. Mr Newman has withdrawn his custom from you. Put up the shutters and solace yourselves, pending the arrival of the broker, with Poe's Ulalume and Lear's Book of Nonsense.

In spite of all this, Mr Newman is a Progressive anti-Wagnerite. He exposes the errors of his predecessors unsparingly; does not complain of Wagner's "ingratitude" to Meyerbeer; and condones his quilted silk dressing gowns. Far from disparaging his musical gift he proclaims that it has "never been equaled among men," an estimate which quite takes my breath away, as if someone had said that Watts was a greater draughtsman than Montegna. When he comes to details, however, he shews curious limitations to his appreciation. For example, the clever passage in The Mastersingers, delightful to a singer who is a comedian, in which Pogner describes the German burgher's reputation for closefistedness, is dismissed by Mr Newman as "recitative of the most wearisome and commonplace order" (it forms, by the way, a perfect musical verse); and he can see no connexion between the sentiment and associations of the whole speech and the charm of the music. He pleads elsewhere rather indignantly that it is a pretty thing that Wagnerians should accuse *him* of a want of humor, when he has proved his possession of it by laughing at the dragon in Siegfried, which they take so seriously.

On the whole, Mr Newman's book is not likely to produce more effect than the late Edmund Gurney's Power of Sound. As Gurney was a clever and cultivated man, writing with a detachment impossible to a true master of his subject, his labor was not altogether in vain; he grew a little parsley crop of accuracies, ingenuities and corrections between his barren furrows, just as Wagner has left us a certain proportion of tares in the plentiful harvest of his wheat. I cannot say that I find in Mr Newman's method any advance on Gurney's. Except that he has fallen under the spell of Wagner's music, and therefore has an intellectual rather than a musical quarrel with him, the procedure is the same; and probably the result will be the same. The book seems to me the last defiant protest of the vanquished, not the first war-cry of the next reaction.

Mr Irvine, as I have already hinted, is a very different sort of person—literally a portentous person. He is a Wagnerite without any previous history. At what age he, exposed to time and chance with vacant mind, open ears, and ready Scotch metaphysical brain, was suddenly seized, body and soul, by Wagner and Schopenhauer, I do not know. But there he is, our first unquestioning apostle of the faith, calling the world, in greenclad volumes only to be interpreted by strenuous spirit wrestlings, to turn aside from the Jewish Jehovah and all other gods; from belief in creation; from subjection to the illusions of time, space, causation, and death; above all, from indelicately wilful methods of perpetuating the species, to ideal manhood with Parsifal in Grail Castles of the fourth dimension. His matter is mystic; but his manner is lively and concrete to the verge of abusiveness and often over it. Of his style I will give two examples. After demonstrating the tragic conflict in which the social pioneer (or Redeemer) necessarily finds himself engaged with his contemporaries, Mr Irvine adds "Everyone that gets kicked cannot be great." And again, "Probably the announcement of Lucifer's crime would not have inconvenienced a garden party at a Bishop's.

In Heaven he had to leave, with fatal consequences to the garden parties held there." This is crisp enough; but when Mr Irvine wants to put his message into one pregnant sentence, he says "What is plainly asserted here is this, that in the light of, or according to, the doctrine and example of Christ, it is known to every one who knows intellectually the drift of Christianity." If I am asked what is the antecedent of "it" in this sentence, I reply that I have not the remotest idea: it might be anything in the preceding 346 pages.

Briefly, Mr Irvine gives in this book the Schopenhauer-Wagner criticism of civilization. He introduces certain obvious topical adulterations, as, for example, when he says that "Titurel is nothing else than that death struggle now taking place of the ritualists to reimpose their ceremonies on an enlightened generation, which can do all its Christianity without such." Here Mr Irvine boldly presents Wagner, who was an arrant ritualist all his life, in the character of the Scotchman to whom a church organ is a blasphemous "kist o' whustles." But in the main he sticks so literally to the Bayreuth creed that he flatly declares that "the creations of the subjective musician are the guarantee of the existence of objective reality of the Ding an sich,"* which may stand as the polar opposite of Mr Newman's auditory nerve theory of music. His chapter on the music of Parsifal is a shade less absurd than the corresponding chapter in his book on The Ring. In that he discovered the most remarkable and significant resemblances between the musical intervals in Wagner's various themes, not knowing apparently that these intervals have become stereotyped in music owing to the fact that for many centuries they were the only intervals playable upon most wind instruments. This time he confines his

* Philosophic term meaning "the thing in itself."

discoveries to Wagner's mannerisms; and though he still makes a mare's nest out of every such trick by assuming that Wagner repeated himself consciously with ulterior intentions, the mares' nests are not uninteresting as a list of the mannerisms. To sum up, Mr Irvine's faith is a significant social symptom; and his book, though it has the faults as well as the qualities of a Scotch sermon, is neither barren nor misleading.

Mr Alfred Forman has completed his labor as a translator of Wagner's music-dramas by a version of Parsifal. It is not possible for a successful translator of The Ring, with its curt, energetic measures, and pointed alliterations, to produce an equally novel and striking effect with Parsifal. Besides, Mr Forman has not this time been first in the field (the danger being over); and certain renderings are so obvious that the first comer cannot miss them. Take for example the best-known passage in the work:

> Durch Mitleid wissend, der reine Thor:
> Harre sein', den ich erkor.

The [Frederick] Corder translation runs:

> By pity lightened, the guileless Fool:
> Wait for him, my chosen tool.

Here, "my chosen tool" is dreadful, and guileless is not the right word; but the phrases fit the music. Mr Forman has:

> The spotless fool, by fellow-pain who knows;
> Wait for him, whom I forechose.

This is better English; but it quite defies the musical setting. On the other hand, many of Mr Forman's lines are better than those of the Corder version, even for the special musical purpose of that version; and he is quite guiltless of the impenitent Wardour-street archaisms of the Corders, and of their flowery suppressions of such vital points in the poem as the self-mutilation of Klingsor. On the whole, it is much the most accurate and scholarly version we have.

I will not go through the usual pretence of criticizing the seventh volume of Mr Ashton Ellis's translation of Wagner's Prose Works, containing the bright journalism, the witty and touching fiction, of the early days in Paris and Dresden. All we who write about music have to pretend that we know as much about Wagner and his writings as Mr Ellis does; but the truth is that we owe all our knowledge to him. We ought to know better than any others the appalling copiousness of Wagner's collected works; the toughness of the matter; the uselessness of mere dictionary transliteration; the difficulty of interpretation; the indispensable preliminary vows of poverty, industry and unremitting devotion imposed on the translator; the certainty that public recognition of the work, not to mention a grant in aid from the Civil List, or even an order of copies from the public libraries, would be granted more readily to the silliest county history; and the probability that the very critics who would make money out of the work done for them would use the translation to conceal their own indebtedness to it. Mr Ellis, facing all this, has fought his way through it for years until he is now within sight of the end; and neither Richter nor Mottl nor Levi has interpreted the scores more convincingly than he the books. I do not presume to criticize: I take off my hat.[U]

A WORD MORE ABOUT VERDI

The Anglo-Saxon Review, March 1901

I have read most of the articles on Verdi elicited by his death, and I have blushed for my species. By this I mean the music-critic species; for though I have of late years disused this learned branch I am still entitled to say to my former colleagues *Anch' io son critico.* And when I find men whom I know otherwise honorable glibly pretending to an intimate acquaintance with Oberto, Conte di San Bonifacio, with Un Giorno di Regno, with La Battaglia di Legnano; actually comparing them with Falstaff and Aïda, and weighing, with a nicely judicial air, the differences made by the influence of Wagner, well knowing all the time that they know no more of Oberto than they do of the tunes Miriam timbrelled on the shores of the divided Red Sea, I say again that I blush for our profession, and ask them, as an old friend who wishes them well, where they expect to go to after such shamelessly mendacious implications when they die.

For myself, I value a virtuous appearance above vain erudition; and I confess that the only operas of Verdi's I know honestly right through, as I know Dickens's novels, are Ernani, Rigoletto, Il Trovatore, Un Ballo, La Traviata, Aïda, Otello, and Falstaff. And quite enough too, provided one also knows enough of the works of Verdi's forerunners and contemporaries to see exactly when he came in and where he stood. It is inevitable that as younger and younger critics come into the field, more and more mistakes should be made about men who lived as long as Verdi and Wagner, not because the critics do not know their music, but because they do not know the operas that Wagner and Verdi heard when they were boys, and are consequently apt to credit them with the invention of many things which were familiar to their grandfathers.

For example, in all the articles I have read it is assumed that the difference between Ernani and Aïda is due to the influence of Wagner. Now I declare without reserve that there is no evidence in any bar of Aïda or the two later operas that Verdi ever heard a note of Wagner's music. There is evidence that he had heard Boïto's music, Mendelssohn's music, and Beethoven's music; but the utmost that can be said to connect him with Wagner is that if Wagner had not got all Europe into the habit of using the whole series of dominant and tonic discords as freely as Rossini used the dominant seventh, it is possible that Falstaff might have been differently harmonized. But as much might be said of any modern pantomime score. Verdi uses the harmonic freedom of his time so thoroughly in his own way, and so consistently in terms of his old style, that if he had been as ignorant of Wagner as Berlioz was of Brahms there is no reason to suppose that the score of Falstaff would have been an unprepared thirteenth the worse.

I am, of course, aware that when Aïda first reached us, it produced a strong impression of Wagnerism. But at that time nothing of Wagner's later than Lohengrin was known to us. We thought the Evening Star song in Tannhäuser a precious Wagnerian gem. In short, we knew nothing of Wagner's own exclusive style, only his operatic style, which was much more mixed than we imagined. Everybody then thought that a recurring theme in an opera was a Wagnerian Leitmotif, especially if it stole in to a *tremolando* of the strings and was harmonized with major ninths instead of sub-dominants; so when this occurred in Aïda's *scena*, *Ritorna vincitor*, we all said "Aha! Wagner!" And, as very often happens, when we came to know better, we quite forgot to revise our premature conclusion. Accordingly, we find critics taking it for granted today that Aïda is Wagnerized Verdi, although, if they had not heard Aïda until after Siegfried and Die Meistersinger, they would never dream of connecting the two composers or their styles.

The real secret of the change from the roughness of Il Trovatore to the elaboration of the three last operas is the inevitable natural drying up of Verdi's spontaneity and fertility. So long as an opera composer can pour forth melodies like *La donna e mobile* and *Il balen*, he does not stop to excogitate harmonic elegancies and orchestral sonorities which are neither helpful to him dramatically nor demanded by the taste of his audience. But when in process of time the well begins to dry up; when instead of getting splashed with the bubbling over of *Ah si, ben mio*, he has to let down a bucket to drag up *Celeste Aïda*, then it is time to be clever, to be nice, to be distinguished, to be impressive, to study instrumental confectionery, to bring thought and knowledge and seriousness to the rescue of failing vitality. In Aïda this is not very happily done: it is not until Otello that we get dignified accomplishment and fine critical taste; but here, too, we have unmistakably a new hand in the business, the hand of Boïto. It is quite certain that Boïto could not have written Otello; but certain touches in Iago's Credo were perhaps either suggested by Boïto, or composed in his manner in fatherly compliment to him; and the whole work, even in its most authentic passages, shews that Verdi was responding to the claims of a more fastidious artistic conscience and even a finer sensitiveness to musical sound than his own was when he tried to turn Macbeth into another Trovatore, and made Lady Macbeth enliven the banquet scene with a florid drinking song. The advance from romantic intensity to dramatic seriousness is revolutionary. Nothing is more genial in Verdi's character than this docility, this respect for the demands of a younger man, this recognition that the implied rebuke to his taste and his coarseness shewed a greater tenderness for his own genius than he had shewn to it himself.

But there is something else than Boïto in Otello. In the third act there is a movement in six-eight time, *Essa t'avvince,* which is utterly unlike anything in the Trovatore period, and surprisingly like a rondo in the style of Beethoven. That is to say, it is pre-Wagnerian; which at such a date is almost equivalent to anti-Wagnerian. In Falstaff, again, in the buck-basket scene there is a lightfingered and humorous *moto perpetuo* which might have come straight out of a Mendelssohn concerto. Unfortunately it is ineffectively scored; for Verdi, brought up in the Italian practice of using the orchestra as pure accompaniment, was an unskilled beginner in German symphonic orchestration. These are the only passages in the later works which are not obviously the old Verdi developed into a careful and thoughtful composer under the influence of Boïto and the effect of advancing age on his artistic resources. I think they would both be impossible to a composer who had not formed an affectionate acquaintance with German music. But the music of Beethoven and Mendelssohn is the music of a Germany still under that Franco-Italian influence which made the music of Mozart so amazingly unlike the music of Bach. Of the later music that was consciously and resolutely German and German only; that would not even write *allegro* at the head of its quick, or *adagio* at the head of its slow movements, because these words are not German; of the music of Schumann, Brahms, and Wagner, there is not anywhere in Verdi the faintest trace. In German music the Italian loved what Italy gave. What Germany offered of her own music he entirely ignored.

Having now, I hope, purged myself of the heresy that Verdi was Wagnerized, a heresy which would never have arisen if our foolish London Opera had been as punctual with Lohengrin as with Aïda, instead of being nearly a quarter of a century late with it, I may take Verdi on his own ground. Verdi's genius, like Victor Hugo's, was hyperbolical and grandiose: he expressed all the common passions with an impetuosity and intensity which produced an effect of sublimity. If you ask What is it all about? the answer must be that it is mostly about the police intelligence melodramatized. In the same way, if you check your excitement at the conclusion of the wedding scene in Il Trovatore to ask what, after all, *Di quella pira* is, the answer must be that it is only a common bolero tune, just as *Stride la vampa* is only a common waltz tune. Indeed, if you know these tunes only through the barrel organs, you will need no telling. But in the theatre, if the singers have the requisite power and spirit, one does not ask these questions: the bolero form passes as unnoticed as the saraband form in Handel's *Lascia ch'io pianga,* wheras in the more academic form of the aria with *caballetto,* which Rossini, Bellini, and Donizetti accepted, the form reduces the matter to absurdity. Verdi, stronger and more singly dramatic, broke away from the Rossinian convention; developed the simpler cavatina form with an integral *codetta* instead of a separated *cabaletto*; combined it fearlessly with popular dance and ballad forms; and finally produced the once enormously popular, because concise, powerful, and comparatively natural and dramatic type of operatic solo which prevails in Il Trovatore and Un Ballo. A comparison of this Italian emancipation of dramatic music from decorative form with the Wagnerian emancipation shews in a moment the utter unthinkableness of any sort of connexion between the two composers. No doubt the stimulus given to Verdi's self-respect and courage by his share in the political activity of his time is to some extent paralleled by the effect of the 1848 revolution on Wagner; but this only accentuates the difference between the successful composer of a period of triumphant nationalism and the exiled communist-artist-philosopher of The Niblung's Ring. As Wagner contracted his views to a practicable nationalism at moments later on, I can conceive a critic epigrammatically dismissing the Kaiser March as a bit of Verdified Wagner. But the critic who can find Wagner in Otello must surely be related to the gentleman who accused Bach of putting forth the accompaniment to Gounod's Ave Maria as a prelude of his own composition.

By this Mascagni-facilitating emancipation of Italian opera, Verdi concentrated its qualities and got rid of its alloys. Il Trovatore is Italian opera in earnest and nothing else: Rossini's operas are musical entertainments which are only occasionally and secondarily dramatic. Moses in Egypt and Semiramis, for example, are ridiculous as dramas, though both of them contain one impressively spendid number to shew how nobly Rossini could have done if the silly conditions of the Italian opera houses had given their composers any chance of being sensible. "I could have achieved something had I been a German" said Rossini humbly to Wagner "*car j'avais du talent.*" Bellini, Donizetti, and the Italianized Jew Meyerbeer pushed the dramatic element in opera still further, making it possible for Verdi to end by being almost wholly dramatic. But until Verdi was induced by Boïto to take Shakespear seriously they all exploited the same romantic stock-in-trade. They composed with perfect romantic sincerity, undesirous and intolerant of reality, untroubled by the philosophic faculty which, in the mind of Wagner, revolted against the demoralizing falseness of their dramatic material. They revelled in the luxury of stage woe, with its rhetorical loves and deaths and poisons and jealousies and murders, all of the most luscious, the most enjoyable, the most unreal kind. They did not, like Rossini, break suddenly off in the midst of their grandiosities to write *excusez du peu* at the top of the score, and finish with a galop. On the contrary, it was just where the stage business demanded something elegantly trivial that they became embarrassed and vulgar. This was especially the case with Verdi, who was nothing if not strenuous, wheras Bellini could be trivially simple and Donizetti thoughtlessly gay on occasion. Verdi, when he is simple or gay, is powerfully so. It has been said, on the strength of the alleged failure of a forgotten comic opera called Un Giorno di Regno, that Verdi was incapable of humor; and I can understand that an acquantance limited to Ernani, Il Trovatore, La Traviata, and Aïda (and acquaintances of just this extent are very common) might support that opinion. But the parts of the Duke and Sparafucile in Rigoletto could not have been composed by a humorless man. In Un Ballo again we have in Riccardo the Duke's gaiety and gallantry without his callousness; and at the great moment of the melodrama Verdi achieves a masterstroke by his dramatic humor. The hero has made an assignation with the heroine in one of those romantically lonely spots which are always to be found in operas. A band of conspirators resolves to seize the opportunity to murder him. His friend Renato, getting wind of their design, arrives before them, and persuades him to fly, taking upon himself the charge of the lady, who is veiled, and whose identity and place of residence he swears as a good knight to refrain from discovering. When the conspirators capture him and find that they have the wrong man they propose to amuse themselves by taking a look at the lady. Renato defends her; but she, to save him from being killed, unveils herself and turns out to be Renato's own wife. This is no doubt a very thrilling stage climax: it is easy for a dramatist to work up to it. But it is not quite so easy to get away from it; for when the veil is off the bolt is shot; and the difficulty is what is to be said next. The librettist solves the problem by falling back on the chaffing of Renato by the conspirators. Verdi seizes on this with genuine humorous power in the most boldly popular style, giving just the right vein of blackguardly irony and mischievous mirth to the passage, and getting the necessary respite before the final storm, in which the woman's shame, the man's agony of jealousy and wounded friendship, and the malicious chuckling of the conspirators provide material for one of those concerted pieces in which Italian opera is at its best.

And here may I mildly protest that the quartet in Rigoletto, with its four people expressing different emotions simultaneously, was not, as the obituary notices almost all imply, an innovation of Verdi's. Such concerted pieces were *de rigueur* in Italian opera before he was born. The earliest example that holds the stage is the quartet in Don Giovanni, *Non ti fidar*; and between Don Giovanni and Rigoletto it would be difficult to find an Italian opera without a specimen. Several of them were quite as famous as the Rigoletto quartet became. They were burlesqued by Arthur Sullivan in Trial by Jury; but Verdi never, to the end of his life, saw anything ridiculous in them; nor do I. There are some charming examples in Un Ballo, of which but little seems to be remembered nowadays.

In Otello and Falstaff there is some deliberate and not unsuccessful fun. When Cassio gets too drunk to find his place in Iago's drinking song it is impossible not to burst out laughing, though the mistake is as pretty as it is comic. The fugue at the end of Falstaff so tickled Professor Villiers Stanford that he compromised himself to the extent of implying that it is a good fugue. It is neither a good fugue nor a good joke, except as a family joke among professional musicians; but since Mozart finished Don Giovanni with a whizzing *fughetta*, and Beethoven expressed his most wayward fits by scraps of *fugato*, and Berlioz made his solitary joke fugally, the Falstaff fugue may be allowed to pass.

However, to shew that Verdi was occasionally jocular does not prove that he had the gift of dramatic humor. For such a gift the main popular evidence must be taken from the serious part of Falstaff; for there is nothing so serious as great humor. Unfortunately, very few people know The Merry Wives of Windsor as it was when Falstaff was capably played according to the old tradition, and the playgoer went to hear the actor pile up a mighty climax, culminating in "Think of that, Master Brook." In those palmy days it was the vision of the man-mountain baked in the buck-basket and suddenly plunged hissing hot into the cool stream of the Thames at Datchet that focused the excitement of the pit; and if the two conversations between Ford and Falstaff were played for all they were worth, Shakespear was justified of his creation, and the rest was taken cheerfully as mere filling up. Now, it cannot be supposed that either Boïto or Verdi had ever seen such a performance; and the criticisms of modern quite futile productions of The Merry Wives have shewn that a mere literary acquaintance with the text will not yield up the secret to the ordinary unShakespearean man; yet it is just here, on Ford and Falstaff, that Verdi has concentrated his attack and trained his heaviest artillery. His Ford carries Shakespear's a step higher: it exhausts what Shakespear's resources could only suggest. And this seems to me to dispose of the matter in Verdi's favor.

The composition of Otello was a much less Shakespearean feat; for the truth is that instead of Otello being an Italian opera written in the style of Shakespear, Othello is a play written by Shakespear in the style of Italian opera. It is quite peculiar among his works in this aspect. Its characters are monsters: Desdemona is a *prima donna*, with handkerchief, confidante, and vocal solo all complete; and Iago, though certainly more anthropomorphic than the Count di Luna, is only so when he slips out of his stage villain's part. Othello's transports are conveyed by a magnificent but senseless music which rages from the Propontick to the Hellespont in an orgy of thundering sound and bounding rhythm; and the plot is a pure farce plot: that is to say, it is supported on an artificially manufactured and desperately precarious trick with a handkerchief which a chance word might upset at any moment. With such a libretto, Verdi was quite at home: his success with it proves, not that he could occupy Shakespear's plane, but that Shakespear could on occasion occupy his, which is a very different matter. Nevertheless, such as Othello is, Verdi does not belittle it as Donizetti would have done, nor conventionalize it as Rossini actually did. He often rises fully to it; he transcends it in his setting of the very stagey oath of Othello and Iago; and he enhances it by a charming return to the simplicity of real popular life in the episodes of the peasants singing over the fire after the storm in the first act, and their serenade to Desdemona in the second. When one compares these choruses with the choruses of gypsies and soldiers in Il Trovatore one realizes how much Verdi gained by the loss of his power to pour forth *Il balens* and *Ah! che la mortes.*

The decay and discredit which the Verdi operas of

the Trovatore type undoubtedly brought on Italian opera in spite of their prodigious initial popularity was caused not at all by the advent of Wagner (for the decay was just as obvious before Lohengrin became familiar to us as it is now that Tristan has driven Manrico from the Covent Garden stage), but by Verdi's recklessness as to the effect of his works on their performers. Until Boïto became his artistic conscience he wrote inhumanly for the voice and ferociously for the orchestra. The art of writing well for the voice is neither recondite nor difficult. It has nothing to do with the use or disuse of extreme high notes or low notes. Handel and Wagner, who are beyond all comparison the most skilled and considerate writers of dramatic vocal music, do not hesitate to employ extreme notes when they can get singers who possess them. But they never smash voices. On the contrary, the Handelian and Wagnerian singer thrives on his vocal exercises and lasts so long that one sometimes wishes that he would sing Il Trovatore once and die.

The whole secret of healthy vocal writing lies in keeping the normal plane of the music, and therefore the bulk of the singer's work, in the middle of the voice. Unfortunately, the middle of the voice is not the prettiest part of it; and in immature or badly and insufficiently trained voices it is often the weakest part. There is, therefore, a constant temptation to composers to use the upper fifth of the voice almost exclusively; and this is exactly what Verdi did without remorse. He practically treated that upper fifth as the whole voice, and pitched his melodies in the middle of it instead of in the middle of the entire compass, the result being a frightful strain on the singer. And this strain was not relieved, as Handel relieved his singers, by frequent rests of a bar or two and by long *ritornellos*: the voice has to keep going from one end of the song to the other. The upshot of that, except in the case of abnormally pitched voices, was displacement, fatigue, intolerable strain, shattering *tremolo*, and finally, not, as could have been wished, total annihilation, but the development of an unnatural trick of making an atrociously disagreeable noise and inflicting it on the public as Italian singing, with the result that the Italian opera singer is now execrated and banished from the boards of which he was once the undisputed master. He still imposes himself in obscure places; for, curiously enough, nothing dumbs him except wellwritten music. Handel he never attempts; but Wagner utterly destroys him; and this is why he spread the rumor through Europe that Wagner's music ruined voices.

To the unseductive bass voice, Verdi always behaved well; for since he could not make it sensuously attractive, it forced him to make the bass parts dramatically interesting. It is in Ferrando and Sparafucile, not in Charles V. and the Count di Luna, that one sees the future composer of Falstaff. As to the orchestra, until Boïto came, it was for the most part nothing but the big guitar, with the whole wind playing the tune in unison or in thirds and sixths with the singer.* I am quite sure that as far as the brass was concerned this was a more sensible system, and less harshly crushing to the singer, than the dot and dash system of using trumpets and drums, to which the German school and its pupils in England clung pedantically long after the employment of valves had made it as unnecessary as it was ugly and absurd. But beyond this, I do not feel called upon to find

* Elgar, the greatest of all orchestral technicians, maintained that the big guitar business has a genuine skilled technique, and that, for instance, such scores as Rossini's Stabat Mater, in the apparently crude and crushing accompaniment to Cujus animam, in performance sound exactly right, and help the singer instead of annihilating him. [GBS]

excuses for Verdi's pre-Boïtian handling of the orchestra. He used it unscrupulously to emphasize his immoderate demands for overcharged and superhuman passion, tempting the executants to unnatural and dangerous assumptions and exertions. It may have been exciting to see Edmund Kean revealing Shakespear "by flashes of lightning," and Robson* rivaling him in burlesque; but when the flashes turned out to be tumblers of brandy, and the two thunder-wielders perished miserably of their excesses, the last excuse for the insufferable follies and vulgarities of the would-be Keans and Robsons vanished. I speak of Kean and Robson so as not to hurt the survivors of the interregnum between Mario and de Reszke, when bawling troopers, roaring Italian porters, and strangulating Italian newspaper criers made our summer nights horrible with Verdi's *fortissimos.* Those who remember them will understand.

But in his defects, as in his efficiencies, his directness, and his practical commonsense, Verdi is a thorough unadulterated Italian. Nothing in his work needs tracing to any German source. His latter-day development of declamatory recitative can be traced back through the recitatives in Rossini's Moses right back to the beginning of Italian opera. You cannot trace a note of Wotan in Amonasro or Iago, though you can trace something of Moses in the rhythms of Wotan. The anxious northern genius is magnificently assimilative: the self-sufficient Italian genius is magnificently impervious. I doubt whether even Puccini really studies Schumann, in spite of his harmonic Schumannisms. Certainly, where you come to a strong Italian like Verdi you may be quite sure that if you cannot explain him without dragging in the great Germans, you cannot explain him at all.

* Thomas Robson (1822?–64) was a remarkable practitioner of farce and burlesque at the Olympic Theatre.

At all events, Verdi will stand among the greatest of the Italian composers. It may be that, as with Handel, his operas will pass out of fashion and be forgotten whilst the Manzoni Requiem remains his imperishable monument. Even so, that alone, like Messiah, will make his place safe among the immortals.

MUTILATED OPERA

To The Times, London, 31 May 1904

Sir,—I am loth to say a word that could hamper Mr Higgins in his plucky, but hopeless, duel with your critic.* When a gentleman explains that in announcing Don Giovanni without cuts he meant Don Giovanni with cuts, he makes his position clear; and there is nothing more to be said except to apologize for having misunderstood him.

But I have a protest to record against the implied doctrine that when a composer or dramatist is driven by circumstances to allow his work to be performed with cuts, or even to make the cuts himself sooner than trust the scissors to somebody else, he thereby publishes the mutilated score or prompt-book as a revised "version" of his work. When the Deutsches Theater of Berlin accepted for production my play entitled Cæsar and Cleopatra, I myself proposed the total omission of the third act in order to bring the performance within the customary limits of time. But I shall be greatly surprised

* A criticism on 3 May by J. A. Fuller-Maitland, the musical critic of The Times, that the Royal Opera, after announcing uncut productions, had not performed them in their entirety, resulted in extended correspondence between manager H. V. Higgins, the critic, and Times readers. Shaw here refers to Higgins's letter of 25 May.

if the Deutsches Theater announces the performance as "without cuts," and unspeakably staggered if Dr Richter describes, or allows it to be said that he describes, the performance without the third act as "the correct version."* A cut score or book is not a "version" at all; for instance, there are two versions of Beethoven's Leonore overture, No. 2 and No. 3 (No. 1 is virtually an independent work); but the old mutilation of No. 3, made at a time when it was considered too long for performance, is not a third version.

Take again Meyerbeer's Les Huguenots, always outrageously mutilated, and now performed at Covent Garden without the last act. Meyerbeer was forced to let the earlier mutilations pass because of the Procrustean tyranny of the fashionable dinner hour. But I venture to say that if he were alive now, and compelled to cut the same number of bars, he would cut the work in a very different way, sacrificing such dragged-in irrelevancies as the chorus of bathers in the third act for the sake of restoring the dramatic coherency of the third. What is performed of any opera at the opera house is only that part of it which survives from the composer's struggle with the public, always ten years behind the composer, and the *impresario,* always twenty years behind the public. To call the result "the correct version" is—well, it is what Mr Higgins accuses Dr Richter of.

No doubt the *finale* to Don Giovanni is "an anti-climax." To the many people who do not wait even for the statue scene, that is an anti-climax too. And the third part of the Messiah is an anti-climax after the Hallelujah chorus. And Bach's St Matthew Passion

* Higgins had written: "No one was induced by our prospectus to believe that we should produce the Prague version of Don Giovanni or the earlier version of Tannhäuser. They expected to hear what Dr Richter considers the correct version in each case, and they have not been disappointed."

should end with the thunder and lightning chorus. For all who sit out the mutilated last scene of Don Giovanni simply because they want to see the ghost, not only should the *finale* be cut, but the preliminary pages also; in fact, a surprisingly compact selection from the opera would satisfy them better than what they get at present. But for those to whom an *impresario* pretends to appeal when he announces Don Giovanni without cuts, and takes it out of the hands of the third-rate conductors by whom this great work has been outraged and insulted for so many years past at Covent Garden, the *finale* is not only indispensable to its integrity, but contains, in its last ecstatic *fugato,* one of the most delightful and intensely characteristic of all Mozart's personal outbursts. We never expected its restoration from Mr Higgins; why should we? But we did expect it from Dr Richter; and I hope that, if his authority is again brought into question in this correspondence, it may not be offered at second hand.

Yours truly,
G. Bernard Shaw

SUMPTUARY REGULATIONS AT THE OPERA

To The Times, London, 3 July 1905

Sir,—The opera management at Covent Garden regulates the dress of its male patrons. When is it going to do the same to the women?

On Saturday night I went to the Opera. I wore the costume imposed on me by the regulations of the house. I fully recognize the advantage of those regulations. Evening dress is cheap, simple, durable, prevents rivalry and extravagance on the part of male leaders of fashion, annihilates class distinctions, and gives men who are poor and doubtful of their social position (that is, the great majority of men) a sense of security and satisfaction that no clothes of their own choosing could confer, besides saving a whole sex the trouble of considering what they should wear on state occasions. The objections to it are as dust in the balance in the eyes of the ordinary Briton. These objections are that it is colorless and characterless; that it involves a whitening process which makes the shirt troublesome, slightly uncomfortable, and seriously unclean; that it acts as a passport for undesirable persons; that it fails to guarantee sobriety, cleanliness, and order on the part of the wearer; and that it reduces to a formula a very vital human habit which should be the subject of constant experiment and active private enterprise. All such objections are thoroughly un-English. They appeal only to an eccentric few, and may be left out of account with the fantastic objections of men like Ruskin, Tennyson, Carlyle, and Morris to tall hats.

But I submit that what is sauce for the gander is sauce for the goose. Every argument that applies to the regulation of the man's dress applies equally to the regulation of the woman's. Now let me describe what actually happened to me at the Opera. Not only was I in evening dress by compulsion, but I voluntarily added many graces of conduct as to which the management made no stipulation whatever. I was in my seat in time for the first chord of the overture. I did not chatter during the music nor raise my voice when the Opera was too loud for normal conversation. I did not get up and go out when the statue music began. My language was fairly moderate considering the number and nature of the improvements on Mozart volunteered by Signor Caruso, and the respectful ignorance of the dramatic points of the score exhibited by the conductor and the stage manager—if there is such a functionary at Covent Garden. In short, my behavior was exemplary.

At 9 o'clock (the Opera began at 8) a lady came in and sat down very conspicuously in my line of sight. She remained there until the beginning of the last act. I do not complain of her coming late and going early; on the contrary, I wish she had come later and gone earlier. For this lady, who had very black hair, had stuck over her right ear the pitiable corpse of a large white bird, which looked exactly as if someone had killed it by stamping on its breast, and then nailed it to the lady's temple, which was presumably of sufficient solidity to bear the operation. I am not, I hope, a morbidly squeamish person, but the spectacle sickened me. I presume that if I had presented myself at the doors with a dead snake round my neck, a collection of blackbeetles pinned to my shirtfront, and a grouse in my hair, I should have been refused admission. Why, then, is a woman to be allowed to commit such a public outrage? Had the lady been refused admission, as she should have been, she would have soundly rated the tradesman who imposed the disgusting headdress on her under the false pretence that "the best people" wear such things, and withdrawn her custom from him; and thus the root of the evil would be struck at; for your fashionable woman generally allows herself to be dressed according to the taste of a person whom she would not let sit down in her presence. I once, in Drury Lane Theatre, sat behind a *matinée* hat decorated with the two wings of a seagull, artificially reddened at the joints so as to produce an illusion of being freshly plucked from a live bird. But even that lady stopped short of the whole seagull. Both ladies were evidently regarded by their neighbors as ridiculous and vulgar; but that is hardly enough when the offence is one which produces a sensation of physical sickness in persons of normal humane sensibility.

I suggest to the Covent Garden authorities that, if they feel bound to protect their subscribers against the danger of my shocking them with a blue tie, they are at least equally bound to protect me against the danger of a woman shocking me with a dead bird.

Yours truly,

G. Bernard Shaw

THE BANDS OF THE SALVATION ARMY

A critical report, written for the Salvation Army on 31 March 1906; published under the caption What the Critic Had to Say, in The Musician of the Salvation Army, 3 December 1960

[U] On Saturday the 7th December 1905 I attended the musical festival at the Congress Hall, Clapton. The bands taking part were the International Staff, Regent Hall, Highgate, Chalk Farm, and Clapton. I am not a member of the Salvation Army, and am not personally acquainted with any of the members of these bands. I do not live in any of the districts they represent. I listened to their performance without any personal or local bias, exactly as in the course of my experience as a professional critic of music I have listened to some of the best professional orchestras and bands in Europe.

DISCIPLINE

In point of discipline, alertness, and conscientiousness, all the bands were first-rate. Professional orchestras never do their best unless they have a good conductor. I have repeatedly heard a vapid, absentminded, careless performance in London under a mediocre conductor, followed in the same week by a splendid performance of the very same work by the very same players under Richter or Mottl. This tendency of professional orchestral players to earn their money with as little trouble to themselves as possible does not exist in the Salvation Army, where the men are playing, not for money, but for the glory of God. All the bands did their best eagerly and enthusiastically. But mere enthusiasm could not have produced the remarkable precision and snap in their execution. They must have worked hard and been well-coached by their conductors. And there were no incompetent conductors—for instance, no gentlemen set to wield a *bâton* because they had won a musical degree at a university. The bandmasters had evidently won their places by their aptitude and efficiency.

SKILL

In point of skill there was naturally more difference between the bands. The International Staff Band was beyond criticism in this respect: it was as skilful and finished as it is possible for a band to be. The Highgate Band found some of its work, especially in the faster passages, difficult enough to make it a little excited and unsteady; but it always succeeded, though not without congratulating itself on having escaped a risk once or twice. The Chalk Farm band was surer; but the balance of tone might have been improved: the cornets overpowered the middle and lower parts, and were too strident. Cornet playing requires a good deal of self-denial if the tone is to have any charm or vocal quality; and the Chalk Farm cornet players were very zealous. The Regent Hall Band, with its well-weighted bass, was better behaved. The cornets were not too edgy, thanks, perhaps, to the excellent example of a soloist with that sweet and feminine tone which is the best a cornet can produce. The Chalk Farm soloist, also a capital player, was a born trumpeter; and the better a trumpeter is the worse example he sets to the cornets. On the whole, skill in execution was in excess rather than in defect. The surprising fluency with which *bravura* passages are executed, especially by the euphoniums, has led to an unnecessarily florid style of scoring which is often far inferior in effect to broad simple chords. It is no doubt good exercise for euphoniums to have their parts figured out into volleys of triplets, and for all the basses to finish a cadence by running down the scale in semiquavers. But exercises are not music, and should be kept out of the public performances of the bands. I respectfully suggest to the Army bandmasters that they should score their pieces solely with a view to the emotional effect of the music, and not to shew off the virtuosity of their executants.

EXPRESSION AND ARTISTIC INDIVIDUALITY

Here we come to the higher criticism. A band may be beyond all fault-finding in point of discipline, equipment, and executive skill; and yet there may be nothing to distinguish it from a first-rate professional or military band. It is not enough for a Salvation Army band to play one of its scores technically well: you have only to hand the band parts to Mr de Sousa's band or to the band of the Grenadier Guards, and they will play it equally well. But there should be an emotional difference. It should be possible for a blindfold critic to say at once which was the Salvation Army band and which was the professional. I kept this test in my mind all through the festival; and the only band which stood it quite unquestionably all through was the Clapton Band. It had the peculiar combination of brilliancy and emotional quality which is and ought to be the distinctive Salvationist musical characteristic. The other bands had it occasionally when playing favorite hymn tunes; but the Clapton band never lost it, and combined it with a joyous vivacity of style and clear jubilant tone which stamped it as *the* Salvationist band *par excellence.*

THE MUSIC

I now come to a matter of great importance on which it is impossible for me to report quite favorably. The Salvation Army very soon finds out whether a hymn is good music or not. With the exception of one insincerely pious ballad sung by a bandsman, with an ugly tune and all the characteristics of ordinary music-shop trash, the religious music was good and effective. But the Salvation Army needs not only hymns, but marches and quick-steps. And here a much purer taste and severer censorship is needed. The Chalk Farm Band began by playing a march which was rowdy to the verge of profanity. Later on the Regent Hall Band played another which, though it had a *quasi* religious title, made me feel at once as if I were in the Hippodrome. It was followed by the announcement of the Band March Competition Award; and I listened with much curiosity to the winning piece. It was a very creditable composition, neatly constructed and effectively scored. But it had absolutely no religious character. It was a military march pure and simple. Anyone hearing it at a Promenade concert, or on the pier at a fashionable seaside place, would never have suspected that it had any religious antecedents. Now the march which was judged second-best, though not so smart, had a trio in which there was an attempt at devotional feeling. The award convinced me that the view of the judges was that the Army's secular music cannot be too secular.

I venture to suggest that this view is a mistaken one. If the only alternative to thoughtlessly secular music were the solemn, churchy, joyless so-called "sacred" music, I should cordially agree that the whole success of the Army depend on its avoiding anything of that kind.

I am also quite alive to the fact that the music must not be over the heads of the people. At the Festival I sat next a laborer who had probably worked half as long again that day as any man should work at heavy physical toil: at all events he was partly stupefied with mere fatigue. If the bands had played very refined music for him—say the Priest's march from Mozart's Magic Flute, the overture to Gluck's Alceste, the Elysian Fields music from Gluck's Orpheus, or the entry to the Castle of the Grail from Wagner's Parsifal—he would have been fast asleep in three minutes. And when the Chalk Farm Band played a piece of empty but exciting circus music for him in the most violently spirited way, he woke up and was pleased, as most of the audience were. But it woke him up at the cost of switching off the current of religious enthusiasm and switching on the current of circus excitement. It woke him up very much as a tablespoonful of brandy would have woken him up. And with all its racket, which was powerfully reinforced by the low roof and the terrific clatter of the overtones set up by the instruments, it was not nearly as stirring as I'm climbing up the golden stairs to glory or When the roll is called up yonder. Music can be impetuous, triumphant, joyful, enrapturing, and very pretty into the bargain without being rowdy or empty. I know the difficulty of keeping up the necessary supply of good marches, and the danger of wearing out the best ones by too frequent repetition. But after making all allowances, I think it is a pity that the Salvation Army, which has produced a distinctive type of religious service and religious life, should not also produce a distinctive type of marching music.

SUGGESTIONS

I think that the bandmasters should make a practice of attending the best concerts of serious orchestral music, especially those at the Queen's Hall under the conductorship of Mr Henry J. Wood and the eminent foreign conductors and composers who visit us occasionally, and the Richter concerts in Manchester. They would very soon learn that the figurations into scales and triplets with which they now decorate the middle parts in their scores are too commonplace and obvious to have any real value. When they take their standards of figuration from the chaconnes of Bach and Handel instead of from each other, they will improve their style of scoring; and their example will react on the bandmasters who do not live in great cities within reach of good concerts.

Also, they will learn the value of certain band effects which they now seem to neglect altogether. They do not make half enough use of the individual character of the instruments and the way in which they can be made to relieve and contrast with each other. I longed to hear a passage for the trombones alone contrasted with a passage for the euphoniums and tubas alone, or similar contrasts between the horns and saxhorns, the trumpets and cornets, &c. They were always mixed up in the same mass of harmony. And the scorers seem to have no idea of the effect of a unison passage for a mass of wind instruments breaking finally into harmony, or of a pedal point. They harmonize all the time in the same way, using all the instruments indiscriminately. In a word, they neglect variety, though variety is far more needed in brass band playing than in orchestral playing, where the use of string and wood instruments, harps and kettledrums, &c., supplies variety and contrast almost automatically.

THE INTERNATIONAL STAFF SONGSTERS

I suggest further that the International Staff Songsters should be trained to sing without an accompaniment. If they are let alone they will sing perfectly in tune, and the touching effect produced by the contraltos will not, as at the Festival, be partly spoiled by the sopranos singing sharp and listening timidly for a harmonium which was supposed to be "supporting" them, but which was really dragging them out of tune. Their conductor should recollect that the tuning of a piano, organ, harmonium, or concertina is only a compromise; so that the instrument *cannot* be played in perfect tune as the human throat can. On the harmonium the effect of the adulterated tuning is specially bad; and the songsters will never do themselves justice until they are rid of it.

In conclusion, let me assure any officers who may read this report, and who may be unfamiliar with the few technical terms I have had to use, that I have suggested nothing that is not quite broad, popular, and easily within the reach of the bands—a simplification, in fact, rather than an elaboration. Also, since it is inevitable in a report of this kind that remediable defects should occupy a larger space and be more energetically pointed out than successes accomplished, I ask the Army officers to remember that I make this report privately, and that in my public references to the music of the Army I have expressed myself in terms of unqualified admiration for its achievements. [U]

STRAUSS AND HIS ELEKTRA

Although the royal obsequies for Edward VII in May 1910 provided Londoners with their most spectacular show of the year, these were rivaled by two controversial events of the first magnitude: Roger Fry's exhibit of Manet and the Post-Impressionists at the Grafton Galleries and the opera season conducted by Thomas Beecham at Covent Garden, highlighted by the first British production of

Richard Strauss's Elektra. At the opening performance on 19 February, we are told, "the excitement of musical London rose to fever-pitch; fantastic prices were offered for seats, and a packed audience, that included the King and Queen and other members of the royal family... greeted the performance with immense enthusiasm." At the end of the evening there were prolonged ovations for Edyth Walker (Elektra), Hermann Weidemann (Orest), Anna Bahr-Mildenburg (Klytemnestra), and Frances Rose (Chrysothemis), "and Beecham was presented with a laurel wreath." (Herbert Van Thal, in Ernest Newman, Testament of Music, 1962.)

On 26 February Ernest Newman published a minority report in The Nation which Bernard Shaw considered to be not only harsh but ill-judged and unreasonable. The result was a memorable correspondence between the two men in the pages of The Nation. Reproduced below is Newman's original article in full, followed by the complete correspondence as published between 12 March and 9 April 1910.

I

26 February 1910

Judging from the tone of a number of last Monday's articles, our musical critics, as a whole, are still a little doubtful as to the propriety of saying what they must really feel about Strauss. They cannot possibly like a great part of what they hear, but at the back of their heads is the thought that, as Wagner was abused by the critics of his own day for extravagances that time has shown to be no extravagances at all, so time may show that Strauss was right in *his* extravagances, and that the critics who objected to them were wrong. So a number of the prudent gentlemen stay the flood of ridicule that is almost on their lips, and, instead, talk darkly of the future showing what it will show, and utter other safe commonplaces. All the while there is no real comparison between the Wagnerian case and the Straussian. All new music, from the mere fact that it *is* new, is apt to be misunderstood, and an idiom may seem wild or incoherent merely because we are not yet accustomed to it. But because the human ear has sometimes disliked a new thing and afterwards liked it, it does not follow that it will some day like everything that today it cordially dislikes.

There are other things to be considered, and one of these is the fact that nowadays we are much better placed than our fathers were for judging new music accurately. They had, for the most part, to listen to it without the slightest previous knowledge of it, and to express an opinion upon it probably after one hearing of the work. In these days we can generally study the score of the work long before we hear it. To talk of hearing Elektra for the first time on Saturday last is nonsensical. The vocal score has been at our service for twelve months or more, and it was open to any critic to have it by heart before he went into Covent Garden on Saturday. A piano arrangement, it is true, does not tell us all about a complex modern work; but it tells us a great deal, and with that knowledge we can listen to a first performance on the stage in a better state of preparation than the Wagnerian critics could do at a tenth performance. All this critical timidity, then, is not very creditable. Anyone who had taken the trouble to study the score of Elektra could easily gather from Saturday's performance whether the parts he had marked out as requiring elucidation sounded as bad as he had expected them to do, or better. And, after the performance, he should be quite able to relieve posterity of the trouble of making up his mind for him on nine points out of ten. Anyhow, it would be better to make the attempt.

All but the Strauss fanatics will admit that, though he is undoubtedly the greatest living musician, there is a strong strain of foolishness and ugliness in him, that he is lacking in the sensitive feeling for the balance of a large work that some other great artists have, and that consequently there is not one large work of his, from Don Quixote onward, that is not marred by some folly or some foolery. If it were not for this strain of coarseness and thoughtlessness in him, he would never have taken up so crude a perversion of the old Greek story as that of Hugo von Hofmannsthal. One does not in the least object to a modern poet looking at ancient figures through modern eyes, so long as he can see them convincingly and make them live for us. But to make a play a study of human madness, and then to lay such excessive stress upon the merely physical concomitants of madness, is to ask us to tune our notions of dramatic terror and horror down to too low a pitch. Strauss, of course, revels in this physical, and therefore more superficial, side of the madness, with the result that, instead of impressing us, he generally either bores us or amuses us. We have only to look at a pathological study of human morbidity such as Dostoievsky gives us in Crime and Punishment, so fine, so unobtrusively true to life, and then listen to the vulgar din by which Strauss tries to convey to us that a woman's brain is distraught, to realize the difference between a man of genius and one who, for the moment, has become merely a man of talent.

For the real complaint against the excited music in Elektra is that it mostly does not excite you at all; you are rather sorry, in fact, that the composer should take so much trouble to be a failure. For he is so violent that, as a rule, you cannot believe in the least in his violence.

He has the besetting Teutonic sin of overstatement, of being unable to see that the half is often greater than the whole; and all this blacking of his face and waving of his arms, and howling "bolly-golly-black-man—boo!" at us leaves us quite unmoved, except to smile and wish he wouldn't do it. One could easily name a hundred passages in ancient and modern music that thrill us far more horribly, and with far simpler means, than all the clatter that breaks out when Orestes, for example, is murdering Aegisthus. The mere recollection of stories of ghosts in the churchyard, or of his own fears when, as a child, he was left alone in a dark room, might have told Strauss that horror and the creeping of the flesh are not necessarily associated with noise and fury. His orchestra doth protest too much.

Nor do we need to wait for posterity to tell us that much of the music is as abominably ugly as it is noisy. Here a good deal of the talk about complexity is wide of the mark. The real term for it is incoherence, discontinuity of thinking. "The three angles of a triangle are equal to two right angles" sounds absurdly simple, but really represents a good deal of complex cerebral working; so does the G minor fugue of Bach. But "the man in the moon is the daughter of Aunt Martha's tomcat," though it sounds very complex, is incoherent nonsense; and so is a good deal of Elektra. Unfortunately, while we have obvious ways of testing the sense or nonsense of the remark about the man in the moon, it is not so easy to test the sense or nonsense of a passage of music; and so a good deal of quite confused thinking gets the credit for being hyper-subtle thinking. What awestruck worshippers call complexity in Elektra would often be more correctly described as impudence at its best and incompetence at its worst. As for the more normally lyrical pages in Elektra, there are very few of them worthy even of a smaller musician that Strauss. The first solo of Chrysothemis, for example, is merely agreeable commonplace; the theme of triumph in the *finale* is so cheap that it must have been picked up on the rubbish-heap of Italian or French opera. Nothing marks so clearly the degeneration of the musician in Strauss from what he was fifteen years ago than the average melodic writing in Elektra.

What saves the opera is, first of all, the wonderful beauty of parts of the scene between Elektra and Orestes, especially when, ceasing to be a maniac and becoming a normal woman, she pours out her soul in love for her brother. There is grandeur again—spasmodic, of course, but none the less unescapable—at a hundred points in the score. It may last merely a moment or two, and then flicker off into ugliness or commonplace, but while it is there we are mastered by it. Elektra's cry of "Agamemnon," whenever it occurs, always holds us in this way. Strauss in Elektra, indeed, is like a huge volcano spluttering forth a vast amount of dirt and murk, through which every now and then, when the fuming ceases and a breath of clear air blows away the smoke, we see the grand and strong original outlines of the mountain. And when Strauss puts forth his whole mental strength, it is indeed overwhelming. We may detest the score as a whole for its violence and frequent ugliness, but the fine things in it are of the kind that no other man, past or present, could have written—the monologue of Elektra just mentioned, for example, or the wailing themes that dominate the section preceding it, or the tense, fateful gloom of the finish of the opera. The result of it all is to give far more pain to Strauss's admirers than it can possibly do to those who have always disliked him. In spite of the pathetic way in which he wastes himself, playing now the fool, now the swashbuckler, now the trickster, you cannot be in doubt that you are listening to a man who is head and shoulders above all other living composers. One still clings to the hope that the future has in store for us a purified Strauss, clothed and in his right mind, who will help us to forget the present Strauss – a saddening mixture of genius, ranter, child, and charlatan. As it is, one would hardly venture to prophesy more than a few short years of life for Elektra, for the public will not long continue to spend an hour and three-quarters in the theatre for about half an hour's enjoyment.

Ernest Newman

II

12 March 1910

Sir,—May I, as an old critic of music, and as a member of the public who has not yet heard Elektra, make an appeal to Mr Ernest Newman to give us something about that work a little less ridiculous and idiotic than his article in your last issue? I am sorry to use [such] disparaging and apparently uncivil epithets as "ridiculous and idiotic"; but what else am I to call an article which informs us, first, that Strauss does not know the difference between music and "abominable ugliness and noise"; and, second, that he is the greatest living musician of the greatest school of music the world has produced? I submit that this is ridiculous, inasmuch as it makes us laugh at Mr Newman, and idiotic because it unhesitatingly places the judgment of the writer above that of one whom he admits to be a greater authority than himself, thus assuming absolute knowledge in the matter. This is precisely what "idiotic" means.

Pray do not let me be misunderstood as objecting to Mr Newman describing how Elektra affected him. He has not, perhaps, as much right to say that it seemed ugly and nonsensical to him (noise, applied to music, can only mean nonsense, because in any other sense, all music is noise) as Haydn had to say similar things of Beethoven's music, because Haydn was himself an eminent composer; still, he is perfectly in order in telling us honestly how ill Elektra pleased him, and not pretending he liked it lest his opinion should come to be regarded later on as we now regard his early opinion of Wagner. But he should by this time have been cured by experience and reflection of the trick that makes English criticism so dull and insolent—the trick, namely, of asserting that everything that does not please him is wrong, not only technically but ethically. Mr Newman, confessing that he did not enjoy, and could not see the sense of a good deal of Elektra, is a respectable, if pathetic, figure; but Mr Newman treating Strauss as a moral and musical delinquent, is—well, will Mr Newman himself supply the missing word, for really I cannot find one that is both adequate and considerate?

When my Candida was performed for the first time in Paris, the late Catulle Mendès was one of its critics. It affected him very much as Elektra affected Mr Newman. But he did not immediately proceed, English fashion, to demonstrate that I am a perverse and probably impotent imbecile (London criticism has not stopped short of this), and to imply that if I had submitted my play to his revision he could have shewn me how to make it perfect. He wrote to this effect: "I have seen this play. I am aware of the author's reputation, and of the fact that reputations are not to be had for nothing. I find that the play has a certain air of being a remarkable work and of having something in it which I cannot precisely seize; but I do not like it, and I cannot pretend that it gave me any sensation except one of being incommoded." Now that is what I call thoughtful and well-bred criticism, in contradistinction to ridiculous and idiotic criticism as practised in England. Mr

Newman has no right to say that Elektra is absolutely and objectionably ugly, because it is not ugly to Strauss and his admirers. He has no right to say that it is incoherent nonsense, because such a statement implies that Strauss is mad, and that Hofmannsthal and Mr Beecham, with the artists who are executing the music, and the managers who are producing it, are insulting the public by offering them the antics of a lunatic as serious art. He has no right to imply that he knows more about Strauss's business technically than Strauss himself. These restrictions are no hardship to him; for nobody wants him to say any of these things: they are not criticism; they are not good manners nor good sense; and they take up the space that is available in the Nation for criticism proper; and criticism proper can be as severe as the critic likes to make it. There is no reason why Mr Newman should not say with all possible emphasis—if he is unlucky enough to be able to say truly—that he finds Strauss's music disagreeable and cacophonous; that he is unable to follow its harmonic syntax; that the composer's mannerisms worry him; and that, for his taste, there is too much restless detail, and that the music is over-scored (too many notes, as the Emperor said to Mozart). He may, if he likes, go on to denounce the attractiveness of Strauss's music as a public danger, like the attraction of morphia; and to diagnose the cases of Strauss and Hofmannsthal as psychopathic or neurasthenic, or whatever the appropriate scientific slang may be, and descant generally on the degeneracy of the age in the manner of Dr Nordau.* Such diagnoses,

* Dr Max Nordau, a German physician, was the author of Degeneration (1892–3), which sought to prove a link between genius and degeneracy. Shaw's reply, A Degenerate's View of Nordau, monopolized virtually the entire issue of Liberty (New York), 27 July 1895. It was later revised as The Sanity of Art (1908).

when supported by an appeal to the symptoms made with real critical power and ingenuity, might be interesting and worth discussing. But this lazy petulance which has disgraced English journalism in the forms of anti-Wagnerism, anti-Ibsenism, and, long before that, anti-Handelism (now remembered only by Fielding's contemptuous reference to it in Tom Jones); this infatuated attempt of writers of modest local standing to talk *de haut en bas* to men of European reputation, and to dismiss them as intrusive lunatics, is an intolerable thing, an exploded thing, a foolish thing, a parochial boorish thing, a thing that should be dropped by all good critics and discouraged by all good editors as bad form, bad manners, bad sense, bad journalism, bad politics, and bad religion. Though Mr Newman is not the only offender, I purposely select his article as the occasion of a much needed protest, because his writings on music are distinguished enough to make him worth powder and shot. I can stand almost anything from Mr Newman except his posing as Strauss's governess; and I hope he has sufficient sense of humor to see the absurdity of it himself, now that he has provoked a quite friendly colleague to this yell of remonstrance.

Yours, &c.,

G. Bernard Shaw

III

12 March 1910

Sir,—A lady once asked Mr Shaw to dine with her. Mr Shaw's answer was "Certainly not: what have I done to provoke this attack on my well-known morals?" or words to that effect. The lady's telegram in reply was as effective as it was quiet: "Know nothing about your

morals, but hope they are better than your manners."*
I, too, hope so; for Mr Shaw's manners, judging from this letter of his, are getting almost as bad as his logic. If I were to respond to his "appeal" to me in a spirit similar to his own, I should appeal to him not to talk so dogmatically and offensively of things he knows nothing about—for he confesses that he has not yet heard Elektra—and to control his bad temper and his vanity to a degree that will save him from too gross a parody of the case he is attacking—one does not expect, of course, too much from the man who has written about Shakespeare and other people as Mr Shaw has done. I nowhere said that Strauss did not know the difference between abominable ugliness and noise, or that he is "the greatest living musician of the greatest school of music the world has produced." Mr Shaw plainly does not know the difference between what he reads and what he dreams. To say that a man at times writes ugly music does not imply that at other times he cannot write beautiful music; and to say that Strauss's large and wonderful previous output, plus the wonderful passages of Elektra, prove him to be the greatest of living composers (the "greatest school of music, &c. &c.," is the product of Mr Shaw's own hectic imagination) is not inconsistent with the opinion that in recent years Strauss has sometimes done vulgar and stupid and ugly things. I hope this is clear, even to Mr Shaw.

I shall be happy to discuss Elektra with Mr Shaw when he knows something about it; and to discuss the general problem of aesthetic judgment with him when he shows some appreciation of the real difficulties of it.

* This is a misquotation of Shaw's "[W]hat have I done to provoke such an attack on my well-known habit?" in response to a luncheon invitation. See The Reminiscences of Lady Randolph Churchill (1908); she was the hostess.

For a man who is always at such pains to inform the world that he is cleverer than most people, he really talks very foolishly—if I may be permitted to copy his own style of adverb. It is wrong for me to object to some of Strauss's music, even after careful study of it; but it is quite right of Mr Shaw to say I am wrong, while confessing that he himself has not heard Elektra! But Mr Shaw's logic was always peculiar. Look at some of the delightful deductions he draws from my article. I said that there was a lot of incoherent and discontinuous thinking in the opera. From this plain ground the industrious Mr Shaw raises the following wonderful crop, which he puts to my credit: (1) Strauss is mad, (2) Elektra is the "antics of a lunatic," (3) Mr Beecham and the singers and the orchestra are insulting the public by performing it. Prodigious logician! How does he do it? Mr Shaw's ingenious theory is that I don't like some of Strauss's music because I can't follow it—his "harmonic syntax," for example. My objection to passages of this kind is not that they are opaque to my poor mind, but too transparent; and my general objection, as a musician, to some of Strauss's later themes and his combinations of them is that they are so ridiculously easy to write. But perhaps I am taking Mr Shaw and his outburst too seriously. I quite agree with him that his letter— so rich in knowledge, so admirable in reasoning, so perfect in taste, so urbane in style!—should teach the musical critics something, even if only in the way that the language and the antics of the drunken helots were held to be useful for teaching the Spartan youths the advantages of sobriety.

Yours &c.,

Ernest Newman

IV

19 March 1910

Sir,—It is our good fortune to have produced in Professor Gilbert Murray a writer and scholar able to raise the Electra of Euripides from the dead and make it a living possession for us. Thanks to him, we know the poem as if it were an English one. But nothing Professor Murray can do can ever make us feel quite as the Electra of Euripides felt about her mother's neglect to bury her father properly after murdering him. A heroine who feels that to commit murder, even husband murder, is a thing that might happen to anybody, but that to deny the victim a proper funeral is an outrage so unspeakable that it becomes her plain filial duty to murder her mother in expiation, is outside that touch of nature that makes all the ages akin: she is really too early-Victorian. To us she is more unnatural than Clytemnestra or Egisthus; and, in the end, we pity them and secretly shrink from their slayers. What Hofmannsthal and Strauss have done is to take Clytemnestra and Egisthus, and by identifying them with everything that is evil and cruel, with all that needs must hate the highest when it sees it, with hideous domination and coercion of the higher by the baser, with the murderous rage in which the lust for a lifetime of orgiastic pleasure turns on its slaves in the torture of its disappointment and the sleepless horror and misery of its neurasthenia, to so rouse in us an overwhelming flood of wrath against it and ruthless resolution to destroy it, that Electra's vengeance becomes holy to us; and we come to understand how even the gentlest of us could wield the axe of Orestes or twist our firm fingers in the black hair of Clytemnestra to drag back her head and leave her throat open to the stroke.

That was a task hardly possible to an ancient Greek, and not easy even to us who are face to face with the America of the Thaw case,* and the European plutocracy of which that case was only a trifling symptom. And that is the task which Hofmannsthal and Strauss have achieved. Not even in the third scene of Das Rheingold, or in the Klingsor scenes in Parsifal, is there such an atmosphere of malignant and cancerous evil as we get here. And that the power with which it is done is not the power of the evil itself, but of the passion that detests and must and finally can destroy that evil, is what makes the work great, and makes us rejoice in its horror.

Whoever understands this, however vaguely, will understand Strauss's music, and why on Saturday night the crowded house burst into frenzied shoutings, not merely of applause, but of strenuous assent and affirmation, as the curtain fell. That the power of conceiving it should occur in the same individual as the technical skill and natural faculty needed to achieve its complete and overwhelming expression in music, is a stroke of the rarest good fortune that can befall a generation of men. I have often said, when asked to state the case against the fools and money changers who are trying to drive us into a war with Germany, that the case consists of the single word, Beethoven. Today, I should say with equal confidence, Strauss. That we should make war on Strauss and the heroic warfare and aspiration that he represents is treason to humanity. In this music-drama

* Harry K. Thaw in 1906 had murdered the famed architect Stanford White for sexual attentions paid to Thaw's showgirl wife Evelyn Nesbitt. A sensational court case followed, in which the millionaire defendant was adjudged to be insane.

Strauss has done for us just what he has done for his own countrymen: he has said for us, with an utterly satisfying force, what all the noblest powers of life within us are clamoring to have said, in protest against and defiance of the omnipresent villainies of our civilization; and this is the highest achievement of the highest art.

It was interesting to compare our conductor, the gallant Beecham, bringing out the points in Strauss's orchestration, until sometimes the music sounded like a concerto for six drums, with Strauss himself bringing out the meaning and achieving the purpose of his score so that we forgot that there was an orchestra there at all, and could hear nothing but the conflict and storm of passion. Human emotion is a complex thing: there are moments when our feeling is so deep and our ecstasy so exalted that the primeval monsters from whom we are evolved wake within us and utter the strange tormented cries of their ancient struggles with the Life Force. All this is in Elektra; and under the *bâton* of Strauss the voices of these epochs are kept as distinct in their unity as the parts in a Bach motet. Such colossal counterpoint is a counterpoint of all the ages; not even Beethoven in his last great Mass comprehended so much. The feat is beyond all verbal description: it must be heard and felt; and even then, it seems, you must watch and pray, lest your God should forget you, and leave you to hear only "abominable ugliness and noise," and, on remonstrance, lead you to explain handsomely that Strauss is "vulgar, and stupid, and ugly" only "sometimes," and that this art of his is so "ridiculously easy" that nothing but your own self-respect prevents you from achieving a European reputation by condescending to practise it.

So much has been said of the triumphs of our English singers in Elektra that I owe it to Germany to profess my admiration of the noble beauty and power of Frau Fassbender's Elektra. Even if Strauss's work were the wretched thing poor Mr Newman mistook it for, it would still be worth a visit to Covent Garden to see her wonderful death dance, which was the climax of one of the most perfect examples yet seen in London of how, by beautiful and eloquent gesture, movement, and bearing, a fine artist can make not only her voice, but her body, as much a part of a great music-drama as any instrument in the score. The other German artists, notably Frau Bahr-Mildenburg, shewed great power and accomplishment; but they have received fuller acknowledgment, wheras we should not have gathered from the reports that Frau Fassbender's performance was so extraordinary as it actually was. A deaf man could have watched her with as little sense of privation as a blind man could have listened to her. To those of us who are neither deaf nor blind nor anti-Straussian critics (which is the same thing), she was a superb Elektra.

Whatever may be the merits of the article which gave rise to the present correspondence, it is beyond question that it left the readers of the Nation without the smallest hint that the occasion was one of any special importance, or that it was at all worth their while to spend time and money in supporting Mr Beecham's splendid enterprise, and being present on what was, in fact, a historic moment in the history of art in England, such as may not occur again within our lifetime. Many persons may have been, and possibly were, prevented by that article from seizing their opportunity, not because Mr Newman does not happen to like Strauss's music, but because he belittled the situation by so miscalculating its importance that he did not think it worth even the effort of criticizing it, and dismissed it in a notice in which nothing was studied except his deliberate contemptuous insolence to the composer. It would have been an additional insult to Strauss to have waited to hear Elektra before protesting, on the plainest grounds of international courtesy and artistic good faith, against such treatment of the man who shares with Rodin the enthusiastic gratitude and admiration of the European republic, one and indivisible, of those who understand the highest art. But now that I have heard Elektra, I have a new duty to the readers of the Nation, and that is to take upon me the work Mr Newman should have done, and put them in possession of the facts.

And now, Ernest, "*Triff noch einmal!*"* Yours &c.,

G. Bernard Shaw

V

26 March 1910

Sir,—Mr Shaw's second letter makes argument with him more possible than the first did. He himself aptly described that as a yell; and discussion with Mr Shaw while he is merely yelling is too much like arguing with a locomotive whistle in full blast. But now that Mr Shaw's manner has lost something of its blend of the patronizing pedagogue and the swaggering bully, we can get more directly to the real matter in hand.

My offence, it seems, is a triple one. (1) I wrote an article upon Elektra in my own way and from my own standpoint, instead of first finding out the way and the standpoint of Mr Shaw, and writing accordingly. This, I own, was unpardonable, and I apologize for it. (2) I took a wrong view of Strauss and Elektra. (3) In expressing this view, I necessarily made use of language that was not always complimentary to Strauss. Let us first look at No. 2.

* Strike again: the cry of Elektra to Orestes as he kills Clytemnestra.

Mr Shaw has now heard Elektra, and he pronounces it very good. I know that this authoritative announcement ought to be enough; but I am still so perverse as to maintain that parts of Elektra are very ugly, and other parts of it a failure. I repeat that there are abundant signs in it of the development of the bad elements that have spoiled so much of Strauss's work during the last few years—ugly, slap-dash vocal writing, which he attempts to carry through by means of orchestral bravado, a crude pictorialism, ineffective violence simulating strength, a general coarsening of the tissue of the music, a steady deterioration in invention, especially on the melody side. Mr Shaw performs an enthusiastic fantasia upon von Hofmannsthal's drama, which, to my mind and the mind of many others, is—beauty of diction apart—a most unpleasant specimen of that crudity and physical violence that a certain school of modern German artists mistakes for intellectual and emotional power. In setting this violence to music, Strauss tries to out-Herod Herod.

I should not blame him so much for this, if the things were only well done. In Salome the subject is a trifle unpleasant, but Strauss has given us a marvellous study of the diseased woman's mind. My complaint against Elektra is that he frequently fobs us off with the merest make-believe. The music (I am speaking, of course, of the bad parts of it now) does not itself cut to the roots of the characters as that of Salome does; Strauss tries to bluff us partly by the tumult of his orchestration and partly by the easy pathos of the theatre. I have no objection to Mr Shaw being bluffed in this way; but I am not going to be bluffed myself by means so transparent. Mr Shaw, in his desperate attempt to justify the ways of Shaw to men, actually tells us that "on Saturday night the crowded house burst into frenzied shoutings, not merely of applause, but of strenuous assent and affirmation, as the curtain fell." The spectacle of Mr Shaw bringing up the opinion of a British audience on a point of art as a support for his own is delicious. Oh, Bernard, Bernard, has it come to this? May not that applause be accounted for in another way? One curious feature of these Elektra performances has been that while many advanced musicians, real admirers of Strauss, have been chilled by the work, the general public has been enthusiastic over it. I take this to be due, roughly speaking, to two causes. Some people have been swept off their feet by the first excitement of the thing; others have been astonished and delighted to find that, so far from the Strauss idiom being so advanced and recondite as they had been led to believe, many of the tunes, such as that of Chrysothemis and that of the final triumph, are of the most friendly and accommodating commonplace.

I ask Mr Shaw to look at the latter theme, on p. 238 of the score, and tell me honestly whether it is not banality itself. It is fit only for third-rate French or Italian opera; you can hear the same kind of tune on the band in the park any Saturday. And, thinking that a theme of this kind is utterly unworthy of Strauss, I have every right to say so. I have a right, again, to speak of the "impudence" of the attempt to bamboozle me into the belief that great music is going on in the orchestra when I know that it is only the big drum banging, or some trick of orchestration sending a shudder under my skin. I have a right to speak of "incompetence" when a composer makes a tremendous show of rising to the supremest heights of a situation, and, in spite of all his mouthing and his violence, falls as far below it as Strauss does in the ineffective noise that accompanies Elektra's digging-up of the axe, or murder of Aegisthus. (*Technical* incompetence I never urged against Strauss, as Mr Shaw seems to think.) I have a right to say that pages such as 36–40, or 53–56 (there are many others like them) are an unblushing evasion of the problem of thinking coherently and continuously in music. I hold, in a word, that much of Elektra is merely frigid intellectual calculation simulating a white heat of emotion.

I find that Mr Shaw once expressed, apropos of Marlowe, the very point I would make here: Marlowe, he says, is "itching to frighten other people with the superstitious terrors and cruelties in which he does not himself believe, and wallowing in blood, violence, muscularity of expression and strenuous animal passion, as only literary men do when they become thoroughly depraved by solitary work, sedentary cowardice, and starvation of the sympathetic centres."* Precisely. I would explain the bogus passion and bogus hysterics of a good deal of Strauss's later music in the same way. He drives furiously at us, with all his enormous cerebral energy and his stupendous technique; but at heart he is cold, for all the whipping and spurring. He reminds me, in moments like these, of the beggars who simulate epilepsy in the streets, producing the foaming at the mouth by chewing a piece of soap. I have no objection to the sympathetic and trustful Mr Shaw believing the fit to be a real one; but he really must not lose his temper because, having learned some of the tricks of the trade, I assure him that I can see the soap.

And now for No. 3. Mr Shaw heatedly objected to the tone of some of my criticism of Strauss. It was "neither good manners" (Mr Shaw is our leading authority on manners) "nor good sense" for "writers of modest local standing to talk *de haut en bas* to men of European reputation"; it was an "intolerable thing, an exploded thing, a parochial, boorish thing," and Heaven only

* "The Spacious Times," in the Saturday Review, 11 July 1896.

knows what else. Very good; but who is this purist who yells so deafeningly for moderation in criticism? Let us look for a moment at a few passages of Mr Shaw's own that he appears to have forgotten. He has lately called Schubert a mere confectioner. He once called Marlowe a fool—"the fellow was a fool." Unless my memory is greatly at fault, he once called Shakespeare an idiot—though I will accept Mr Shaw's correction here if I am wrong. But he certainly wrote that Cymbeline "is for the most part stagey trash of the lowest melodramatic order, in parts abominably written, throughout intellectually vulgar, and, judged in point of thought by modern intellectual standards, vulgar, foolish, offensive, indecent, and exasperating beyond all tolerance."

Again, the same poor Shakespeare, "in his efforts to be a social philosopher," can only "rise for an instant to the level of a sixth-rate Kingsley"; but Mr Shaw cannot stand "his moral platitudes, his jingo claptraps, his tavern pleasantries, his bombast and drivel, his incapacity for following up the scraps of philosophy he stole so aptly," nor "his usual incapacity for pursuing any idea." He tells us frankly that his own Cæsar and Cleopatra is an improvement on Shakespeare. In fact, says Mr Shaw, "With the single exception of Homer, there is no eminent writer, not even Sir Walter Scott, whom I can despise so entirely as I despise Shakespeare when I measure my mind against his."* Some unkind people might say that this was a case of a writer of modest standing talking to a man of European reputation *de haut en bas.* Shakespeare's reputation, I fancy, is European; and if I say nothing about the modest local

* All of the foregoing Shaw quotations are drawn from Saturday Review drama criticisms: "The Spacious Times," 11 July 1896; Blaming the Bard, 26 September 1896; Toujours Shakespear, 5 December 1896.

standing, it is solely because I hesitate to incur the responsibility of mentioning modesty and Mr Bernard Shaw in the same sentence.

I know what he will say to this—that all these dicta of his upon Shakespeare were based upon a study of his drama, and that while blaming Shakespeare for many things he praised him for others. But that is exactly my attitude towards Strauss. If, then, it is right for Mr Shaw, it cannot be wrong for me; if it is wrong for me, it cannot be right for him. At all events, if he is going to set out to prove the contrary he will need a better equipment than a penful of scurrilous impertinence and a disgracefully bad memory for his own past.

Yours, &c.,

Ernest Newman

VI

2 April 1910

Sir,—Mr Shaw, by talking at such length about von Hofmannsthal's drama, has switched this discussion on to a side track; and "H.W.M.'s" article* in last week's Nation, acute and illuminative as it is on the literary points it touches, shows the necessity of bringing the discussion back to its starting-point. To myself and hundreds of other people there is a good deal that is crude and melodramatic in von Hofmannsthal's play. He is not content, for example, with having Aegisthus slaughtered at one window, but must needs have the poor man chased to another window and the agony prolonged there—for all the world, as one American

* H. W. Massingham wrote on Elektra as a play in The Nation for 26th March 1910, signed with his initials.

critic put it, like a bullock in a Chicago stock-yard. But if other people like this and similar melodramatic effects, I am quite content that they should. My concern is not with the drama, but with the music. Surely the real question is not "What kind of a drama has von Hofmannsthal written?" but "What kind of music has Strauss written?" It is the music alone that will save the opera or damn it, as history abundantly proves. Fifty composers have set Goethe's Faust to music; but the greatness of the drama has not sufficed to save fortyfive of these works from destruction. And if Smith writes another Faust tomorrow, the literary critics may rhapsodize as they please about Goethe's genius; but if Smith's music is not good his work will not have the ghost of a chance of keeping the stage. The Elektra question, then, is purely a musical one. My article, indeed, was entitled "Strauss and his Elektra": it was Strauss the musician that I mostly fell foul of; and it was for daring to speak in that way of Strauss as a musician that Mr Shaw got so absurdly angry with me. Now, are we not all more likely to come to some kind of agreement on the matter if we make sure that we are all talking about the same thing?

Let me put my own position in a nutshell. No one admires the bulk of Strauss's work more than I do. But it seems to me indisputable that for some years now his musical faculty has been deteriorating. The first sure signs of this were to be seen in certain parts of the Symphonia Domestica. In Elektra I hold it to be most marked. It takes four main forms. (1) Instead of getting to the very heart of the situation in his music, as he used to do, he is inclined to illustrate the mere externals of it; hence the facile and foolish pictorialism of such things as the "slippery blood" motive in Elektra or the orchestral delineations of Clytemnestra's jewels, the sacrificial procession, and so on. He sometimes does wonders of virtuosity in this way with the orchestra, but it is all as far from real music as a pianist's or violinist's display of technique for technique's sake can be. (2) He is degenerating into a bad and careless builder. Mr Shaw may object to the phrase, but I repeat that it is ridiculously easy to put a score together as Strauss now does for pages at a time—flinging out a leading motive of three or four bars' length, and then padding unblushingly for twenty or thirty bars until another salient motive can be introduced. (2) He is often downright ugly. There were some shocking examples of this in the Symphonia Domestica. In Elektra I do not know who would not call the opening scene ugly; even Mr Kalisch,* the most loyal Straussian in England, wrote that a second hearing did not alter his view that the music was "needlessly ugly." (4) His thematic invention is sometimes positively wretched now. This may not be so evident to one who hears Elektra for the first time, with all the excitement of the stage action and the orchestration to distract him, as it will be when he knows the music better. Thus "H.W.M." speaks of being carried off his feet as the opera swept to its end. I venture to say that when he has played through the final scene a hundred times, as I have done during the past twelve months, he will be appalled at the banality of the bulk of it; even the theme of the "recognition" is spoiled. He will hardly know whether to laugh or cry—laugh at the barrel-organ jingle of some of the themes, or cry that a man like Strauss should have sunk so low. The solo of Chrysothemis is even worse in parts—let anyone, for example, play or sing pages 45 and 50–51 half a dozen

* Alfred Kalisch, who at this time was, by Shavian coincidence, musical critic of The Star and of The World, was the translator into English of Elektra and several other Strauss operas.

times, and say if a tune like this is fit for anything but musical comedy or the music halls. It is thus not a case, as Mr Shaw imagines, of Strauss's art rushing ahead and myself being too slow to follow, but of his art worsening in quality and my declining to call five shillings a sovereign. It is not a case of the Wagner of Lohengrin developing into the Wagner of Tristan, and so thinking far ahead of his old admirers, but of the Wagner of Tristan being smitten with a withered hand and degenerating every now and then into the melodic banalities of Rienzi. There is great stuff in Elektra—the recognition scene, for instance, and a score or two of isolated pages here and there; but there is much that is mere orchestral bunkum—if I may use that word—and much that is downright commonplace.

And who are they who are most conscious of these things? Not the non-Straussians, but those who of old took Strauss for their leader! He began as a genius, as Bülow said of Mendelssohn, and is ending as a talent. If Mr Shaw was dying to strike a blow for Strauss he should have done it years ago, when Strauss was worth fighting for; but to sing his praises now, when he has lost half the power, the originality, the resource, the fund of genuine feeling that made him so great, reminds me of the people in Mark Twain's story* who valorously broke their night's rest, as they thought, to see the sunrise on the Rigi, and only discovered when the other people in the hotel were laughing at them that they had overslept themselves, and it was the sunset they were watching.

Yours, &c.,

Ernest Newman

* A Tramp Abroad (1880), Chapter XXVIII.

VII

2 April 1910

Sir,—Just a last word with Mr Newman. I make no apology for bullying him: the result has justified me. I leave it to your readers to say whether I have not wakened him up beneficially, as well as put a very different complexion on the case of Strauss and Elektra. The anti-Strauss campaign was so scandalous that it was clear somebody had to be bullied; and I picked out Mr Newman because he was much better able to take care of himself than any of the rest. Most of them I could not have attacked at all: as well strike a child or intimidate an idiot.

I will now repeat my amusing performance of knocking Mr Newman down flat with a single touch. He asks me, concerning a certain theme in Elektra to look at it honestly and tell him whether it is not banality itself. Certainly it is. And now will Mr Newman turn to the hackneyed little "half close" out of which Handel made the Hallelujah Chorus, and tell me honestly whether it is not—and was not even in Handel's own time—ten times as banal as the Chrysothemis motif? Strange how these men of genius will pick up a commonplace out of the gutter and take away our breath with it; and how, as they grow older and more masterful, any trumpery diatonic run, or such intervals of the common chord as have served the turn of thousands of postboys, dead and alive, will serve their turn, too!

Fancy trying that worn-out banality gambit on an old hand like me!

Now for Mr Newman's final plea, with its implicit compliment to myself, which I quite appreciate. That plea is that he did to Strauss only as I did to Shakespear. Proud as I am to be Mr Newman's exemplar, the cases are not alike. If the day should ever dawn in England on a Strauss made into an idol; on an outrageous attribution to him of omniscience and infallibility; on a universal respect for his reputation accompanied by an ignorance of his works so gross that the most grotesque mutilations and travesties of his scores will pass without protest as faithful performances of them; on essays written to shew how Clytemnestra was redeemed by her sweet womanly love for Egisthus, and Elektra a model of filial piety to all middle-class daughters; on a generation of young musicians taught that they must copy all Strauss's progressions and rhythms and instrumentation, and all the rest of it if they wished to do high-class work; in short, on all the follies of Bardolatry transferred to Strauss, then I shall give Mr Newman leave to say his worst of Strauss, were it only for Strauss's own sake. But that day has not yet dawned. The current humbug is all the other way. The geese are in full cackle to prove that Strauss is one of themselves instead of the greatest living composer. I made war on the duffers who idolized Shakespear. Mr Newman took the side of the duffers who are trying to persuade the public that Strauss is an impostor making an offensive noise with an orchestra of marrow-bones and cleavers. It is not enough to say that I scoffed, and therefore I have no right to complain of other people scoffing. Any fool can scoff. The serious matter is which side you scoff at. Scoffing at pretentious dufferdom is a public duty; scoffing at an advancing torchbearer is a deadly sin. The men who praised Shakespear in my time were mostly the men who would have stoned him had they been his contemporaries. To praise him saved them the trouble of thinking; got them the credit of correct and profound opinions; and enabled them to pass as men of taste when they explained that

Ibsen was an obscene dullard. To expose these humbugs and to rescue the real Shakespear from them, it was necessary to shatter their idol. It has taken the iconoclasm of three generations of Bible smashers to restore Hebrew literature to us, after three hundred years of regarding the volume into which it was bound as a fetish and a talisman; and it will take as many generations of Shakespear smashers before we can read the plays of Shakespear with as free minds as we read the Nation.

Besides, what I said about Shakespear, startling as it was to all the ignoramuses, was really the classical criticism of him. That criticism was formulated by Dr Johnson in what is still the greatest essay on Shakespear yet written. I did not read it until long after my campaign against Bardolatry in the Saturday Review; and I was gratified, though not at all surprised, to find how exactly I had restated Johnson's conclusions.

Yours, &c.,

G. Bernard Shaw

(On the broader issue raised here, is not the trouble precisely this: that Mr Shaw appears to claim for himself the possession of a perfect criterion for distinguishing "duffers" and "torchbearers" and for naming other persons qualified to perform the same task of discrimination? Ed., The Nation).

VIII

9 April 1910

Sir,—As Mr Shaw has said his last word in this pleasant little controversy, may I now say mine? I should not like to lose this opportunity of thanking Mr Shaw for his lucid explanation of the difference between my criticism of Strauss and his of Shakespeare. The thing is now simplicity itself. Artists, it seems, fall into two categories—the "duffers" and the "torchbearers." You can be as rude as you like to the former, but must be very polite to the latter. But how to know which is which? How to know whether we should bless a given artist for a torchbearer or damn him for a duffer? That, also, is simplicity itself: find out on which side Mr Shaw is, and bless or damn accordingly. "Any fool," as he wisely says, "can scoff; the serious matter is which side you scoff at." The necessity of being on the right side is self-evident; therefore, when in doubt, write or wire to Mr Shaw. (Telegraphic address: "Infallibility," London.)

"He knows about it all; HE KNOWS; HE KNOWS."

And now, just a word on what he calls his amusing performance of knocking me down with a single touch. He has looked at the passage in Elektra to which I drew his attention, and he agrees with me that it is banality itself. But, he says, "strange how these men of genius will pick up a commonplace out of the gutter and take away our breath with it"—instancing Handel. I am sure that on reflection Mr Shaw will see how confused his thinking is here. What he has in his mind is the way in which a great composer will sometimes take an apparently insignificant germ-theme and work it up into wonderful music; as Beethoven does, for example, with the very plain theme of four bars' length that opens the Eighth Symphony, or the mere G and E flat that form the basis of most of the first movement of the Fifth Symphony. No musician here would dream of quarrelling with the theme itself for being "banal" (which it is not, by the way; it is only modest). It is like the unprepossessing bulb that will some day give us the glory of form and scent and colour of the flower. I blush to have to point out to Mr Shaw that the melody to which I drew his attention is not a theme of this kind at all. It is not a germ-theme; it is a long melodic passage, meant to speak for itself there and then. It is, in fact, intended for a piece of portraiture—Elektra, according to the stage directions, dancing about "like a Mænad." And the objections to it are two—first, that it is a wretchedly cheap melody, such as no other great musician in history has ever written at the height of his career; and second, that it is hopelessly inappropriate and ineffective as a piece of characterization. This a Mænad! It is only Salvation Sal, or Jump-to-Glory-Jane.

But note that Mr Shaw, in the act of trying to palliate the banality of the theme, admits that it is banal; these great geniuses, he cries, have a way of turning to gold what they pick out of the gutter. So the theme was picked up in the gutter, was it? And the man who makes this incautious admission is the same man who a few weeks ago cursed me by all his false gods for saying that Strauss must have picked it up on a rubbish heap! Or is there some superiority of the gutter over the rubbish-heap that only Mr Shaw's subtle brain can distinguish? It is as I hinted in a previous letter. The cheap gilding on the button takes Mr Shaw in; and so he gets furious with those of us who, having fingered the button a hundred times to his once, are more conscious of the impudent brass of which it is really made. Anyhow the fact remains that on the solitary point on which Mr Shaw has come down from his sublime generalities and deigned to discuss the actual music of Elektra— which I have been vainly trying to get him to do all along—he agrees with me. I have, therefore, every reason to hope that when his knowledge of the score is a little more profound than I suspect it to be at present, he will agree with my indictment of Strauss on the other counts.

Yours, &c.,

Ernest Newman

THE REMINISCENCES OF A QUINQUAGENARIAN

Shaw's improvized address was delivered before the meeting of the Musical Association on 6 December 1910. As it "unfortunately defied verbatim reporting," Shaw provided the following report for the Proceedings, 37th Session, 1910–11. This was reprinted in The New Music Review, New York, August 1912, but the verbatim report of the ensuing discussion and of Shaw's rebuttal was omitted

A good deal of what I said need not be reported. It served its purpose of keeping the audience in good humor for the moment; and there is no reason why it should survive.

The important points were these:

That musical reminiscences are usually valueless except as anecdotage, and even at that are seldom witty unless they are also incredible. They might, however, be made really instructive and supply material for genuinely scientific treatises on art, if musical veterans, instead of mentioning that they once played a pianoforte duet with Chopin, and that the night they first heard Jenny Lind sing was the wettest they can remember, would try to recall faithfully what things in the music that was new in their time sounded strange to them, or even scandalous and intolerable. It is not easy for a musician today to confess that he once found Wagner's music formless, melodyless, and abominably discordant; but that many musicians now living did so is beyond all question. I myself was deeply interested in Wagner's music, and I supported him enthusiastically to the utmost of my opportunities; but I had to listen to his music and that of his successors for many years before I could say, as I can say now, that the overture to

Tannhäuser sounds as hackneyed, as far as its chords and progressions and modulations are concerned, as the overture to William Tell did forty years ago.

The technical history of modern harmony is a history of the growth of toleration by the human ear of chords that at first sounded discordant and senseless to the main body of contemporary professional musicians. By senseless I mean, in the case of a discord, that you cannot foresee its resolution or relate it to a key. Great composers anticipate the rank and file of us in this sort of perception, and consequently in the toleration of combinations which seem unbearable in the absence of any such perception. Musicians had to confine themselves to thirds and fifths until somebody—we used to say it was Monteverdi—ventured to pile a minor third on top of the fifth in a very cautious way, introducing the new note first as a third, fifth, or unison in the previous chord, and letting it sweeten itself into a concord again in the following one: preparation and resolution, as we call it. It took quite a long time before the battle over the toleration of this discord of the seventh was so thoroughly won that it could be exploded without preparation on an audience in any position. I can still remember the time when its last inversion—with the seventh in the bass—sounded strange and dramatically momentous, as in the first *finale* in Don Giovanni, and especially in Beethoven's early Prometheus overture, which opens with an abrupt third inversion of the seventh, *fortissimo.* By that time, however, minor ninths, then called diminished sevenths, were familiar; and Wagner's battle began with unprepared major ninths, which, joyously blared forth in the second act of Tannhäuser, sounded as scandalous as anything in Richard Strauss's Sinfonia Domestica does today. Who cares about an unprepared major ninth now, or an eleventh, or a thirteenth? Yet when you have accustomed people to these, you have conquered the whole diatonic scale, and may sound every note in it simultaneously, leaving nothing for future generations to discover but the art of making chords out of combinations of different keys, an art in which we are already making experiments.

Parallel with this line of advance goes the training of our ears and minds in alertness in passing from key to key: that is, from mood to mood. Formerly we needed to have a change of key broken to us very gently, by modulation, and even then only to a very closely related key: that is, a key consisting as nearly as possible of the same notes. As an example of the violent throwing off of such precautions, let me cite the point in the third act of Lohengrin, where the full close of the Wedding Chorus in B flat is succeeded without a note of warning by a discord belonging to the key of E natural. Nowadays this produces no effect except that of its admirable dramatic propriety. We are accustomed to such changes. We are even beginning to consider effects like the alternations of the common chords of A flat and A natural in The Ring as cheap and pretty. But I assure you that when I first heard Lohengrin I literally did not know where I was when I was flung into that sharp key out of the flat one without modulation. I thought Wagner had invented some novel and extraordinary chord, undreamt of by Mozart or even by Bach, who anticipated everybody and everything in music.

I submit that this sort of reminiscence has some real historical value. If we would all make notes of the progressions that puzzled or surprised, startled or shocked us, when we first heard them, and that we have lived to see added to the commonplaces of the music hall, we should be providing materials for a really scientific history of music, and, what is more, for a really vital way of teaching students. I do not know how they are taught now; but in my time nobody except Stainer did anything but explain that Wagner's practice was "wrong," and that everything depended on your having correct views as to the true root of the chord of the supertonic, all this nonsense about roots being the result of a wildly absurd attempt to dress up the good old rule-of-thumb thoroughbass with Helmholtz's discovery of overtones, partial tones, combination tones, and the like.

But what is of far greater importance than the theoretical instruction of the musician—for, after all, the follies of the academic treatises did not prevent academy students from writing music if they had it in them—is the question of the practical training of composers. I want to make an earnest protest against the gentleman amateur in music and all other arts. I do not deny that gentlemen amateur artists have done remarkable and even great things since artists unfortunately became gentlemen—more or less—in the XVII century. Though Hogarth was the last English painter who could boast of being a skilled tradesman until the Pre-Raphaelite revival began, yet Reynolds was a fine artist and Turner a very great one indeed, even when they daubed and smudged in a way that would have thrown Van Eyck or Memling into ecstasies of derisive laughter. Nonetheless, if a carriage builder were to daub a brougham or a house painter a hall door as crudely as most of our gentlemen painters daub their Academy pictures, he would be bankrupt in a fortnight. Have we anything analogous in the musical profession? Certainly we have. As far as I know, there is only one way in which an orchestral composer can become a really skilled tradesman, in the Van Eyck sense of the word, in this country, and that is by working in the theatre. In the theatre, when I want a piece of music for a certain purpose, I can get it. If I want it a certain length, I can get it exactly that length. If in the course of rehearsal I want it altered to suit some change in the stage business of my play, I can get the alteration made. The conductor does not say that his inspiration cannot be controled in this way, and that he must work his movement out as his genius prompts him and as its academic form demands. He does not tell me that he cannot do what I want without eight horns and four tubas, half a dozen drums and a *contra fagotto.* He has to do it with one oboe generally. He is really master of his materials, and can adapt them at a moment's notice to any set of circumstances that is at all practicable. And it is precisely because he can do these small things when other people want them that, if he has talent enough, he can do great things when he himself wants them. This is the way of the true master.

Mozart was able not only to write Don Giovanni to please himself and his friends: he was also able to sit in a tavern garden with Schikaneder* and write Die Zauberflöte just as Schikaneder wanted it for the stage, and cut it about without spoiling it when it did not fit. This did not prevent him from telling the king who complained that there were too many notes in his scores that there were just the right number, or from having his own way when he knew it was the right way. My point is that he was master of his trade and of his materials, and could do a thing in a dozen different ways and on a dozen different scales according to circumstances. If you want to know who was the greatest master of the orchestra in London in the days when I was a critic of music, I can tell you at once. It was Mr James Glover,† of Drury Lane Theatre. I tried to induce him

* Emanuel Schikaneder and Johann Georg Metzler were co-librettists of Die Zauberflöte.

† Dublin-born orchestra conductor, composer, theatre manager, musical critic for several journals, and Mayor of Bexhill.

once to write a treatise on orchestration for the benefit of those who have to arrange full concert scores for small theatre bands, and, above all, to explode the superstitions of the big standard treatises as to the limitations of wind instruments. Yet I doubt whether Mr Glover ever wasted an hour over the pages of Berlioz or Gevaërt.* You all know the drum and trumpet parts of Mozart and Beethoven—the quaint writing in dots and dashes forced on those composers by the gaps in the scale on the old horns and trumpets. I have heard these ridiculous dot and dash passages conscientiously imitated by our gentlemen amateur composers and professors when Mr Glover was not only handling his cornets with the freedom of a military bandmaster, but was producing effects of extraordinary brilliancy in the Drury Lane pantomime by filling the stage with a battery of the modern instruments known as Bach trumpets. He had also, in a ballet at the Palace Theatre, written an accompaniment for a scene representing a Channel crossing which for humor and daintiness of handling could not have been surpassed by any English composer. Yet this was all in his night's work. It was never performed as a concert piece. Nobody wrote solemn criticisms of it any more than of the work of the scene-painters, who, by the way, are also masters of their art. We read the story, quoted by Ruskin, of the Pope's messenger who asked Giotto for a sample of his skill, and to whom Giotto replied by lifting his hand and drawing a perfect circle on the wall. Our gentlemen painters are deeply impressed by this anecdote; but I have seen Mr Hemsley, the scenepainter, raise his hand like Giotto and do this very same thing in sketching a

* Berlioz had published his Traité d'instrumentation et d'orchestration modernes in 1844, François Gevaërt his Traité d'instrumentation in 1863.

plan of a scene for me in his studio. Now I do not know whether Mr Glover will ever want to write a symphony or a mass or an opera, or any of the things that our academic musicians aim at; but of this I am certain, that if he does, he will make his orchestra do what he wants, and not let it make him do what the text books say it ought to do. If Sir Charles Stanford and Sir Hubert Parry had graduated by occupying for four or five years the posts held by Mr Glover at Drury Lane and the late Mr Jacobi (an equally skilful if less original bandmaster) at the old Alhambra, I venture to say that they would have expressed themselves not only more copiously but much more fully and freely in their essays in the highest class of composition. I repeat, until a composer has learnt how to turn out music to order for other people and for practical use, he will not be able to turn out work to his own order, no matter how many exercises he may have labored through. And though this generation has many more opportunities of hearing orchestral music, and even of practising it, than existed thirty years ago, it is still true that the theatre is the only place where a young man who aspires to mastery of the orchestra can make himself what I call a real tradesman.

This is the more important as England is now taking her old place, after an interval of two centuries, as a productive nation musically. Sir Edward Elgar, whose genius, like that of Burne-Jones, achieved a finished technique by study and by making opportunities of practice, produces neither second-hand Handel like Arne, second-hand Mozart like Bishop, [nor] second-hand Mendelssohn like Bennett—to come no nearer our own time—but music which is as characteristically English as a Shropshire country house and stable are characteristically English. I am not here raising the question whether it is good music: that is to say, whether you happen to like it or not (though as a matter of fact

I like it myself). My point is that, whether you like it or not, it is the characteristic expression of a certain type of English breeding, and very good breeding at that. Before Elgar came such a thing did not exist on the symphonic plane in England. You had to go back to Purcell for it.

Before concluding, let me say that there is still, as there has always been in England, a huge body of mere brute musical faculty, and a sort of connoisseurship which is exactly like that of the football field and cricket pitch. Our musical festivals are for the most part horribly unmusical. Our notion that you can give majesty to Handel's music by having it roared and growled and wheezed and screamed simultaneously by 4000 people who do not know how to sing is too silly for human patience. But the people who go to hear this sort of thing are often quite keen critics of certain points of execution. They will listen to a tenor singing Deeper and deeper still to discover whether he can sing the ascending passages without an obvious break and change of register; and if he achieves this feat as successfully as Santley in Honor and Arms they will applaud him, though he will please them all the more if he interpolates a high note at the end that would infuriate any really cultivated musician. But silly as these people are, they are musical, and only need plenty of opportunities of hearing good music, especially real English music like Elgar's (not sham English music produced by simply writing in the old English dance forms), to provide a demand which will give all our young composers as much practice as they want without having to choose between the theatre band or the church organ and no practice at all.

DISCUSSION

The Chairman [W. H. Cummings].—On my own behalf, and I am sure I may add on yours also, I tender most sincere thanks to Mr Shaw for the very entertaining and eloquent discourse he has given us. I remember we have had comic histories of England, and I was sometimes reminded of these when Mr Shaw was speaking; but we must remember that a comic presentation of facts may nevertheless enforce great truths, and at the back of Mr Shaw's remarks there are many important lessons to be learned. A few years ago I happened to be at a country town, and the Mayor apologized for the feebleness of an "octogeranium." I hope you will make some allowance for me on the same grounds. The last subject discussed was Elgar. He had told an audience that he taught himself to compose by taking a score of Mozart and filling it up with his own parts bar by bar. That shews we must build on the old foundations. Mr Shaw has made an amusing reference to our unfortunate orchestras, but he told us how we afterwards learned to play Wagner. There was a great deal of truth in his remarks. Wagner was at first abhorred; but that is nothing wonderful. If you take up a Greek book—say Homer's Iliad—and do not know the alphabet, could you appreciate it? So you have to learn the language of Wagner, and you may find it good or bad. I do not think Mr Shaw's history of English music is quite correct. There is one man who might have done great things in the direction Mr Shaw has indicated—Sir Henry Bishop. When at Drury Lane he tried to copy Mozart and Beethoven. Mr Shaw's final sentences are the best we can take away with us. We want our own language, our own thoughts, our own expressions, our own brutality if you like; and if he can help us to that I am sure we shall all be delighted.

Mr [James] Glover.—As you seem to be amused by the reminiscences of one Irishman, perhaps you will hear a few words from another. I am the Mr Glover to whom reference has been made. Mr Shaw has spoken of the practical side of the more or less trifling or important music for which I have been responsible. With respect to trumpets, I was limited. I found very few trumpet players, and those who had only a few notes invariably played them out of tune. But my manager insisted on engaging twelve trumpets. You know that to have twelve trumpets blowing the same few notes all through the night is too awful. I did have a trumpet with a valve attachment which gave us all those chromatic beauties of which Mr Shaw has spoken. I remember Sir Arthur Sullivan sending round to me between the acts, and asking how I did it. There is one phase of Mr Shaw's remarks that I should like to enlarge on, and that is the apathy of eminent musicians to popular demands during the last twentyfive or thirty years. I formed a musical association, and tried to encourage the better class of musicians—I mean the musicians who compose—to give us something more for a smaller orchestra. Nine-tenths of the populace know Sir Edward Elgar's Pomp and Circumstance. This was published in Germany with a French title. Sir Edward did not write impossible orchestration; it is scored for a small orchestra by Adolph Schmidt, who did the same for Madame Wagner in order to popularize her husband's works. If I ask about the first violin part of a composition, and am told there are eight first violin parts, it is evident I can have no use for it. There are hundreds of things of Sir Charles Stanford's I would gladly introduce into the pantomime, but I cannot because I am barred by the complications of the instruments. Everybody for the last thirty years has been complaining that the better class of music gets no encouragement from the State. But, as I have pointed out where I am allowed to write, an Act of Parliament was passed in 1907 entitling every borough to charge a penny rate for music; and there are not three towns that have taken advantage of it. I do not complain of this; but what I do complain of is that there is not a single person connected with the higher music of London who has called a meeting for promoting the adoption of the Act. A penny rate in the little town of Bexhill, where I go for my weekends, means £428. If I can get Bexhill to take it up I will see that the £400 is spent on music. If you add up the rateable value of the entire country there is £500,000 waiting for English music, and there is not a person in London who is prepared to stand up for it. It is waiting for every member who writes works that nobody wants to hear. Many years ago, when I was at Covent Garden, and had the pleasure of first introducing the Valkyrie, a man from over the way said "This is the place for you"; but I said "Not for me." But it does seem to me that what we want is the education of the public taste, not in a too academical sense. Those who are at the head of affairs have not the pluck or the commonsense to agitate for it.

Dr [Thomas Lea] Southgate.—I should like to call attention very briefly to an inconsistency on the part of our lecturer. He commenced by deprecating reminiscences, and he has given us reminiscences. He reminded me of an ancient hero who was called in to curse, and remained to bless! His reminiscences practically took the form of one branch of history. History is always entertaining, especially to old members, and the Chairman and I are among the oldest. I remember very well those reminiscences to which our lecturer has referred, and can name the gentleman he has in mind, Mr G. A. Osborne: he has long been dead, so we need not mind mentioning his name. I must say I found his experiences very interesting, because he had had a wide range of knowledge of music and musicians in many parts of the world. I should like to make one protest, and that is against the lecturer's statement that in his early days composers did not write English music. Now when I think of Sir Sterndale Bennett, who has sometimes been ignorantly represented as an imitator of Mendelssohn, but was nothing of the kind; of Macfarren, whose Chevy Chase overture I still remember; of Sullivan, whose music was distinctly English; of Hatton; and of Bishop, to whom our Chairman has referred, I think his stricture that these men did not write English music is not justified. He has forgotten one branch of music of which we are all justly proud—I mean our English church music; surely Sir John Goss wrote noble cathedral music! The moral to be deduced from the lecture we have heard is a very old one: Practice makes perfect. According to the theory laid down, the music heard at the Crystal Palace and elsewhere did not give satisfaction because the players did not master the parts! I was surprised to hear that assertion about Manns' orchestra. We must remember that those Saturday concerts were only the weekly ones. There were also the daily ones, so the orchestra had plenty of opportunities of practising together. May I set Mr Shaw right on one point? He thought Ouseley and Stainer belonged to different Universities, though I daresay the remarks he made with regard to the views of each on chords and harmony were true. But I rather think he referred to the idea that, when Macfarren was Professor at Cambridge, not many got through on Stainer's book on Harmony. Macfarren, who believed so passionately in Day's theory, was not in sympathy with the theories that obtain at Oxford.

A Member.—Mr Shaw suggests that we are dependent on the machinery we find. Does not the artist often invent his own machinery?

Mr Bernard Shaw.—It is, of course, true that artists

are inventive. I suppose every great artist does add a brick or so to the general structure of art. But even if you take the case of Wagner at Bayreuth, I think you must admit that if there had been no orchestras or theatres in Paris or elsewhere, it would not have been possible for him to construct his theatre. Had he been a Sandwich Islander he could have done nothing. He could not have done the work he did if the way had not been prepared by all the great modern musicians from Bach onward. He simply took the structure that had been raised by other great men and added his own little contribution. You must take up the art at the particular point to which it has been built up.

Why did Dr Southgate get up and give Osborne away? I did not mention his name. I do not know that I particularly disliked his reminiscences, because there was always a sort of dramatic touch about his accounts of Berlioz and Chopin, and those whom he had known. I cannot agree that Sir Sterndale Bennett wrote English music. Of course it is quite possible that his most characteristic work was written before he saw any of Mendelssohn's, but he must have come across a good deal that was inspired by Mendelssohn, such as some of Spohr's works. His music was very charming, and I wonder why one or two of his compositions are not more frequently performed; but they are in no sense English. The May Queen appears to me to express what is not English. There is a certain feeble sentimentality about it; but if you are an Englishman and can get up and say you find everything that is characteristic of your country in the music of Sterndale Bennett, I shall really wonder whether you have any clear idea as to what English music is. I do not say that English characteristics do not occasionally shew themselves in Sterndale Bennett and Macfarren, *e.g.* in Tis jolly to hunt, or the end of the Chevy Chase overture; but that is not exactly what I am talking about. I was thinking of the soul of England. If you were to present Tis jolly to hunt to a man from Asia, he would fail to recognize the soul of England in it.

I have a certain sympathy for the way in which Dr Southgate contended for Sterndale Bennett and Macfarren; but if one really thinks that is English music, he does not know what English music is. I remember how Goetz sent over to the Philharmonic Society a Spring Overture, and Macfarren had to write an analytical program—a very terrible thing it is when you have to write an analytic program for a Society. Yet here Macfarren said "This seems to me a collection of consecutive 7ths." What he meant was that Goetz had no right to compose in consecutive 7ths; and I say a man who is in that frame of mind has lost sight of what music really is. One of the secrets of the success of Chevy Chase was that Macfarren in his early youth had learned to play a brass instrument, and consequently for once he got a genuine inspiration. I make Dr Southgate a present of Sullivan, and Hatton, and the rest of them; they wrote very nice things. I need not speak against Goss. But if I want to speak well of English music, I have to go further back. I cannot rise to any enthusiasm about Goss. A real omission I made was in speaking of the theatrical conductors as the only musicians; I should have mentioned another class of practical men—the church organists. I did not mean to speak disrespectfully of the Crystal Palace band, because they were thoroughly practical men; but whenever they essayed pieces that were very seldom played, they could not do them well. A performance under Manns of a Mozart symphony was deplorably like two young ladies at Brixton playing a pianoforte duet. Mozart is the test; he is the master of masters. I am obliged to Dr Southgate for setting me right about the rival examiners.

THE VALUE OF VIENNESE OPERETTA

Reply to an inquiry "concerning the values and the possibilities of development of the contemporary operetta," which remained stupendously successful despite critical attacks on it as inferior to the works of Strauss and Karl Millöcker. Die Zeit, Vienna, 25 December 1910; retranslated from the German by Dr Felix F. Strauss

[U] What is the artistic value of Viennese operettas? Exactly that value which delights the public that fills the theatres in which it enjoys itself. And just this pleasure which they give to the public is the cause of their success. To the question whether these operettas have a corruptive influence upon the public I can only say: No! The public corrupts the artist, not the artist the public.[U]

CAUSERIE ON HANDEL IN ENGLAND

Shaw's causerie was written to be read to a society of musicians in France, in a translation by Augustin Hamon. It was never published in England, but Shaw sanctioned American publication in Ainslee's Magazine, May 1913. An unauthorized reprint, under the title Bernard Shaw on Handel, appeared in The Boston Evening Transcript, 21 June 1913

Handel is not a mere composer in England: he is an institution. What is more, he is a sacred institution. When his Messiah is performed, the audience stands up, as if in church, while the Hallelujah chorus is being sung. It is the nearest sensation to the elevation of the

Host known to English Protestants. Every three years there is a Handel Festival, at which his oratorios are performed by four thousand executants, collected from all the choirs in England. The effect is horrible; and everybody declares it sublime. Many of the songs in these oratorios were taken by Handel from his operas and set to pious words: for example, *Rendi'l sereno al ciglio, madre: non pianger più* has become Lord, remember David: teach him to know Thy ways. If anyone in England were to take the song from the oratorio and set it back again to secular words, he would probably be prosecuted for blasphemy. Occasionally a writer attempts to spell Handel's name properly as Händel or Haendel. This produces just the same shock as the attempts to spell Jehovah as Jahve. The effect is one of brazen impiety.

I do not know of any parallel case in France. Gluck, almost unknown in England until Giulia Ravogli made a success here some twenty years ago in Orfeo, was, and perhaps still is, an institution in France; but he was an operatic, not a religious, institution. Still, there is some resemblance between the two cases. Gluck and Handel were contemporaries. Both were Germans. Both were very great composers. Both achieved a special vogue in a country not their own, and each of them remained almost unknown in the country which the other had conquered. I can think of no other instance of this.

Handel's music is the least French music in the world, and the most English. If Doctor Johnson had been a composer he would have composed like Handel. So would Cobbett.* It was from Handel that I learned that

* William Cobbett (1763–1835), English essayist and political writer, was noted as a vigorous literary stylist. Shaw anonymously reviewed a new edition of his Rural Rides (1830) in the Pall Mall Gazette on 27 July 1885.

style consists in force of assertion. If you can say a thing with one stroke unanswerably you have style; if not, you are at best a *marchand de plaisir*; a decorative *littérateur*, or a musical confectioner, or a painter of fans with cupids and *cocottes*. Handel has this power. When he sets the words Fixed in His everlasting seat, the atheist is struck dumb: God is there, fixed in his everlasting seat by Handel, even if you live in an Avenue Paul Bert, and despise such superstitions. You may despise what you like; but you cannot contradict Handel. All the sermons of Bossuet could not convince Grimm that God existed.* The four bars in which Handel finally affirms "the Everlasting Father, the Prince of Peace," would have struck Grimm into the gutter, as by a thunderbolt. When he tells you that when the Israelites went out of Egypt, "there was not one feeble person in all their tribes," it is utterly useless for you to plead that there must have been at least one case of influenza. Handel will not have it: "There was not one, not one feeble person in all their tribes," and the orchestra repeats it in curt, smashing chords that leave you speechless. That is why every Englishman believes that Handel now occupies an important position in heaven. If so, *le bon Dieu* must feel toward him very much as Louis Treize felt toward Richelieu.

Yet in England his music is murdered by the tradition of the big chorus! People think that four thousand singers must be four thousand times as impressive as one. This is a mistake: they are not even louder. You can hear the footsteps of four thousand people any day in

* Jacques Bossuet (1627–1704), French Roman Catholic prelate, was a renowned pulpit orator. Friedrich Melchior, Baron von Grimm (1723–1807), German-born critic and freethinker philosopher, was associated with Rousseau and Diderot in France.

the Rue de Rivoli—I mention it because it is the only street in Paris known to English tourists—but they are not so impressive as the march of a single well-trained actor down the stage of the Théâtre Français. It might as well be said that four thousand starving men are four thousand times as hungry as one, or four thousand slim *ingénues* four thousand times as slim as one. You can get a tremendously powerful *fortissimo* from twenty good singers—I have heard it done by the Dutch conductor, De Lange—because you can get twenty people into what is for practical purposes the same spot; but all the efforts of the conductors to get a *fortissimo* from the four thousand Handel Festival choristers are in vain: they occupy too large a space; and even when the conductor succeeds in making them sing a note simultaneously, no person can hear them simultaneously, because the sound takes an appreciable time to travel along a battle front four thousand strong; and in rapid passages the semiquaver of the singer farthest from you does not reach you until that of the singer nearest you has passed you by. If I were a member of the House of Commons I would propose a law making it a capital offence to perform an oratorio by Handel with more than eighty performers in the chorus and orchestra, allowing fortyeight singers and thirtytwo instrumentalists. Nothing short of that will revive Handel's music in England. It lies dead under the weight of his huge reputation and the silly notion that big music requires big bands and choruses. Little as Handel's music is played in France, the French must be better Handelians than the English—they could not possibly be worse—as they have no festival choirs. Perhaps they even know his operas, in which much of his best music lies buried.

The strangest recent fact in connexion with Handel in England is the craze he inspired in Samuel Butler. You do not yet know in France that Samuel Butler was one of the greatest English and, indeed, European writers of the second half of the XIX century. You will find out all about him in a couple of hundred years or so. Paris is never in a hurry to discover great men; she is still too much occupied with Victor Hugo and Meyerbeer and Ingres to pay any attention to more recent upstarts. Or stay! I am unjust; there are advanced Parisians who know about Delacroix and the Barbizon school, and even about Wagner; and I once met a Parisian who had heard of Debussy, and even had a theory that he must have been employed in an organ factory, because of his love of the scale of whole tones.

However, I am forgetting Handel and Butler. Butler was so infatuated with Handel that he actually composed two oratorios, Narcissus and Ulysses, in the closest imitation of his style, with *fugato* choruses on the cries of the Bourse, the oddest combination imaginable. Butler's books are full of references to Handel, and quotations from his music. But, as I have said, what do the French care for Butler? Only Henri Bergson can understand the importance of his work. I should explain that Mr Bergson is a French philosopher, well known in England.* When he has been as long dead as Descartes or Leibnitz, his reputation will reach Paris. Dear old Paris!

* Bergson was the author of Matière et Mémoire (1897) and L'Évolution Créatrice (1906), which paralleled a number of Shaw's philosophic concepts in Man and Superman (1903).

A NEGLECTED MORAL OF THE WAGNER CENTENARY

The New Statesman, 31 May 1913; unsigned

Last week the London press descanted on the fact that Richard Wagner stands with Bach and Beethoven as one of the greatest composers of all time. It also reported a naval court martial at which, among other matters, it transpired that a battleship, in a department needing eighteen men for its full equipment, put to sea with three.

What, it may be asked, is the connexion between these two items? The connexion is that they were both symptoms of our national weakness for writing and speaking without the smallest reference not only to facts, but to our own previous utterances on the same subjects. How did the London press treat Wagner during his lifetime? As an impostor, a charlatan, a musical ignoramus who, being unable to compose a bar of melody, produced a hideous *charivari* by a monstrous abuse of the orchestra and called it "the music of the future." When for one season, by some strange accident, he became conductor of the Philharmonic Society, he was, in spite of the support of Queen Victoria and her Consort, driven off and replaced by a musician [Hans Richter] whom no one now supposes worthy to black his shoes. Not since Handel had a composer written so healthily for the human voice; yet he was said to smash all the voices, though Verdi and even Gounod, with their trick of writing for the upper fifth of the singer's compass alone (the pretty part), were filling Europe with the wrecks of shattered goat-bleaters whilst the Wagner veterans were roaring cheerfully a quarter of a century after their great-grandchildren had started in life and were presumably imploring them to stop. Mr Ashton Ellis devoted his life to the translation of Wagner's prose works; and it was with the greatest difficulty that, after years of effort, a wretchedly inadequate Civil List pension was procured for him in the face of the sedulously inculcated conviction that Wagner was an abominably bad musician, and that, being only a composer, he could not possibly have written books, or if he did they could not be proper ones. Nearly two generations of Englishmen were deprived of the pleasure and edification of Wagner's music, and filled with a purely mischievous contempt for a very great man for no mortal reason whatever, and with no countervailing benefit to any human being. In round figures, we had to do without Wagner's compositions for thirty years because they were not performed here at all; and we were by that time so prejudiced against them that it was another thirty years before we became really familiar with them.

And now, when the Wagner Centenary comes, all the papers say what a great man he was, without making the smallest reference to the fact that they did all that in them lay to blast his reputation and starve him to death. Some of the very men who have written the Centenary articles thought no stone too jagged and no mud too dirty to throw at him; though their only quarrel with him was that the Niblung's Ring was not written in the style of Mendelssohn's Elijah.

Just about the time when even editors of newspapers, though densely ignorant of music, and divided between their Philistine contempt for it as a subject and their deep awe of their critics' jargon about the chord of the supertonic (which did not then suggest a Nietzschean heresy) and "a smoothly contrasted second subject in the dominant," were at last beginning to wonder, with the Richter concerts at the height of their vogue, with

Lohengrin more hackneyed at the opera than Il Trovatore had ever been, with Bayreuth almost as fashionable as Goodwood,* with Europe, in short, saturated with an enormous popularity such as no musician before had ever attained or dreamt of, whether it could really be the correct thing to go on explaining that Wagner was an obscure and infamous impostor who could not compose a melody, and whose reputation was a passing craze got up by a few long-haired and unwashed victims of neurasthenia, Ibsen reached us. And then it began all over again. Wagner was hastily snatched from the pillory and perfunctorily shoved among the immortals; and Ibsen was thrust into his vacant place of disgrace. And he was treated worse than Wagner, though that seemed impossible. It was, however, easy. We had at least not accused Wagner of obscenity, nor called for the prosecution of Her Majesty's Theatre as a disorderly house after the first performance of Lohengrin. But we did that to Ibsen. And in due course, when we come to Ibsen's Centenary, we shall calmly treat him as the greatest dramatist since Shakespear, hardly even excepting Goethe, without the smallest reference to the fact that at the moment when he delivered his message to mankind we assured the English nation that he was an illiterate, diseased, half-crazy pornographer, and wanted to prosecute the people who performed his plays in spite of the prohibition of the Censor, who actually declared, at a Parliamentary inquiry, that the plays which were not censored were only passed over in contempt as not mattering.† And

* An English private park, the property of the Duke of Richmond, containing a popular racecourse, noted for its annual Cup race (since 1812) the last Thursday in July.

† See Report of the Select Committee appointed by the House of Commons . . . relating to the licensing and regulation of theatres . . . (London, 1892).

the French kept us in countenance by the now incredible folly of the rejection of the magnificent monument to Balzac by Rodin, glaringly the mightiest sculptor since Michael Angelo.

The latest victim of this sort of stupidity is Richard Strauss; but Strauss is a man of business, and in his case, as in that of the Post-Impressionists, a much more energetic commercial exploitation than Wagner or Ibsen ever enjoyed has met and stemmed the torrent of abuse. The press, which never felt its master in Wagner or Ibsen, bows at once to a well-advertized commercial vogue; and the fossilized critics have been forced, sulkily enough, to take their heads out of their sacks and the cotton-wool out of their ears, and to recognize high prices if they cannot recognize fine art. But nobody can doubt that if the newest developments were as unfriended in the City as the old ones were, their fate would be no better.

The other side of the banner is the one that Ibsen tried so hard to turn towards us. For we seem compelled by Destiny not only to vilify what is great, but at the same time to idealize and flatter what is rotten. And of that the court martial is a very mild instance. Take for instance our ideal navy. This navy—the navy of our hopes and dreams—though never large enough to secure that command of the sea to which we have as much right as to the command of the moon and stars, is nevertheless, as far as it goes, perfect in equipment and discipline, ready, aye, ready for anything that may confront it. An inquiry brings out the fact that the real navy puts to sea with three men to do the work of eighteen. We hear such stories on holiday airings at Portsmouth, when we meet the inevitable man who points to our floating fortresses and assures us that "her full complement is eight hundred men; and there aint not a man more nor 123 aboard her if the Germans come over." Which of us has ever dreamt of believing such tales? And yet here is a court martial, solemnest of official inquiries, at which it comes out that six per cent. of the full complement is considered too ordinary a proportion to excite any surprise or comment. We ask ourselves, with misgiving, is Our Navy as imaginary as the Wagner who could not write a melody, or the Rodin whose Balzac was "unfinished," or the Ibsen who deserved to be prosecuted under Lord Campbell's Act?* If so, the matter is serious; for it is one thing to imagine you have a duffer and a blackguard and find you have a prophet and a hero, and quite another to imagine you have a strong tower of defence and find you have only a paper boat. And if we are living in a fool's paradise as to these things—these fleets that cover miles of the sea, and these geniuses whose glory blazes throughout Europe—what is likely to be our condition as to the obscurer things, the unromantic dirty commonplace things, the dry details of Minority Reports, which are nevertheless at the root of all our fortunes? What sort of place does the man in the street conceive England to be? And what sort of place *is* England? Can it be possible that the fact that the man in the street is so much less sensible and direct than a dog is due to the fact that the dog does not read newspapers, does not listen to speeches, and does not make them?

If so, this paper will get into trouble presently through its occasional references to the actual facts of our civilization, and its sense of the value of Ibsen's warning against ideals that correspond to nothing on earth, and of Wagner's Wotan's hint to Alberic, the outwitted capitalist, *Alles ist nach seiner Art: an ihr wirst du nichts ändern.*

* Libel Act of 1843, drafted by the British jurist John Campbell (1779–1861), 1st Baron Campbell.

THE STRANGE CASE OF RICHARD STRAUSS

When Serge Diaghileff's Russian Ballet made its June 1914 visit to London the repertory included, fresh from its Paris première in April, a new ballet The Legend of Joseph by Richard Strauss, with a libretto by Count Harry Kessler and Hugo von Hofmannsthal, a setting by J. M. Sert, and costumes by Léon Bakst. Choreographed by Michel Fokine, danced by Léonide Massine in his début with the Diaghileff troupe, and conducted by Strauss himself, the performance generated as much anticipation as had that of Elektra nearly four years earlier. The ballet, unfortunately, proved to be lavish, pretentious, and dull, with Strauss's score a somewhat banal symphonic poem that only occasionally offered glimmers of his greatness.

Ernest Newman, in his review in The Nation on 27 June, was predictably negative; moreover the notice was designed, as he later confessed, to draw out Shaw again. Another delightful correspondence ensued, in which this time Newman, on stronger ground than in his previous encounter with Shaw, was clearly the victor. Reproduced below is Newman's original article in full, followed by the complete correspondence as published between 4 July and 8 August 1914.

I

27 June 1914

[U] For some of us the sitting out of Strauss's new ballet at Drury Lane the other evening was like attending the funeral of a lost leader. For apparently Strauss is now quite dead so far as music is concerned. Hanslick used to say that in England—he might with equal truth have said the whole artistic world over— it is difficult to win a reputation and impossible to lose one. Strauss may congratulate himself on this trait of canine fidelity in the public. The music of The Legend of Joseph is bad enough to ruin any man's reputation but his; had one of the younger German composers written it, everyone would have been talking contemptuously of the German vein being exhausted. Whether it is or is not, it is hard to say. Threatened nations, like threatened men, have a way of living long. It is nearly forty years now since Tchaikovsky gave it as his opinion that German music had come to the end of its resources. Well, since then we have seen Brahms—the Brahms whom Tchaikovsky could never understand—taking more and more confidently his place in the great Teutonic line; and we have seen Richard Strauss—the Strauss whom we used to know as a man of genius—enriching music with a new vocabulary, a new idiom, and a new psychology. German music may yet renew its youth, perhaps in the person of some composer sealed of the tribe of Schönberg. But one vein of German music is certainly used up—the post-Lisztian-Wagnerian vein; and in exhausting that, Strauss has evidently exhausted himself also. He is now one of the dullest and at the same time one of the most pretentious composers in Germany.

It is not pleasant to have to say things like this of a man who was once our leader. The obvious *riposte* from the Straussians— of whom there are probably a few still surviving— is that the degeneration may be in the critic rather than in the composer. Mr Bernard Shaw suggested, when he and I were exchanging compliments over Elektra three or four years ago, that I failed to see the true inwardness of that work because I could not follow Strauss's new harmonic language; whereby Mr Shaw simply demonstrated his comical ignorance of Strauss, of modern music, and of me. Strauss's harmonic idiom in Elektra presented no more difficulties to any ordinarily good musician than a page of average German prose does to a linguist; while in the works that have followed Elektra—especially Ariadne auf Naxos, the Festliches Præludium, and Joseph—the harmony is for the most part relatively as simple as Mozart's. Our complaint against the present Strauss is not that he is a wild pioneer hustling us against our will along an unknown and terrifying road that may lead anywhere, but a tired and disillusioned mediocrity lagging behind his fellows and behind us and beckoning us back to the road that leads nowhere. We can forgive anything in an artist but commonplace. Strauss is now virtually nothing but commonplace. In Salome, Elektra, and the Rosenkavalier there are quarters-of-an-hour of dazzling genius; in Ariadne auf Naxos there are moments of genius not quite so dazzling; in Joseph there is not a page of genius, or even of a talent beyond that of a good hundred composers whom one could name.

What will save Joseph, if it can be saved, is the splendour of the *décor*, the beauty of the dancing, and, it may be, the quality of the old story and the suggestiveness of the action. It is true that the authors of the scenario, with a typically Teutonic childishness, have tried to overlay the simple story of Joseph and Potiphar's wife with a bastard sort of symbolism; but on the stage the symbolism does not carry, even to those who have taken the trouble to wade through Count Kessler's super-solemn preface to the score. All that the authors and composer have done is to exploit the naked story for every penny that it is worth, and by transporting it from Egypt to the Venice of the XVI century, to give it an almost insolent magnificence of colour. Ten years ago Strauss would probably have treated the subject ironically, as Fielding did in Joseph Andrews. Today he talks pseudo-philosophy about it with Count Kessler and Hugo von Hofmannsthal. At one point, and one only, have the German authors added a really effective touch to the story. The greater part of the first scene is a mere quasi-dramatic excuse for dancing; the temptation scene is just what one might have expected it to be; the final scene, with the angel leading Joseph away, is a combination of the last act of Gounod's Faust and the British Christmas card. But the ballet of the women venting their rage and horror on Joseph after the catastrophe—a kind of outward projection of the despair and frenzy of Potiphar's wife after her repulse—not only intensifies the action just at the point where it might have been in danger of thinning out, but has inspired Mr Fokine to one of his most expressive pieces of mimetic invention.

The Russians, indeed, have done their part of the work magnificently. It is only Strauss who has failed us. It is no question of failing to see his meaning or disagreeing with his bent, as in the case of some of the real leaders of the musical thought of the day. One's objection to The Legend of Joseph is very simple: look where one will, the score is a mass of unredeemed banalities. The writing is the merest journalese of music, the self-satisfied, platitudinous orotundity of the leading article and the party speech. The opening theme, and all the subsequent developments of it, are simply the eleventh-fold chewing of a ten-times masticated German standing dish. The paradoxical tonalities of the first dance promise well for a moment, but the interest of the dance is exhausted in less than a dozen bars. The music for the boxers is simply the usual late-Straussian bluff; the noises in the moments of great dramatic intensity are simply the usual late-Straussian bluster; the affected theme of Joseph is simply the third-rate attempt of a dull mind to invent something "characteristic"; the *finale* is imposing only in virtue of its piling up of orchestral color, not of any value in the ideas themselves. Even Strauss's technique seems to have deserted him; from the mere point of view of effect the new work is a perpetual disappointment. He has obviously written himself out, whether for good or only for the moment remains to be seen. It is pitiable to think that all that is left of the man who wrote Don Quixote is the platitudinarian and futilitarian who has written The Legend of Joseph.

Ernest Newman

II

4 July 1914

Sir,—Mr Newman opportunely reminds you that when Richard Strauss's Elektra was produced in London by the enterprise of Sir Joseph Beecham, he encouraged that public-spirited gentleman by assuring the public, in effect, that Elektra was despicable trash, and that it was just like the impudence of an inferior person from Germany to attempt to impose on him, Ernest Newman, with such stuff. Whereupon, I contradicted Mr Newman with extreme flatness. And now Mr Newman assures us that Elektra contains "quarters-of-an-hour of dazzling genius." He adds that Joseph, which has now succeeded to Elektra, is bad enough to ruin any man's reputation; that Strauss is now one of the dullest and, at the same time, one of the most pretentious composers in Germany; that he is a tired and disillusioned mediocrity; not to mention that he is now quite dead as far as music is concerned; after which it is hardly worth adding that he is a platitudinarian and futilitarian, that the score of Joseph is a mass of unredeemed banalities, the merest journalese of music, the eleventh-fold chewing of a ten-times masticated German standing dish, the third-rate attempt of a dull mind to invent something characteristic, an attempt baffled by the fact that even Strauss's technique seems to have deserted him.

As before, I flatly contradict Mr Newman. He kept paying out all that ill-mannered nonsense about Wagner after even the Daily Telegraph (remonstrated with at last, it is said, by Royalty) had dropped it. I contradicted him flatly; and now he thinks Wagner, on the whole, rather a great composer. He paid it out about Elektra. I contradicted him flatly, with the result recorded above. He will say it about Strauss's next masterpiece. I will contradict him flatly (in fact, I do so now in advance), with the same sequel; for Mr Newman's erroneousness is almost certain enough to be accepted as a law of nature; and his death-bed repentances may be as confidently looked forward to as the revivals of Peter Pan.

But from the point of view of journalism, they are open to exception. How many people realize that a whole generation of the English people was deprived of the enjoyment of Wagner's music solely because the critics went on about Wagner exactly as Mr Newman is now going on about Strauss, and as he formerly went on about Wagner until the grossness of his error was too much even for English editors? The extent to which we are kept out of our inheritance of contemporary culture by mere inconsiderate offensiveness in the mask of criticism is appalling. If Mr Newman does not like Strauss's music, nobody wants him to pretend that he does. If he is bored by simple diatonic themes such as all the great composers abound in shamelessly, and is so weary of his business that he has no appetite for anything but the very interesting technical experiments of what he calls "composers sealed of the tribe of Schönberg," let him say so by all means. But do not let him suppose that his weariness justifies him in assailing Strauss or anyone else with libellous insolence seasoned with disgusting metaphors. A gentleman may say that the opening theme of Joseph has done service before in The Minstrel Boy, in one of the *entr'actes* in Bizet's Carmen, and probably in many other compositions besides, just as Handel's O thou that tellest had done duty in God Save the King! He may poke a little goodhumored fun at Strauss over it if he does that sort of thing amusingly, and does not forget Strauss's dignity and his own. But to call the theme the eleventh-fold chewing of a ten-times masticated German standing dish is not criticism but simple obscenity. It is not amusing, as obscenities sometimes are. It is laboriously and intentionally offensive; and the fact that it is addressed to a foreign visitor of great distinction and of extraordinarily attractive personality, who has impressed Europe as a genius of the first order, by an English journalist who has some past errors of judgment to apologize for does not make it any pleasanter.

Since The Times set the example, paragraphs of the news of a hundred years ago have become familiar in our older newspapers. If the Nation could devize some means of printing the opinions which Mr Newman will have some years hence, instead of his first impressions, your readers would be spared the irritation of being told, at the moment when a masterpiece is being performed, that it is not worth hearing, and learning after the performances are over that it contains quarters-of-an-hour of dazzling genius.—Yours, &c.,

G. Bernard Shaw

(Mr Newman can (and no doubt will) defend his own taste in music. But we see nothing obscene in his metaphors.—Ed., The Nation.)

III

11 July 1914

Sir,—It was a voluptuous joy to find I had drawn Mr Shaw again; but his angry letter about Strauss and myself—mainly myself—was a disappointment to me. Mr Shaw is going off sadly as a controversialist. He has lost his punch along with his temper; and now he is obviously losing his memory, as I shall show. In my article on The Legend of Joseph I referred to Mr Shaw's comical ignorance of Strauss, of modern music, and of me. I must apologize. Comic isn't the word: I should have said tragic.

Mr Shaw's misunderstanding of Strauss and his position in modern music need not detain us long. He objects to my speaking as I did of "a foreign visitor of great distinction and of extraordinarily attractive personality." Strauss's personality—about which I know nothing at first hand—has nothing to do with the matter. The fact that Strauss happens to be in this country when his work comes up for criticism has nothing to do with the matter. And that Strauss is now "of great distinction" I deny. He is not, on the basis of his present work, a distinguished musician at all. He is simply a distinguished financier who deals in music.

Mr Shaw calls The Legend of Joseph a masterpiece. I call it a mass of banalities, a re-hash of the stalest German ideas and most conventional German formulas. To hear Mr Shaw talk, anyone would think I was the only person in Europe with the temerity to suggest that Strauss is now writing a good deal of poor music. I invite Mr Shaw to read the press of England and Germany, *passim*, on the subject of The Legend of Joseph, and to have a few conversations about it with some leading English and Continental musicians, as I have done. If Mr Shaw likes commonplace, or if he dabbles so superficially in modern music as to mistake a well-worn platitude for a stroke of originality, that is his affair. It does not concern the rest of us, and all his bellowing will not move us.

I wish Mr Shaw would make up his mind as to what sort of person I really am in music. During the Elektra affair his first view was that I was an old fogey who could not keep pace with the rapid developments of Strauss's harmony. I had to point out to him that my complaint against Strauss was not that he was too advanced—for indeed he is as simple as Mozart in comparison with some other modern composers—but that of late years he has written an appalling amount of music that is mere commonplace, bluff, bluster, make-believe, padding, call it what you will. He is not in front of us now, but behind us. Mr Shaw's latest view of me is as a sort of musical *roué* whose wearied nerves can respond to nothing but extreme and unnatural titillations. He imagines me to be "bored by simple diatonic themes such as all the great composers abound in shamelessly," and "so weary of my business" that I have "no appetite for anything but the very interesting technical experiments" of "composers sealed of the tribe of Schönberg." It may cheer Mr Shaw up to know that I am not a bit like that. I am perfectly well and happy, and enjoying good music of all sorts and schools, old and new. I have not the slightest objection to diatonic music if it is good, any more than I object to a story told in words of one syllable if the words are put together by a man who has something of his own to say. I pass by with a smile Mr Shaw's reference to Schönberg. He evidently does not understand what my original sentence meant, because he as evidently does not know his Schönberg. If he did, he would know that there is another Schönberg than the one who indulges in "interesting technical experiments."

Mr Shaw imagines that I have recanted over Elektra. I must disabuse him of that notion. If he will refresh his memory, he will see that from the beginning I admired certain parts of it. I can assure him that those are still the only parts I admire. My opinion of the work as a whole remains unchanged: quite recently I wrote of it, after hearing yet another performance, that three people seem to have had a hand in the score—a man of genius, a man of talent, and a fool. Mr Shaw's discovery is only another of his mare's nests.

And now, Mr Shaw having had his say about me, let me have a word or two with him. He declares that Joseph is a masterpiece, and that I will some day recognize it to be such, when I have corrected my "first impressions." It will be remembered that Mr Shaw fell foul of me over Elektra before he had heard the opera. There was no need for me to prove it: he admitted it. There is no need for him to admit that he does not know The Legend of Joseph: I can prove it. He was at a rehearsal of the ballet, but for all that he does not know the music, or he would not have made the howler to which I am about to draw attention. "A gentleman," he says—*i.e.*, some person other than myself—"may say that the opening theme of Joseph has done service before in The Minstrel Boy." A gentleman might, but a musician would not. I puzzled for a good hour over Mr Shaw's strange saying. Had he quite lost his reason, and would he be telling us next that the opening phrase of Tristan is the same as God Save the King? And then a light dawned on me. There *is* a theme in Joseph that bears, in its first few notes, a superficial resemblance to the tune of The Minstrel Boy; but it is not the opening theme. I have not my score of Joseph with me where I am writing this, but the theme occurs, I think, in the middle of the second page.

Now this is instructive. No man who had played or read through even the first couple of pages of the score could possibly have said that the Minstrel Boy melody is "the opening theme." Mr Shaw plainly does not know the work; he is, as usual, merely dogmatizing on a matter he imperfectly understands. And the cocksure amateur who thus publicly demonstrates his ignorance of Joseph has the assurance to talk of *my* "first impressions" of a work which, before writing about it, I had played through at least a dozen times in the course of a month, and of which I had heard two rehearsals and one public performance!

Mr Shaw on Joseph and myself is only "a joke and a sore shame." Mr Shaw on Wagner and myself is a perverter of the truth. According to him, I "kept paying out all that ill-mannered nonsense about Wagner after even the Daily Telegraph (remonstrated with at last, it is said, by Royalty) had dropped it. I contradicted him flatly; and now he thinks Wagner, on the whole, rather a great composer." This is definite enough: Mr Shaw charges me with being a one-time ill-mannered disparager of Wagner as a musician. Now when a controversialist possessing the public ear is so lost to literary decency as to attempt to put into circulation so gross a falsehood as this concerning me, I refuse to mince my words with him. I simply give Mr Shaw the lie direct. Wagner as a composer has always been one of the three supreme gods to me. Mr Shaw has in mind my Study of Wagner, which was published in 1899. At that time I was less near Bach and Beethoven than I am now, and I wrote about Wagner's musical gifts in terms of almost idolatrous admiration. I could easily fill a couple of columns of the Nation with quotations to prove this, but I will content myself with referring the reader to pages 42, 47, 48, 249, 250, 257ff., 289, 291ff., 296ff., 305, 312ff., 317ff., 355, 357ff., 364ff., 379, 384, 392 and 393.

So great was my admiration for Wagner's music, indeed, that a reviewer of my book thought it his duty to abate it a little. "Far from disparaging [Wagner's] musical gift," he wrote, "[Mr Newman] proclaims that it has 'never been equalled among men', an estimate which quite takes my breath away, as if someone had said that Watts was a greater draughtsman than Mantegna." I had "fallen under the spell of Wagner's music," he went on to say, "and therefore had an intellectual rather than musical quarrel with him." Where and when did this review appear, Mr Shaw may ask. In the Daily Chronicle of 9th June 1899. And the writer of it? None other than George Bernard Shaw!!* So that the very man who is now trying to spread the malicious fiction that I have only arrived at my present stage of Wagner appreciation through an earlier stage of "ill-mannered" Wagner depreciation is the same man who, fifteen years ago, had his breath taken away by what *he* thought my excessive admiration for Wagner!

Not content with this primary mendacity, Mr Shaw adds that "a whole generation of the English people was deprived of the enjoyment of Wagner's music because the critics went on about Wagner exactly as Mr Newman is now going on about Strauss, and as he formerly went on about Wagner, until the grossness of his error was too much even for English editors." Again I give Mr Shaw the lie direct. If he objects to my handling him thus roughly, let him give the readers of the Nation some proof of his charge that I ever "went on about Wagner" in such a way as to turn English people against him; and let him name the "English editors" for whom the grossness of my imaginary error became in time "too much."—Yours, &c.,

Ernest Newman

* See III, 560ff.

IV

18th July 1914

Sir,—I should perhaps apologize to your readers for not having warned them that my first thanks for rescuing them from Mr Newman's misdirection would be a demonstration by him that I am an abandoned liar. I had better rectify the omission by explaining how it is done.

When a barrister is pleading for the conviction of an educated forger or swindler, or when the judge is summing up (which usually comes to the same thing), they invariably lay great stress on the prisoner's amazing cleverness, on the excellent education he received from his parents, on the hopes that were built on his early promise, on what he might have done but for the fatal perversity which enables the judge to finish with the traditional "Instead of which you go about stealing ducks." Mr Newman never neglects this old and trite method of securing a conviction. But he goes further than any judge has ever gone. When you say to a judge "You put X away for ten years, though he was as honest a man as yourself," he does not say "You lie; nobody could have spoken more highly of X than I did at the trial." He stands to his guns. Not so Mr Newman. If, a year hence, I accuse him (as I very likely shall) of having abused Strauss, he will say: "You lie in your dastardly throat. If you turn to The Nation of 27th June 1914, page 488, column 1, line 1, you will find that I described Strauss as a composer of dazzling genius." And if (as is not at all probable) I cite Mr Newman as one of Strauss's admirers, he will exclaim: "The mendacity of Mr Shaw is a public scandal. If you turn to The Nation of 27th

June 1914, page 487, column 2, last line but five, you will find Strauss denounced as a tired and disillusioned mediocrity in an article signed Ernest Newman (*moi qui vous parle*); and nobody knows it better than Mr Shaw, as he protested angrily against it at the time."

Let it rest at that. Strauss, according to Mr Newman, is a tired and disillusioned mediocrity of dazzling genius. It is a fine day; but the weather is extremely rainy and tempestuous.

The fact that in our old controversy in the Daily Chronicle I quoted Mr Newman's implication that Wagner was a greater musician than Sebastian Bach (for instance) needs no further explanation. But Mr Newman has raked up that controversy to prove that in those days he was an enthusiastic champion of Wagner, and I his opponent. If he did not mean this, the raking-up is an irrelevance. Yet his quotation makes it clear that the controversy was about his "quarrel" with Wagner. So he *was* quarreling with Wagner then. Out of my own mouth he has proved my good faith. On that occasion I was defending Wagner's greatness against Mr Newman's disparagements of it exactly as I am now defending Strauss's greatness against Mr Newman's disparagements of it. This is the essential truth of the matter; and if Mr Newman is ashamed of having been on the wrong side then as he is on the wrong side now, the fault is not mine. I did, and am doing, my best to convert him.

I admit frankly, however, that my opinion of Joseph was based on half an orchestral rehearsal and two performances, all three conducted by Strauss, the last one (the second public performance) a triumph of conducting and of response to it from the band. I have since heard another performance; and, though at some points I missed Strauss's conducting, I was confirmed beyond redemption in my opinion that Joseph is a magnificent piece of work, and that any lover of music among your readers who has been prevented from hearing it by Mr Newman has been very cruelly deprived of one of the rare opportunities of a lifetime.

Mr Newman objects to a judgment based on such experiences. He declares that his own opinion is based on a dozen performances by himself. As Mr Newman is not a walking orchestra, I presume he played Joseph on the piano, unless, indeed, his theory of the excessive simplicity of Strauss's harmony led him to resort to the accordion. Now, I am bound, in all candor and fair dealing, to confess at once that if I had played Joseph twelve times on the piano and judged the work thereby, it is only too probable that my opinion would have been the same as Mr Newman's. I conclude that Mr Newman's accomplishments as an executant bear a melancholy resemblance to my own. And I thought, somehow, that he was a fine player. Another illusion gone!

I must apologize for having misled Mr Newman by calling the Minstrel Boy theme the opening theme. Let me indicate its position more exactly by saying that the work begins with it. It is recognizable as a rhythm before the end of the third bar, though it is repeated several times before it passes, by an irresistible gravitation, into the actual notes of the old tune. When I was a professional critic, we used to describe a theme so situated as the opening theme. I do not know what Mr Newman calls it; but, at all events, he now knows where it is.

I accept Mr Newman's explanation that when he alluded to Schönberg he did not mean Schönberg, but another composer of the same name. But I had rather not accept his invitation "to read the press of England and Germany, *passim*, on the subject of The Legend of Joseph" and to have a few conversations with some leading English and Continental musicians, as Mr Newman has done. If I had done that in the days of the Wagner controversy, I should have arrived at the same conclusions as to Wagner that Mr Newman has arrived at as to Strauss. I am glad to know now, on his own authority, how he has been led into his errors. My own plan is to listen to a piece of music and say what I think of it. I recommend this method to Mr Newman as, on the whole simpler, and more satisfactory in its results, than the one he recommends to me.

Mr Newman's memory betrays him as to Elektra. I did not criticize that work before I had heard it. I criticized Mr Newman years before it was composed; but that is not quite the same thing. Mr Newman now says he knows nothing at first hand of Strauss personally, and that Strauss's personality has nothing to do with the matter. I confess I did not understand this: I thought that calling a man "a tired and disillusioned mediocrity" with "a dull mind" was meant as a personal criticism. I seem to be always misunderstanding Mr Newman. I am very sorry.

"I wish" says Mr Newman "Mr Shaw would make up his mind as to what sort of person I really am in music." I have.

Sans rancune

G. Bernard Shaw

V

25 July 1914

Sir,—In my former letter I deplored the failure of Mr Shaw's memory. I have now to lament the failure of his eyesight; at least it is to some such failure that I may perhaps attribute his having omitted to read my letter to the end. I accused him, you will remember, of having told two fibs about myself, and I gave him the choice of either justifying them or withdrawing. He has done neither. Has he read what I said to him and about him, or does he think that by keeping silence on these points he will cause the public and myself to forget them? I can assure him that having got him in a corner from which all the dialectical ingenuity in the world will not enable him to escape I am not going to walk away and let him slip out. Not likely! But I will return to this anon. It is no use our continuing to bandy words over Joseph. Mr Shaw says it is "magnificent," "a masterpiece." I say it is platitudinous Teutonic tosh that any decently schooled German musician could have turned out, and that the more thoughtful of them will pray that they may never turn out. Obviously I cannot *prove* this to Mr Shaw, any more than he can *prove* to me that the work is a masterpiece. Let us then leave it for the next five or ten years to show who has blundered. Today I want to have a little fun with Mr Shaw's desperate attempts to score a point off me here and there.

1. According to him, I have said that "Strauss is a tired and disillusioned mediocrity of dazzling genius." "It is a fine day"—runs Mr Shaw's comment—"but the weather is extremely rainy and tempestous." It apparently does not occur to Mr Shaw that though it is rainy today there may have been fine moments last Tuesday. It is surely possible for a man to write a work that has some pages of genius in it, and *four years later* to write another that shows no genius whatever. I hope this is clear even to Mr Shaw.

2. Mr Shaw would fain persuade your readers that I formed my opinion of Joseph from "the press of England and Germany," and from "conversations with some leading musicians." I cannot believe he is so stupid as not to have seen the plain meaning of what I said—not

that I had derived my opinion from anyone, but that if Mr Shaw would take the trouble to look into the matter he would find that I was not the only person with a supreme contempt for Joseph.

3. Mr Shaw objected to my speaking as I did of Joseph, seeing that the work was by "a foreign visitor of extraordinarily attractive personality." I rejoined that the attractiveness or repulsiveness of Strauss's personality had nothing to do with the question of whether his music was good or bad; and now Mr Shaw plaintively says he thought that "calling a man a tired and disillusioned mediocrity with a dull mind was meant as a personal criticism." Cannot Mr Shaw see that if a critic has never spoken to Strauss in his life, what he says about him can only be an artistic, not a personal criticism? What in the name of reason has "attractive personality," in the sense in which Mr Shaw originally used the words, to do with the matter? I believe that Strauss as an artist—as a thinker, let us say—is at present tired, disillusioned, and mediocre; but he may still refrain from beating his wife, or forging a friend's name, or drinking his soup from a sponge.

4. Mr Shaw would have your readers believe that no idea of Joseph can be had from the piano score, even after a dozen readings of it. If that is so, I shall sue Strauss for having got sixteen shillings out of me under false pretences; for if the pianoforte score is not intended to give people an idea of the music, why is it published? As a matter of fact, such a score tells us a good deal; it makes us familiar, for one thing, with the thematic contours of the work; and we can then listen more intelligently to an orchestral performance. I am told that Mr Shaw was once a musical critic. It seems incredible, but I am assured it is so by people whom I have found truthful in other matters. In those days did Mr Shaw ever study the piano score of a new work before he heard

it and criticized it? If he did—and it certainly was his duty to do so—he ought to know better than to talk the cheap nonsense he is now retailing. If he did not, then he must have criticized new works on the basis of a single performance—that is, he trusted to those "first impressions" which he censured me, wrongly as it happens, for trusting to in the case of Joseph.

I pass over in charitable silence Mr Shaw's grotesque attempt to make out that when he spoke of a certain theme as the "opening theme" he did not mean the theme that opens the work, but a totally different theme that occurs some time later. I lave him to God. "I do not know what Mr Newman calls it," he says; "but at all events he now knows where it is." This to me, after I had shown *him* where it is!

Is all this display of damp fireworks intended to make the public and myself forget that I have a crow to pluck with Mr Shaw over Wagner? I wish to draw him back, gently but firmly, to his first letter. He accused me of "paying out ill-mannered nonsense" about Wagner years ago, "after even the Daily Telegraph (remonstrated with at last, it is said, by Royalty), had dropped it." I challenged him to prove this. He makes only a passing reference to the matter—a reference that in its turn is deliberately dishonest, as I shall show in these columns if Mr Shaw provokes me to pursue the subject. He knows perfectly well that my arguments in A Study of Wagner (1899) were directed against Wagner the metaphysician, Wagner the historian, and half a dozen other minor Wagners—not against Wagner the musician. But that it was Wagner the composer whom he accused me of disparaging is clear from his own words—"and now he" (*i.e.*, myself) "thinks Wagner, on the whole, rather a great composer" (the "on the whole" is merely another gratuitous impertinence). It was Wagner the composer against whom the Daily Telegraph used to fulminate;

nor can we imagine "Royalty" intervening on behalf of Wagner the metaphysician. Mr Shaw will excuse me, then, if I insist on his either producing his evidence for his charge against me, or apologizing for having fibbed about me.

His other libel was that I ran down Wagner the composer "until the grossness of [my] error was too much even for English editors." This charge he must either publicly prove or publicly withdraw. Once more I ask him for the names of those editors. Nay, sorry as I am for Mr Shaw, I will set him an easier task. According to him, I pursued my career of crime against Wagner for some time before the editors revolted. Presumably, then, the damning articles that caused the revolt are in print somewhere. If Mr Shaw cannot name the editors who protested, and the articles that were refused, surely he can cite the articles that were printed? But he may save himself the trouble of research. There were no such articles, there were no such editors. Will Mr Shaw climb down, or must I bring him down?

Ernest Newman

VI

1 August 1914

Sir,—Allow me one word more. I cannot leave Mr Newman to be soured and maddened by an imaginary injustice. He believes that your readers may infer from my first letter that he was once dismissed from the staff of a newspaper for abusing Wagner after our editors had discovered that Wagner was a very considerable composer. If anyone has actually drawn such an inference, they have mistaken me. I do not even suggest that Mr Newman's editors ought to have dismissed him; for though I think that his judgments of his greatest contemporaries are on the whole erroneous, and his critical manners towards them hardly those of one gentleman to another, yet he is too clever and entertaining to be dispensed with; and when great men are in question, the *advocatus diaboli* is useful: indeed I have myself taken that brief in the case of Shakespear with much benefit to English literary mankind.

Further, I take a sort of paternal interest in Mr Newman's championship of the delightful toy symphonies of Stravinsky, and the very useful and sometimes exquisite experiments and novelties of Scriabin and of that school generally which was encouraged by the success of Debussy's scale of whole tones, long familiar to organ builders, but strange to the musical public. It is perhaps natural that Mr Newman should have got into a state of taste in which Strauss's procedure seems so hackneyed that he writes as if you could take the double-bass part from the score of Joseph: turn it into a figured bass by writing six-four, four-to-three, six-three, &c., under it; and hand it to any bandmaster or church organist to fill up accordingly and reproduce the harmonic effect of the entire work. Mind: I do not say that Mr Newman has said this in so many words (he will be rude to me again if I do); but if he does not mean this, I respectfully submit that he does not mean anything. The truth that he overlooks in his craving for more Stravinsky is that the greatest artists always belong to the old school; and that the simplicity which is common to Handel's Hailstone Chorus and the exordium of Strauss's Zarathustra is the result, not of ignorance or resourcelessness, but of the straightforwardness of the great man who, having something to say, says it in the most familiarly intelligible language, unlike the smaller man who, having little or nothing to say, very properly secures interest by a curious way of saying it. Thus you have Handel, Mozart, Beethoven, Wagner and Strauss denounced as madmen, even by eminent musicians, whilst their personal mannerisms were still strange, and then denounced by the amateurs of strangeness as platitudinous, sententious, and even by such exceptionally hardy and fanatical amateurs of strangeness as Mr Newman, mediocre.

I now leave the verdict to the good sense, including the sense of humor, of your readers. I should not have begun the controversy (on express provocation from Mr Newman, who must not complain if he has got more than he bargained for) but for my strong sense of the vast public mischief done by our campaigns of stupid abuse against supreme geniuses like Wagner, Ibsen, and Rodin, with the result that whole generations are robbed of their birthright of culture by the misleading and intimidation of the *entrepreneurs* whose business it is to supply the public demand for the highest art. My sole object was to make it clear to your readers that Mr Newman's remarks about Strauss need not deter them from attending performances of his music, nor *entrepreneurs* from venturing their capital upon it, nor public-spirited gentlemen like Sir Joseph Beecham from devoting their fortunes to it.

But, of course, I note Mr Newman's denial to Wagner of all the qualities that distinguished him from eminent musicians like his contemporaries, Sir Frederick Gore Ouseley and Dr Stainer (not to mention men still living). To Mr Newman's mind, this is a handsome acknowledgment of Wagner's position as a composer. To my mind, it represents the extremest length to which anti-Wagnerism can safely go now that no one, without making himself publicly ridiculous, can question Wagner's technical ability. In short, there is a difference between Mr Newman's mind and mine; and as nothing that we can say or write will alter that difference, we must remain content with having given the readers of The Nation and, incidentally, oneanother, a piece of our minds on the subject.

Mr Newman's last letter proves, especially in his references to pianoforte scores and opening themes, that the more delicate nuances of controversy, however entertaining to the bystanders (for whose sake I hope he will excuse my little attempts), are apt to escape him. I propose, therefore, that we drop it. If he will cease asking me for the name of that imaginary editor who did not dismiss him, I, on my side, will not press him for the names of the hundred composers who could easily have composed Joseph and magnanimously refrained, though we should all dearly like to know them. And so I leave the last word with Mr Newman.—Yours &c.,

G. Bernard Shaw

P.S. I see by a rather jolly article of Mr Newman's in the Birmingham Post* that his hundred men in buckram have now more than doubled their numbers. By the time this appears they will no doubt have run into four figures; but that will not affect my estimate of his critical powers.

VII

8 August 1914

Sir,—As Mr Shaw is kind enough to leave me with the last word—a right that I think would have been mine in any case—I shall repay his courtesy by talking more about him than about myself. I propose today to analyze his technique of controversy.

* The Recent Position of Richard Strauss, signed E.N., Birmingham Daily Post, 27 July 1914.

But first of all let me set Mr Shaw's mind at rest on one point, and apologize in connection with another. Mr Shaw rightly opines that I gave him "express provocation" to begin this controversy. I did indeed, and of malice aforethought. For three years I have been trying to decoy Mr Shaw into another argument. After each article I have written on Strauss I have said to myself: "This will draw him"; but Mr Shaw has refused to be drawn. When Joseph came along I saw a special opportunity and made a special effort. I knew this was the poorest long work that Strauss has ever written. I knew I had only to say so in picturesque language to goad Mr Shaw into committing himself irrevocably to the opinion that it is a masterpiece; but to make quite sure I baited the trap with an almost too obvious hint to Mr Shaw that it was his bounden duty to contradict me. The bait took: the unwary Mr Shaw rushed into the trap: and here we are.

On one point, I admit, he has me; I might have expected, indeed, that his eagle eye would detect the one weak spot in my armor. I was rash enough to say that some two hundred European composers could easily have written a work so commonplace as Joseph. But on reflection I see that I was wrong. Not one of them could. I am not like some people I could name: when I recognize that I have done anyone a gross injustice I admit my fault. I apologize to the two hundred.

And now let me display the anatomy of Mr Shaw's technique. His first great dodge is to turn a blind eye to every awkward question and every dilemma that is presented to him. He reminds me of Montaigne's story of the two Greek wrestlers.* One of them was not much

* Montaigne, Of the vanity of words, Complete Essays, Book I, No. 51, tr. Donald M. Frame (Stanford, 1958).

good at wrestling, but was a great rhetorician; and each time his antagonist threw him he volubly demonstrated to the spectators that he really had not been thrown at all. I point out to Mr Shaw that a theme incautiously called by him "the opening theme" does not, in fact, appear until some time after the opening. Does Mr Shaw admit that he has blundered? Not a bit of it! Even before he has risen from the mat he assures the spectators that while in one sense the theme is not the "opening theme" because it does not open the work, in a higher, subtler sense it *is* the opening theme, inasmuch as the music passes into it by "an irresistible gravitation." Mr Shaw's week, I suppose, begins with Tuesday afternoon; for on an enlightened consideration of the calendar it is clear that the whole of Monday and Tuesday morning are merely "irresistible gravitations" into Tuesday afternoon. And when I chuckle, as many other musicians have done, over his delicious conundrum of "When is an opening theme not an opening theme?" Mr Shaw gravely tells the spectators that "the more delicate nuances of controversy" are "apt to escape me." The rhetorician, in fact, has only been "downed" by his opponent's ignorance of the more delicate nuances of wrestling.

Mr Shaw's other most familiar trick is to paint a gross caricature of his adversary's opinions, and then argue, not against the man, but against the caricature. I tell Mr Shaw, for example, that plenty of musicians besides myself despise Joseph. Whereupon Mr Shaw appeals to the crowd: "You see, ladies and gentlemen, this abandoned person actually confesses that he *derived his opinion* of Joseph from other people." The only exercise I have had throughout this controversy has been chasing round after Mr Shaw, putting my foot through one after another of his imaginary portraits of me, and substituting a genuine photograph for it. I would not go so far as to say that this inveterate practice of his is primarily conscious and purposive; it seems to derive ultimately from a congenital inability to see what is plain before him without first running round the corner and standing on his head. But this copious natural faculty for seeing truth from an angle that hopelessly distorts it has been developed by the dire necessity of extricating himself, at any cost, from the difficulties into which his many controversies land him—controversies often begun by his incurable mania for lecturing professional people on subjects in which he is only an amateur. (The amateur is writ large over Mr Shaw's latest remarks on Scriabin and Debussy.) In the end it is hard to say where the natural unconscious impulse ceases and the conscious exploitation of it begins. Always there is the unblushing attempt to be the interpreter not only of his own views but of his opponent's; always the opponent's views are grotesquely manipulated to suit Mr Shaw's purposes; always from this welter of absurdity is drawn the inference that Mr Shaw wants.

"Joseph contains a lot of diatonic music," runs one of his preposterous syllogisms. "Mr Newman dislikes Joseph; therefore Mr Newman dislikes diatonic music." Which is like saying that I never, never, never eat fruit, because Mr Shaw has seen me decline to have a rotten apple forced down my throat. "Elektra seems to me music of an advanced harmonic idiom," was a former syllogism of Mr Shaw's: "Mr Newman does not like some parts of Elektra; therefore Mr Newman, plodding old fogey that he is, does not like advanced harmonic idioms." Then the tune changes. When Strauss writes another work, so obvious in idea that the brain of a musical rabbit could grasp the bulk of it, Mr Shaw elaborates an antithetical syllogism: "Joseph is simple and rather old-fashioned music; Mr Newman does not think much of Joseph; therefore Mr Newman is a furious foe of simple and old-fashioned music." The next misrepresentation follows as a matter of course. "If Mr Newman detests simple music of the 'old school,' he must necessarily lust after the 'strange' music of the 'new school.' Now Stravinsky, in my opinion, writes strange music; therefore Mr Newman's god is Stravinsky."

This is the latest caricature through which I have to put an avenging foot. In all my life I have not written ten sentences about Stravinsky. What Mr Shaw has in his mind is clearly a recent article of mine on Strauss in the Birmingham Daily Post, which he admits having read. After expressing my regret that our one-time leader Strauss should have lost our confidence by degenerating into a platitudinarian, I said that "in works like Joseph he has no message that can interest us; and so we turn to younger men like Stravinsky, who, *though we cannot always see eye to eye with them*, yet give us the impression that they are personalities, that they have something of their own to say that is worth saying, that they thoroughly well know how to say it, and that something big *may some day come of one of them.*" Observe the extreme caution of the phrasing. I have not given my artistic conscience into Stravinsky's keeping; he is simply a young composer who, though he sometimes puzzles me, always interests me—a composer who, in my opinion, is worth keeping one's eye on. How does Mr Shaw translate this guarded declaration for your readers? "You have Handel, Mozart, Beethoven, Wagner, and Strauss denounced as madmen, even by eminent musicians, whilst their personal mannerisms were still strange, and then denounced by the amateurs of strangeness as platitudinous, sententious, and *even by such exceptionally hardy and fanatical amateurs of strangeness as Mr Newman*, mediocre." I will not ask Mr Shaw where I have "denounced" the eminent old musicians he mentions; he is not good at giving his authority for his charges. I merely ask the reader to glance once more at my own remark about Stravinsky, and to try to discover, if he can, what ground there is in it for Mr Shaw's description of me as a "hardy and fanatical amateur of strangeness." Mr Shaw is really incorrigible. I beg anyone who may do me the honour to be interested in my opinions on music to get them direct from me, not from Mr Shaw, who is simply not to be trusted in these matters.

For the last time I would remind your readers that Mr Shaw, in spite of many appeals from me, has neither substantiated nor withdrawn the statement he made concerning me in connection with Wagner. With touching solicitude, he hopes I will not complain if I have "got more than I bargained for." My only complaint, my only regret, at the end of this controversy is that it leaves me with a grievously diminished opinion of Mr Shaw's sense of honour.—Yours, &c.,

Ernest Newman

TORQUAY'S NEGLECTED OPPORTUNITY

Torquay Directory, 1 September 1915

[U] May I, in my double capacity of a visitor to Torquay and an old municipal councillor, give vent in your columns to my unbounded astonishment on learning that Torquay proposes to reduce and impair its most valuable asset, the Municipal Orchestra, at the very moment when any sensible townsman would expect the municipality to double, if not triple, the public expenditure on it.

The war, which has brought disaster to so many cities, has given Torquay the chance of its lifetime. Whilst we were at peace, and our upper and upper-middle classes were becoming richer at an unprecedented rate, it was almost impossible for an English watering-place, however favored by climate and situation, to intercept and retain the flood of gold that streamed to the Continent every year. German and Austrian hotelkeepers—all along the Mediterranean, in the Tyrol, in the Black Forest, in every spot in Europe which was intelligent enough to cultivate its attraction for visitors—gathered English money in millions. In places not to be compared with Torquay in climate and natural beauty, and accessible only by railway journeys of intolerable length and heat and dustiness, or by a whole week of motoring, I have seen crowds of English people paying for rooms and meals sums that no Torquay hotel would dream of charging, sometimes for accommodation that no Torquay hotel would care to offer.

These places had military bands, promenade bands, casino orchestras and symphony orchestras, employing musicians by the hundred. "What extravagance!" some of your Torquay councillors will exclaim. If they had aired that opinion in the places I refer to they would have run quite a respectable chance of being lynched, and none at all of being re-elected. This does not mean that the lynching ratepayers would be devoted lovers of music. Many of them would not know God Save the King from Deutschland über Alles, or ever dream of entering a concert room. They would be acting simply on their experience of the fact that when the public expenditure on music went up their incomes went up much more, whether they lived on rents, profits, or wages.

Almost all the mistakes of municipal government are made by councillors who think they are practical men of business because they are experienced in conducting private business successfully for forty years by simply doing what your father did before you, without ever learning the principles of business; and you are not found out until you are taken out of your father's business and put into a different one. You are found out very thoroughly when you venture out of private business into public business, because the test of success in public business is exactly the opposite of the test of success in private business. If a business pays in the commercial sense, the municipality can leave it to take care of itself. The duty of the municipality is to undertake the businesses that do not pay commercially, because they are the most valuable and indispensable of all the businesses.

Unfortunately, the councillor whose notions are merely the habits of private business objects to everything that does not pay commercially. For example, the enforcement of the Public Health Acts is to him a dead loss. He tries to keep down the salary of the Medical Officer of Health, or to get a private doctor to do the work as a half-timer. He resists the appointment of every additional sanitary inspector. If it were not for the compulsion of the Local Government Board, he would make the Acts a dead letter, and thus save thousands a year "in the interest of the ratepayers." In private life he would complain of his doctor's bills, and of his employees being devitalized slackers losing weeks in the year through illness, without ever connecting that expense with his own folly on the Council, or calculating what the annual loss amounted to when all his neighbors' losses were added to his own. When an epidemic came and ruined the town for twenty years by giving it the reputation of a plague spot, he would catch the disease and die in the full conviction that he had done his duty to the ratepayers as a practical man of business. Elect a majority of such penny wiseacres and pound fools to the Torquay Town Council, and in five years Torquay will be a less attractive place than Wigan or Hanley, which have at least their manufactures to fall back on. There will not even be a paved road in the town, because roads "do not pay."

But the councillor who will do nothing that does not pay is not half so dangerous as the councillor who will do nothing that does pay. If the Council wishes to make the Pavilion pay, nothing is easier. Mr Basil Cameron* can be provided with a proper orchestra of from seventy to a hundred players at a roaring profit. A gambling table, a few bars, a dancing saloon, and an indulgent attitude on the part of the police will be sufficient. No managing committee will be needed: a contractor, backed by a syndicate, will take the Pavilion over at a handsome rent, which will go to reduce the rates. Respectable women will cease to frequent the Pavilion, and presently cease to frequent Torquay; but what of that? The disreputable women will spend money freely, and their money is as welcome at the bank as anyone else's. Business is business! If the Torquay Town Council is really on the paying tack, the old wide way is open before it. It can sell its soul for quite a lot of money. Business is far brisker nowadays in that department than it was in the Middle Ages; and the terms are much the same: twentyfive years or so of riotous living, with big profits, ending in hell.

There is a third sort of councillor who is the worst of all. He will not do the things that do not pay because they do not pay, and he will not do the things that pay because they ought to be left to private enterprise. So he does nothing at all except come late to committees to sign the attendance book, and vote against everything. Please remember that I am a stranger in Torquay. Do

* Concert violinist, who since 1913 had been conductor of the Torquay Municipal Orchestra.

not accuse me of aiming at Mr So-and-So or Mr Whatshisname, because this description exactly fits him. I know the species: that is all.

Now for some details about the orchestra. When I came to Torquay for the first time last year I saw an advertisement by the Town Council of an orchestral concert. The program included a symphony by Beethoven. I paid 2/- for Beethoven. I was swindled—swindled by the Torquay Town Council. A Beethoven symphony, though written for what now ranks as the simplest and smallest orchestra, requires for the bare performance of the notes in the score four horns. There were only two. It requires two oboes and two bassoons. There was one oboe and one bassoon. The 2/- program included works by Wagner, Liszt, and Tchaikovsky. I was swindled again. These works require, in addition to the Beethoven orchestra, three trombones. There was only one. They require a third flute, a bass clarinet, an English horn, a contra bassoon, a third trumpet, and a tuba. Liszt writes in his scores that the violin parts are to be played by a least fifteen first violins and fifteen seconds: a number which involves about twelve cellos and six or eight double basses. One very popular modern orchestral piece, Wagner's Funeral March from Die Götterdämmerung, demands eight horns, six drums, and four tubas. Quite simple modern trifles like Mr Percy Grainger's Shepherd's Hey require xylophones, celestas, and all sorts of novelties. Strauss demands, for wind instruments alone, twelve more players than the Torquay Town Council grudges to Mr Cameron for his whole orchestra, not to mention an organ, two harps, bells, and more percussion instruments than Mr Cameron's resourceful six-handed drummer dare tackle!

To sum up the case in figures, the very smallest number of players that can, without dishonesty, be announced as an orchestra for symphonic and classical work (the cheapest sort of work as well as the best) is thirtytwo, and such an orchestra can play nothing later than XVIII century music. To 1850 you can manage with fifty performers, though Beethoven, who died in 1827, wanted seventy. For modern work, such as the public taste demands from Mr Cameron at the Pavilion, he should have eighty players; and on special occasions a hundred. I furnish these figures, not because I expect the Council to rise to them for a year or two yet, but to give those councillors who provoked the town to tell them to "Go to Bath!" and who went there and unfortunately did not stay, some idea of the absurd exhibition of musical ignorance they are giving when they offer Mr Cameron twenty performers to play even Mozart, much less Tchaikovsky and Wagner.

As it was, I was swindled; and it was my public duty to take proceedings against the Council for obtaining money from me under false pretences. Two considerations restrained me. First, Mr Cameron had made such extraordinarily good use of the stinted resources placed at his disposal, and his excellent players had worked so well in spite of all the disadvantages, that the performances had really given me a great deal of pleasure. Second, I was afraid that if the Council engaged extra players they would try to save the cost by dismissing Mr Cameron and having the band conducted gratuitously by the aldermen, who could take it in turns. After all, it is only waving a stick. At least, that is what it looks like. I, who know better, shudder when I think of the toil and ingenuity which Mr Cameron must face to make twenty men pretend to do the work of fifty with any sort of plausibility. And even he cannot do impossibilities. Imagine Beethoven's Pastoral Symphony with one double bass! I had to do more than imagine it: I had actually to listen to it. And we were not even admitted at half price!

But when the war came I thought all would be well. For now at last Torquay was freed from the competition of the Continent. People who had never before dreamt that they could spend their holidays in England asked me where they could go; and I recommended Torquay as a place where there is an Italian sky, a Mediterranean climate, an Ionian Sea, cultivated people, first-rate music, and a really gifted conductor. I said nothing about the band being too small, because I concluded that the Council would grasp the opportunity to throw its last penny into seizing and holding its new visitors. I confidently expected to see the orchestra doubled, and the Council, full of public spirit and pluck, shewing the Germans that Torquay is not reduced to war bread and potatoes, either materially or spiritually.

I need not dwell on what I actually found. Thirtyfive thousand people so frightened that they cannot afford 2/- per head per annum to increase their incomes by attracting the best sort of people to their town, and to enable their children to grow up as cultivated citizens, with the finest of the fine arts to interest them and satisfy their imagination during the dangerous years of adolescence, instead of performances of "Splash Me"!

Well, it cannot be helped. After all, there are cheaper things than that Bath band of twenty at starvation salaries. There is the gramophone. And there are orchestral players among the German prisoners. Why not make use of them, and let the present band go into the workhouse? [U]

GLUCK IN GLASTONBURY

The Nation, London, 6 May 1916

Perfection is inextinguishable. If ever a nation tried hard to extinguish Gluck, one of the attainers of perfection, by the simple British method of ignoring him, that nation is ourselves. At long intervals some dramatic singer, Giulia Ravogli or Marie Brema, has revived Orpheus. Nearly forty years ago there was a Gluck Society conducted by Malcolm Lawson; and I still recollect very distinctly a performance of Alceste at which Theo. Marzials was the Hercules, and the call of Charon was played, as it should be, on one of the most unnatural notes of the old horn without valves, with the player's hand stuffed up the bell. But how many of our inhabitants have ever heard Iphigenia in Tauris? Not I, for one, until I stumbled on it at Easter in a village called Street, close to Glastonbury, the last place on earth where I should have expected it.

It was in some vital respects a better performance than ever Sir Thomas Beecham could have afforded in London. I guessed that it had been rehearsed for three months; I found on inquiry that it had been rehearsed for four. In London musical performances consist mostly of people playing and singing music they do not really know, helped out by the occasional *virtuoso* playing or singing one of the three or four *rôles* or pieces he or she knows far too well. It is a hard and joyless way of earning a living; and the way of the critic who makes his by listening to it is much harder. There was nothing of this mixture of the perfunctory and the stale at Street. The Somerset folk know Iphigenia through and through. Nothing could shake them as they delivered the English version of it (such English as is possible in translations which have to fit music made to fit a French text) in their native dialect. They were utterly unlike that ageless, deathless miracle, the metropolitan opera chorus, with its hollow square of motley nondescripts who have made some unholy compact with the devil, by which they are to live forever without growing older or younger on condition that they sing perpetually in masterpieces of dramatic music without ever becoming musical or dramatic. The Somerset Scythians and Achaians were both musical and dramatic. Like all natural people on the stage, they tried to be as conventional as an Imperial ballet; for to be natural on the stage in the realistic manner is the last accomplishment of artifice, and, to the performer, the most revolting of all outrages on Nature. They waved their arms and moved with convulsive strides; but they were full of illusions about it, and really meant it and felt it. And the Covent Garden chorus could by no means have shouted them down. Their tone was close, unadulterated with bawling and blowing and wheezing; their attack was prompt, confident, and solid; and every bar sounded as if it meant something.

The principals did not disgrace their parts. Iphigenia (Miss Gladys Fisher) sang very agreeably, and with adequate power and presence, without suggesting that her part presented the slightest difficulty. The audience did not know that there were even any high notes in it. When she becomes a thoroughly sophisticated *prima donna*, and learns to shriek every note above the treble staff as if it were her last gasp, the audience will wonder at her prowess; but she will no longer be Iphigenia. Her costume carried village simplicity a little too far. No doubt Diana and her priestesses were so chaste that nothing could do their virtue justice in Somerset but the white muslin of the British village maiden trimmed with silver foil. Nevertheless, I contend that the village maiden always gets married in the end, and looks it, wheras a priestess of Diana should chill the future as icily as the present. Miss Lillah McCarthy in her wonderful costumes* looked ten times chaster than the Somerset maidens, who tend to buxomness, in their muslin frocks; and at the fall of the curtain we all felt that Iphigenia's hand and heart were a sure thing for Pylades. If I were Miss Fisher, I should stand out for a less native and more imaginative dress next time.

Pylades (Mr Louis Godfrey), an excellent tenor, hit off the amiability and sincerity of that almost too virtuous friend to a marvel, singing very agreeably indeed; and Thoas (Mr Bernard Lemon), a good rough *basso cantante*, was a very presentable tyrant.

Orestes had been reached at the last moment by the voice of patriotic duty, and had gone to face a sterner music in Flanders or Salonika. The result was that the conductor had to take up the part; and it may be that some of the freshness and excellence of the performance were due to the fact that there was no conductor. At all events, Mr Rutland Boughton, to whom, and to his collaborator, Miss Christina Walshe, in the scene dock and wardrobe, this whole unexpected organization of the latent artistic resources of the countryside is due, had saved the situation by hurling himself suddenly on the stage in the vestments of Orestes. I do not know what Orestes was like, and so cannot say whether Mr Rutland Boughton resembled him; but he certainly did resemble a wellknown portrait of Liszt so strongly that I felt that Pylades should have been made up as Wagner; and yet when I looked at Pylades he reminded me so

* Designed by Norman Wilkinson for Gilbert Murray's translation of Euripides' Iphigenia in Tauris, produced by Miss MacCarthy in March 1912.

strongly of Mr Festing Jones* that I felt that Orestes should have been made up as Samuel Butler.

Mr Rutland Boughton did astonishingly well under the circumstances. His ability as a composer stood him in good stead; for when his memory gave out, he improvized Gluck recitatives with felicitous ease, though his modern freedom of modulation occasionally landed him in keys from which the orchestra (Mr Clarence Raybould at a grand piano) had to retrieve the others as best it could. I do not know whether Mr Boughton's voice is a tenor or a bass, nor even whether he can be said to have any voice at all for *bel canto* purposes; but it was all the more instructive to hear how he evaded all such questions by attacking the part wholly and simply from the dramatic point of view.

There was fortunately no scenery and no opera house: in short, no nonsense; but there was a shrine of Diana and sufficient decoration by Miss Walshe's screens and curtains to create much more illusion in the big schoolroom than I have ever been able to feel in Covent Garden.

In the evening there was a performance of Mr Boughton's Snow White (mostly dancing), which has been seen in London. Miss Florence Jolley, of the Margaret Morris school, was extremely wicked and extremely seductive, a popular and delightful combination. Miss Morris has really achieved something in the study of what people who cannot dance, as stage dancing is understood by Fokine and Karsavina,† can be made to do without a more arduous training than most earnest amateurs are willing to face. The result was a very enjoyable evening.

* Henry Festing Jones was Samuel Butler's longtime friend, traveling companion, musical collaborator, and editor.

† Tamara Karsavina was a Russian ballerina who had performed in London with the Imperial Russian ballet. Michel

Altogether, this Easter exploit of the Glastonbury Festival School, as it is called, was very successful and pleasant. Allowances have to be made in judging such performances; and London critics might exaggerate them because, as they are new allowances, they would be much more conscious of them than of the prodigious allowances that have to be made in grand opera houses in great capitals. But the truth is that there was far less to suffer and far less to excuse and allow for at Glastonbury than at the usual professional performances, which, just because rehearsals are so enormously expensive in money, and all operatic stars are wandering stars, are necessarily all scratch performances. And, anyhow, the London critics who have so far been devoted enough to go to Glastonbury have tended towards idyllic infatuation rather than to hypercriticism.

If the opera is repeated, may I suggest to the writer of the synopsis of Iphigenia in the program that the total omission of any mention of the pursuit of Orestes by the Furies must, to the Somerset folk who were not familiar with classic tradition, have reduced the Eumenidean scenes to mere madness? Alas! I stand out for snakes in the hair of the Furies. The Glastonbury Furies looked like Macbeth's witches, strayed into the classic drama by mistake. They made great play with skinny fingers; but there was not half a snake among the lot of them.

Fokine was a dancer and choreographer, director of Diaghilev's Ballets Russes, and creator of the ballet Petrouchka. Shaw had seen both of them dance in London in July 1913. Margaret Morris, who ran a school of interpretive dancing, had collaborated with Rutland Boughton for several years, at Glastonbury and elsewhere.

SPOOF OPERA

BY A GHOST FROM THE 'EIGHTIES

The Nation, London, 7 July 1917

The institution called variously a busman's or a stage-doorkeeper's holiday has never been called a musical critic's holiday. The musician who has been a professional critic knows, better even than Wagner, that music is kept alive on the cottage piano of the amateur, and not in the concert rooms and opera houses of the great capitals. He will not go to public performances when he is no longer paid for his soul-destroying sufferings. I wonder how many of our critics at last become quite clearly conscious that what they have to listen to in these places is not music. Sometimes the horrible thought comes that perhaps some of them have never heard music in their lives, but only public performances, and therefore honestly believe that these sounds, produced for so many guineas a week, and synchronized by an official called a conductor, really make music, and that there is no other sort of music. But such a state of damnation is hardly possible; for it happens from time to time within the experience of every opera- or concert-goer that the pentecostal miracle recurs, and for a few bars, or a whole number, or even for a whole evening, the guineas' worth of notes organize themselves into living music. Such occasions are very rare; but they are frequent enough to give every critic some moments of the real thing to compare with the simulacrum. Yet the critics seldom venture to face the conclusion that the difference is not between a bad performance and a good one, but between the waste and heartbreak of a vain search, and the supreme satisfaction of a glorious discovery.

Still, the miracle being always possible, there is hope, as long as the performers are really trying. Sometimes, if only for a moment, there is success. But they are not always trying. Worst of all, they are sometimes guying. Our orchestras become so stale with their endless repetitions of work which contains no durably interesting orchestral detail nor presents any technical difficulty, that nothing but a high standard of artistic self-respect and honesty in their public obligations will make them do their work seriously if the conductor either sympathizes with their attitude or lacks the authority which is not to be trifled with. When these saving conditions are lacking, you get spoof opera. The accompaniments are a derisive rum-tum. The *fortissimo* chords are music hall crashes, pure *charivari*, in which the players play any note that comes uppermost, and then laugh to one another. The joke is kept from the audience, partly by its own ignorance, and partly by the fact that as the *farceurs* are in a minority, most of the players are playing the notes set down in their parts because that is the easiest thing to do, and because they are not all in the humor for horseplay, not to mention that some of them are artists to whose taste and conscience such tomfoolery is detestable.

Verdi was the victim of a riot of this sort which lately came under my ghostly notice. I haunted a famous London theatre one evening in time to hear the last two acts of what was the most popular opera of the XIX century until Gounod's Faust supplanted it: an opera so popular that people who never dreamt of going to the opera as a general habit, and never in all their lives went to any other opera, went again and again to hear Il Trovatore whenever they had a chance.

Il Trovatore is, in fact, unique, even among the works

of its own composer and its own country. It has tragic power, poignant melancholy, impetuous vigor, and a sweet and intense pathos that never loses its dignity. It is swift in action, and perfectly homogeneous in atmosphere and feeling. It is absolutely void of intellectual interest; the appeal is to the instincts and to the senses all through. If it allowed you to think for a moment it would crumble into absurdity like the garden of Klingsor. The very orchestra is silenced as to every sound that has the irritant quality that awakens thought: for example, you never hear the oboe: all the scoring for the wind that is not mere noise is for the lower registers of the clarinets and flutes, and for the least reedy notes of the bassoon.

Let us admit that no man is bound to take Il Trovatore seriously. We are entirely within our rights in passing it by and turning to Bach and Handel, Mozart and Beethoven, Wagner and Strauss, for our music. But we must take it or leave it: we must not trifle with it. He who thinks that Il Trovatore can be performed without taking it with the most tragic solemnity is, for all the purposes of romantic art, a fool. The production of a revival of Il Trovatore should be supervised by Bergson; for he alone could be trusted to value this perfect work of instinct, and defend its integrity from the restless encroachments of intelligence.

The costumes and scenery need to be studied and guarded with the most discriminating care. For example, there is only one costume possible for the Count di Luna. He must wear a stiff violet velvet tunic, white satin tights, velvet shoes, and a white turban hat, with a white puggaree falling on a white cloak. No other known costume can remove its wearer so completely from common humanity. No man could sit down in such a tunic and such tights; for the vulgar realism of sitting down is ten times more impossible for the Count di

Luna than for the Venus of Milo. The gypsy must be decorated with sequins and Zodiacal signs: as well put a caravan on the stage at once as relate her by the smallest realistic detail to any gypsy that ever sold uncouth horses at St Margaret's Fair or kept a shooting-gallery. The harp of Manrico must be, not "the harp that once," but the harp that never. It should be such an instrument as Adam* decorated ceilings with, or modern piano-makers use as supports for the pedals of their instruments. Give Manrico an Erard harp—a thing that he could possibly play—and he is no longer Manrico, but simply Man; and the unplumbed depths of the opera dry up into an ascertained and disilluding shallow. And the scenes in which these unbounded and heart-satisfying figures move must be the scenery of Gustave Doré at his most romantic. The mountains must make us homesick, even if we are Cockneys who have never seen a mountain bigger or remoter than Primrose Hill. The garden must be an enchanted garden: the convent must be a sepulchre for the living: the towers of Castellor must proclaim the dungeons within.

I should say that a production of Il Trovatore is perhaps the most severe test a modern *impresario* has to face; and I suggest that if he cannot face it he had better run away from it; for if he pretends to make light of it no one will laugh with him.

Well knowing all this, I haunted, as aforesaid, half a performance of this wonderful opera a few nights ago. It cost me six-and-sixpence.

Let the six-and-sixpence go: I do not ask for my money back, except perhaps the sixpence that went as tax to the Government, which might have stopped the

* Robert Adam (1728–92), famed architect, who with his three brothers built the Adelphi, which became Shaw's home from 1898 to 1927.

performance by virtue of Dora,* and didnt. But except for the unorganized individual feats of the singers, it was not worth the money. The Count of Luna not only wore an ugly historical costume (German, I think), in which he could have sat down, but actually did sit down, and thereby killed the illusion without which he was nothing. The scenery was the half playful scenery of the Russian opera and ballet. The soldiers, instead of being more fiercely soldierly than any real soldiers ever were on sea or land, were wholly occupied in demonstrating their unfitness to be combed out; and though, unlike the old Italian choristers, they had voices, they seemed to have picked up their music by ear in the course of a demoralizing existence as tramps. Worst of all, the humorists of the orchestra were guying what they regarded as the poor old opera quite shamelessly. There was some honorable and fine playing in the woodwind: Leonora could not have desired a more dignified and sympathetic second than the flute in her opening of the last act; but there were others, of whom I cannot say that they treated Verdi, or the audience, or their own professional honor, handsomely.

In their defence, I will say just this: that the cue was given to them by mutilations of the score for which the management must be held responsible. In the wedding scene, Verdi demands that Leonora shall wear a bridal veil and make it clear that her intentions are honorable. But here Leonora scandalously wore her walking dress. Manrico shamelessly sang his love song; and then, instead of giving Leonora a chance in the touching little antiphony which introduces the organ and gives the needed ritual character to the scene, besides saving the

* Acronym from initial letters of the Defence of the Realm Act (1914), which curbed liberty of speech during the Great War through myriad regulations. It survived until 1921.

lady's character, he went straight on to the final war song with the bolero accompaniment, and thus made the whole scene a licentious concert. The end of it was quite senselessly botched in a way that must have given somebody a good deal of unnecessary trouble. The first interlude between the bolero blood-and-thunder song and its repetition was cut out, and replaced by the second; yet the song was repeated, so that when it ended there was nothing to be done but set the chorus and band to demonstrate at random, in the key of C or thereabouts, whilst the tenor brought down the curtain and the house by delivering that note "all out," as motorists say, above the din. If there was any more design in the business than this, all I can say is that it was not discernible: the finish seemed to me to be pure spoof. In any case, I see no reason why any gentleman employed about the theatre should have been called on to improve Verdi, who knew how to arrange that sort of climax very well. As the thrown-open window, and the blaze of red fire which tells the audience that Manrico's high C is extracted from him by the spectacle of his mother at the stake, were omitted (too much trouble in the hot weather, doubtless), nobody had the least notion of what he was shouting about.

Again, in the prison scene, when one was expecting the little *stretto* for the three singers which leads to Leonora's death, and which is happily not a stunt for any of them, but a very moving dramatic passage which completes the musical form of the scene, the lady suddenly flopped down dead; the tenor was beheaded; and the curtain rushed down: this barbarous cut announcing plainly that the object was to get the silly business over as soon as possible when there were no more solos for the principals.

Yet that is not the worst thing of the kind I have heard lately. I went to hear Figaro's Wedding, by

Mozart, at another theatre a few weeks ago*; and they not only made a cut of several pages in the *finale* of the last act, including one of the most beautiful passages in the whole work, but positively stopped the music to speak the words set to the omitted music, and then calmly resumed the *finale*, leaving me gasping. They had much better have taken a collection. There would have been some sense in that. And they began the proceedings with the National Anthem, which almost makes the matter one of high treason.

And now may I ask the critics why they, the watchdogs of music, suffer these misdemeanors to pass unmentioned and unreproved? They may know so little of Italian opera, and have so low an opinion of it, that the cuts in Il Trovatore may escape them; and they may really believe that all that spoof and *charivari* is genuine Verdi. But if they know anything about the forms of music at all, they must know that the interruption of a Mozart *finale* for a spell of dialogue is as impossible as a step-dance by a dean in the middle of an anthem. Several numbers of the opera were also omitted; but the omission of complete separate numbers is not mutilation: circumstances may make it reasonable; for instance, the artists may not be able to sing them, or it may be desirable to shorten the performance. But if such cuts as I have just described are allowed to pass without remonstrance, we shall soon have all the connective tissue of opera either left out or supplied by spoof, the residue consisting of star turns. Needs there a ghost from the criticism of the eighteen-eighties to tell the public that they are not getting full measure? Why, even the dramatic critics only the other day missed Polonius's blessing from Hamlet when Mr Harry Irving

* The Carl Rosa Company's production at the Garrick Theatre.

cut it. When his father omitted about a third of King Lear, the critics of that day did not miss a line of it, and only wondered mildly what on earth the play was about. If dramatic criticism can progress, why should musical criticism, which used to be the senior branch, be left behind?

What makes me touchy about Il Trovatore is that the materials for a better performance than I have ever heard were present. In the XIX century, Verdi, Gounod, Arthur Sullivan, and the rest wrote so abominably for the human voice that the tenors all had goat-bleat (and were proud of it); the baritones had a shattering *vibrato*, and could not, to save their lives, produce a note of any definite pitch; and the sopranos had the tone of a locomotive whistle without its steadiness: all this being the result of singing parts written for the extreme upper fifth of voices of exceptional range, because high notes are pretty. But today our singers, trained on Wagner, who shares with Handel the glory of being great among the greatest writers for the voice, can play with Verdi, provided they do not have to do it too often. There was no spoof about the singing of Leonora and Manrico: they threw about high Cs like confetti, and really sang their music. I have never heard the music of the prison scene sung as it was by the tenor. He was, by the way, remarkably like Mr Gilbert Chesterton, who would certainly have a very pleasant voice if he took to opera (I hope he will); and the illusion was strongly reinforced by the spectacle of Mr [Hilaire] Belloc seated in a box in evening dress, looking like a cardinal in mufti. A better Leonora was impossible: there is nothing more in the part than she got out of it. Though the opera was supposed to be in English, they all exhorted her to lay a Nora whenever they addressed her; and I am afraid they thought they were pronouncing her name in the Italian manner. I implore them to call her Leeonora, like Sir James Barrie's heroine,* in future; for that is at least English. Layanora is nothing but simple mispronunciation. I do not think either the conductor or the chorus knew much about the opera except the tunes they had picked up from the ghosts of the old barrel-organs (where they heard them, goodness only knows); but the Count knew his part; and the result in the *trio* at the end of the third act, where there is a very jolly counterpoint to be pieced out in mosaic by the Count, Ferrando, and the chorus, was amusing, as the Count got in his bits of the mosaic, whilst the bewildered chorus merely muttered distractedly, and the conductor raced madly to the end to get it all over and enable the gypsy to cover his disgrace by answering repeated curtain calls, which she deserved, not only for her courageous singing against a very unsympathetic accompaniment, but for the self-restraint with which she refrained from committing murder.

England's musical obligations to the artistic director† of this enterprise are so enormous that it seems ungrateful to ask him to add to them by taking Il Trovatore in hand himself next time I drop in. But I really can say no less than I have said above. Even at that, I am surprised at my own moderation.

By the way, incredible as it may seem, there really was a Manrico in the XV century who fought a Di Luna, who was not a Count, but a Constable (not a police constable). Di Luna was not his brother, and did not cut his head off; but as Manrico was the founder of Spanish drama, perhaps it would have been better if he had.

* In Barrie's play The Adored One (1913), subsequently retitled Legend of Leonora.

† Thomas Beecham.

MOZART WITH MOZART LEFT OUT

The Nation, London, 28 July 1917

Everyone who has seen the new production of Figaro's Wedding at Drury Lane will agree that it is quite the most delightful entertainment in London. It may without exaggeration be described as ravishing. To all Londoners who are at their last shilling and are perplexed as to how to spend it most economically I say unhesitatingly, Spend it at the Drury Lane paybox when next Figaro is in the bill. Can a critic say more? Can a gentleman say less?

And yet see what has just occurred. An able musical critic,* well known to the readers of these columns, and with every reason to make the utter best of Sir Thomas Beecham's enterprise (as indeed what lover of music has not?), volunteers the curious suggestion that Sir Thomas should revive the operas of Paisiello and Cimarosa, in order to teach the public that what they are admiring and enjoying in the Drury Lane performance is a sweetness and a neatness, a featness and discreetness (pardon the vile jingle) that belongs to all the best XVIII century composers no less than to Mozart. This is a shot that hits Sir Thomas between wind and water. It means that he has given us the charm of the XVIII century, but not that strange spell by virtue of which Mozart, being dead, yet liveth, whilst Paisiello and Cimarosa are in comparison as dead as mutton. It means that the same success might have been achieved by a revival of Paisiello.

* Ernest Newman.

The wily critic aforesaid has no difficulty in illustrating his suggestion by citing several numbers in Mozart's opera which might have been written by any of his popular contemporaries without adding a leaf to their now withered laurels. If you doubt it, turn to Don Giovanni, and pretend, if you can, that the contemporary specimens preserved in the supper scene by the Don's restaurant band are any worse than, or even distinguishable in style from, *Ricevete O padroncina* or any of the numbers mentioned in Mr Newman's article. The truth is that the XVIII century produced a good deal of the loveliest art known to us; and any of its masterpieces adequately presented to us now could not fail to make us ashamed of our own violent and vulgar attempts to entertain ourselves. When you are enchanted at Drury Lane, you must not say "What a wonderful man Mozart was!" but "What a wonderful century Mozart lived in!"; and so it was, for persons of quality, comfortably mounted on the backs of the poor.

Turn now to the XVIII century opinion of Mozart. Far from finding his contemporaries listening with half-closed eyes to his delicious strains of melody, and to the melting supertonic cadence that Wagner made fun of in Die Meistersinger, you are stunned and amazed by complaints of the horrible noisiness of his instrumentation, of having to climb an arid mountain of discord to pluck a single flower of melody, of "the statue in the orchestra and the pedestal on the stage," of "too many notes," of assaults on the human ear and [on] the human tendency to slumber in the stalls after dinner. They suggest the Tannhäuser fiasco in Paris in 1860 or the reception of Ibsen's Ghosts in London in 1890 rather than *Voi, che sapete* and *Deh vieni alla finestra.* What has become of all this disturbing power? In the case of Tannhäuser we can explain it by the fact that we have only lately become quite accustomed to the unprepared major ninths which made the joyous music of Elisabeth sound so horrible to our grandfathers' ears. But the harmonies which disgruntled Mozart's contemporaries were not new. Mozart could take the common chord and make you jump by just doubling the third in the base; or he could put the hackneyed discord of the dominant seventh in a form so cunningly distributed and instrumented that it would sound as if it came straight from hell or from the Elysian fields across the Ionian Sea, according to his purpose. It is hardly an exaggeration to say that as far as mere grammar and vocabulary go, there is nothing more in the statue scene from Don Juan, which threw open the whole magic realm of modern orchestration first explored by Mozart's forerunner Gluck, than in the exquisite little song of Cherubino, *Non so più.* All the effects are still there, as fresh, and, on occasion, as terrible as the day they were composed: handle them properly, and Lohengrin and Tristan will taste like soothing syrup after them. Unfortunately, nobody seems able to handle them properly. After a long experience of many conductors and many composers, I have come to the conclusion that Mozart and Berlioz are, among the moderns, by far the most elusive and difficult in performance.

As I am only half a critic now, I act up to that character by going to only half an opera at a time. As in the case of Il Trovatore, I did not see the first two acts of Figaro's Wedding. When I entered, Sir Thomas Beecham struck up, by way of instrumental prelude to the third act, the fandango (at least Mozart, who had never been in Spain and can certainly never have heard a note of Spanish music, called it a fandango) from the wedding scene. What Mozart would have said if he had heard himself thus held up as a miserable XIX century composer, so barren of invention as to have to fall back on tunes out of his opera for preludes, I will not try to imagine, though I hope he would simply have expressed a mild wish that people would not do silly things. However, I was not sorry to hear the fandango twice; and I suppose nobody else was, in spite of the bad form involved. Only I began instantly to suspect that Sir Thomas is very fond of XVIII century music and does not care twopence about the specific Mozart. When the great duet came presently, he treated the few eloquent notes of exordium as if they were merely pianist's chords to fix the key; and of the wonderful opening-out of feeling which comes with the first words of Susanna I could not detect a trace. The first section was just dapper and nothing else: not until the concerted part came did the conductor warm to it. But the conclusive test was the sestet following Figaro's discovery of his parentage. How fine a piece of music that is, and how much it makes of a rather trivial though affectionate situation Sir Thomas will never know until he has fulfilled his destiny by conducting some of Mozart's greatest church music: say the grand Mass in C which lay so long undiscovered. Nothing came of the sestet, absolutely nothing at all: it might just as well have been omitted, as it was by the Carl Rosa company. But when it came to *Dove sono*, the conductor was really great: he squeezed every drop of nectar it contains out for us to the very last drop, and never relaxed his care, not even for the tiniest fraction of a bar. I will not blame the singer for putting in a little *liaison* of her own at the reprise, though I hope she will creep up to it diatonically instead of chromatically in future; for the chromatic progression is a mannerism of Meyerbeer's, and a patch of Meyerbeer on Mozart does not match nicely.

All the rest was like that. The sentimental parts were nursed with the tenderest care; but the dramatic and rhetorical parts were treated as so much purely decorative music, kept going very tightly and strictly and rapidly, and played with perfect precision and prettiness: that is to say, for Mozart's purpose, not played at all. The singers, in these rhetorical and dramatic passages, could do nothing but hold on hard lest they should find themselves in the last bar but one. Mr Newman's complaint that he could find none of the bitterness Beaumarchais gave to Figaro in the air *Aprite un po' quegl' occhi* was therefore not Mozart's fault. It is true that Mozart made no attempt to write political music in the sense of expressing not only wounded human feeling but the specific rancor of the class-conscious proletarian; but the wounded feeling is provided for very plentifully if only the conductor will allow the singer to put it in instead of treating him as if he were one of the second violins. That unlucky power of juggling with music which enabled Mozart to force dramatic expression upon purely decorative musical forms makes it possible for a conductor to treat any of his numbers as merely a sonata or rondo or what not; and this is very much what Sir Thomas Beecham does except when he comes to the beauty bits which appeal to him by their feminine sweetness. In conducting Wagner or Strauss he could not do so, because if he ignored the dramatic element there would be nothing left but senseless-sounding brass and tinkling cymbals. In Mozart's case what is left is a very elegant and pretty sonata movement; and with this Sir Thomas is quite satisfied. But even whilst securing a spirited and polished execution of the music on this plane, he shews a curious want of appreciation of Mozart's personal quality, especially his severe taste. After strangling his singers dramatically, he allows them to debase the music by substituting for what Mozart wrote what he no doubt might have written if he had been, not a great composer, but a conceited singer. Sir Thomas thinks that his singers are better composers than Mozart; he allows Susanna not only to transpose passages an octave up, as if he could not stand her quite adequate low notes, but to alter wantonly the end of *Deh vieni non tardar*, a miracle of perfect simplicity [and] beauty, into what seems by contrast a miracle of artificial commonplace, not to say vulgarity.

After conducting Basilio's aria—that quaint pæan of meanness which only a great actor could make intelligible—so completely in the spirit of abstract music that not even the roar of the tempest or the growl of the lion is suggested by the orchestra, he allows him to perpetrate the most third-class of all operatic tricks, the bawling of the last note an octave up in order to beg a foolish *encore* by a high B flat. As this is not weakness on Sir Thomas Beecham's part, for he is strict to tyranny in getting what his artistic conscience demands, he must really consider that his singers are improving Mozart. He actually lays himself open to the suspicion of having suggested the improvements. In that case there is nothing more to be said. What is clear so far is that he likes XVIII century music in its XVIII century form; and that this taste of his, highly creditable so far as it goes, has brought him accidentally into contact with Mozart; but of and for the specific Mozart who was not for the XVIII century but for all time he knows and cares nothing.

Now this opinion of mine is only an opinion unless it can be brought to the test of experiment. Who am I that I should criticize a conductor of Sir Thomas Beecham's experience, and an artistic director of his proved enterprise and popularity? Simply nobody but a man of letters of no musical authority at all. Well, I propose an experiment, and a very interesting one. Let Sir Thomas Beecham induce Sir Edward Elgar to take over Figaro for just one night. Elgar has not only the technical tradition (which is being so rapidly lost that I wish the Government would at once commission him to edit all

Mozart's operas for State publication) but he understands the heroic side of Mozart, which includes the dramatic side. It is sometimes rather a rough side; but Elgar would not be afraid of that. If Sir Thomas does not, after one hearing, blush to the roots of his hair and exclaim "Great Heavens! And I took this great composer for a mere confectioner!" I will pay a penny to any war charity he likes to name.

Mozart's opera scoring does in truth need some editing; for our conductors are spoiled by the copious and minute instructions which have been provided for them ever since they ceased to be a socially humble, professional caste fortified with an elaborate technical tradition instead of coming in from the general body of cultivated gentlemen amateurs. Mozart jotted down *f* or *sf* in his score where Meyerbeer would have written *con esplosione*. He wrote *p* where Verdi would have written *pppppp*! He did not resort to abbreviations to anything like the extent that the XVII century and earlier composers did; but compared to XIX century composers, who wrote down every note they meant to be sung, he used conventional musical shorthand to a considerable extent; and we want someone to fill in his scores as Arnold Dolmetsch has filled in the scores of Mozart's predecessors. Sir Thomas Beecham, relying on the existing scores, seems to have no conception of the dynamic range of Mozart's effects, of the fierceness of his *fortepianos*, the *élan* of his whipping-up triplets, the volume of his *fortes*. Even when Mozart writes *pp*, by which he means silence made barely audible (as in the first section of the Wedding March, for instance), we get at Drury Lane the same *mezzo forte* that prevails, except at a few blessed moments, during the whole performance. When the audience should be holding its breath to listen, or reeling from the thunder of the whole band and all the singers at their amplest, it still gets the same monotonous pretty fiddling that is neither high nor low, loud nor soft.

Yet on Thursday night, when I returned to hear the first two acts, I was carried away by the superb virtuosity of the orchestral execution, and the irresistible vigor and brilliancy of the great *finale* to the first act. Everything except this *finale* was far too fast even for all the instrumental effects, not to mention the dramatic ones; but I could not grudge the conductor his musical triumph; and I was positively grateful to him for audaciously forcing on us between the acts a slow movement for strings that had nothing to do with the opera, so finely was it played. It was pathetic and delightful to see the extraordinary pleasure of the audience, many of whom seemed to be discovering Mozart and going almost silly with the enchantment of it.

I repeat, the Drury Lane performance is charming; and very little additional care and understanding would make it great. It is, by the way, partly a performance of Beaumarchais' Mariage de Figaro; and I think it probable that if Mozart could be consulted as to the propriety of this attempt to make the best of both theatrical worlds, he would say that what he had taken from Beaumarchais he had taken and ennobled, and what he had left he had left for good reasons. To drag the Countess of *Porgi amor* and *Dove sono*, and the Cherubino of *Non so più* and *Voi, che sapete* back into an atmosphere of scandalous intrigue was dangerous, but it is not unsuccessful: Mozart carries everything before him. The scenery and costumes are rich and amusing. The idea seems to have been to do something in the style of Mr Charles Ricketts*; and the rose-pink crinoline

* Artist and stage designer, who had created the set designs and costumes for Shaw's productions of Don Juan in Hell (1907) and The Dark Lady of the Sonnets (1910). His greatest achievement was Saint Joan (1924).

petticoats are certainly as much in the style of Mr Ricketts as the sestet was in the style of Mozart: that is, Ricketts with Ricketts left out. Mr Nigel Playfair* did what a man could in looking after Beaumarchais; but it was Mozart that needed looking after, and Mr Playfair could not supersede the conductor. However, I cannot bear to grumble; only I wish a little more thought had been added to all the money and time and trouble lavished. That last scene, for instance, which should be so cunningly fitted to the music, and is not fitted to anything at all but a vague idea that it would make a pretty picture cover for a summer number of something. When I think of—but there! I think too much to be a reasonable critic.

SCRATCH OPERA

The Nation, London, 22 June 1918

Last week my old professional habit of opera-going reasserted itself for a moment. I heard the last two acts of Don Giovanni at the Shaftesbury Theatre by the Carl Rosa company, and The Valkyrie (Hunnishly known as Die Walküre) at Drury Lane. There was an immense difference between the two performances. One of them might have been an attempt on the part of an opera company, a conductor, and a number of bandsmen, all perfect strangers to oneanother and accidentally marooned in the Shaftesbury Theatre, to wile away the time by reading at sight a bundle of band parts and vocal scores of a rather difficult opera which they had never heard before by a young and very puzzling composer. The other had been rehearsed to the point of achieving,

* Popular actor-manager and frequent performer in Shaw's plays. He had staged The Marriage of Figaro at Drury Lane.

at its best moments, a superb fulfilment of the composer's intention; and the repeated storms of applause which broke out, until the conductor was forced to make several reluctant appearances before the curtain, were not, and could not have been, more generous than he deserved.

And yet they were both scratch performances.

When I was a child I heard certain operas rehearsed by a company of amateurs who, having everything to learn, could not have achieved a performance at all if they had not been coached and trained and rehearsed with a thoroughness impossible in professional music. It would cost too much. These amateurs rehearsed an opera for six months. There were all sorts of weaknesses about their performances; and yet I have never since, even in the course of several years' experience as a professional critic in London, with occasional excursions to Paris, Italy, and the German capitals, heard any performances as perfect, except some of the most thoroughly prepared productions at Bayreuth and Munich. I may be asked whether the brothers de Reszke, playing Gounod's Faust for the fifty millionth time at Covent Garden, did not display a tolerable familiarity with that work; and, of course, I cannot deny that they did; but the Valentins and Marguerites and Siebels came and went; and there was always the scratch habit which is so hard to throw off. In the ordinary theatre, where thorough rehearsal is the rule, and the conductor (called the producer) and the company have nothing else to do for six weeks or more than to work at the play, I have sometimes had to deal with an actor whose lot has been cast in theatres where a new play had to be presented every week or even every night. In such actors the scratch habit is an incurable disease. At the first rehearsal they astonish everyone, just as London orchestras always astonish foreign conductors and composers, by being almost letter-perfect, and giving such a capable and promising reading of their parts that one feels that after a fortnight's work they will be magnificent, and leave all the others nowhere. And they never get a step further. The fortnight's work is to them useless, unnecessary, and irritating. Even the letter-perfection vanishes; it deteriorates into appeals to the prompter or appalling improvizations.

The same thing occurs with opera singers. You hear a performance of some hackneyed opera by singers who have sung in it hundreds of times. It is never accurate. The individual singers are not so accurate, or even nearly so accurate as when they performed the part nervously and anxiously for the first time, and were much too young to have found out how little accuracy they could make shift with. They could no more give such a performance as Mr [Gerald] Du Maurier's company at Wyndham's Theatre gives of [Barrie's] Dear Brutus than a hotel waiter can behave like an old family servant. All experienced travelers have noticed that, however generously they may tip, hotel servants get tired of them if they attempt to reside in the hotel instead of passing on like all the others. There is a hotel psychology, a stock company psychology, and an opera psychology; and all three are modes of the scratch psychology, which is incompatible with thorough excellence.

I sometimes ask myself whether a thorough representation of an opera is worth while. I do not mean commercially: commercially it is impossible under existing conditions. But suppose money were no object, would the final degrees of perfection be worth the trouble they would cost? I go further than merely saying baldly that I think they would. I am strongly of opinion that nothing but superlative excellence in art can excuse a man or woman for being an artist at all. It is not a light thing in a world of drudgery for any citizen to say "I am not going to do what you others must: I am going to do what I like." I think we are entitled to reply "Then we shall expect you to do it devilish well, my friend, if we are not to treat you as a rogue and a vagabond." I have a large charity for loose morals: they are often more virtuous than straitlaced ones. But for loose art I have no charity at all. When I hear a fiddler playing *mezzo forte* when his part is marked *pianissimo* or *fortissimo* (as the English orchestral fiddler is apt to do if he can trifle with the conductor), or a trombone player shirking the trouble of phrasing intelligently, I hate him. Yet I could forgive him quite easily for being a bigamist.

The difference between the Don Giovanni and the Valkyrie performances was that the Carl Rosa company had better not have played Don Giovanni at all than played it as they did, wheras it would have been a positive national loss to us if we had not had the Beecham performance. I grant that there are extenuating circumstances. Mozart's music is enormously more difficult than Wagner's; and his tragi-comedy is even more so. With Mozart you either hit the bulls-eye or miss; and a miss is as bad as a mile. With Wagner the target is so large and the charge so heavy that if you get the notes out anyhow, you are bound to do some execution. It takes a Coquelin, combined with a first-rate *basso cantante*, to play Leporello; but any heavyweight bass, with the voice of a wolf, and very little more power of vocal execution, can put up a quite impressive Hunding. Roll Forbes-Robertson* and Vladimir Rosing into one, and you will have an adequate Don Juan; but which of all the famous Wotans could have touched Don Juan

* Johnston Forbes-Robertson, who had recently retired, was the greatest Hamlet of his generation. He also created Shaw's Cæsar.

with the tips of his fingers? It is the same with the conducting: what conductor of any talent, with the tradition of Wagner and Richter to prompt him, could fail with the scene between Siegmund and Brynhild in the second act of Die Walküre, or with the fire music at the close? Try him with the two symphonic scenes in which Don Juan invites the statue to supper, and in which the statue avails himself of the invitation, and he is as likely as not to be hopelessly beaten. Felix Mottl was one of the very best Wagner conductors produced by Bayreuth. I have heard him conduct Mozart's Nozze di Figaro, Così fan tutte, and Clemenza di Tito to perfection in Munich. But he was utterly beaten by Don Giovanni. Senor de la Fuente, the Carl Rosa conductor, when he conducted Le Nozze di Figaro last year, handled it brilliantly. It is an easily learnt work: the execution may require exquisite delicacy and immaculate taste; but there is no touch of tragedy in it, nor any touch of passion of the tragic quality.

Now, Don Juan is a tragic hero or nothing: his destiny is announced by Mozart from the very first chord of the overture. That the opera is called a *dramma giocosa*, and that there was an early Don Juan who was only a squalid drunkard and libertine, does not weigh against the evidence of the score. Before Shakespear touched Hamlet there was a zany Hamlet who mopped and mowed, and nailed down the courtiers under the arras and set them on fire, going through all the pitiable antics with which the village idiot amused heartless visitors when he was one of the sights of the village instead of an inmate of the county asylum. Well, Mozart abolished the drunken Don Juan as completely and finally as Shakespear abolished the zany Hamlet. Unfortunately, the operatic conductors and stars do not seem to have found this out. When the singer who impersonates Don Juan happens to be a gentleman, he takes the greatest pains to make himself a cad for the occasion. Leporello's agonies of terror are replaced by silly and ineptly executed buffooneries which the Brothers Griffith could do, in their proper place,* artistically and funnily. Everyone, the conductor included, is nosing through the score for the vulgar fun which is not there, and overlooking the tragic and supernatural atmosphere which is there. And the result is that they all feel that the thing is not going, that they are missing instead of hitting. They do not know what is the matter, and yet know that something is the matter. They find the music frightfully difficult; cling with their eyes to the conductor; become rattled and flurried and panic-stricken; until at last their passages sound like nothing at all. The conductor has to keep up an air of assurance, but is secretly almost equally puzzled: you know it by the infirmity of the rhythm. Even the ruthless march of the statue music, a rhythm which no conductor ever misses in the music of Wotan or of Rossini's Moses, dwindles into an irresolute buzzing. For example, the terrible address of the statue, which begins *Tu m'invitasti a cena*, is preceded by two ominous bars in which this rhythm is thundered through dead vocal silence as emphatically as the opening of Beethoven's symphony in C minor. The conductor must mark this with Handelian conviction and power; for it is quite as necessary to the effect as the more sensational orchestration of the hellish blasts which follow it, and which only a deaf conductor could underrate. But Senor de la Fuente noticed nothing in it but commonplace rum-tum, which he was too worried to attend to. That is only one instance of the sort of thing that went on all through the symphonic numbers, and that always will go on until some conductor will take the work in tragic seriousness, search the score for what

* The Brothers Griffith were music hall comics.

Mozart put into it and not for what he made his reputation by leaving out of it, and finally rehearse it hard for a year or so before letting the public in.

He will find other things besides the tragic intensity of the overture and the statue music. He will find that the window *trio Ah, taci, ingiusto core,* is not a comic accompaniment to the unauthorized tomfoolery of Don Juan making a marionet of Leporello, but perhaps the most lovely nocturne in the whole range of musical literature. And he may also be led to the discovery, greatly needed by all English conductors, and apparently by one Spanish one, that six-eight time does not always mean that the piece is a country dance. In German music it often means an *andantino* of intense and noble sentiment.

I must in fairness make it clear that the shortcomings in the Carl Rosa performance were not the fault of the singers. They were asked to perform under scratch conditions a work which has never yet been satisfactorily or even decently performed under such conditions, and never will. At Covent Garden the directors used to throw it over to some *ripieno* conductor to run through once a season as an easy routine job, and were perfectly successful in making it appear worthy of the ignorant contempt with which they were treating it. The Carl Rosa company at least know it to be an important work; but as they know little else about it except the mere notes, and some of its silliest would-be comic traditions, the result is no better. Why not leave Don Giovanni in peace on the shelf? It is so easy not to perform it.

By the way, there was one original point made. Mr James Pursail is the first Don, as far as I know, to notice that, as Don Juan was not a professional singer, however masterfully he may sing all the dramatic music, he should sing the serenade like an amateur. And this was just what Mr Pursail did. I do not mean that he sang it badly: on the contrary, he sang it very nicely; and I do not quarrel with his unauthorized F sharp at the end, because, for a high baritone with an F sharp which is better than his low D, it is a pardonable flourish, and is not in any case a vulgarity like shouting the last note an octave up, with which Mr Edward Davies discredited an otherwise excellent performance of *Il mio tesoro.* I mean that Mr Pursail sang it, not in the traditionally ardent and accomplished manner, but in the manner of a modest amateur. This is a real new reading which deserves to be noted.

Die Walküre was a very different affair. The singers and the conductor knew much more about the work, and the execution was remarkably accurate. And yet the scratch quality came out sometimes just where the accuracy was closest and the skill most perfect. Take, for example, the sword theme. The seven notes of which it consists are all over Die Walküre. They present no difficulty to such wind players as Sir Thomas Beecham commands; and they are scored so as to give them the prominence of a constellation in the orchestral heaven. Well, a lady who is not unfamiliar with the music made the astounding remark to me that she had detected the sword theme *once.* Before Sir Thomas dismisses that lady as a deaf imbecile, I advise him to engage a mathematician to calculate how many different phrasings can be put upon a seven-note theme. Then let him call a wind rehearsal, and try all the different phrasings. He will be interested to find that whenever the third note is included in a slur, the theme will become unrecognizable as Wagner's sword theme. A single *portamento* in the wrong place will put off any listener who does not know the score. It will veil the star which gives the constellation its characteristic form, and turn it into a mere strip of the milky way. Clearly, in a performance prepared up to the best Bayreuth point, an understanding would be established with all the wind players as to the exact phrasing of this and every other theme. On Saturday night hardly any two wind players gave the same version of it; and the result was that it lost its identity. That is why I reluctantly put this very splendid and valuable revival under the heading of Scratch Opera.

Sir Thomas Beecham was the star of the evening, but the singers ran him close. Miss Agnes Nicholls sang the music of Brynhild beautifully; but I ask how any woman can be expected to look like a Valkyrie, or feel like one, or move like one, in the skirt of an ultra-womanly woman of the period when a female who climbed to the top of an omnibus would have been handed [over] to the police as a disgrace to her sex. If Sir Thomas or anyone else imagines that the situation is saved by adding to the womanly skirt a breastplate and a barmaid's wig of that same period, he errs. In 1876, when this ridiculous dress was "made in Germany," it could at least be said that when Brynhild left the theatre in her private character, she wore a long skirt. But before Miss Agnes Nicholls leaves her dressing room for the street she has to put on a short skirt, and to find even that conspicuous for its length in the crowd of knickered *chauffeuses* and booted and breeched female war workers of all sorts. Why on earth does not Sir Thomas throw all this ragbag rubbish of fifty years ago into the dustbin, and make his Valkyries look like Valkyries and not like Mrs Leo Hunter? This thing is beyond patience; I pass on.

Fricka I did not hear, because I dined, Bayreuth fashion, between the first and second acts. Miss Miriam Licette did as much with Sieglinde as a soprano with a mezzo-soprano part could do against the competition (where there should have been contrast) of Brynhild. Mr Robert Parker was in a similar difficulty: his bright hard voice is not of the right color for Wotan, "the melancholy Dane" of the modern stage. And he really should not dance at Brynhild as if he were going to kick her unless he seriously reads the part that way. He was more Herod than Wotan; but his articulation was the best in the company, and he put in some fine singing. It would be unreasonable to ask for a richer Siegmund than Mr Walter Hyde, who was deservedly very popular. The English version, as far as it got across the footlights, was very helpful to the English audience; but why are the German epithets retained in such passages as *Friedmund darf ich nicht heissen; Frohwalt möcht' ich wohl sein: doch Wehwalt muss ich mich nennen?* Polyglot nonsense, I call it. The performance was described in the program as having been "produced." I saw no evidence of the process. The old routine was carried out in all its sacred staleness. The scenery made Old Drury feel young again. Wings, sky-borders, set pieces: nothing was missing. Granville-Barker must have chuckled.

The house was crammed from floor to ceiling, and the applause prodigious. This, for a work of which the hero and heroine are within the tables of consanguinity, written and composed by one classed by our patriotic papers as a congenital scoundrel with a specific lust for the blood of women and children, would probably be accounted for by the patriots on the ground that Old Drury, huge as it is, does not hold 47,000,000 people. I will therefore conclude by mentioning that I never saw a more normal and native British musical audience in my life, or a more enthusiastic one. And now bring along your Dora and hale me to the Tower.

THE FUTURE OF BRITISH MUSIC

British Music Society Bulletin, June 1919, under the title Starved Arts Mean Low Pleasures; reprinted in The Outlook, 19 and 26 July 1919, under its revised title

It has never been possible for modern British composers to live by the practice of the higher forms of their art in their own country; but until 1914 Germany provided a market which enabled them to produce a symphony with at least some hope of having it performed and even published. That is now at an end. Performances of British music in Germany have ceased; and remittances are cut off. Thus British composers who have obtained a hearing in that country are suffering seriously from a closing of the most important source of their incomes from classic work; and the economic inducement to our younger composers to keep British music in the front rank of culture no longer exists.

This situation is not creditable to us as a nation. And it has arisen at a moment when the introduction of compulsory military service and the waging of a long war has dealt a heavy blow to the fine arts. To realize the weight of that blow it is necessary to consider what the state of music would have been if Sebastian Bach had been engaged in the Thirty Years War, and Mozart, Beethoven, and Wagner sent to the trenches for the few years (no longer than the duration of the present war) during which they produced, respectively, Don Giovanni, Figaro, the Jupiter Symphony and its successors in G minor and E flat, the Eroica Symphony and the Emperor Concerto, and the Ring Poem and the scores of Das Rheingold and Die Walküre. Such a sacrifice to militarism would have left the world three centuries behindhand in musical development. Yet an instalment of that sacrifice befell British music during the war. We were so little conscious of it that attempts to persuade tribunals that the composition of serious music is work of national importance were received with derision. Almost in the same week we saw one energetic young composer and organizer of musical festivals [Rutland Boughton] sneered at and sent into the army by the tribunal in a leading English city, and another exempted elsewhere with something like awe because he had once composed a popular waltz.

Such a state of public opinion is inexcusable in a civilized country once famous throughout Europe for the quality of its music. Yet it has lasted for two centuries, which may be reckoned as the dark ages of British music. During that time musicians have supported themselves by giving piano lessons to young ladies without serious musical intentions, or by composing drawing-room ballads, or as church organists by accompanying hymns and "sacred music" which seldom rose above the level of Jackson's Te Deum. Sterndale Bennett, for example, with a promise as bright and a character as high as Mendelssohn's, was sterilized by a lifetime of drudgery as a piano teacher.

The notion that musical genius is independent of the substantial encouragements which attract men towards other careers is strikingly contradicted by the history of music in England. It is true that British composers of a sort survived when the overwhelming pecuniary temptations of the industrial revolution turned the genius of England to commerce in the XVIII century; but the outstanding fact about them is that they wrote no British music except trivial drawing-room music or vulgar dance music with less national character than their knives and forks. In the higher departments they produced shoddy Handel, a little Mozart and water, and, finally, a great deal of secondhand Mendelssohn and Spohr. They expressed nothing of the British character or the British imagination: all that their scores convey to us is their love of foreign music and their vain ambition to become great composers by imitating it. With the exception of a few sturdily unfashionable Britons like Pearsall, who kept up the old tradition in his motets and madrigals, our composers posed as Germans as ridiculously as our singers posed as Italians. And the main reason clearly was that it is not in the British character, if indeed it be in any sound character, to accept success in art at the cost of poverty and contempt in the common life of the nation. Under such circumstances art will be practiced only by those who are infatuated with their love of music (the character of the amateur), or who are good for nothing else—and it is a disastrous mistake to suppose that the great artists are good for nothing else. Yet it is a very common mistake: it is even considered a mark of soulful enlightenment in artistic matters to believe that if Phidias had been born an Andaman Islander and Beethoven a Patagonian, they would have produced the Parthenon and the Ninth Symphony by inspiration. Genius, it is supposed, will bridge all chasms and vanquish all difficulties, the inevitable result being that England tends towards the condition of Patagonia or the Andaman Islands as far as the higher forms of music are concerned. Under this false, mean, lazy, and stupid assumption that it is sordid and Philistine to regard music as a product of national respect for it, and national practical encouragement of and inducement to it, classical music is left to "irresistible vocation," and perishes accordingly. Even the really irresistible vocations, such as Mozart's or Elgar's, are dependent on the quite easily resistible ones. Mozart could not have occurred except in a Europe in which there had been many generations of thousands of commonplace musicians whose vocation was by no means irresistible, and many of whom had been driven to the first study of their art by blows. Michael Angelo could not have occurred in the England of his day, and did not. He was the product of a great craft of masonry, and of a magnificent patronage of its artistic application. There is not a single case in the whole history of art in which artists have produced the greatest work of which art is capable except as a final step in an elaborate civilization built up and maintained by a multitude of citizens, mostly amateurs employing professional artists of whom not one-tenth [of one] per cent. were original geniuses, but all accepting fine art as an indispensable element in the greatness of States and the glory of God.

Public opinion must be roused to the need for providing in England the conditions in which it will be possible for Englishmen, after a lapse of two centuries, once more to express themselves in genuinely British music with a weight and depth possible only in the higher forms of music. Here there is no question of the sort of "national music" that is produced by forcing music into local dance forms, or into the pseudo-modes which can be imitated by omitting those intervals of our scale which could not be played on primitive forms of the bagpipe or the harp. All such *bric-à-brac* already receives more than enough encouragement. The language and instrumentation of music are now international; and what is meant by British music is music in which British musicians express their British character in that international language. When Elgar startled us by suddenly reasserting the British character in music he did it in an idiom which was no more distinctively English than the idiom of Schumann; but Schumann could not, or rather would not, have written ten bars of an Elgar symphony.

The needs of the situation may be roughly summed up as more performances, more publication, and more advertisement. Taking the [last] first, how many people are aware of the fact that the British Isles can put into the field about forty living composers of serious music without counting those XIX century composers whose names are well known to the public, such as Elgar, Stanford, Parry, Cowen, Bantock, Delius, and others? It is not only possible to find enthusiastic musical amateurs who do not know this, but positively difficult to find any who do know it. Our resources must be advertized.

The most effective advertisements of the fine arts are the performances and exhibitions attended by the critics who deal with them in the press. Mere commerce is never up to date in this matter. The pioneering must be done by societies of enthusiasts. If our critics of the drama know something more of modern dramatic literature than can be picked up by attending commercial performances, they owe their knowledge to the efforts of private societies such as the Stage Society and the Pioneer Players. If there were no other picture exhibitions than those of the Royal Academy, the modern developments of painting would not exist either for the critics or for the public. If the commercial concert givers are ever to insist on their conductors undertaking the labor of studying new works by troublesome young men, they must be sharply criticized for their neglect, and made to feel that programs without a single novelty, whether British or foreign, are ridiculous. Before the critics can be expected to do that, societies like the British Music Society must bring the new work to their knowledge.

And the performances cannot be followed up unless the music is published at reasonable prices in vocal score or in transcription for the piano in two-handed and four-handed arrangements or in pianola rolls; for it remains as true now as when Wagner said it that music is kept alive on the cottage pianos of the amateurs, and not by commercial performances.

What the British Music Society may be able to do in these directions will depend on the support it receives. It is impossible to feel very sanguine in the face of such facts as the influentially launched Shakespear Memorial National Theatre scheme with, as a result of years of expensive agitation, a single subscription of £70,000 from a German gentleman, or the ruthless seizure during the war of the public picture galleries throughout the country for the commonest office purposes, culminating in a shameless attempt, which fortunately collapsed through some accident at the last moment, to crown the sacrifice by the seizure of the British Museum. These things, be it noted, happened at a moment when we were claiming to be the champions of European civilization against Hunnish barbarism. When at last the Armistice came, what was it that sprang to the front to demand restoration and reconstruction as the first relief and recreation brought by our victory? Racing, hunting, football, cricket. Not a word about music, though perhaps the most ridiculous incident that relieved the tragedy of the war had been the demand for the instant exclusion of German music from the programs of the Promenade Concerts, which, being at once effected amid patriotic cheers, resulted in empty concert rooms for a week, at the end of which an unparalleled outburst of Beethoven and Wagner crowded them again. It need not be said harshly and uppishly that all this is disgraceful to us. But it will be said, and indeed must be said, that it makes our pretensions to be a cultured nation (not, to be quite just, that we often make such pretensions, or seem to be the least bit ashamed of ourselves) so absurd that we ourselves have to laugh heartily at them like the cheerful savages we are on that plane.

During the war we borrowed our music not only from Germany but from Russia. This is a sort of borrowing for which an honest nation should pay in kind. If we have to borrow tea from China and pay for it in hardware, we can at least plead that our soil will not produce tea. Now music it *can* produce. It has done it before and can do it again. The stuff is there waiting for a market to make it worth mining. It is kept waiting because we are a people of low pleasures. And we are a people of low pleasures because we are brought up to them: the British workman finds the public-house and the football field offering themselves to him insistently at every turn; and the British gentleman is actually forced to spend his boyish leisure at cricket and football before he enters an adult society in which he cannot escape hunting, shooting, bridge, and billiards, though he can go through life as a complete gentleman without hearing a Beethoven sonata in any other form than that of a disagreeable noise which he forbids his daughters to make in the schoolroom except during the hours when he is usually out of doors. If you eliminate smoking and the element of gambling, you will be amazed to find that almost all an Englishman's pleasures can be, and mostly are, shared by his dog.

Why is this state of things described always as "healthy"? Simply because there are worse pleasures in ambush for human leisure in our civilization. Compulsory perpetual athletics at school are to send the boy to bed too tired for mischief. The meet in the hunting field is better than the meet in Piccadilly Circus. But what is the worth of a society which has to resort to such barbarous shifts? Are not the Muses always there to give our leisure the most delightful entertainment, and to refine our tastes and strengthen our intellects at the same time? We banish them, and then find that we must resort to the occupations of greyhounds and ferrets, and the migrations of birds, to rescue us from the snares of the pestilential rivals of the Muses.

It is a pitiful state of things; and I, for one, wish the British Music Society luck in its resolve to educate, agitate, and organize against it in the sacred names of Euterpe and Polyhymnia, Thalia and Terpsichore. I am tired of being suspected of being no gentleman because I am more interested in these goddesses than in the mares in the stables of those of my friends who represent the culture of the Empire.

SIR EDWARD ELGAR

I

Music and Letters, January 1920; Harper's Bazar, April 1920

Edward Elgar, the figurehead of music in England, is a composer whose rank it is neither prudent nor indeed possible to determine. Either it is one so high that only time and prosperity can confer it, or else he is one of the Seven Humbugs of Christendom. Contemporary judgments are sound enough on Second Bests; but when it comes to Bests they acclaim ephemerals as immortals, and simultaneously denounce immortals as pestilent charlatans.

Elgar has not left us any room to hedge. From the beginning, quite naturally and as a matter of course, he has played the great game and professed the Best. He has taken up the work of a great man so spontaneously that it is impossible to believe that he ever gave any consideration to the enormity of the assumption, or was even conscious of it. But there it is, unmistakable. To the north countryman who, on hearing of Wordsworth's death, said "I suppose his son will carry on the business," it would be plain today that Elgar is carrying on Beethoven's business. The names are up on the shop front for everyone to read. ELGAR, late BEETHOVEN & CO., Classics and Italian & German Warehousemen. Symphonies, Overtures, Chamber Music, Oratorios, Bagatelles.

This, it will be seen, is a very different challenge from that of, say, Debussy and Stravinsky. You can rave about Stravinsky without the slightest risk of being classed as a lunatic by the next generation. You can declare the Après-midi d'un Faune the most delightful and enchanting orchestral piece ever written without really compromising yourself. But, if you say that Elgar's Cockaigne overture combines every classic quality of a concert overture with every lyric and dramatic quality of the overture to Die Meistersinger, you are either uttering a platitude as safe as a compliment to Handel on the majesty of the Hallelujah chorus, or else damning yourself to all critical posterity by a *gaffe* that will make your grandson blush for you.

Personally, I am prepared to take the risk. What do I care about my grandson? Give me Cockaigne. But my recklessness cannot settle the question. It would be so much easier if Cockaigne were *genre* music, with the Westminster chimes, snatches of Yip-i-addy,* and a march of the costermongers to Covent Garden. Then we should know where we are: the case would be as simple as Gilbert and Sullivan.

But there is nothing of the kind: the material of the Cockaigne overture is purely classical. You may hear all

* Song by John H. Flynn, with lyric by Will D. Cobb, popularized by Blanche Ring in America in 1908. Max Beerbohm described it as "banality raised to the sublime."

sorts of footsteps in it, and it may tell you all sorts of stories; but it is classical music as Beethoven's Les Adieux sonata is classical music: it tells you no story external to itself and yourself. Therefore, who knows whether it appeals to the temporal or the eternal in us; in other words, whether it will be alive or dead in the XXI century?

Certain things one can say without hesitation. For example, that Elgar could turn out Debussy and Stravinsky music by the thousand bars for fun in his spare time. That to him such standbys as the whole-tone-scale of Debussy, the Helmholtzian chords of Scriabin, the exciting modulations of the operatic school, the zylophone and celesta orchestration by which country dances steal into classical concerts, are what farthings are to a millionaire. That his range is so Handelian that he can give the people a universal melody or march with as sure a hand as he can give the Philharmonic Society a symphonic adagio, such as has not been given since Beethoven died. That, to come down to technical things, his knowledge of the orchestra is almost uncanny.

When Gerontius made Elgar widely known, there was a good deal of fine writing about it; but what every genuine connoisseur in orchestration must have said at the first hearing (among other things) was "What a devil of a *fortissimo*!" Here was no literary paper instrumentation, no muddle and noise, but an absolutely new energy given to the band by a consummate knowledge of exactly what it could do and how it could do it.

We were fed up to the throats at that time with mere piquancies of orchestration: every scorer of ballets could scatter pearls from the *pavillon chinois* (alias Jingling Johnny) over the plush and cotton velvet of his harmonies; but Elgar is no mere effect monger: he takes the whole orchestra in his hand and raises every separate instrument in it to its highest efficiency until its strength is as the strength of ten. One was not surprised to learn that he could play them all, and was actually something of a *virtuoso* on instruments as different as the violin and trombone.

The enormous command of existing resources, which this orchestral skill of his exemplifies, extends over the whole musical field, and explains the fact that, though he has a most active and curious mind, he does not appear in music as an experimenter and explorer, like Scriabin and Schönberg. He took music where Beethoven left it, and where Schumann and Brahms found it. Naturally he did not pick up and put on the shackles that Wagner had knocked off, any more than he wore his trumpet parts in tonic and dominant *clichés* in the XVIII century manner, as some of his contemporaries made a point of honor of doing, for the sake of being in the classical fashion. But his musical mind was formed before Wagner reached him; and his natural power over the material then available was so great that he was never driven outside it by lack of means for expressing himself.

He was no keyboard composer: music wrote itself on the skies for him, and wrote itself in the language perfected by Beethoven and his great predecessors. With the same inheritance, Schumann, who had less faculty and less knowledge, devotedly tried to be another Beethoven, and failed. Brahms, with a facility as convenient as Elgar's, was a musical sensualist with intellectual affectations, and succeeded only as an incoherent voluptuary, too fundamentally addleheaded to make anything great out of the delicious musical luxuries he wallowed in. Mendelssohn was never really in the running: he was, in his own light, impetuous, and often lovely style, *sui generis,* superficial if you like, but always his own unique self, composing in an idiom invented by himself, not following a school and not founding one.

Elgar, neither an imitator nor a voluptuary, went his own way without bothering to invent a new language, and by sheer personal originality produced symphonies that are really symphonies in the Beethovenian sense, a feat in which neither Schumann, Mendelssohn, nor Brahms, often as they tried, ever succeeded convincingly. If I were king, or Minister of Fine Arts, I would give Elgar an annuity of a thousand a year on condition that he produce a symphony every eighteen months.

It will be noted, I hope, that this way of Elgar's, of accepting the language and forms of his art in his time as quite sufficient for anyone with plenty of courage and a masterly natural command of them, is the way of Shakespear, of Bach, of all the greatest artists. The notion that Wagner was a great technical innovator is now seen to be a delusion that had already done duty for Mozart and Handel: it meant nothing more than that the born-great composer always has the courage and commonsense not to be a pedant.

Elgar has certainly never let any pedantry stand in his way. He has indeed not been aware of its academic stumbling blocks; for, like Bach, he has never been taught harmony and counterpoint. A person who had been corrupted by Day's treatise on harmony once tried to describe a phrase of Wagner's to him by a reference to the chord of the supertonic. Elgar opened his eyes wide, and, with an awe which was at least very well acted, asked "What on earth is the chord of the supertonic?" And then, after a pause, "What *is* the supertonic? I never heard of it."

This little incident may help to explain the effect produced at first by Elgar on the little clique of devoted musicians who, with the late Hubert Parry as its centre, stood for British music thirtyfive years ago. This clique was the London section of the Clara Schumann-Joachim-Brahms clique in Germany, and the relations between the two were almost sacred. Of that international clique the present generation knows nothing, I am afraid, except that when Madame Schumann found that Wagner's Walküre fire music was to be played at a concert for which she was engaged, she declined to appear in such disgraceful company, and only with great difficulty was induced, after anxious consultation with the clique, to make a supreme effort of condescension and compromise herself rather than disappoint the people who had bought tickets to hear her.

This is too good a joke against the clique to be forgotten; and the result is that poor Clara and Joachim and company are now regarded as a ridiculous little mutual-admiration gang of snobs. I entreat our snorting young lions to reconsider that harsh judgment. If they had heard Clara Schumann at her best, they could not think of her in that way. She and her clique were snobs, no doubt; but so are we all, more or less. There are many virtues mixed up with snobbery; and the clique was entirely sincere in its snobbery, and thought it was holding up a noble ideal on the art it loved. Wagner was about as eligible for it as a 450 h.p. aeroplane engine for a perambulator.

It was much the same at first with Elgar and the London branch of the clique. A young man from the west country without a musical degree, proceeding calmly and sweetly on the unconscious assumption that he was by nature and destiny one of the great composers, when, as a matter of fact, he had never heard of the supertonic, shocked and irritated the clique very painfully. It was not, of course, Elgar's fault. He pitied them, and was quite willing to shew them how a really handy man (they were the unhandiest of mortals) should write for the trombones, tune the organ, flyfish, or groom and harness and drive a horse. He could talk about every unmusical subject on earth, from pigs to Elizabethan literature.

A certain unmistakably royal pride and temper was getatable on occasion; but normally a less pretentious person than Elgar could not be found. To this day you may meet him and talk to him for a week without suspecting that he is anything more than a very typical English country gentleman who does not know a fugue from a fandango. The landlady in Pickwick whose complaint of her husband was that "Raddle aint like a man" would have said, if destiny had led her to the altar with the composer of the great symphony in A flat, "Elgar aint like a musician." The clique took Mrs Raddle's view. And certainly Elgar's music acted very differently from theirs. His Enigma Variations took away your breath. The respiration induced by their compositions was perfectly regular, and occasionally perfectly audible.

That attitude towards him was speedily reduced to absurdity by the mere sound of his music. But some initial incredulity as to his genius may be excused when we recollect that England had waited two hundred years for a great English composer, and waited in vain. The phenomenon of greatness in music had vanished from England with Purcell. Musical facility had survived abundantly. England had maintained a fair supply of amazingly dexterous and resourceful orchestral players, brass-bandsmen, organists, glee singers, and the like. But they lacked culture, and could not produce a really musical atmosphere for the local conductors who tried to organize them. And the only alternatives were the university musicians who made up the metropolitan cliques, gentlemen amateurs to a man, infatuated with classical music, and earnestly striving to compose it exactly as the great composers did. And that, of course, was no use at all. Elgar had all the dexterities of the bandsmen; sucked libraries dry as a child sucks its mother's breasts; and gathered inspiration from the skies. Is it any wonder that we were skeptical of such a miracle? For my part, I expected nothing from any English composer; and when the excitement about Gerontius began, I said wearily "Another Wardour-street festival oratorio!" But when I heard the Variations (which had not attracted me to the concert) I sat up and said "Whew!" I knew we had got it at last.

Since then English and American composers have sprung up like mushrooms: that is, not very plentifully, but conspicuously. The clique is, if not dead, toothless; and our Cyril Scotts and Percy Graingers, our Rutland Boughtons and Granville Bantocks and the rest pay not the smallest attention to its standard. The British Musical Society offers to name forty British composers of merit without falling back on Elgar or any member of his generation. But, so far, Elgar alone is for Westminster Abbey.

As I said to begin with, neither I nor any living man can say with certainty whether these odds and ends which I have been able to relate about Elgar are the stigmata of what we call immortality. But they look to me very like it; and I give them accordingly for what they may prove to be worth.*

* Although Elgar was flattered and moved by Shaw's tribute, he quickly published, in the second number of Music and Letters in April, a denial that Hubert Parry had led a clique with the principal aim of keeping him down. He hoped, he said, "to make known all I owe to his ungrudging kindness at some future time." After Elgar's death, in 1934, Ralph Vaughan Williams also refuted the charge, in the same journal.

II

To The Daily News, London, 9 June 1922

The Leeds Choral Union gave a superb performance of Sir Edward Elgar's fine work, The Apostles, yesterday at Queen's Hall in aid of the Westminster Abbey Restoration Fund.

So scanty was the audience that the neglect of such a British masterpiece was a matter of general comment, and Mr Bernard Shaw expresses his feelings in characteristic terms in the letter below. [Editor, DAILY NEWS.]

Sir,—I have just heard at Queen's Hall the finest performance of Sir Edward Elgar's masterpiece, The Apostles, that our present executive resources at their choral best in the North, and their solo and orchestral best in London, can achieve.

It is only at very long and uncertain intervals that such a performance is possible.

The Apostles is one of the glories of British music: indeed it is unique as a British work. Its quality is such that German music at its highest in this form can put nothing beside it except the St Matthew Passion of Bach, a few samples from the Messiah of what Handel could have done with the same theme, and Beethoven's great Mass in D.

It places British music once more definitely in the first European rank, after two centuries of leather and prunella.

It would be an exaggeration to say that I was the only person present, like Ludwig of Bavaria, at Wagner's *premières*. My wife was there. Other couples were visible at intervals. One of the couples consisted of the Princess Mary and Viscount Lascelles, who just saved the situation as far as the credit of the Crown is concerned, as it very deeply is.

I distinctly saw six people in the stalls, probably with complimentary tickets.

In the cheaper seats a faithful band stood for England's culture.

It was not, as days go this month, an oppressively hot day. The season was at its height.

The occasion was infinitely more important than the Derby, than Goodwood, than the Cup Finals, than the Carpentier fights, than any of the occasions on which the official leaders of society are photographed and cinematographed laboriously shaking hands with persons on whom Molière's patron, Louis XIV, and Bach's patron, Frederick the Great, would not have condescended to wipe their boots.

The performance was none the less impressive, nor the music the less wonderful.

My object in writing this letter is simply to gratify an uncontrolable impulse to let Sir Edward Elgar and the Leeds Choral Union know that I am unspeakably ashamed of their treatment.

I apologize to them for London society, and for all the other recreants to England's culture, who will, I fear, not have the grace to apologize for themselves.

I think the enormous expenses of the performance should be repaid to the public-spirited Yorkshireman on whom, I understand, they will fall.

And, finally, I apologize to posterity for living in a country where the capacity and taste of schoolboys and sporting costermongers are the measure of metropolitan culture.

Disgustedly yours,
G. Bernard Shaw

III

In February 1931 a letter signed by eighteen representative musicians and music lovers, including William Walton, Augustus John, Emile Cammaerts, Philip Heseltine, John Ireland, and Shaw, was sent to the Press Association, emphatically protesting against "the unjust and inadequate treatment of Sir Edward Elgar" by Professor E. J. Dent in an article on modern music published in Germany in the new edition of Adler's monumental Handbuch der Musikgeschichte. "The fact that the learned Professor devotes 66 lines to Parry, 41 to Stanford, and only 16 to Elgar is perhaps hardly a matter for criticism, but the statement that 'for English ears Elgar's music is much too emotional and not free from vulgarity,' the summary dismissal of all his orchestral works as 'lively in colour, but pompous in style, and of a too deliberate nobility of expression,' and his chamber music as 'dry and academic' cannot go unchallenged." The letter concludes: "Professor Dent's failure to appreciate Elgar's music is no doubt temperamental, but it does not justify him in grossly misrepresenting the position which Sir Edward Elgar and his music enjoy in the esteem of his fellow-countrymen." To this statement Shaw added his own postscript. The letter and Shaw's postscript were published in The Manchester Guardian on 6 February 1931

[U] I wish, however, to add that Professor Dent's undervaluation is much more serious than our protest suggests. Elgar holds the same position in English music as Beethoven in German music. The "vulgarity" of his more popular tunes is the vulgarity of Handel's See the Conquering Hero, or the *finale* to Beethoven's Fifth Symphony. The Kingdom and The Apostles are not oratorios in the Handelian sense: they are a new form of symphonic art involving a "literarischen Bildung" of which Parry and Stanford never dreamt. Professor Dent should not have made them ridiculous by such comparison and should not have belittled his country by belittling the only great English composer who is not dwarfed by the German giants. [U]

IV

To The Times, London, 20 December 1932

Sir,—I have occasionally remarked that the only entirely creditable incident in English history is the sending of £100 to Beethoven on his deathbed by the London Philharmonic Society; and it is the only one that historians never mention.

Thanks to Sir John Reith* it is no longer unique. His action in commissioning a new symphony from Sir Edward Elgar, the first English composer to produce symphonies ranking with those of Beethoven, is a triumph for the B.B.C.

But is it not a pity that Sir Edward has had to wait so long for the advent of a public administrator capable of rising to the situation? The forthcoming symphony will be his third†: it should be his ninth. It is true that we have loaded him with honors. I use the word loaded advisedly, as the honors have the effect of enabling us to exact much gratuitous work from him. He has given us

* Sir John C. W. (later Baron) Reith was Director-General of the British Broadcasting Corporation.

† Elgar was fifty before he completed his first symphony in 1908. The second followed three years later. The third was left in fragmented form at the time of his death in 1934.

a Land of Hope and Glory*; and we have handed him back the glory and kept all the hope for ourselves.

I suggest that we make a note not to wait until our next great composer is seventy before guaranteeing his bread and butter while he is scoring his Eroica.

Yours truly,

G. Bernard Shaw

THE MUNICIPALIZATION OF MUSIC

Speech in a debate sponsored by the British Music Association, 5 May 1920. British Music Bulletin, July 1920

[U] Ladies and gentlemen, I am an old municipal hand; and I think it will be convenient if I open the debate not by dealing with any of the specific points on the agenda, but by a word or two generally on the municipal situation, because I am sorry to say that most musicians, though keenly interested in music and in artistic questions, have very vague notions of the political constitution of their country. Now our object here is to get music taken up in this country as a matter of public importance. We want to have it financed by public money: in other words, we want the English people to organize their own music for themselves, and not always have to go to concert agents and commercial syndicates for it. Our view is that the value of the artistic culture of a country cannot be tested by commercial methods. The ordinary business view, that if a thing will not pay

* Land of Hope and Glory originated as a melody in Pomp and Circumstance March No. 1 in D Major (1901). It was later incorporated in Coronation Ode (1902), with lyrics by A. C. Benson, this version becoming virtually a second English national anthem.

commercially it is not worth doing, is a view which we energetically repudiate. Such a view is entirely impossible in municipal affairs—not that many municipal councillors do not hold it, but then they ought never to have been elected. You see, a municipality could not possibly keep the town which it controls in existence if it did not undertake such services as public lighting and the maintenance of roads and bridges, which do not pay at all in the commercial sense. For instance, you do not take a ticket to pass though Oxford-street: you use it quite freely! Oxford-street costs a lot of money; but it is paid for out of the rates because it is important to the life of the country that there should be roads open to everybody, and because the bedridden and the people who never set foot in Oxford-street benefit by its existence as much as the people who have to trudge up and down it.

And since we take the position that it is equally important that there should be in every centre of population in this country a competent symphonic orchestra and opera theatre, and that no child in this country should be brought up without abundant and free means of access to the best music, we have to reject the commercial standpoint. Now the moment you reject the commercial standpoint you are thrown back either on performances got up by private subscription (and they, as you know, are few and far between), or you must have the matter organized by your public authority with rating powers. Municipal action was formerly hampered by the fact that there was not enough municipal machinery in the country. But about thirty years ago a series of Acts of Parliament gave us a municipal system of county councils, borough councils, district councils, and parish councils in addition to the old city corporations. Through these bodies it has been possible to organize many public services which formerly could not be organized at all; and one of the many things which we aim at in this Society is to get music organized in that way. These bodies can not only raise rates but obtain money from Parliament through grants in aid. Parliament in certain circumstances will pay half the cost of a municipal service, and by doing so retain the right to make the municipality keep the service up to a certain standard, and protect officials against arbitrary or corrupt dismissal by the local body.

Another advantage these bodies have which is not very well understood is this. They are entirely free from the party system. I do not mean that there are not Progressives and *soi-disant* Municipal Reformers and Unionists and Conservatives and Liberals and Laborists and Socialists and so forth on these bodies; but the party system is quite a different matter. In Parliament when a question comes up, no Member of Parliament can vote on the merits of that question. He must always vote on the entirely different question of whether his party shall remain in power or not. If, for example, the Government of the day brought up in Parliament a measure to establish and endow a great national opera house, the unfortunate members of the House of Commons, instead of being able to rank themselves into musicians and anti-musicians, into Philistines and cultivated people, and so on, and voting accordingly, would have to vote on an utterly unmusical issue. All the followers of the Government, even if they were deaf, even if they hated music, would have to vote for the opera house lest their Government should be defeated and consequently have to resign; and on the other hand the Opposition, though its members might be enthusiastic musicians to the last man—I wish they were, by the way—would still have to vote against the proposal, because they must always vote against the Government and throw it out if they can.

Now that necessity does not exist in a municipality, because of the different way a municipal body is worked. Municipal bodies work through committees. One committee will deal with finance, another with electric lighting, another with sanitation, and so on, each committee drafting a series of proposals and then going to the general meeting and recommending the proposals for adoption by the whole municipal body, which decides for or against them. Suppose a municipal committee—say a Parks and Bands Committee—proposes the establishment of a municipal orchestra. There is nothing farfetched in this, by the way. Somebody might point out: "We have a town hall which we let for concerts. We also have in that town hall an organ; and we let that organ, when we let the hall, for a certain charge. We have a municipal cemetery; we have a municipal chapel and organ in that cemetery; we let that chapel and organ for funeral services for a certain charge. Why not add to these a permanent municipal symphonic orchestra, and give municipal symphonic concerts in our town so that our children may not grow up in savage ignorance of the best music?" He might point out that the London County Council has had bands performing in all the parks. Before the war they used to perform every night for months at a time right under my windows; so that it was impossible for me ever to have any music in the evening in my house. Well, if a band, why not an orchestra? Why not, instead of having a fit-up put into a town hall by a traveling theatrical company, have a theatre; and why not let a municipal symphonic orchestra or a portion of it be the band of that theatre; and why not, instead of letting it to traveling companies, organize a permanent municipal opera company? A committee might quite well be persuaded to put forward a proposal of this kind.

And now comes my point about the party system.

That proposal would be presented to the general meeting of the whole municipal body; and the members would vote on it according to their artistic consciences. If the proposal were defeated, nothing would happen. The Chairman of the Committee who brought up the resolution would not have to resign. There would not be a dissolution of the Council followed by a general election sending everybody back to pay the expenses of a candidate and risk the loss of the seat. The body would go on undisturbed for the remainder of the three years for which it was elected. In short, neither an adverse vote nor a favorable one would entail the consequences of the party system as it exists in Parliament; and consequently, in making a propaganda of municipal music, we can go to the municipal councillors and urge them to vote for our schemes without being pulled up by the objection that they must vote with their party, rightly or wrongly. The municipal councillor, in fact, enjoys the extraordinary luxury of being able to vote exactly according to his conscience. All of you, both ladies and gentlemen, presumably have votes for your municipality; and as the municipal councillor looks to votes, and votes only, to maintain him in his dignity, you can press him accordingly.

The only other thing I want to say is that in this propaganda we shall not be met by esthetic objections, but by the objection which half strangles our municipal life. No matter what our opinions are on the subject of music, or on any other subject, there is one point on which we are all sensitive, and that point is the rates. The resistance will come, not from people with musical views or anti-musical views, but from the ratepayer's dread of the rates going up. Therefore we must take care to point out that musical culture, and artistic culture of all kinds, pays in the long run. You see, the municipalities have charge of the morals of the districts of which they have control; and they know by experience that the punitive measures they are obliged to take to control immorality are worse than futile: they actually give the municipality a share of the profits of vice. If you want really to raise the morals of a city or county you must remember that their population consists largely of young persons who are growing up. These young persons are adolescent for some years before they are mature enough or earning enough to get married; and during these years it is useless to pursue with them a policy of what is rather inaccurately called Puritanism: that is, a policy of strict repression of all their adolescent impulses. The real remedy is provided by Nature, or, as some of us would say, by God. There is an outlet for all those impulses in art, and especially in the art of music.

If your young men have music to interest them, if they have pictures to interest them, if they have the powers and beauties of art to engage and satisfy their impulses and refine their tastes, they will not resort to the low pleasures of the streets. They will become too fastidious for that. But if you leave your towns in the state of barbarism and Philistinism with regard to art that too many of them are in at present, then the profit will go to the people who exploit the vices of the streets, and the loss to the general citizen who pays the rates. That is seldom mentioned in this country; and yet it is the vital centre of the whole thing. Coarse pleasures bring disease, drunkenness, and degradation of character; and all these things are a loss to the community; that is, they put up the police rates and the hospital rates, besides producing a lowering of personality and personal stamina that results in untrustworthiness and poor work, and is, in effect, a heavy tax levied on all who employ labor or are dependent on it. We cannot escape that tax by being too thoughtless to count it or complain of it, as we complain of the rates. Therefore, if you will only master that side of the subject, you will have plenty of arguments to persuade even the most parsimonious sparer of the rates that it would be really in the long run far better, and make the town healthier and wealthier, and keep the rates lower, if he would vote for an abundant and generous provision for art. I hope we can now proceed to details without losing our grasp of the general municipal situation. [U]

THE NEEDS OF MUSIC IN BRITAIN

Address delivered before the National Conference of the British Music Society, 6 May 1920. British Music Bulletin, November 1920; reprinted in Platform and Pulpit, 1961

The branches of the British Music Society and musical people generally throughout the country have before them absolutely unlimited opportunities of gathering together a few persons with very high ideas in music, and elaborating schemes whereby *if* the municipality could be induced to grant them a couple of thousand a year, and *if* Lord Howard de Walden* would give them twenty thousand pounds, they could build a handsome concert room or opera house, get the best artists from every part of the world, and effect an extraordinary elevation of the culture of the neighborhood. The number of such schemes brought before me personally I can hardly count. Lord Howard de Walden probably finds at least a dozen of them every morning on his breakfast table. It is pure waste of time to add to their number. My advice to you is, have nothing to do with them.

* President of the British Music Society and a frequent contributor to theatre and allied arts.

We have now to ask ourselves what else the projectors of these schemes can do. We have already discussed what can be done through the municipalities in a public way. This morning we come to what can be done by individuals. I know something about that, because, though I was brought up in a town where there were practically no official or commercial opportunities of hearing music, nevertheless before I was ten years old I was so accustomed to good music that I had to struggle with a strong repugnance to what is called popular music. Strauss's waltzes, which were rampant at that time, positively annoyed me. This familiarity with serious music I owed altogether to a man [Vandeleur Lee] who, like most musicians, had no private resources, and made his living by giving lessons in singing and playing the piano. But this did not satisfy him. He walked through the streets of the city, and whenever in passing a house he heard some person scraping a violoncello inside, he knocked at the door and said to the servant "I want to see the gentleman who is playing the big fiddle." He did the same when he heard a flute, when he heard a violin, when he heard any instrument whatsoever—simply knocked at the door and insisted on seeing the poor terrified amateur, to whom he said "I am forming an orchestra; you must come and play in it." And being a determined person he usually had his way.

Finally he managed to get together a small orchestra. Remember, he was not one of those men who forget that better is the enemy of good, and that he who waits for perfection waits forever. He did not say "I cannot begin until I have two flutes, two oboes, two clarinets, two bassoons, four horns, two trumpets, three trombones, kettle drums, and a good string quartet." He did not consider it vandalism to touch a work of Mozart or Beethoven with anything less than that. Still less did he think about English horns or bass clarinets or a battery of tubas. He took what he could get, conducted from a vocal score or a first-violin part, and filled out with the piano or in any way he could. As to four horns, he never dreamed of such a luxury in his life: he was only too glad to get two, and one of them was generally a military bandsman picked up for the occasion. He just took the materials at hand, and found the singers among his own pupils. He taught them to sing, and organized them as a choir. For instance, he taught my mother to sing. She led the chorus; she sang the principal parts; she copied out the band parts; and, I grieve to say, if there was no money to hire the authentic band parts she composed them herself from the vocal score on general assumptions as to the compass of the instruments.

Well, what has been done once can be done again. If you can get somebody in a town to begin in that way, and go ahead with the means that are available, a great deal can be done; and the children who have the luck to be within earshot, like me, will not grow up as musical barbarians. Of course, it will not be always pleasant, because at every concert that is given the daring conductor will be ruined, and will have to begin his teaching next day in debt; but he will have had some satisfaction out of it, not to mention the advertisement. He may even make the thing pay in the end. This enterprise which educated me musically did finally manage to give big oratorio festivals, and to achieve performances of operas by amateurs; and although the opera singing was not always of the Covent Garden class, still the singing had an extraordinary quality owing to the fact that all the performers knew the music thoroughly from beginning to end, a thing you have never heard at Covent Garden.

Such things can be done wherever there is an energetic musician with some natural gift for conducting. It is easier now than it was in Dublin sixty years ago because, through the spread of the pianola and the gramophone, you can now find plenty of people who have discovered what serious music is like, and acquired a taste for it. Take the case of our friend Mr Rutland Boughton. In Glastonbury he has done exactly the sort of thing I am advocating. He is one of those happily constituted men who can never see any reason for not doing anything, and he started with whatever means he had and whatever people he could find. Having no band, he accompanied on the piano. There being no theatre, his partner [Christina Walshe] made a fit-up, painting the decorations on anything that was lying about, and making the dresses out of fabrics of all sorts. The result is that they have given performances which have given me much more pleasure than I used to have when I was a professional critic in London. And the rehearsing, the social atmosphere of the thing, creates no end of interest and fun: in short, the jolliest kind of social life instead of the deadly dulness of country-town life. Need I draw the moral—go thou and do likewise.

BEETHOVEN'S CENTENARY

The Radio Times, 18 March 1927; reprinted in Pen Portraits and Reviews, 1932

A hundred years ago a crusty old bachelor of fiftyseven, so deaf that he could not hear his own music played by a full orchestra, yet still able to hear thunder, shook his fist at the roaring heavens for the last time, and died as he had lived, challenging God and defying the universe. He was Defiance Incarnate: he could not even meet a Grand Duke and his court in the street without jamming his hat tight down on his head and striding through the very middle of them. He had the manners of a disobliging steamroller (most steamrollers are abjectly obliging and conciliatory); and he was rather less particular about his dress than a scarecrow: in fact he was once arrested as a tramp because the police refused to believe that such a tatterdemalion could be a famous composer, much less a temple of the most turbulent spirit that ever found expression in pure sound. It was indeed a mighty spirit; but if I had written the mightiest, which would mean mightier than the spirit of Handel, Beethoven himself would have rebuked me; and what mortal man could pretend to a spirit mightier than Bach's? But that Beethoven's spirit was the most turbulent is beyond all question. The impetuous fury of his strength, which he could quite easily contain and control, but often would not, and the uproariousness of his fun, go beyond anything of the kind to be found in the works of other composers. Greenhorns write of syncopation now as if it were a new way of giving the utmost impetus to a musical measure; but the rowdiest jazz sounds like The Maiden's Prayer after Beethoven's third Leonore overture; and certainly no negro corobbery that I ever heard could inspire the blackest dancer with such *diable au corps* as the last movement of the Seventh Symphony. And no other composer has ever melted his hearers into complete sentimentality by the tender beauty of his music, and then suddenly turned on them and mocked them with derisive trumpet blasts for being such fools. Nobody but Beethoven could govern Beethoven; and when, as happened when the fit was on him, he deliberately refused to govern himself, he was ungovernable.

It was this turbulence, this deliberate disorder, this mockery, this reckless and triumphant disregard of conventional manners, that set Beethoven apart from the musical geniuses of the ceremonious XVII and

XVIII centuries. He was a giant wave in that storm of the human spirit which produced the French Revolution. He called no man master. Mozart, his greatest predecessor in his own department, had from his childhood been washed, combed, splendidly dressed, and beautifully behaved in the presence of royal personages and peers. His childish outburst at the Pompadour "Who is this woman who does not kiss me? The Queen kisses me" would be incredible of Beethoven, who was still an unlicked cub even when he had grown into a very grizzly bear. Mozart had the refinement of convention and society as well as the refinement of nature and of the solitudes of the soul. Mozart and Gluck are refined as the court of Louis XIV. was refined; Haydn is refined as the most cultivated country gentlemen of his day were refined: compared to them socially Beethoven was an obstreperous Bohemian, a man of the people. Haydn, so superior to envy that he declared his junior, Mozart, to be the greatest composer that ever lived, could not stand Beethoven. Mozart, more farseeing, listened to his playing, and said "You will hear of him some day"; but the two would never have hit it off together had Mozart lived long enough to try. Beethoven had a moral horror of Mozart, who in Don Giovanni had thrown a halo of enchantment round an aristocratic blackguard, and then, with the unscrupulous moral versatility of a born dramatist, turned round to cast a halo of divinity round Sarastro,* setting his words to the only music yet written that would not sound out of place in the mouth of God.

Beethoven was no dramatist: moral versatility was to him revolting cynicism. Mozart was still to him the master of masters (this is not an empty eulogistic superlative: it means literally that Mozart is a composer's

* High Priest of the Temple of Isis in Die Zauberflöte.

composer much more than he has ever been a really popular composer); but he was a court flunkey in breeches whilst Beethoven was a Sansculotte; and Haydn also was a flunkey in the old livery: the Revolution stood between them as it stood between the XVIII and XIX centuries. But to Beethoven Mozart was worse than Haydn because he trifled with morality by setting vice to music as magically as virtue. The Puritan who is in every true Sansculotte rose up against him in Beethoven, though Mozart had shewn him all the possibilities of XIX century music. So Beethoven cast back for a hero to Handel, another crusty old bachelor of his own kidney, who despised Mozart's hero Gluck, though the pastoral symphony in the Messiah is the nearest thing in music to the scenes in which Gluck, in his Orfeo, opened to us the plains of Heaven.

Thanks to broadcasting, millions of musical novices will hear the music of Beethoven this anniversary year for the first time with their expectations raised to an extraordinary pitch by hundreds of newspaper articles piling up all the conventional eulogies that are applied indiscriminately to all the great composers. And like his contemporaries they will be puzzled by getting from him not merely a music that they did not expect, but often an orchestral hurlyburly that they may not recognize as what they call music at all, though they can appreciate Gluck and Haydn and Mozart quite well. The explanation is simple enough. The music of the XVIII century is all dance music. A dance is a symmetrical pattern of steps that are pleasant to move to; and its music is a symmetrical pattern of sound that is pleasant to listen to even when you are not dancing to it. Consequently the sound patterns, though they begin by being as simple as chessboards, get lengthened and elaborated and enriched with harmonies until they are more like Persian carpets; and the composers who design these patterns no longer expect people to dance to them. Only a whirling Dervish could dance a Mozart symphony: indeed, I have reduced two young and practised dancers to exhaustion by making them dance a Mozart overture. The very names of the dances are dropped: instead of suites consisting of sarabands, pavanes, gavottes, and jigs, the designs are presented as sonatas and symphonies consisting of sections called simply movements, and labeled according to their speed (in Italian) as *allegros, adagios, scherzos,* and *prestos.* But all the time, from Bach's preludes to Mozart's Jupiter Symphony, the music makes a symmetrical sound pattern, and gives us the dancer's pleasure always as the form and foundation of the piece.

Music, however, can do more than make beautiful sound patterns. It can express emotion. You can look at a Persian carpet and listen to a Bach prelude with a delicious admiration that goes no further than itself; but you cannot listen to the overture to Don Giovanni without being thrown into a complicated mood which prepares you for a tragedy of some terrible doom overshadowing an exquisite but Satanic gaiety. If you listen to the last movement of Mozart's Jupiter Symphony, you hear that it is as much a riotous corobbery as the last movement of Beethoven's Seventh Symphony: it is an orgy of ranting drumming tow-row-row, made poignant by an opening strain of strange and painful beauty which is woven through the pattern all through. And yet the movement is a masterpiece of pattern-designing all the time.

Now what Beethoven did, and what made some of his greatest contemporaries give him up as a madman with lucid intervals of clowning and bad taste, was that he used music altogether as a means of expressing moods, and completely threw over pattern-designing as an end in itself. It is true that he used the old patterns all his life with dogged conservatism (another Sansculotte characteristic, by the way); but he imposed on them such an overwhelming charge of human energy and passion, including that highest passion which accompanies thought, and reduces the passion of the physical appetites to mere animalism, that he not only played Old Harry with their symmetry but often made it impossible to notice that there was any pattern at all beneath the storm of emotion. The Eroica Symphony begins by a pattern (borrowed from an overture which Mozart wrote when he was a boy), followed by a couple more very pretty patterns; but they are tremendously energized, and in the middle of the movement the patterns are torn up savagely; and Beethoven, from the point of view of the mere pattern musician, goes raving mad, hurling out terrible chords in which all the notes of the scale are sounded simultaneously, just because he feels like that, and wants you to feel like it.

And there you have the whole secret of Beethoven. He could design patterns with the best of them; he could write music whose beauty will last all your life; he could take the driest sticks of themes and work them up so interestingly that you find something new in them at the hundredth hearing: in short, you can say of him all that you can say of the greatest pattern composers; but his diagnostic, the thing that marks him out from all the others, is his disturbing quality, his power of unsettling us and imposing his giant moods on us. Berlioz was very angry with an old French composer who expressed the discomfort Beethoven gave him by saying "*J'aime la musique qui me berce*," "I like music that lulls me." Beethoven's is music that wakes you up; and the one mood in which you shrink from it is the mood in which you want to be let alone.

When you understand this you will advance beyond the XVIII century and the old-fashioned dance band (jazz, by the way, is the old dance band Beethovenized), and understand not only Beethoven's music, but what is deepest in post-Beethoven music as well.

OLD MEN AND NEW MUSIC

Unpublished fragment of an undated essay (British Library Add. Mss. 50662, ff. 5–10), possibly intended for inclusion in the Collected Edition (1930–2) as a preface or postscript to Music in London.

[U] When I was a lad (this suggests Gilbert and Sullivan; but for the moment I am flying at higher game) Beethoven had been dead for little more than a quarter of a century; consequently the Moonlight Sonata was recorded as a profound example of his latest and sublimest style. The Ninth Symphony was unthinkable, and the playing of the Hammerklavier Sonata Opus 106 by Arabella Goddard was ranked with the latest record in weight lifting. Lohengrin was composed before I was born, and was actually performed in London when I was fourteen. It sounded horrible to all trained musicians (organists and Musical Doctors and such like) because unprepared major ninths blared all over it, and a full close in B flat was followed by a discord, equally unprepared, in the totally unrelated key of E major. To us, who were accustomed to have remote keys broken to us gently, this was an outrage. But the mob, knowing no better, liked Lohengrin; Wagner got his nose in in spite of every possible warning and denunciation; and things went from bad to worse until Tristan reached Covent Garden when it had barely turned thirty.

Tristan was stuffed with "false relations"; and the acts began mostly by flinging at your ears unprepared discords compared to which dominant major ninths were as the cooing of doves. But the mob did not object to the relations being false as long as they were not poor; and as to discords, even professional masters were beginning to forget that they were not concords, or that they had ever been prepared and resolved as carefully as composers were baptized and confirmed. Once, when Richter conducted Isolde's Liebestod at the old St James's Hall (which to musicians seemed as sacred a place as Westminster Abbey), I saw an elderly gentleman on the platform spring to his feet and wave his clenched fist at the conductor in an ecstasy of hissing, which finally yielded, not to the visible indignation of Richter, who would in another moment have ejected the brawler with his own hands, but to the elderly gentleman's stupefaction as it dawned on him that instead of leading an irresistible popular demonstration of resentment against such unbearable cacophony he was not only alone in his wrath, but in considerable danger of being quoited downstairs as ignominiously as Pistol by Falstaff.* Englishmen had been known to rush frantically out of German theatres after twenty bars of the overture to Die Meistersinger; and I myself saw a British party routed by the second scene of Das Rheingold at Bayreuth. Queen Victoria stood up valiantly for Wagner when the Philharmonic Society, in a moment of madness, engaged him as conductor for a season; but she could no more save him from the wrath of the critics and the professional musicians than Napoleon III. and Princess Metternich could save him in Paris in 1860 from the wrath of the Jockey Club.

The present generation knows nothing of these things, and is even unable to conceive them. They can believe anything about Wagner except that his harmony, or his

*Shakespear's Henry IV, Part 2.

instrumentation, or any part of his technical procedure can ever have sounded in the least out of the common. If you play the music of, say, Henry Smart, to them, they will admit that it is ridiculously quaint and Victorian. Champagne Charlie* tickles them because of the evident derivation of the middle section from Hymns, Ancient and Modern. But Wagner is neither new nor old for them: he wrote, they think, as everyone wrote from Philipp Emanuel Bach† to Brahms and Elgar. They can see that the style of Handel and Bach is not that of Strauss; but then, they say, the style of Mozart is not that of Beethoven, and surely you are not going to pretend that they were not playing the same game, now called the old game, writing in two modes only, major and minor, committing themselves to definite keys by key signatures, satisfying themselves with thin common chords consisting merely of keynote, third and fourth, and generally dancing in chains. It was astonishing what they managed to do within their convention of tonality, and with their squeamish ears: but after all, did they ever get beyond the Swanee River‡ business; and in Heaven's name in what way is Wagner less of a back number than Beethoven, or as daring and individual as Mozart at his best?

Strauss did not break the tradition in the least. Like Mozart he indulged in sallies that made us laugh and sit up, and even bothered us completely at first hearing; but he did not shock the academic conventions as Wagner did, because Wagner had left none of them to shock; and it was now clear that you might write any

*A catchy music hall ditty of the 1860's, written and sung by George Leybourne, with music by Alfred Lee. Another of their compositions was The Man on the Flying Trapeze.

†Son of Johann Sebastian Bach; a pioneer of note in the sonata and symphony forms and in orchestration.

‡Stephen Foster's Old Folks at Home (1851).

progression or modulation or combination you pleased provided it had sense enough to make it possible for the public to tolerate it and finally acquire a taste for it. But having some sense in it meant that it had some musical grammar in it: that in spite of every license and every caprice its syntax was that of the keys or tonalities in which Mozart and Beethoven expressed themselves. Strauss did not violate this condition in the least. His Also Sprach Zarathustra, in C major, ended with a still small B natural persistently challenging its close on the key note; and the connoisseur-poseurs saw in this an audacious novelty; but those who knew Beethoven's mighty Mass in D, where a last echo of military music protests in exactly the same way against the Give Us Peace, only congratulated Strauss on being clever enough, like Molière, to take his goods where he found them.

Besides, there were the older hands, like myself, who knew their Donizetti; and Strauss's melody was so Donizettian that we could almost believe that the forgotten composer had risen from his marble chair in Bergamo, like the commander in Don Giovanni, and resumed operations with a German training, a German audience, the ground cleared for him by Wagner, and a resolution (again Molièresque) to make music deal with the thoughts of modern men instead of the adventures of Franconian Knights and their golden haired dames, or with figures from the myths of Vikings. This last was a needed change; but it was not a departure from the Beethoven tradition. Beethoven's music was the expression of the moods of his own age, and even of modern atomic physics.

The first attempt at what I call the new music must have been due, as I surmise, to the accident of a musical Frenchman named Debussy living next door to an organ factory, or perhaps being employed in one. In an organ factory all the tuning that goes on proceeds by whole tones; so that anyone within earshot soon becomes accustomed to a scale which you can play on your piano as C, D, E, F sharp, A flat, B flat, C. Once you are used to it it is as good a scale as the familiar major and minor mode, or any of the old modes of which you can produce passable imitations by playing scales on the white notes only, except that your mode will always have eight notes in it from key note to key note inclusive, wheras the whole tone scale will have seven only. But for that matter if you make a scale of the black notes only you have only six notes, and yet they make excellent bagpipe music. Debussy wrote music in the whole tone scale, melody, harmony and all; and immediately there was a genuine new music. Its instant success was partly due to the fact that Debussy could compose charming music in any mode. But the novelty had a great deal to do with it. The beauty and interest and power of the masterpieces of the old school had prevented us from noticing that we were tired of its tonality; but the secret was given away by the prodigious relief given by such a simple departure as the whole tone scale.

Very soon the scale system and the harmonic practice founded on it broke up altogether. Scriabin took the [U]

The fragment ends abruptly here

SIR ARTHUR SULLIVAN: A RE-EVALUATION

A response to a charge that Shaw, in 1889, had been "very wrong" in his criticism of the Gilbert and Sullivan comic operas. News Chronicle, 13 October 1933

[U] Sullivan's music in this genre has risen in value by keeping. When it was first heard it was heavily underestimated because it was English, and because, challenging as it did the extraordinary effervescence of Offenbach, who was then in supreme command of the stage as a composer of *opéra bouffe,* and such masterpieces of light opera as Auber's Fra Diavolo, its harmonies sounded 'churchy.' That contrast no longer troubles us.

Nobody remembers Sullivan as the organist of Chester Square; and very few know that the composer of Trial by Jury was also the composer of Onward Christian Soldiers.

We compare the score of The Mikado today not with the score of Les Brigands and La Grande Duchesse but with that of Die Meistersinger; and can now appreciate its delicacy and the tenderness which redeems its witty levity and preserves the more ephemeral topicalities of Gilbert from perishing.[U]

SIBELIUS

Statement on the occasion of Sir Thomas Beecham's Sibelius Festival in London. The Manchester Guardian, 1 November 1938

[U] Sibelius is unquestionably a leader in the front rank of symphonic composers. He has got out of the ruts worn by his predecessors far more completely than Brahms got away from Beethoven, or even Richard Strauss from Wagner. If someone would only burn Finlandia he would come to our young people as an entirely original inventor of a new art form and a new harmony technique. To them Mendelssohn and Schumann are drawing-room composers, Bruckner and Mahler expensively second-class, and Elgar so tremendously English as to be *hors concours.* Sibelius is now the head of the great symphonic dynasty, to the best of my judgment.[U]

HANDEL'S MESSIAH

To The Times, London, 14 October 1941

Sir,—Mr Hubert Langley's letter* in your issue of September 24 was a very welcome distraction of our attention from the war and the personality of Mr Hitler to the infinitely more important though less pressing subject and greater personality of Messiah and its composer.

But his demand for a performance "as Handel wrote it" is not so simple a matter as he assumes. A composer in writing a score is limited by the economic conditions and artistic and technical resources at his disposal. He must take what he can get and make the best of it. Had the Albert Hall, the B.B.C. orchestra, and the Salvation Army's International Staff band been within Handel's reach the score of Messiah would have been a very different specification. The music would not and could not have been better, but the instrumentation would have been very much richer and more effective. The money taken at the doors would have far exceeded the utmost that the room in Fishamble-street, Dublin, where the first performance took place, could hold at the prices charged for admission in those days. Suppose Handel had all this money to play with. Suppose his trumpets and horns could play chromatic scales instead of the few scattered notes of a posthorn. Suppose he had clarinets as well as oboes (hautboys), and tubas as well as trombones. Suppose he had an equally tempered modern

* Langley, an actor-singer who devoted much of his life to producing forgotten early British opera and theatre music, was founder of the Thomas Arne Society in 1922.

cinema organ to which all keys are alike, instead of a comparatively simple organ in mean tone temperament in which only a few of the twelve major and minor keys were available. Suppose he could count on sixty strings instead of twenty, on four horns, or eight, instead of two, on woodwind in Wagnerian groups of three instead of two, on the chords from kettledrums used by Berlioz in his Fantastic Symphony. Would his score have been anything like as poor as it stands in his manuscript? Is there no excuse for the conductors and composers who have ventured to guess how Handel would have enriched it under such conditions?

Mr Langley may say that Mozart went beyond this. He certainly did. Take for example the bass air The people that walked in darkness. It is not too much of an exaggeration to say that Handel did not harmonize it at all: he scored it in hollow unisons, perhaps with some intention of conveying an impression of darkness and void. Mozart filled up these hollows with harmonies so enchanting that every musician longs to hear them again and again. I believe Handel would have been delighted with them. And is it certain that he did not anticipate them? Elgar, who adored them, pooh-poohed the purists by reminding them that Handel was at the organ, and must have put in all sorts of harmonic variations, being a great improvizer. Handel's variations are lost; but are we to throw Mozart's after them?

Handel and his contemporaries wrote trumpet parts that became impossible when the pitch rose as it did until they became unplayable. The trumpets had to be replaced by clarinets until at the first performances of our Bach Society Kosleck arrived with a new two-valved Bach trumpet on which all the impossible passages are now brilliantly played. That was a glorious restoration; but its success does not justify a deliberate reduction of our Messiah performances within XVII century limits.

Only, the changes must be made by a master hand. Wagner provided Gluck's Iphigenia overture with a very beautiful ending to replace the conventional rum-tum *coda* which was considered *de rigueur*, and which still spoils Mozart's Don Giovanni overture at concert performances. Who wants to have the rum-tum back again? When Wagner wrote trombone parts for a chorus in one of Spontini's operas, the composer, instead of being outraged, sent for the parts when he was producing the opera in Berlin, and was kind enough to say it was a great pity Wagner could never become a great composer, as he (Spontini) had exhausted the possibilities of music. Wagner, when he conducted Beethoven's Ninth Symphony, a sacred masterpiece if there ever was one, found that certain themes which were evidently meant to be heard as principal melodies were smothered by their accompaniments. He rescored the passages to correct this. Gounod accused him of sacrilege; but Wagner's version is now played instead of that left by the deaf Beethoven. Passages in which the brass was left idle because it could not play the chromatic intervals have been reinforced by it without anyone protesting.

I could multiply instances; but enough is enough. Besides, I must confine my assent to changes made by master hands like those of Mozart, Wagner, and Elgar. Genius alone has the right to tamper with genius.

I am myself a composer: that is, a planner of performances, in the special capacity of a playwright. When I began, I had to keep production expenses within the limits of, say, £2000 at a London West End manager's bank, and £20 in the provinces. The invention of the cinema has placed capitals running to a quarter of a million at my disposal for modern revivals of my old cheap plays. This enormous economic change enables me to do things I should never have dreamt of in the XIX century. A cinema production which confined itself to the old version would be an imbecility. But I do not allow the additions to be made in Hollywood by the nearest Californian barman.

Finally, take the case of Shakespear. He did not write original plays: he wrote "additional accompaniments" to old ones. Has anyone on earth except Tolstoy, who had no ear for English word music, ever suggested that we should go back to the original Lear? Could Mr Langley endure a performance of the old Hamlet after tasting Shakespear's version?

Fifty years ago The Times, greatly daring, ventured to hint, through its music representative the late J. A. Fuller-Maitland, that the Handel Festivals at the Crystal Palace, where 4000 performers created an uproar which would have infuriated the irascible composer, were barbarous orgies which had no more to do with Handel's intentions than the Cup Ties. Naturally Costa, the once famous but now forgotten conductor, piled up all the brass and blare and percussion he could muster for these occasions. I agree warmly with Mr Langley that these additions should be ruthlessly scrapped. At the same period Shakespear himself was known to playgoers only by horribly mutilated "acting versions" which made Mr Granville-Barker's uncompromising restorations of the real Shakespear seem surprising novelties even to the professional critics. I agreed with Mr Granville-Barker as heartily as I do with Mr Langley; but that did not prevent my reconditioning the last act of Cymbeline* to an extent that would have surprised Shakespear. Some changes are inevitable: I can even

* Shaw's Cymbeline Refinished, written for the Shakespeare Memorial National Theatre at Stratford, was never produced there. It was first performed at the Embassy Theatre, Swiss Cottage, London, 30 November 1937, and is published in Vol. VII (1974) of The Bodley Head Bernard Shaw Collected Plays with Their Prefaces.

imagine Mr Augustus John touching up a Goya. It all depends on how it is done.

Yours truly,
G. Bernard Shaw

RADIO MUSIC

The Musical Times, January 1947

Radio music has changed the world in England. When I made my living as a critic of concerts and of opera in London fifty years ago I heard a Beethoven symphony once in a blue moon in the old St James's Hall or the Crystal Palace as part of a musical set of perhaps a thousand people who could afford to pay and were quite accidentally musical in their tastes. My own familiarity with the orchestral classics was gained by playing arrangements of them as piano duets with my sister. As to the Ninth Symphony, performances of it were extraordinary events separated by years.

Today, with radio sets as common as kitchen clocks, the Eroica, the Seventh, the Ninth, are as familiar to Tom, Dick, and Harriet as Nancy Lee used to be when it was played increasingly on every street piano. So also are Mozart's three greatest symphonies. Haydn, no longer forgotten, is alive again. Highbrow music is everywhere, as audible in the slums as in the squares. And it is all due to radio.

I affirm this because I am going to criticize the B.B.C., and must not be set down as a Philistine unconscious of the revolution it has made. Only those who, like myself, are old enough to remember the pre-radio London can have any conception of what we owe to it.

But this does not mean that radio music is less in need of the severest criticism than XIX century performances.

On the contrary, such criticism has become a matter of national importance. That is why I am induced to return for a moment to my old *métier* and note a few points on which the B.B.C. goes wrong occasionally.

Its worst concessions to popular bad taste, real or imaginary, are very horrible. I switch them off so promptly that I am hardly qualified to condemn them. But I protest against the notion that because there are vulgar people with such low tastes that all orchestral wind instruments have to be degraded by mutes to please them, radio music should condescend to a propaganda of musical obscenity instead of musical beauty. I can trace this evil to its source, because when I was an *ex-officio* member of the B.B.C. [General Advisory] Council, in virtue of my chairmanship of its Spoken English Committee,* I urged that the most critical care should be taken of what were called the music hall programs. The Council was horrified. I was actually proposing that its members should be on speaking terms with the low class of persons from which our red-nosed comedians and players of freak instruments were mostly drawn. Against this snobbery I could do nothing. Within its limits the Council was an excellent one; but they were ladies and gentlemen first and last, and would not mix with charladies' and costermongers' entertainers on any terms.

But later on they did meddle. The elderly members who had fallen to the charm of music hall singers, like Marie Lloyd, Bessie Bellwood, and Vesta Tilley, tried to revive them by broadcasting their songs. Now these songs, with their interpolated patter, were not only

* Shaw was appointed by the British Broadcasting Corporation to its Advisory Committee on Spoken English in 1926. He succeeded to the chairmanship on the death of Robert Bridges in 1930, continuing in the post until his resignation from the committee in 1937.

vulgar but so silly as to be hardly intelligible. And the B.B.C. made the outrageous mistake of thinking that the secret of their popularity lay in their vulgarity, though a moment's consideration should have convinced them that vulgar and silly girls could be picked up in any poor street for a few shillings a week. The real secret was that their intonation and rhythm were so perfect as to be irresistible. When Marie Lloyd sang Oh Mister Porter,* what shall I do? I want to go to Birmingham and theyre taking me on to Crewe, nobody cared twopence about Birmingham or Crewe; but everybody wanted to dance to Marie's exquisite rhythm, and found the sensation delightful. Bessie Bellwood's patter, assuring us that she was not going to gow on the stije and kiss her ijent, did not draw sixpence into the pay-boxes; but she, too, could sing in perfect tune and measure. Chirgwin earned his salary, not for his make up as the White-Eyed Kaffir or his substitution of a kerosene tin with one string for a Stradivarius, but for his infallible musical ear, which kept him always exactly in tune. Sir Harry Lauder, still with us, triumphed, not because of his Scotch accent, but because he has a very fine voice and never sings a false note nor misses a beat. The sham Maries and Bessies strove their hardest, not too successfully, to be vulgar in the cockney manner, and took their passable intonation for granted. The revival was a disgraceful failure.

Let us shift to the classics, where this elementary blundering was also apparent. What does singing or playing in tune mean? Most people who sing or play can do so passably in tune with a piano or orchestra to keep them to the pitch. But between that and being really in the middle of the note there is a world of difference. Experiments by physicists have shewn that if two

* Well-loved comic song by George Le Brunn.

instruments are tuned to the same pitch and one of them gradually sharpened or flattened, listeners do not at first detect the variation, and they differ in the degree of it they can observe. The effect of these differences is that when a choir of people who can sing only passably in tune are not kept to the pitch by an organ or band and are set to sing motets, madrigals, and glees, they make a most disagreeable noise, because they are all singing in different keys. The fact that the differences are much less than a semitone makes the discord worse. Yet, tested individually, they can all sing passably in tune and are selected, even at an advanced age and with poor voices, because they are good readers and good starters. And however unmusical their performances may be, they are endured, because it is supposed that the music, being old, must be quaint.

Besides, they do not all sing the same scale. Joachim and Sarasate, the greatest fiddlers of their time, had respectively a German scale and a Latin scale. Had they ever attempted to play in unison they would have accused oneanother of being out of tune.

Of all this the B.B.C. seems to know nothing. Because its choir can sing hymns and anthems acceptably to an organ accompaniment, it thinks that it must be equally available for motets by Byrd or Orlandus Lassus. It takes years of practice to train a group of good readers to sing in tune not only passably but exactly, and in the same scale. Not since we were visited half a century ago by De Lange's wonderful Dutch choir have I heard the treasures of XV century music pleasurably performed. Vaughan Williams's orchestral handlings of Byrd and Tallis are delightfully harmonious. Who can say as much for the B.B.C. choir cavorting desperately through a struggle to "read" the original work of these composers?

Singing in tune is not the only consideration in broadcasting. The microphone gives away all singers' and speakers' secrets: the gutter from which they may have sprung, the cocktails and too recent meals they may have swallowed, their ages and what not. In casting plays to be performed by invisible actors the contrasts of soprano, alto, tenor, and bass are indispensable to an intelligible and agreeable performance. A cast in which all the voices have the same pitch and pace is as disastrous as it would be in an opera.

On broadcast opera generally may I note that one act at a time, thoroughly done without cuts, would often be better entertainment than scrambling through scraps of the whole work. For example, take the operas of Meyerbeer, treated by the B.B.C. as extinct. The Huguenots, a really great opera of its class, raved about by Goethe, Balzac, and even Wagner in his youth, is so long that after its first performance in Paris it was cut to ribbons and has never since been heard in its entirety. Every act is a complete piece by itself, full of numbers that need the intimacy and finish of the radio and are not on the scale of the Paris Grand Opera into which all operas were then forced. It should be given one act at a time, carefully studied and uncut.

And why are such masterpieces as Goetz's Taming of the Shrew, Mozartian in its melody, and Peter Cornelius's Barber of Bagdad, with its delightful *Salamaleikum* at the end and a great *basso profundo rôle*, shelved for operas by Rossini which our vocalists cannot sing?

I could put other questions; but enough is enough for once. With daily concerts, an orchestra to which the scores of Wagner and Berlioz are child's play, a bevy of first-rate native conductors and two-thirds of a penny for listening in comfort at home: is there any limit to these possibilities?

They stagger my old-fashioned imagination.

BASSO CONTINUO

To The Times, London, 25 October 1948; reprinted under the title G.B.S. and Orchestral Basses, in Musical America, February 1949

Sir,—It would be a pity to let this correspondence* drop without emphasizing the ever-pressing need for remedying the weakness of the orchestral bass. I do not greatly care whether *recitativo secco* is accompanied by scraps of the cello or by piano or harpsichord. I should rather like to hear the *tromba marina*; but I shall lose no sleep if I do not. Seventy years ago I filled up the figured basses in Stainer's textbook of harmony quite correctly. Any fool could, even were he deafer than Beethoven.

What has worried me through all these years is that I could never hear Beethoven's No. 3 Leonore Overture as he meant me to hear it; and I never shall until his florid basses can hold their own against the thunder of the full orchestra *fortissimo.* When his impetuous figuration rushes down from top to bottom of the orchestra, the first half of it rings out brilliantly and the rest is a senseless blare. When the bass should tremble and rattle nothing is heard but a noisy growl and a thump.

I have inquired again and again how the bass could be made audible. Elgar thought it could be done by a group of Belgian trombones with five valves which enabled

* Basso Continuo, an article by the musical critic of The Times on 17 September, concerning the baffling problem of Bach's accompaniments, was a subject of discussion in the correspondence columns during most of September and October.

them to play the most florid passages *prestissimo*. But the ophicleide, a giant-keyed bugle with a peculiar tone which moved Berlioz to denounce it as a chromatic bullock, is as agile as five valves can make (and spoil) the trombone. My uncle played it, so I know.

The expense of extra players daunts many conductors: I know one who, when he pleaded to the municipality for third and fourth horns, was told to make the first and second play twice as loud. But nowadays, when Wagner in The Dusk of the Gods and Strauss in Hero Life require eight horns, and bass clarinets, English horns, hexelphones, and other luxuries undreamt of by Beethoven have to be available for every callow composer, the B.B.C. can afford to damn the expense.

The purists who want the original score and nothing but the score, not even the music, have no case. Elgar defended Mozart's rescoring of the Messiah on the ground that Handel at the organ could improvize equivalent descants and harmonies (and who can believe that in The People that walked in darkness he played only the written unisons and hollow octaves in the score?); but I am all for the replacement of Mozart's clarinet parts by the new Bach trumpet on which they are no longer unplayable. Trumpeters in Mozart's time were a bumptious lot; he hated them and loved the clarinet. Wagner had to rescore passages in the Ninth Symphony to bring out the parts that Beethoven evidently meant to be prominent, but which, great master of the orchestra as he was, he was too deaf to balance for himself. Schumann was no such master; nobody has yet complained of Mahler's rescoring of his symphonies. But it is the Beethoven basses above all that I want to hear; and we have not heard them yet.

Yours faithfully,

G. Bernard Shaw

MUSIC TODAY

A Questionnaire in The Stage, 20 April 1950

Do you think there has been any appreciable development in musical interest and understanding in this country since the days when you were a musical critic?

Yes, of course. Enormously. The radio has made Beethoven's Ninth Symphony familiar to millions of people who did not know that such a thing as a symphony existed.

Has the radio had an important influence, one way or the other, on musical appreciation?

It has worked both ways. It has corrupted musical taste and degraded musical instruments by the most obscene sort of jazz as well as reviving Haydn's vogue and making Bach a popular composer.

Now that the day of the patron is over, in what way could, or should, the Government assist musicians, orchestras, &c.?

The Government supports the British Museum, the National Gallery, and the cathedrals. What is to prevent it supporting municipal orchestras and festivals?

Do you think that the Arts Council, for example, is doing the right sort of work to foster musical taste and to cultivate talent?

It is doing what it can within the limits of its tastes and resources. Its existence is an advance towards a Ministry of Fine Arts.

Do you think there has been any notable change in the quality of instrumental playing during the last, say, forty or fifty years?

Yes, a prodigious change for the better. Not only do *virtuosi* such as Heifetz and Menuhin and Kentner surpass Joachim, Sarasate, and Rubinstein technically and have much wider repertories, but the average orchestral player is superior as an artist—I had almost written more of a cultured gentleman (or lady)—than in my time.

Do you agree that musical criticism today is not of a high enough standard?

No. Musical criticism can never be high enough, but the proportion of musically unqualified reporters praising every performance and enjoying unlimited free tickets is much smaller, if not practically extinct.

What significance, if any, do you think may be attached to the wartime enthusiasm for music, when concerts and recitals were more patronized than for many years?

Most concerts used to be advertisements paid for by the artists and attended by their deadhead friends. As I have not been in practice as a critic for fifty years I cannot say how far this still goes on. My impression is that the wartime enthusiasm was for dancing, and was so crazy as to be pathological.

Would you favor any sort of Government aid for individual composers or instrumentalists who require help if they are to develop without wearing themselves out first or being forced to write music for films, &c.?

It depends on the cases helped. Film music has the highest possibilities, and at its worst is better than academic cantatas and sham oratorios manufactured for prestige at the Three Choirs Festival.

Can you account for the rarity of really front-rank British conductors?

What do you call rarity? In my time we had Stanford, Barnby, Mackenzie, and Cusins, none of whom could conduct. Now, without stopping to think, I can reel you off Adrian Boult, Malcolm Sargent, Basil Cameron, Clarence Raybould, Stanford Robinson, Charles Groves, Ian Whyte, &c. &c. &c., all of them as competent as Furtwängler. If they had foreign names nobody in England would question their eminence.

WE SING BETTER THAN OUR GRANDPARENTS!

Everybody's Magazine, 11 November 1950

The notion that singing has deteriorated in the present century is only a phase of the Good Old Times delusion. It has, in fact, enormously improved.

Fifty years ago the singers whose voices lasted because they knew how to produce them were the de Reszke brothers, taught by their mother, Santley, an ex-choir boy from Liverpool, Adelina Patti, and Edward Lloyd.

Every musical period suffers from the delusion that it has lost the art of singing, and looks back to an imaginary golden age in which all singers had the secret of the *bel canto* taught by Italian magicians and practiced *in excelsis* at the great Opera Houses of Europe by sopranos with high C's and even higher F's, tenors with C sharps, baritones with G sharps, and *bassi profundi* with low E flats. Their like, we think, we shall never hear in our degenerate days.

We are now idolizing the singers of sixty years ago in this fashion. This does not impose on me: I have heard them. The extraordinary singers were no better than ours; the average singers were much worse. At the predominant Royal Italian Opera, Mr Heddle Nash would have been impossible so-called; but Signor Edele Nascio would have been as much in order and at home with Signor Foli and Signor Campobello as with Mr Santley, Mr Sims Reeves, Mr Lyall, Miss Catherine Hayes, and the other indispensables who refused to have their names and nationalities disguised. Edward Lloyd alone was excluded because he would not sing in any language but his own.

As to the robust tenors who came between Mario and Jean de Reszke, the educated and carefully-taught ones sang so horribly that they were classed as "Goatbleaters": Heddle Nash is an Orpheus compared to the once famous Gayarré. The rest were proletarians who had developed stentorian voices as newsboys, muffinmen, infantry sergeants, and humble, vociferous cheapjack auctioneers, who mostly shouted their voices away and are forgotten. De Reszke seemed a prince in comparison.

When I was first taken to the opera in my boyhood and heard Il Trovatore, I was surprised to hear in the second scene a voice from behind the scenes: Manrico singing the serenade. I asked the adult [Vandeleur Lee] who had brought me (a teacher of singing) "What is that?" He replied, "A pig under a gate." I forbear to rescue that tenor's name from oblivion.

Voice production in general is now immeasurably better than it was fifty years ago.

Voices so strained by singing continually in the top fifth of their range that they could not sustain a note without a *tremolo*, nor keep to the pitch, like those of Faure and Maurel; sopranos Garcia-trained to sing nothing but high C's on the vowel Ah, and [who] soon had to have their C's transposed to B flats, were rife in those days; now they are extinct. Genuine Italian singers and conductors to whom Wagner was not music at all (bar perhaps Lohengrin) are dead; and Toscanini is better at German music than at Rossini.

The notion that Wagner's music broke voices, and that opera singers should sing only that of Rossini, Donizetti, Bellini, and Meyerbeer, has been replaced by the truth that Wagner, Mozart, and Handel, who wrote for the middle of the voice with very occasional high notes for exceptional singers, never broke a properly produced voice.

In Don Giovanni, the greatest opera in the world, there are two baritones and two basses, not one of them having a note to sing that is not easily within the compass of Tom, Dick, and Harry.

Where we fall short is in *roulades,* shakes, and *gruppettos,* which many of our singers simply cannot sing at all, though the B.B.C. puts them up to sing Rossini, making them ridiculous when they could be better employed on such neglected masterpieces as Goetz's Shrew and Cornelius's Barber. As to Meyerbeer, whose Huguenots should be broadcast seriously without cuts one act at a time, the B.B.C. has apparently never heard of him.

Let us hear no more of a golden age of *bel canto.* We sing much better than our grandfathers. I have heard all the greatest tenors (except Giuglini) from Mario to Heddle Nash, and I know what I am writing about; for, like de Reszke, I was taught to sing by my mother, not by Garcia.

INDEXES

BIOGRAPHICAL INDEX

This index of musical personages is not intended to be comprehensive, but to provide data (when available) on persons figuring significantly in Shaw's criticism who may not be familiar to today's reader.

ALBANI, (Dame) EMMA (1847–1930), Canadian-born soprano, made her *début* as Amina in La Sonnambula at Messina, later appeared in same *rôle* in London, 1871. Sang all the great soprano *rôles* of Italian opera, but was especially acclaimed for her Elsa in Lohengrin, Elisabeth in Tannhäuser, Senta in Fliegende Holländer.

ALBÉNIZ, ISAAC (1860–1909), concert pianist and composer of Iberia Suite, the opera The Magic Opal (1893), and over 200 piano works, was court pianist to queen of Spain. Celebrated exponent of "New Spanish" school of nationalistic composers.

ALVARY, MAX (1856–98), Wagnerian tenor, was first American Siegfried at Metropolitan Opera. Sang Tristan and Tannhäuser at Bayreuth (1891) and in Ring cycle at Covent Garden under Mahler a year later. Illness forced retirement in 1897.

BACKER-GRÖNDAHL, AGATHE (1847–1907), Norwegian pianist, student of Bülow and Liszt, whose repertoire consisted primarily of works of masters of the Romantic school. Baker's describes her as "unquestionably the foremost woman-composer of Scandinavia."

BANTOCK, (Sir) GRANVILLE (1868–1946), composer and conductor, introduced Sibelius to England, was professor of music at Birmingham University, 1908–34. Many of his most successful compositions were built on Oriental themes, and virtually all had programs. Best-known opera is Caedmar.

BARNBY, (Sir) JOSEPH (1838–96), organist, conductor, composer, founder of choral society named after himself. Succeeded Gounod as conductor of Royal Albert Hall Choral Society.

BAUERMEISTER, MATHILDE (1849–1926), German-born English soprano, *protégée* of Tietjens, studied at Royal Academy of Music and first sang at Covent Garden as Siebel in Faust. Performed more than 100 *rôles* before her "Grand Benefit" farewell organized by Melba, 1905.

BENNETT, JOSEPH (1831–1911), musical critic (Daily Telegraph, Pall Mall Gazette, &c.), writer, translator. Annotated Philharmonic Society and Popular Concerts programs. Furnished librettos to A. C. Mackenzie (Dream of Jubal), Arthur Sullivan (Golden Legend), Frederic Cowen (Thorgrim).

BENNETT, (Sir) WILLIAM STERNDALE (1816–75), considered by many of his contemporaries one of England's greatest composers. Founded Bach Society in 1849, conducted London Philharmonic and Leeds Musical Festival. Composed symphony, four piano concertos, an oratorio (Woman of Samaria).

BEVIGNANI, ENRICO (1841–1903), Italian composer and opera conductor, came to London as *répétiteur* at Her Majesty's, 1863. Conducted at Covent Garden, 1868–87, 1890–6, including London's first Aïda (1876), Gioconda (1883), and Pagliacci (1893).

BISPHAM, DAVID (1857–1921), American-born dramatic baritone, performed over 100 oratorio parts before making *début* at Covent Garden in 1892. Later became star of Metropolitan Opera, 1896–1903. Despite late start, sang more than fifty opera *rôles* before retirement in 1909.

BOUGHTON, RUTLAND (1878–1960), composer who sought at Glastonbury, unsuccessfully, to create English school of Wagnerian music-drama. Maintained his faith despite all obstacles, and was rewarded by one immensely popular opera, The Immortal Hour (1922).

BREMA, MARIE (1856–1925), first English operatic singer to perform at Bayreuth. Sang Gluck's Orfeo and Brünnhilde in London, the Ring and Tristan at the Metropolitan Opera under Mottl and Seidl.

BURNS, GEORGINA (*c.* 1862–1932), one of Carl Rosa's most popular singers, appeared as Messenger of Peace in Wagner's Rienzi, Catherine in Meyerbeer's L'Étoile du Nord, and in title *rôle* in Wallace's Lurline. Later toured provinces with husband Leslie Crotty and a company of their own.

CALVÉ, EMMA (1858–1942), French-born soprano, noted for her dramatic ability, excelled in Carmen and Massenet's Sappho and as Santuzza in Cavalleria Rusticana. Endeavored to interpret her *rôles* with great realism.

CAPOUL, VICTOR (1839–1924), French tenor of Opéra Comique company, 1861–89. Toured America with Christine Nilsson. First appeared in England, 1871, as Faust, singing at Drury Lane until 1875, then at Covent Garden until 1879.

COSTA, (Sir) MICHAEL (1808–84), Italian composer and conductor, of Spanish parentage. Wrote several successful operas (including Don Carlos), oratorio (Eli). Directed Handel Festival, 1857–80. From 1871 was "director of the music, composer and conductor" at Her Majesty's.

COWEN, (Sir) FREDERIC (1852–1935), composer of operas (Pauline, Thorgrim), oratorio (Ruth), cantatas (Corsair, St Ursula). Conducted Promenade Concerts at Covent Garden (1880, 1893), Royal Philharmonic (1888–92, 1900–07), Hallé Concerts (1896–9).

CUSINS, (Sir) WILLIAM GEORGE (1833–93), conductor and composer, professor of piano at Guildhall School of Music, Master of the Music to Queen Victoria. Conducted London Philharmonic, 1867–83.

DAVIES, BEN (1858–1943), Welsh tenor, whose voice was of a rich, solid tone, almost baritone in its lower reaches. First appeared with Carl Rosa Opera in The Bohemian Girl (1881), later joined New English Opera Company, creating title *rôle* in Sullivan's Ivanhoe. Equally at home at Covent Garden and in West End musical comedy.

DOLMETSCH, ARNOLD (1858–1940), French-born specialist in early music and ancient instruments (many of which he reconstructed), created new interest in work of many neglected composers, including Matthew Locke, through sponsorship of concerts and recitals in which he performed with his Dolmetsch Trio.

D'OYLY CARTE, RICHARD (1844–1901), successful theatre manager, had the prescience to commission Gilbert and Sullivan to write Trial by Jury. Built Savoy Theatre (1881), in which most of the Gilbert and Sullivan (Savoyard) comic operas were performed. Attempted disastrously in 1891 to establish English Grand Opera.

DUFRICHE, EUGÈNE, French baritone, sang at Covent Garden, 1890–1905, and at Metropolitan Opera, 1898–1908 (though he had made his *début* there in 1893 on the same night as Emma Eames and Pol Plançon, in Gounod's Philémon et Baucis).

EAMES, EMMA (1865–1952), American soprano, made her *début* as Juliet (chosen by Gounod) in Paris, 1889. First sang at Covent Garden as Marguerite in Faust (1891), and for ten years was Melba's chief rival. Retired prematurely in 1912.

ELLIS, WILLIAM ASHTON (1853–1919), physician who became pioneer translator of Wagner's prose writings into English. Was a founder and secretary of London branch of the Wagner Society.

FANCELLI, GIUSEPPE (1833–87), Italian tenor, for many years a member of Mapleson's company at Drury Lane. Sang Radames at La Scala in first Italian performance of Aïda. Lacked personality and was a poor actor, but quality of his voice was superb and his intonation unfailing.

FAURE, JEAN-BAPTISTE (1830–1914), principal baritone at Paris Opéra for seventeen years. In London sang Mephistopheles in Faust (1863–6), Iago in Rossini's Otello (1870), Lotario in Thomas's Mignon. Frequent performer in London in the 1870's.

FILLUNGER, MARIE (1850–1930), Viennese concert soprano, outstanding interpreter of German lieder, especially Schubert's. First sang in London, with spectacular success, in 1889, soon made her home there. After retirement from concert platform, taught at Manchester Royal Academy of Music.

FOLI, SIGNOR [ALLAN JAMES FOLEY] (1835–99), outstanding Irish *basso profundo*, began career as a youth singing in church choirs in America, later studied in Naples. Made operatic *début* in 1862 in Rossini's Otello. Had repertoire of over sixty operatic *rôles*, but in later years sang principally in oratorio and concert.

GARCIA, MANUEL (1805–1906), Spanish voice teacher, trained Jenny Lind, invented laryngoscope to inspect vocal cords while they were in use. Was professor at Royal Academy of Music, 1848–95.

GAYARRE, JULIAN (1844–90), Spanish tenor, formerly a blacksmith, the Caruso of his day, sang in every great opera house of Europe. His Trovatore and Favorita were considered achievements without equal in the art of singing.

GERSTER, ETELKA (1855–1920), Hungarian coloratura soprano, one of the most remarkable of her time. Scored instant success in London *début* at Her Majesty's, 1877, as Amina in Sonnambula, remained for four seasons. Retired in 1890 after suddenly losing her voice.

GODDARD, ARABELLA (1836–1922), one of the most imposing pianists of her generation, first played publicly at age of four. After performing successfully all around the world, she retired due to illness in 1880.

GOLDSCHMIDT, OTTO (1829–1907), pianist, pupil of Mendelssohn and Chopin, accompanist and conductor in America for Jenny Lind, whom he married in Boston, 1852. Founded Bach Choir and was its conductor, 1875–85.

GROVE, (Sir) GEORGE (1820–1900), distinguished critic and editor, prepared analytical programs for Crystal Palace concerts for more than forty years. Most significant work was four-volume Dictionary of Music and Musicians (1879–89), now an institution.

GYE, FREDERICK (1810–78), opera *impresario*, managed the old and, after a fire, the new Covent Garden, 1849–77. Greatest coup was introduction of Patti to London in 1861. Under his aegis the first Wagner operas were performed in London, 1875–6.

HALLÉ, (Sir) CHARLES (1819–95), founded Hallé Orchestra in Manchester, 1857, conducted its concerts until his death. Married popular violinist Wilma Norman-Neruda.

HARRIS, (Sir) AUGUSTUS (1852–96), theatre manager and *impresario*, produced spectacular melodrama and elaborate pantomime at Drury Lane, then undertook to restore grand opera in England to its former exalted position after long decline. Invited Richter and German opera company to London in 1882, brought Carl Rosa Opera to London for first time in 1883, and managed Royal Italian Opera (later Royal Opera) at Covent Garden until his early death.

HENSCHEL, (Sir) GEORGE (1850–1934), concert baritone and composer, born at Breslau. Conducted symphonic concerts in Boston, 1881–4, later directed London Symphony and was first conductor of Scottish Orchestra. Composed a Stabat Mater (1894) and operas A Sea Change (1884) and Frederick the Great (1899).

JOACHIM, JOSEPH (1831–1907), Hungarian violinist, first appeared in London (on recommendation of Mendelssohn) in 1844. Was principal attraction for many years at Crystal Palace concerts and Popular Concerts. Organized celebrated quartet that bore his name.

KLAFSKY, KATHERINA (1855–96), Hungarian soprano, came to London with Leipzig touring company of Wagnerian operas in 1882, singing Wellgunde in Rheingold and Waltraute in Walküre. Returned in 1892 to sing Leonore in Fidelio, Brünnhilde, Isolde, Elisabeth in Tannhäuser, Agathe in Freischütz, and Elsa in Lohengrin. Died prematurely, at peak of her artistry.

KREBS, MARIE (1851–1900), brilliant German pianist, performed publicly from age of eleven. Retired on her marriage in 1885 after many years of popularity in England.

LABLACHE, MME DEMERIC, Italian mezzo-soprano, daughter-in-law of Luigi Lablache, made London *début* at Covent

Garden in 1849, later sang for Mapleson at Her Majesty's in the 1860's and 1870's. Was still going strong in the 1880's.

LAGO, ANTONIO, employed in 1869 as prompter for Gye-Mapleson opera season at Her Majesty's, later sponsored rival seasons of opera productions in Italian at Covent Garden and in several London theatres (as well as in New York), 1886–93. Introduced the Ravogli sisters, and first presented Cavalleria Rusticana, Eugène Onegin, and Glinka's A Life for the Tsar, in London.

LANNER, KATTI (1829–1908), Austrian ballet star, became director of London's National Training School of Dancing. Choreographer for opera productions at Her Majesty's, 1877–81, and thirty-six ballets at Empire Theatre, 1887–97.

LASSALLE, JEAN-LOUIS (1847–1909), a great French baritone, made his *début* at Paris Opéra at nineteen. Sang leading *rôles* in Thomas's Hamlet, Huguenots, Aïda, L'Africaine, William Tell, and Mozart's Ascanio.

LAWSON, MALCOLM (1849–?), organist and composer, whose works include an opera, several symphonies, and much sacred music.

LEHMANN-KALISCH, LILLI (1848–1929), German *prima donna*, daughter of famed dramatic singer Maria Loewe-Lehmann, from whom she received earliest instruction. Especially popular at Bayreuth and in America, her phenomenal range and fine acting shewed to especial advantage in such *rôles* as Brünnhilde, Fidelio, Carmen, Norma, Isolde.

LEMMENS-SHERRINGTON, HELEN (1834–1906), made first appearance in London in 1856, soon became leading English soprano both in sacred and secular music. Appeared in opera from 1860, singing in Norma, Giovanni, Martha, Huguenots.

LESLIE, (Sir) HENRY (1822–96), founded in 1855 a choir of over 200 voices, whose performances of unaccompanied music were of an excellence unmatched in England; disbanded in 1880. A prolific composer of cantatas, oratorios, and orchestral works, Leslie is not to be confused with the frequently-mentioned (by Shaw) Henry J. Leslie (d. 1900), London theatre manager.

LEVI, HERMANN (1839–1900), German orchestral conductor and noted Wagnerian interpreter, directed first performance of Parsifal at Bayreuth in 1882. Also champion of Mozart and, later, Bruckner. Came to England in 1895, but conducted only one concert in London.

LIEBAN, JULIUS (1857–1940), Austrian tenor of Hamburg Opera Company, sang at Bayreuth (1882–1912), was first heard at Covent Garden as Mime in Siegfried in 1892. Repeated the *rôle* in 1893 and 1897; does not appear to have sung anything else in London.

LLOYD, EDWARD (1845–1927), tenor trained in Westminster Abbey choir, gained international reputation as singer in concert and oratorio. Created tenor *rôles* in oratorios by Gounod, Sullivan, Elgar; also sang popular ballads. Star tenor piece in concert was "The Holy City."

LUDWIG, WILLIAM (1847–1923), Irish baritone, sang for several years in chorus at Old Gaiety Theatre, London. Gained prominence through performance in Fliegende Holländer when in 1877 he succeeded Santley as Carl Rosa's principal baritone. Noted for Wagnerian *rôles*, in which, says Grove, "the sombre tone of his voice was exactly suited to the music."

LUSSAN, ZÉLIE DE (1861–1949), American soprano, engaged by Harris in 1888 for his first Covent Garden season, appeared as Carmen, a *rôle* she sang over 1000 times during quarter century on opera stage. Appeared with Carl Rosa Opera, 1890–1900. Greatest *rôles* were Zerlina in Giovanni, Mignon, Cherubino in Nozze di Figaro, and Nedda in Pagliacci.

MAAS, JOSEPH (1847–86), principal tenor for Carl Rosa, 1878–80, singing Raoul in Huguenots, Faust, Radames in Aïda, Rienzi. Sang Lohengrin at Covent Garden in 1883, and was the Chevalier des Grieux in first London production of Massenet's Manon, 1885.

MacCUNN, HAMISH (1868–1916), Scottish composer, pupil of Parry, at twenty became professor of harmony at Royal Academy of Music. A prolific composer of operas, cantatas, and orchestral pieces, his works were performed by Manns when he was only nineteen.

MACFARREN, (Sir) GEORGE ALEXANDER (1813–87) music theorist, composer of operas, oratorios, and a symphony, blind from 1860. Longtime professor of harmony and composition at Royal Academy of Music, of which he became Principal in 1876.

M'GUCKIN, BARTON (1852–1913), Irish tenor, first appeared at Crystal Palace concert in 1875. Made opera *début* under Carl Rosa in 1880, soon became popular fixture of the troupe, principal *rôles* including Lohengrin, Faust, Des Grieux in Manon, Don José in Carmen. Also well known in oratorio.

MACINTYRE, MARGARET (1865–1943), Scottish soprano, was instant success in *début* at Covent Garden in 1888, playing Micaela to Nordica's Carmen. Also scored as Margaret in Boïto's Mefistofele, Inez in L'Africaine, Marguerite in Faust, but career as a leading singer was rather brief.

MCNAUGHT, WILLIAM GRAY (1849–1918), music director of Bow and Bromley Institute, 1876–1900, was assistant inspector of Music Education Department of London Board Schools, 1883–1901, and frequent adjudicator at music competitions.

MALTEN, THERESE (1855–1930), principal soprano at Dresden for thirty years, sang Kundry in Parsifal at Bayreuth in 1882 and 1884. Heard rarely in London: in Fidelio at Drury Lane (1882), concert version of Parsifal in Albert Hall (1884), and in Richter concert (1886). Her voice had an extraordinary compass and her acting prowess matched her singing skill.

MANCINELLI, LUIGI (1848–1921), Italian composer of operas, oratorios, and songs who, after remarkable *début* at London concert in 1886, was a principal conductor at Covent Garden for twenty years.

MANNS, (Sir) AUGUST (1825–1907), German bandmaster and conductor, engaged in 1855 as conductor at Crystal Palace, where he led Saturday Concerts until 1901. Succeeded Costa as conductor of Handel Festival. Fostered work of German composers, notably Schumann.

MAPLESON, (Col.) JAMES HENRY (1830–1901), opera *impresario*, managed Italian seasons, 1861–89, at Drury Lane, Her

Majesty's, Lyceum Theatre, and Covent Garden, as well as at New York Academy of Music. Introduced Faust to London in 1863 and Carmen in 1878, and engaged Patti in 1881.

MARIO [GIOVANNI MATTEO] (1810–83), Italian tenor, descended from nobility. First appeared in London in 1839 in Lucrezia Borgia, was considered most perfect stage-lover ever seen. The beauty of his voice has become legendary. Retired in 1867, but returned to Covent Garden for farewell in 1871.

MATERNA, AMALIE (1844–1918), celebrated dramatic soprano of German opera, gained worldwide reputation at Bayreuth in 1876 when she created *rôle* of Brünnhilde. Sang in Wagner Festival at Albert Hall in 1877; was Parsifal's first Kundry at Bayreuth in 1882.

MAUREL, VICTOR (1848–1923), French baritone, student of Faure, made his *début* at Paris Opéra in Huguenots, 1868. First appeared at Covent Garden as Renato in Ballo in Maschera, 1873. Greatest *rôles* were Iago and Falstaff; sang first Telramund (Lohengrin) and Wolfram (Tannhäuser) in England.

MELBA, (Dame) NELLIE (1861–1931) idolized silvery-voiced Australian soprano, with vocal range of 2½ octaves, made her London *début* as Lucia di Lammermoor in 1888 at Covent Garden, where she reigned as undisputed queen until retirement in 1926. Studied Faust with Gounod, Otello with Verdi, Bohème with Puccini, and was coached in acting by Sarah Bernhardt.

MENTER, SOPHIE (1846–1918), German pianist, student of Tausig and Liszt, made first appearance in England in 1881. Was married (1872–86) to the noted cellist David Popper.

MOTTL, FELIX (1856–1911), Austrian conductor and composer of three operas, pupil of Bruckner, took part in first Bayreuth performances of the Ring, 1876. Conducted Tristan at Bayreuth in 1886, Ring cycle at Covent Garden in 1898, Parsifal at Metropolitan Opera in 1903–4. Edited vocal scores of all Wagner's operas.

MURSKA, ILMA DI (1836–89), legendary Hungarian dramatic

soprano possessed of remarkable compass of nearly three octaves. Made London *début* at Her Majesty's in 1865 as Lucia di Lammermoor, soon rivaled Patti in popularity in same repertoire.

NACHÉZ, TIVADAR (1859–1930), Budapest-born violinist, pupil of Joachim and Hubert Léonard. After initial success in Paris, settled in London in 1889, quickly gaining reputation as virtuoso soloist and composer of violin works. Retired in 1926 after extended residence in California.

NASH, HEDDLE (1896–1961), Milan-trained English tenor, scored immediate success at Old Vic in 1925 as the Duke in Rigoletto. Acclaimed at Covent Garden in 1929 for his Ottavio in Giovanni. Grove calls his David in Meistersinger "incomparable."

NEWMAN, ERNEST (1868–1959), musical critic (Manchester Guardian, Birmingham Post, Observer, Sunday Times 1920–59), wrote brilliant study of Hugo Wolf, "definitive" biography of Wagner, books on Richard Strauss, Elgar, Gluck.

NICOLINI, ERNEST (1834–98), French dramatic tenor of undistinguished accomplishment, first sang at Drury Lane in 1871 and a year later at Covent Garden. Was married to Adelina Patti in 1886.

NILSSON, CHRISTINE (1843–1921), sweet-voiced Swedish soprano, first appeared in London in 1867 as Violetta in Traviata. Outstanding *rôles* included Martha, Queen of Night in Zauberflöte, Ophelia in Thomas's Hamlet (which she created), Donna Elvira in Giovanni, Cherubino in Nozze di Figaro. Retired in 1887.

NORDICA, LILLIAN (1857–1914), American soprano, came to Covent Garden in 1887 after initial success in New York. First American singer to appear at Bayreuth (Lohengrin, 1894), noted for performances as Brünnhilde and Isolde in New York and London. Equally successful as Violetta in Traviata and similar Italian *rôles*.

NORMAN-NERUDA, WILMA [LADY HALLÉ] (1839–1911), Moravian-born violinist, one of London's most popular soloists, performed every season from 1869 to 1898 at Philharmonic, Crystal Palace, Popular Concerts. Married Sir Charles Hallé in 1888. Alexandra appointed her "Violinist to the Queen."

PADEREWSKI, IGNACE JAN (1860–1941), famed Polish pianist and composer, taught by Leschetitzky under sponsorship of actress Helena Modjeska. Made London *début* as soloist in 1890, followed by spectacularly successful tour of over one hundred concerts. No pianist of his generation attained such triumph—or such critical hostility. Became first Premier of Polish Republic, 1919, but retired from politics a year later to resume musical career.

PARRY, (Sir) CHARLES HUBERT H. (1848–1918), composer, author, teacher. Bach Choir's performance of his chorale Blest Pair of Sirens established him as master of choral writing. Composed five symphonies, unproduced opera Guinevere, four oratorios, several treatises on music.

PATEY, JANET (1842–94), outstanding Scottish contralto, member of Henry Leslie's choir, later became leading contralto concert singer. Most noted operatic *rôle* was Blanche of Devan in Macfarren's Lady of the Lake. Has been compared favorably as a singer with Marietta Alboni.

PATTI, ADELINA (1843–1919), Spanish-born daughter of Italian parents, one of greatest of all coloraturas. *Début* in New York as Lucia di Lammermoor in 1859, in England as Amina in Sonnambula in 1861. Repertoire included Violetta in Traviata, Zerlina in Giovanni, Martha. Sang annually, 1861–84, at Covent Garden in repertory of about thirty operas. Career lasted 56 years.

PIATTI, ALFREDO CARLO (1822–1901), outstanding cello *virtuoso*, was from 1859 a leading performer in London's Monday and Saturday Popular Concerts of chamber music. A profound musician, he had enormous influence on contemporary cellists.

PLANÇON, POL (1854–1914), superb French basso, sang at Metropolitan Opera, 1893–1908. First appeared at Covent Garden in 1891 after eight years at Paris Opéra, and for the next decade was a reigning star on both sides of the Atlantic. Most esteemed *rôle* was Mephistopheles in Faust, but had large repertoire of Italian and German *rôles* in which he also excelled.

RANDEGGER, ALBERTO (1832–1911), settled in London in 1854, where he became a noted singing-teacher, after early career as composer and theatre conductor in Italy. In England he continued to compose, and eventually conducted Carl Rosa Opera, 1879–85, going on to Drury Lane and Covent Garden, 1887–98.

RAVOGLI, GIULIA (1866–?), Italian-born *prima donna*, whose sister Sofia (d. 1910) was also a well-known singer. Repertoire included Gluck's Orfeo, Lohengrin, Aïda, Gioconda, Carmen. Very popular with American audiences, in Europe was hailed as one of the greatest dramatic sopranos; much admired by Shaw.

REEVES, SIMS (1818–1900), revered tenor, started career as second tenor in Macready's company at Drury Lane, later sang Edgardo in Lucia at La Scala with marked success. Same *rôle* at Drury Lane, 1847, earned him position of actor and singer of first rank. Greatest reputation came from oratorio, particularly performances in Handelian repertory and in Bach's St Matthew Passion.

RESZKE, ÉDOUARD DE (1853–1917), Polish basso, brother of Jean de Reszke, who taught him singing. A favorite at Covent Garden for two decades, noted particularly for Wagnerian *rôles*, considered outstanding singer and actor of lyric stage.

RESZKE, JEAN DE (1850–1925), Polish baritone who developed into a tenor, generally regarded as best tenor since Mario. Principal *rôles* included Faust, Romeo, Radames, Tristan, Tannhäuser, Lohengrin, Siegfried, Samson. Founded operatic singing-school in Paris in 1905 and became celebrated teacher.

RICHTER, HANS (1843–1916), Austro-Hungarian conductor, friend of Wagner, conducted first performance of Ring cycle at Bayreuth, 1876. Frequently conducted concert and operatic performances in England, particularly Hallé concerts in Manchester, 1900–10. Was an early interpreter of Bruckner.

RIGBY, GEORGE VERNON (1840–1928), tenor who first appeared as concert singer. After study in Milan and Berlin, sang Handel's Samson at Gloucester Festival, replacing Sims Reeves. Appeared frequently in opera and concert, but never developed into a firstrate performer.

ROSA, CARL (1842–89), German violinist and conductor, came to London in 1866, later (1875) organized English opera company, with Rose Hersee and Charles Santley as principal artists, which met with instant success. Introduced to London the operas Manon, Rienzi, Cowen's Pauline, Goetz's Taming of the Shrew.

ROZE, MARIE (1846–1926), French soprano, began career at Opéra Comique, 1865–8, was great favorite at Drury Lane and Her Majesty's, 1872–81. Joined Carl Rosa Opera in 1883.

SANTLEY, (Sir) CHARLES (1834–1922), sometimes called king of English baritones, performed title *rôle* in Mendelssohn's Elijah for half a century. Introduced Fliegende Holländer to London, 1870, but retired from opera in 1877, appearing thereafter only in concerts and oratorio. At 81 sang with perfect intonation and much of the quality he had revealed half a century earlier.

SAPELLNIKOFF, VASSILY (1868–1941), Russian pianist and composer, toured Europe with great success for many years, briefly serving (1897–9) as professor of piano at Moscow Conservatory.

SARASATE, PABLO DE (1844–1908), Spanish violinist, performed on two Stradivari. First appeared in London at Crystal Palace in 1861. Grove says he had "purity of style, charm, brightness of tone, flexibility, and extraordinary facility." Favored works of Saint-Saëns and Lalo, frequently performed exquisitely-played solos of his own composition.

SCHUMANN, CLARA (1819–96), Austrian wife of composer Robert Schumann and one of most celebrated pianists of the century. First performed and toured as child prodigy; was a popular artist in England, appearing regularly from 1856 to

1888, lauded as a sound musician of all the best piano repertoire from Bach to Brahms, whose work she championed.

SCHUMANN-HEINK, ERNESTINE (1861–1936), operatic contralto, born near Prague. English *début* at Covent Garden, 1892, as Erda in Siegfried (and a few nights later in Rheingold), a *rôle* she sang at the Metropolitan Opera in 1932—at the age of 71! Sang at Bayreuth, 1896, and for several seasons (from 1898) at the Metropolitan. Created *rôle* of Klytemnestra in Strauss's Elektra, 1909. Noted also for lieder singing.

SHAKESPEARE, WILLIAM (1849–1931), composer, conductor, voice teacher, popular tenor in oratorio and concert. Member of teaching staff of Royal College of Music.

SLIVINSKI, JOSEPH VON (1865–1930), Polish pianist, studied under Leschetitzky and Anton Rubinstein, first performed in London in 1893. After touring with Leipzig Symphony, settled down to teaching career.

STANFORD, (Sir) CHARLES VILLIERS (1852–1924), Irish composer, conductor, teacher, best known for Irish Rhapsodies and "Irish" Symphony. Conducted Bach Choir, 1885–1902, Leeds Triennial Festival, 1901–10. Composed nearly a dozen operas, including Savonarola and Much Ado About Nothing.

STAVENHAGEN, BERNHARD (1862–1914), spectacularly successful pianist, rivaled only by Paderewski, first toured Europe, England and America in 1894–5. Within a few years turned to conducting, notably in Munich and Geneva from 1907 until end of his life.

STERLING, ANTOINETTE (1850–1904), American contralto, possessed voice of extraordinary range. Although she sang classical music (Mendelssohn, Schumann, Bach), was best known as ballad singer of such works as "Three Ra'ens," "Sands of Dee," and "The Lost Chord."

SUCHER, ROSA (1849–1927), German soprano, appeared with Hamburg Opera, 1878–90. Came to London in 1882 as first Isolde and first Eva in Meistersinger, as well as in Tannhäuser, Lohengrin, and Weber's Euryanthe. Sang again at Covent

Garden in 1892 as Brünnhilde and Isolde, and at Bayreuth, 1886–94.

SULLIVAN, (Sir) ARTHUR (1842–1900), organist and choir master of St Michael's, Chester Square, in London, first attracted attention in 1862 for incidental music to Shakespear's The Tempest. After brief period of teaching composition became successful composer of comic opera, notably with W. S. Gilbert. Continued to compose oratorios, cantatas, and one grand opera, Ivanhoe, and conducted several principal orchestras.

SVENSDEN, OLUF (1832–88), Norwegian flautist, joined Crystal Palace orchestra in 1856. Later performed with Philharmonic and, for ten years, in orchestra at Her Majesty's.

TAMBERLIK, ENRICO (1820–89), Italian tenor, first appeared in England in 1850 as Masaniello in Auber's Muette de Portici, remained with Royal Italian Opera until 1864, later sang at Covent Garden and Her Majesty's. Most important *rôles* were Florestan in Fidelio, Don Ottavio in Rigoletto, title *rôle* in Rossini's Otello, Manrico in Trovatore.

THOMAS, ARTHUR GORING (1850–92), opera composer of limited talent, whose most accomplished works were Esmeralda (1883) and Nadeshda (1885). Also wrote cantatas, odes, and songs.

TREBELLI-BETTINI, ZÉLIA (1838–92), Paris-born mezzo-soprano, made her *début* at Madrid, singing Rosina to Mario's Almaviva in Il Barbiere. One of her greatest *rôles* was Orsini in Lucrezia Borgia, which she sang to thunderous ovation in London *début*, 1862. One of London's best-loved singers until retirement in 1889.

VAN DYCK, ERNEST (1861–1923), Belgian Heldentenor, gave up law studies for vocal career. Made first success in Bayreuth in 1888, continuing to sing there as Parsifal and Lohengrin until 1912. First heard at Covent Garden in 1891. Shaw was one of first to predict greatness for the later-celebrated singer.

VIANESI, AUGUSTE (1837–1908), Italian-born conductor and composer, came to London in 1858 to conduct Drury Lane orchestra. Later conducted Italian opera at Covent Garden for twelve years, until chosen in 1887 to be principal conductor of Paris Opéra.

VIARD-LOUIS, JENNY (1832–1904), French pianist and *impresario*, presented now-historic series of concerts in St James's Hall, 1878–9, with Joachim and Weist Hill, which included Massenet's Scènes pittoresques and Bizet's L'Arlésienne Suite. Shaw frequently alluded to her adventurousness and abilities.

WALLACE, WILLIAM VINCENT (1812–65), Irish violinist, became prodigious composer of operas, the most popular of which were his first, Maritana, at Drury Lane in 1845, and Lurline, at Covent Garden in 1860.

WEIST HILL, THOMAS H. (1823–91), violinist, conductor, teacher, became member of Costa's orchestra at Royal Italian Opera in 1849. Was conductor at Alexandra Palace, 1874–6, conducted Viard-Louis's orchestral concerts, 1878–9. Later was Principal of Guildhall School of Music.

YSAŸE, EUGÈNE (1858–1931), Belgian violinist and conductor, studied under Wieniawski and Vieuxtemps, first appeared in London at Philharmonic concert, 1889. Composed "Variations on a Theme of Paganini" and six violin concertos, popularized Franck's violin sonata, which was dedicated to him.

ZIMMERMANN, AGNES (1847–1925), German-born pianist and composer, resident in London, studied at Royal Academy of Music and made first public appearance in 1863. Her name, says Grove, "became for many years a household word for purity of interpretation and excellent musicianship." Limited her performance to works of classical school, especially sonatas of Mozart and Beethoven and complete piano works of Schumann, which she edited.

INDEX

to the entire edition
compiled by Ralph Bateman

Personages whose names are preceded by an asterisk are included in the Biographical Index